The Poetry Demon

STUDIES IN EAST ASIAN BUDDHISM 29

The Poetry Demon

SONG-DYNASTY MONKS ON VERSE AND THE WAY

Jason Protass

A KURODA INSTITUTE BOOK

University of Hawai'i Press
Honolulu

Library of Congress Cataloging-in-Publication Data
Names: Protass, Jason, author.
Title: The poetry demon : Song-Dynasty monks on verse and the way / Jason Protass.
Other titles: Studies in East Asian Buddhism ; no. 29.
Description: Honolulu : University of Hawai'i Press, 2021. | Series: Kuroda Institute studies in East Asian Buddhism ; 29 | Includes bibliographical references and index.
Identifiers: LCCN 2021012122 | ISBN 9780824886622 (cloth) | ISBN 9780824889074 (pdf) | ISBN 9780824889081 (epub) | ISBN 9780824889098 (Kindle edition)
Subjects: LCSH: Chinese poetry—Buddhist authors—History and criticism. | Zen poetry, Chinese—History and criticism. | Monks' writings—History and criticism.
Classification: LCC PL2308.5.B8 P76 2021 | DDC 895.11009—dc23
LC record available at https://lccn.loc.gov/2021012122

ISBN 9780824889104 (paperback)

The Kuroda Institute for the Study of Buddhism is a nonprofit, educational corporation founded in 1976. One of its primary objectives is to promote scholarship on the historical, philosophical, and cultural ramifications of Buddhism. In association with the University of Hawai'i Press, the Institute also publishes Classics in East Asian Buddhism, a series devoted to the translation of significant texts in the East Asian Buddhist tradition.

University of Hawai'i Press books are printed on acid-free paper and meet the guidelines for permanence and durability of the Council on Library Resources.

Cover art: "Reading a Sutra by Moonlight," Unidentified Artist, ca. 1332, The Metropolitan Museum of Art, New York, Edward Elliott Family Collection, Purchase, The Dillon Fund Gift, 1982.

For all my Teachers

Contents

Acknowledgments

THE PATH to this book began years ago, crossed several countries, and was made possible by support from many people and organizations. I first want to thank my mom and dad for nourishing my interests and for encouraging me to chase my passions.

I thank my advisors at Stanford, John Kieschnick, Carl Bielefeldt, and Paul Harrison, my teacher of poetry, Stuart Sargent, as well as Ron Egan, who joined my dissertation committee. Thanks, too, to Kinugawa Kenji at Hanazono University, Kyoto, and Liao Chao-heng at Academia Sinica, Taipei, each a true *kalyāṇamitra*. Words cannot convey how thankful I am for their generosity and dedication to transmitting the lamp of learning. As a student at Yale and Stanford I had the fortune of studying with Stephen Bokenkamp, Bernard Faure, Griffith Foulk, Robert Gimello, Peter Gregory, Paul Groner, Fabrizio Pregadio, John McRae, Morten Schlütter, Stanley Weinstein, and Mimi Yiengpruksawan. I hope this book can be a small token of my gratitude to all my teachers.

At Brown University, Janine Sawada has been an incredible senior colleague. She offered written comments on a draft of the whole manuscript. My friend Tom Mazanec generously commented on each chapter in spite of the demands of his own strenuous schedule. This book was substantively improved by both of the anonymous readers, to whom I am much obliged for their rigorous and constructive feedback. To Peter Gregory, Robert Buswell, and the Kuroda editorial board, my thanks for your support and detailed suggestions. Patricia Crosby was wonderful to work with and her copyediting clarified the text. All remaining errors and infelicities are, of course, my own.

This project was enriched by countless conversations with many colleagues and friends. I would like to specifically thank the following people for their critical support. Norihisa Baba facilitated my visits to Tokyo and made introductions to Zen studies scholars. Sarah Babcock corresponded with me about Huihong. James Benn read an early draft and pointed me in the right direction. Ben Brose was a true *senpai* in Taiwan, California, and Rhode Island. Rafal Felbur generously critiqued my translations and shared his unpublished work. Alex Hsu read drafts of chapters, shared his insightful research, and indulged me in meandering conversations that deepened my thinking. Genine Lentine dared to read my translations as poetry and introduced me to her inspiring world. George Keyworth graciously offered comments on the *wenzi chan* chapter. Kida Tomoo made possible my two very productive years of research in Kyoto. Kid Lam offered inspiration and friendship in Taipei. Jeffrey Moser provided intellectual support and collegial warmth during the latter stages of revision. Nishitani Isao shared his unpublished research and insights about the Song. James Robson offered encouragement wherever we happened meet. Hal Roth discussed several important passages and terms. Morten Schlütter read my doctoral dissertation and offered important guidance on revisions for this book. Aaron (Haifeng) Shang read translations of poems by Zhiyuan as well as all of Chapter Two. Student assistant Shen Yanqing organized my research notes for Chapter Two. Dan Stevenson carefully critiqued Chapter Four. Molly Vallor read Daoqian with me at the start of this project. Nick Witkowski introduced me to Chinese translations of Vinaya. Yanagi Mikiyasu patiently shared his erudite knowledge on the history of Chan. Ven. Yifa created many of the causes and conditions that made the work possible.

The contents of this book were refined based on learned feedback from audiences at lectures delivered at Academia Sinica, Columbia University, Hanazono University, Harvard University, Nanjing University, and University of Tokyo. My thanks also to the following conference organizers and thoughtful attendees for their comments and debate and to the conference hosts: Center for Buddhist Studies at the University of Arizona (Albert Welter and Jiang Wu); Hong Kong Confucius Institute, Hong Kong Polytechnic University (Jia Jinhua); Dharma Drum Institute of Liberal Arts, sponsored by FROGBEAR (Chen Jinhua); and Zen Reading Group at the Annual Meeting of the American Academy of Religion (Steven Heine). My thanks also to the attendees of the "Princeton Workshop on Chinese Religious Poetry for Junior Scholars" and to Stephen Teiser and Anna Shields for their support thereof.

My wonderful colleagues in the Department of Religious Studies at Brown have been inspiring, encouraging, and understanding. I could not have imagined a better community in which to finish this book.

Gratefully, I acknowledge the financial and administrative support, so critical to the research and writing of this work, from the following institutions: Bukkyō Dendō Kyōkai; Research Institute for Buddhist Culture, Ryukoku University; Fulbright Taiwan; Institute of Chinese Literature and Philosophy, Academia Sinica; the ACLS Robert H. N. Ho Family Foundation Program in Buddhist Studies; the Ho Center for Buddhist Studies at Stanford University; and the Department of Religious Studies at Brown University. Thank you to Stephanie Chun and the team at UH Press for skillfully guiding this book to publication.

My brother, Adam, lent me his constant and enthusiastic support. My dear friends Alex, Bathsheba, and Murphy took me hiking these past few years, giving me space to think, and were always tolerant of detailed perseveration on the Song dynasty. My beloved dog, Trumble, never failed to lift my spirits. My wife, Seguin, ever willing to talk about the Song dynasty early in the morning, helped me refine my thoughts in the course of our daily lives, moved to several countries in support of this project, and never stopped articulating the necessity of the humanities.

Conventions

INFORMATION ON the conventions for citing *Taishō shinshū daizōkyō* and *Shinsan Dai Nihon zoku zōkyō* are given in the list of abbreviations that follows this section. An explanation of citation styles for traditional xylographic printed texts and modern critical editions of sources can be found at the beginning of the bibliography.

Poems in translation are set off from the main text. Even-numbered lines are enumerated for the benefit of the reader. Unless noted, transcription of rhyme words follow the Baxter-Sagart Middle Chinese reconstructions. Early Chinese reconstructions preceded by an asterisk (*) are based on another source given in the notes. All other Chinese terms are romanized using the Hànyǔ Pīnyīn system, adapted to omit diacritical marks that indicate standard tones in Mandarin. Words are the basic units, not individual characters, and two- or three-syllable concepts are transcribed together. Quotations of texts containing Wade-Giles romanization have been altered to conform to this Pinyin convention; Wade-Giles in the titles of publications has not been altered. Japanese is romanized according to the Revised Hepburn system. Sanskrit terms preceded by an asterisk (*) are scholarly reconstructions derived from Chinese sources. Traditional Chinese characters are used throughout the manuscript; this includes quotations, author names, and publication titles originally published in simplified Chinese.

All years are converted from traditional reign dates to the corresponding Western calendar year. Months and days are not converted. The names of persons and places are romanized, not translated. The titles of books are translated at first appearance in the main text and are given in romanization in footnotes and the bibliography. Except where noted, all translations are by the author.

Abbreviations

T	*Taishō shinshū daizōkyō. Citations are to T, followed by volume number, page number, register, and line number(s).*
ZZ	*Shinsan Dai Nihon zoku zōkyō. Citations to the revised Tokyo edition are to ZZ, followed by volume number, page number, register, and line number(s).*
SBCK	*Sibu congkan*
SKQS	*Siku quanshu*

Introduction

IN HIS POEM "The Poetry Demon" 詩魔, the Tiantai monk Gushan Zhiyuan 孤山智圓 (976–1022) depicts his impulse to versify as an interruption of his evening religious practice.[1]

	My *chan* mind is vexed by the poetry demon,	禪心喧撓被詩魔
2	"The moon cold and a gentle breeze"—what to do about it?	月冷風清奈爾何
	All night I try to subdue [the demon, but] subdue I cannot!	一夜欲降降不得
4	A horde of [Māra's] minions come and come.	紛紛徒屬更來多

The poetry demon (*shi mo*) is a metaphor for an irresistible urge to compose verse. In this poem, just as the poet begins to still his mind for evening meditation, the muse descends upon him.[2] The beauty of the moon calls to the monk, who begins actively contemplating poetic phrases instead of concentrating his mind. As fragments of poetry interfere with the poet's religious duties, he recalls Śākyamuni Buddha encountering Māra on the night before awakening. The poet battles his thoughts as if they were demons, minions of Māra, the enemy of liberation. In "try to subdue, subdue I cannot," a caesura punctuates the repetition of "subdue" (*jiang* 降), and the poem turns to describe defeat in the face of an unrelenting desire. Zhiyuan's poem itself performs his succumbing to poetic temptation. The poem is a clever depiction of a devout Buddhist monk encountering the pleasures of verse. It is a poem about the intersections of the Buddhist path and Chinese poetry.

Buddhist monks in China's Northern Song (960–1127) and Southern Song (1127–1279) dynasties wrote prodigious amounts of poetry. At the same time, they propagated prohibitions, warnings, and canonical exhortations against monks engaging in literary endeavors. How did this discourse about the dangers of poetry shape historical poetic practices? During the Song, most Buddhists still understood Chinese poetry to be an "outer" form of knowledge, not part of the "inner learning" essential to the path of awakening.[3]

---

1. *Xianju bian* (ZZ56.934a24-b2).

2. I treat Chan as a proper noun in reference to the Chan lineages and the literature and teachings associated with the people who identified with that lineage; lowercase *chan* denotes *dhyāna,* or meditation. Zhiyuan, a Tiantai monk, was referring to the latter. Following guidelines in Foulk, "Histories of Chan," 28.

3. This topic is detailed in Chapter 4. The indigenous Chinese use of "inner" and "outer" asserted innate hierarchical relations, as explained in Campany, "Very Idea of Religions," 307–309.

Such an understanding underpins Zhiyuan's depiction of poetry as Māra. Poetry itself is not the Way. At the same time, hymns and songs celebrating the joys of liberation were recited in daily liturgies, and Buddhist teachers were expected to use poetic forms to propagate the dharma. This book is about how Song-dynasty monks understood and navigated the multiple relationships between poetry and the Way.

The Song era was a watershed in Chinese Buddhist history. The received traditions of earlier times were reshaped into forms, sects, and literatures that greatly influenced later traditions and mediated their understanding of the pre-Song past. This distinctive period was the time when a new literati culture bloomed. Following the violent demise of the Chinese aristocracy in the final decades of the Tang dynasty (618–907), the power of patronage shifted first to regional rulers and then to the scholar-officials and other educated elites.[4] During the Song, a class of literati bureaucrats attained positions of authority and exerted broad influence over cultural productions.[5] Leading monks often belonged to this new class of cultured men and were active participants in the exchange of poetry and letters. At times, monks wrote poetry addressed directly to literati supporters,[6] but judging from extant collections, Buddhist abbots and monastic officers most often exchanged poetry among themselves, not in appeals to lay patrons. These poems exchanged within monastic communities are especially worthy of our attention for what they reveal about how monks understood and practiced poetry with one another.

Most monks' poems were composed in Buddhist monasteries, which during the eleventh to fourteenth centuries underwent significant reformations. A new kind of monastic legal code known as the "rules of purity" (*qinggui* 清規) became widely adopted from the eleventh century on through the Yuan dynasty (1271–1368).[7] Along with the classic Buddhist disciplinary rules, or Vinaya, these Chinese monastic codes instilled values and regulated many aspects of Chinese monks' daily lives as well as their social and religious rites. In addition, new printed primers, encyclopedias, lexicons, and other educational materials for monks propagated normative attitudes to poetry as well as knowledge of literary forms and conventions within monasteries. Monks themselves put these attitudes into practice, visible especially in paratexts,

---

4. See Brose, *Patrons and Patriarchs,* on regional patronage in the tenth century, which reconfigures Buddhist history from the late Tang to early Song, following insights from Tackett, *Destruction of the Medieval Chinese Aristocracy.* Chen, "The State, the Gentry, and the Local Institutions," summarizes how the Hartwell-Hymes hypothesis about the rise of "local gentry" during the Southern Song has been revised in recent monographs and essays.

5. Gregory and Ebrey, "Religious and Historical Landscape," sets the Tang-Song transition as a framework for making sense of both the changes and continuities in religious traditions. Among the many works on Song history and the new class of literati, a source helpful for thinking about the education of young men is Bol, "The Sung Examination System."

6. The use of poetry to win patronage is discussed in Schlütter, *How Zen Became Zen,* 7–10, 62–77; and Heller, *Illusory Abiding,* 336–348.

7. Foulk, "*Chanyuan qinggui* and Other 'Rules of Purity,'" 298–306, surveys extant *qinggui* from the eleventh to fourteenth century.

that is, the colophons, prefaces, headnotes, and titles that bracket their poetry. From these various monastic sources we can reconstruct Song monks' own assumptions about poetry and verse, its many genres, and their relationships to the Buddhist path.

"Buddhist poetry" during the Song dynasty ranged from anonymous didactic hymns to landscape poems with clearly identified individual authors. Overall, about 30,000 verses by Song-era monks survive. This is more than 10 percent of all extant Song-era *shi* 詩, "(regulated) poetry," which numbers around 240,000 poems.[8] Compared to Song poetry, Tang-era poetry has been well studied, even though only about 49,000 have been transmitted in the *Complete Poems of the Tang* 全唐詩 (published 1707). Quantity is an imperfect measure of significance; the relatively large corpus of 30,000 poems by Song monks are rarely read. This in part may be because monks' poems historically were viewed as peripheral to the mainstream of Chinese literature, and within Buddhist traditions, they were treated as second-order phenomena. Similar biases are perpetuated in modern academic disciplines.

On the one hand, some scholars have been quick to dismiss Song monks' poetry as not very literary. Iriya Yoshitaka, for example, has remarked that "in the poet-monks of the Song dynasty we see...adulation for the poems by literati, or to the contrary a propensity to 'stink' of Zen."[9] Elsewhere, Iriya has made clear that he is echoing the ubiquitous Song literati critique of monks' poetry as having "the whiff of vegetables" (*cai qi* 菜氣), usually connoting bland and passionless poetry.[10] In contrast, Iriya has praised the poetry of Hanshan 寒山 (Cold Mountain) as well as of Tao Yuanming 陶淵明 (365?– 427), arguing that each captured the spirit of Zen in literary form.[11] The former is a semi-legendary figure and the latter lived before the historical beginnings of Chan, however. The poems of historical monks, on the other hand, were for Iriya either too similar to those of the literati or not literary enough.

Stephen Owen is among those who have criticized the poetry of China's monks as not sufficiently rich in something "truly 'religious,'" by which he means a poem that crystallizes "a possible flash of faith experienced while

---

8. The quantities and sources of monks' poetry are reviewed in Jin, "Songdai Chanseng shi zhengli yu yanjiu de zhongyao shouhuo." The *Quan Song shi* includes an estimated 20,000 poems authored by monks; 1,000 more monks' poems in *Quan Song shi dingbu.* Zhu and Chen, in *Songdai Chanseng shiji kao,* gathered an additional 7,800 poems by monks. Chinese scholars continue to publish newly recovered poems.

9. Iriya, *Gūdō to etsuraku,* 90, 末代の詩僧には [...] 士大夫の詩に対する媚びと、それの裏返しである禅臭の露出があるだけである. Translation adapted from Norman Waddell in Iriya, "Chinese Poetry and Zen," 65.

10. Iriya, *Gozan bungaku shū,* 327–331. I have discussed this topic at length in Protass, "Flavors of Monks' Poetry."

11. Iriya here has performed the kind of "Buddhist readings" later advocated in Rouzer, *On Cold Mountain.* For an excellent overview of current scholarship on Hanshan, see Rouzer, *On Cold Mountain,* chaps. 1 and 2.

visiting a temple."[12] Owen also decries a work by poet-monk Lingyi 靈一 (727–762), writing that "exactly the same poem might have been written by a secular poet."[13] In scholarly modes such as this, conclusions are predetermined by the search for something matching what is assumed to be religious. Responding directly to some of Owen's comments, Paul Kroll has elucidated how several Li Bo poems are intelligible only when we understand their "precise Daoist diction and imagery."[14] That is to say, the *traces* of Shangqing and Lingbao Daoism are fundamental to grasping the meaning of Li Bo's poems.[15] Kroll describes his approach as a tripartite relationship among received conventions, social uses, and rhetoric.[16] Owen, on the other hand, observes that "Li Bo was even less a religious poet than Wang Wei."[17] Owen's ideas about religious poetry are revealed in his praise of the poetry of monk Qingjiang: "It is his self-doubt about his own religious conviction that makes him perhaps the most religiously serious of the southeastern poet-monks."[18] Here, what is foregrounded is the *tension* of an individual grappling with his religious ideals, a conclusion that resonates with a view once espoused by Anthony Yu that "China has no poet with an explicit religious commitment and concern comparable to the stature of a Dante, Milton, Donne, or T.S. Eliot."[19] It becomes clear that these scholars have in mind different *kinds* of religious poetry. Kroll focuses on the uses of scripture by poets in medieval China. Owen and Yu have searched for analogues to the Western canon and judged the poetry written by Buddhist monks to be insufficiently "religious."

Owen's critiques about what the poetry of Buddhist monks *should be* has been taken up by historians discussing what such poetry *was.* John Kieschnick, for example, has observed that Tang poet-monks saw poetry as "for the most part secular" while, for scholar-monks, the arts like poetry, calligraphy, and painting were somehow "less *Buddhist*" than doctrinal exegesis.[20] This scholarly classification of the poetry of Tang monks as somehow not religious is predicated on a sense that it ought to be religious in a way recognizable to us and distinct from so-called secular poetry. It is the case, however, that both poets and monks wrote verse that crossed such boundaries. The difficulty with which we apply a distinction between religious and secular poetry to the

---

12. Owen, "How Did Buddhism Matter?" 390.

13. Owen, *The Great Age,* 282–283. This idea is echoed in Kieschnick, *Eminent Monk,* 117–118. For more on Lingyi, see Mazanec, "Invention of Chinese Buddhist Poetry," 37–40, 382.

14. Kroll, "Li Po's Transcendent Diction," 99n1; and Kroll, "Verse from on High," 232n39.

15. Felstiner, *Paul Celan,* xvi–xviii, distinguished between the "traces" and "tensions" of Judaism found in the German-language poetry of Paul Celan. For more on how this offers an analogous way of thinking about transliterated or technical terms as traces and tensions in Chinese Buddhist monks' poetry, see Protass, "Buddhist Monks and Chinese Poetry," 2–4.

16. The tripartite division given in Diehl, *Medieval European Religious Lyric,* cited in Kroll, "Daoist Verse," 983n65.

17. Owen, *The Great Age,* 140.

18. Owen, *The Great Age,* 287.

19. Yu, *Comparative Journeys,* 104.

20. Kieschnick, *Eminent Monk,* 116, 117–118, emphasis in the original.

Song dynasty is a sign that we are wrongly framing the question and distorting historical realities.

For a multiplicity of reasons, then, we have either overlooked or misunderstood the large body of poetic literature produced by monks. This book takes this religious literature seriously on its own terms—beginning with wide reading in the Song texts—and not from preconceptions about Buddhist poetry. To do so, I examine in Part 1 the pre-Song and Song contexts of *jisong* 偈頌, a Chinese term that at first referred to the author-less, Indic *gāthā* in Buddhist scripture, and by the Song was a genre for Chinese-language verses by Chan masters. I illustrate how *jisong* intersected with Chan monks' textual practices of manuscripts, collation, and printing, and to a lesser extent orality. I ask, in other words, how Chan monks in the Song dynasty constructed genres and how these ideas shaped practices. Part 2 demonstrates that poetry itself was not the path to liberation for Song monks. Looking beyond just Chan, we can observe monastic norms in encyclopedias, primers, legal codes, and other prescriptive literature, and I will argue that these norms circulated widely enough that they conditioned monks' poetic practices. In Part 3, I offer interpretations of poems based on monastic rituals, Buddhist doctrines, and literary conventions. Here, I juxtapose analysis of poems by Chan masters, a Tiantai teacher, and poet-monks. As these Song Buddhist monks wrote poetry, how did they negotiate tensions between the expectations of mainstream poetry and their commitments to the higher calling of Buddhist monasticism? In the remainder of this introduction I offer a synoptic overview and introduce some key concepts.

Poetry and Buddhist Cultures

Poetry is found both among the earliest Buddhist texts and across most of today's Buddhist cultures. One may wonder if there ever was a Buddhism without poetry. At the same time, every literature has its own horizons, bound by local literary traditions, conventions, and social contexts. Some patterns that emerge from Song-era Buddhism are similar to those of literatures of other Buddhist cultures while other aspects are particular to the Song.

In the investigation of South Asian Buddhist cultures, for example, scholars have observed a tension between monastic education and the expression of emotions through poetry.[21] One medieval Lankan text asserted that the only appropriate subject for Sinhala *kāvya* poetry should be the lives of the Buddha.[22] This pious topic and its conventional aesthetics are very narrow compared with the rich possibilities of the broader Sanskrit *kāvya* tradition. Similarly, in China, admonishments to use poetry only for edification are found

---

21. Berkwitz, *Buddhist Poetry and Colonialism,* 13, 81.
22. Hallisey, "Works and Persons in Sinhala Literary Culture," 703–706. On poetry and reader and audience response among late medieval Sri Lankan Buddhists, see Berkwitz, *Buddhist History in the Vernacular,* 233–234.

in moralistic primers and monastic etiquette guides, including those composed and circulated during the Song. This also seems to resonate with an early North Indian *kāvya*, Aśvaghoṣa's *Saundarananda,* in which the poet concludes that literary embellishments are merely honey that encourage people to consume the bitter medicine of moralistic literature. Aśvaghoṣa says, "I have told here under the pretext of a poem the truth, namely that liberation is what matters."[23] We might call this the instrumental use of literary form for Buddhist purposes. Here, we find a similarity across Buddhist poetries. Some defenders of Chinese Buddhist literary culture also argued that poetry can best spread the word of the Buddha to those who are inclined to listen to poetry.

Other South Asian literatures by contrast seem to establish their moral vision precisely through the evocation of emotions. Anne Monius, for example, in her analysis of the long poetic narrative of *Maṇimēkalai,* produced by a Tamil Buddhist community in the first millennium of the common era, illustrates the very techniques by which the text is at once "religious or philosophical teaching and sophisticated literary art."[24] A similar insight animates Charles Hallisey's introductory essay to his recent translation of the *Therīgāthā,* songs attributed to the earliest Buddhist nuns. He singles out a verse by Ambapali that was composed in a meter often used for love songs and paeans to female beauty.[25] This meter would evoke in the listener associations with both well-known songs of youthful splendor and social conventions about gender. Ambapali's poem instead depicts the aging of her body, a direct challenge to what a contemporaneous listener would have expected. Our understanding of this poem's power depends on our familiarity with such conventions and the audience's foreknowledge. In an analogous way, Chinese monks' poems written in standard Chinese poetic meters evoked certain expectations in their contemporary audiences. I focus in Part 3 on monks' writing in genres of parting and mourning, both types of poems that grapple with sorrow.

Scholars have observed structural similarities between Buddhist literary cultures of South Asia and China, but the extent and nature of direct sharing of literary forms or poetics remain a matter of debate.[26] Buddhist poetry of China differs from that of other Buddhist cultures largely because the indigenous traditions of learning and literature were well-developed in China before the arrival of Buddhism. Although Buddhist contributions to Chinese poetry and literature were woven from language and patterns of thinking rooted in pre-Buddhist traditions, there were outspoken and influential men of letters who viewed Buddhism as a foreign tradition.[27] These well-positioned

---

23. Salomon, "Aśvaghoṣa's Saundarananda," 190.

24. Monius, *Imagining a Place for Buddhism,* 13.

25. Hallisey, *Therigatha,* xiii–xix.

26. Mair, "Buddhism in *The Literary Mind,*" surveys some of the international debate. Partly in response to the strong position of Mair and Mei, "Sanskrit Origins of Recent Style," Klein offers useful perspectives in "Indic Echoes."

27. In addition to poetry, Buddhism was important in the development of vernacular performance literatures at least as early as *bianwen* from Dunhuang.

defenders of a lettered nativist tradition often enjoyed cultural hegemony, and their anti-Buddhist rhetoric was an inescapable part of the historical contexts of Buddhist literature in China. This feature of Chinese Buddhist poetry distinguishes it from that of Tibet, for example, wherein belles-lettres developed from the reception of Indian traditions such as Daṇḍin's *Kāvyādarśa*.[28] The well-educated masters of lettered traditions in Tibet were mostly ordained monks. Prominent literary figures belonging to the elite monastic class fashioned even the supposedly low genre of "song" (*glu*), found in Dunhuang and in later Treasure literature, and celebrated these coarse verses as an autochthonous literary tradition.[29] By contrast, the most influential and well-read figures in Chinese belletristic traditions were infrequently Buddhist monks, with notable exceptions in the Tang and early Qing, something that distinguishes Chinese Buddhist poetry from that of Tibet, or even premodern Japan.[30]

In Japan, too, many important literary figures belonged to the learned monastic class. Japanese and Chinese attitudes toward the relationship between Buddhism and poetry diverged despite close and sustained historical contacts between communities in each country.[31] Continental learning in Japan was often led by elite Buddhist monks, for example, the monks of the so-called Gozan, or Five Mountains, Zen temples from the late Kamakura period (1185–1333) until at least the early Edo period (1603–1868), when Confucian scholars successfully vied for authority over Chinese erudition.[32] During preceding centuries, aristocrats, courtiers, and monks sometimes discussed their composition of poetry as a Buddhist practice with liberative power.[33] As early as the eleventh century, imperial anthologies of *waka* 和歌, Japanese poetry, included sections of *shakkyō-ka* 釈教歌, that is, poems on the teachings of the Buddha.[34] These poems exemplified the late-Heian formula that "the path of poetry is none other than the path of the Buddha" 歌道即

---

28. van der Kuijp, "Tibetan Belles-Lettres."

29. Jackson, " 'Poetry' in Tibet."

30. For example, on the mid-Tang monk Jiaoran, see Williams, "Taste of the Ocean." Mazanec, "Networks of Exchange," 330, demonstrates that during the cultural Late Tang (ca. 830–960) "Buddhist monks were hubs of literary activity." See Liao, *Zhongyi puti*, for a study of the seventeenth-century style of the renaissance of monks' poetry that resulted after learned Ming loyalists refused to join the Qing government and instead took refuge in monastic cloth.

31. Rouzer, "Early Buddhist Kanshi," 437–438, observed similar differences between Heian Japan and Tang-Song China.

32. For a general introduction to the Five Mountains, see Collcutt, *Five Mountains*. On the place of Gozan Zen monks in continental learning and foreign diplomacy, see Murai, "Chūsei Nitchō kōshō no naka no kanshi," as well as the monographs by Asakura Hisashi listed in the bibliography. On the early Edo period, see Park, "Vehicle of Social Mobility." On later Edo-period conflicts, see Sawada, "Religious Conflict in Bakumatsu Japan." On the relatively diminished but not insignificant positions of Zen and émigré monks among Edo belles-lettres, see Liao, "Huangbo zong yu Jianghu zhongqi sengshi lunxi."

33. See Plutschow, "Is Poetry a Sin?" and Rambelli, *Buddhist Theory of Semiotics*, 175.

34. Yamada, "Poetry and Meaning."

佛道.[35] This formula has no parallel in China. One touchstone for this Japanese understanding was an inscription by the Tang poet Bai Juyi 白居易 (772–846), who lamented his "karma of words" and imagined that his worldly poems might somehow participate in the Buddhist moral economy.[36] This idea was reframed in the literary practices of the Heian court. There, imperial students concerned about the karmic consequences of studying "ornate phrases" (kigo 綺語; Ch. qi yu)—one of the "ten unwholesome [acts]" (shi'e 十惡)—in 964 formed a confraternity, visited Mount Hiei, and ritually intoned Bai's words to alleviate their karmic burden.[37] In China, no similarly creative interpretations of Bai Juyi's phrase can be detected. The moral conflict between literature and Buddhist teachings in Japan was generally resolved by the twelfth and thirteenth centuries with the widespread understanding that the production of waka delighted kami and buddhas and could lead to liberation.[38] I will show that during this same period in China, poetry, though created by monks in profusion, was still understood as incidental to the Buddhist path.

What, then, were the distinctive traits of the Chinese Buddhist literary culture? I want to focus this question by shifting away from Buddhist poetry and toward the historical practices of monks. Chinese monks' poetry, that is, the corpus defined by the author's monastic identity, is not the equivalent of our term "Buddhist poetry." Closer to the latter, the early Song-dynasty anthology Blossoms from the Garden of Literature 文苑英華 (completed after 980) included a section of poetry under the heading "Buddhism" (shimen 釋門). Therein, only seven of the ninety-one authors were monks.[39] The majority of these "Buddhist" poems were written by mainstream poets during temple visits or as gifts to monks.[40] They are Buddhist because of their subject matter, not because of a didactic message, ritual function, or the identity of the author. This kind of Buddhist poetry, sensu lato, did include writing by monks and so was neither mutually exclusive nor categorically equivalent to monks' poetry.[41]

In the following chapters I focus on the Buddhism and literature of mo-

---

35. Miller, Wind from Vulture Peak, 5.

36. Waley, Life and Times of Po Chü-i, 107, 207; and LaFleur, Karma of Words, viii, 8–9, 91.

37. Kamens, Three Jewels, 295–298. Cited with further analysis in Klein, "Wild Words and Syncretic Deities," 181–182.

38. Jamentz, "Buddhist Affirmation of Poetry," 58. Bushelle, "Joy of the Dharma," 9 and 180, translates relevant texts by Jien 慈円 (1155–1225).

39. See Wenyuan yinghua, fascs. 219–224, 1093–1126. Additional poems by monks are found elsewhere in this same text, including in the section on "Daoist poetry" (daomen 道門), 225/1136–1137, 228/1148. These details in Rouzer, "Early Buddhist Kanshi," 434.

40. Such temple-visit lyrics and the place of Buddhist thought in the intellectual and personal lives of China's famous poets have been productive subjects of research. An incomplete list of Anglophone scholarship might include Ronald Egan, Word, Image, and Deed in the Life of Su Shi; Kroll, Meng Hao-jan; Schmidt, Stone Lake; Grant, Mount Lu Revisited; Zhiyi Yang, Dialectics of Spontaneity; and Chennault, "Representing the Uncommon."

41. I have in mind the distinctions between sensu stricto and sensu lato introduced by Martin, "Buddhism and Literature."

nastic clerics rather than that of the lay literati. This is in part because the latter, with respect to Buddhist learning, "love books, but do not live by books," to borrow the words of Robertson Davies.[42] The Buddhist monastery was a place of leisure for laypeople, who could repair from official duties to quiet gardens and forested complexes. For the priesthood who pledged to live by the rules of the monastic order, the monastery was a site of discipline.[43] Communal monastic life was regimented, designed to quell the passions, and followed a rhythm of meritorious activities.[44] Monastic rule books outlined major and minor rituals, explained correct attitudes for cultivation, included monthly and annual calendars, and relegated the study of literature and poetry to gaps in the schedule. The disciplinary apparatus of Buddhist monasticism shaped the literary lives of those who strictly adhered to the Buddhist path. As I will show, the disciplinary and educational apparatus of Buddhist monasticism can be detected in the poetry of Chinese monks.

I see parallels in the English- and Japanese-language scholarship that productively troubled the category "Zen art," still widely used to refer to some mystical spirit of Zen.[45] Scholars of this inclination shifted their focus to the uses of objects and themes within monastic visual cultures. Similarly, I want to shift away from thinking of so-called Buddhist poetry and toward analyses of poetic objects within monastic literary cultures. Instead of looking only for what we think Buddhist poetry should be, we might turn our gaze toward what monks actually wrote in tremendous quantities. If we do so, we are likely to ask more and new questions about still more intriguing poetry.

Monastic Literary Culture

Buddhist monasteries in China's Northern and Southern Song dynasties were, among other things, centers of literary activity and education. Verse permeated the lives of children, young adults, and both lay and monastic officials. For example, Buddhist tunes with sing-song rhymes and with straightforward didactic messages are evidence that postulants, generally children who could ordain when they came of age, were through songs instructed in basic literacy as well as proper deportment for communal life in the monastery.[46] In the Tang and to at least some extent in the Song, non-religious education existed

---

42. Davies, *Voice from the Attic,* chapter on "Defining the Clerisy," 6–7.

43. Robson, "Introduction" 17n28, similarly depicts the practices of Chinese monasteries as a disciplinary apparatus.

44. On the ideals of the monastery as an apparatus of diminished sense pleasures, see, for example, the lucid explanation in Heim, *Forerunner of All Things,* 170; on the relevant ideals of a Ming Chinese monastery, see Yü, *Renewal of Buddhism in China,* 192–222.

45. Hisamatsu, "On Zen Art," promulgated an insider, or normative, account. In response, see Shimizu, "Zen Art?" More recently, Asami, "Kamakura," vii–viii, focuses on the limitations of Hisamatsu's constructive approach. My comments echo Levine, "Two (or More) Truths," 59.

46. Details in Chap. 4 below. Additional information and fragmentary evidence for the education of postulants in Yü, "Ch'an Education in the Sung."

as well in Buddhist monasteries, where young men could study for civil service examinations.[47] Monasteries also housed aspiring junior monks who refined their learning and practices through itinerant wandering, occasionally engaging in poetic exchange. Abbots and senior officers were the heart of a monastery's literary life, whether corresponding with civil officials, entertaining and ministering to important lay visitors, or admonishing novices and pilgrims. A large public monastery was the site of a complex of different literatures for multiple audiences.

Verse was woven into the fabric of a Buddhist monk's life. Verses for daily, monthly, and occasional ritual life of a monastery were given in rule books such as the *Rules of Purity for Chan Monasteries* 禪苑清規 (preface dated 1103).[48] The verse sections of sūtras and verses by Chan ancestors suffused monastic life.[49] At a large monastery, a postulant might also learn by watching senior monks exchange poems with visiting officials. Abbots regularly included verses in their sermons and presented farewell poetry to departing itinerant monks. A new monk could observe poetic practices and adopt the habitus of the monastic order.[50] The dispositions inculcated by these communities were reinforced by the explicit precepts that survive in prescriptive texts, for example, the various rule books of the Song.

Our direct knowledge of the library holdings for individual Song monasteries is sparse, but many libraries likely contained the primers, encyclopedias, and dictionaries that were frequently reprinted between the eleventh and fourteenth centuries.[51] Monks also created personal collections of books, often by making manuscript copies. Some monastic leaders in addition compiled guidebooks for novices, one such being *Master Wuliang [Zong]shou's Smaller Rules of Purity for Daily Use* 無量壽禪師日用小清規 (colophon dated 1209), also known as *For the Daily Use of Those Entering the Assembly* 入眾日用.[52] Prescriptive texts such as this are especially useful for the modern historian as a kind of archive of social memory.[53] Prescriptive texts, of course, told people what they *should* do and are not descriptions of what people *did* do. These normative texts were a means by which such conventions were dissemi-

---

47. See Zürcher, "Buddhism and Education," as well as Galambos, "Confucian Education in a Buddhist Environment."

48. See Yifa, *Buddhist Monastic Codes,* 127, 129, 137, 176, 196, 201, 206, 213.

49. For a study of the ritual verses in *qinggui,* see Matsuura, *Zenshū kojitsu gemon no kenkyū*; on sūtras recited by Song Chan monks, see Matsuura, *Zenshū shoyō kyōten no kenkyū.*

50. Bourdieu, *Outline of a Theory of Practice,* 88.

51. The extant Buddhist catalogues of the Song period, listed in Shiina, *Sō Gen ban,* 115–116, were mostly created for imperial collections or large printed canon projects. They do not reflect the idiosyncratic holdings of individual libraries, which generally included numerous manuscript books.

52. *Ruzhong riyong* (ZZ63.556b7) gives the alternate titles; (558c17) has the dated colophon by Zongshou.

53. My thinking about what I refer to as "prescriptive texts" has been enriched by Campany, *Making Transcendents,* 32–33, which suggests "social memory" as a fruitful approach to religious texts such as hagiographies.

nated. Evidence in subsequent chapters suggests that many monks were knowledgeable about the conventions recorded and handed down in prescriptive texts. This discourse was not disconnected from practices.

Despite, or perhaps because of, the prevalence of literary activity in monasteries, Chinese poetry occupied an ambivalent position in rule and etiquette books, study guides, and primers. At one extreme, the apocryphal but authoritative bodhisattva precept text *Fanwang jing* 梵網經 (**Brahmajālasūtra*) prohibited altogether the study of non-Mahāyāna literature as a danger to progress on the bodhisattva path, a rule interpreted by some later commentators as forbidding categorically the study of poetry.[54] Other texts made allowances for literature if used for proselytization, an exception that I above referred to as instrumental. The influential Tiantai monk Jingxi Zhanran 荊溪湛然 (711–782) and the Song Tiantai monk Zhiyuan both asserted that worldly literature and its composition *should* be studied, but only after attaining the fifth bodhisattva *bhūmi*.[55] This significant level of attainment would ensure that one could help others without creating more karma for oneself.

What did monks know about the Chinese poetic tradition? We may infer the level of monastic knowledge from sources like monastic primers as well as from the poems themselves. Beginning with the latter, to judge from the erudite allusions and quotations in the poetry of elite monks, we know that some read a great deal of mainstream poetry. Zhiyuan, for example, composed poems of appreciation after reading the collected works of Bai Juyi, Du Mu 杜牧 (903–852), Luo Yin 羅隱 (833–910), Qiji 齊己 (864–937?), and others. The Southern Song Chan monk Yayu Shaosong 亞愚紹嵩 (fl. 1229–1232) created hundreds of poems that quoted from the works of 108 Tang and 137 Song poets.[56] At the opposite extreme, an illiterate monk might be able to recite songs and orally create verse, as Huineng is depicted doing in the *Platform Sūtra*. What is likely is that fully ordained monks were generally familiar with at least the basic formal traits of regulated poetry, including tonal prosody, end rhyme, and couplets of single line length, and, to a lesser extent, the rich tradition that informed literary allusions. Song monastic primers included concise explications of the histories and conventions of genres, literary allusions, and historical precedents. The appearance of similar materials in both primers and poems suggests coherence within the broader monastic literary culture. Song monks were enthusiastically collecting, circulating, and composing all these works, thus creating and fueling a monastic audience for poetry.

A range of individual knowledge is reflected in other kinds of sources as well, including those recounting the lives of eminent monks. Precocious boys

---

54. *Fanwang jing* (Funayama 164–165, 384–385; T24.1006c19–23) and the Southern Song commentary *Fanwang pusajie jing shu zhu* (ZZ38.113a16).

55. In their respective exegeses of *Vimalakīrtinirdeśa*, Zhiyuan's *Weimojing lüeshu chuiyuji* (T38.761a25-b9) draws directly from Zhanran's *Weimo jing shu ji* (ZZ18.892a1–4).

56. See *Yayu Jiang Zhe jixing jiju shi*. These numbers are from Zhang Fuqing, "Cong Shaosong." Shaosong appears to have quoted poems that he had committed to memory.

ostensibly learned thousands of Tang poems before they were fully ordained, as was the case with Hongzhi Zhengjue 宏智正覺 (1091–1157). Other monks, such as the eminent Chan master Dahui Zonggao 大慧宗杲 (1089–1163), famously did not display such literary aptitude in their initial learning.[57] The uneven landscape of monks' poetry was in part the result of individual talent and circumstances. Particularly well-educated clerics such as Daoqian 道潛 (1043–after 1111?) could write poems that were indistinguishable from those of any other member of the literati.[58] Already in the Song, literati interlocutors sometimes referred to those who were especially talented as "poet-monks" (*shiseng* 詩僧), a term of Tang-era origins, in part to distinguish them from the merely competent monastic officer or abbot. The moniker "poet-monk" was not entirely complimentary, however, as I explain below. For the most part, monastic knowledge of Chinese poetry ranged from capable familiarity to masterful command of the tradition.

To look again at Zhiyuan's "Poetry Demon," we can see that the poem participated simultaneously in religious and literary contexts. In pursuing a method that draws together Buddhological and poetic analyses, I hope to avoid reducing the study of religion to an analysis of literary techniques; nor do I wish to limit the study of literature to that of a history of Buddhist thought and institutions. I am convinced that literary studies and Buddhist studies can inform one another. As an object of historical analysis, the term "monastic literary culture" has the salutary effect of drawing our attention toward thinking about how poetry was understood by and functioned for Buddhist monks in the Song dynasty. By "literary culture" I am referring to the intersections of ideals, conventions, and norms with practices of learning, writing, and literary production. These textual practices were manifested by historical people as they negotiated several simultaneous cultural expectations. My approach is not unlike the recent examination of Zhongfeng Mingben 中峰明本 (1263–1323) by Natasha Heller, who has considered the multiple media and genres deployed by Mingben as part of the cultural repertoire or toolkit of a Chan master.[59] While her approach could fruitfully be expanded to take stock of the particular approaches of monks throughout the Northern and Southern Song, my work is focused on genres rather than individual biography. Productive

---

57. The literary education of Hongzhi and Dahui and other monks is discussed in Yü, "Ch'an Education in the Sung," 80–81.

58. The date of Daoqian's death is debated. Kong, "*Song shiseng Daoqian shengping kaolüe*," 181–182, has persuasively proposed that Daoqian died within two or three years of returning from Kaifeng to Jiangnan in 1105. I, however, found in the early Yuan edition of *Canliaozi shiji* held at National Central Library in Taipei, that the front of each fascicle reads: "Recompiled by Zonghui, a latter heir of Canliao from Tianning of Ningbo" 四明前天寧參寥後裔宗譓重集. Tianning Temple in Ningbo was so called only after an edict in 1111 and until it was destroyed in the Song-Jin wars in ca. 1130; the reconstructed temple was re-named in the early S. Song (see *Baoqing Siming zhi*, 11/5130). If this edition compiled by Zonghui (n.d.) accurately names Daoqian's position, then Daoqian would have resided at the temple and not retired before 1111.

59. Heller, *Illusory Abiding*, 309–310, 336–348, developing ideas found in Campany, "On the Very Idea of Religions."

pathways through literary cultures have been suggested by recent studies that understand genres as creative resources for living traditions.[60]

Before explaining what I mean by genre, I want to alert the reader that this book is not a survey, or comprehensive history, of all monks' poetry and verse of the Northern and Southern Song dynasties. Scholars have noted that the study of a literary culture is not compatible with an ambition to comprehensiveness.[61] Nor is this book a history detailing a series of breakthroughs and presented as a teleological evolution of ideas. I am moreover not proposing a definition or a checklist for what is or is not Buddhist poetry. I do not frame arguments about Buddhist contributions to Chinese literary history, and I do not intend to discuss a transhistorical "Buddhist reading of poetry."[62]

This project would of course be impossible but for pioneering and erudite studies on Buddhist poetry in China.[63] I nonetheless depart from several methodological assumptions of that earlier work. First, I avoid taking normative rhetoric as a guide for historical practices. For example, I do not assume that Chinese poetry *should* be better suited to expressing ineffable truths than other forms of language. Song monks did not think that *shi* somehow naturally escaped the limitations of all language to express the ineffable. Second, I do not conflate the rhetoric of Song-era literati—who depicted the intellectual pleasures of suddenly completing a couplet as equivalent to a deep insight gained through *samādhi*—with the practices of monks. A lay poet's appropriation of Chan rhetoric should not be mistaken for descriptions of historical practices by Chan monks. These same poets, after all, often held monks' writing in low regard. Third, I do not rely directly on later interpretations by Ming-dynasty monks, who re-imagined Song-era Buddhism to support their own convictions. Such retrospective projections are not transparent windows onto Song practices. Works by medieval Japanese Zen monks likewise offer important but partial views of these same practices.[64]

I avoid these pitfalls by thinking about how individual monastic writers

---

60. Hallisey, *Therigatha,* and Salomon, "Aśvaghoṣa's Saundarananda."

61. Tian, *Beacon Fire and Shooting Star,* 4. Similarly, Pollock's introduction to his *Literary Cultures in History,* 14.

62. Rouzer, *On Cold Mountain,* 11. The reading practices advocated by Rouzer are laudably grounded in the historical reception of Hanshan, primarily that of Hakuin's insightful commentary to the Hanshan corpus.

63. Pioneers in Japan include the monastic scholars Shaku Seitan 釋清潭 (fl. 1892–1938) and, later, Hata Egyaku 秦慧玉 (1896–1985). Significant modern Japanese scholarship includes works by Iriya Yoshitaka and Kaji Tetsujō 加地哲定. Taiwanese scholarship can be traced to Ba Hutian 巴壺天, then Du Songbo; historical cultural analysis began with Hsiao Li-hua, *Tangdai Shige yu Chanxue,* which one can compare with Sun Changwu, *Chansi yu Shiqing,* published on the mainland that same year. The Chinese field has grown exponentially. Volumes written or edited by Zhou Yukai are especially noteworthy. In English, important positions were laid out by Bernard Faure, Robert Gimello, and Richard John Lynn. Works by these authors are listed in the bibliography.

64. For a skillful overview of the relationship between Song literature and Zen, see "The Kōan and the Chinese Literary Game" in Hori, *Zen Sand,* 41–61.

learned genre norms and selectively put them into practice. These days, genres are often thought of as boxes into which we can pigeonhole texts or speech acts. I have tried to set aside preconceptions about Buddhist poetry and instead begin with the Song-era texts themselves.[65] This inductive kind of genre studies is useful because it is not about pigeonholes so much as about the pigeons.[66] Poems do not belong to genres so much as participate in propagating, modifying, and expanding them. The genre, then, should be analyzed for its social functions as well as for its role in transmitting cultural know-how. In other words, I also pay attention to how Song writers imagined pigeonholes, or genre norms, in order to understand how this influenced their production of verse. The eager acolyte of Song Buddhism would garner knowledge of conventions and expectations, which could then inform his textual practices. My method here is to cycle between monastic literature that espouses ideals about poetry and monks' actual practices of poetry. This kind of genre studies, then, is about norms and practices. The relationships of literary norms and practices being analogous to those of religious norms and practices, I am convinced that this is a fruitful way to study religion and literature together. As a result, the book before you participates in the sociology of literature in addition to Buddhist studies.

Texts and Contexts of Monasticism in the Song Dynasty and After

This book includes in translation about equal numbers of poems and writings in prose. I compare works by Chan masters, a Tiantai monk, and several poet-monks, all of whom differed both in their attitudes to language as a medium for teaching Buddhist truths and in their explanations regarding the usefulness of poetry. I will introduce several major figures whose poems appear most frequently; however, the dramatis personae assumes a certain amount of knowledge about Song monasticism, the differences between Chan and Tiantai (which I refer to as sects of Chinese Buddhism), and the shared heritage of all Buddhist monastics in the Song.

Tiantai and Chan monks generally resided in separate public monasteries and had relatively strong sectarian identities that correlated to distinct sets of textual knowledge, doctrinal positions, and modes of praxis. Other monks lived in smaller private temples; they did not necessarily have strong sectarian identities and might adhere only to more mainstream monastic norms. The different institutional contexts varied widely in ways that impacted the creation of verse. The poetry written at a large public institution like Lingyin Monastery 靈隱寺 of Hangzhou differed from the contemporaneous poems written at a small private hermitage on nearby West Lake. Although sectarian identities and institutional contexts were significant in many respects,

---

65. This and subsequent ideas about "genre" reference Culler, *Theory of the Lyric*, 39–90.
66. Newsom, "Pairing Research Questions," citing the vivid metaphor of Fowler, *Kinds of Literature*, 37.

common values were shared by many, if not all, elite monks in the Song dynasty. One among the numerous sources that give us insight into these mainstream norms is the *Essential Reading for Buddhist Monks* 釋氏要覽. This encyclopedic primer compiled by the monk Daocheng 道誠 (fl. 1009–1019) was frequently reprinted throughout the Song and was referenced by writers across all sects. Further to the matter of sectarian distinctions, as Griffith Foulk has noted, the buildings and layout of so-called Chan public monasteries were largely similar to those of later Tiantai and Vinaya public monasteries. The latter two sects followed their own "rules of purity" codes that were modeled closely on the earlier Chan "rules of purity." The result was that, for the general assembly of monks, most daily practices, training, education, and regimens within large Buddhist monasteries were similar regardless of sect. Differences mattered more among elite monks; still, the monks' poetry in this book was written by men who shared general assumptions about deportment and education. Following Foulk, I will call this "mainstream" monasticism.[67] For advanced students and monastery leaders, this mainstream monastic education coexisted with their specialized sectarian learning.

Already in the Northern Song, large public monasteries in the lower Yangzi River region housed well over a thousand monks at a time.[68] In addition to the public monasteries of various sizes, smaller private monasteries, which I will refer to as temples, dotted the landscape of the Song. Also called "hereditary temples" (*jiayi si* 甲乙寺) or sometimes "Vinaya temples" (*lüsi* 律寺), these private temples constituted the majority of the thirty-nine thousand officially registered Buddhist monasteries in the middle of the Northern Song.[69] The legal distinction between public and private corresponded to the mechanisms of patronage for an abbot.[70] Living in a small temple could determine what kinds of verse a monk might write. For example, Daoqian, who was celebrated for his poetry in his own lifetime, lived mostly in private temples. His poetry often reflects life at a smaller temple with only a handful of monks near an urban cultural center. His collected poems are like mainstream literati poetry, with almost no verses comparable to those in the collections of Chan masters. He did not have a strong sectarian identity, and sectarian learning is not readily visible in his poetry. Some monks living in private temples, on the other hand, did practice sectarian Buddhism. In 1016, near the end of his life, Gushan Zhiyuan raised funds to purchase land for a

---

67. Foulk, "Myth, Ritual, and Monastic Practice," 150, 167.

68. For example, Lingyin Monastery of Hangzhou had over one thousand monks, *Chanlin sengbao zhuan* (ZZ79.515a8–10). Schlütter, *How Zen Became Zen* (99–101), and Protass, "Geographic History" (148n136), give additional examples.

69. These numbers from Schlütter, *How Zen Became Zen*, 36.

70. The abbot of a public monastery was decided by imperial officials, sometimes in consultation with local Buddhist leaders. Control of private temples passed directly from master to disciple, without involving government officials, and were thus called "hereditary." The name "Vinaya temple" referred to the idea that succession would follow Buddhist canon law rather than Song public law. In practice, local patronage could be a significant determinant.

private temple on West Lake, where he instructed his disciples in Tiantai teachings.[71] Zhiyuan had a strong sectarian identity, and, I argue, his Tiantai learning is visible in his poetry. Another example of a monk outside the public monastery system is the eccentric Jingduan 淨端 (1031–1104), who watched over the private merit cloister for the family of Zhang Dun 章惇 (1035–1105).[72] Such "merit cloisters" (gongde yuan 功德院) were built and controlled by families or local stakeholders, with the karmic benefits directed to parents and forebears. Jingduan's verses include didactic songs as well as occasional poetry exchanged with literati. With an itinerant career in and out of sectarian spaces, his verse reflects the changing social and ritual contexts of his life.

The public monasteries that developed during the Song, on the other hand, were centers of sectarian learning for elite students. This context mattered for poetry composed by Chan or Tiantai abbots of public monasteries. Public, or literally a temple "of the ten directions" 十方, was a legal status granted by the imperial government, which conferred, along with legal standing, both privileges and obligations.[73] Unlike private temples that were under local control and did not require sectarian identity, every public monastery had an official sectarian designation, classified either as a "Chan public monastery" 十方禪院, the first and most numerous of the designations; "Teachings public monastery" 十方教院, dedicated to either Tiantai or Huayan;[74] or "Vinaya public monastery" 十方律院, after an official Vinaya lineage was created. These designations restricted the monastery's abbacy to recognized members of the designated sect. Only a Chan master could be the abbot of a Chan public monastery. An abbot's sectarian identity correlated with the specialized rituals he performed several times each month, as well as his private training of advanced students. These advanced students might hold positions in the monastery bureaucracy. For the vast general assembly of ordinary monks, however, these monasteries inculcated mainstream monastic education. But here I am dealing with poetry, and poetry was written largely by abbots and monastic officers. Buddhist sectarian differences therefore often mattered.

The public monastery system as a form of monasticism had standardized daily routines and rituals that were codified in "rules of purity." As detailed in

---

71. Tam, "Life and Thought of Zhiyuan," 187–193.

72. Earlier, he was abbot of a small temple that Liu Yi 劉誼 (jinshi 1067) converted into a public monastery. Jingduan was considered an outsider by his contemporaries, according to three biographies (a hagiographic zhuan 傳, a eulogistic xingye ji 行業記, and a necrography muzhi 墓誌) and the S. Song preface in Wushan Jingduan chanshi yulu (ZZ73.71a22–24).

73. Throughout this section, I draw on Schlütter, "Vinaya Monasteries, Public Abbacies, and State Control."

74. On successful efforts by Zhili and Zunshi to establish Tiantai public monasteries, in 1012 and 1020, respectively, see Getz, "Siming Zhili," 129–163, and Stevenson, "Protocols of Power," 347–350. Based on these Tiantai precedents, "A petition to [the prefectural government of] Hangzhou seeking Huiyin Chan Cloister be converted into a [public] ten-directions teachings cloister and abbatial seat" 謹奏杭州乞將慧因禪院改為十方教院住持事 sought a public teaching abbacy dedicated to Huayan in 1088. A stele inscription also from 1088 commemorated its success. Yucen shan Huiyin Gaoli Huayan jiaosi zhi, fascs. 9, 6.

Chapter 4, these prescriptive texts supported a tradition of norms regarding the monastic uses of literary learning. Their widespread circulation is reflected in the preface to a 1202 edition of the foundational *Rules of Purity for Chan Monasteries*, a text completed nearly a century earlier in 1103, which contained a note that previous woodblocks had been used so often that many words had worn away. By the late twelfth century, these new rule books had gained an authoritative status in public monasteries "equal to that of the Vinaya," as Foulk writes.[75] Moreover, we can see that many of the rites and protocols prescribed in these rule books closely match the activities described in other sources from the eleventh to fourteenth centuries. Rule books reflected widespread protocols regarding verse culture and in turn became the means by which procedures at public monasteries were further standardized.

Additional rule books were compiled over the succeeding centuries and evince deep and sustained intertextuality. Some focused on daily life in the general assembly and were addressed to newcomers. A second type of rule book, addressed primarily to monastic officers, expanded on details that were known from or could be found in the *Rules of Purity for Chan Monasteries* and included model texts one could copy out for rituals and bureaucratic procedures. A third type consisted of local supplements for a single monastic community. These Song texts persisted into the Yuan, and *Baizhang's Rules of Purity, revised by imperial order* 勅修百丈清規, compiled between 1335 and 1338 under Yuan imperial direction, was based on the 1103 *Rules of Purity for Chan Monasteries* together with the later addenda.[76] Additional Yuan-era publications of *Rules of Purity for Teachings Monasteries* 教苑清規 (preface 1347) and *Rules of Purity for Vinaya Monasteries* 律苑事規 (preface 1324) further illustrate the hegemony of the Song-Yuan *qinggui* model for public monasteries that began in the eleventh century.[77]

Taken together, these interrelated "rules of purity" texts underpinned a general contiguity of monastic culture across public monasteries from the eleventh to fourteenth centuries. Historians of Chinese religions such as Barend J. Ter Haar have argued that the period from 1100 to 1340 was "a single coherent period" in the history of Buddhist lay movements.[78] I have observed a similar coherent period for the poetry by elite Chan abbots and monastic officers from the Northern Song through the Yuan, at least at the well-endowed public monasteries. Yuan sources can and should, of course, be studied to analyze the history of the Yuan as a distinct period in Chinese

75. Foulk, "*Chanyuan qinggui* and Other 'Rules of Purity,'" 297, limits his claim to the Zhejiang area.

76. The *Chixiu* text effectively displaced the others over the coming centuries. On this text, see Foulk, "*Chanyuan qinggui*," 304, and Yifa, *Buddhist Monastic Codes*, 49.

77. The writings of the Japanese pilgrim Shunjō 俊芿 (1166–1227) strongly suggest that some similar rules were already in place at Teachings and Vinaya public abbacies in the late twelfth century, over a century before the official *qinggui*.

78. Ter Harr, "Buddhist Inspired Options," 96, observes continuities in the history of lay Buddhist movements. Cited in a relevant passage of Heller, *Illusory Abiding*, 14.

Buddhist history. Here, however, I am primarily interested in Yuan-dynasty manuscripts of individual poems that were written in the lower Yangzi area and that evince similarities with earlier Song Chan culture.[79] I will avoid sweeping conclusions about Yuan Buddhism and will be transparent about the methodological challenges of using Yuan sources to hypothesize about traces of Song Buddhist monasticism.

I have, moreover, generally avoided the backward projection of later developments. For example, when interpreting poetry from the very early Northern Song written by Gushan Zhiyuan, I have given preference to pan-sectarian normative texts of that period, in addition to Zhiyuan's own exegetical writing, rather than texts from later centuries. The Tiantai monasteries of the early Northern Song did not compile "rules of purity" *per se*. Still, Ciyun Zunshi 慈雲遵式 (964–1032) did set down a code of regulations for Tianzhu Monastery 天竺寺 in Hangzhou.[80] When Foulk examined the similarities between Zunshi's regulations, Chan rules, and the Yuan dynasty Tiantai rule book, he concluded "that the monastic rules they used were nearly identical at both the early and the late phases of that development."[81] Here, Foulk is highlighting those shared aspects of mainstream Buddhist monasticism across this period. At the same time, because poetry was written by elite monks, these sectarian differences mattered. Stevenson describes the distinctive halls constructed in Northern Song Tiantai monasteries for specialized practice, as well as Song practicum for contemplation and repentance, both of which would have been unfamiliar to a monk in a Chan monastery.[82] In other words, Chan and Tiantai monks differed in substantial ways that we must take into account when reading their poetry, and yet they had enough in common that their poems are worth comparing.

When I emphasize the general contiguity among "rules of purity" from Song to Yuan, I wish to draw a contrast with the monastic legal texts from later periods that reflect dramatic transformations within Chinese monasticism. For example, the nineteenth-century *Verified Exegeses of Baizhang's Rules of Purity* 百丈清規證義記, although a valuable commentary, often includes explanations that can be traced to late-Ming reformations. Shifts in monastic forms are also evidenced in late-Ming rule books like *Essential Extracts of Rules and Rites for the Novitiate* 沙彌律儀要略, by Yunqi Zhuhong 雲棲株宏 (1535–1615), as well as the *Huangbo [Ōbaku] Rules of Purity* 黃檗清規, compiled by the émigré monk Yinyuan Longqi 隱元隆琦 (1592–1693). Some continuities with the earlier periods are present; however, these late Ming rule books

---

79. Heller, *Illusory Abiding*, 7–10, 175–188, notes that during the Yuan dynasty, Chan monasteries in the eastern region around Jiangnan were still organized in a manner similar to that of the preceding Song period.

80. Yifa, *Buddhist Monastic Codes*, 35–37. For a detailed overview of the life and importance of Zunshi, see Stevenson, "Protocols of Power."

81. Foulk, "*Chanyuan qinggui*," 306.

82. Stevenson, "Where Meditative Theory Meets Practice," 74–75, 84–85, 119–121. Stevenson, "Hall for the Sixteen Contemplations," 148, 156, 157–171, 174.

reflect a new literary culture with new and different attitudes toward poetry.[83] This new attitude toward poetry is also visible in Ming-era collections of writing by Chan masters, which began to include genres of poetry that had been excluded from Song collections.

The primary sources of Song monks' poetry can be divided into four types. The Song-era construction of these disparate types, and the stabilization of titling practices, was itself important for creating a monastic audience for poetry. These texts also mirrored some of the above-mentioned institutional contexts. First, verses were included in individual collections of religious writing by Chan masters known as *yulu* 語錄, "recorded sayings"; these collections consist of specialized Chan teaching literature that includes sermons, dialogues, and other writing. As early as the Song, some *yulu* were admitted to the imperially sponsored printed Buddhist canons, but for the most part these texts circulated independently during the period. Second, belletristic collections of an individual monk's poetry are mostly found in the imperial or sinological collectanea, such as *Sibu congkan* or *Siku quanshu*, and were generally excluded from Buddhist canon projects. The titles of such collections are often marked *shiji* ("The collected poems of..."). Some are available only in rare premodern editions. Third, in addition to printed collections, monks' poetry is found in manuscripts. To my knowledge, most manuscripts of individual poems by Song and Yuan Chinese monks are preserved in Japan. Fourth, multiauthor anthologies preserve thousands of verses not found in individual collections. Anthologies are found in the modern Buddhist canons, in sinological collectanea, or rare woodblock editions. I draw on examples from all four types of source material and analyze each to understand the social values that informed how it was constructed, what kinds of verse were included in each text, and how compilers fashioned genre distinctions.

To answer questions about the construction of genres by textual communities of the Song, it is important to attend to historical editions. Over one hundred *yulu* survive for individual Chan masters from the Song and Yuan dynasties; however, I prioritize texts for which direct witnesses to a Song recension are available.[84] I also consulted the early Japanese Gozan editions thought to most closely represent a Song recension.[85] My conscientious use of editions is particularly salient when analyzing paratextual elements such

83. Liao, *Zhong-bian, shi-chan, meng-xi*, offers a foundation for late-Ming Buddhist literary culture.

84. I follow the distinctions between text, recension, edition, ancestral redaction, and witness outlined in Roth, "Text and Edition." Unless otherwise noted, I take the *Taishō shinshū daizōkyō* and *Dai Nihon zoku zōkyō* as *textus receptus*. I use "modern critical edition" to refer to contemporary books with a critical apparatus of either annotations and/or a comparison of editions.

85. I use "Gozan editions" to refer to Japanese editions from the Kamakura or Muromachi period. Gozan is sometimes used to refer to early Edo editions; however, I refer to these as "Edo editions." See an overview of Gozan print culture by Sumiyoshi Tomohiko 住吉朋彦 in Shimao, *Higashi Ajia no naka no Gozan bunka*, 132–150.

as titles of individual poems and genre categories in sectional headers.[86] I have found that paratexts and genre boundaries were frequently altered by the compilers of new editions from the sixteenth and seventeenth centuries and onward. In addition to early printed materials, manuscripts offer opportunities to circumvent the work of even a Song-dynasty editor.

As for belletristic collections, surviving sources from the Southern Song are more numerous than those from the Northern Song. Zhou Yukai enumerates forty-two titles of Northern Song belletristic collections listed in catalogues, most of which do not survive.[87] Huang Ch'i-chiang has collected the titles of forty-six belletristic collections by individual monks from the mid-to-late Southern Song, several of which are extant.[88] Huang Ch'i-chiang has argued that this is evidence of a sudden increase in the number of monks who wrote mainstream poetry from the mid-Southern Song on.[89] This apparent increase was at least in part also the result of a twofold historiographic problem. First, widespread print culture did not develop until at least midway through the Northern Song, and many more printed books were created in the Southern Song. Second, one Southern Song official estimated that between 40 to 50 percent of all Chinese books in existence were missing after the fall of Kaifeng in 1127, which gives an impression of significant losses, even if likely exaggerated.[90] Southern Song texts were also more likely to survive in part because of the bibliomania of the Japanese pilgrims who arrived in significant numbers from the late twelfth century on. We simply have much more material from the Southern Song and need to adjust our analysis accordingly when comparing the Northern and Southern Song dynasties.

In the monastic literary culture from the eleventh to fourteenth centuries, the major genres of prescriptive texts, *yulu*, and poetry collections show a remarkable level of contiguity. Finer periodization is possible and warranted when analyzing an individual writer, however. The above-described intellectual, institutional, and sociological variations provide the structure of the dramatis personae. I return throughout the book to the terms introduced here for specificity and nuance within the broader landscape of monastic literary culture.

---

86. My terms are developed from Genette, *Paratexts*, with adaptations for sinology.

87. Zhou, *Fayan yu shixin*, 95–98.

88. See Huang Ch'i-chiang, *Yiwei Chan*, 3–7. Aside from the pioneering research by Huang and by Xu Hongxia, the literary collections of Southern Song monks have been little studied. Many of these books were reproduced in the *Chanmen yishu* series, although not always the best edition.

89. Huang Ch'i-chiang, *Yiwei Chan*, 38.

90. See De Weerdt, "Discourse of Loss in Song Dynasty Private and Imperial Book Collecting." De Weerdt argues that the memory of the loss of books was often noted during the later development of private and commercial printing and cannot be taken at face value. See also Chia and De Weerdt's introduction to *Knowledge and Text Production*, 14, on the limitations of our sources for quantitative analysis.

Dramatis Personae

The following figures, Buddhist monks whose works most often feature in this book, are Chan abbots, a Tiantai master, and poet-monks, mostly from the Northern Song period. Extant manuscripts and printed books from the Northern Song are few, and thus works by Chan masters from the late Southern Song are foregrounded in Chapters 2 and 5, where I emphasize these kinds of evidence. These elite monks had much in common in terms of their general monastic education as well as their assumptions about monastic etiquette and deportment. We can nevertheless distinguish them as Chan, Tiantai, or poet-monks, for these distinctions mattered for their institutional horizons, sectarian rituals, and specialized textual learning. My selections, though necessarily limited by the constraints of space, are intended to convey several important perspectives.

Tiantai monk Gushan Zhiyuan, whose poem opened this chapter, is only one of many Tiantai monks who wrote poetry in the Song dynasty. The poems by Zhiyuan offer a valuable counterbalance to an examination of Song Chan monks. In general, Northern Song Tiantai monks both wrote *shi* in mainstream literary modes and composed verse for rituals. Ciyun Zunshi was reputedly a talented writer. Xu Duanfu 許端夫 (act. late N. Song) compared Zunshi's poetry favorably to that of both the earlier poet-monk Guanxiu 貫休 (832–913) and his contemporary Gushan Zhiyuan.[91] Despite his poetic talent, less than twenty *shi* from Zunshi's belletristic poetry collections survive, and only the two collections of didactic and liturgical verse are extant.[92] Another prominent Tiantai monk, Jingjue Renyue 淨覺仁岳 (992–1064), composed a suite of nineteen verses about the life of the Buddha for use in annual observances of the Buddha's *parinirvāṇa*. He noted that he was inspired by the suites composed by Zhiyuan and Zunshi.[93] The Vinaya revivalist Lingzhi Yuanzhao 靈芝元照 (1048–1116) wrote verse compositions that resemble these broader Tiantai trends.[94] Selections of poetry by other Song Tiantai monks survive in anthologies and local gazetteers. In contrast to these fragmentary or lost collections, Zhiyuan stands out as a Tiantai monk of the Song for whom a large corpus of *shi* survives. Nearly four hundred poems fill fifteen fascicles of *Compilation of Idle Dwelling* 閑居編 (hereafter *Xianju bian*), a collection of

---

91. *Fozu tongji* (T49.209a15–23).

92. The collections of didactic verse are *Tianzhu bieji* 天竺別集 and *Jin yuan ji* 金園集; the lost collections of poetry are entitled *Ling yuan ji* 靈苑集 and *Cai yi ji* 采遺集. Only seventeen complete poems and three fragments of couplets attributed to Zunshi are in *Quan Song shi*, 2:1111–1114. For information and analysis of Zunshi's poems, see Shi Guojing, "Ciyun Zunshi yu Tianzhu si," 124–138.

93. *Shijia rulai niepan lizanwen* (T46.964a1–6). Stevenson, "Buddhist Ritual," 347n23, notes the ongoing use of Renyue's liturgy.

94. Yuanzhao's preface to his mixed prose and verse *Lanpen xiangong yi* (ZZ74.1069a8–16) notes that he modeled the ritual on a text by Zhiyuan. The verses in Yuanzhao's sing-song *Daoju fu* (ZZ59.603c6–604b7) resemble edifying songs for children.

Zhiyuan's essays, epistles, poems, and miscellaneous writing. Across twelve extant books, 108 fascicles of writing by Zhiyuan survive (of an estimated 150 in total output), including lengthy commentaries on *Vimalakīrtinirdeśa* and *Mahāyāna Mahāparinirvāṇasūtra*. This makes it possible to interpret his poetry against his own sūtra exegesis, as I do in Chapters 4 and 6. I include additional information about Zhiyuan's life in Chapter 6, including his place in what became known as the "home mountain" and "off mountain" factions. The juxtaposition of *shi* by Tiantai monks against *jisong* by Chan monks highlights important differences between them in terms of Buddhist doctrine as well as literary qualities.

A large majority of monks' poetry from the Song dynasty was written in Chan public monasteries by abbots, monastic officers, and itinerant students. Most poems in this book were composed by Chan monks, at least twenty-five of them abbots. An abbot was the administrative head of a monastery compound and religious teacher of the community of monks that resided there. A Chan monk earned the moniker Chan master when he received his first abbatial appointment. The abbot of a Chan public monastery was necessarily from a Chan lineage, an heir of the ineffable Buddha mind, the awakening transmitted from master to disciple. Chan abbots performed daily and monthly rituals in a distinctive Chan style, and instructed advanced students in specialized Chan learning. I provide the name of the particular lineage, or Chan family, to which each Chan master belonged, but I do not use Chan lineages as analytic categories. Nearly all Chan abbots wrote poetry, with differences manifesting mostly in rhetoric and poetics along a spectrum. Among the poetry of Chan monks, I distinguish the two impulses toward language described by Robert Gimello as the "more radical" and the "conservative."[95] Radical interpretations of the dicta "do not rely on the written word" (*buli wenzi* 不立文字) or "do not rely on written or spoken language" (*buli wenzi yuyan* 不立文字語言) led to poetry that employed the apophatic rhetoric of subitism, or the sudden teaching.[96] Humor and misdirection, clever allusions, and literary techniques were used to instruct students. Many of the parting poems analyzed in Chapter 5 are examples of this style. Individual Chan abbots did not, however, necessarily maintain a single philosophical position on the utility or dangers of poetry and might take variously radical and conservative positions in different situations. Poems written with a conservative attitude regard Chinese poetry more positively, viewing the literary tradition as a valuable medium for communication. I intend these distinctions not as hard-and-fast categories, and certainly not as sociological groups, but rather as relative inclinations by individuals toward the usefulness and limitations of poetry.

---

95. Gimello, "Mārga and Culture," 374–379.

96. Buswell, "Ch'an Hermeneutics," 241–245. See Gimello, "Apophatic and kataphatic Discourse," on the philosophical underpinnings of negative versus positive registers of discourse in Buddhist China.

Works by four Northern Song Chan masters appear often. First is Xuedou Chongxian 雪竇重顯 (980–1052), a Yunmen lineage Chan abbot who was quite a popular teacher in his own lifetime, active especially in the eastern coastal areas near Hangzhou Bay, and very influential on the later tradition. More than 250 of his poems are extant. Chongxian was a talented literary stylist with a playful style. Collections of his writing were already circulating widely in his lifetime and afterward went on to become a fixture in the Chan canon. The second Chan master is Huanglong Huinan 黃龍慧南 (1002–1069). A Linji abbot of public monasteries of Hunan and Jiangxi, he maintained by comparison a relatively radical attitude toward poetry, so much so that there are only fourteen poems in his *yulu*. The two of Huinan's verses that I translate engage in straightforward subitist rhetoric and poetics. Here I want to affirm that we should not confuse the iconoclastic rhetoric of cenobitic abbots like Huinan—what Bernard Faure calls "domesticated" radicalism meant to challenge students and lead them toward liberation—with actual radical behavior and eremitism.[97] Huinan's verses served ritual and social functions within an established monastic context. The least known today is the relatively conservative figure Cishou Huaishen 慈受懷深 (1077–1132). A Yunmen lineage Chan abbot, he headed several prominent monasteries in Jiangnan. He then spent six years in Kaifeng as abbot of the prestigious Huilin Chan Cloister 慧林禪院, one of two public Chan institutions within the enormous Xiangguo Monastery 相國寺 located footsteps from the imperial palace. An early imprint dated 1135 of one of his *yulu* survives. Cishou crafted songs for children, fashioned imitations of Hanshan poetry, and was generally fond of poeticizing. The fourth figure is the important Linji lineage Chan master Yuanwu Keqin 圓悟克勤 (1063–1135), best known for creating *Blue Cliff Record* 碧巖錄. I focus, however, on his extant *jisong* and funeral verse, poetic writing by Keqin that addressed social and ritual situations. Keqin generally maintained a radical attitude toward language, his rhetoric focused on didacticism, with frequent allusions to Chan lore. These four figures are useful guides to the range of attitudes by Chan masters between 1020 and 1130, before the Song-Jin wars precipitated the collapse of the Northern Song.[98]

Of the numerous mid-to-late Southern Song Chan masters, I focus most on Xutang Zhiyu 虛堂智愚 (1186–1270), the Linji lineage abbot of several prominent public monasteries in the Lower Yangtze region during the waning decades of the Southern Song. As an abbot in Ningbo, Xutang encountered numerous pilgrims from abroad and is remembered as the teacher of several important Japanese Zen monks. Xutang is a useful example for at least four reasons. Most important is that a redaction of his *yulu* dated 1269, compiled and printed shortly after his death, survives in a Southern Song edition, of

---

97. Faure, *Rhetoric of Immediacy*, 24–31.

98. See Protass, "Geographic History," 143–156, on some effects of the Song-Jin wars on the demise of certain Chan lineages.

which there is also a faithful Gozan reproduction dated 1313.[99] In other words, a collection of his poetic verse survives in an early xylographic edition created by his own community, and not a subsequent redaction that might have been altered by later editors. Second, the genres and modes of Xutang's poetry offer us a view of the poetic life of a Chan abbot at the twilight of the Song dynasty. Third, because he had numerous Japanese disciples, including Nanpo Jōmin 南浦紹明 (1235–1309), additional poems by his community circulated and survived in Japan, making possible analysis of an authorial community. A collection of sixty-eight poems created by his disciples and other associated monks offers us a coherent set of texts composed by a clearly defined local community. Fourth, examples of Xutang's poetry written in his own calligraphy survived in Japan, enabling the comparison of his poetry in manuscript and printed forms. It is unusual for so many types of material for one Song-era figure to survive. One may compare Xutang's radical rhetoric and strict monasticism with the conservative attitude toward literature of Beijian Jujian 北磵居簡 (1164–1246) and his disciple Wuchu Daguan 物初大觀 (1201–1268), Linji masters in the lineage of Dahui. Beijian and Daguan were part of a network of what modern Chinese scholars call "literary monks" 文學僧.[100] These Southern Song literary Chan monks are distinguished by their production of lengthy collections of belletristic writing, each containing many hundreds of poems, and relatively brief *yulu*. In contrast, Xutang Zhiyu left a comprehensive *yulu* and no belletristic writing. Although I discuss the collected works of literary monks in Chap. 2, and briefly analyze some of their writing in Chap. 4, given the constraints of space, a detailed consideration of the voluminous output by this group of Southern Song monks is beyond the scope of this book. To review the range of monkish writers associated with Chan public monasteries, in addition to these above-mentioned Northern Song and Southern Song Chan abbots, who displayed a range of attitudes toward language itself, I also translate poems by lesser-known abbots and monastic officers.

Compared with Tiantai and Chan abbots, a third group of poeticizing monks wrote verses that do not reflect strong institutional identities. This is likely because they did not serve as abbots of public monasteries and instead relied on their poetry and scholarship for patronage. Some monks of this type rose to fame as *shiseng*, "poet-monks," a term often used to deprecate, and from the mid-eighth century on, members of the literati wrote about poet-monks who were not poets in the full sense of that term.[101] This critical denotation continued in the Song. Ye Mengde 葉夢得 (1077–1148), for

---

99. See the text notes in *Gozan-ban Chūgoku zenseki sōkan*, 8.738–743. The only known Song edition at Seikidō bunko 成簀堂文庫 with a colophon dated 1269 is partially damaged. Per Shiina, the 1313 Gozan edition accurately reproduces the content and structure of the Seikidō bunko edition, except for the section clearly appended at the conclusion after the Song colophon.

100. See especially Huang Ch'i-chiang's recent Chinese-language monographs, including *Nan Song liu wenxue seng jinian lu*, which establishes this group's sociological connections.

101. Mazanec, "Invention of Chinese Buddhist Poetry," 33–82, explicates the genealogy of

example, offered sweeping criticisms of even the most well-known Tang poet-monks and their numerous Song imitators, as well as disparagement of the "monastic style of poetry, still unrefined, that [monks] make for themselves" 自作一種僧體，格律尤凡俗, and which others referred to as "monks' poetry" (*sengshi* 僧詩).[102] Song-era critics, moreover, described a succession of poet-monks active from the mid-Tang through to the Song as if they formed some kind of social institution. The bands of Tang and Song poet-monks in these lists did not, though, constitute a Buddhist lineage in any formal sense.

Because of the negative connotations in emic usage, I avoid the term "poet-monk" as a critical category and use it only as shorthand to refer to this third type of monk. The primary representative of this third type is Daoqian. Although Daoqian is not well-known to modern readers, he enjoyed wide fame as a monastic poet in his own lifetime. Several Qing scholars judged Daoqian's poems to be the finest of any monk in the Song.[103] Most modern scholars still assume that Daoqian belonged to the Yunmen Chan lineage, as implied by Chen Shidao 陳師道 (1053–1102) in an epistle that became the preface to Daoqian's collected works. But Daoqian never became the abbot of a Chan monastery or otherwise participated in the institutional life of any large public abbacy. His own disciples were known for composing poetry more than for teaching the dharma.[104] To the extent one may judge by comparing his poetry with that of figures like Xuedou Chongxian and Xutang Zhiyu, Daoqian only occasionally hosted itinerant students and seldom participated in the kinds of religious learning that occurred at large public monasteries.

Daoqian and his poetry can be better understood, I would argue, as part of mainstream Buddhist monasticism as well as through his relationships with local monks across sects, scholar-officials, and Kaifeng aristocracy. The most consequential of these associations was his twenty-five-year friendship with Su Shi 蘇軾 (1037–1101), the most celebrated literary figure of the Song dynasty. When Su Shi was once again in exile in 1094, Daoqian sent him an icon of Amitabha.[105] Daoqian's own writing demonstrates that he also associated with Hangzhou-area Tiantai monks. From all this we see that Daoqian was no sectarian partisan. Daoqian's monastic career in general differed markedly from the successful abbots of public monasteries. These differences mattered because they influenced the kinds of poems Daoqian wrote, which are categorically different from much of the verse found in Chan *yulu*.

"poet-monk" as a term of disparagement in the mid-Tang. For continued use in the Song era, see Protass, "Buddhist Monks and Chinese Poetry," 116–158.

102. *Shilin shihua*, 1.31a–b, translated in Protass, "Flavors of Monks' Poetry," 137–138.

103. As in the Qing editors' bibliographic notice, "Tiyao," in *Canliaozi shiji*, SQKS.

104. More on his disciple Faying in Chap. 2 below. Another monk named Congxin 從信 (n.d.) also studied literature with Daoqian and later met Su Shi's son Su Guo 蘇過 (1072–1123), who wrote, "Presented to poet-monk Congxin (who studied poetry with Canliao)" 贈詩僧從信 (信學詩于參寥), *Quan Song shi*, 23:15464.

105. Su thanks Daoqian in a letter, *Su Shi wenji*, 61/1863.

Although Daoqian's poems resemble mainstream poetry, he, too, wrote about a tension between the ascetic commitments of monasticism and the worldly aesthetics of poetry.

I also treat as one of the third type of monastic writer Qisong 契嵩 (1007–1072). Qisong was an erudite Chan monk whose poetic writings were well-regarded in his own time. He is often remembered today as a Buddhist interlocutor for prominent scholar-officials, including Ouyang Xiu 歐陽修 (1007–1072), and has often been interpreted as a key figure in historical Confucian-Buddhist interactions.[106] Although he was an active participant in the Yunmen lineage as a social network, because he did not serve as the abbot of a public monastery, he was not strictly speaking a full-fledged member of the lineage. More important for us, his poetry does not resemble that of a Chan abbot. Qisong's poetry is more like that of a poet-monk or mainstream literati.

Juefan Huihong 覺範惠洪 (1071–1128), a son of Jiangxi-area Buddhism, can be compared with these poet-monks. He was, however, also a more complex figure and was deeply engaged in sectarian learning. Although he was a student of Chan teachers, he had a penchant for traditional sūtra exegesis, mainstream literary pursuits, and socializing. His views and their possible significance have become the topic of scholarly debate in recent years. In Chapter 3, I review this scholarship and offer a new interpretation of Huihong's use of the term *wenzi chan* 文字禪, often translated as "literary Chan" or "lettered Chan."

Taking a step back and looking across this dramatis personae, I distinguish these three types of monks—Chan abbots and officers, Tiantai masters, and poet-monks—to clarify the social, institutional, and ritual contexts of monks' poems, and thereby to provide a framework for doctrinal interpretation. I hope to show that our ability to interpret Song monks' poetry is enhanced by attending to the particulars of monastic life. It is in this way that we might reveal how religious ideals shaped individual monks' poetic practices. It should be clear that the focus of this project is on the place of poetry in the lives of historical Song monks rather than of eccentrics or legendary figures. Most monks' poetry was written by those in the mainstream of monastic history. It is that poetry that awaits attention and to which this book is a small contribution.

Chapter Overviews

How did monastic communities in the Song dynasty construe monks' poetry? How did monks themselves understand the relationship between poetry and the Buddhist path? And how did they negotiate the perceived tension between

---

106. Morrison, *Power of Patriarchs*, 5–7 and 115–120, gives a critical overview of such scholarship. My understanding of Qisong and his career builds on Morrison's lucid analysis throughout her monograph.

worldly aesthetics and the asceticism of men who vowed to live under monastic rule? By answering these questions, I hope to rebut the idea that monks' poetry was meant to be impenetrable nonsense, a Zen riddle, or even necessarily that their poems were expressions of enlightenment. Modern popular writing depicts Chan literature as an instrument for overcoming discursive thought. But Robert Sharf has noted, on the contrary, that "the 'obscurity' and 'inscrutability' often attributed to Zen writings is merely an indication that they were intended for an educated elite and presume familiarity with a vast and sophisticated literary canon."[107] The same must be said of monks' poetry.

The following chapters of this book are arranged in three parts. Part 1 looks at the construction of Chinese *gāthā*, or *jisong*, as a genre of poems authored by Song Chan monks. Chapter 1 begins with Chinese poetry and the pre-Song and Song understandings of *gāthā*, including explicit definitions in lexicons and sūtra exegeses. The latter part of the chapter considers the implicit working definitions of *jisong* used by Chan monks that can be recovered from surveying the genres and modes of verse found in Song *yulu*. Chapter 2 describes *jisong* in practice, focusing on manuscripts and early recensions of printed texts. I analyze manuscripts of Chan monks' poetry from the Southern Song and Yuan that include a preface or colophon by the author. These paratexts illustrate how writers themselves participated in the construction of *jisong* as a form of religious poetry. I then compare manuscripts with printed collections to reveal new details about textual practices. Finally, although we lack direct evidence of the Chan manuscript culture of the Northern Song, I reveal how the forewords to Northern Song *yulu* show how disciples collected and edited manuscripts of their master's verses to create printed editions. In general, these forewords also worked to construct *jisong*, encouraging readers to treat them as a kind of poetry of their own.

Part 2 reconsiders relationships between poetry and the Way. Chapter 3 critically reexamines the idea that there was a monastic movement to compose poetry as a Buddhist path beginning in the Song dynasty. A progressive historical development in which Chan monks developed literary ways of being is associated with the term *wenzi chan* and its supposed proponent, the monk Juefan Huihong. Huihong was a talented literary stylist who composed Chan histories, poetic criticism, and sūtra exegesis. Over a thousand poems by Huihong survive. To my surprise, when I examined Huihong's actual usage of the phrase *wenzi chan* in context, the evidence for the most part did not support this idea of writing poetry as a vehicle for enlightenment. On the contrary, I believe *wenzi chan* was used by Huihong as a term of self-disparagement. It was part of his rhetoric of foolishness and the residual karma of his *juvenilia*. *Wenzi chan* was not a monastic movement in any institutional sense during the Song dynasty. Rather, it was in the late Ming that a debate began when Zibo Zhenke 紫柏真可 (1543–1604) republished the

---

107. Sharf, review of *Eloquent Zen*, 433.

works of Huihong and added a positive reevaluation of *wenzi chan* in his new preface. I conclude in this chapter that we should not project this Ming-era movement backwards onto the Song dynasty and should instead place Song uses of the term *wenzi chan* within Song-era contexts.

Developing this idea that poetry itself is not the Way, Chapter 4 follows a prescriptive idea, namely, poetry as "outer learning" (*waixue* 外學) and traces it onto two poetic topoi. I first closely examine numerous mainstream and sectarian disciplinary and educational texts in order to historically ground this idea in prescriptive sources of the Song. I then interpret poems about enjoying poetic pleasures during leisure time in the monastic schedule. Finally, I closely read poems about the poetry demon. This chapter illuminates direct connections between prescriptive texts and poems.

In each of the final two chapters of Part 3 of this book, I shed light on monks' literary sociality by focusing on two genres of verse. Chapter 5 concerns parting poetry by Chan monks. One of the most conservative genres, mainstream parting poems were written by literati to bid farewell to departing friends, disciples, and loved ones. Parting words would remain with a traveler, who might send back a poem from the road. Like other *propemptikon,* these poems offered benedictions and expressed nostalgia. Monks, by contrast, imbued their parting poems with doctrinal and philosophical meaning, often completely contravening the common expectations of sentimental words and warm affirmations of social relations. I argue that monks' parting poetry used these social norms by subverting them and thereby gave Buddhist significance to the ordinary social practice of saying farewell.

Chapter 6 considers various kinds of mourning poetry in the Northern Song. First, I analyze ritual verses composed by Chan abbots for monastic funerals (such as "on lowering the flame" mentioned above). "Rules of purity" manuals prescribed the performative context for intoning these verses amid funeral liturgies. I incorporate these ritual contexts into my literary analysis. Ritual funerary verses were written by an abbot to address the sangha's communal grief at the loss of a member and were in contrast to poems that expressed personal grief. These funerary verses ritually transformed a moment of death into a potent teaching on Buddhist values. I next turn to analyzing personal lamentations written in an overtly emotional genre. These poems of grief were not as common among monks, who were meant to have transcended the vagaries of life and death. Monks created multiple poetic strategies in response to the all-too-human emotional reactions to mortal loss. This series of analyses illustrates some differences among Chan monks, Tiantai monks, and poet-monks. Together, these two chapters use genre and social historical contexts to illustrate several ways that poetry and ritual verse figured in the lives of Buddhist monks in the Northern and Southern Song.

Monks' poetry of the Song dynasty was a negotiation, at least in part, of the animating tensions between monastic asceticism and literary genre conventions. Emblematic of this dynamic are poems about "the poetry demon." This non-canonical demon, a minion of Māra the tempter, emerged in late-medieval China to describe the unbidden muse who excites the passions of poetry. As a metaphor, the phrase depicts word craft as karmic residue and ascribes the fashioning of literary ornamentation to unresolved mental inclinations detrimental to the Buddhist path. Ironically, most references to the "poetry demon" are made directly in the poems themselves. Such a self-deprecating image in a monk's literary composition tells us as much about historical social expectations as it does about monastic literary practices. Conversely, nuanced interpretation of such poems depends on our knowledge of the contexts of their production. If we are to develop new lenses through which to interpret the poetry of monks, we must first learn about the literary subcultures from which monastic poetry emerged.

PART ONE

A Poetry of Their Own

1

Gāthā *in Pre-Song and Song Contexts*

THROUGHOUT THE NORTHERN AND SOUTHERN SONG DYNASTIES, poems written by Chan masters were often referred to as *ji* 偈, the Chinese word for Indic *gāthā*. The use of *gāthā* as a generic label for Chinese poetry was not unprecedented. During the late Tang, *gāthā* became a creative genre for new compositions, which were no longer just anonymous hymns in the sūtras. In the Song the practice of writing Chinese *gāthā*, or *jisong* 偈頌, became ubiquitous among abbots of Chan public monasteries. Chinese *gāthā* did not, however, merely denote Buddhist poetry. Song-era primers, commentaries, and scriptural texts drew distinctions between Chinese *gāthā* as verse with salvific power and the literary arts of mainstream poetry. These explicit definitions parallel the textual practices found in other Chan texts.

Readers in the eleventh to fourteenth centuries could encounter the story of Huineng, the sixth Chinese patriarch of the Chan lineage, in the *Jingde-Era Record of the Transmission of the Lamp* 景德傳燈錄 (hereafter *Jingde chuandenglu*). This version of the famous story, much like the now well-known Dunhuang editions of the *Platform Sūtra,* narrates a contest of verses. The fifth patriarch, Hongren, would recognize the winner as the sole heir to the Chan lineage. A Song reader of the *Jingde chuandenglu* might imagine Shenxiu, the foremost learned disciple and obvious heir apparent, inscribing his verse on the temple wall, a *jisong* in four lines with five characters each.[1] The couplets rhyme and the words alternate between rising and deflected tones in a standard regulated pattern. In terms of form, Shenxiu's verse is identical to a *jueju* 絕句, or "quatrain," a type of *shi*-regulated poem that will be introduced in more detail below. Though the verse looks like a poem, it is treated as a *gāthā*. Hongren tells the community that if they use Shenxiu's verse and "practice in accord with it" 依此修行, good karmic results will follow. In other words, looking at form alone, this verse is not different from poetry, but the figures in this text revere the verse as a religious teaching and use terms like *gāthā* to refer to it. Monks in the assembly begin to recite Shenxiu's verse. One of them

---

1. *Jingde chuandenglu* (T51.222c20–22). Shenxiu's verse in the Dunhuang and received *Platform Sūtra* is a regulated *jueju* poem.

is overheard by the illiterate Huineng, who then, we are told, spontaneously composes a response in verse form with matching rhymes. Huineng's matching verse is a *prajñāpāramitā* critique of Shenxiu's conventional diligence and in contrast emphasizes the emptiness of all phenomena.[2] Huineng, of course, wins this dramatic contest.

Turning to poetic form, Huineng's response repeats the same end rhymes selected by Shenxiu, constituting a formal echo. Unlike Shenxiu's verse, however, Huineng's *gāthā* does not completely adhere to the tonal patterns of regulated poetry.[3] Huineng's verse is more conversational than Shenxiu's and departs from the formal conventions of mainstream poetry. A reader of the text might think these infelicities reflect Huineng's supposed illiteracy. Indeed, if this verse were not composed in Huineng's lifetime, as scholars currently believe, it would be reasonable to think that "the Huineng verse" was intentionally crafted to appear unpoetic.[4] Huineng wins the contest because his verse more fully expresses the Chan teachings, regardless of the deficiencies in his poetic meter. The learned Shenxiu's respectable poem is bested by a verse from the reputedly illiterate spiritual genius Huineng. The clear message of this narrative is that literary form and aesthetic concerns, though not irrelevant, are subordinate to the conveyance of religious truth. The Dunhuang editions of the *Platform Sūtra* also name these verses as *ji* and reflect one of the earliest texts in which a historical Chinese monk created a *jisong*.

Jisong had become by Song times a creative genre for new works that could be authored by Chinese writers. Distinctions between *jisong* and *shi* were not, however, based on literary form. Some, but not all, *shi* by monks were regarded as *jisong*; *jisong* often, though not necessarily, were carefully composed *shi*. Literary devices used in Song *jisong* are often similar to or adapted from those of *shi*. If not a formal genre distinction, then what made these differences meaningful? Tentatively, the Song distinction between *jisong* and *shi* bears a similarity to our distinction between "the religious" and "the worldly." But what did that mean to Buddhists in the Song? Furthermore, what kinds of verse did monks write and in what relative numbers? What literary forms did they use? And last—though an answer to this question will have to wait until later chapters—how did normative definitions of monks' poetry influence its practices?

---

2. McRae, *Seeing through Zen,* 64, offers a different reading of Huineng's verse as critique that "could not stand alone." The two verses form "an indivisible pair . . . a single polarity, not two separate teachings." *Prajñāpāramitā,* or "Perfection of Wisdom," is the name of both the philosophical tradition associated with emptiness and the class of Mahāyāna texts that expound this teaching.

3. Huineng's verse in *Jingde chuandenglu* (T51.223a6–7) has a tonal error in line 1, as does the received *Platform Sūtra* known as *Liuzu dashi fabao tanjing* (T48.348b24–25). The second couplet is nice; however, it is undesirable that the two couplets repeat the same tonal pattern. The earlier Dunhuang texts have not one, but two verses attributed to Huineng, both of which have more prosodic errors than Song and Yuan editions. Yang Zengwen, *Dunhuang xin ben Liuzu tan jing,* 14.

4. McRae, *Seeing through Zen,* 62–63.

Some Song readers would have encountered this distinction between worldly poetry and religious verse as it was given in the tenth-century encyclopedia *Six Books of the Śākya Clan* 釋氏六帖, a text sufficiently popular that it was issued several times during the Northern Song dynasty.[5] When a new recension was published in 1103, a colophon was added that described how the text had been used in monastic education.[6] Students made personal copies that introduced numerous errors, which the sponsors of the 1103 edition sought to correct. The erudite monastic administrator (*sengzheng* 僧正) of Suzhou oversaw emendations to the text prior to its publication. *The Six Books* encyclopedia entry entitled "poetry and hymns" (*shisong* 詩頌) quotes a short passage from the Xuanzang 玄奘 (602–664) translation of the extensive *Abhidharma-mahāvibhāṣa*.[7]

> If you ask, "Among the many kinds of literary verse, what is poetry and what is not poetry?" then you will get this response: The words of buddhas are not poetry. Frivolous speech is poetry. Many masters have explained "the inner teachings are not poetry, but rather the outer teachings are poetry." For such exegetes, when a text and its meaning are in accord, they can benefit others, and so it is not called "poetry." They use "poetry" to gloss literary verse of worldly types.[8]

> 問於諸文頌何者是詩，何者非詩，有作是說。佛語非詩。餘語是詩。有餘師說，內教非詩，外教是詩。如是說者，文義相稱能引義利，不名為詩。詩謂翻此世間文頌。

This passage distinguishes the poetry of the world from the religious words of a buddha. That which is articulated by buddhas—here *foyu* 佛語, likely translated from the Sanskrit *buddhavacana*—must not be conflated with the merely ornamented language of worldly poets. Song readers of *The Six Books of the Śākya Clan* would likely have interpreted this passage as reflecting their own concerns and a Chinese conception of worldly poetry. Indeed, similar distinctions between ordinary poetry and religious verse are found in Song paratexts, such as forewords to Chan masters' collected verses and colophons appended to individual verses in extant manuscripts, both of which are addressed in the next chapter. These examples illustrate how the discourse distinguishing *jisong*

---

5. Colophon at the end of *Shishi liutie,* 436b9, indicates that an edition was printed in 973 during Song Kaibao era, which Shiina speculates was the first printed edition. A second colophon dated 1103 describes creation of the new recension. An extant Song edition owned by Tōfukuji follows the format of the 1103 recension. Shiina suggests in *Zengaku tenseki sōkan* 6, pt. 2, 532, that it was possibly produced from Northern Song blocks. The initial compilation is described in Toleno, "Skilled Eating," 70–74.

6. *Zengaku tenseki sōkan* 6, pt. 2, 437b.

7. *Apidamo dapiposha lun* (T27.660c20–28). The Xuanzang passage is cited with some abbreviations in *Shishi liutie,* 10/112a.

8. On "literary verse," elsewhere this text explains, "that which is depicted by literary verses sometimes is so and sometimes is not, but the words in many kinds of literary verses frequently miscontrue reality" 文頌所說或然不然，諸文頌者言多過實. *Apidamo dapiposha lun* (T27.361c3–4).

from poetry was put into practice. In the present chapter, I illustrate the conceptual categories as explained by Song Buddhists themselves.

The sections below continue to examine how Song Buddhists explained the distinction between Chinese poetry and Chinese *gāthā*. I examine how these issues were framed in prescriptive texts, a set of sources I call "explicit definitions." The Northern Song lexicographic *Chrestomathy from the Ancestors' Halls* 祖庭事苑 (hereafter *Zuting shiyuan*), compiled by the Chan scholar-monk Mu'an Shanqing 睦庵善卿 (fl. 1108), is especially important for showing connections between mainstream Buddhist learning and Chan learning. This reading aid for a small corpus of Chan texts incorporated earlier exegetical traditions to provide a Chan definition of what *jisong* were supposed to be, who could write them, and how were they to be read. *Zuting shiyuan* is valuable for us today in part because it says things plainly so that even a student could understand. But it gives only one interpretation (albeit a well-informed one) of what a *jisong* should be and does not directly tell us what *jisong* actually were. That being the case, I will survey here the major poetic genres commonly found across *yulu,* the collections of "recorded sayings" of Song Chan monks. I regard these genres and modes as conveying implicit definitions. Both explicit and implicit definitions of *jisong* illustrate how Chan monks constructed their own verse culture. First, however, I give two poetic examples to illustrate the strict form of *shi* and the formal flexibility of *jisong*.

Chinese Poetry and Buddhist Verse

The Chinese word *shi* is often glossed in English as "poetry," but the two words are not one-for-one equivalents. When monks in the Song discuss poetry, they are almost always discussing the genres of *shi*, not all verse. The rise of *shi* has long been traced to the final years of the Han dynasty during the Jian'an reign (196–220).[9] During the Tang dynasty, *shi* developed into a mature tradition with well-established conventions and themes. As early as the opening decades of the Song dynasty, when learned men disputed the traits of fine poetry, the Tang was heralded as a golden age.[10] The modern preference to read and study Tang poetry is indebted to the tastes of these Song men. Turning to *shi* written in the Song, scholars from late imperial times down to today have looked for general comparisons with the Tang. Seen in the shadow of Tang poetry, Song *shi* appear more philosophical, more concerned with daily life, and more enmeshed in social relations.[11] Though it is a hackneyed stereotype, there is some truth to this generalization. The persistence of this stereotype is one reason Tang poetry remains better studied. Other qualities of Song poetry remain topics for investigation. Recent scholarship has shown how

---

9. Such origin tales are largely inherited from the Six Dynasties (220–589) compilers of the extant anthologies. See Owen, *Making of Early Chinese Classical Poetry*, 33–66.

10. Shields, "Defining the 'Finest.'"

11. Yoshikawa, *Introduction to Sung Poetry,* 6–38.

Song-era writers themselves generally valued innovation, freshness, and precision in *shi*.[12] Moreover, the genres of *shi*, even the relatively intellectual poems of the Song, remained vehicles for emotional and moral expression, and these aspects of Song *shi* must be taken seriously.

In literary history the Song dynasty is most often associated with the emergence of new genres such as *ci* 詞, "lyrics," however, for writers of the period, the various forms of *shi* remained the center of poetic life and the most important literary genre.[13] This is reflected in the large total number of extant *shi* from the Song, which is more than ten times greater than the total number of *ci*, which number fewer than twenty thousand in the *Complete Song* Ci 全宋詞. One reason for the voluminous output of *shi* is that *shi* was still the preferred genre for serious poetry. *Ci* were associated with desire, loss, and romantic love. It is unsurprising that, when monks wrote poetry, they mostly chose to do so using the genres of *shi*.[14] *Shi* as a genre was respectable and traditional, appropriate for social occasions and the exchange of poetry. The *shi* form was conservative, rule-bound, and prestigious. It was also broadly accessible, owing to the stabilization of conventions in the Tang, as well as being circulated via poetry handbooks. With rare exceptions, amounting to roughly 150 extant examples, monks did not experiment with *ci*.[15] Here, we see a divergence from Daoist authors, as most of the extant *ci* from the Jin dynasty were written by Quanzhen Daoists.[16] *Shi* was appropriate for the relatively conservative social occupation of a monk.

How did monks think about *shi*? I have found misleading the Romantic-Transcendentalist conception of the poet as a speaker of truth, or as "one who offers epiphanies."[17] This was not how Song monks thought of the work of poetry. I have instead found it useful to reflect on Viktor Shklovsky's idea that "making strange" or "defamiliarization" (*ostranenie*) is something that distinguishes poetry from other kinds of language.[18] That poetic art may counteract habitual perception, making ordinary things fresh or new again, seems to resonate with the pleasures of poetic wit that delighted Song poets.

---

12. A generalization found in Zhang Gaoping, *Chuangyi zaoyu*, 2–9; and Sargent, *The Poetry of He Zhu*, 453.

13. On the relative status of the *ci* in the Song and among later scholars, see Owen, *Just a Song*, 1–5.

14. The *ci* had romantic undertones and probably was considered inappropriate for a monk. Among the *ci* of Juefan Huihong, the first of three written to the tune of "Moon over the West River" 西江月 stands out for playing with the language of desire, beginning: "ten fingers gently pull at sprouts of spring bamboo" 十指嫩抽春筍. *Quan Song ci*, 710–714.

15. *Quan Song ci* contains approximately 142 distinct lyrics composed by nineteen different monks. Most prolific is Zhongshu 仲殊 (fl. 11th c.), for whom more than 70 lyrics survive. Analyzed in Zhang Ruolan, "Shi Zhongshu."

16. Komjathy, *Cultivating Perfection*, 384–397.

17. For sources on Romanticism, see Taylor, *Sources of the Self*, 423. On the twentieth-century creation of what McMahan calls "hybridized Buddhist-Romantic" arts, see McMahan, *Making of Buddhist Modernism*, 76–87, 117–147.

18. Shklovsky, *Theory of Prose*, chapter on "Art as Device."

In the language of Shklovsky, the work of poetry is achieved by roughening language through poetic devices (such as rhyme, rhythm, and meter) and thereby drawing attention to objects anew—to make the world visible again. We may study a poem's formal traits as traces of the one who made it and of the world in which that maker lived. Stepping inside a poem moves us toward, as Owen says, "a limited window on a full world."[19]

What makes a *shi* "poetry" cannot be separated from its literary devices and formal structures, and yet it cannot be reduced simply to devices and forms. And yet the genres of *shi* are nonetheless often delineated by formal properties. A distinction between "ancient poetry" 古體詩 and "regulated poetry" 律詩, also known as poetry of the "recent style" 近體, emerged in the late seventh century, with these naming conventions being established by the early eighth century.[20] These forms mattered in part because they conveyed the weight of precedent, which may be why Song writers distinguished between "ancient poetry" and "regulated poetry."[21] Note that Song monks often wrote in the style of regulated poetry, though not exclusively.

In ancient poetry, the total number of lines is not restricted, end rhymes may alternate within a single poem, and tonal sequences within lines are not rigidly fixed—though awkward sounding patterns are still avoided. Ancient-style lines may be intentionally coarse or roughened, or what Stuart Sargent characterizes as "the noticeable rejection rather than indifference to rules."[22] By contrast, regulated poetry has a fixed line length and a single rhyme. And regulated poetry has rules governing tonal patterns for each line. Set tonal sequences ensure euphony by avoiding awkward or repetitive sounds. A *line* may be regulated if it accords with one of four basic sequences. A proper sequence of such regulated lines creates a regulated *poem*. The correct sequence creates a pleasant tonal counterpoint within a couplet and adhesion between sequential couplets. The basic unit of regulated poetry is two lines, or a couplet.

As Sargent has painstakingly illustrated, a regulated poem often contains unregulated lines.[23] Such lines possess "violations" of tonal conventions, which may be artfully deployed to emphasize a poetic device or to draw attention to certain words. These violations done intentionally might open paths of interpretation. Conversely, a regulated poem without any tonal violations would conform entirely to conventions. It would sound predictable. Although I transcribe Chinese characters with the modern *pinyin* romanization system, I analyze sonic qualities like tone and rhyme with the standard Song pronunciations given in the imperially sponsored rhyming dictionary *Guangyun* 廣韻

---

19. Owen, "Transparencies," 239.
20. Jia, "Pearl Scholars," 16–20.
21. Much of the summary that follows is based on Sargent's monograph *Poetry of He Zhu*, which Fuller calls "a systematic 21st Century *shihua*" about Song-dynasty poetry. Sargent, on p. 2, translates He Zhu's comments pertinent to ancient and recent style.
22. Sargent, *Poetry of He Zhu*, 12–13.
23. Sargent, *Poetry of He Zhu*, 8–9.

(completed 1008).[24] Though many Song poets used the standard pronunciations found in *Guangyun*, regional variations based on historical dialects have also been detected by scholars.[25]

Regulated poetry possesses several additional formal elements. End rhyme in regulated poetry occurs in even lines, at the end of each couplet. As a variation, the first line may also have end rhyme, a practice especially common among monks. In general, line length is fixed at either five or seven characters. A full regulated *shi* is eight lines long, while the *jueju* form of *shi* is half as long, with four lines, which I will also refer to as a "quatrain." Beginning in the Song, most monks' poems were seven-character *jueju*, that is, four-line *shi* that observe tonal regulations.

These various rules and patterns are most easily gleaned from a simple example. The following is a well-regarded seven-character *jueju* poem, one of ten entitled "Miscellaneous Thoughts on a Spring Day" 春日雜興, composed during the Northern Song. Because some of the seven-character lines are rather dense with meaning, I have enjambed each line of English to accommodate my translation, which corresponds to the natural caesura in each line of the Chinese that usually separates the first four characters from the latter three characters.[26]

	From the dense base of the bamboo hedge 　　purple shoots push up	戢戢籬根紫筍長 ●●○○●●○
2	The peach and plum blossoms that fill the city 　　cease their alluring scents.	滿城桃李罷芬芳 ●○○●●○○
	Though spring wind may 　　be an unfeeling thing,	東風雖是無情物 ○○○●●○●
4	It sends off spent [blossoms], welcomes new growth, 　　and is yet more busy.	送謝迎繁亦更忙 ●●○○●●○

This is the ninth poem of a suite of ten contemplating springtime. "Miscellaneous thoughts" (*za xing* 雜興) was a common trope for poetic rumination in the Tang and Song. The first couplet describes sights and smells of the enlivening flora and the second couplet comments on the workings of spring. The poet's vision expands from seeing a small shoot on the ground to imagining the whole city filled with a floral aroma and then turns to consider how the wind rustles and shakes the trees. I could mention other allusions at work to add further depth and nuance, but first let us consider the elements of form.

The poet's control over rhymes and tones provides a sonic structure that sustains the poem. I have marked these tonal patterns beneath each line with

---

24. Here and throughout the present book, tonal prosody is analyzed with *Guangyun* via *Yintong;* rhyme words are presented in the Middle Chinese reconstructions from Baxter and Sagart, *Old Chinese.*

25. For example, Kinugawa, "Sodōshū no kiso hōgen."

26. *Canliaozi shiji,* 5.7a-b; 76–77.

a filled circle ● for "deflected" (ze 仄) tones and an empty circle ○ for "level" (ping 平) tones. These determinations are based on the standard Song pronunciations given in *Guangyun*. Following Sargent's model, where there are tonal violations in a line, a filled square ■ would indicate a deflected tone where one expected a level tone, and an empty square □ the reverse. In this poem, however, each line is regulated and without tonal violations.[27] In addition to tone, rhymes are carefully controlled. The final words rhyme in the first, second, and fourth lines, while the third line does not rhyme. Because the first line rhymes, a reader familiar with the conventions of regulated poetry would expect the very sequence of lines that follow. In other words, in addition to each line being regulated, the sequence of lines is also regulated.[28] With correct sequence, the middle two lines "adhere" with matching tones in the second, fourth, and sixth positions of each line.[29] Moreover, within each couplet (lines 1 and 2, and lines 3 and 4), tonal antithesis is balanced in the second, fourth, and sixth positions. The poet demonstrates his knowledge of the poetic tradition with these subtle manipulations of sonic texture.

In addition to manipulating sounds, for a poem in the Song to participate in the *shi* poetic tradition, it also should engage with earlier poetic precedents in meaningful ways. Through clever allusions, the poet expects his reader to have some knowledge of the *shi* tradition; he then participates in that tradition by making a further comment on an established topic. The above poem alludes to a well-known line by Han Yu 韓愈 (768–824), part of a suite entitled "Moved by Springtime" 感春. In the opening line in Han's series the gaze goes upward to see the first blossoms atop a magnolia tree, thus marking the start of spring. In the final couplet, Han imagines that as spring "welcomes new growth, then sends off spent [blossoms], it has a particular intent; / Why do I linger and pace around again?" 迎繁送謝別有意，誰肯留戀少環迴.[30] Han Yu focuses on the human fondness for beauty in the face of unrelenting impermanence. A Southern Song commentary explicates this couplet with reference to a poem by Yuan Zhen 元稹 (779–831), also written about the same magnolias outside Han Yu's home.[31] Yuan proposed in this poem that Han himself pluck the blossoms to share with a friend before they are snatched by the wind.[32] Both of these Tang poems focus on human appreciation of fleeting beauty in nature. Our Song poet has added his own voice to this poetic conversation.

---

27. Though the poem is regulated, one can still debate its prosody. For example, the third line begins with three level tones, which is often undesirable. The third word in that line might have been better if a deflected tone. However, the lines and sequence are regulated regardless of this possible infelicity.

28. See Sargent, *Poetry of He Zhu*, 9–10, for an English-language introduction to the system of denotation developed by Qi Gong 啟功 (1912–2005), *Shi wen shenglü lungao*, here B1, D1, A3, B1.

29. Sargent, *Poetry of He Zhu*, 138.

30. *Han Changli shi xinian jishi*, 7/732.

31. Song commentary quoted in *Han Changli shi xinian jishi*, 7/732, no. 4.

32. "Magnolia Blossoms, Inquiring with Han Yu" 辛夷花問韓員外, *Yuan Zhen ji*, 26/308, and noted in McMullen, "Han Yü," 615n19.

The Song poet arrives at a comparatively intellectual conclusion about the effects of spring wind on flowers. He describes the sensorium of spring as well as the wind that first shakes blossoms open and then knocks them down. This wind, though without intentions of its own, nonetheless is actively involved in the transformations of spring. A similar idea about the agency of wind is found in an earlier Tang poem by Wang Wei 王維 (701–761) that asks, "If you say the winds of spring do not understand intent, / why do they blow us falling flowers?" 若道春風不解意，何因吹送落花來.[33] Our Song poet does not go as far as Wang, who playfully questions whether it is the wind that has intent or if it is only from a human perspective that the wind appears to be blowing flowers toward us. The Song poet instead states that springtime wind is unfeeling and yet participates in the movement of the physical world. Recalling that the modern scholar Yoshikawa Kōjirō generalized that Song *shi* are more intellectual than the passions of Tang poetry, in this case his assessment proves accurate.[34] This Song poem, "Miscellaneous Thoughts on a Spring Day," in general simultaneously draws on, elaborates, and embellishes knowledge of the mainstream Chinese poetic tradition.

To further illustrate distinctions separating Buddhist verse from *shi*, we may briefly explore contrasts with a didactic verse that circulated widely during the Song. Below is one of the "*gāthā* on eight graduated [steps]" 八漸偈 found in the final fascicles of *Jingde chuandenglu*. I have translated the sixth in the series, entitled "Unhindered [superpowers]" 通.[35] This is no *shi*.

	When wisdom is perfected it is illumination,	慧至乃明
		●●●○
2	This illumination is without darkness.	明則不昧
		○●●●
	When illumination is perfected it is the unhindered,	明至乃通
		○●●○
4	This unhindered is without obstacles.	通則無礙
		○●●●
	What is without obstacles?	無礙者何
		○●●○
6	To be self-mastered among transformations!	變化自在
		●●●●

This verse addresses Buddhist doctrine and practice in an edifying manner. The author composed in couplets with a consistent line length of four characters, a square rhythm that would sound archaic. Each line repeats two deflected tones at its middle. The rhythm of each couplet is punctuated by

---

33. "Playfully Inscribed on a Large Boulder" 戲題盤石, *Wang Wei ji jiaozhu*, 93; translation by David Lattimore, in Minford and Lau, *Classical Chinese Literature*, 717.

34. Yoshikawa, *Introduction to Sung Poetry*, 9–10, 21, 28–29.

35. *Jingde chuandenglu* (T51.455a10–12). Tones given only for comparison.

an end rhyme in the *dui* 隊 (*dwojH*) family in line 2, a close-slant rhyme with those in the *dai* 代 (*dojH*) family in lines 4 and 6. These rhyme words end in "departing" (*qu* 去) sounds, which are deflected tones. Rhyming in deflected tones itself is not unusual but is less common in regulated poetry. The use of rhyme exhibits basic craft and intentional design. In terms of imagery, the diction is straightforward and instructive. This does not mean that the author did not consider the effects of tonal textures. Perhaps the force of four deflected tones repeated in the final line was intended as a serious-minded admonitory flourish. We might refer to this short text as a hymn or didactic verse. The compiler of the *Jingde chuandenglu* referred to it as a *ji*, the Chinese designation for Indic *gāthā* here used to refer to a Chinese Buddhist composition. Numerous formal qualities distinguish this verse from the *shi* above.

It might surprise the reader that the above example *shi* was written by a Buddhist monk, Daoqian, and conversely that the *gāthā* was written by a mainstream poet, Bai Juyi. I juxtapose these two by way of cautioning against simple associations of Buddhist genres with an author's putative Buddhist identity. I would instead encourage a more dynamic interpretive rubric that considers both the conventions of the genres as well as what social norms it was incumbent on each writer to know, to the extant they could be known. In what ways might our interpretations of the above examples be informed by knowledge of the personal identities of their authors?

Bai Juyi was a prolific Tang writer and aristocratic statesman.[36] He was at times a composer of pious verse who frequently wrote with tongue in cheek. The above *gāthā* was effectively canonized by its inclusion in the formative *Jingde chuandenglu,* one of five Song Chan "Flame Record" 燈錄 anthologies. Similar hymns and verses were written by Song literati as well. The hymns, encomia, and *gāthā* (*ji*) written by Su Shi were gathered into the anthology of his collected writings, not into his collected poetry.[37] Buddhist verse did not become *shi* simply because the author was a poet—an observation that resonates with the American critic John Hollander's dictum that "most verse is not poetry"—and should not be lumped together with poetry.[38] Lettered people of the Song would likely agree. Verses with prosodic forms or singsong rhymes—like many Buddhist hymns and popular verses—were not the same as poetry. For the well-educated of discerning taste, the word poetry meant something grander.

More questions are raised by the *shi* written by monk Daoqian, a lifelong friend of Su Shi. Does our interpretation shift now that we know the author was a Buddhist monk? For example, whereas Han Yu remarked that flowers were shaken from trees "with a particular intent," Daoqian reworked the image by calling the gusty wind "an unfeeling thing." Daoqian's phrase is cleverly ambiguous. On the one hand, he may mean the wind is a thing

---

36. The verse appears in *Bai Juyi ji,* 39/885–887.
37. *Su Shi wenji,* 20–22/583–649. The division of *shi* from the other genres of writing is seen already in Song-era printed editions of Su Shi's works.
38. Hollander, *Rhyme's Reason,* 1.

without emotions (*wuqing*), a reading suggested by our knowledge of Tang poems. But Daoqian also left open the possibility of this as a reference to the Buddhist concept of "insentient things" (*wuqing wu*). In this latter vein, Daoqian's poem seems to wade into the heated Chinese Buddhist debate over whether insentient things possess buddha-nature, become buddhas, or preach the dharma.[39] We have no writing from Daoqian apart from his poetry that could shed more light on his understanding of this doctrinal issue. We are, in other words, left with matters of interpretation. How does this mainstream poem by the poet-monk Daoqian compare with the many modes of verse written by other monks at the time? When we turn to Chan monks, frequently their poems were referred to as "Chinese *gāthā*," *jisong*, or "*gāthā*," *ji*, the term used for the didactic verse above. To better understand the Song idea of *jisong*, we begin with the pre-Song history of the Chinese word itself.

Origins of *Jisong*

In the Song, *jisong* became a widely available creative genre. Chan monks composed original verses that possessed salvific efficacy equivalent to that of *buddhavacana*. These religious verses were referred to as *jisong*. While often characterized today as a Chinese translation of the Sanskrit word *gāthā*, the word *jisong* and its semantic drift from scriptural *gāthā* to Chinese-authored *gāthā* has a complex history.

The rich Sanskrit vocabulary for poetic verse could be both transliterated and translated into multiple Chinese terms. The words *ji* 偈 and *song* 頌 superseded other phrases and began, from at least the Tang, to be used to refer to newly composed Buddhist monks' *shi* poetry. This development occurred at the same time that a new conception of *buddhavacana* was developing, one in which the words of an awakened Chan master were understood to be those of an awakened being. It was widely accepted by Song times that Chan monks' verse, frequently in the regulated poetic form of *jueju*, were participating in an established *jisong* genre. I turn to Song-era explications of *jisong* in the following subsection, but first offer a brief history of the changing Chinese terms for and conceptions of Buddhist verse and its relationship to *buddhavacana*.

The earliest Buddhist verses in China were integral parts of translated Indic texts. Tremendous formal variation exists in early translations; for example, *gāthā* were rhymed or unrhymed and rendered in many line lengths.[40] Early translators also employed several strategies for rendering the names of the types of verse found in the sūtras. For example, the Sanskrit term *geya* was transliterated as *qiye* 祇夜 (*gjie-yae)[41] to approximate the sound;

---

39. Sharf, *Coming to Terms*, 247–249.

40. For line length and rhyming preferences in early texts, see Nattier, *Guide to the Earliest Chinese Buddhist Translations*, 119–120; and Saitō, *Kango Butten*, 525–610.

41. This reconstructed pronunciation from Baxter and Sagart, *Old Chinese*; all others in this section as given in Saitō, *Kango Butten*.

it was also translated as "reiterating verse" (*chongsong* 重頌). These verses are defined by their function: they follow prose and reiterate its meaning. Many other kinds of verse appear frequently in the sūtras. For example, hymns of praise, often directed toward the Buddha, are embedded directly in the narrative as spoken utterances, unlike the reiterating verses that follow prose passages. These paeans are referred to in Sanskrit as *stotra*, often rendered with the native Chinese word *zan* 讚. Both transliteration (yielding foreign-sounding esoteric terms) and translation (domesticating Buddhist ideas) were used to represent the genres of verse in sūtras. In practice, both transliteration and translation often appear within individual texts, as in the alternation between *ji* and *song* for *gāthā*.[42] Bodhiruci (d. ca. 535) in his translation of the *Laṅkāvatārasūtra* even used more than one transliteration within a single sentence.[43]

The Indic word *gāthā* was rendered into Chinese in multiple ways. I follow Saitō Takanobu's proposed history for the development of these terms.[44] The early translator An Shigao 安世高 (2nd c. CE) used the word *jue* 絕 and sometimes the compound *jueci* 絕辭. The rendering of *gāthā* as *jue* remains a topic of debate, with some evidence suggesting that it conveyed semantic meaning; however, it seems likely to have also been a representation of Indic sound. Saitō, considering the late Han pronunciation **dzwiat*, argues that the final consonant *t* enabled this single character to represent the two-syllable *gāthā*. A similar example from the An Shigao corpus is the single word *jie* 劫, or **kjap*, for the two-syllable Sanskrit word *kalpa* (an eon).[45] In the end, the term *jue* was soon superseded by *ji* as the preferred Chinese word to transliterate *gāthā*.

One might think that because the Indic word *gāthā* has two syllables, that the word *ji* developed as an abbreviation for the Chinese phrase *jituo* 偈陀. This would be yet another case of the well-documented tendency of Chinese to abbreviate foreign-sounding terms. But after *jue*, the next earliest rendering of *gāthā* into Chinese was the single character *ji* 偈 by Lokakṣema (2nd c. CE). Saitō demonstrates that the pronunciation known to Lokakṣema may have been either **gjiadh* or **gjiat*, and argues, as in the case of **dzwiat* above, that this single Chinese character 偈 adequately conveyed with its final consonant the sound of the word *gāthā*. In the next centuries, final consonants softened and **gjiadh* shifted to **gjäi*. Only after the final consonant disappeared did it become necessary to use two Chinese words to represent the Sanskrit sound gāthā. It is possible that the earliest two-character transcription was *jita* 偈他 (**gjäi-t'a*). The most common transliteration, however, was *qietuo* 伽陀 (**gja-t'a*), first attested in a text by Kumārajīva (344–413). Judging from examples from the seventh century, Xuanzang observed that *jita* / **gjäi-*

42. This practice continued in Chan literature, such as alternately using *ji* and *song* in *Zutang ji*, fascs. 8, 9.

43. *Ru lengqie jing* (T16.515a26–27).

44. Saitō, *Kango Butten*, 147–198, also includes a critical review of earlier scholarship. On An Shigao and Lokakṣema, see also Nattier, *Guide to the Earliest Chinese Buddhist Translations,* 38–89.

45. Coblin, *Handbook of Eastern Han*, 241.

t'a was not an accurate representation of what he heard when traveling in South Asia and therefore concluded that *ji* was an erroneous abbreviation; he conceded that the Chinese translation as *song* was correct.[46] Xuanzang proposed *qieta* 伽他 (**gja-t'a*) as the best representation of the pronunciation that he himself had learned. Despite such attempts to standardize a two-character Chinese transliteration for *gāthā*, the single word *ji* continued to be used often in Chinese Buddhism in translated (or apocryphal) sūtras, commentaries, and other literature.

As for the compound expression *jisong* 偈頌, it may have resulted from a penchant in Chinese for two-character terms.[47] In many early translations, *gāthā* is translated with the word *song* 頌, both as a verb (to eulogize) and a noun (a panegyric). The history of the word *song* can be traced back to the "Eulogia" sections of *The Classic of Poetry* 詩經. While *The Classic of Poetry* played a significant role in the self-mythologizing of Chinese poetry, *song*, or "hymns," were not the most prestigious form of verse therein. The association of Buddhist *gāthā* with hymns was likely because the latter were generally directed toward the spirit world and, as observed by Tom Mazanec, "are as performative as much as they are aesthetic."[48] This likely seemed analogous to the prominent functions of *gāthā* in the sūtras, in addition to any aesthetic concerns. The resulting two-character word *jisong* is an example of what Zürcher called "hybrid compounds" that combine one character from a transliterated foreign term with one native Chinese word.[49] As a compound, *jisong* connotes verses written with Chinese words (*song*) that possess a foreign aura (*ji*). Similarly, An Shigao's compound *jueci*, above, probably drew upon the *Songs of Chu* 楚辭 in order to combine one word of transliteration (*jue*) with a familiar Chinese word for poetry (*ci*). These hybrid compounds yielded Chinese terms that appeared foreign, a strategy that marked these literary objects as Buddhist.

In contrast to the complexity of nomenclature and diversity of Indic terms present in this early period, from at least the Song and on *jisong* came to be ubiquitous. Already in the Tang era, the word *gāthā* more than other Indic terms became the center of theoretical discussions about the propriety of poetry for monks. Numerous other Sanskrit terms relevant to verse, its functions and forms, naturally had also been rendered into Chinese. For example, the Sanskrit *pāṭha*, which could mean a passage of text as well as its recitation, became *bai* 唄, which as part of a compound appears in Chinese texts as a noun, "hymn" (as in *fanbai* 梵唄), and a verb, "to recite," (as in *baizan* 唄讚).

---

46. *Da Tang Xiyuji* (T51.882c24–883a1).

47. Zürcher, "Late Han Vernacular Elements," 29–34.

48. Mazanec, "Medieval Chinese *Gāthā*," 110–112, which also includes a lengthier explanation of these affinities.

49. Zürcher describes *chanhui* 懺悔 as another example of a "hybrid compound" in "Buddhist *Chanhui*," 612n6. *Fayuan zhulin* (T53. 574b9-c5) offers a traditional etymology of another example of a "hybrid compound," *baizan* 唄讚, concluding that one word comes from the West, and one from the East, and "though different in name, they are the same in substance" 名異實同.

When the word *bai* does appear in Chinese poetry, it generally denotes the sounds of a monastery or a muttering monk. The Chinese understanding of *gāthā*, too, may have begun as a genre defined by its function in religious texts more than by its aesthetics. By the end of the Tang, however, it was *gāthā* that retained a religious air and yet was associated with Chinese poetry. From the Song dynasty and on, Chan monks wrote voluminous quantities of verse, mostly *jueju* quatrains, and referred to them in general as *jisong*. Several scholars have traced the broad historical brushstrokes of this transformation.[50] I would add that Tiantai monks and poet-monks, by contrast, wrote poems that they regularly referred to as *shi*.

For clarity, I use the Chinese term *jisong* to refer to poems authored in Chinese by Song Chan monks. The terms *ji* and *jisong* were widely used in Song Chan texts in reference to but distinguished from verses found in sūtras. A *jisong* originally composed in Chinese should resonate with Chinese cultural connotations.[51] To refer to such Chinese verses with an unmodified Sanskrit name obscures the fact that they were composed in the Chinese language by people in a historical, geographic entity, China. The Chinese-language expression for "Chinese *gāthā*," on the other hand, elicits the complexity of Buddhist culture in China. Or, akin to the felicitous explanation of Lucas Klein, these are Chinese innovations with Indic echoes "that refer to Indic culture without necessarily representing 'actual' India or its poetries."[52]

Scriptural *gāthā* were thought to possess authority and power as the words of the Buddha. As Chinese masters began writing original *jisong*, it was understood that they were not the words of the historical Buddha. In what manner were they *gāthā*? Could these new verses manifest soteriological power? The doctrinal issues in the Chinese creation of *jisong* recapitulated, perhaps unintentionally, an earlier Indic dispute about scripture. In general, debates between Indic schools about canonicity revolved around the scope of the concept *buddhavacana*, or "words of the Buddha," translated variously into Chinese as *foyu* 佛語 or *foyan* 佛言.[53] Roughly speaking, *buddhavacana* could be taken in either a strict or a broad sense. Strictly speaking, *buddhavacana* is taken literally to mean only words spoken directly by the historical Buddha. The implications of adhering to the strict sense are visible, for example, when texts of the *Khuddaka-nikāya*—including material putatively

---

50. The sequence established by Mazanec, "Medieval Chinese *Gāthā*," is most convincing. Additional details of the convergence of *gāthā* and poetry is also documented in Suzuki, *Tō Godai Zenshū shi*, 530–560. Less clarity is achieved in narratives that foreground the "poetification" 詩化 of *gāthā*, for example, Tan Zhaowen, *Chanyue shihun*, 7–15, which mirrors other narratives of the Sinification of Buddhism.

51. This is in part an extension of Sharf, *Coming to Terms*, 19, who argued that "whatever 'dialogue' transpired took place largely among the Chinese themselves," and is intended to shift the focus of scholarly attention toward understanding the agency of Chinese actors in creating local or vernacular Buddhisms.

52. Klein, "Indic Echoes," 76.

53. For a review of the role of *buddhavacana* in differences over canonicity, see Salomon, "Unwieldy Canon," 166.

authored by the Buddha's disciples, such as the *Therīgāthā,* poems attributed to the first Buddhist nuns—are classified outside of literal *buddhavacana* in some iterations of the canon.[54] On the other hand, *buddhavacana* in the broad sense extends to include "what the Buddha would have said, had he been there, or sayings about the Buddha, or sayings in accordance with Buddha's teaching."[55] As Paul Harrison has helpfully suggested, the conceit that "all that the Buddha has said is well said … [can be] turned around: Whatever is well said (i.e., true) is the word of the Buddha."[56] This broad conception of *buddhavacana* could mean that if a Chinese master composed verse with the insight of a buddha, that verse had a status similar to scripture. The broader sense of *buddhavacana* is fundamental to understanding the large body of Chan literature.

This broad interpretation of *buddhavacana* already appears in some Tang-dynasty Chan writing. To my knowledge, the earliest text in which a Chinese-authored *shi* is referred to as a *gāthā* is the Dunhuang versions of the *Platform Sūtra.*[57] This same principle underlies the "dharma transmission *gāthā*" 傳法偈 delivered by Chan patriarchs, established in the *Transmission of the Jeweled Grove* 寶林傳 (comp. 801; hereafter *Baolin zhuan*). Studies of Dunhuang materials suggest that the composition of regulated *shi* as *jisong* became widespread no later than the ninth century.[58] The number and geographic distribution of communities of poeticizing monks increased around this time, especially during the late ninth and tenth centuries, as recently documented by Wang Xiulin.[59] Probably in response to this expanded production, elite poet-monks hardened the boundary between *gāthā* and *shi,* establishing themselves as authorities on the latter and casting the former as an amateurish literary genre for mere "*gāthā*-scribblers."[60] In spite of such literary criticisms, *jisong* was a popular practice in need of some explanation.

Religious expatiations on Chan *gāthā* emerged around this same time. The earliest may be the critical assessment by the monk Guifeng Zongmi 圭

---

54. On when the *Khuddaka-nikāya* was regarded as within the *sutta-piṭaka* "basket" of *buddhavacana,* and when a separate fifth "basket" as *Kṣudraka-piṭaka* or *Kṣudraka-āgama,* see Salomon, "Unwieldy Canon," 165–167. The sectarian rivalries and politics of the construction of the Pali canon are explored in Collins, "On the Very Idea of the Pali Canon."

55. Norman, *Philological Approach to Buddhism,* 178; cited in Salomon, "Unwieldy Canon," 166.

56. Harrison, "Canon," 112.

57. Shenxiu's verse is a perfectly regulated *jueju* referred to as a *ji.* Yang Zengwen, *Dunhuang xin ben Liuzu tan jing,* 11–12. Huineng's responses are also called *ji.* Saitō, *Kango Butten,* includes earlier examples of rhyming five-character lines in early Chinese Buddhist texts; however, these are anonymous verses in scripture and not individually authored verse à la Chinese poetry.

58. See Mazanec, "Medieval Chinese *Gāthā*," 127–135. Mazanec, 117–119, suggests that earlier origins are possible depending on how one dates the title given to the works of Pang Yun 龐蘊 and other "vernacular Buddhist poetry," as well as whether one regards them as poetry.

59. Wang Xiulin, *Wan Tang Wudai shiseng,* 136–193; also 341–342 for brief comments on the relationship between these communities and the composition of *gāthā.*

60. The latter term was artfully coined by Mazanec, "Medieval Chinese *Gāthā*," 142–144. He analyzes the criticisms by Qiji and Guanxiu regarding *gāthā* as an amateurish genre. They understood themselves to be writing *shi* and to be "poets" in the full and prestigious sense of that term.

峰宗密 (780–841). As is well-known, Zongmi was a Huayan and Chan scholar interested in both doctrinal and practical matters whose writings were widely read in the Song.[61] Zongmi compiled a separate "Chan basket" 禪藏 to equal the mainstream Buddhist canonical *piṭaka,* which he entitled *Collected Writings on the Source of Chan* 禪源諸詮集. Only the preface written in 833 survives.[62] In that preface, Zongmi described gathering numerous "*gāthā* of various types of *chan*" 諸禪偈, consisting entirely of Chinese-authored verses on topics ranging from meditation to awakening.[63] According to Zongmi, these Chinese-authored *gāthā* were especially well-suited for the capacities of people like himself in China. Buddhist sūtras, by comparison, were difficult to apply because they comprehensively included myriad teachings for manifold beings across the cosmos.[64] In other words, the numerous types of Chan *gāthā* were useful for propagating the dharma in China.

Zongmi, however, distinguished Chan *gāthā* from *buddhavacana* in the narrow sense and explicitly maintained a difference between the words of a Chan master and the words in the sūtras. Zongmi wrote, "Sūtras are the words of a buddha. Chan is the intention of a buddha. The minds and mouths of buddhas surely do not contradict one another!" 經是佛語，禪是佛意。諸佛心口，必不相違。[65]Although Chan and the sūtras ought to agree, only the latter was reserved by Zongmi as one of the three means of valid knowledge (*liang* 量; Skt. *pramāṇa*) that can confirm truth.[66] Profound personal experiences are not adequate measures of Buddhist truth. If something based on personal experience does not accord with the Buddha's words transmitted in the sūtras, then they are unreliable. Zongmi's technical distinction between Chan writing and *buddhavacana* was debated by some Chan monks in the Song.[67]

Zongmi also held that Chan *gāthā* had salvific power. In a discussion about

---

61. Peter Gregory's writings on Zongmi provide background on Zongmi's achievements. Yanagi, *Eimei Enju to Sugyōroku no kenkyū,* traces numerous threads of intellectual history from Zongmi to Song Chan figures. Sub-commentaries on Zongmi's writing and liturgies were also newly composed in the Song.

62. On this lost collection as an autochthonous Chan *piṭaka* and its "comprehensive preface," see Gregory, "Bridging the Gap." When preparing my translations below, I also consulted Broughton, *Zongmi on Chan.*

63. Zongmi distinguishes between verses focused on practice that "instruct others" 示人, guiding them toward liberation; verses that explain the teachings in an accessible way that "gathers an assembly" 攝眾; verses that "admonish deluded beings" 警策群迷, like those by Fu Dashi and Wang Fanzhi; and verses about monastic comportment or "exemplary monks" 軌範僧侶, such as by Lushan Huiyuan; see *Chanyuan zhuquan ji duxu* (T48.412a1 and c16–25).

64. *Chanyuan zhuquan ji duxu* (T48.400a23–25). In a note regarding this passage, Broughton, *Zongmi on Chan,* 244–245n13, leaps to the poetic but untenable conclusion: "In short, *Chan literature is a form of Chinese poetry.*" (Emphasis in original.)

65. *Chanyuan zhuquan ji duxu* (T48.400b10–11). This passage by Zongmi re-appears in the biography of Tiantai Deshao in *Song gaoseng zhuan,* (T50.790a6–7), and in *Zongjing lu* (T48.418b6). Cf. translation in Welter, *Yongming Yanshou's Conception of Chan,* 249.

66. *Chanyuan zhuquan ji duxu* (T48.401a8–21)

67. This passage plays a role in the biography of Fayun Faxiu 法雲法秀 (1027–1090), *Chanlin sengbao zhuan* (ZZ79.543b20).

sudden awakening, his imagined interlocutor cleaves to this distinction of *buddhavacana* in the narrow sense, proposing that "if sūtras are words of the Buddha, and Chan is the talk of monks, I do not think I can oppose the Buddha to follow monks" 經是佛語，禪是僧言，違佛遵僧竊疑未可. Zongmi assures this straw man of the reality of sudden awakening and that "when one awakens, one becomes a buddha" 悟即成佛.[68] He also explains that *jisong* are transmitted by "wholesome companions" 善知識 (Skt. *kalyāṇamitra*), a term sometimes translated as "good friend," an epithet for Buddhist teachers.[69] From comments like these, we may infer that Zongmi understood the salvific power of Chan *gāthā*, even though he himself reserved the epithet *buddhavacana* for use in its narrow denotation.

In the Song, a major touchstone for this broader interpretation of *buddhavacana* was another supposed Tang-era view, a comment attributed to the iconic Chan monk Mazu Daoyi 馬祖道一 (709–788). In a well-known sermon, he famously taught that the mind itself is the Buddha.[70] Two exegetical problems concerned a different phrase in that sermon, however: "The essence of that which was spoken by the Buddha is our principle" 佛語心為宗. First, Mazu's remark was frequently misunderstood to be a quote directly from the *Laṅkāvatārasūtra* (misunderstood to be the direct teaching of the Buddha, thus making it *buddhavacana* in the narrow sense) from at least the tenth century.[71] But the adage is not in any edition of the *Laṅkāvatārasūtra* and clearly in context should be treated as a comment by Mazu about the *Laṅkāvatārasūtra* and its association with the mind-to-mind transmission of early Chan.[72] Second, a hermeneutical challenge focused on the referent of the Chinese word *xin* 心, which might denote "essence" (Ch. *xin;* Skt. *hṛdaya*) or "mind"

---

68. Doubt about sudden awakening as merely the words of monks and not found in *buddhavacana sensu stricto* is raised in *Chanyuan zhuquan ji duxu* (T48.401a27–29) and then answered several passages later (T48.402a10–19).

69. *Chanyuan zhuquan ji duxu* (T48.399c16–22).

70. On the several versions of this sermon, see Poceski, *Records of Mazu*, 83–85, 242–243, 248–249.

71. The misattribution is found in both the *Zutang ji* and in works by Yongming Yanshou, including *Zongjing lu* and *Xinfu zhu* (ZZ63.117c1–2). The conspicuous absence of the phrase from any known edition of the *Laṅkāvatārasūtra* was noted by Iriya, *Baso no goroku*, 18–19, who suspected that a transposition error from *yi* 以 to *yun* 云 led to a misunderstanding in some early texts. *Yi* also appears in many prominent Song texts, *pace* Welter, *Yongming Yanshou's Conception of Chan*, 328n79, who inexplicably cites an early Qing commentary by the Ming loyalist turned monk Jingting 淨挺 (1615–1684).

72. Poceski, *Records of Mazu*, 204, suggests Mazu summed up the pith of the sūtra. I, however, conjecture that Mazu's sermon alludes to the well-known alternative title of the sūtra. The use of 佛語心經 as an alternative title is attested by Mazu's contemporary Zongmi, *Zhonghua chuan xindi chanmen shizi chengxi tu* (ZZ63.33b14), and by some later commentaries such as *Butsugoshinron* 佛語心論 by Kokan Shiren 虎關師鍊 (1278–1346). Among Chinese translations of *Laṅkāvatārasūtra*, the alternate title is found only in *Lengqie abaduoluo baojing* (T16.480a16) by Guṇabhadra (394–468). The Guṇabhadra text was associated with early Chan per McRae, *The Northern School*, 15–29. Thus, the Mazu passage might be glossed as "the *Laṅkāvatāra* is our shared inheritance [*zong*], and the gateless is our dharma-gate."

(Ch. *xin;* Skt. *citta*).[73] Ishii Kōsei has suggested that Mazu intentionally conflated these two meanings of *xin*.[74] When we compare the reception of this phrase in texts from the Tang and Song, we see that "the essence of what the Buddha spoke" 佛語心 would become "the mind of *buddhavacana*."[75] By the Song, it was generally agreed that Mazu had remarked, "As for what was spoken by the Buddha, the mind is fundamental; the gateless is the dharma gate" 佛語心為宗，無門為法門.[76] In other words, the awakened mind was given priority over any written word.

This adage was taken up in the Song. The important Linji lineage Chan master Yuanwu Keqin 圓悟克勤 (1063–1135) in a letter explicated the pith of Mazu's saying "To put it another way, it is that my words right now really are *buddhavacana*" 更言只如今語便是佛語.[77] This does not mean that the words of a master are the words of the historical Buddha. The Chan master says, to borrow K. R. Norman's phrase, "what the Buddha would have said, had he been there."[78] This is a broad interpretation of *buddhavacana* that identifies the words and deeds of an awakened Chinese master with the words and deeds of a buddha.

If the Chan master is a buddha, then his poetic writings are Chinese *gāthā*, or the verses of a buddha. This idea also is found in Song texts. For example, the literatus Xu Fu 徐俯 (1075–1141), a nephew of Huang Tingjian 黃庭堅 (1045–1105), composed a preface for *Recorded Sayings of Chan Master Foyan* 佛眼禪師語錄, extant in an early printed edition.[79] Regarding this collection of works by the Linji lineage master Foyan Qingyuan 佛眼清遠 (1067–1120), Xu Fu wrote that although the collection is comprised of eight distinct genres including *jisong*, "their purpose is unitary, the very meaning of 'What is spoken by a buddha, the mind is fundamental; the gateless is the dharma gate'" 其義則一也：所謂「佛語心為宗，無門為法門」也.[80] The meaning is that the

---

73. Fazang 法藏 (643–712), *Ru lengqie xinxuanyi* (T39.430a27-b2), argued the meaning must be essence and not faculty of thought. Similarly, Suzuki, *Studies in the "Lankavatara Sutra,"* xliii–iv, 39–40, and 222, gives "The Essence of the Teaching of all Buddhas" for the Sanskrit *sarvabuddhapravacana-hridaya* reconstructed from 一切佛語心.

74. Ishii Kōsei "Baso ni okeru *Ranka kyō, Ninyū shigyōron* no iyō," 114.

75. For example, Chan records like *Yuanwu Foguo chanshi yulu* (T47.784a5–9) as well as sūtra commentaries from the Song and on will give this new interpretation, whereas the earlier commentary by Fazang did not. On the importance of Fazang's commentary, see Deleanu, "*Laṅkāvatārasūtra,*" 23.

76. Some of this is conveyed in Poceski, *Records of Mazu,* 203–204, which gives "According to the Buddha's teaching the mind is the essential principle." Cf. Welter, which renders this as "the mind that the Buddha spoke of," in *Yongming Yanshou's Conception of Chan,* 80, 172–177, 243, 250–251.

77. Keqin quotes the same version of this saying found in *Zong jing lu* (T48.418b16–17). "For Chan postulant Yuanzhang" 示元長禪人, *Yuanwu Foguo chanshi yulu* (T47.787a22–23). The same text appears in *Foguo Keqin chanshi xin yao* (ZZ69.495b19–22).

78. Norman, *Philological Approach to Buddhism,* 178.

79. *Shuzhou Longmen Foyan heshang yulu,* 1.1a-b; also in *Gu zunsu yulu* (ZZ68.173b4–6). On Xu Fu, see Fuller, *Drifting among Rivers and Lakes,* 114–118.

80. *Gu zunsu yulu* (ZZ68.173b5–6).

various kinds of words and deeds, including those in verse, are all words and deeds of a buddha. Later in this very *yulu* Foyan Qingyuan himself began a sermon thus: "Students these days [think they] do not investigate the words of buddhas [*buddhavacana*], and only investigate the words of ancestors and masters. Who doesn't know that the words of ancestors and masters are precisely the words of buddhas?" 今時學者不究佛語，祇究祖師語，殊不知祖師語即是佛語.[81] We may infer that this sermon was responding to the general enthusiasm in the Northern Song for studying the words of Chan masters. Both the sermon and the preface frame Chan texts as possessing the soteriological efficacy of *buddhavacana*.

It is notable that the terms *ji* and *jisong* were used so often in the Song that they also had a more common denotation meaning simply a verse or poem written by a monk. But when we examine the textual practices of elite monks and their disciples during the Song era, the technical connotation above becomes relevant. A Chan abbot's poems written in *shi* forms were included in *yulu*, usually in the concluding fascicles and often under a section entitled *"Jisong."* The placement of a master's poems at the end of a *yulu*, after those teachings recorded in prose, appears to be homologous to the classical structure of a sūtra in which the Buddha's teachings are given first in prose and then in verse.[82] *Jisong* here only loosely refers to Sanskrit *gāthā*; rather, it was used creatively as a label for the Chinese poems (often *shi* carefully observing tonal meter) written by well-regarded Chan teachers. Using the term *jisong* conferred on these poems the religious reverence accorded Indic verse. Song monks themselves offered explicit definitions of the word *gāthā* in this vein, based in part on Tang-dynasty sūtra commentaries, translated in the next section.

Tang and Song Definitions of *Jisong*

Although Chinese monks had begun to compose what they called *gāthā,* the term's origins in the sūtras remained important to Buddhist monks and the educated elite. The connotations of *gāthā* when used to describe Chinese-authored verse drew on knowledge of scripture. In Buddhist sūtras, *gāthā* include several kinds of verse that fulfilled a number of functions. Most Song-era Tiantai and Huayan exegetes defined *gāthā* using two sets of observations that were formulated by the important Huayan scholar-monk Chengguan 澄觀 (738–839).[83] These glosses also informed the Chan lexicon *Zuting shiyuan*, a primer intended for use by monkish students of Chan literature, to which we will return below.

---

81. *Gu zunsu yulu* (ZZ68.184c6–7). Foyan was among the illustrious students of Wuzu Fayan. For a useful overview of Foyan's life and works, see Hasegawa, "Butsugen Shōon no shisō."

82. This observation made by Shang, "*Xuedou lu* Song Yuan ben," 8.

83. It is likely that some Song readers were familiar with these two lists through Zongmi, who quotes the entire passage in *Yuanjue jing da shu* (ZZ9.351c12–352a5).

Chengguan observed both formal literary qualities as well as the functions of verse in the sutras. The list of "four types" 四種 includes four types of "verse" (*song* 頌). First are verses that adhere to the classical Indic meter of four *pāda*, or metrical feet, with eight syllables each, for a total of thirty-two syllables. Chengguan calls this *anousudupo* 阿耨窣覩婆, a transliteration of the Sanskrit *anuṣṭubh*. It is a definition by form; in this case, one recognizes a *gāthā* by formal qualities of language. The second type Chengguan calls *qietuo* 伽陀, or "*gāthā*," in which the dharma is expounded in verse form directly and not as a reiteration of some preceding narrative. Here, *gāthā* refers to liberating speech in verse form, marked by soteriological function. This meaning is picked up by Shanqing in *Zuting shiyuan*. Third are the *qiye* 祇夜, or *geya*, the hymnal reprises that follow sections of prose within a sūtra. These verses repeat what had already been spoken or explained in non-poetic language. This definition derives from the narrative structure of the sūtras. The fourth type consists of those verses that serve as mnemonic devices, a definition that focuses on another function of verse.

The second list is set of observations in which Chengguan focuses on functions, what he calls "eight purposes" 八義. The list begins with an elaboration of how *gāthā* serve as an aid to memory.[84]

> What is the reason that sūtras often depend on verse? Generally, there are eight purposes. The first is because so few words convey so much meaning; second is because those who praise mostly do so with *jisong*;[85] third is to repeat an explanation for those with dull faculties; fourth is for the sake of devotees who arrived late;[86] fifth is to adapt to what is desired [by a living being];[87] sixth is to facilitate acceptance and memory; seventh is to make more lucid what was preached; and eighth is because the *gadya* (prose) had not yet explained something.

> 為何意故經多立頌。略有八義。一少字攝多義故。二諸讚歎者多以偈頌故。三為鈍根重說故。四為後來之徒故。五隨意樂故。六易受持故。七增明前說故。八長行未說故。

---

84. *Da fangguang Fo Huayan jing shu* (T35.543a28-b3).

85. These are drawn directly from commentarial gloss in the *Shidi jing lun* (T26.127c13–15), the Chinese translation by Bodhiruci et al. of Vasubandhu's **Daśabhūmikasūtra-śāstra*. "What is the reason [Vimukticandra 解脫月] used *jisong* to ask [Vajragarbha 金剛藏 to keep preaching]? Because so few words convey so much meaning. Also because those who praise mostly do so with *jisong*" 何故偈頌請？少字攝多義故。諸讚歎者多以偈頌故. This passage also quoted with citation in the related section of the earlier Fazang commentary, *Huayan jing tanxuanji* (T35.137c18–19).

86. Jizang 吉藏 (549–623) in his commentary *Jingang bore shu* explains that those who arrive first may hear an extensive explanation and those who arrive late will hear an abbreviated explanation in verse form (T33.118a23-b5).

87. Chengguan does not clarify this terse phrase in the relevant section of his auto-subcommentary *Da fangguang Fo Huayan jing shu yanyi chao* (T36.154a23-b18). My tentative translation is based on Chengguan's explanation in another section of this commentary.

Among this set of potential purposes for scriptural *gāthā,* all but one reference the benefits for the audience. *Gāthā* are terse and powerful. *Gāthā* are didactic. The purpose of a *gāthā* is to create benefits and to lead others to liberation. This is likely the meaning of the fifth purpose of *gāthā,* "to accord with what is desired" (*sui yile*). In another section of this commentary, Chengguan explains that expedient means may respond to ordinary wishes or hopes: "One adapts to what will delight the many living beings, each of which is different, then accords with what is desired as an expedient means to open and reveal [the way]" 隨諸眾生意樂各異，順彼所欲方便開示.[88] Chengguan does not give an example in which a *gāthā* responds to the wishes or hopes of a pupil; nonetheless, in the above text it is clear that a skillful teacher may use verse to teach people who are disposed to learn from poetry. Verses may also facilitate memorization or be of special benefit for those of lesser faculties.

The Chan lexicon *Zuting shiyuan,* compiled by monk Mu'an Shanqing, glosses the meaning of Chan *gāthā* with reference to Chengguan's sūtra commentary. Shanqing generally wrote his glosses plainly so that they could be understood by students. The colophon dated 1154 appended to a Southern Song re-publication discusses the importance of this lexicon as a resource for monastic education.[89] Shanqing's glosses today are invaluable for their straightforward, readily understandable manner. Few Chan texts from this period state their meaning so plainly. The *Zuting shiyuan* is a Northern Song example of what I call a normative or prescriptive text. The text prescribes definitions that reflect the norms that preceded its compilation and that in turn were given to later students, thus perpetuating those cultural and intellectual norms.

The *Zuting shiyuan* was intended as a reading guide to accompany a set of Chan texts. Though properly a lexicon, it is like a Song dictionary for difficult terms selected from Shanqing's working canon of nineteen items.[90] The entries in the lexicon appear in the same order as in the target texts; one

---

88. *Da fangguang Fo Huayan jing shu* (T35.572a9–11). Chengguan has several extended passages on *yile* in the commentary and auto-sub-commentary that also support this reading of *yile* as a single phrase, in the vein of a mental inclination, to be the object of the verb *sui,* including T35.661c15–21. Alternatively, one could also read this phrase as *suiyi le* describing "the joy of following one's inclinations." This would shift focus to the blissful mind of the maker of a *gāthā,* instead of how *gāthā* please the target audience. I am not aware of other instances in which Chengguan advanced the idea, and it would depart from the other items on this list.

89. *Zuting shiyuan* (ZZ64.434b4–10). The related Gozan edition discussed by Kawase, *Gozan ban no kenkyū,* 1:409.

90. Here I use "working canon" to refer to the more limited body of texts an individual or community read for interpretation in distinction to the normally larger "ritual canon" that could be used in multiple ways in addition to reading. In addition to his target texts, Shanqing quotes from *Pinaiye zashi* (*Mūlasarvāstivāda-vinaya,* given as 毗柰耶雜事); *Shisong lü* (*Sarvāstivāda-vinaya*); the Dharmagupta four-part Vinaya, *Sifen lü;* and the *Wufen lü* 五分律 (*Mahīśāsaka-vinaya*); as well as Zanning's *Seng shi lüe* (which he calls *Zanning seng shi* 贊寧僧史). *Zuting shiyuan* itself provides evidence of the circulation of these kinds of texts and their readership.

could keep a copy of *Zuting shiyuan* open next to a primary text and have Shanqing's glosses appear in sequential order as one read along. Each of the roughly 2,400 entries is on a technical term, some jargon in local dialect, or an obscure allusion. An entry might include Shanqing's gloss, a scriptural reference, or both. The target texts include the well-known *yulu* of Yunmen and Xuedou Chongxian and, in addition, texts less studied today, such as a Northern Song book of *gong'an* 公案 (J. *kōan*) entitled *A Collection of the World's Pearls and Jade* 八方珠玉集, as well as the otherwise altogether lost *Hundred Inquiries at Chiyang* 池陽百問, attributed to the prominent Yunmen lineage Chan master Tianyi Yihuai 天衣義懷 (993–1064).[91]

Shiina Kōyū has observed that Shanqing appears to have associated with masters of the Yunmen lineage, begun his studies in Jiangnan, and been active in the Northern Song capital of Kaifeng.[92] Shanqing did not receive an abbatial appointment at a public monastery, however, and was not a full member of a Chan lineage.[93] Little is known about Shanqing beyond what can be gleaned from his comments in *Zuting shiyuan* and the preface by a monk named Faying 法英 (n.d.).[94] According to Faying's preface, he encountered Shanqing at a monastery in the Northern Song capital of Kaifeng in 1108. At that meeting, Shanqing told of his itinerant study at numerous large Chan monasteries and with many masters and revealed his personal manuscript draft of *Zuting shiyuan*. He began his erudite lexicon in response to witnessing fellow students' rote study of Chan records. These students were not well-educated enough to understand their teachers' explications, so they fabricated erroneous interpretations of their own.[95] Faying, deeply impressed, worked with a prominent layman to have the book published.[96]

Neither sectarian bias nor geographic distance appears to have dampened the later reception of the *Zuting shiyuan*. The text was republished in Sichuan several times during the Southern Song.[97] It was also quoted as an authority in numerous Song and Yuan Chan records, including broadly influential texts such as the *Blue Cliff Record;* a collection of pithy Chan sayings entitled *Eyes of Humans and Gods* 人天眼目 (comp. 1188); and the Yuan-era monastic rules *Baizhang's Rules of Purity, revised by imperial order.* The lexicon

---

91. Huang Yi-hsun, *Songdai Chanzong cishu,* methodically analyses each of the target texts in sequence. Note that the complete *Bafang zhuyu ji* is preserved in the *Nian Bafang zhuyu ji,* a set of *gong'an*-style commentaries begun by Fojian Huiqin 佛鑑惠懃 (1059–1117) and posthumously completed by his dharma brother Yuanwu Keqin nearly simultaneously with the publication of his *Blue Cliff Record.* See Keqin's preface dated 1125 to *Nian Bafang zhuyu ji* (ZZ67.634a5-b1).

92. *Gozan-ban Chūgoku zenseki sōkan,* 3:712–713.

93. Huang Yi-hsun, *Songdai Chanzong cishu,* 9. On the relationship between an initial abbatial appointment and "full membership" in a Chan transmission lineage, again see Schlütter, *How Zen Became Zen,* 65–66.

94. Huang Yi-hsun, *Songdai Chanzong cishu,* 12–14, identifies Faying as Damei Zujing 大梅祖鏡, a Chan abbot in the Yunmen lineage.

95. *Zuting shiyuan* (ZZ64.313a21–22).

96. The circumstances of publication in Huang Yi-hsun, *Songdai Chanzong cishu,* 15–18.

97. *Gozan-ban Chūgoku zenseki sōkan,* 3:713–715.

also circulated in Japan.[98] The frequency of its reproduction suggests that there was likely some ongoing readership.

The *Zuting shiyuan* includes two entries pertinent to a discussion of *jisong*. One is for the word *qietuo*, a transliteration of *gāthā*, as used in a Northern Song recension of the *yulu* of Fayan Wenyi 法眼文益 (885–958).[99] The second is for the term *jisong* as part of the explanation of terms from *The Extensive Records of Master Yunmen* 雲門廣錄. In the first of these glosses Shanqing begins with ideas inherited from the Chengguan commentary.[100]

> *Qietuo* [according to Chengguan] "are known as 'chanted verses' and as 'non-versifying verses' because they do not make verses of sūtra prose. Some people call these 'direct verses' because one directly uses a *gāthā* (*ji*) to explain the dharma."[101] These days the term "chanted verses" is used by Ruists to refer to the praise of moral conduct and extolling of success, [hence we do not use the phrase anymore]. "Direct verses" can only be composed if one has illuminated the mind-ground and attained the insight of a buddha. In our current generation, many people think that hymns (*song*) are not "sensuously intricate" and thus can be dashed off quickly. Such people do not realize that hymns are far more difficult than poetry of the world. This is the meaning of Qiji's preface to [the *jisong* by] Longya, which says "the form may be a poem, but the aim is not poetry." Thus, we know that the poetic Elegantiae and Laude[102] of the world are absolutely different from the *gāthā* [*qietuo*] of the Buddhists.

> 伽陀 此云諷頌，亦云不頌頌，謂不頌長行故。或名直頌，謂直以偈說法故。今儒家所謂游揚德業、褒讚成功者，諷頌也。所謂直頌者，自非心地開明達佛知見，莫能為也。今時輩往往謂頌不尚綺靡，率爾可成。殊不知難於世間詩章遠甚。故齊己龍牙序云，"其體雖詩，其旨非詩者，"則知世間之雅頌與釋氏伽陀固相萬矣。

Shanqing here explicitly states that the necessary condition for composing *jisong* is awakening.[103] His statement implies that to be awakened is to be able to function as a buddha. Thus, just as when a buddha teaches in a "direct verse," so, too, when an enlightened master teaches directly in poetry, the result is a "Chinese *gāthā*." By this definition, a Song text's reference to the

---

98. On Mujaku Dōchū and his critiques of *Zuting Shiyuan,* see Yanagida, "Mujaku Dōchū no gakumon."

99. Shanqing used a text that does not correspond to the extant *Jinling Qingliang yuan Wenyi chanshi yulu* 金陵清涼院文益禪師語錄 (T47, no. 1991), based on a late-Ming recension. See Yanagida, "Zenseki kaidai," 447, no.15, and 476, no.127.

100. *Zuting shiyuan* (ZZ64.404c5–11; *Gozan-ban,* 348).

101. Cf. the passage by Chengguan in *Da fangguang Fo Huayan jing shu* (T35.543a21-b3).

102. "Elegantiae" 雅 and "Laude" 頌 are the titles of sections of the *Classic of Poetry* 詩經, here a synecdoche for mainstream Chinese poetic traditions.

103. Yanagida, *Goroku no rekishi,* 425–433, outlines scriptural sources for Chan understanding of mind-ground in the context of transmission verses (*chuan fa ji*).

literary output of a Chan monk as *jisong* venerates the person as an awakened being with the insight of a buddha.[104]

Shanqing defended these verses against criticisms by men of the world. Here and elsewhere, monks noted that literati readers were critics of monks' poetry. In response, Shanqing drew a genre distinction as a way of arguing that monks' verse should not be read as *shi*. Though Shanqing appears to address potential critics of monks' verse, the intended readership named in the preface to *Zuting shiyuan* was other monks, a fact corroborated by our knowledge of the publication history of the book. Shanqing made a distinction between poetry and Buddhist verses by way of exhorting monks to read the verses of Chan ancestors as religious writing and not to judge them by the literary standards of poetry.

Shanqing summoned a particular image of worldly poetry by invoking the phrase "sensuously intricate," or *qimi. Qimi* literally describes finely patterned fabric and here surely alludes to a well-known idea about poetry. The locus classicus is a line from *Wen fu* 文賦 by Lu Ji 陸機 (261–303), which reads, "the poem (*shi*) follows from the affections (*qing*) and is sensuously intricate" 詩緣情而綺靡.[105] The term *qimi* describes, as Owen puts it, "something brightly colored, intricate, and alluring," qualities associated with strong feelings.[106] The idea that monks' poetry lacks these qualities of *qimi* does correspond to other Song descriptions of monks' verse. Zheng Xie 鄭獬 (1022–1072), for example, wrote a preface for a lost collection of poetry by the monk Wenying 文瑩 (fl. 1058–1078),[107] observing that "where Buddhist masters excel at poetry [...] they use mostly solitary, enfeebled, or lifeless words" 浮屠師之善於詩 [...] 多幽獨衰病枯槁之辭.[108] Zheng defended the quality of Wenying's poetry by declaring it an exception to widely held stereotypes regarding monks' poems. According to Song literary criticism, monks' poetry was marked by bland or sour flavors, possessing "a whiff of pickled stuffing" 酸餡氣 or "a whiff of vegetables and bamboo" 蔬筍氣, and was not sensuous or passionate.[109] Back in Shanqing's gloss, we see that a Northern Song monk also regarded the embroidering of feelings into text, or *qimi,* to be extraneous to monks' poetry. *Qimi* as a metonym stood for a certain idea about the mainstream *shi* tradition that Shanqing distinguished from those *jisong* crafted with didactic aims.

The distinction between mainstream poetry and Buddhist verse is underscored by a quotation from the preface to a set of ninety-five verses by Longya

---

104. The intellectual history of the Chan master as a living buddha is nicely presented in Buckelew, "Becoming Chinese Buddhas."

105. Translation from Owen, *Readings in Chinese Literary Thought,* 130.

106. Owen, *Readings,* 131.

107. Wenying's miscellanies *Xiang shang ye le* 湘山野錄 and *Yu hu ye shi* 玉壺野史 are extant today. Aside from what can be gleaned from these texts and in the writings by literati, there is little known about Wenying's life.

108. "Preface to the collected poetry of master Wenying" 文瑩師詩集序, from *Yunxi ji,* 14.12b-14a.

109. See Protass, "Flavors of Monks' Poetry."

Judun 龍牙居遁 (835–923).[110] The preface—authored by the monk Qiji 齊己 (ca. 864–937), one of the most famous poets of his generation[111]—contains the epigrammatic comment that "the form may be that of poetry, but the aim is not that of poetry," which emphasizes that anyone who tries to understand Judun's *jisong* as poetry will miss the point.[112] This is a back-handed compliment implying that Longya's verses are not very good as poetry *per se*.[113] Shanqing, on the other hand, extracts this comment to argue that because *jisong* were not written as *shi* but with another purpose in mind, they should be read as such. The word *zhi* 旨, translated as "aims" or the intentions of the poet, also had a religious resonance meaning "principles" or fundamental teachings. We may read both meanings into Shanqing's text to understand that the principles of *jisong* differ from the aims or intent of *shi* even when *jisong* are constructed in *shi* poetic forms. Regardless of whether we, today, might consider this to be a naïve hermeneutic focused on authorial intent, the distinction mattered to historical authors and compilers. The sources reveal to us Song-era hermeneutics and reading strategies.

The second relevant lexical entry in *Zuting shiyuan* also addresses this issue of authorial intention and situational context. Shanqing explains the term *jisong* as found in his copy of *The Extensive Records of Master Yunmen*.[114] In his gloss, Shanqing states that Song scholars had misinterpreted these verses because they erroneously evaluated them as mainstream poetry. He argues that correct interpretation comes from understanding the context and pedagogic spirit in which Yunmen's verses were produced.[115]

> Not all of the *jisong* written by Yunmen are titled [and so the context is absent]. Some [verses] propagate the cardinal meaning and others exhort his descendants.[116] These are not the same as works by a poet, who waits for a topic and only then writes his poem.[117] As a result, the judgments of later scholars [concerning

---

110. Preface and ninety-five poems were included in the anthology *Chanmen zhu zushi jisong* (ZZ66.726c5–729a20). A modern critical edition is in *Quan Tang shi bubian*, 1472–1479, including a ninety-sixth poem from *Chanlin sengbao zhuan*. A summary of traditional accounts of Longya Judun's life is in Kirchner, *Record of Linji*, 99n31.

111. Many of Qiji's works are analyzed throughout Mazanec, "Invention of Chinese Buddhist Poetry"; see 384–387 for a biographical sketch.

112. Shanqing's quotation conveys the gist of, but does not perfectly match, Qiji's preface as recorded in *Chanmen zhu zushi jisong* (ZZ66726c9), which reads, "although the form is identical to a poem, its aim is not poetry" 雖體同於詩，厥旨非詩也.

113. My interpretation improved by Mazanec, "Medieval Chinese *Gāthā*," 134, 144–149.

114. The received *Yunmen guanglu*, as well, has *jisong* as the title of the collection of verse.

115. *Zuting shiyuan* (ZZ64.318a13-b3; *Gozan-ban*, 184)

116. Some express ultimate meanings, some are an expediency.

117. Shanqing seems to be referring to poetry banquets, or perhaps the exams at which prompts and topics for poems were presented. Among the ample evidence that elite monks also participated in such poetic games is manuscript no. 25 in *Zenrin Bokuseki*. The manuscript's author, Chan master Mieweng Wenli 滅翁文禮 (1167–1250), noted that he composed the poem to the rhyme word *tsyuw* 舟 (boat), as would happen in games where lots were drawn to determine either topoi or rhyme categories.

Yunmen's *jisong*] have been inconsistent, some puffed up with conjecture and losing the truth of the Way. I could find only a few examples of Yunmen's *jisong* in [*Jingde*] *Chuandenglu,* [Tiansheng] *Guangdenglu* and *Xuefeng guanglu* that also include their context. [...] [Shanqing's three examples here omitted. Trans.] Once scholars examine these [examples in] context, there will be no need to fabricate overwrought interpretations!

雲門所著偈頌，皆不立題目，或舉揚宗旨，或激勸後昆，非同詩人俟題而後有作。然後世學者議論不一，或多臆說，亡失道真。愚嘗讀傳燈・廣燈并雪峯廣錄，有其緣者唯一二偈，未聞其它。［...］是故後世學者因覩此緣，遂妄生穿鑿，然何必爾也！

Shanqing notes that the *jisong* in his copy of *The Extensive Records of Master Yunmen* do not include titles—neither does the *textus receptus* have individual titles for verses. Shanqing insists that a reader of these *jisong* should understand them as the product of a masterful teacher with a didactic purpose. He is prescribing a religious reading strategy, which resonates with other movements in the Song toward demonstrating genius or sagacity not by expressing absolute truth but by responding appropriately to changing phenomena in an ever-changing world.[118]

Other functions of Song-era Chan verse mimic canonical *gāthā*. Verses often appear in Chan sermons as rhetorical flourishes to round off a line of thought. This function resonates with Chengguan's enumeration of the uses of scriptural *gāthā* to conclude sermons. Chan *gāthā,* too, can summarize, re-iterate, emphasize, or elucidate what has just been said. Or the function can be as a mnemonic device to recall a more comprehensive teaching, and, as such, citing a verse could function as shorthand to evoke an entire discourse. Similarly, some Chan sermons begin with a condensed and allusive verse. Because a verse of a few words may be dense with meaning, this technique invites an audience to follow along to the subsequent unpacking of the subtle meanings contained therein. These novel adaptations of *jisong* in Song texts show structural similarities with the earlier scriptural *gāthā*. From the above explicit definitions of Chinese *gāthā*, we now turn to the genres of *jisong* in the Song and consider the implicit definitions therein.

Genres by the Numbers: Collections and Anthologies

Song monks' verse and poetry survive in individual collections and anthologies. Bearing in mind the likelihood that most of the verse written by monks during the Song and Yuan dynasties has not been preserved, among extant texts, a great many verses are found in *yulu,* collections produced on behalf of individual Chan monks. Anthologies, or selected multiauthor collections,

---

118. Regarding the views from the Northern Song on what it meant "to act as a sage" that Zhu Xi rejected, see, for example, Bol, "Chu Hsi's Redefinition of Literati Learning."

are fewer in number and offer a different perspective that, as I will show, can corroborate or challenge the impression created by *yulu*.

The development of a mature *yulu* genre was one of the most important contributions of Song Chan literature. *Yulu* for individual masters continued to be compiled for centuries across East Asia. The genre was also adapted by Neo-Confucians.[119] Important modern research has focused on the antecedents and early history of the *yulu* genre.[120] In recent years, studies of Song texts about Tang-era masters have exposed the hagiographic processes, competition for patronage, and other factors that influenced the construction of these texts. Song Chan texts about contemporary Song monks, on the other hand, are far more numerous, though less often studied. In Anglophone scholarship, an important exception is found in Morten Schlütter's analysis of *The Extensive Records of Hongzhi* 宏智廣錄 as a case study on the structure of Song *yulu*. I agree with Schlütter's observation that many details in Song *yulu* correspond to the regulations for daily life in a Chan monastery as found in the "rules of purity" monastic codes.[121] For that reason, as much as is possible I read verses from *yulu* together with the Chan monastic codes.

Modern scholarship, since at least Henri Maspero's 1914 article, has concentrated on the medieval colloquial language in these *yulu*.[122] The entextualization of colloquial language has long been considered their most distinctive and important element.[123] Each *yulu* is a bricolage of many distinct types of writing, however, including literary representations of colloquial speech acts as well as numerous formal compositions and verse. In Chan public monasteries beginning in the Northern Song, formal compositions in parallel prose such as "petitions" (*shu* 疏) were vocalized in ritual performance.[124] Other formal documents were sent to distant interlocuters. Sermons, dialogues, and comments on "old cases" are not uniformly colloquial or literary. These texts wove together different literary registers, high and low, elite and vernacular. In addition to all these, multiple genres and modes of verse were generally included in the final fascicles of Song *yulu*.

To invoke Hollander again, "It is nonetheless common and convenient for most people who don't read carefully to use 'poetry' to mean 'writing in

---

119. See Gardner, "Modes of Thinking and Modes of Discourse in the Sung."

120. The modern study of *yulu* began with the discovery of manuscripts in the Dunhuang Cave 16. Significant development in the postwar period was led by Yanagida Seizan, including his monograph-length essay "Goroku no rekishi." See also in English, Yanagida, "'Recorded Sayings' Texts of Chinese Ch'an Buddhism." The phrase "encounter dialogue" was coined by John McRae to translate a concept introduced by Yanagida, and which McRae further developed in "Encounter Dialogue and the Transformation of the Spiritual Path in Chinese Ch'an." Reviews and responses to these arguments can be found in Welter, *Linji lu,* and Poceski, *Recorded Sayings of Mazu.*

121. Schlütter, "*Record of Hongzhi*," 187–188.

122. Maspero, "Sur quelques textes anciens de chinois parlé."

123. See Schlütter's richly informed comments on what he terms "*yulu* proper" in "*Record of Hongzhi.*"

124. Nishio, *Chūsei zensō no bokuseki*, 1–19, 156–176.

some kind of verse.' "[125] We as careful readers know that not all verse written by monks was, strictly speaking, poetry. It is for this reason that I do not analyze *songgu* in these pages. Already in Song texts, *songgu* 頌古, or "eulogizing the old [precedents]" were distinguished from the other forms of monks' verse, with occasional poems and other topical poems collected under the rubric *jisong*. *Songgu* was a didactic mode of Buddhist verse and a distinctive innovation of Chan Buddhism during the Song dynasty that was practiced by Chan monks across lineages.[126] The word *song* as used in Song texts was sometimes a noun, as in "verses on old [precedents]," and sometimes a verb, as in "to eulogize an old [precedent]." These *song* verses were composed in response to *gu*, that is "old precedents" (*guze* 古則), anecdotes depicting the awakened behavior of "old worthies" (*gude* 古德). This Chan genre of commenting on established precedents imitates Chinese legal writing, hence the related term "public cases" (*gong'an*).[127] *Songgu* were often delivered as part of sermons, sometimes anthologized, and could later accumulate further commentary. An important example is a collection of Xuedou Chongxian's verses that became the foundation of the famous Chan *gong'an* collection *Blue Cliff Record* 碧巖錄 (colophon dated 1125) composed by the Linji lineage master Yuanwu Keqin.

An explanation for this basic division between *jisong* and *songgu* was provided by Chan master Foguo Weibai, the compiler of the imperially sponsored anthology *Jianzhong Jingguo Era Record of the Continuation of the Flame* 建中靖國續燈錄. Weibai organized the anthology into five broad categories, including two categories of verse: *songgu* in one fascicle and *jisong* in two fascicles. Many of the *songgu* employ rudimentary literary techniques, such as couplets with end rhyme and fixed line length, and one can fruitfully employ literary studies methods to analyze them,[128] even explore which Chan masters used superior literary skills in their crafting of *songgu*.[129] But the purpose of *songgu* was not to appeal to higher standards of poetry; rather, it was a vehicle for propagating Chan principles. This is the key difference between *songgu* and *jisong* according to Foguo Weibai.[130]

> The teachings of *songgu*: Bring forth the profundities of former worthies through eulogizing, and though expressions have parameters, the cardinal principles do not err.

---

125. Hollander, *Rhyme's Reason*, 1.

126. The earliest collection of *songgu* are in *Fenyang Wude Chanshi yulu*, followed by those of Xuedou Chongxian. For evidence that Chongxian was aware of the earlier text, see Huang Yi-hsun, *Xuedou qiji*, 214–216.

127. Sharf, "How to Think with Chan '*Gong'an*,' " 207–210.

128. Such as Hsieh, "Poetry and Chan '*Gong'an*.' "

129. Zhou, *Chanzong yuyan*, 125.

130. *Jianzhong jingguo xudenglu mulu* (ZZ78.622a10–11). Regarding the historicity of this "table of contents," note that it was included with the petition to the throne by Weibai and is named several additional times in documents appended to *Jianzhong jingguo xudenglu* (ZZ78.827b2, 828a8, 829a16); a Northern Song witness for the *mulu* survives as well.

The teachings of *jisong*: Good friends [i.e., teachers] across time who have eluci-
dated both inner [Buddhist] and outer [Confucian learning], sing about the Way
and compose literature, which we record to serve as a future guide.

頌古門：先德淵奧，頌以發揮，詞意有規，宗旨無忒
偈頌門：古今知識，內外兼明，唱道篇章，錄為龜鑒

Following these Song-era distinctions, the mainstream Chinese poetic tradition
was understood to inform so-called Chinese *gāthā* and was often absent from
songgu. On the one hand, *songgu* are a form of commentary with a primary
purpose of illustrating the awakened intentions of the Chan ancestors. On the
other hand, *jisong* are pieces of literature that both proclaim Buddhist truth
and participate in Chinese literature, which Chinese Buddhists often referred
to as "outer learning." The *summum bonum* of Buddhist teaching was known as
"inner learning," as in other Buddhist cultures.[131] As used by Chinese Buddhists,
inner learning referred to Buddhist texts and teachings and outer learning to
worldly knowledge such as literature and other Confucian learning. Chapter
4 will return to outer learning. Here, it is important to emphasize that Weibai
categorized as *jisong* the verses by Chan monks that most resembled poetry.
Similarly, I exclude *songgu* from my discussion focused on monks' poetry. *Songgu*
and *gong'an* were of course important in the history of Chan texts, but they ap-
peared in separate collections, were discussed in different terms, and were
generally treated as phenomena separate from either *jisong* or *shi*.

Poems appear in almost every *yulu* from the mid-Northern Song on. Within
these corpora of monks' verse, certain modes appear to have been written with
greater frequency. Quantity is an imperfect indicator of significance, but a glance
at relative numbers can suggest the kinds of poetry Buddhist abbots wrote most
frequently. The breakdown of explicit modes of verse in five *yulu* collections as
found in the received editions of *Taishō Daizōkyō*, volume 47, is shown in the table
below. This quantitative survey of monks across time period and lineage provides
us, albeit in a limited manner, a starting point for further analysis. It may be sur-
prising, for example, that a combination of social poems and encomia was the
category that appeared most often in these *yulu*, distantly followed by dharma
instructions and funeral verse. Chongxian's collections are unusual for includ-
ing very few encomia. By contrast, encomia make up the most numerous mode
in the collected works of Yuanwu, Xutang, and Mi'an. The numbers are based
on the individual titles found in these texts. Many verses have ambiguous titles
and do not explicitly participate in one of these modes. Despite its limitations,
quantitative analysis quickly illustrates that some modes of verse were more
common than others. For that reason, rather than focus only on those verses
that we assume should be ideologically important to Buddhist monks, I priori-
tize the kinds of verse that were most numerous in Song monastic literary culture.

---

131. Gyatso, *Being Human in a Buddhist World,* 102. Again, on the innate hierarchy expressed
by declaring "inner and outer" and other metaphors of spatial arrangement in the Chinese
imagination, see Campany, "On the Very Idea of Religions," 307–309.

Modes of Verse* in Five *yulu* from *Taishō Daizōkyō*

	Xuedou Chongxian (980–1052)	Wuzu Fayan (1024?–1104)	Yuanwu Keqin (1063–1135)	Mi'an Xianjie (1118–1186)	Xutang Zhiyu (1185–1269)
Encomia (讚)	9 (3.3%)	6 (10.7%)	48 (77.4%)	27 (57.4%)	95 (28.0%)
Funeral Verse (佛事)	0	4 (7.1%)	7 (11.3%)	2 (4.3%)	37 (11.0%)
Parting Poems (送)	126 (45.5%)	11 (19.6%)	8 (12.9%)	12 (25.5%)	56 (16.5%)
Other social verse (次韻, 寄, 贈, 謝)	58 (21.0%)	19 (33.9%)	2 (3.2%)	6 (12.8%)	36 (10.6%)
Dharma instructions (示)	7 (2.5%)	3 (5.4%)	8 (12.9%)	6 (12.8%)	10 (2.9%)
Inscriptions (銘)	2 (0.7%)	0	1 (1.6%)	1 (2.1%)	0
Songs (歌)	4 (1.4%)	0	1 (1.6%)	0	0
Total number of verses	277	56	62	47	339

* Numbers for each mode are based on terms explicitly indicated in titles of individual verses or subsection headers; verses with ambiguous titles are not included in a mode but are counted toward the "total number of verses." Note that the total numbers of verses exclude *songgu* and any verses within sermons. Percentages given in parentheses indicate the portion of the total number for each author.

Monks across Chan sects wrote in similar modes of verse. It is not the case that any one genre is associated with any one lineage. Each individual monk instead drew on a shared repertoire of modes. A systematic quantitative analysis of verse in other Song and Yuan *yulu* would probably yield similar results. For example, Christopher Byrne's recent analysis of verse by Hongzhi Zhengjue 宏智正覺 (1091–1157), a Caodong lineage master, includes a series of tables indicating that 279 of the total of 1,314 verses in *The Extensive Records of Hongzhi* were composed in modes of social or occasional poetry, including parting poems, poems sent from afar, and poems presented to a person.[132] While the total number of verses is extraordinarily high for a Chan teacher, the relative proportion of occasional verse is in keeping with the broader

132. That is the total *jisong* in the sixth folio, per Byrne, "Poetics of Silence," 54–56, 60–61, 155–156.

practices of mainstream poets of the Song dynasty. The collected poems of a figure like Su Shi likewise include a large proportion of occasional writing, though the types of occasions generally differed from those that took place in a Buddhist monastery.

The relative frequency of modes of verse among Song and Yuan monks is corroborated by anthologies, one such being the medieval Japanese *Newly Issued Jōwa-Era Collection of Verse from the Ancestral Garden Arranged by Type* 重刊貞和類聚祖苑聯芳集 (hereafter *Jōwa-shū*), compiled by Zen monk Gidō Shūshin 義堂周信 (1325–1388).[133] Many of the Song and Yuan books that were Gido's sources no longer survive, making this an invaluable source. Over some decades, Gidō organized 2,999 complete poems by Song and Yuan monks—mostly five- and seven-character *jueju*—into sections according to his own sixty-five types.[134] The "sending off wandering" 送行 section has 204 poems, a number second only to the 262 "encomia" 讚. Both of these types exceed the 100 verses "eulogizing the old [precedents]" 頌古 included by Gidō. Compare these with the mere 7 poems about "awakening to the way" 悟道. Additional social poems, including epistles and matching poetry, total 248, a number that exceeds the 178 dharma instructions addressed to monastic officers and disciples. Of similar magnitude to the latter are poems about "grief" 哀悼, which total 123. It is surprising to see that various kinds of occasional poems often exceed explicitly didactic verses. These relative quantities to some extent reflect Gidō's personal interests. It is nonetheless significant that so many poems written by Song and Yuan monks in these modes were considered important enough that they circulated as far as Japan. These numbers moreover reinforce the observations in the table, which similarly illustrate the prominence of social poetry in Chinese sources of *yulu*.

Chinese anthologies of Song monks' poetry include *Wind and Moon [Poems] from Chan Groves of the [Song] Renaissance* 中興禪林風月集 (comp. 1230s or 1240s) and *Wind and Moon [Poems] from the Rivers and Lakes* 江湖風月集 (late Song–early Yuan). The former was compiled by a layperson and comprises one hundred poems by sixty-three different monks. The collection

---

133. Gidō's colophon signed in 1388 only weeks before his death explains that his lifelong endeavor to collect, correct, and organize Song and Yuan monks' poems began when he was a student during the Jōwa period (1345–1349). Gidō referred to this deathbed edition as a "recompiled edition" (*jūhen* 重編)—first in his diary *Kūge roshi nichiyō kufū ryakushū* 空華老師日用工夫略集 under the date Kakei 2/2/12 and then in the colophon signed 3/14. He references an earlier compilation lost to a fire at Tenryū-ji in 1358. Thus, the 1388 edition itself is known as *The Newly Issued Jōwa-shū* 重刊貞和集. He died that year on 4/6. Keene, *Seeds in the Heart,* 1069–1073, and Parker, *Zen Buddhist Landscape Arts,* 65–67, give thumbnail sketches of Gidō's life, influence, and later reception. For more, see Kageki, *Gozan shishi no kenkyū,* 240–274. On the editions of *Jōwa-shū* authorized by Gidō, see Kawase, *Gozan ban no kenkyū,* 1:149–150 and 165–168. For the latest scholarship on *Shinsen Jōwa-shū* 新撰貞和集, once thought to be a later forgery, see Asakura, "Gozan-ban *Shinsen Jōwa bunrui kokon sonshuku geshu shū* kō."

134. This total calculated from the *mokuroku* added to the edition in *Dai Nihon Bukkyō zensho,* 143:1–2. Gidō in his colophon suggests he had not been able to collate eight-line regulated poems, however, examples of eight-line poems do appear, among which are *Jōwa-shū,* 9.29a-30a.

begins with Daoqian and includes monastic writers with diverse backgrounds across Chan and Tiantai as well as those without a strong sectarian identity.[135] These poems reflect those found in belletristic "poetry collections" (*shiji*) such as that of Daoqian. *Wind and Moon from Chan Groves* is a collection, in other words, that reflects literati interests and situates elite monks as participants in broader literati culture. The *Rivers and Lakes* collection, which was compiled by monks and includes 264 verses by seventy-six Southern Song Chan monks, incorporates the kinds of verses that are found in *yulu*. Nearly all of the authors belonged to Yangqi branches of the Linji lineage, which implies either that it was a sectarian collection or that the selection was representative of a local time and place where this lineage was predominant.[136] These two compilations were not widely commented on in Chinese letters, and we know little about their reception or readership in China.[137] Still, one collection represents a literati perspective on monks' poetry that differs from that presented in Chan *yulu* while the other gathers together the kinds of *jisong* one might find in *yulu*.

Another anthology, *Selected Poems by Eminent Monks of the August Song* 聖宋 高僧詩選, was created and published by a Hangzhou book merchant, Chen Qi 陳起 (ca. 1186–ca. 1256). It is noteworthy that this book was commercially produced, indicating Chen either anticipated a market for such a volume or hoped to create one. Chen is better known for his publication of a collection of "Rivers and Lakes" poets that resulted in his banishment from the capital from 1227 until 1233.[138] After his return, his Hangzhou workshop became a hub for the dissemination of texts and ideas. The *Selected Poems* collection preserves an important recension of the nearly lost anthology *Poems of Nine Monks* 九僧詩, first compiled by Chen Chong 陳充 (944–1013).[139] The latter text was re-published several times in the Qing dynasty.[140] Chen's collection is more like *Wind and Moon from Chan Groves*, a collection of poems by monks with diverse sectarian identities.

---

135. On this volume and its numerous Japanese commentaries, see Huang Ch'i-chiang, *Yiwei Chan*, 42–116, and Xu, *Zhenben Song ji wu zhong*, 1:265–267. Huang, *Yiwei Chan*, 47–48, surveys explanations of the book's title from Japanese commentaries.

136. These numbers and the two possibilities are considered in Suyama, "*Gōkofūgetsu shū no Zen sōtachi*."

137. By contrast, the two texts soon circulated to Japan and engendered a large commentarial tradition and frequent republication down to today. Numerous Edo commentaries still circulate, and modern translations of the *Gōkofūgetsushū* 江湖風月集 were authored in 1969 by Shibayama Zenkei 柴山全慶 (1894–1974) and in 2003 by Yoshizawa Katsuhiro 芳澤勝弘.

138. My discussion here draws on Fuller, *Drifting among Rivers and Lakes*, 408–411.

139. Ouyang Xiu, in *Liuyi shihua*, lamented that all but a few lines of poetry had been lost in the decades since his own youth. Sima Guang later found and republished many of the poems. The collection, originally with 110 poems, was expanded by Chen Qi 陳起 to a total of 134 poems. See Chi, "Songchu jiuseng shiji kaoshu."

140. An expanded recension in the mid-Qing is known as the *Yiqiuguan* 宜秋館 edition, available in *Congshu jicheng*. This was the basis for a further expanded late-Qing recension, known as the *Shizhu Youlanshi* 師竹友蘭室 edition, which, despite being marred with textual errors, is widely available in *Chanmen Yishu, xu bian*, 1:1–19. See Chi, "Songchu jiuseng shiji kaoshu."

New anthologies of monks' poetry were compiled in later Chinese dynasties as well as in Edo Japan.[141] Modern anthologies frequently build on Qing collections that reflect Qing preferences rather than Song practices. Likewise, the literati that compiled Song and Yuan anthologies of monks' poetry excluded formal ritual verse, such as that for funerals, and instead collected poetic quatrains on landscapes, seasons of the year, flowers, animals, objects, and numerous social occasions. The selections in these anthologies tell us about the preferences of their compilers for poetry over ritual hymns.

Song Chan abbots wrote many distinct types of verse. On the whole, in many *yulu* and in some anthologies, occasional poetry and encomia stand out as most numerous. In the next section, I conclude this chapter with a qualitative survey of the major modes and genres written by abbots of Chan public monasteries of the Song.

Major Functions of *Jisong* in the Song

I have devised five categories to illustrate the major forms and functions of verse in Song-era *yulu*. These functions often span multiple genres. The categories are (1) verses defined by their use in rituals, such as funerals; (2) popular songs and hymns, such as *ge* 歌, likely for edification; (3) "encomia" (*zan* 讚), verses in praise and usually inscribed on a painting; (4) occasional poetry in which a primary quality is a social interaction or an event, such as parting poetry; and (5) explicit doctrinal expositions, such as "dharma instructions" (*shi* 示).

This typology captures the plural contexts and functions of the different kinds of verse that were collectively referred to as *jisong*, in its broader sense (see p. 95). This is a heuristic model with some obvious limitations, addressed below and in Chapter 2. The categories, then, are only useful if they help us disambiguate the types of Chan verse and therefore aid our understanding of how to read in different genres. From this broad survey, I focus in later chapters on ritual verse and occasional poetry.

1. Ritual *jisong*

In *yulu*, a collection of *jisong* may include ritual verses composed by the Chan master. By this, I mean verses primarily composed for use in a ritual setting. Often a set of ritual *jisong* are grouped under the subheading "affairs of a buddha" (*foshi* 佛事), a euphemism for funeral rites. Other kinds of ritual verse found in *yulu* include deathbed *gāthā*, hymns for recitation or liturgical use, and verses of dharma transmission.

A general example of a verse used in Song Chan funeral rites is the "*gāthā* of impermanence" 無常偈 that opens with "all phenomena are impermanent" 諸行無常, thought to have been spoken by the Buddha shortly before his

---

141. See Liao, "Huangbo zong yu Jianghu zhongqi sengshi lunxi," and other works by this author on Ming and Qing collections of monks' poetry.

parinirvāṇa.[142] Several "rules of purity" texts dictate that, in the case of a dead monk, the verse be either written and displayed near the coffin or recited.[143] One encoffinment liturgy that combined poetry, parallel prose, and vernacular elements was written by Fohai Huiyuan 佛海慧遠 (1103–1176), a popular Linji master of the early Southern Song, for the funeral of the last Southern Song Yunmen lineage master Yuetang Daochang 月堂道昌 (1089–1171).[144] Fohai's single-use liturgy for Daochang iconoclastically inverted the "*gāthā* of impermanence." A similarly well-crafted ritual funeral liturgy with verse is translated in full and analyzed in Chapter 6.

The composition of a ritual verse at the deathbed was widely attested during the Song and often referred to as "bequethed *gāthā*" (*yiji* 遺偈) or "*gāthā* on departing the world" (*cishi ji* 辭世偈). Such verses continued a long tradition of Chinese deathbed poetry.[145] Paul Demiéville has suggested that this practice by monks was an imitation of the Buddha's final sermon,[146] a scene well-known to Song communities from the oft-recited apocryphal *Sūtra of the Instructions Left Behind by the Buddha* 佛遺教經.[147] A deathbed verse naturally had weighty significance, but it necessarily constituted a small proportion of the total quantity of poetry.[148]

Another kind of ritual verse composed by Chan masters of the Song consisted of hymns to the Pure Land. Chan masters like Changlu Zongze composed new hymns for recitation that reflected then-current debates about the

---

142. In Chinese translations of the mainstream *Mahāparinirvāṇasūtra,* the verse is sometimes spoken by the Buddha before the *pariṇirvāṇa,* as *Da banniepan jing* (T1.204c23–24), translated by Faxian 法顯 (337–422); and in some translations the verse is spoken by one of the heavenly devas immediately after the *pariṇirvāṇa,* as in *Pinaiye zashi* (T24.399c29–400a1). In the Mahāyāna *Mahāparinirvāṇasūtra,* it is in a previous lifetime that Śākyamuni, hearing half a *śloka* from a *rākṣa* ogre, gives his life to hear the second half. *Da banniepan jing* (T12.450a16), translated by Dharmakṣema 曇無讖 (385–433). Per Chan traditions, in Śākyamuni's hagiography from *Jingde chuandenglu* (T51.205c9), his deathbed verse is referred to as the *wuchang ji.*

143. A written display is the method in *Chanyuan qinggui* (ZZ63.541a15), with similar instructions in *Huanzhu'an qinggui* (ZZ63.586a6). Chanting is prescribed in *Chanlin beiyong qinggui* (ZZ63.653a14).

144. See "Encoffinment of Venerable Yuetang" 為月堂和尚入壙 in *Xiatang Huiyuan Chanshi guanglu* (ZZ69.596b13). On these two masters as well as the survival of the Yunmen lineage in northern regions under Jin control, see Protass, "Geographic History."

145. The longer Chinese tradition was a focus of Demiéville's *Poemes chinois d'avant la mort* and its adaptation in Japanese Zen in his "Stances de la fin."

146. Demiéville, "Langue et littérature chinoises," 280.

147. For general background on this text, see Frederick Chen, "*Deathbed Injunction Sutra.*" *Rentian baojian* (ZZ87.19c17–18) records that the recitation of the *Fo yijiao jing* was a prerequisite for ordination under Chan master Cihang Liaopu 慈航了朴 (12th c.). The *Fo yijiao jing* was recited as part of the annual observance of the Buddha's *pariṇirvāṇa,* according to Yuan-era *Jiaoyuan qinggui* (ZZ57.304c18). Song-era Chan *qinggui* describe a similar rite, but do not give the title of the sūtra recited, which I speculate was likely the *Fo yijiao jing.* Centuries later, the Qing-era commentary *Baizhang qinggui zhengyiji* (ZZ63.39519-b2) identified the sūtra in the Chan annual rite as the *Fo yijiao jing.*

148. A thoughtful examination of the visual elements and significance of deathbed verses is found in Levine, "The Faltering Brush."

status of the Pure Land.[149] Readers in the Song would have been familiar with earlier anonymous Pure Land verses as well as those by Shandao 善導 (613–681), known as "*Gāthā* for Worshipful Praise for the Six Periods of Each Day" 六時禮讚偈.[150] Many Chan masters of the later Northern Song advocated both the practice of "mind-only Pure Land" 唯心淨土 in this world as well as death-bed practices leading to salvation by birth in the western paradise of Amitābha.[151] Upholding both positions—mind-as-Pure Land as well as salvation by birth—was especially common among the Yunmen lineage Chan masters descended from Yuanzhao Zongben 圓照宗本 (1020–1100).[152] Cishou Huaishen also wrote in this genre.[153] Pure Land poetry was reinvigorated in the Yuan with works by Zhongfeng Mingben and Tianru Weize 天如惟則 (1286–1354),[154] and flourished in the early Ming with 110 "Poems of Longing for the Pure Land" 懷淨土詩 by the Chan master Chushi Fanqi 楚石梵琦 (1296–1370).[155] Based on his study of the Qing anthology *Selected Poems of the Lotus Land* 蓮邦詩選, Liao Chao-heng concluded that only beginning with Fanqi did Pure Land verse depart from didactic ritual hymns and instead approach a poetry of the Pure Land.[156]

One kind of ritual verse generally *not* practiced in the Song was the "dharma transmission gāthā" (*chuanfa ji* 傳法偈 or *fufa ji* 付法偈), found mostly in classical Chan literature. These didactic verses signify the formless mind-to-mind transmission from one Chan patriarch to the next. The earliest transmission verses appear in the Dunhuang editions of the *Platform Sūtra*.[157] A full set of verses for all twenty-eight Indian patriarchs became integral to the narrative of mind-to-mind transmission no later than the composition of the *Baolin zhuan* in 801. Transmission verses presented at the moment of a student's awakening were almost never created or bestowed by

149. Zongze's Pure Land hymns circulated as far as Xixia and are found in codices TK132, TK323, and B2, with facsimile reproductions in *Ecang Heishuicheng wenxian*, vols. 3, 5, 6.

150. Shandao's verse is one of several texts in the two-fascicle *Ji zhujing lichanyi*, also listed in *Lebang wenlei* (T47.151b11).

151. On the moniker "mind-only Pure Land" in the Song and its relation to Chan, see Sharf, "On Pure Land Buddhism," 309–314. See also Yi-hsun Huang, *Integrating Chinese Buddhism*, 106–159, for a more traditional intellectual history.

152. Satō Seijun, *Sōdai Bukkyō no kenkyū*, 259–278.

153. See six verses titled "Hymns on Recollecting Amitābha" 念彌陀頌 in *Cishou Huaishen chanshi guanglu* (ZZ73.109a22-b10).

154. On the importance of Tianru Weize's writing for late-Ming monks and laypeople, see Eichmann, *Chinese Buddhist Fellowship*, 224–225.

155. *Xizhai jingtu shi*, fasc. 1. A later recension with seventy-seven poems selected by Ouyi Zhixu 蕅益智旭 (1599–1655) with interlinear comments and colophons is in *Jingtu shi yao* (ZZ61.725b18–730c07).

156. Liao, *Daochui wukongdi*, 451–456.

157. For a review of essential scholarship on Chan transmission verses, see Ishii Shūdō, "Denpō ge," 281–305. For more on the structure and influence of the *Baolin zhuan* verses, see Yanagida, *Shoki Zenshū shisho no kenkyū*, 396–397. A later review of the topic is Tanaka, "Zenshu toushi no katen," 108–113. See also Adamek, *Mystique of Transmission,* 163, 292; and Morrison, *Power of Patriarchs,* 72–76.

living Buddhists during the Song dynasty.[158] A practice of transmission verses was, though, revived in the Ming.[159] Song monks did sometimes write "verses of awakening" (*wudao ji* 悟道偈), though these, too, were fewer in number than one might suppose. In other words, in the Song dynasty, transmission verses and verses of awakening were generally scriptural categories and seldom genres for creating new verses.

2. Edifying Songs

A second type of verse in Song *yulu* consists of songs, simple rhymed verse probably intended for popular memorization. Such rhyming songs seem to have enjoyed wide circulation, as demonstrated by the popular songs found at Dunhuang to the northwest and Japan in the east.[160] These sing-song verses are often categorized as "songs" (*ge* 歌) or "chants" (*yin* 吟), both referring to vocalization.[161] Less common, though historically significant, are *ming* 銘, "inscriptions," and *zhen* 箴, literally, "lancets," denoting a shart rebuke, also in simple rhyming lines and serving edifying functions.[162] I briefly review the salient traits of these genres as found in Song *yulu*.

Popular songs, such as the many variations of "Songs for Twelve Periods of the Day" 十二時歌 and "Turning the Five Watches of the Night" 五更轉, plainly state their meaning and seldom use subtle allusions.[163] Though the popular song may be considered a low and vernacular genre, it is important to recall that these songs may have been the most widespread forms of Buddhist verse. Early examples are anonymously authored and likely reflect broader communal concerns.[164] Several earlier songs, like *Song of Realizing the Way* 證道歌, were quoted frequently and enjoyed authority in the Song Chan community.

New songs were also produced by Song-era Chan masters. When we turn to examine these new songs, the distinction between high and low is complicated by the fetishization of vulgar speech in Chan literature. Some new songs are depicted as emerging spontaneously from the "joy of the Way," the literal

---

158. Cf. Anderl, "Zen Rhetoric," 15n25.

159. See *Wudeng quanshu* (ZZ82.233b1–3, 236c22–23, 241c5–6), for verses of awakening by Wuji Mingwu 無際明悟 (1381–1446), his disciple Yuexi Cheng 月溪澄 (n.d.), and Cheng's disciple Fangning 方寧 (d. 1491). In the early Qing, Faxi Zhengyin 法璽正印 (fl. 1660s–1670s) wrote at least thirty-two dharma transmission verses for his disciples, in *Faxi Yin chanshi yulu,* 812c24.

160. The introductory chapter of Wang Zhipeng, *Dunhuang Fojiao geci yanjiu,* provides a thorough review of major Chinese secondary literature. Kaji, *Chūgoku Bukkyō bungaku kenkyū,* 186–216, surveys the fundamentals. Tanaka and Tei, *Tonkō zenshū bunken bunrui mokuroku,* gives an overview of current scholarship. In addition, the titles of many songs and verses are in the catalog of documents Ennin 圓仁 (794–864) retrieved from his voyage to China.

161. Tanaka and Tei, "Shūdō ge ichi," 259–261.

162. Tanaka and Tei, "Shūdō ge ichi," 246–251.

163. See Kawasaki, "Shūdō ge ni," for an overview.

164. Jia, *Hongzhou School,* 89–92, proposes a convincing theory concerning Baozhi's 寶誌 (ca. 418–514) putative authorship of the *Shi'er shi song* 十二時頌. Her conclusions are based in part on the presence of mid-Tang rhyme words that did not rhyme in the Qi-Liang period when Baozhi was alive. She views the poems attributed to the famous Baozhi as works of an anonymous Hongzhou monk(s).

meaning of *ledao ge* 樂道歌.[165] Songs could be rhymed and follow some rules of meter. Audiences in the Song were generally disposed to regard such popular songs as old-fashioned. The familiar feeling of songs may have made this mode an effective vehicle for domesticating iconoclastic rhetoric.[166]

Two additional genres found in *yulu* also consisted of simple rhymes and served an edifying purpose. The Chinese genres of *ming* and *zhen* pre-date Buddhism in China. According to the early sixth-century text *Wenxin diaolong* 文心雕龍, the difference between *ming* and *zhen* is that while the latter are oral and critical, the former are written and encouraging.[167] According to *Wenxin diaolong*, the *ming* originated in high antiquity as admonitions engraved by emperors on high-status objects like chariots and bronze bells. By the Eastern Han (25–220), virtues were inscribed on stone, and from the second century the *muzhi ming* 墓誌銘, or stone tomb inscription, consisted of prose followed by a verse in rhyming couplets (commonly in four- or six-character lines) to extol the deceased.[168] In addition, as early as Cui Yuan's 崔瑗 (78–143) well-known poem "Inscription Placed to the Right of My Seat" 座右銘, *ming* emerged as a genre of poetic verse in an admonitory mode. Similarly, in later Chan literature *ming* were adapted into a genre for didactic songs or exhortations. The *ming* as an inscription was transformed into a metaphor: a verse to be engraved on the heart, as in *Exhortation to Faith in Mind* 信心銘, attributed to the third Chan patriarch. *Zhen* are less numerous in Chan literature; they also seem to have indefinite line lengths and employ irregular end rhyme. The best-known *zhen* may be the *Lancet on Seated Meditation* 坐禪箴 by Hongzhi Zhengjue.[169] Such songs were meant to be memorized and served an edifying purpose.

3. Encomia and painting inscriptions

A third type of verse in *yulu* consists of *zan* 讚 (encomia), praise poems usually inscribed on paintings.[170] These differ from the *zan* as popular songs that are found in Dunhuang literature.[171] In Chan literature, many *zan* were written

165. Sun, *Chansi yu shiqing*, 293–315, gives inspiring readings of interesting sources as a survey of these kinds of poems from the late Tang and early Song.

166. On the strategies and impulses toward the domestication of radical Chan, see Faure, *Rhetoric of Immediacy*, chaps. 5 and 6.

167. *Wenxin diaolong*, 3.2b. My thanks to Tom Mazanec for suggesting *Wenxin Diaolong* and Cui Yuan's *ming*.

168. Brashier, "Eastern Han Commemorative Stelae."

169. Translated in Bielefeldt, *Dōgen's Manuals*, 199–203. Bielefeldt plays with the oldest meaning of *zhen* as a needle when he renders the title "Lancet of Seated Meditation."

170. Both in medieval texts and in modern scholarship, *zan* are frequently written or printed as 贊. Shaku Seitan, *Kozen rishi*, 10, notes a philological distinction between 讚 and 贊 (also written 賛), in which the latter maintains the pre-Buddhist meaning of *lunzan* 論贊, "to evaluate." In historical writing and printing, however, the characters were often used interchangeably. The problem is compounded by the modern simplified character 赞 used to render both traditional characters 讚 and 贊.

171. For an overview of *zan* as found in Dunhuang literature, see Wang, "*Zan zhen*." Cf. Cartelli, *Five-Colored Cloud*, 87–88.

as *jueju*, although *zan* were also written with irregular line lengths or in a series of four- or six-character lines. The *zan* type was therefore defined by function rather than form. If quantity is any indicator of significance, it is worth remembering that *zan* comprise the largest single mode of poetry in the *Jōwashū* anthology as well as in many *yulu*.[172] I do not focus on *zan* in the later chapters of this book and therefore linger here on several examples to illustrate their contribution to monastic literary culture.

Zan can most broadly be divided into two types. The first is encomia in praise of a subject. By the Song era, *zan* were written with tremendous frequency about buddhas, arhats, and bodhisattvas (especially Guanyin), on semi-legendary people such as Hanshan and Shide, as well for historical teachers of the near or distant past. In addition to portraits of individuals, Chan *zan* were sometimes inscribed on depictions of landscapes, flowers, and birds. A careful reader may find allusions to Chan lore and literature within these verses, as well as allusions to mainstream literature.[173]

The second type is the "self-encomium" (*zizan* 自讚), a verse inscribed on a portrait (*zhen* 真 or *dingxiang* 頂相) prepared by a disciple, honored guest, or donor.[174] By the end of the Northern Song, in addition to writing inscriptions on depictions of buddhas, bodhisattvas, and ancestors, it had become common for students to make and present portraits of the master himself for self-encomia. In some collections, such as *Yuanwu fogou chanshi yulu* and *Xutang heshang yulu,* these self-encomia are gathered under the header "portrait encomia" (*zhenzan* 真讚), and each individual verse is entitled with the name of the disciple who requested the inscription, indicated by the words *qingzan* 請讚 or *qiuzan* 求讚. Previously, scholars understood inscribed portraits to play a role in dharma transmission and lineage propagation,[175] but we now understand them to have been used as gifts and exchanged or sold in fundraising campaigns.[176] Portraits were also displayed during funeral rituals and could be kept afterward in a monastery's "ancestor's hall" (*zutang* 祖堂), where they would serve as the locus for ongoing memorial rites.

The Chan poetics of self-encomia were well-developed. Praising oneself would be improbable hubris; therefore, self-encomia deployed self-abasing rhetoric and directly engaged the viewer's expectations.[177] An extant portrait bearing a self-encomium by Xutang, now in the Daitoku-ji collection, specifi-

---

172. It is also clear from material evidence that the middle-period Chinese practices of inscribing *zan* on portraits spread to Japan.

173. For such careful readings, see Shimada and Iriya, *Zenrin gasan.*

174. See Foulk and Sharf, "Ritual Use of Ch'an Portraiture," 196.

175. In their extensive survey, Foulk and Sharf "failed to uncover a single instance in which an abbot presented his own portrait to an advanced disciple as a certificate of enlightenment or dharma transmission." "Ritual Use of Ch'an Portraiture," 200.

176. Following Foulk and Sharf, Heller, in his *Illusory Abiding*, expands this mode of analysis to works by Zhongfeng Mingben. *Illusory Abiding*, 358–360, 394–396.

177. Zhang Peifeng, *Song shi yu Chan,* includes a deft analysis of the poetry of *zizan*, with parallels to mine here.

cally addresses the student Nanpo Jōmin.[178] Xutang's colophon that followed his verse adds that "[Nanpo] painted this old monk's ugly character and then sought a praise-poem" 繪老僧陋質請讚.[179] Such rhetoric is common among self-encomia.

The poetics of *zan* generally mobilize play between visual and literary elements.[180] The earliest self-encomium I am aware of is by Tiantai Deshao 天台德韶 (891–972). The inscription turns on the multiple possible meanings of the single word *zhen* 真 as "portrait," "authentic original," and "truth." The meaning is ambiguous in places: "Who is the *zhen* and who is the depiction? The only authentic original (*zhen*) is me, so my portrait (*zhen*) is not true (*zhen*), and any depiction is actually you!" 誰真誰寫，真唯我，我真不真，寫者你也.[181] A portrait, no matter how like the thing it depicts, is never the same as the thing itself. The informal second person pronoun "you" (*ni* 你) could refer to Qian Hongyi 錢弘億 (929–967), who created the portrait and sought the inscription; but at the same time, the pronoun could address any viewer.

This playful idea is common in later Song and Yuan *zizan*.[182] A close look at two more examples will elucidate the general contours of this mode of religious verse. First, writing in the eleventh century, Huanglong Huinan composed a colophon that read, "This student depicted my likeness and requested my praise. Ai! To depict it was surely a mistake, and to praise it would be doubly deluded!" 禪人圖吾真請吾讚，噫！圖之既錯，讚之更乖. Immediately after the colophon, Huinan added a self-encomium on the painting with lines like, "You call this my *zhen*, but it is my thief!" 謂吾之真，乃吾之賊.[183] The logic here is similar to that in the verse by Deshao.

A second example of a "self-encomium" was written by the Southern Song Linji lineage Chan monk Fohai Huiyuan, who was introduced above. Huiyuan, who was from a family of Sichuanese scholars, followed his older brother into the novitiate at age twelve. It is said that after years of study, in 1135 he finally had a great awakening when listening to a lecture by Yuanwu Keqin. Huiyuan devoted himself to Keqin until Keqin's death only months later and thereafter journeyed to the Huainan region, where he enjoyed patronage and received a series of abbatial posts. In 1171 he was called to Lingyin Monastery 靈隱寺 near the capital, where in 1176 he wrote a farewell *gāthā* shortly before

178. The same text is found in *Xutang heshang yulu* (T47.1061c8–10). The portrait is reproduced (no. 12) in Fukuoka-shi Bijutsukan, *Daiō kokushi to Sōfukuji*, 47, 183.

179. The colophon is not in *Xutang heshang yulu* and is only found on the painted object. It is signed 1265.

180. See Winfield, *Icons and Iconoclasm*, chap. 4, for an analysis of poetics between word and image in Dogen's *jisan*. Adamek, "The Impossibility of the Given," well analyzes precedents in Tang *zan*.

181. *Zuting shiyuan* (ZZ64.412b1), quoting from the long-lost collection *Lianhua feng yulu* 蓮華峯語錄.

182. Heller, *Illusory Abiding*, 388, describes Zhongfeng Mingben's inscriptions and "the problematization of depiction."

183. *Huanglong Huinan chanshi yulu* (T47.636a8–10). Eight-line verse, six lines of four-characters, two lines of seven-characters. Two rhymes: *tok* 德 and *yang* 陽.

his death.[184] The following text is undated and found in the *yulu* along with thirty other self-encomia under the general header "Chan students depicted the master's likeness and sought encomia" 禪人寫師真請讚. Some of Hui-yuan's self-encomia were composed in poetic meters; others incorporated parallel prose and vernacular elements.[185]

	Painting won't get it. Encomia won't get it.	畫也錯，讚也錯。
2	You don't recognize the shrimp catcher,	不識蜆子笊籬，
	And call him Puhua with wooden clacker!	喚作普化木鐸！
4	So to sum up,	而今要且，
	This head is not a head, and this foot is not a foot.	頭不是頭，脚不是脚。
6	I fear people will not believe it, and set this inscrip-tion as a guideline.	恐人無信，立此為約。

The master inscribed this admonition on a painting of his own likeness. This is typical of Song *zizan,* in which Chan masters purposefully wrote coarsely rhymed lines. Huiyuan elevates the painting with the rhetoric of negation and thereby invites the viewer to reconsider the relationship between repre-sentation and reality. The opening line declares this very painting to be "a mistake" (*cuo* 錯). In another self-encomium, Huiyuan wrote, "It cannot be painted, you've abandoned wisdom for the sundry poisons" 畫出不堪，棄智雜毒, and in another, "If I myself were ten parts, you've painted one-half" 幸自十分，畫出一半.[186] Such inscriptions circulated along with the image itself. The full meaning of these texts depended on the presence of the image, and the presence of this encomium thereby transformed a painting into a vehicle for promulgating a master's teachings.

The poetics of such *zan* anticipate the ordinary ways of appreciating an image. When Huiyuan declares that the head in the painting is not in fact his own fleshy head, it may seem an insipid comment. But the purpose of this self-evident critique is to draw attention to the habitual ways in which people mistake mental representations for the things themselves. The apparently trite insight about the portrait can therefore be extrapolated to other sensate experiences including thoughts as objects of mind. The suggestion is that to see things as they are would require a departure from the ordinary judgments of the discriminating mind. This is also the message of Huiyuan's allusion to the shrimp-catching monk.[187] This loutish monk goes down to the stream each day to eat his fill. Though he seems unrefined, he is in fact a fount of

184. See the dated petitions in *Xiatang Huiyuan Chanshi guanglu* (ZZ69.571a2, 597b6) and "Pagoda inscription for [Hui]yuan, Chan Master Fohai of Lingyin" 靈隱佛海禪師遂公塔銘 by Zhou Bida 周必大 (1126–1204) in *Wenzhong ji,* 40.15a–18a.

185. *Xiatang Huiyuan Chanshi guanglu* (ZZ69.595a19–20). Two rhymes: *dak* 鐸 and *yak* 藥.

186. *Xiatang Huiyuan Chanshi guanglu* (ZZ69.595b18 and c24).

187. See the story of "Venerable Xianzi of Jingzhao" 京兆蜆子和尚 in *Jingde chuandenglu* (T51.338a27-b6). Although *xianzi* 蜆子 are clams, the story tells of eating both clams and shrimp. Later paintings depict the eccentric monk about to devour a wriggling shrimp.

wisdom. Similarly, the eccentric Puhua appears in *The Record of Linji,* and his wild behavior is easily misunderstood as boorish.[188] To mix up the identities of these two monks means to not recognize them. To think that a painted foot is a real foot means to misunderstand the relationship between reality and the sensate representations in the mind. Mistaking feet or mistaking eccentric monks, both are errors, the workings of a deluded mind. At the same time, to see things as they are does not mean one altogether abandons seeing. The master sets down his inscription to exhort a viewer toward a proper view of things.

Some *zan* follow *shi* regulated form, while others do not. This mode of writing was marked by function, not by literary form. Encomia had the religious function of propagating Chan teachings. Chan encomia, moreover, were composed in reference to images, often produced by students and patrons. Encomia can be best understood as negotiating these social, material, and religious contexts.

4. Occasional poems as *jisong*

The fourth type of Chan verse is constituted of those occasional poems found throughout *yulu.* Occasional verses are common in mainstream poetry. Broadly speaking, such poems were written for a particular event or named occasion, or they somehow involved named people. Such poems are seldom found in Chan texts before the Song, and yet they became the most numerous in many collections of writing from the Song on. I analyze many examples of these occasional poems throughout later chapters. Chapter 2 will give examples of *yulu* in which *jisong* refers specifically to a collection of occasional poems.

Occasional poetry is a family of modes rather than a single genre. Common modes of occasional writing include "parting poems" 送 and poems sent as "missives" 寄. Poems were also "written in response," 酬 or 答, sometimes using another's "rhymes in sequence" 次韻, or as "thanks" 謝 for a gift. Because social relationships were affirmed and negotiated through occasional poetry, the social lives of abbots can be understood by reading them. Another subset of occasional poetry addresses a topographic place, a temple, or a single room or building. The occasions for monks' poetry parallel those for the literati, except that the former reflect the settings of a monastery and its daily rhythms. During the life of a Song-dynasty monk, he might write verse for events such as gatherings with friends or disciples, scenes of parting, and missives received and sent afar. These occasional poems often create a poetics of circumstance, in which the social and material contexts are incorporated into the text of the poem.[189]

Some *jisong* may participate in this mode of writing as well as in another

---

188. On Puhua, see the essay by Yanagida Seizan in Kirchner, *Record of Linji,* 71, 97.

189. I borrow the term "poetics of circumstance" from an analysis of Stéphane Mallarmé's *vers de circonstance* in Sugano, *Poetics of the Occasion.*

of the categories outlined here. Xutang, for example, composed a verse entitled "Winter Night, Shown to Attendant [Wei]jun" 冬夜示俊侍者. This edifying verse was written to a particular person at a particular time and therefore should be understood as both "dharma instruction" and "occasional poem."[190] An abbot would also compose verses for formal ritual events, such as funerals, with the stages of encoffinment, cremation, and interment each potentially occasioning a verse. These ritual *gāthā* may in one sense also be considered "occasional writing," even though their primary quality is best understood in light of the performative contexts of funerals.

What I foreground as "occasional poetry" are those social poems that most closely resemble the contemporaneous mainstream *shi* tradition, such as parting poetry or songs of grief. It is these *jisong* that bore a resemblance to mainstream poetry and that therefore have much to reveal to us about how monks negotiated the literary space between cenobitic life and the world out of the cloister.

5. Dharma-instruction *gāthā*

Some verses in *yulu* texts are explicitly didactic. These may be organized into two types. One type is marked by the verb *shi* 示 and usually includes the name of the recipient of the dharma instructions. The recipient may be a specific person, a set of people, or even the general assembly of monks (*shizhong* 示眾). Many dharma instructions do not acknowledge the circumstances of composition; neither are they addressed to a person or explicit social relationship nor do they refer to a specific event.

A second type of dharma instruction verses found in *yulu* are written on a topic and do not mention a recipient. One common topos among *jisong* is "recuperating from illness" 病起.[191] Such poems were written after recovering from a malady. But it is likely that many monks in good health would imaginatively take up the common human experience of illness as a topic. A topic of interest not only to Chan monks, the Tiantai monk Gushan Zhiyuan also wrote a long poem entitled "Self-Narrative on Recuperating from Illness" 病起自敘.[192] Chan masters, too, sometimes took their illness or convalescence as the cause for a sermon;[193] and on occasion, the illness of another monk could lead to such public reflection.[194] These poems commonly allude to the manifestation of illness by Vimalakīrti as an expedient means, followed by a

---

190. *Xutang heshang yulu* (T47.1036b16). This monk is probably Tiantai Weijun 天台惟俊 (fl. 1245–1269), who appears again in later chapters.

191. See Antje Richter, "Teaching from the Sickbed." In Pierce Salguero and Andrew Macomber, eds. *Buddhist Healing in Medieval China and Japan* (2020), 57–90.

192. *Xianju bian* (ZZ56.939c4).

193. Numerous examples from the Song and Yuan are gathered under the header *bingqi tiwang* 病起提綱, in the Qing-era compilation *Liezu tiwang lu* (ZZ64.137c23). Additional examples may be found in individual *yulu*.

194. For example, an aristocratic patron sponsored a sermon by Yuanwu Keqin on behalf of a recuperating monk. *Yuanwu Fogou chanshi yulu* (T47.734b15).

discussion of the emptiness of all phenomena, health and illness alike. Chan monks could thus transform their own illness into an opportunity to teach their disciples. We may infer that such sentiments made compilers regard these verses as *jisong* and not as poetry.

To review, the five functions of *jisong* frequently included in *yulu* are ritual verses, edifying songs, encomia, occasional poetry, and dharma instructions. These etic types are intended to be heuristic devices and are not exclusive categories or generic pigeonholes. Indeed, many monks' poems can be interpreted fruitfully from more than one of these perspectives. I also surveyed in this chapter emic genre categories and common literary forms and themes. The poetics may differ within each genre, but as *jisong*, all point the listener or reader toward liberation. Only some of these five types, however, frequently resemble mainstream *shi*. In the chapters that follow, therefore, I focus my inquiry on those *jisong* that were written in the forms of *shi*, those verses that a person in the Song might think, "the form may be a poem, but the aim is not poetry."

Coda

According to Chinese exegetes, *gāthā* were verses in Buddhist scriptures that served multiple functions. A teaching spoken directly in verse by the Buddha was *buddhavacana*. By the eighth century, the words and deeds of a Chan master were understood to be the words and deeds of an awakened being. Increasingly from the ninth century on, Chan verses were treated as Chinese *gāthā—jisong—*autochthonous *buddhavacana,* possessing salvific power. From the mid-eleventh century until the end of the Northern Song, as the literary culture of Chan abbots more and more came to resemble that of mainstream literati, the production and collection of *jisong* likewise expanded. Occasional poetry, encomia, and dharma instruction verses became increasingly common. Such verses are ubiquitous in texts from the Southern Song and Yuan. At the same time, Song-era monks distinguished worldly literary qualities from religious functions. Some *jisong* were *shi*, but not all. And some of the *shi* by monks became *jisong*, but not all. *Jisong* was not a single genre and was not limited to a single poetic form.

The distinctions between Buddhist verse and worldly poetry that existed in normative discourse were also put into practice in multiple ways. To better understand how and why these distinctions mattered, we should examine the practices by which textual communities in the Song made *jisong*. In the next chapter, I analyze how this distinction appears first in manuscript colophons by authors and then in the textual practices of disciples who compiled *yulu*.

2

Jisong in Practice

CHAN MONKS and monastic communities made *gāthā*.[1] By this I mean the literary composition of new Chinese *gāthā*, or *jisong*, as well as its reading, collecting, and publishing practices. My phrase "made *gāthā*" is a reference to the work of W. C. Smith, who proposed a focus on how "people—a given community—make a text into scripture, or keep it scripture: by treating it in a certain way."[2] Song-era writers and readers transposed the scriptural genre of anonymously authored hymns (*gāthā*) into a creative genre for individually authored religious poetry. As seen in Chapter 1, this shift was noted at the time and Song writers themselves proffered theoretical explanations. The doctrines and positions in prescriptive texts shaped the poetics of individual poems and the paratexts that framed collections of verse. "Monastic literary culture" refers to this web of connections between normative texts and the practices of individual poems.

Studies of manuscripts and the history of books can allow us to see the practical contexts in which Chan monks' verse was written and circulated. Throughout this chapter I will emphasize paratexts, by which I mean any element except the main text itself. Paratexts may include a chapter title, subtitle, section header, an individual poem's title and attached headnote, a preface, colophon, inscription, marginalia, or a signature.[3] Using an architectural metaphor, these paratexts form the vestibules through which a reader passes to enter the principal text; they thereby offer opportunities to explicitly establish an interpretive framework for readers on the part of the bookmaker.[4]

In the first half of this chapter, I closely examine manuscripts of verse written by Southern Song and Yuan monks, especially those works with colophons by the author himself.[5] I have selected texts for which we have both an early woodblock edition as well as a manuscript. Comparison of the paratexts

---

1. Note that conventions and practices differed in Tiantai and other non-Chan communities, about which more research remains to be done.

2. Smith, *What is Scripture?*, 18–19.

3. My terms for paratexts developed from Genette, *Paratexts,* and modified below to established conventions in the field of sinology.

4. Genette, *Paratexts,* 1–4.

5. Similar ideas were introduced in Heller, "Between Zhongfeng Mingben and Zhao Mengfu," though with different emphases.

of manuscripts with those of the received printed editions sheds light on the practices of poetry.[6] Most Song and Yuan monks' poems that survive in manuscript form are poems of parting wherein physical objects serve as tokens. I address the poetics of parting poetry more fully in Chapter 5. Here, my focus is on how writers used colophons to signal a difference between religious verse and literary poetry.

In the second half of this chapter, I examine Song *yulu* (collections of recorded sayings) to understand the role of compilers in making the verses of an abbot into *jisong*. This includes the historical descriptions of bound manuscript books as well as some of the earliest extant printed Chan *yulu* from the Northern Song. Again focusing on paratexts, I will analyze and translate the prefaces appended by compilers and consider the strategic use of genre categories to examine how Chinese *gāthā* were made by editorial processes. As Hilde De Weerdt has observed, it is these "features that turn texts into books and other types of publications."[7] These details concerning collecting and publishing will contribute to our understanding of how the monastic literary culture of the Song worked to make Buddhist verse distinct from poetry.

By focusing this chapter on manuscript materials alongside printed *yulu*, I seek to complement the emphasis other scholars have placed on print in the development of Chan. The broader field of Chinese studies, too, has emphasized the rise of print culture in the Song dynasty. In her influential essay, Susan Cherniack observes that printing "fundamentally chang[ed] the conditions of textual transmission that had shaped earlier book culture" because "print books exerted an influence disproportionate to their number."[8] She argues that authors began to interact differently with texts and new editorial strategies emerged to attempt to control texts. As scholars have continued to debate the complex cultural and intellectual changes wrought by the commercialization of printing, some, including Joseph McDermott, have argued for the sustained importance of manuscripts. On balance, to borrow the apt description by Chia and De Weerdt, "printed books 'co-habited' easily with manuscript[s]."[9] The development of a print culture in the Song did not displace hand copying and manuscripts.[10] By the same token, manuscripts and printed books "cohabited" in Song-dynasty Buddhist monasteries. It is therefore important to regard manuscript cultures of the Song alongside those of print.

Before beginning, I want to single out the fundamental research published by Shiina Kōyū. Shiina has meticulously documented the print history of Chan

---

6. Some of these Song manuscript practices show continuities with Tang practices of poetic circulation and collection, described in Nugent, *Manifest in Words,* see below n. 102.

7. De Weerdt, "Cultural Logics of Map Reading," 247.

8. Cherniack, "Book Culture and Textual Transmission," 32.

9. Chia and De Weerdt, "Introduction," 12n34—borrowing the image of co-habitation from David McKitterick—and referring to McDermott, *Social History of the Chinese Book,* 47.

10. For a thoughtful and critical synthesis of these recent debates, see Brokaw, "Book History in Premodern China," 259–262.

books of the Song and Yuan dynasties and has suggested the important role of bound manuscript books in the production of Chan texts.[11] My contribution here is my focus on monks' verses both as constituents of a living manuscript tradition and as objects of collecting, editing, and printing. I argue that across manuscript- and book-making processes, Chan monks and their communities regularly treated poems in certain ways to make them *gāthā*.

Jisong in Manuscripts

Individual Chan masters could distinguish between mainstream *shi* and *jisong* in their own writing. The distinction, in other words, was not limited to normative texts like dictionaries and monastic codes. Traces of the master's discernment can be found in his own writing and is best observed in calligraphic colophons, paratexts in which an author could explicitly state his intentions. Poems did not always have significant ancillary texts: a couplet by Wuchu Daguan, for example, is merely signed "Abbot of Ayuwang, Daguan," and bears three seals; a poem about plums by Beijian has only a simple signature, "Beijian."[12] Song and Yuan manuscripts did not necessarily require colophons, but manuscripts with colophons offer evidence for how Chan monks understood their own verse.

There are few examples today of Chinese collections of the calligraphy of Song monks.[13] On the other hand, collections in Japan of *bokuseki* 墨蹟, literally, "ink traces," a term that came to denote the calligraphy of Chan and Zen monks, include hundreds of original manuscripts written by Southern Song and Yuan Buddhist monks. Very few examples of monks' calligraphy survive from the Northern Song.[14] It is likely that the destruction of the capital and Grand Canal region during the Song-Jin wars of the 1120s and 1130s resulted in a significant loss of Northern Song written culture.[15] Calligraphy surely was produced, collected, and appreciated in the Northern Song—for example, colophons of appreciation by Huihong attest to numer-

---

11. Shiina, "Tōdai zenseki no Sōdai kankō ni tsuite," 528–529. Similar questions about the importance of a "print revolution" are raised in the erudite notes of Ahn, "Who Has the Last Word?" 4n7, 7n15.

12. *Zenrin bokuseki,* figs. 10 and 9.

13. For an overview of extant Song monks' calligraphy, see Hu Jianming, *Chūgoku Sōdai Zenrin kōsō bokuseki.*

14. Northern Song calligraphy includes several works by Daoqian as well as well-studied works by Yuanwu Keqin. Hu, *Chūgoku Sōdai Zenrin kōsō bokuseki,* builds on Nakajima, *Shodōshi yori miru zenrin no bokuseki.* To these I add the previously overlooked letter by Daoqian, "To Abbot Ning of My Hometown" 山主寧師鄉友, in *Yingyin Mingta Tingyunguan fatie,* 2.368–371; cf. variants in *Quan Song wen,* 101:311–313. Additional Northern Song brushwork in Huihong's hand in *Fengshu tie* 鳳墅帖, *Zhongguo fatie quanji,* 8:90–91, 126–134.

15. On the loss of books, see Lee, "Books and Bookworms," 204–205. De Weerdt, "Discourse of Loss in Song Dynasty Private and Imperial Book Collecting," has shown that quantitative descriptions of book loss cannot be taken at face value.

ous private collections by other monks in the Hongzhou area.[16] We can rely on additional colophons composed in the twelfth and thirteenth centuries by Chan masters when viewing the calligraphy of earlier monks, often incidentally noting the collecting practices of fellow monks and pious laypersons as indirect witnesses to Northern Song manuscript texts and their reception during the Southern Song.[17]

Japanese *bokuseki* are not, however, representative of all Southern Song and Yuan practices across all regions of China. *Bokuseki* collections disproportionately preserve writing by monks revered as ancestors by Japanese Zen schools; the Rinzai Zen school in particular had a preference for Linji lineage Chan masters.[18] The collections therefore represent Chan masters from the Jiang and Zhe areas, and especially from the large monasteries where Japanese students lived and studied. Furthermore, the most active period of Japanese pilgrimage to Song China began in the late twelfth century, one possible reason that extant manuscripts of monks' verse in Japanese collections are mostly from the Southern Song on.

Manuscripts in these *bokuseki* collections include pieces produced within Chinese contexts (such as domestic epistolary) that later were obtained or purchased by Japanese travelers, works addressed directly to a Japanese pilgrim often as a parting poem to send him on his way home, and works by Chinese émigré monks residing in Japan. When the same verse also appears in a master's *yulu*, it likely was not collected directly from a manuscript that had traveled to and survived in Japan. Multiple copies of a single poem could be written on a single occasion, allowing the recipient to have at least one copy of the poem and one for the writer to keep.[19]

In addition to poetry, *bokuseki* include other genres of writing, such as letters, formal documents like petitions, and encomia inscribed on paintings. The collections also include Southern Song "sermons" 上堂 and "dharma talks" 法語 written out by Chan masters. These other genres of writing

---

16. Fasc. 26 of *Shimen wenzi chan* includes numerous inscriptions, such as "Inscribed after the copy of Lingyuan Weiqing's [calligraphy] in the collection of Venerable Cai" 題才上人所藏昭默帖 and "Inscribed on a small convocation in Lingyuan Weiqing's own writing" 題昭默自筆小參. Zhaomo was a sobriquet of Lingyuan Weiqing, who retreated to convalesce at Zhaomo Hall 昭默堂 on Mount Huanglong in ca. 1101.

17. See, for example, several of the "prefaces and colophons" 序跋 in *Fojian chanshi yulu*. Wuchu Daguan composed numerous colophons, among them "Colophon on ink traces of four venerable elders" 跋四老墨跡, in which he contrasted the calligraphy of Daoqian as "a fine blossom of calligraphy" 翰墨之英華 and that of Hongzhi Zhengjue as having "not yet escaped the commonplace" 未能免俗. Xu, *Zhenben Song ji wu zhong*, 2:834. Xu, 2:834, 838, 856, also concern pieces of calligraphy by Hongzhi; 2:845 records a layperson visiting with a scroll containing seven compositions.

18. Levine, *Daitokuji*, 351nn17–18, notes that not all *bokuseki* were regarded as equal; privileged status was bestowed on calligraphy by those ancestors in Linji lineages favored by Japanese Rinzai communities. A quantitative analysis in Jiang, *Ri cang Song Yuan chanseng moji xuanbian*, 6, corroborates that a majority of extant *bokuseki* are by Linji monks.

19. Murck, *Poetry and Painting*, 153–156.

illustrate additional contexts in which manuscripts were produced and used in monasteries. A Chan abbot's preparation of a clean manuscript copy of his sermon was part of the broader literary life of the monastery. Although printed *yulu* may portray a Chan master as ascending the hall and spontaneously delivering his sermon, implying that his sayings and doings were transcribed by a student, manuscript evidence shows that a master might record his own sermons. In addition to the words of the sermon, a master could write out actions and behaviors, such as "look left and right." These action words were not necessarily added later by the master's disciples when they edited a *yulu*. For example, on the annual memorial for Bodhidharma, Xutang Zhiyu (1186–1270) made a ritual sermon known as "Raising Incense on the Bodhidharma Memorial" 達磨忌拈香. It survives both as a manuscript by Xutang and as part of the edited and printed *Recorded Sayings of the Venerable Xutang* 虛堂和尚語錄 compiled by his disciples.[20] The content of the two texts is identical except for one minor character variant: the manuscript *doulou* 兜婁 is printed as *doulou* 兜樓. Included in Xutang's manuscript are the performative aspects of the sermon, not just the words of the sermon itself. Xutang wrote action verbs on the manuscript —"then he said, ..." 且道 and "lifting incense, he said, ..." 插香云—that, like stage directions, were not spoken. The Xutang manuscript is evidence of the circulation of Chan sermons, which included descriptions of the Chan master's action, prior to and outside of their collation into printed books. It is possible that he created this clean copy sometime after the sermon, either as a personal record or to serve as a gift for a disciple or donor. In this case, the manuscript does not have colophons that would provide direct evidence of whether Xutang wrote it before or after his sermon.

Few surviving *bokuseki* can be demonstrated to have been written in preparation for a ritual event. One clear example is the sermon by Chijue Daochong 癡絕道沖 (1169–1250) prepared to honor the annual memorial of Wuzhun Shifan 無準師範 (1178–1249).[21] Wuzhun died in the third month of 1249. Later that year in the tenth month, Chijue succeeded him as the abbot of Jingshan 徑山. Chijue thereafter composed a sermon, to be delivered in 1250, for the first annual memorial of Wuzhun's death. The sermon was never delivered, however. On the manuscript, Chijue Daochong noted that it was "a memorial sermon for Wuzhun, written at the request of Librarian Yuan" 無準忌辰上堂源藏主乞書. Chijue signed the note on the twenty-fifth day of the second month,[22] before the memorial to be held on the eighteenth day of the third month.[23] While the idea of preparing a sermon was not unusual (a

---

20. *Zenrin bokuseki*, fig. 33. *Xutang heshang yulu* (T47.1049b20–24; *Gozan-ban*, 116b).

21. *Zenrin bokuseki*, fig. 22.

22. Librarian Yuan is a fairly common name, and little more can be known for certain. He is possibly the Librarian Jueyuan 覺源 written about by Xueyan Zuqin 雪巖祖欽 (1216–1287). *Xueyan Zuqin chanshi yulu* (ZZ70.631a24-b7).

23. This sermon was not included in *Chijue heshang yulu*, published in 1251. In *Zenrin bokuseki kaisetsu*, 3:15a, Tayama Hōnan incorrectly speculated that the sermon had been deliv-

Southern Song *qinggui* describes how to prepare for an approaching memorial day),[24] sometime between the writing of the sermon and Wuzhun's memorial, Chijue foresaw his own death. He wrote out an autobiographic text to be displayed during his own encoffinment and "then dictated dharma words to be sent to Wuzhun's pagoda, which said: 'Wuzhun's memorial is on the eighteenth; I will have departed on the fifteenth; I will not be able to manage the offering of incense'" 且口占法語寄無準塔所曰：無準忌在十八，吾以十五即行，不得瓣香修供矣.[25] Chijue passed away, as he had predicted, three days before the memorial. The prepared sermon went undelivered, but the surviving manuscript is evidence of a Chan master composing a sermon in advance of the event. This may seem to depart from the idea that a Chan master awakens others through spontaneous debate and actions. In Chijue's case, we might compare his preparation to that of a great actor who relies on a script, internalizes his lines and stage directions, and delivers a brilliant performance. Though a script is prepared, each individual performance is a live situation.

Bokuseki of poetry reveal numerous details about historical social practices. They also aid our understanding of the thousands of individually titled verses preserved in printed Song and Yuan *yulu*. Small details in these titles reveal the diversity and ubiquity of occasions and topics on which a master would write poetry. Similar details are in the paratexts of manuscripts. Verses could be "sent" (*ji* 寄) from afar or "shown to" (*shi* 示) a postulant. Thus, the reader knows who is the teacher and who is the student, who is near and who is far, who is staying to continue studying and who is departing in search of something. The distinction between who is the master and who the student is plainly revealed in poems that inscribe the practice of the acolyte's "requesting a *gāthā*" (*qing ji* 請偈), thereby providing the means to record that the master has been elevated to the status of one who produces *jisong*. The prevalence and consistency of these kinds of titles in printed *yulu* from the Northern and Southern Song and Yuan dynasties suggest a broadly shared literary culture that put into practice the norms found in "rules of purity" monastic codes, the lexicon *Zuting shiyuan*, and other prescriptive texts.

Comparing the *bokuseki* manuscripts and printed *yulu*, I found that the content of the poems did not vary significantly. It was, on the other hand, quite common for paratexts to have been altered in the textual processes from separate manuscripts to collected works. This is especially the case with the poem titles and author colophons. These differences reveal practices that otherwise cannot be seen by looking only at the received printed text or the

---

ered in 1249. No memorial (忌辰) sermon would be given the very day Wuzhun died in 1249. The text of the sermon begins "this morning, on the eighteenth day of the third month" 今朝三月十八, indicating that the sermon must be for the annual memorial, not for a ceremony on the day of cremation nor on the initial seven seventh-days or one hundredth day.

24. *Conglin jiaoding qinggui zongyao* (ZZ63.615a2-b17) gives, in addition to instructions for day-of ceremonies, instructions on what to do prior to the day of observance.

25. *Chijue heshang yulu* (ZZ70.75c11–14).

manuscript. We might say that, although these appear to be "the same poem," they are framed by paratexts that differed, sometimes radically so.

In this section, I present three arguments. The first is that Chan masters used inscriptions to state that their main purpose was religious and not artistic. Manuscripts reveal that Chan masters in their own writing participated in perpetuating a distinction between *shi* and *jisong*. Second, I will consider in what ways colophons reflected that the autographed manuscript as a physical object had social capital and served social functions beyond the literal meaning of the words on the page. Third, I will show how Chan masters wrote poems as gifts and might repeat the same lines in new poems or even re-use whole poems for new recipients.

Distinguishing Poetry and *Gāthā* in *Bokuseki*

Among *bokuseki*, the poems given to departing Japanese pilgrims are laden with details about their composition.[26] These parting poems are known by different names, among them *songbie* 送別, *songxing* 送行, and *zengbie* 贈別. Parting poems were a regular part of an abbot's repertoire and constitute a large percentage of the overall corpus of extant monks' poems.[27]

I begin with a relatively late example (fig. 1), one especially rich with textual details, written by Jixiu Qiliao 即休契了 (1269–1351).[28] The poem is addressed to Guchū Shūkyū 愚中周及 (1323–1409), who traveled to Yuan China at age nineteen and stayed for approximately ten years. This is a case where both a manuscript and an edited book survive. The same verse also appears in a supplemental collection of Jixiu's teachings, compiled by Guchū, known as *Gathered Omissions* 拾遺集 (hereafter *Shiyi ji*).[29] Guchū completed a copy of the *Shiyi ji* by the spring of 1350 and showed it to Jixiu, who added a colophon. Guchū took leave of Jixiu some months later, near the end of that year, and then waited in Ningbo before sailing in the third month of 1351. It is unclear when the parting poem was written; nor do we know when it was added to the *Shiyi ji*.[30]

The verse proper in the *Shiyi ji* and in the manuscript are identical.[31] The paratexts accompanying each verse are not the same, however. The *Shiyi ji* has only an abbreviated title before the verse, "Seeing Off Librarian [Shū]kyū

---

26. Huang Ch'i-chiang, "Canfang mingshi," discusses the role of *jisong* in the interactions between Japanese pilgrims and Chinese monks.

27. Repertoire here is intended to echo the uses by Heller, *Illusory Abiding*, who cites the influence of Campany, "On the Very Idea of Religions."

28. On Jixiu's death, see *Buttoku Daitsū Zenji goroku* (T81.96a25-b19). According to the colophon appended to *Shiyi ji*, he was eighty-two *sui* in 1350.

29. *Jixiu Qiliao chanshi shiyi ji* (ZZ71.99b6–9).

30. *Guchū Shūkyū nenpo* in *Buttoku Daitsū Zenji goroku* (T81.96a5–24) records that in the final month of 1350 Jixiu took ill and bid Guchū farewell. The parting verse is included there with most of the inscription intact. More details in *Kaisan Nenpo shō* 開山年譜鈔 by Guchū's disciple; see Kinugawa, "*Guchū Shūkyū nenpo* to Isshō Zenkei *Nenpo shō*."

31. There are variant renderings of 詮 and 銓, 遊 and 游. See *Jixiu Qiliao Chanshi shiyi ji* (ZZ71.99b6–9).

Figure 1. Parting poem from Jixiu Qiliao to Guchū Shūkyū. Source: *Zenrin bokuseki*, no. 81.

on his Return Home Japan" 送及藏主歸里日東.[32] The word "librarian" (*zangzhu*) indicates that Guchū had become a monastic officer.[33] Each officer had specific responsibilities to ensure the proper functioning of the monastery. They were generally literate and received additional training from the abbot. There was also the possibility that they could rise through the ranks and receive an invitation to become an abbot of a Chan temple, thereby joining the Chan family tree as a full-fledged member of the lineage.

Compare the short title in the edited *Shiyi ji* with the inscription by Jixiu written directly on the manuscript reproduced in figure 1. In the original authorial inscription, the old master wrote out his intentions for his young assistant.[34]

> Librarian Shūkyū of Japan, from the time he served as the incense keeper up until head of the scriptures,[35] in all these roles he helped this old man to peruse and read. I commend his hard work! Now, on his return home, may this *gāthā* [*ji*] exhort him onward.
>
> Qiliao, the old man of Zijin [Jinshan]

日東周及藏主，／自侍香典教至，／居間皆得，以代／香耄檢閱之／勞，可嘉也。今其／歸里，偈以／勸進。／紫金老人契了

---

32. The characters for "Japan" were carved half-sized to clarify that the *li* 里 (home) to which the person returns is a foreign country.

33. The colophon appended to *Shiyi ji* attributed to Jixiu is also addressed to "Librarian [Shū]kyū from Japan" 日東及藏主 (ZZ71.109b16–21). Guchū Shūkyū likely was holding this office at the time of his departure.

34. Following the transcription in *Zenrin bokuseki kaisetsu*, 3:51–52, emending 屋 to 至 as attested in *Buttoku Daitsū Zenji goroku* (T81.96a11–13). The slash / in the Chinese indicates line-breaks on the manuscript.

35. The compound *dianjiao* 典教 is not well-defined but grammatically seems like *dianzuo* 典座 (cook), and I gloss it as "responsible for the sūtras" and a synonym for "librarian." A similar use of *dianjiao* appears in Jixiu's colophon, *Shiyi ji* (ZZ71.109b16–21).

The inscription details Guchū's service as an assistant aiding the old man to read. It concludes with a declaration of its double purpose. When Jixiu ends with "may this *gāthā* exhort him onward," he is marking the event of a young man beginning his travels homeward while at the same time transforming the journey itself into a metaphor for the Buddhist path, thereby encouraging the young man in his religious pursuits. The didactic intentions of the writer are clear: this verse was a *gāthā*, a *ji*, not meant to be read as an ordinary *shi*.

Despite the author's assertions, Jixiu's verse in fact follows the tonal prosody of a regulated *shi* and has a single rhyme.[36] Jixiu wrote in a conservative literary mode. This is not to say that crafting the poem did not require skill, but rather that it was not experimenting with form.[37] In other words, this verse is a regulated poem in form and a *gāthā* in its author's stated intent. Jixiu's colophon encouraged that the poem be read as *gāthā* based on Buddhist values and perhaps was meant to discourage a reader from judging the verse as lackluster literati poetry.

The Social Function and Social Capital of *Gāthā*

The social dynamics surrounding a Chan master's composition of poetry are illustrated by an autographed parting poem from Xutang Zhiyu to his disciple Dewei 德惟 (n.d.) (fig. 2), signed and dated 1254.[38] Xutang was a successful abbot in the latter half-century of the late Southern Song serving as head of several prominent temples in the Jiangnan area. He hosted numerous students from Japan and Korea, with the result that both an early edition of his *yulu* as well as numerous pieces of calligraphy survive.

In the manuscript reproduced in figure 2, the columns of text read from right to left, as is most common. The right side of the manuscript begins with a quatrain, written in a manner that occupies the full height of the paper. To the left, an inscription is positioned at a lower register; it reads,

The Chan student Dewei on pilgrimage about to head east asked for a *gāthā* [*ji*]
Autumn of the Jiayin year of the Baoyou reign
Signed by the codger Xutang Zhiyu

德惟禪者巡 / 禮請偈東行 / 寶祐甲寅秋 / 虛堂叟智愚書

The author's paratextual element confirms that his verse is an example of occasional poetry. The occasion is the departure of a monk for itinerant practice. Note that the poem is addressed to a named individual, a Chan practi-

---

36. One rhyme: *hjuw* 尤. With first-line rhyme, follows the common B D A B C D A B pattern, based on Sargent's adaptation of Qi Gong's system, cited in the previous chapter.

37. Experiments with form and breaking conventions were ways a poet could distinguish himself. See Silbergeld, "Origins of Literati Painting," 483. On conspicuous clumsiness to affect ancientness, see Sargent, *Poetry of He Zhu,* 188.

38. *Zoku Zenrin bokuseki,* fig. 26.

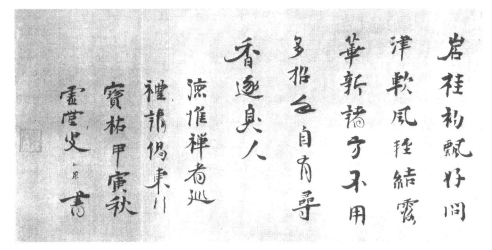

Figure 2. Parting poem from Xutang Zhiyu to Dewei, signed 1254. Source: *Zoku Zenrin bokuseki,* no. 26.

tioner with the dharma name Dewei, and that it was written in response to Dewei's request. Indeed, the quatrain itself addresses the young man about to embark on the next leg of his itinerant study.[39]

	Since gusts of [fragrant] clifftop osmanthus, you favor inquiring on the road;	巖桂初飄好問津
2	When a soft breeze gently stops, the pearls of dew will renew.	軟風輕結露華新
	Wherever you go there is no need to ask others too often;	諸方不用多招手
4	You yourself are the perfume chaser pursuing foul odors.[40]	自有尋香逐臭人

The verse offers advice for a person on a journey. Dewei surely began his itinerant study because he caught a whiff of the truth. But Xutang explains that what Dewei is seeking cannot be found by dashing about in the world asking for it from others. If he chases after his conception of truth, it will yield only more delusion.

Focusing on the inscription by Xutang, compare this manuscript with the same poem within the edited compilation *Recorded Sayings of the Venerable Xutang.* In the latter, the paratext is positioned before the verse, offset from

---

39. *Zoku Zenrin bokuseki,* fig. 26; *Xutang heshang yulu* (T47.1039b2–3; *Gozan-ban,* 103b).

40. "Perfume chaser" is a literal Chinese translation of *gandharva,* the Indian spirit thought to subsist on fragrances. In Buddhist cosmology, the *gandharva* is a lesser deity. *Gandharva* is also the name of the intermediary being that exists between death and future birth. In an extended meaning, both "perfume chaser" and "pursuing foul odors" appear often, though separately, in Chan literature to describe itinerant students who seek awakening outside of themselves. Xutang several times used 自有 or a similar construction to address students as "you yourself are [such a person who]" in *Xutang heshang yulu.*

the top of the printed page beneath white space. Here, it is the title of the poem, "For Attendant Dewei Going on Pilgrimage" 德惟侍者巡禮.[41] The author's manuscript colophon appears to have been abbreviated and transformed into a title. The abbreviated title excludes the word *gāthā*, or *ji*, which is found in the manuscript. Instead, the poem was placed within a subsection collectively entitled "*Jisong*."[42]

In the manuscript, Xutang himself wrote that the verse was a *jisong*. He used paratext to frame the verse as a response to a situation in which someone approached him. The manuscript preserves the traces of this encounter with a student. The manuscript is also evidence of Xutang's acquiescence to the request. Through this tacit acceptance, Xutang does not have to explicitly assert his own status as a teacher. He instead affirms that the verse is a *jisong*, even though the verse has perfect end rhyme and neat tonal patterns. Xutang moreover knew that this was not a private document and that it might be viewed by people Dewei encountered on his journey. The document could, then, serve as proof that Dewei had in fact met Xutang, without (in this case) necessarily signaling any spiritual accomplishment. The crafted rhetoric of the inscription addresses multiple audiences, allows Xutang to situate himself as someone who is regarded as a teacher, and offers a teaching apposite to this student's situation.

Comparing the manuscript and later printed edition, the recipient Dewei has been promoted from "a Chan student" (*chanzhe*) in the manuscript to "an attendant" (*shizhe*) in the printed version, reflecting the higher status Dewei attained between the composition of the manuscript and the compilation of a book. Dewei was indeed eventually a close disciple and served as one of the editors of Xutang's *yulu*, specifically for the section containing sermons delivered at Guangli Monastery outside Ningbo.[43] Additional details about the situation in which the manuscript was composed and presented as a gift can be gleaned from the manuscript inscription, which includes the year and season of composition. The regnal period of Baoyou (1253–1258) and sexagenary cycle correspond to the year 1254, before Xutang served as abbot of Guangli Monastery from 1256 to 1258. Satō Shūkō has reasoned that beginning in 1249, Xutang lived in reclusion in a small cloister above Lingyin Monastery of Hangzhou, then under the abbatial control of a Caodong lineage monk named Donggu Miaoguang 東谷妙光 (d. 1253).[44] It therefore seems

---

41. *Xutang heshang yulu* (T47.1039b1; *Gozan-ban,* 103b). On the titles of poems in Song collections, see Owen, "Manuscript Legacy of the Tang."

42. *Xutang heshang yulu* (T47.1034b13; *Gozan-ban,* 94b).

43. The full section title is "Recorded Sayings of Guangli Chan Monastery of Mount Ayuwang in Qingyuan" 慶元府阿育王山廣利禪寺語錄, in *Xutang heshang yulu* (T47.1003c04; *Gozan-ban,* 39b).

44. Satō Shūkō, "Kidō Chigu to Nansō matsu zenrin," 101. Xutang refers to the cloister as Jiufeng'an 鷲峯庵. Located along the ridge *Beigao feng* 北高峰, it was associated with the funeral site of Songyuan Chongyue 松源崇岳 (1131–1202); *Songyuan Chongyue Chanshi yulu* (ZZ70.109c12) and *Genkō shakusho,* 95.b7.

likely that when this manuscript was written, Dewei was about to depart from Lingyin Monastery after the summer retreat and had requested the verse from Xutang, even though Xutang was not the presiding abbot at the time. The monastic culture of parting poetry included prominent monks in residence, not just the abbot.

There are further examples of Southern Song parting poems to be found in the *Zenrin bokuseki* collections. Constraints of space do not allow me to exhaustively analyze them, but I can offer a few examples. A verse by Xisou Shaotan 希叟紹曇 (d. after 1275), a disciple of Wuzhun Shifan, includes a colophon that reads, "The Japanese Venerable Toku'e about to return home had paper up his sleeve and sought some [parting] words, and thus I responded to his request" 日本德會上人、歸鄉袖紙求語，因其請酬.[45] The same poem appears in a printed collection of his works without the colophon.[46] Similarly, a verse composed by Chijue Daochong in 1246 survives in manuscript with a detailed colophon, but the verse is not included in his *yulu*.[47] A colophon to a verse by Yuepo Puming 月坡普明 (fl. late S. Song), also a disciple of Wuzhun Shifan, identifies the addressee as a layman surnamed Tao 陶 who is en route home from a pilgrimage to Mount Putuo.[48] No collection of writings by Yuepo survives, however. These examples of colophons convey the numerous relationships had by Song Chan masters.

An especially clear illustration of the circulation of parting poetry comes from two poems written during the Yuan dynasty by Liao'an Qingyu 了庵清欲 (1292–1367). Both were addressed to the same Japanese pilgrim, Mubō Issei 無夢一清 (1294–1368), who stayed in China for roughly thirty years.[49] The first verse (fig. 3) was written in 1335. It is followed by an inscription that reads, "The librarian [Is]sei of Baizhang requested a *ji* on his return home, and I wrote this to see him off" 百丈清藏主徵偈還 / 鄉書以贈之.[50] The same verse appears in the printed *yulu* with the abbreviated title, "Sending Off Librarian [Is]sei of Baizhang" 送百丈清藏主. This ten-line verse alternates line length, does not follow tonal prosody, and has both rhymed and unrhymed

45. *Zoku zenrin bokuseki,* fig. 36.

46. *Xisou Shaotan chanshi guanglu* (ZZ70.470b13–15) gives the title "The Venerable Chō from Japan" 日本澄上人. It is unclear if this was the result of a copyist's error or was because the same poem had been given to two different Japanese monks.

47. *Zenrin bokuseki,* fig. 21.

48. *Zenrin bokuseki,* fig. 42.

49. His name is sometimes given as "Mumu Issei." The evidentiary record is contradictory concerning the year Mubō traveled to Yuan China. Some evidence suggests an earlier date and that he remained for about forty-five years. However, Mubō himself remarked that he stayed for about thirty years, which I prioritize. For a detailed and current study on Mubō Issei, see Kyūshū Kokuritsu, *Chūgoku o tabishita zensō no sokuseki,* 32.

50. The verb-noun phrase *zheng ji* 徵偈 is not common. One meaning of *zheng* is to seek out (as in the compound *zhengqiu* 徵取). This meaning of *zheng* appears throughout *Liao'an Qingyu chanshi yulu,* suggesting a pattern by Liao'an Qingyu.

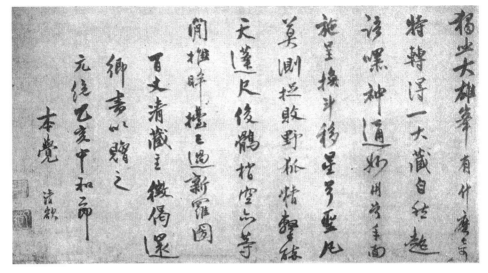

Figure 3. Parting poem by Liao'an Qingyu to Mubō Issei, signed 1335. Source: *Zenrin bokuseki*, no. 78.

lines.[51] The first four lines, a pair of rhyming couplets, include a clever reference to the responsibilities of the monastery librarian.[52]

	[When Baizhang said,] "sitting alone on Daxiong peak,"	獨坐大雄峯
2	What rare ability was that?[53]	有什麼奇特
	You turned the great canon,	轉得一大藏
4	And spontaneously transcended speech and silence.	自然超語默

The allusion in the first couplet refers to an awakened mind within ordinary life. Qingyu praises Issei as a librarian, the man in charge of maintaining scriptures, for overcoming the limits of language without falling into silence. The practice of "turning" 轉 might refer to vocalized chanting of only a few lines rather than every word, sometimes called *zhuanjing* 轉經 or *zhuandu* 轉讀; or, it might refer to physically turning the canon on a revolving library case, known as *lunzang* 輪藏.[54] Either way, this reference to the everyday work of a librarian

---

51. The manuscript includes an additional couplet not in the *yulu:* 捉敗野狐精，擊碎天蓬尺. Five of six couplets end in an entering tone, the first two couplets in the *tok* 德 rhyme family (translated in the main text), one each in *tsyik* 職 and *sjek* 昔, and the final couplet repeats the *tok* rhyme. One couplet ends with a word in the *tshjeng* 清 rhyme family.

52. *Zenrin bokuseki*, fig. 78; *Liao'an Qingyu chanshi yulu* (ZZ71.356b1–4).

53. A reference to a dialogue in which a student asked Baizhang Huaihai 百丈懷海 (749–814) what superpowers he could display; *Tiansheng guangdenglu* (ZZ78.450c6–7). See also case 26, *Biyanlu* (T48.166c26–29).

54. On revolving bookcases see Jiang Wu, "Cult of the Book," 53–58, also 60–63, where the vocalized reading practice is described.

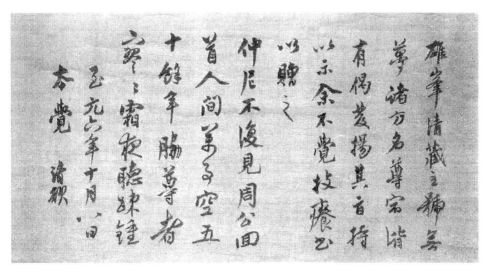

Figure 4. Parting poem from Liao'an Qingyu to Mubō Issei, signed 1350. Source: *Chūgoku o tabishita zensō no sokuseki*, no. 9.

would be obvious to a reader who saw the abbreviated title in the printed collection. The title provides important contextual information. The *yulu,* however, does not mention that the verse was for a Japanese pilgrim. This information, which appears only in the manuscript's paratext, provides further context for interpreting the references to pilgrimage and travel to a foreign country in the latter lines of this verse, which I will not analyze in detail.

This document, moreover, had significance as a physical object. It bore written traces of the master that were transported by Mubō Issei first around China and later to Japan. The manuscript served as proof that the student had worked as a monastic officer under an illustrious teacher. It was a common practice for itinerant students to "request a *gāthā*" when departing from a monastery. Itinerant study had many names, among them *xunli* 巡禮, *youfang* 遊方, and *xingjiao* 行脚, during which an aspiring postulant would go from teacher to teacher "to inquire about the Way" 訪道 or "to practice and learn" 參學. The *Zuting shiyuan* lexicon glosses *xingjiao* as "seeking a teacher and inquiring about the Way is to practice Chan" 尋師訪道為參禪, a line from *Song of Realizing the Way.*[55] A Chan master's calligraphy was not a substitute for actual travel documents while on public roads, but if upon arriving at a new temple, an itinerant monk could show calligraphy from a well-known teacher to his new colleagues and abbot, the newcomer might receive a more favorable reception.

Mubō Issei collected poems and showed them as he traveled, as also

---

55. *Zuting shiyuan* (ZZ64.432c19–433a3; *Gozan-ban,* 400–401).

attested in the additional manuscripts addressed to Mubō not analyzed here due to space. Although Qingyu's first manuscript (fig. 3), signed in 1335, includes a colophon stating it was written for Issei as he departed for home, Mubō Issei did not return to Japan until 1350.[56] His activities in the intervening years are hinted at by the second manuscript presented to him by Qingyu in 1350 (fig. 4).

In the 1350 manuscript, Qingyu recounted that Mubō Issei had traveled widely and wrote, "[He] was carrying *ji* that propagate the teachings of well-known honored elders from all corners of the world, and when he showed them to me I couldn't help feeling the urge to use my craft and wrote the following to present to him" 諸方名尊宿，皆有偈，發揚其旨，持以示余，不覺技癢，書以贈之.[57] This exposition of the circumstances in which the poem was composed incidentally recorded the fact that Mubō Issei was a vehicle for the circulation of poetry. Mubō Issei showed to his old teacher poems by other abbots. As any calligrapher would expect, a Chan master wrote poetry knowing that the physical traces could travel and be viewed by others. These poems, in other words, were not private addresses. They were written for a public readership and therefore should be interpreted as such.

Qingyu moreover showed his respect for verses by other abbots by referring to them as *jisong*, verses with salvific power. He described his own composition as a worldly "urge to use literary craft," a phrase unusual in Buddhist texts but a common literary Chinese phrase.[58] In his use of it Qingyu demonstrates his humility as a Buddhist monk, referring to his own worldly word craft and not claiming for himself a higher soteriological purpose. By juxtaposing *gāthā* and literature, he foregrounds the very issue of religious intent. He implies that it is the religious aspect of monks' poetry that he holds in higher regard and to which he wishes to draw the reader's attention. Qingyu surely expected that his poem would be read by others. If Mubō showed Qingyu's manuscript to others, those viewers would know that Mubō had met an orthodox master who elevated Buddhism over worldly literary pursuits.

A Repertoire of Prepared *Gāthā*

When a Chan master received a request for a poem, he could respond by using pre-prepared poetic lines. We may speculate that even when using prepared phrases, a master would spontaneously arrange and complete a final composition. Shorter set phrases appear regularly throughout Chan *yulu*. It is thus not entirely surprising that a Chan master might use the same seven-character line across many poems. I, however, will show below examples in

---

56. The *Entairyaku* 園太暦 records that Mubō did not return until 1350, per Ueda Takeshi as translated in Fogel, "Sino-Japanese Shipping Connections," 71.

57. Kyūshū Kokuritsu, *Chūgoku o tabishita zensō no sokuseki,* 20–21.

58. The "urge" is more literally "an itch" 癢. One might compare this with Bai Juyi referring to his poetry as "an addiction" 癖 and an affliction or "disease" 病, as discussed in Owen, *End of the Chinese "Middle Ages,"* 104–106, 119.

Figure 5. "*Gāthā* to send off a monk, written for layman Xu," by Xutang Zhiyu, signed 1268. Source: *Zenrin bokuseki*, no. 32.

which a master presented the same poem in its entirety to two different people. The multiple uses of a single poem on different social occasions, to my knowledge not discussed by other scholars, offers new insights into the poetry practices of Chan masters.

I will give as an example another verse by Xutang Zhiyu, which survives in both manuscript form and in printed *yulu*. The manuscript (fig. 5) proceeds in vertical columns from right to left, beginning immediately with the words of the verse on the right, followed by the colophon at left. The symmetry of the calligraphy is striking. Two lines of three characters each appear in the middle of the manuscript. On the right are the final three words of the poem. On the left are the three characters *song seng ji* 送僧偈 ("a *gāthā* to send off a monk"), which is functionally the title of the verse. These three characters are separated visually and grammatically from the words that follow, which consist of a personal inscription recording the name of the recipient, the year and month, the location at Jingshan for the occasion of the poem's writing, and Xutang's own name similar to that reproduced in figure 2 above. In addition to these basic elements—the time, place, and people involved—there is that terse explanation of the intention of the author. Xutang wrote the words "a *gāthā* to send off a monk," inviting readers to understand that though this may look like a *shi* in its form—the entire quatrain adheres to tonal prosody[59]—the author understood himself as participating in the tradition of *jisong*. Similarly, Yuan-era Chushi Fanqi 楚石梵琦 (1296–1370) wrote the phrase "a *gāthā* to send off" (*ji song* 偈送) on an extant manuscript as a kind of titular paratext.[60] The recipient of Xutang's manuscript entitled "*Gāthā* to Send Off a Monk," however, turns out to be Layman Xu.

---

59. The verse includes first-line rhyme and follows the common B D A B line structure described by Qi, *Shi wen shenglü lungao.*

60. *Zenrin bokuseki shūi*, fig. 124; the compounds *gjejH-suwngH* 偈送 and *gjejH-zjowngH* 偈頌 are almost homophonous; the first words are identical, and the second words both have a "departing tone" with the same final, closely related medial vowels, and related initial consonants—voiced (z) and voiceless (s) sibilants.

The manuscript in Xutang's hand reveals another practical aspect of writing occasional poetry. Once an abbot had composed a verse, he could address and present it to more than one recipient. The same quatrain in figure 5 is also found in *Recorded Sayings of the Venerable Xutang*, where it is addressed to a different person and entitled "Presented to the Chan Student Zugong" 示祖躬禪人.[61] This is a simple title that perhaps was abridged from a longer inscription on a manuscript given to Zugong. The title is nonetheless enough for us to determine that two distinct textual objects were created on discrete occasions using the same twenty poetic words in the same order, that is, the "same" poem was used on multiple occasions.

In this case, we can determine that the original composition was addressed to Zugong. The first line of the poem begins *zu* 祖 ("ancestor") and ends *gong* 躬 ("body" or "oneself"), the same words that constitute Zugong's dharma name. The line reads, "*Ancestral* intentions gleam in your very *body*" 祖意明明在爾躬. This is unlikely to be a coincidence. Xutang likely used the characters of Zugong's name so that the poem would have deeper personal significance. Such a poem would have had additional social capital for Zugong as well. By contrast, when Layman Xu received a copy of this poem, Xutang's inscription indicated that the content of the verse was not addressed to the layman. From this manuscript, a viewer would know that the layman may have visited the master and received a memento, but he had not garnered a personal poem of his own. This personal inscription could nonetheless be more significant than receiving calligraphy with no inscription at all, suggesting that it might have been purchased or otherwise acquired secondhand. The reasons for Xu's receiving a recycled verse are obscure. It nonetheless seems likely that possessing a recycled verse conveyed less social capital than receiving a composition addressed directly to the bearer and that a Chan master could affirm social distances through such subtleties in the gift-giving of calligraphy.

A further example of a single poem extant in manuscript and in print, addressed to different recipients in each, is a parting poem written by Shixi Xinyue 石溪心月 (d. 1256 or after). In the manuscript, Xinyue addressed this poem to Mushō Jōshō 無象静照 (1234–1306) and signed it 1256, and the same poem appears in his *yulu* with a title indicating it was a teaching intended for a layman.[62] The contents of the two poems are identical, and they can be differentiated only by the paratextual inscriptions.

In addition to the repurposing of entire poems, another common practice was the repeated use of a single line in multiple circumstances. The manuscript by Fanqi mentioned above, also a parting poem, is not found in Fanqi's

---

61. *Xutang heshang yulu* (T47.1036c15–17; *Gozan-ban*, 99a).

62. *Zenrin bokuseki shūi*, fig. 10, and *Shixi Xinyue chanshi yulu* (ZZ71.62c20–22). The two verses are identical, with one variant synonym: *qi* 齊 in the *yulu* reads *dou* 都 in the manuscript. A preface to the *yulu* reports that Xinyue died six years earlier, which would be 1254. However, several texts in the *yulu* are dated 1255. This manuscript to Jōshō signed and dated 1256 provides the *terminus post quem* for Xinyue's death.

yulu, but its last line, "a man from Japan tilling Shaanxi fields" 扶桑人種陝西田, was used as the final line of a different poem entitled "Seeing Off Librarian Yan of Jingci to Visit Mount Lu" 送淨慈顏藏主游廬山.[63] This same seven-character line was used yet again, this time in a dialogue purportedly spoken by Fanqi in response to a student.[64] In other words, this seven-character phrase was part of Fanqi's repertoire, used repeatedly to respond to different circumstances. Christopher Byrne recently noted a similar example of repetition of images and themes in the poetic writing of Hongzhi Zhengjue.[65] In Chapter 5 of this book and elsewhere I discuss the community of monastic authors that composed *Yifanfeng* and shared imagery and poetic logic. We see from these examples evidence that communities of writers as well as individual authors drew on repertoires of images to craft particularized poems in response to events.

Insights based on the above examples can, with caution, be extended back to the earlier Northern Song. Northern Song *yulu* contain a large archive of verse, including occasional poetry. Examples include relatively large collections of verse by the aforementioned Xuedou Chongxian, as well as by Wuzu Fayan 五祖法演 (1024?–1104). More modest numbers of occasional verse are found in collections of other Northern Song masters across Chan lineages, including Fenyang Shanzhao 汾陽善昭 (947–1024),[66] Shishuang Chuyuan 石霜楚圓 (986–1039), Huilin Zongben 慧林宗本 (1021–1100), Huanglong Zuxin 黃龍祖心 (1025–1100), Touzi Yiqing 投子義青 (1032–1083), and Changling Shouzhuo 長靈守卓 (1066–1124). Taken together, these collections show that occasional poetry was already a part of the Chan abbot's occupation from the early eleventh century and clearly well established by the mid-Northern Song.

In these *yulu,* a verse's title and sometimes an appended headnote convey the details of the various encounters and social interactions that prompted the verse. In some examples above, a poem's printed title was abbreviated from a manuscript colophon. Similarly, headnotes (*xu* 序) likely originated as colophons written on a manuscript, as also seen above. I use the English word "headnote" to distinguish these paratexts from the "preface" (*xu* 序) to the entire collection. The above examples should also, in my view, suffice to illustrate that we should assume that many, if not most, of these paratextual elements like titles and headnotes do not transparently convey the paratext directly from the master's manuscript. Even if they were simplified or appended by compilers, titles of occasional verse offer a window onto the likely circumstances of production. These conclusions about monastic manuscript

---

63. *Zenrin bokuseki shūi,* fig. 124; *Chushi Fanqi chanshi yulu* (ZZ71.638c4–17).

64. *Chushi Fanqi chanshi yulu* (ZZ71.576a13).

65. Byrne, "Poetics of Silence," 273–274.

66. To the extent that the surviving recension is an indication, this was the first *yulu* to include verse and occasional poetry. Yanagida, "Zenseki kaidai," no. 158, suggests that both of the now-lost 1101 and 1310 editions likely incurred significant alterations. On the correct dates for Shanzhao's life, see Yang Zengwen, *Song Yuan Chanzong shi,* 259–260.

culture and its relationship to printed books will inform my analyses based
on titles and headnotes in later chapters.

The processes of collection, collation, and dissemination generally in-
volved a master's disciples. The compilers of *yulu* were responsible for setting
the correct text. They in addition made numerous book-making decisions,
such as what title to give a poem and whether to add a preface or colophon
for the entire collection. Compilers also selected genre terms to use in the
internal titles of collections of verse. The term *jisong* could be used as a category
by anthologists post facto, regardless of whether every individual manuscript
included paratext by the writer himself. In other words, a disciple could shape
future readings by placing his master's poems within "a collection of *jisong*."

Making Collections of *Jisong*

Very few monks' poems survive today in forms like the manuscripts discussed
above. Most extant monks' verses come to us through processes just outlined.
Printed collections of individual Chan monks' poetic works generally belong
to one of two broad types: belletristic collections of poetry similar to those of
mainstream literati and religious collections most often included as the final
section of a Chan master's *yulu*. My main focus here will be on Chan *yulu*, the
construction of which provided opportunities for the compilers to inscribe
the intentions and values of their communities. Fascicles with verse collec-
tions often include an internal title to indicate the genre of the section's con-
tents (such as "*gāthā* and encomia"). In addition to these internal section
titles, a preface or colophon for the entire *yulu* is generally found at the front
or back of the text.

In the previous chapter, I surveyed the major poetic genres found in
varying proportions across Song and Yuan *yulu*. Here, I focus on the con-
struction of the image of a Chan master in the paratextual elements—
prefaces, genre categories, headnotes, and afterwords—added by the *yulus'*
compilers. These are the supposedly ancillary textual and visual components
of a physical book through which a reader passes to enter the principal text.
I am particularly interested in how these textual vestibules explicitly suggest
interpretive strategies to readers.[67] I argue that through the addition of
paratexts—prefaces, colophons, and genre markers—the compilers of these
collections conveyed what they felt was an important distinction between
worldly and Buddhist literatures. The following series of examples suggests
that in the Northern and Southern Song the distinction between the two was
widespread among the textual communities that produced most of the col-
lections of Chan monks' verse we have today. I will first examine genre terms
and then analyze prefaces and colophons.

Disciples were most often the responsible parties for producing a *yulu*.
Some collections were compiled and printed only after the master had died.

---

67. Again, on paratext as vestibule, see Genette, *Paratexts*, 1–4.

Others were produced during a teacher's lifetime, in which case we must assume that the master was involved in authorizing and disseminating texts.[68] In general, verses form the final main section of a *yulu*. There, the internal titles informed readers what genre the verses *should* be (and not necessarily what they *were*). That genre usually was *jisong*, or sometimes a combination of *jisong* together with other genres like encomia (*zan*). This textual practice was one way that communities in the Northern Song and after made *jisong*.

To my knowledge, none of the surviving *yulu* from the Northern or Southern Song dynasties categorized verses with the word *shi* ("poetry" or "poem") as part of an internal title for a collection of verses.[69] The one apparent exception I could find appears on the outer wrapper of an Edo-period hand-copied edition, but not within the text itself.[70] In some cases, the word *shi* appears in the title of individual verses. In *yulu* collections from the Song, however, the sections are categorized and titled only with *jisong* or one of the related terms explained below.

Two organizational structures are most common in these texts. First, in some Song *yulu*, a collection of diverse genres are subsumed under the term *jisong*. This is the case for the woodblock print edition of *Recorded Sayings of Chan Master Foyan* posthumously created for Foyan Qingyuan (1067–1120), likely in the 1130s.[71] The collection of sermons ends on page 60.b, and a paratextual note states "here ends sermons" 上堂終. On the next page, the section's title reads "*jisong*" 偈頌. This section extends across twenty-five printed sheets containing various genres of verse. At the end of the fascicle, on page 85.b, the diverse section concludes with a note, "here ends *jisong*" 偈頌終.[72] The various genres of verse run together within a broader *jisong* section that includes a subsection for "portrait encomia" 真賛 with its own internal subtitle. The preface to Chan master Foyan's *yulu*, written by Xu Fu (1075–1141) and analyzed in the previous chapter for its references to *buddhavacana*, also reinforced this textual architecture by enumerating the eight sections of the

---

68. As clearly argued in Schlütter, *"Record of Hongzhi*," 198.

69. I reviewed *yulu* for Song-era Chan Masters found in the *Taishō* and *Zoku zōkyō* canons (some derived from late-Ming editions); Song-era editions in the collections of the Japanese National Diet Library and Imperial Household Agency (in *Kokuritsu Kokkai Toshokan Dejitaru Korekushon* and *Kunaichō shoryōbu shūzō kanseki shūran*); as well as the early Gozan Japanese reproductions of Song texts, photo-reproduced in *Gozan-ban Chūgoku zenseki sōkan*, vols. 6–9.

70. The section title "poetic inscriptions" 題詩 is found once on the outside wrapper of the *Xisou Shaotan chanshi guanglu*. This section title is not found within the fascicle, however, suggesting that it was added by the Edo copyist. Note that a separate Song-era *yulu* exists in an early Gozan print and has a section of verse titled "*Jisong*." *Gozan-ban Chūgoku zenseki sōkan*, 8:751, where Shiina raises other questions about the two Xisou texts.

71. The following page numbers refer to the Southern Song edition of *Shuzhou Longmen Foyan heshang yulu*.

72. *Shuzhou Longmen*, 1.61a-85b. The text was initially compiled by the senior disciple Shanwu 善悟 (1074–1132), per the colophon dated 1125. This second edition was produced by another of Qingyuan's disciples, Zhu'an Shigui 竹庵士珪 (1092–1146), active in Fuzhou in the 1130s; see Yanagida, "*Kosonshuku goroku kō*," 31. This text also added to later Song expanded editions of *Gu zunsu yulu* (CBETA.64b1–89a3).

printed text, with *jisong* encompassing all verse apart from *songgu*, "verses on old [precedents]." A similar structure was also used in *The Recorded Sayings of Chan Master Fachang Yiyu* 法昌倚遇禪師語錄, created posthumously for Fachang Yiyu 法昌倚遇 (1005–1081), for which an 1105 imprint may be the earliest surviving direct witness of a *yulu* for a Song Chan master.[73] This collection was created by a monk named Zongmi, likely referring to the Hongzhou-area Linji lineage Chan master Longya Zongmi 龍牙宗密 (fl. 1100s).[74] As creator of this edition, Zongmi arranged three sections of text: Fachang's "sermons" (*shangtang* 上堂), followed by a section of "critical examinations" (*kanbian* 勘辯), and finally Fachang's verses all in a single section entitled *"jisong."* The collection brought together diverse genres of parting and epistolary poems addressed to individuals, landscape poems like "Climbing a Mountain" 登山, as well as didactic songs. Also included were verses about famous Chan tales, which later anthologists re-categorized as *songgu*, "verses on old [precedents]."[75] Not all, but many of Fachang's verses have end rhyme and tonal prosody, especially the social and landscape poems.

Again, a similar structure was used in the posthumous 1133 edition of records for Cishou Huaishen, which includes a fascicle entitled *Cishou's Gāthā and Encomia* 慈受偈讚.[76] I have translated the characters *ji* and *zan* as separate words, *"gāthā* and encomia," rather than reading them together, which yields the single idea "verses that praise." Inside the collection, encomia praising Chan ancestors are distinguished from quatrains with individual titles indicating that a postulant "sought a *gāthā*" (*qiu ji* 求偈). This fascicle of *"gāthā* and encomia," however, also includes other kinds of verse such as "hymns in praise of recollecting Amitabha" 念彌陀頌. Included as well is a suite of twelve short verses—each composed to rhyme with one of the twelve earthly branches—which in a headnote Cishou refers to as "these 'twelve *gāthā* of Dongting,' which I show to the sangha for daily use" 洞庭十二偈，以彰眾生日用.[77] Such headnotes, as well as individual titles, give the impression that the writer himself had referred to his verses as *jisong*. These paratextual ele-

---

73. N. Song imprint dated 1105, entitled *Hongzhou Fenning Fachang Chanyuan Yu chanshi yulu* 洪州分寧法昌禪院遇禪師語錄. On extant N. Song imprints of Chan texts, see Shiina, *Sō Gen ban,* 24–25, 93–100. Other extant texts include *Flame Record* anthologies and texts attributed to pre-Song Chan masters. Fachang Yiyu's death in 1081 based on *Zongtong biannian* (ZZ86.219c22). I calculate year of birth from a poem written one day before his death, in which he recorded his age as seventy-seven *sui, Fachang Yiyu chanshi yulu* (ZZ73.70b20–21).

74. The compiler had to be known to Lingyuan Weiqing 靈源惟清 (d. 1117), who reviewed the text and added a colophon shortly before printing. Longya Zongmi's teacher was Letan Yingqian 泐潭應乾 (1034–1096), part of the Huanglong branch.

75. An example of the re-categorization of Fachang's verse as *songgu* is in *Jiatai pudenglu* (ZZ79.459b7–22), which also maintained some of Fachang's verses as *jisong* (ZZ79.473a23-b18).

76. This is the title of the undated manuscript edition in the catalog *Kenninji Ryōsokuin zōsho mokuroku,* 985b. The full title in the received text is "*Gāthā* and Encomia of Venerable Cishou [Huai]shen from Huilin Chan Monastery of the Eastern Capital [Kaifeng]" 東京慧林禪寺慈受深和尚偈讚.

77. *Cishou Huaishen chanshi guanglu* (ZZ73.110c21–22).

ments, then, work in concert with the broader framing of the entire collection of verses as "*gāthā* and encomia."

A second common structure divided verses among smaller collections by genre. This can be seen in several extant Southern Song woodblock print editions. The posthumous collection for Wuzhun Shifan entitled *Recorded Sayings of Chan Master Fojian* 佛鑑禪師語録 (preface dated 1251) includes a series of separate sections. Figure 6 is a reproduction of two pages of an early Gozan edition dated 1370 in which the layout is identical to the Southern Song imprint.[78] Following six printed sheets of *songgu*, is a section of nine printed sheets of *jisong* separate from the next section of "encomia for buddhas and ancestors" 讚佛祖. As seen in figure 6, the section of *jisong* concludes on page 9.b with a closing paratextual marker, and the next section begins on a separate sheet with a new section title and is numbered 1. *Recorded Sayings of Chan Master Fojian* subsequently includes a separate section of funeral verses entitled "affairs of buddhas" 佛事, followed by a section of "prefaces and colophons" 序跋. The beginnings of a similar structure can be found in earlier Southern Song texts, such as the woodblock edition of *Recorded Sayings of Chan Master Fohai* 佛海禪師語録 (preface dated 1177), a posthumous collection for Fohai Huiyuan 佛海慧遠 (1103–1176).[79] This Southern Song text includes several separate collections, beginning with "encomia for buddhas and ancestors," then "*jisong*," followed by "encomia on [portraits of] oneself" 自讚, and finally a section of funeral verses—here untitled, but with contents identical to those elsewhere entitled "affairs of buddhas." Again, each of these sections begins and ends with its own internal title, and new sections begin separately at the start of a new woodblock page. The genres and their sequence were not fixed across *yulu*; other genres were sometimes added, but the categories we find in *Recorded Sayings of Chan Master Fohai* and *Recorded Sayings of Chan Master Fojian* (fig. 6) were common.

Among the genres of verse included in this second type of organizational structure, one does not find in Song-era texts a section of *shi*. Instead, social and occasional verses, those kinds of verse most likely to be considered poetry (*shi*), were placed in a section entitled "Chinese *gāthā*" (*jisong*). Based on the poetic contents, a contemporaneous reader might have expected the section title to be *shi*, but in Song and Yuan *yulu* this section of poem-like verse is entitled *jisong*. The section title *jisong* indicates that these poems of social exchange were the responses of an awakened master, not merely poetry. Many

---

78. I note only one difference in this 1370 Gozan edition, namely, the addition of a running page number in the top left corner of each sheet; fig. 6 here shows it at right, "page 164." The Southern Song edition in the Kunaichō collection has only the discontiguous page numbers that begin anew with each section, such as is visible here for the pages reproducing *jisong* 3.9b and *zan fozu* 3.1a. The Southern Song edition is available online via *Kunaichō shoryōbu shūzō kanseki shūran*. See Shiina's essay in *Gozan-ban Chūgoku zenseki sōkan*, 7:536–538, on the close relationship between the Southern Song and Gozan editions.

79. All details here refer to the Kunaichō edition, bibliographic information is given under *Xiatang Huiyuan Chanshi guanglu*.

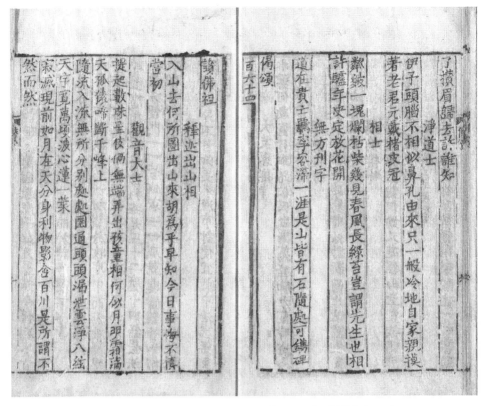

Figure 6. *Recorded Sayings of Chan Master Fojian,* Gozan ed. of 1370, based on Southern Song ed. dated 1251. At right, the conclusion of the *jisong* section, and at left the start of *zan* section. Source: National Diet Library website.

yulu from the late Ming on, by comparison, specifically included a section of *shi* in addition to other genres. The exclusion from Song *yulu* of a section of "poetry" surely was an intentional decision by the Chan communities that produced these texts.

Indeed, it was possible for monks in the Song to produce a poetry collection for a fellow monk if they so desired. Already in the tenth century, printing blocks were carved posthumously for the *White Lotus Collection* 白蓮集 of *shi* written by Qiji and edited by his disciple Xiwen 西文 (n.d.). Additional collections of monks' *shi* circulated as bound manuscript books in the eleventh century, and by the twelfth century it was common for belletristic collections of individual monks' poetry to be compiled and printed in a manner similar to other mainstream poetry, as, for example, was the case with the poet-monk Daoqian.

The poems of Daoqian were collected and published as *Collected Poems of the Lofty and Distant Master* 參寥子詩集. Faying 法英 (n.d.), one of Daoqian's only known disciples, compiled the first recension of the "collected poems" (*shiji*), of which imprints from the late Northern Song survive.[80] Every fascicle begins and ends with the book's title and the words "collected poems." Faying, who like Daoqian focused his energies on literature and calligraphy, was learned enough for Chen Shidao to once refer to him as "the heir of Canliao's dharma and a monk of the Su Dongpo school" 參寥乏法孫，東坡之門僧.[81] Rather than seek fulfilment within public Buddhist institutions or sectarian learning, Daoqian chose the life of a pious monk, albeit one with a refined aesthetic who participated in the *shi* poetic tradition. Roughly four hundred poems were gathered and included in this twelve-fascicle collection. Most of the works are social, occasional, or landscape poems, frequently without obvious Buddhist themes. Some of the poems, such as Daoqian's lovely "On the Road to Linping" 臨平道中, circulated especially widely.[82]

	Wind over stalks of rush, rustling, playing light and soft,	風蒲獵獵弄輕柔
2	The dragonflies wish to alight but cannot do as they please.	欲立蜻蜓不自由
	On the low road to Linping beneath mountains in May,	五月臨平山下路
4	Innumerable lotus flowers cover a small stream shoal.	藕花無數滿汀洲

This poem was included in Song literary anthologies and works of literary criticism;[83] it also inspired numerous literary responses.[84] It was later re-situated within anthologies of Chan literature and quoted by Chan figures in *gong'an* literature.[85] In cases like these, where a poem was later placed in a religious anthology, the apparent genre of a verse was not fixed. It could change depending on the contexts established by later readers and compilers.

A contrary case is one where a *jisong* from a *yulu*, a collection of "recorded sayings," could be placed in a collection of poetry and thus assigned to a different genre, *shi*. The following *jueju* by Chongxian was incorporated into his

---

80. The earliest extant exemplars of *Canliaozi shiji*, reproduced in *Zhonghua zaizao shanben*, are also the basis for the *Sibu congkan* edition. This redaction includes taboo characters that would have been excluded in later editions, including the taboo characters *huan* 桓 for Emperor Qinzong 欽宗 (r. 1126–1127) and *shen* 慎 for Emperor Xiaozong 孝宗 (r. 1162–1189); as noted in Sichuan daxue, *Song ji zhenben congkan shumu tiyao*, 62–63.

81. "Ying shi zi xu" 穎師字序, *Houshan jushi wenji*, 16.3b-5a/498–499. Faying, from Qiantang and surnamed Zhu 朱, was effectively orphaned at seven or eight, when his father died and his mother took the tonsure. He demonstrated a precocious literary aptitude and was adopted by Daoqian. See also *Su Shi wenji*, 72/2302, and an inscription in Qin Guan, *Huaihai ji jian zhu*, 30/1000–1002.

82. *Canliaozi shiji*, 1.9a; 18–19. Per tradition, this poem circulated orally and thus came to the attention of Su Shi, thereby inaugurating their friendship.

83. It was included in Song literary anthologies such as *Sheng Song gaoseng shixuan* and *Zhongxing chanlin fengyue ji* 中興禪林風月集, the latter in Xu, *Zhenben Song ji wu zhong*, 1: 350–351. The poem is found throughout Song *shihua* literary criticism.

84. Even outside China, the poem was a topic of painting and discussion in Joseon Korea, per *Gugan-Sihwa* 龜磵詩話 by Nam Hui-Chae 南義采; and by Japanese Gozan monks as a subject of painting and poems, *Gozan bungaku shinshū*, 7:1037–1038.

85. *Chanzong za du hai* (ZZ65.77b2–4) and anonymously quoted in *Linquan laoren pingchang Danxia Chun* (ZZ67.365a10).

yulu. Yet in the Southern Song, this same verse was included as a *shi* in Chen Qi's *Selected Poems by Eminent Monks of the August Song*. The *jueju* is entitled "Sending off Layman Yu as He Returns to Sichuan" 送俞居士歸蜀.[86]

	Where is the sequestered perch that summons my dream-spirit with such haste?	何處深棲役夢頻
2	It is the Qingcheng Mountains casting mist into countless gullies.	青城拋却數溪雲
	Now in old age, it is hard to go back,	如今老大歸難得
4	I can only set down the feelings I have when seeing you off so far.	秖寫情懷遠送君

Nostalgia for one's home was a time-honored poetic theme. Chongxian was born in Sichuan and ordained in Chengdu at the age of twenty-two following the deaths of his parents.[87] After some years of study, he left Sichuan in search of a teacher and had a long career at Mount Xuedou outside Ningbo. He never returned to Sichuan. In this verse, he depicts longing as an act of the mountains themselves, an external force that calls in his dreams. A compiler could treat a verse such as this as a *jisong*, a Chinese *gāthā*, by placing it in a *yulu*, a recorded-sayings collection. At the same time, Chen Qi could make it into a poem by placing it in an anthology of poems. In later dynasties as well, Song verses could be re-contextualized, as, for example, when Li E 厲鶚 (1692–1752) selected three fascicles of verse with superior literary qualities written by renowned Chan masters, including Chongxian and Dahui Zonggao, for his hundred-fascicle encyclopedic poetry anthology, *Recorded Occasions of Song Poetry* 宋詩紀事, some poems of which still bear Chinese words for *gāthā* in their titles.[88]

The porous boundaries between worldly and religious types of collections were often hardened by later cataloguers. Nonetheless, when we turn to the Song-era authors and compilers themselves, we see they also drew distinctions between the poetry of ordinary literature and the verses that served Buddhist aims. This distinction itself conveyed a commitment to propagating the dharma. Such commitments are more pronounced in *yulu*, but they are visible in belletristic collections as well. Huang Ch'i-chiang's exhaustive research on several large collections of poetry by Southern Song monks of Jiangnan has illustrated how monastic authors could present themselves when participating in worldly literature. These monks, including Beijian, referred to their own literary activity as "outer learning."[89] Similarly, when Beijian's disciple Wuchu Daguan compiled his master's *yulu*, he differentiated these religious

---

86. *Zuying ji*, 2.16a-b; *Mingjue chanshi yulu* (Gozan ed., 94; T47.708c22–24); the *Taishō* canon has 只 for 秖. *Sheng Song gaoseng shixuan*, 22a-b.
87. Huang Yi-hsun, *Xuedou qiji*, 18–33.
88. *Songshi jishi*, 91.30b.
89. On Beijian and *waixue*, see Huang Ch'i-chiang, *Yiwei Chan*, 208–211.

collections with *jisong* from literary collections of Beijian's *shi* and belletristic writing.[90] The oeuvre of Wuchu Daguan, too, was divided into these two types of collections.[91] The first, a small one-fascicle *Recorded Sayings of Venerable Wuchu* 物初和尚語録, is a work of inner learning, with sermons, instructions to disciples, "verses on old [precedents]" (*songgu*), encomia (*zan*), funeral verses, and *jisong*; the second is an enormous twenty-five fascicle anthology entitled *Wuchu's Superfluous Sayings* 物初賸語.[92] This second, ostensibly outer, collection contains hundreds of poems as well as "commemorative inscriptions" 記, epistolary correspondence, colophons, "pagoda inscriptions" 塔銘, and various official petitions (疏、表、榜).[93] Yet, despite the apparently neat boundaries between inner and outer collections, one finds numerous exceptions within the collections themselves. In addition to numerous poems addressed to monks, Daguan's encomia on classical Buddhist topics such as the eighteen arhats are unexpectedly included in his so-called superfluous writing, not with his other encomia in the *yulu*.[94] The generic distinctions between a literary collection and a Buddhist collection were living and dynamic concepts that needed to be repeatedly negotiated in practice by writers and compilers throughout the Song.

Prefaces to Collections of *Jisong*

Prefaces to *yulu* might narrate the processes of collection, collation, and dissemination and thereby affirm the values of a textual community. Prefaces frequently foreground that the gathering and editing of a master's verses into a collection would establish an authorized text, increase the likelihood of preservation, and make possible further circulation. Some colophons,

---

90. See Daguan's preface (dated 1250) and the appended biographic *xingzhuang* 行狀 for Beijian (dated 1251), on the *Beijian heshang waiji;* Xu, *Zhenben Song ji wu zhong,* 1:23, 94–97, and 2:984–986. In addition to *Beijian heshang yulu* compiled by Daguan in 1248—which includes Chinese *gāthā,* encomia, and funeral verses—a second collection of "inner writing" titled *Beijian heshang waiji* is divided into Chinese *gāthā* (*jisong*), encomia (*zan*), colophons (*tiba*), and dharma instruction (*fayu*). According to Daguan's preface, the supplemental collection included those texts composed before Beijian's first abbatial appointment, which meant that they had fallen outside the initial *yulu* collection.

91. On Daguan Wuchu, his career, literary output, and associates, see Huang Ch'i-chiang, *Yiwei Chan,* 284–371.

92. *Wuchu heshang yulu* is in *Gozan-ban Chūgoku zenseki sōkan,* 7:437–463. *Wuchu shengyu* in Xu, *Zhenben Song ji wu zhong,* 2:529–1033.

93. Published toward the end of his life, *Wuchu's Superfluous Sayings* begins with a preface by Daguan himself. The self-deprecatory title, he explains in his preface, points to the fact that his prolific literary output, composed in response to the needs of others, far outnumbered the sermons he gave as an abbot. When his disciple first presented the collection, Daguan rebuked him: "Our [Chan] school has never exalted this [kind of writing]; do not revere my transgressions" 吾宗素不尚此，毋重吾過. As he tells it, once his disciple reminded him of the tradition of expedient means, Daguan laughed at himself and began to refer to the collection as a record of "superfluous" sayings. Xu, *Zhenben Song ji wu zhong,* 2:29.

94. Xu, *Zhenben Song ji wu Zhong,* 2:687–690.

another form of paratext, explicate how verses are distinct from *shi*. The rhetoric in these prefaces and colophons also reflects a broader ambivalence about the production of books in Chan communities. Printed books could reach wider audiences to spread the dharma or secure patronage, but such broad dissemination would also entail a loss of control over interpretation. In addition to printed books, manuscript books, too, were important in how communities made *jisong*.

Starting well before the Song, various records of Chan teachings were gathered, collated, and circulated. At least by the late Tang, manuscript books and hand-copied fragments as well as memorized texts moved with itinerant monks and students. Building on the landmark work of Yanagida Seizan,[95] Jia Jinhua recently demonstrated that between the 880s and 930s, encounter dialogues were carved into Korean and Chinese stone stele inscriptions, illustrating the wide circulation of such tales.[96] These diverse sources of sermons and dialogues would become the basis for larger Chan anthologies compiled in the tenth and eleventh centuries, among which is the *Annals of the Ancestral Halls* 祖堂集, first completed in 952. In addition to sermons and encounter dialogues, many verses were collected and included in these anthologies. The *Annals of the Ancestral Halls* contains 345 verses attributed to 132 different authors.[97]

Many kinds of monks' verse circulated via manuscripts and oral performance.[98] One collection of singly authored verses was created by the disciples of Longya Judun 龍牙居遁 (d. 923), who "arranged and collected the master's *gāthā*" 編集師偈, according to a preface by poet-monk Qiji.[99] Some Dunhuang manuscripts brought together verses from eclectic sources. One example is S2165.v from the Stein collection, which is a single-sheet multi-poem manuscript with a running transcription of nine different verses across genres, both authored and anonymous.[100] Scholars have noted other Dunhuang manuscripts in which monks' poetry was copied out alongside apotropaic liturgies and spells, raising questions about how such manuscripts were used.[101] As a rule, Buddhist verse could be collected into multi-poem manuscripts like

---

95. Yanagida, "Goroku no rekishi," 229–246.

96. Jia, *HongzhouSchool*, 52.

97. Cai Rongting, *Zutangji Chanzong shiji yanjiu*, 11–38.

98. The diversity of verse forms at Dunhuang have been widely studied. For an overview, one might begin with Wang Zhipeng, *Dunhuang Fojiao geci yanjiu*. Oral performance and circulation is well-known. For example, the oral dissemination of Guanxiu's poetry is discussed by Nugent, *Manifest in Word*s, 228–232, 246.

99. A translation of the complete preface in Mazanec, "Medieval Chinese *Gāthā*," 144–145. *Chanmen zhu zushi jisong* (ZZ66.726c5–729a20). Qiji stated that the completed collection contained ninety-five verses, the same number found in an extant Southern Song printed edition of *Chanmen zhu zushi jisong*.

100. The recto also has a selection of eclectic verses. Another example of a multi-poem manuscript from Dunhuang analyzed in Mazanec, "Medieval Chinese *Gāthā*," 129–131.

101. For example, see the discussion of P2104 and S4037 in Mazanec, "Invention of Chinese Buddhist Poetry," 344–353.

those found in Dunhuang as well as into separate collections like that of Judun's *gāthā*.

Most of the early Song *yulu*, which included the verses of masters, were disseminated as manuscript books. Such books are known to have existed in the form of a clean copy, that is, an edited and corrected final form, sometimes known as a "fair copy" 繕寫. Christopher Nugent has described the practice of making fair copies during the Tang dynasty.[102] The practice of a clean hand copy continued in the Song and through later imperial times.[103] According to the early Song Chan anthology *Jingde chuandenglu*, the records of Fayan Wenyi 法眼文益 (885–958) included "collections of dharma [sermons] from three abbotships, as well as compositions of *jisong*, portrait encomia, inscriptions, commemorations, expositions, and others, totaling several tens of thousands of words; fair copies by students circulate throughout the world" 三處法集，及著偈頌、真讚、銘、記、詮注，等凡數萬言，學者繕寫傳布天下.[104] Fayan's records circulating in the tenth and early eleventh centuries had the same structure seen in later *yulu*, with sermons arranged by abbotship, followed by written compositions and verses. Already in these hand-written copies of Fayan's *yulu*, it is evident that the verses were not regarded as poetry *per se*, but instead were placed into a genre of *jisong*.

Manuscript books were in monastic libraries, where students and visitors could peruse and create whole or partial copies.[105] While a student, Juefan Huihong in the late eleventh century made a copy of the record of Huangbo Xiyun 黃檗希運 (d. 850), noting in a colophon that he had "personally transcribed and kept it" 手校而藏之.[106] Textual evidence suggests that in addition to codices, scrolls remained a popular format.[107] Transcribed copies of manuscript books or fragments could enter monks' or scholars' personal collections, which later collectors might seek out for emendations and new editions. In 1274, Weimian recorded his process of collecting and collating numerous manuscript copies. "Reconciling their differences and preserving their similarities, I made a correspondence, then personally drafted a fair copy" 參其異，存其同，而會焉，親手繕寫親手繕寫.[108] These practices parallel many aspects of the broader manuscript culture of the period.[109]

In Chan communities the work of compiling a finished *yulu* text was

---

102. Nugent, *Manifest in Words*, 215, 253–254, 274.

103. For example, Struve, "Deqing's Dreams," 12.

104. *Jingde chuandenglu* (T51.400a10–11); see also the Gozan edition.

105. Nugent, *Manifest in Words*, 260–261.

106. "Inscribed on the *Recorded Sayings of Chan Master Duanji*" 題斷際禪師語錄, *Shimen wenzi chan*, fasc. 25, 2:1470–1471; Zhou Yukai, *Songseng Huihong xinglü*, 41, estimates this colophon was written in 1099.

107. In this collection are at least ten colophons written on scrolls, for example, "Inscribed on the compiled poems of Venerable Bi" 題弼上人所蓄詩, *Shimen wenzi chan*, fasc. 26, 2:1518.

108. *Conglin jiaoding qinggui zongyao* (ZZ63.592a6–9). The book was only printed a decade later, when a second colophon written in 1284 was added. See *Gozan-ban Chūgoku zenseki sōkan*, 5:655.

109. Cherniack, "Book Culture," 33; and Owen, "Manuscript Legacy," 301-312.

often completed by a disciple, who could be responsible for steps including the transcription of things said as well as the gathering of dispersed manuscripts. As important, students were often responsible for collating, editing, and finalizing the text. Once done, they almost certainly consulted the master, were he still alive.[110] These roles assigned to an abbot's attendant were later codified in a Southern Song *qinggui*.[111] In practice, however, the roles a disciple might take on varied, depending on the attitude of the individual master.

Many details about book-making processes are found in prefaces to Chan texts. I focus here on one example of a preface to a manuscript book and one for a printed book. The first is a preface to a manuscript book, dated 1032, which was appended to *Blossoms of the Ancestors* 祖英集 (hereafter *Zuying ji*), one of the seven collections of Xuedou Chongxian's works that circulated in his lifetime. As a counterexample of a posthumous collection, only one year earlier, in 1031, Chongxian wrote a preface for a collection he created of teachings by his recently deceased teacher, Zhimen Guangzha 智門光祚 (ca. 950–1030). The posthumous editorial process was based on mismatched manuscript fragments, "Therefore to give the text shape, I culled[112] and corrected, valuing only what concisely epitomizes [his dharma]" 輒形刪定但貴其簡略而已.[113] Chongxian created his master's records after Guangzha's death. The *Zuying ji* verses, on the other hand, were arranged into Chongxian's collection during his own lifetime. Shang Haifeng has recently convincingly reasoned that the *Zuying ji* circulated only as a manuscript book for many decades.[114] The first explicit reference to a printed edition comes in the *Zuting shiyuan*, published in 1108. Be that as it may, the *Zuying ji* collection circulated widely and was soon read outside the monastery by such people as the Daoist Zhang Boduan 張伯端 (987?–1082), who wrote the verse "On Reading Chan Master Xuedou's *Zuying ji*" 讀雪竇禪師祖英集, translated elsewhere by Joshua Capitanio.[115]

According to its preface, *Zuying ji* contained 220 verses at the time it was compiled. This collection of Chongxian's verse was compiled while the master was still alive, and the author of the preface, Wenzheng 文政 (n.d.), crafted his rhetoric accordingly. Wenzheng's *Zuying ji* preface is perhaps the earliest dated Northern Song preface or colophon to invoke a distinction between

---

110. Again, see Schlütter, *"Record of Hongzhi,"* 198.

111. See the description of duties in *Conglin jiaoding qinggui zongyao* (ZZ63.604c13).

112. The act of "culling" is an allusion to Confucius' purported creation of the *Classic of Poetry*, explained by Nugent, *Manifest in Words,* 248–249.

113. *Gu zunsu yulu* (ZZ68.258c16–259a9); cross-referenced with the Kunaichō early Southern Song edition of *Gu zunsu yuyao*. For more on Guangzha's teachings and the history of printed editions, see Huang Yi-hsun, *"Zhimen Guangzha yulu zhi yanjiu."*

114. Shang, *"Xuedou lu Song Yuan ben."*

115. Found in several editions of Zhang's *Wuzhen pian* 悟真篇, and analyzed with full translation in Capitanio, "Portrayals of Chan," 129–131.

jisong and *shi*.[116] A Song reader who encountered the *Zuying ji* would open it and be introduced to the work as follows:[117]

> The master gives form to words, but his is different from [the lofty melodies of] "bright spring" or "white snow," "blue clouds" or "gentle winds." Indeed, the great tablet, unadorned, is esteemed for its essential nature, and the greatest speech, unembellished, is admired for its inherent truth. And so, among the scales and mirrors [for discerning value] in the world, what can compare with a great teacher? Ever since the master arrived at Cuifeng and Xuedou, he sometimes made verses about the profound and subtle in the words of former worthies; others he made in response to situations, when parting, or sent as epistles. They are many, indeed. There was [one among his students] who loved the Way and would [after hearing the verses] both record them and tuck them away [in a satchel for safekeeping]. One day, he gathered and arranged a complete 220 verses. He then wrote out a copy and presented it to the master. The master said, "I composed these works when I was spontaneously inspired, and though I will allow the verses to survive in an edition [i.e., as a text], I will not allow them to circulate this way." The disciple responded, "Once every thousand years from our ancestor's gates come such resplendent achievements, do not abandon them so lightly!"[118] The master examined the fact that the devotee's honest intentions could not be restrained and withdrew [his unwillingness to circulate the text] and followed the man's [plan]. I, the fortunate attendant Wenzheng, then composed this preface. I applied myself[119] on this day in the first month of the tenth year of the Tiansheng reign of the Great Song Empire.

> 師之形言也，且異乎陽春白雪碧雲清風者也。夫大圭不琢貴乎天真，至言不文尚於理實，乃世之衡鑑豈智識而擬議哉。師自戾止翠峯雪竇，或先德言句淵密，師因而頌之，或感興懷別貽贈之作，固亦多矣。其有好道者並錄而囊之。一日總緝成二百二十首，乃寫呈師。師曰：「余偶興而作，寧存于本，不許行焉。」禪者應曰：「乃祖閫千載之芳烈也，勿輕舍諸！」師察其慤志勉弗獲已抑而從之。文政幸侍座机，輒述序引。用識歲時炎宋天聖十年孟陬月，文政謹序

Wenzheng expresses in his preface both the values and concerns of his monastic community, including the still-living master Chongxian. According to this preface, which, recall, was written in Chongxian's lifetime, the master was reluctant to give his approval to the collection and its dissemination. Chongxian's concern was not textualization *per se*, for he does not tell the compiler to destroy the finished text. His concern, at least as expressed in

---

116. The preface is described in Berling, "Bringing the Buddha Down to Earth," 80. Berling rightly notes that the master "discouraged their publication."

117. *Zuying ji*, 1.1a-b. Punctuation mostly follows *Kokuyaku Keigen-fu Setchō Myōgaku daishi Soei-shū.*

118. Reading *she* 舍 as *she* 捨 and *zhu* 諸 as *zhi* 之 or *zhi hu* 之乎, as given in *Hanyu dacidian.*

119. The use of *yong shi* 用識 in the signature of a letter is attested elsewhere in Buddhist texts, though still uncommon.

this preface, was focused on controlling circulation and discerning the disciple's motivations. The disciple's intentions were not about reputation or personal gain but rather the preservation and propagation of the dharma and so were deemed worthy. The creation of the text depended on the disciple as a compiler, and so the compiler's moral integrity and grasp of the dharma were essential to the success of written teachings.

The preface opens with a pertinent distinction: that the collection is not the same as a collection of mainstream poetry. The "bright spring" and "white snow" are names of ancient melodies, commonly an allusion to high poetry in contrast to popular songs. "Blue clouds" and "gentle winds" were also names of elegant tunes, though less well-known.[120] By 1032, these four tunes were metonymy for a conservative idea of poetry. Wenzheng's preface invokes this traditionalist vision of poetic craft in order to state that the master's verses are not that. The preface distances Chongxian's verses from poetry *per se* and instead insists that they reflect something beyond ordinary words. This is an appeal for the reader to appreciate some religious quality in the verses. They are not poetry but rather the spontaneous responses of a great master to everyday situations in the monastery. Wenzheng also distinguishes between two major types of verse, *songgu* and the occasional or social types of *jisong*. Chongxian's *songgu* were collected separately; the *Zuying ji* largely contains his occasional poetry.[121]

Prefaces like Wenzheng's anticipated that readers might believe the collection to be a volume of poetry. Indeed, as the *Zuying ji* continued to circulate independently, later cataloguers at times did treat it as a poetry collection. The Qing scholars responsible for compiling *Zuying ji* into the imperial *Siku quanshu* praised Chongxian's writing as poetry. They noted that his verses avoided the telltale "whiff of vegetables" common to writings by Chan monks and insisted instead that the poems possessed "a literary quality that is pure and restrained, like the fine sound of jade, [indeed] they can be sung" 風致清婉琅然可誦.[122] But the Qing editors also distanced the simple diction in Chongxian's writing from the more intricately patterned works of poet-monks like Daoqian and Huihong. Such literary evaluations of the *Zuying ji* would run counter to the intentions of the original textual community as outlined in the preface and also suggested in other paratextual elements.

Unlike the *Taishō daizōkyō* edition and its Ming source, no internal title to indicate genre category appears in the Southern Song editions of this text in *Xuedou si ji* or the Gozan edition of *Mingjue chanshi yulu*.[123] Instead, the preface is immediately followed by the first poem's title, "Seeing Off the Elder Bao-

---

120. As glossed in *Zuting shiyuan* (ZZ64.342a3–10; *Gozan-ban,* 231). A similar usage is found in a verse in *Xutang heshang yulu* (T47.1032c8–10; *Gozan-ban,* 91b).

121. See Huang Yi-hsun, *Xuedou qiji,* 207–232, for the history of Xuedou's *Songgu ji* 頌古集.

122. The "tiyao" 提要 dated 1778 is appended at the front of *Zuying ji,* SKQS ed. On the use of vegetal metaphors to evaluate monks' poetry, see Protass, "Flavors of Monks' Poetry."

123. The word *jisong* as an internal title appears in the Yongle Northern Canon and all later canon editions.

xiang" 送寶相長老, a set of five verses addressed to Chongxian's heir, Baoxiang Yunhuan 寶相蘊歡 (n.d.).[124] We may assume the choice of the poem for this important position was deliberate. After the title but before the five verses proper, a reader first encounters the headnote by Chongxian himself.[125]

> Great Master [Yun]huan, a Chan worthy, is about to head to Cinnabar Hill[126] for an appointment that will make resplendent the cardinal tenets. When the time arrives for him to leave, we must not urge him to tarry or stay, but rather [give him] an appropriate composition to mark the beginning of a distant journey. Though one remains and one goes; one will be there, and one here; still, what space is between us? I hurriedly stitched together some uncultivated words to use as a token to bid farewell.

> 大師歡禪德，將赴丹丘辟命光闡宗乘，蓋時應必行，固不可抑留者也。且撫會之作肇曠絕之道，雖一凝一流一彼一此又何間然。率織蕪辭以代贐別。

Chongxian's headnote is positioned directly after Wenzheng's preface so that, before the reader encounters the first poem, the note reinforces the rhetorical thrust of the preface. Chongxian first asserts that this set of parting poems was intended to accompany the one leaving and to encourage him as he went off to propagate the dharma. The community should not make his leaving difficult. Accordingly, the headnote and poems do not directly express the kinds of melancholy one might expect in a parting poem. Second, Chongxian describes his own verse as uncultivated, literally, as "overgrown weeds" 蕪, a learned term for a turgid literary style. We assume that the headnote is by Chongxian, there being no evidence to the contrary, but the placement was the prerogative of the text's compiler, who chose to put this additional paratext near the beginning of the collection.

Chongxian's concerns about the dissemination of manuscript books produced by his disciples prefigured their printed form. In 1065, thirteen years after Chongxian died, the scholar-official Lü Xiaqing 呂夏卿 (*jinshi* 1042) wrote that his disciples had compiled "seven collections" 七集.[127] The *Cascading Falls Collection* 瀑泉集, one of the seven, had its own preface composed by its compiler, Chongxian's disciple Yuanying 圓應, and dated 1030.[128] Yuanying

---

124. Yunhuan in *Jianzhong jingguo xudenglu* (ZZ78.668c7). In many later records, his name is erroneously printed as Yunguan 蘊觀.

125. *Zuying ji*, 1.1b; *Mingjue chanshi yulu* (Gozan ed., 75; T47.698a13-b9). This poem with the preface was also the first to be annotated in *Zuting shiyuan* (ZZ64.342b6), meaning Mu'an's text began with the same sequence.

126. Several locations named Cinnabar Hill existed in the Song. Internal references in the poems suggest probably that outside Taizhou, near Tiantai.

127. *Mingjue chanshi yulu* (Gozan ed., 23-25; T47.712a3–4). Note that the Gozan text here consists of a hand-written emendation to fill a several-page lacuna.

128. Note that the Southern Song *Xuedou si ji* edition includes three "petitions" 疏 from government officials requesting that Chongxian become abbot, not preserved anywhere in the *Taishō* or *Zoku zōkyō* canons; also found in the Gozan text, *Zengi gemon shū*.

noted that three collections were already circulating at that time. The preface to Chongxian's *Songgu ji* 頌古集, another of the seven, noted that the compiler of the text, a disciple named Yuanchen 遠塵, had produced a "fair transcription" 繕錄.[129] Later, some of the seven collections were printed separately, and a single integrated *yulu* was created and printed by the time of the Southern Song.

Additional verses and sermons written by Xuedou Chongxian after the *Zuying ji* was completed were later gathered and printed under the title *Gathered Omissions of Xuedou* 雪竇拾遺.[130] The compiler, Shanqing, who included the texts in his *Zuting shiyuan*, wrote in an explanatory note, "I here record about twenty-nine pieces obtained from local Ningbo manuscript books, and from both far and near inscriptions, as well as autographed manuscripts in the personal collections of Chan monks, which were not included in the *Records of Xuedou*" 即雪竇錄中所未編集者，得於四明寫本，或諸方石刻及禪人所藏手澤凡二十九篇，謹錄于左.[131] He estimated that the twenty-nine manuscripts included a total of fifty new poems.[132] The process by which Shanqing collected manuscript books as well as individual manuscripts and inscriptions probably mirrored the processes of compilation for many collections, including the original *Zuying ji*.

The case of *Zuying ji* illustrates that even before printing, a collection as a set text already presented possibilities and aroused concerns. A collection could disseminate teachings in their own time as well as preserve a corrected edition for future generations. The power of writing and circulation allowed textual communities to reach wider audiences and made possible the broader propagation of the dharma. An awakened master could use written words as expedient means to edify broader audiences. These virtues, as well as some concerns, would continue—and perhaps multiply—as an increasing number of *yulu* were produced in printed form.

Moving to printed books, scholars of Chinese print history, especially that focused on non-Buddhist books, have noted that commercial printing had a presence in select urban areas beginning in the 1060s or 1070s and that commercial publishers became a significant force in the book trade from the early 1100s on.[133] Somewhat in parallel, but with a few significant exceptions, the printing of individual collections for a Chan master became more numerous beginning in the 1060s or 1070s and clearly increased from the early 1100s on. A second wave of widespread and increased book printing—including

---

129. *Xuedou si ji*, 1.1b. This term in the edition seen by Shanqing for *Zuting shiyuan* (ZZ64.333c19).

130. On the *Zuying ji* and *Xuedou shiyi*, see Huang Yi-hsun, *Xuedou qiji*, 158–160, who altogether counts a total of 262 verses.

131. *Zuting shiyuan* (ZZ64.374b6–7; *Gozan-ban*, 291).

132. *Zuting shiyuan* (ZZ64.342a21–22; *Gozan-ban*, 231).

133. Chia, *Printing for Profit*, 65–67. See also Ronald Egan, "To Count Grains of Sand," 36–37, and "The Northern Song," 424.

for Chan *yulu*—emerged in the latter half of the twelfth century, after the demise of the Northern Song.

Members of the educated elite had several concerns about printed books. They complained that younger students no longer truly read or revered individual books but merely collected them.[134] They also were concerned that the reproducibility of a printed edition would broadly disseminate errata.[135] In addition, many keenly felt the loss of control over secondary uses of these texts, especially commercialization—a problem known at the time from the role of unauthorized printed materials in the "Poetry Trial at Raven Terrace," a record of the indictments against Su Shi for *lèse-majesté* in 1079.[136] I have not seen in colophons of Chan texts a concern for commercial uses or political consequences. Other parallels can be seen, however, especially when the compilers of Chan printed texts wrote that they wished to establish a corrected edition in print. Chan masters were also concerned that students would commit their energies to collecting and printing as a way to enhance their master's reputation rather than focusing on the "proper" study of Chan. They worried, too, that readers might regard written words as fixed statements to be superficially collected as objects. These concerns reveal what kinds of reading were important to these textual communities and underscore the important role of disciples as compilers in the creation of what we now know about Chan literature.

Based on current evidence, the first Song Chan master for whom a *yulu* was printed was Fenyang Shanzhao 汾陽善昭 (947–1024), likely in 1015 or 1016 in the north near Kaifeng.[137] The internal title of the third fascicle is "Songs and Verses" (*ge song* 歌頌), at least in the *textus receptus,* a 1709 Japanese edition, from which the *Taishō* canon text is derived.[138] Section titles frequently were altered in later editions, and it is unlikely this title comes directly from the first edition. Regardless of the section title, Song-era references to this

---

134. Ronald Egan, "To Count Grains of Sand," 38. For additional examples, see Zhang Gaoping, *Tiaoxi yuyin conghua,* 119–123.

135. Cherniack, "Book Culture," 65.

136. Ronald Egan "Su Shi's Informal Letters," 479–480. Egan translates the relevant part of a forceful rebuke sent by Su Shi to a commercial printer.

137. An 1101 colophon for a second edition refers to "the old print from Fenzhou" 舊版 在汾州, *Fenyang Wude chanshi yulu* (T47.629b29-c4). The official Yang Yi 楊億 (974–1020) composed a preface, probably after leaving Ruzhou in 1015, though possibly during his one-year appointment as prefect there. Yang Zengwen, *Song Yuan Chanzong shi,* 259–260. See also Welter, *Linji lu,* 69. On Yang Yi's experiences and his role in the creation and promotion of Chan texts at the early Song court, see Welter, *Monks, Rulers, and Literati,* 175–186.

138. Lacunae and critical notes in the *Taishō* canon match the lacunae and headnotes of the 1709 edition at National Diet Library. Yanagida, "Zenseki kaidai," 482, no. 158, notes that all extant editions descend from the 1310 Yuan ancestral redaction. Song or Yuan prints are not included in Shiina, *Sō Gen ban,* suggesting that none are known to survive. I am not aware of Ming or Qing Chinese editions.

yulu attest to a readership, and we know that Shanzhao's verses were later quoted and commented upon.[139]

In addition to the *yulu* of Song masters, at least five *yulu* for Tang Chan masters were compiled, edited, and then printed between 1021 to 1083, based on clearly dated colophons.[140] Two of these *yulu* were produced in Fuzhou in 1080 under the initiative of the prefect Sun Jue 孫覺 (1028–1090), a prominent scholar-official. Sun's prefaces were written after the dangerous case of the "Poetry Trial at Raven Terrace," which for his complicity Sun was convicted and fined.[141] Amid the political disgrace that followed, the patronage of local cultural heroes was a means for Sun to project his moral virtue. Sun estimated that from six incomplete manuscript books, he had collected no more than 80 percent of the teachings of Xuansha Shibei 玄沙師備 (835–908). His prefaces to the printed texts are addressed to elite audiences in the capital and prefectural cities.[142] The *yulu* created in the Song dynasty for contemporary masters differed in some ways.

Many of the *yulu* for Song figures were compiled by disciples and published by local communities. Most were not part of the Buddhist canon projects that received imperial support. In addition to collating the textual contents, these individually circulating books required fundraisers, financial donors, and then the labor to carve woodblocks and print on paper. Fenyang Shanzhao aside, few *yulu* for Song masters were printed before the 1070s. The titles of some lost books from this period are known from orphaned colophons that survive in literati collected works. Zhou Yukai recently compiled a list of 117 prefaces composed by literati for *yulu* during the Northern and Southern Song, illustrating the breadth of textual production by Chan communities.[143] Surviving editions from the Northern Song are rare, however. Whereas Shiina has enumerated more than fifty extant Southern Song imprints of texts for individual Chan masters, only one Northern Song xylographic imprint of an individual Song Chan master's *yulu* survives, *The Recorded Sayings of Chan Master Fachang Yiyu* introduced above. This difference is probably a combination of book loss during the Song-Jin wars as well as a further increase in carving and printing during the Southern Song.

The prefaces to printed texts echo religious values similar to those for

---

139. For example, Juefan Huihong read the *yulu* in 1099 and then wrote a colophon and two poems. Zhou, *Songseng Huihong xinglü*, 48. The 1101 colophon also names the local Hongzhou 洪州 man Chen Zheng 陳政 as the printer 印行 and Lushan Yuantong Yuanji 廬山圓通圓璣 (1036–1118), an heir of Huanglong Huinan, as the editor 校勘.

140. Shiina, "Tōdai zenseki no Sōdai kankō ni tsuite," 516–527. I do not include the printed *Platform Sūtra* here. The *Chuanxin fayao* printed in 1109 as part of the Dongchan Canon; Shiina, *Sō Gen ban*, 584. See App, "Making," on 11th c. editions of *Yunmen guanglu*.

141. *Dongpo wutai shi'an*, 289; and *Xu Zizhi tongjian changpian*, 301/7333.

142. On the uses of local patronage while in exile and intended audience, see Halperin, *Out of the Cloister*, 14, 16.

143. Zhou, *Fayan yu shixin*, 81–84.

manuscript books, though perhaps somewhat more amplified. By the 1100s, the practices of recording, collecting, and compiling had become so widespread that the literatus Xu Fu bemoaned a glut of mediocre *yulu* literature. Xu composed the preface to *The Recorded Sayings of Fachang Yiyu* in 1105 to celebrate the belated publication of the *yulu* of the eccentric Fachang Yiyu several decades after his death. Too often, Xu noted, earnest disciples regarded their abbot as a great master and "as for his everyday sermons and dialogues, the disciples without fail transcribe them, then call [the collection] a *yulu*. The language of recorded sayings now fills the world, but does little good for the buddhadharma" 其平居舉揚問答之語，門人弟子必錄之，號曰語錄。語錄之言滿天下而佛法益微. Xu dismissed such collections as "painted cakes that cannot satisfy hunger" 畫餅不足以充飢耶.[144] The record of Fachang, in his view, was a rare exception. When he received a request by mail, Xu replied with a preface stating that they ought "to proceed to print and circulate it" 遂刊而傳之. He emphasized that preservation was important, and a number of Xu's personal interactions with Fachang in verse form were included.[145] Xu implied that the reason for preservation was that Fachang was a superior teacher and that a written record could benefit students. This text would satisfy a hunger. The colophon does not explicitly discuss the collection of verses; however, as described above, the various genres of verse were all printed under the section title "*jisong*." Together with the preface, these paratexts suggest a mode of reading that was meant to differ from that of a belletristic collection of poetry.

Another of the earliest surviving examples of a preface printed from Song woodblocks is one for a *yulu* compiled posthumously to honor Cishou Huaishen 慈受懷深 (1077–1132). This preface, which I treat in detail below, explicitly compares *jisong* to the words of the Buddha. Shortly after Cishou's death, two different *yulu* were compiled, first in 1133 and then again in 1135. Imprints from the original 1133 edition do not survive, and the received text in the modern *Dai Nihon zoku zōkyō* likely was based on undated Japanese hand-copied editions.[146] An imprint from the 1135 *yulu* is extant. Quotations from both texts are found in anthologies already beginning in the Southern

---

144. Xu's preface is in *Fachang Yiyu chanshi yulu* (ZZ73.55c5–17) and in the 1105 imprint held in the Harvard-Yenching Library. Note that some lacunae in the Harvard direct witness to the text do not match those reproduced in the *Zoku zōkyō* edition. The latter may be derived from a text once held in Kyoto, which is referenced in the Harvard-Yenching library catalogue entry.

145. The content of *yulu* includes a dialogue between Xu and Fachang, several poems from Fachang to Xu, and a *zan* by Xu in honor of Fachang. We cannot determine if they were originally included by the compiler, who induced Xu to compose the preface, or if Xu himself added these to the collection.

146. The 1133 preface by Han Ju 韓駒 (1080–1135) reflects his correct title and position at that time. *Cishou Huaishen chanshi guanglu* (ZZ73.92a8–20). *Kenninji Ryōsokuin zōsho mokuroku*, 984a and 985b, catalogues two hand-copied texts, one entitled *Cishou lu* 慈受錄 and the other *Cishou jizan* 慈受偈讚, each one a separate folio (*satsu* 冊). These catalogue titles correspond to the internal titles of fascicles 1 and 2 of the *Zoku zōkyō* text.

Song, suggesting some circulation of both texts in the period immediately after their production.[147]

The 1135 *yulu* begins with "A Preface to the *Extensive Records of Cishou of Dongjing Huilin*" 東京慧林慈受廣錄序.[148] The preface invites the reader to consider how the text came into existence. I translate here only the first few sentences.[149]

> When Master Cishou would preach the dharma or [compose] *jisong*, he was like the great king of doctors,[150] dispensing medicines in response to illnesses, never careless [in his speech]. Men of his generation appreciated his learning and delighted in his Way. While the master was still wandering the earth, his community already wished to carve and issue [a *yulu*]. Cishou adamantly forbade it and ordered his attendants to burn all their personal notes. Thus, a *yulu* was not published in the master's own lifetime. After he passed away, several of his dharma heirs collected sayings from the master's six abbatial seats, selectively judged and arranged them to make this two-fascicle record of the things said to postulants within those temples. If the master chanced on a situation he would respond effortlessly,[151] present unrestrained explanations, and could cause any living being to obtain liberation. Most of these were not recorded.

> 慈受和尚，說法偈頌，如大醫王應病用藥，無苟然者。世同喜聞而樂道也。師住世日，眾欲鏤板，師力止之，因命侍者盡取私記焚棄。故終師之身，語錄未聞刊行也。師圓寂後，有得法沙門，聚師六處住持之語，銓簡編次，為上下錄，悉與衲子林下語也。若其逢場游戲，放言肆說，俾眾生隨類得解者。多不見錄。

The central message of this preface is that the master, whether in a vernacular sermon or the structure of a *jisong*, was always responding to situations for the sake of liberating others. The writer of the preface explicitly compares Cishou with Śākyamuni Buddha.[152] The preface would signal to the reader that in the

---

147. From the 1133 text, six quatrains in *Lebang wenlei* (T47.220a20-b3), and three verses in *Chanmen zhu zushi jisong* (ZZ66.757c21–758a5). From the 1135 text, see *Chanzong songgu lianzhu tongji* (ZZ65.492b17). Additional passages quoted in Ming texts.

148. *Dongjing Huilin Cishou guanglu,* 56b, includes a different title, "Venerable Cishou [Huai]shen's Sermons and Verses on Old [Precedents]" 慈受深和尚陞堂頌古. Some details in Shiina, *Sō Gen ban,* 563. This text corresponds to the third and fourth fascicles of the *Zoku zōkyō* text; however, lacunae on 44a-b are not consistent with those in *Cishou huaishen chanshi guanglu* (ZZ73.130b12–21).

149. The author of the preface is unclear. The *Zoku zōkyō* edition notes lacunae, where the Kunaichō edition includes two additional characters, *lin shu* 霖述, perhaps "written by Lin."

150. A common epithet for the Buddha.

151. Taking *youxi* 游戲 as "responding effortlessly." For more Song-dynasty background on *youxi sanmei* 游戲三昧, see Zhou, "Youxi sanmei." Also consider the more common expression *feng chang zuo xi* 逢場作戲, "[like an actor] encountering a stage and so acting," to describe spontaneous response.

152. Cishou himself once described the Buddha as "great king of doctors" in a poem "In imitation of Hanshan" 擬寒山詩. Several hundred of these poems by Cishou survive appended

main text that follows it, the primary mode of reading should focus on soteriological efficacy.

Cishou, like many teachers, had forbidden such a project as an outward sign of attachment and thus not a means to liberation. There were cases in which this prohibition may have been a polite fiction, given that some *yulu* did appear within a teacher's lifetime. In other cases, students were forced to wait to issue a record posthumously. Cishou's own opposition to the compilation of a *yulu* is corroborated by a verse included in the 1133 collection. Possibly derived from an original manuscript colophon, the poem is entitled "On Account of a Postulant Wishing to Compile a *Yulu*, I Stopped It with this *Gāthā* [*ji*]" 因禪者欲編語錄以偈止之.[153]

	When our ancestor[154] arrived, he did not possess a single word,	吾祖初來字脚無
2	His later descendants vie to compile writings!	兒孫後代競編書
	Now, don't trouble yourselves by becoming attached to words and letters,	子今莫苦著文字
4	Seize the perfect luminous *uṣṇīṣa* pearl![155]	秘取圓明頂顋珠

Cishou's *gāthā* was the medicine for a student suffering from an attachment to collecting written words. Cishou's wishes were respected in his lifetime, and it was only after his passing that his verse would be compiled into a *yulu*.

Later readers have been fortunate that so many students created collections against their master's stated intentions. Indeed, the possible benefits for future readers was a common justification for compilations. This idea is dramatized in the preface to the 1135 *yulu*, wherein the writer describes a dialogue in which he accuses the compiler Pushao of betraying the wishes of his late master. The disciple is said to have responded with a reference to a popular eleventh-century story about Yunmen Wenyan's two students, who, prohibited from note-taking, "fashioned robes out of paper" so that they could furtively transcribe what the master said.[156] Pushao added that "if [the disciple] Mingjiao had obeyed Yunmen's directions, then Jianfu Chenggu [d. 1045] would not have had the basis for awakening [by reading the record], and we in monasteries today could not once again hear what had been said at that time." 使明教從雲門言，則古塔主無因以悟，今日叢林不復聞當時所

---

to a 1301 edition of *Hanshan shi*, reproduced in *Sibu congkan*. See *Hanshan ziliao leibian*, 249–250 for this poem. Cishou's preface to his Hanshan poems, dated spring of 1130, also survives.

153. *Cishou Huaishen chanshi guanglu* (ZZ73.113c18–20). It is also possible *yin* is the name of the monk and may refer to one of the monks named Yin mentioned elsewhere in the *guanglu*.

154. From the context, "our ancestor" who arrived without words is Bodhidharma.

155. *Ding ning* 頂顋 is glossed in *Yiqie jing yinyi* (T54.667c8). *Ding ning zhu*, or "pearl of *uṣṇīṣa*," is synonymous with the more common *ding zhu* 頂珠. The phrase was likely expanded to three words here to fill out the poetic meter. See also the gloss for *ding zhu* in *Zuting shiyuan* (ZZ64.360b8–10; *Gozan-ban*, 265–266).

156. App, "Making of a Chan Record," 20–22.

說也. So, too, they argued, did the words of Master Cishou need to be preserved despite the master's prohibitions. For a text produced against the wishes of the purported author, it was important to announce proper motivations. The disciples in this case did not seek to enhance the reputation of their master nor their own personal standing or financial gain. What the master had said could be the basis for liberation, they asserted, and could benefit future students. Such a tale of defiance lent a further aura to the collection, suggesting that the reader has been let in on a secret.

It was well-known that some Chan teachers forbid such record-keeping altogether, likely out of concern that a student's eagerness to compile *yulu* would have deleterious effects. Upon visiting the funeral stupa of the Southern Song master Zhi'an 直菴 (12th c.), Yuejiang Zhengyin 月江正印 (1267–after 1350)[157] wrote, "It is such a shame that we are without any records of his enlightened responses to the world! Surely it is not because he was not prominent among his contemporaries. Either he did not permit taking notes or his disciples did not circulate them, and thus there was this loss!" 惜乎應世機緣，無所記載！豈非當時門庭高峻。不許記錄，抑弟子不為流通，有此失耶.[158] Zhengyin suggests here that as a good teacher, the abbot did not let his disciples become distracted by collecting notes instead of studying the dharma. It appears that Zhengyin himself did not practice this virtue, as extant prefaces attest to a series of *yulu* produced during his own lifetime.[159] He favored preservation and circulation.

Though some masters successfully forbid the practice, it appears to have been common for monks to furtively keep personal notes and manuscripts. One practice was memorization followed by transcription. The preface by Xu Xi 徐禧 (1035–1082) written in 1070 to accompany *Recorded Sayings of Chan Master Baojue Zuxin* 寶覺祖心禪師語錄 makes clear that the initial collection was initiated soon after the master's passing. At that time "his disciples gathered and then collected and transcribed what they had once heard" 其徒子和乃集錄其所嘗聞.[160] The *yulu* of Yangqi Fanghui 楊岐方會 (992–1049), also from the eleventh century, survive in a later Southern Song anthology together with Northern Song colophons.[161] The earliest inscription preserved here is the preface by the monk Wenzheng 文政 (n.d.) dated 1050, one year

---

157. I derive these dates from the autographed inscription on *Zenrin bokuseki,* fig. 97, a series of seven untitled quatrains by Zhengyin, signed and dated 1350 and stating his age as eighty-four *sui.*

158. *Yuejiang Zhengyin chanshi yulu* (ZZ71.157b14–17). Zhi'an was a contempory of Mi'an Xianjie (1118–1186), see *Xu Gu zunsu yuyao* (ZZ68.447a22-b3).

159. Colophons appended at the beginning and end of *Yuejiang Zhengyin Chanshi yulu* dated 1317, 1322, 1323, 1335, and 1340 refer to numerous editions circulating in his own lifetime.

160. *Baojue Zuxin chanshi yulu* (ZZ69.213a5–18).

161. This colophon is found in the 1267 edition of the *Gu zunsu yulu* in the collection of National Central Library (Taiwan), but not in the Kunaichō early Southern Song edition of *Gu zunsu yuyao;* also in the Ming recensions of *Yangqi fanghui heshang yulu* 楊岐方會和尚語錄. See Shiina, *Sō Gen ban,* 377, 597.

after Fanghui died.[162] The 1050 text was likely the initial posthumous collection and probably is the printed "old text" referred to in a second colophon dated 1088 composed by Yang Jie 楊傑 (*jinshi* 1059) to mark re-publication.[163] Wenzheng, though not a disciple of Fanghui, was from the nearby Hunan region. Wenzheng describes how he came to view a finished manuscript of the collection, still in scroll form, and lit incense before reading. He credits production of the text to Fanghui's prominent disciple Baiyun Shouduan 白雲守端 (1025–1072). But "[Fanghui] did not allow anyone to record his sayings in manuscript, yet Venerable Shouduan of Hengyang memorized [his words] and wrote them down later, then compiled them in a single scroll" 不許抄錄，衡陽守端上人默而記諸，編成一軸.[164] Fanghui was right to be worried about his listeners' talent for memorization and furtive written records. Many people possessed the ability to remember and transcribe from memory.[165] Posthumous collections like those where the master did not personally authorize the collection or its circulation, created a situation that necessitated a different preface.[166] Especially with posthumous collections, the compiler's honorable intentions as a sign of his grasp of the dharma might be foregrounded. Likewise, a Chan master's actual or purported refusal to permit such collection or its dissemination was a way to present the late master's commitment to the correct dharma and abnegation of worldly fame.

Such displays of virtue could naturally also be fruitful for inspiring patronage—whether for oneself or for the next generation—from members of the literati or imperial court who enjoyed these texts.[167] Even Emperor Renzong, it was said, delighted in reading *yulu*.[168] The fundamental form of patronage provided by these officials and the imperial court was the ability to determine abbatial appointments to public monasteries. This was surely an important factor in the creation of Chan literature. But colophons

---

162. With little biographical information on Wenzheng, we can only guess whether he was or was not the same monk who wrote a preface for *Zuying ji,* noted in the main text earlier this chapter. The preface to Fanghui's text is attributed to Wenzheng "bhiksu from Xiangzhong" 湘中苾蒭, the *Zuying ji* is signed by Wenzheng "the junior monk and disciple" 參學小師.

163. Entitled "Epigraph to *The Recorded Sayings of Elder Hui of Yangqi*" 題楊岐會老語錄. Cf. Berling, "Bringing the Buddha Down to Earth," 79, who confuses the two colophons and mistakes the compiler, Shouduan 守端, for a lay official.

164. *Gu zunsu yulu,* fasc. 32 (CBETA.859b9–860a7).

165. Nugent, *Manifest in Words,* 71–97, details tales of extraordinary as well as ordinary textual memory; on 245–247, he notes that the compiler of Guanxiu's poems regarded those "who silently remembered them" as one of his reliable sources.

166. Here I agree with Berling, "Bringing the Buddha Down to Earth," 79. I disagree with her assertions about monks and laymen, which appear to be based on an untenable reading of the text.

167. Schlütter, "*Record of Hongzhi*," 198–199.

168. Emperor Renzong and Chan master Dajue Huailian 大覺懷璉 (1010–1090) exchanged "matched rhyme poems" 次韻詩 about a particular passage, of which one pair survives, *Luohu yelu* (ZZ83.378b2–4). According to *Luohu yelu,* Renzong was reading *Touzi yulu* of Touzi Datong 投子大同 (819–914), a text first printed in 1021; the passage in question is in *Gu zunsu yulu* (ZZ68.233c20).

composed by monks, such as those by Huihong translated in the next chapter, document that Chan literature, including verse, also circulated directly among monks, without literati intermediaries. That the reading aid *Zuting shiyuan,* compiled in the early 1100s, was directed at monastic students to assist in reading a set of *yulu* is further affirmation that aspiring Chan monks were a primary audience for *yulu.*

I would argue that the intentional act of distinguishing *jisong* from *shi* was addressed to both of these audiences, educated lay elite as well as fellow monks. For the elite lay readers, paratexts signaled that their ordinary ways of reading poetry would not yield what was important here. At first glance, a collection of *jisong* could look like a collection of poetry. Indeed, Song literati who read *yulu* also criticized monks' poetry for having the "whiff of vegetables." For fellow monks, these texts modeled a correct attitude toward poetry. Other components in a monk's education about the proper role of "outer learning," detailed in Chapter 4, would resonate with injunctions to read a Chan master's verse as *jisong* and not poetry *per se.* These paratexts for the most part encouraged reading for the purpose of understanding Buddhist teachings, not for ordinary aesthetic achievements.

Coda

I have focused in this chapter on Chan texts to illustrate the "co-habitation" of manuscript and print during the Song dynasty. Although more remains to be said about collecting and printing, I have emphasized how monks' verses were made into *gāthā* across mediums. The Japanese collections of *bokuseki* were constituted of writings largely from the Southern Song and Yuan. Printed collections of Chan monks' verses, on the other hand, date earlier, to the Northern Song period. Northern Song narratives about giving, receiving, viewing, and collecting individual manuscripts of verse nonetheless strongly suggest that manuscript practices were contiguous with Southern Song and Yuan manuscript practices. For example, wandering monks collected the calligraphy of their masters, transcribed whole and partial copies of texts from libraries or friends, and then physically carried these objects around and showed them to others. Compilers made collections of verse from manuscripts in circulation, across temple and private holdings. For us today, viewing manuscripts alongside printed texts brings into view the sociology of this premodern literature.

Throughout the textual lives of a given verse, Chan monks and their monastic communities used various paratexts to make verses into *jisong.* That Song-era communities did so with such frequency indicates that the distinction between a *shi* and a *jisong* was one that needed to be regularly affirmed. These genre distinctions were known to the writers of verse, to the compilers of collections, and to the readers who added colophons. Examples at all levels of textual production exhibit a concern with distinguishing *gāthā* from poetry. Though the boundary was porous at times, this conceptual difference appears to have been widely known. Future work may also show the role this distinction played in shaping decisions about belletristic collections. In this chapter, however, my focus has been to understand how insiders of this monastic literary culture distinguished between literary and religious ways of writing as well as literary and religious ways of collecting or anthologizing. In the next chapter, I draw on my understanding of Song normative distinctions between religious and literary writing to offer a new interpretation of the concept "literary Chan" (*wenzi chan* 文字禪) as found in the writings of the charismatic and outspoken figure Huihong.

PART TWO

Poetry and the Way

3

Poetry Is Not the Way

With mind deluded, you are turned by the *Lotus;*   心迷法華轉
With a mind awakened, you turn the *Lotus.*   心悟轉法華

   — *Jingde chuandenglu*

A POPULAR Song-era narrative of Huineng 慧能 (trad. 638–713), the Sixth Pa-triarch of Chan, recounts that a monk named Fada 法達, who after studying the *Lotus Sūtra* for seven years, sought the illustrious Huineng to resolve his confusions about the text.[1] Because Huineng could not read, he had to ask Fada to recite the *Lotus* so that he could explain its significance. To exhort Fada to further realize the profound meanings of his interpretation, Huineng spoke a *ji* 偈, a Chinese *gāthā*, that included the lines of the epigraph that begins this chapter. The illiterate Huineng could not read, but he performed his ability to "turn" the text and not be turned by it. The erudite Fada, on the other hand, had found himself still turned by the *Lotus* after seven years of study, a condi-tion that only ended with his awakening at Huineng's exegesis.

The compilers of the Song *locus classicus* inserted a comment that "Fada hereafter grasped the profound tenets but did not abandon his recitation and upholding [of the *Lotus*]" 師從此領玄旨，亦不輟誦持.[2] Though the key to Huineng's Chan teaching was not to be found in any sūtra, this vision of Chan awakening did not preclude reading and interpreting sūtras after awak-ening. Though not a Chan figure, in his abbreviated encyclopedia *Great Song Historical Digest of the Buddhist Order* 大宋僧史略, Zanning 贊寧 (919–1001) expressed the similar view that if "one obtains the Way and verifies the fruit" 得道證果, one could then engage in worldly activities "effortlessly with super-normal powers and thereby carry out deeds of a buddha" 游戲神通而作佛事.[3] Likewise, "The Instructions to the Scribe" in the *Chanyuan qinggui* rule

---

1. Here I emphasize the Song reception of this narrative. A related passage is found in the Dunhuang editions of the *Platform Sūtra*. Yang Zengwen, *Dunhuang xinben Liuzu tan jing,* 56, cor-responding to Yampolsky, *Platform Sutra,* 167. The popular *Jingde chuandenglu* narrative matches that found in the twelfth-century Buddhist encyclopedia *Dazang yilan* (581c18–24) as well as the Yuan-era *Platform Sūtra.*

2. *Jingde chuandenglu* (T51.238b19–20).

3. *Seng shi lüe* (T54.253a26–27). On the Song-dynasty valences of *youxi,* see Zhou, "Youxi sanmei." Welter, *Administration of Buddhism,* gives an extensive introduction and complete translation.

book, translated in the next chapter, exhorts a monk to use brush and ink—his literary writings—for the buddhadharma and not to benefit his personal affairs.

The present chapter lays out a parallel set of attitudes toward poetry found in the writings of Juefan Huihong 覺範惠洪 (1071–1128). Huihong was the author of a thirty-fascicle collection of poetry and belles lettres titled *Shimen wenzi chan* 石門文字禪 in addition to well over a hundred fascicles of Chan annals, poetic criticism, and sūtra commentary. Huihong is well-known today as the reputed founder of a nonexistent historical movement known as *wenzi chan* 文字禪, "literary" or "lettered Chan." My hypothesis is that Juefan Huihong did not regularly advocate that monks study and write poetry as a way to achieve liberation and that he did not found a new school under the banner of *wenzi chan*. Rather, his mature position seems to have been the much more modest assertion that poetry and writing could not fundamentally be outside the Way and that if awakening is to be expressed through expedient means, language may be used. When he wished to refer to such Buddhist uses of writing, Huihong relied on phrases like "using brush and ink to carry out deeds of a buddha" 以翰墨為佛事. He did not use the term *wenzi chan* as a synonym for literary expressions of awakening. Here, I am offering a sharp break with the prevailing scholarship on this topic.

Chan teachers of the Song dynasty did not advocate that their monastic students write poetry as a means to Buddhist liberation. No social movement existed by which a monk should attempt to poeticize his way to awakening. Instead, in the Song, writing and linguistic production, including any kind of verse, were not excluded from the toolkit, or "cultural repertoire," for the awakened Buddhist teacher in his instruction to students. In other words, although poetry is not outside the Way, poetry *per se* is not the Way. This Chinese position is the opposite of the roughly contemporaneous Japanese notion that "the path of poetry is none other than the path of the Buddha" (*kadō soku butsudō* 歌道即佛道).[4] Most monks in Song China viewed poetry as a Confucian pursuit: one could engage in it, but it would not of itself lead to Buddhist insights or liberation. Despite these normative ideas, of course, many historical monks took part in the entangling vines of writing and discursive thinking. In this context, the term *wenzi chan* was a pejorative used for the erroneous views of a monk who mistook such discursive ideation for Chan.

I suspect that it was during the Yuan that the relationship between Chan monasticism and poetry changed, but I have so far found evidence only of traces and not yet an explicit statement to that effect. In the Yuan, the term *wenzi chan* appears to have been used ambiguously, often with a derogatory connotation. Unambiguously explicit statements about poetry as the way to Chan liberation, on the other hand, appear in the Ming dynasty beginning in the 1500s. The idea that *wenzi chan* refers to this union of poetry and Chan was posited by the monk Zibo Zhenke 紫柏真可 (1543–1604). Zhenke's novel

---

4. Miller, *Wind from Vulture Peak*, 5.

exegesis accompanied his reprinting of Huihong's works. The movement led by Zhenke was not without controversy and opposition, however, as I will show below. More to the point is that modern scholars have been projecting this Ming-era movement backward onto the Song and disregarding Song-era understandings and uses of the term *wenzi chan*. It is not merely a case of anachronistic terminology; such historiography has fostered misunderstandings. We have, in effect, relied on Ming-dynasty ideas about *wenzi chan* to misrepresent Song-dynasty phenomena.

The Ming ideas tally with our own presuppositions that poetry and Buddhism should be compatible. Bernard Faure has pronounced on the signal importance of the role of poetry within "literary Chan" as a Buddhist movement associated with Song Chan. "A recurrent theme in 'literary Chan' is that, despite appearances, the words of poetry, being the expression of Chan awakening, have a higher status than ordinary language. They are not the language of a deluded subjectivity that would create a hiatus in the natural flow of things, but rather the language that nature speaks through man."[5] I believe, on the contrary, that *wenzi chan* was understood during the Song to mean exactly the opposite; it was a name for the understanding that literary language and especially poetry do not transcend the ordinary, deluded world. The notion of the poet as a medium for natural truths, an ideal of poetry associated with Western Romanticism,[6] does not match the Song Buddhist discourse on poetry as expedient means. This Song attitude to poetry also appears to have anticipated analogous claims made by Southern Song *Daoxue* people that would strip poetry of the possibility of speaking to truths imminent in the world.[7]

I want to make clear from the outset that I am not arguing that monks did not write poetry. Nor am I arguing that monks did not debate the relationship between language and ineffable awakening. I believe monks understood themselves to be writing poetic verse in at least three ways. First, monks wrote verse to express joy in the dharma, the Way; such poetry was presented and understood to be an expression of an awakened mind. The genres to which these verses were assigned varied—as I reviewed in the latter portion of Chapter 1—but were not regarded as *shi*. Second, monks wrote verse for pedagogical purposes; such poems were often said by writers and readers to be *jisong* (Chinese *gāthā*) and frequently excluded from mainstream *shi*. Such didactic verses balance aesthetics against religious purpose but will generally resolve a tension or reconcile conflicting norms by prioritizing Buddhist goals over aesthetic concerns. Third, monks wrote *shi* in the same manner as did mainstream literati; doctrine, teachings, and "Buddhist perspectives" are

---

5. Faure, *Chan Insights and Oversights*, 210–211.

6. McMahan, *Making of Buddhist Modernism*, 119–120, where he draws on the mid-century work of historian M. H. Abrams, *The Mirror and the Lamp* (Oxford: Oxford University Press, 1953). On the Romantic sources of this notion, see Taylor, *Sources of the Self*, 423.

7. Fuller, *Drifting among Rivers and Lakes*, 299–404.

subordinate to the aesthetics and concerns of genre. This "monks' poetry" (*sengshi* 僧詩) by so-called poet-monks, to use the parlance of Song society, occupied a third space somewhere between literati and monastic communities. *Sengshi* was subject to criticisms from members of both communities and sometimes rose to a level of prominence in one or both. Among the poems and verse by Huihong were those that participated in each of the three categories, with a majority in the third category. All of the kinds of monks' poetry just discussed are worth studying as possible formations of religious literature. I am not arguing against the existence of any of these phenomena nor their value as objects of inquiry.

I focus in this chapter on the term *wenzi chan* because it has been at the center of the prevailing scholarly model, which I contend has hindered further research. Zhou Yukai anticipated similar arguments with his early remarks that Huihong himself used *wenzi chan* only in "a narrow sense," whereas modern scholars use *wenzi chan* "in a broad sense" to describe the many kinds of writing and language deployed by Chan teachers.[8] Since Zhou published this correct observation, however, the broad sense of the term has become normalized in Chinese scholarship with mixed results.[9] Although most of the evidence given below has appeared in Chinese scholarship, I advocate against our continued use of *wenzi chan* in any loose sense because it creates ambiguity and obfuscation where precision and clarity are needed. I contend that only after we clarify what *wenzi chan* did and did not mean in the Song can we begin to ask more useful questions about how to make sense of monks' poetry. I have carried out a careful reading of each usage of the phrase *wenzi chan* in Huihong's own writings. For Huihong, *wenzi chan* refers to poetry expressing the mind of one who has not yet achieved liberation and was often a term of self-effacement.

Some Background on Huihong and *Wenzi Chan*

Some modern scholars of Song-dynasty Chan have assumed that there was a movement within the monastic establishment by which literary creativity could spark awakening. This supposed movement is thought to be Wenzi Chan, treated as a proper name and often rendered as Lettered Chan or Literary Chan. I take the term to mean something more like "Chan of written words," and so treat it as a common noun, *wenzi chan*. This supposed movement is said to have begun with an archetypical founder in the figure of Juefan Huihong and in his collection of writings entitled *Shimen wenzi chan* 石門文字禪. *Shimen wenzi chan* is constituted largely of *shi*, with over one thousand poems organized by form, and followed by inscriptions, petitions, colophons, and other occa-

---

8. Zhou, *Wenzi chan yu Songdai shixue,* 46.
9. Wu Ching-yi, "Huihong wenzi chan zhi shixue neihan yanjiu," provides a detailed review of Chinese scholarship from the 1990s until 2004. Another critical review in Hsiao, "*Wenzi chan*" *shixue de fazhan guiji.*

sional writing. There are in addition a few sections of "inner learning," including one fascicle of *jisong*. In terms of structure, the collection is more akin to the collected works of a literary figure than to a Chan *yulu*.

The relationship between Buddhism and literature in the Northern Song has often been conceived of with the term *wenzi chan*. Several prominent scholars have tried to find some ideology behind this *wenzi chan* that could fit within the well-established contours of Buddhist doctrinal developments in the Song. Shortly after Huihong's death, the eminent monk Dahui Zonggao allegedly sounded the death knell of *wenzi chan*, an event dramatized in the legendary tale of his burning the original woodblocks of his master's *Blue Cliff Record* collection of *gong'an*. Scholars have sought for reconciliation between the Chan polemics of "do not rely on written words" (*buli wenzi* 不立文字) and Huihong's supposed advocacy of "Chan of written words" (*wenzi chan*). In this way, *wenzi chan* in scholarly writing has tended to signify any type of Chan that includes writing, as opposed to a radical rejection of language.

Robert Gimello has written that the Northern Song was a period in which Chan was not marked by "simple rejection of traditional Buddhist text, doctrine, and path but its intensification, enhancement, and experimental fulfillment of the orthodoxy conveyed therein."[10] He aptly describes this as two sides of a story, two vectors in tension. Today, as when Gimello was writing, we are more familiar with the story of Chan as a renegade school of Buddhism. On the other hand, as Gimello notes, "the strains of Chan predominant during the eleventh and early twelfth centuries in one way or another rejected extreme or literalist interpretations of the standard Chan self-image as 'a special transmission outside the theoretical teachings.' "[11] He remarks that the term that best captures this "sober Chan conservatism" is *wenzi chan;* here my view departs from Gimello. He writes, "The term 'Wenzi Chan' is especially associated with the life and thought of the late Northern Song Linji Chan monk Huihong, who used it to characterize his own combination of Chan practice, Buddhist learning, and secular belles lettres."[12] Gimello seeks an intervention against the unsavory reputation of *wenzi chan*, which he attributes to the judgments of later Japanese Zen reformers against the flourishing artistic culture of Muromachi-period Gozan Zen.[13] He proposes that Huihong may have coined the term before such derogatory connotations began to coalesce and that it remained for Huihong as originally intended to describe "the role of literature and learning in Chan practice."[14] Gimello has placed his finger on one of the primary religious tensions of Buddhism in the Song period. Nonetheless, several assertions may need to be qualified.

George Keyworth, in his 2001 dissertation, criticizes Gimello for not going

---

10. Gimello, "Mārga and Culture," 377.

11. Gimello, "Mārga and Culture," 377–378.

12. Gimello, "Mārga and Culture," 415n17.

13. Gimello, "Mārga and Culture," 417n28. Sawada, *Practical Pursuits,* 127–129, analyzes the low regard for *moji zen* in the Tokugawa period.

14. Gimello, "Mārga and Culture," 409.

far enough in asserting that "fundamentally, Chan not only rejected the phrase 'not setting up the written word' [*buli wenzi*] but instead stood as a Buddhist school which did not reject the written word."[15] Keyworth proposes that *wenzi chan* "implied that [monks] could openly engage in literary endeavors."[16] Keyworth's approach to *wenzi chan* ultimately leads him to conclude that it meant "language was a cornerstone of Chan practice."[17] In my view, Keyworth has brought together interesting evidence that supports a conclusion about the term *wenzi chan* contrary to his own. By following similar evidence, my reading also runs against some of the broader brushstrokes painted by literary historians. Ronald Egan has remarked that "Huihong is of particular interest as the leader of the 'Lettered Chan' (*wenzi chan*) movement, which eschewed the traditional mistrust of words and writing of the Chan school and sought to reconcile Chan practices with scholarly reverence for texts of all kinds."[18] I have not found evidence of a Wenzi Chan movement. The phrase *wenzi chan* was seldom used in the Song period, and when it was, it most often referred to Huihong's book.[19] No group, faction, or community called itself Wenzi Chan. Rather, *wenzi chan* was used as a derogatory or ironically self-abasing phrase.

From the perspective of his diverse literary output, Huihong's identity is at once more interesting and variegated than the typical Chan master. Indeed, as a historical personage, Huihong, whose career spanned the waning decades of the Northern Song, cuts a fascinating figure. He thrived as a literary figure in the capital; endured more than one period of imprisonment or exile; produced copious amounts of mainstream poetry, poetic criticism, Chan hagiography, and sūtra exegesis; and passed away as the Northern Song empire crumbled under repeated Jurchen invasions. Though a man of many accomplishments, Huihong's legacy was not as an institution builder. He was not, to my knowledge, an abbot who trained students who in turn later became abbots in a family-style succession within Chan.[20] He neither developed liturgies or standard rituals that persisted in institutions nor engaged in other activities that would create a monastic lineage. On the contrary, he was a prodigiously social man who offered advice to numerous young men, as documented in his hundreds of occasional poems. He achieved a degree of fame in his own lifetime and many of his contemporaries among monastics were eager to associate with him judging from the many people who appear in his

---

15. Keyworth, "Transmitting the Lamp," 3.
16. Keyworth, "Transmitting the Lamp," 4.
17. Keyworth, "Transmitting the Lamp," xv.
18. Ronald Egan, "The Northern Song (1020–1126)," 426–427.
19. Based on digital searches through a database of *Quan Song Shi* published by Beijing University; through the CBETA 2016 edition of CBReader; and through the Scripta Sinica database of Academia Sinica.
20. The impact of the Song-Jin wars should not be discounted as a factor here. Nonetheless, Huihong is a bare branch on the family tree of the "lamp record" lineage charts created during the Song, Yuan, and Ming.

Shimen Wenzi chan. He was popular for his writing, in other words, but he did not build an institution in which to train others.

Huihong's legacy in the world of Chinese Buddhism was his many books. Huihong did not leave a *yulu*, nor did he create Chan-style commentaries on *gong'an*. In addition to his poetry, Huihong wrote commentaries on Buddhist sūtras. In this light, his intellectual output may seem more like that of a Song-era Tiantai or Huayan monk than a typical Song Chan monk, but his was a vision of combined study of sūtras and Chan. At the same time, he compiled two important Chan histories, *Biographies of the Sangha Jewel in the Forests of Chan* 禪林僧寶傳 (hereafter *Chanlin sengbao zhuan*) and *Records from within the Forests [of Chan]* 林間錄. Huihong's literary works, including his poetry and poetic criticism, circulated mostly outside of the cloister, finding an audience among the literati, judging by their inclusion among literary works in imperial collectanea bearing colophons by non-monastic readers and the relative absence of references in later Buddhist monastic texts. Huihong was a remarkably talented writer with the ability to code-switch when addressing different audiences.

Turning now to the history of the term *wenzi chan,* at least two Northern Song texts antedate those by Huihong. I will review each in detail. Possibly the earlier of the two is the undated poem by Huang Tingjian, "An Inscription on Boshi's Painting of Tao Yuanming beneath Pines" 題伯時畫松下淵明, on a painting by Li Gonglin 李公麟 (1049–1106).[21] Though a painting of Tao Yuanming, Huang's poem used the phrase *wenzi chan* to depict the activities of the so-called Lotus Society 蓮社, the group of late Eastern Jin (317–420) loyalists that gathered around the teacher Huiyuan 慧遠 (334–416) at Mount Lu.[22] In the Northern Song, it was thought that Tao's love of drink and freedom was the reason he refused to join an austere and disciplined society like the Lotus. The poem references the zealous Liu Yimin 劉遺民 (354–410; given name Chengzhi 程之), a lay leader among the Mount Lu group, who took up residence in a hermitage on the mountain for the last fifteen years of his life.[23] Liu composed the celebrated vow of the society dated 402, by means of which 123 men declared their collective intention to achieve salvation after death through birth in the Pure Land.[24] Liu and others wrote poetry

21. On Li Gonglin's relationship to the story and image of Tao Yuanming, see An-yi Pan, *Painting Faith,* 185–191. This poem by Huang Tingjian is not in Pan's book, but my understanding was enhanced by Pan's discussion of how Northern Song literati figured Liu Yimin's invitation to Tao Yuanming and the latter's refusal.

22. On Huiyuan and Liu Chengzhi (Yimin), see Zürcher, *Buddhist Conquest of China,* 217–223. On the distant relationships between the history of this society, the Northern Song legends about the society, and the later popular movements also known as Lotus Societies, see Ter Haar, *White Lotus Teachings,* 90–93.

23. These dates per the Northern Song biography in *Lushan ji* (T51.1039b28). If one follows the Qing compiler of *Jushi zhuan* (ZZ88.187c5), that yields a birth year of 352. See also Zürcher, *Buddhist Conquest of China,* 217.

24. Translated by Zürcher, *Buddhist Conquest of China,* 244–245.

during their gatherings, a typical activity of learned men in the Jin.[25] It is not clear which of these writings Huang Tingjian had in mind when he wrote "Huiyuan's society of incense offering, / and the *wenzi chan* of Liu Yimin, / although these were not for the old man [Tao], / his reclusive tendencies are also praiseworthy" 遠公香火社，遺民文字禪，雖非老翁事，幽尚亦可觀.[26] Huang used *wenzi chan* in this poem to describe the activity of Liu, a lay practitioner. In the Northern Song, the society at Mount Lu was associated with Pure Land practices generally and with the practice of visualization known as *nianfo sanmei* 念佛三昧 (*buddhānusmṛti-samādhi*) specifically. Liu is said to have excelled at these visualization techniques.[27] Huiyuan wrote that Liu "focused his thoughts in seated *chan,* and within half a year from starting, saw a buddha while in concentration" 專念禪坐始涉半年定中見佛. He also suggested that Liu in his final moments achieved a vision of Amitabha Buddha of the Western Pure Land.[28] This auspicious death was still being recounted in Song sources.[29] It was also thought in the Song that Liu Yimin contributed to the lost *Collection of *Buddhānusmṛti-samādhi Poems* 念佛三昧詩集.[30] When Huang Tingjian refers to Liu's *wenzi chan,* the reference is likely to this Pure Land concentration practice and to either Liu's composition of poems about *nianfo sanmei* or the collective vow. Whatever this *wenzi chan* referred to, it was at the same time something that Tao Yuanming avoided. *Wenzi chan* here does not, therefore, refer to literary activity in general nor to the spirited spontaneity that Tao was understood to embody. Huang Tingjian was not, of course, making historical arguments with this inscription; the real subject of his comments may have been lay and clergy literati that gathered at Li Gonglin's mountain villa.[31] This poem is thought to be from around 1088, though the date is debated.[32] If it is correct, then a member of the literati, not a monk, coined the term *wenzi chan. Wenzi chan* in Huang's poem does not refer to a

---

25. A set of poems is recorded in *Lushan ji* (T51.1042c3) under the heading *feng he* 奉和, indicating the poem was "offered in response" to the prior poem, titled "Wandering on Mount Lu" 遊廬山, authored by Huiyuan.

26. In twelve lines with a single rhyme, these are lines 5 to 8 of the poem; *Huang Tingjian shi ji zhu,* 9/325–327.

27. The Chinese understanding of **buddhānusmṛti-samādhi* focused on Pure Land visualization develops several strains of early Chinese Buddhist thought. On the introduction to China of *buddhānusmṛti,* see Harrison, "*Buddhānusmṛti* in the *Pratyutpanna-buddha-saṃmukhāvasthita-samādhi-sūtra*." For a related description of *buddha-darśana* and early Chinese Buddhist texts, see Harrison, "Commemoration and Identification in *Buddhānusmṛti,*" 224–226.

28. Quote from *Guang hongming ji* (T52.304b8–9), partially translated in Zürcher, *Buddhist Conquest of China,* 221.

29. On the significance of such visions, see Zürcher, *Buddhist Conquest of China,* 221–222, as well as Stevenson, "Buddhist Ritual in the Song," 363–364, 404.

30. The collection of poems known as *Nianfo sanmei shi ji* is no longer extant, but Huiyuan's preface was preserved in *Guang hongming ji* (T52.351b10-c7). The Song historian Zhipan also thought Liu contributed to the collection, as he noted in *Fozu tongji* (T49.261c17).

31. Paintings of these gatherings in Gimello, "Mārga and Culture."

32. *Pace* Hsiao Li-hua, I follow the dating given by Zhou Yukai, *Wenzi chan yu Songdai shixue,* 32.

monastic movement nor to the Chan lineages but instead refers to the activities of lay people.

The earliest date for a related term comes in 1091. The phrase "the written word [*wenzi*] is not separate from *chan*" 文字不離禪 emerges from a spontaneous composition by the Tiantai master Longjing Biancai 龍井辯才 (1011–1091).[33] Biancai's poetic response survives because Su Shi brushed a copy and added a colophon, found in Su's collected prose.[34] The complete paratextual inscription makes clear that the original poem was by Biancai, written when he was the age of eighty-one *sui*. We know a good deal more about this poem that corroborates its authorship by Biancai. We know that the poem matches the rhymes of a poem composed by Daoqian, which also survives. Daoqian frequently visited Biancai during the latter's dotage, and during one such visit Daoqian composed a poem after evening meditation. He must have shown it to Biancai, who responded with his own poem, using Daoqian's original rhymes. This was likely one of the last poems Biancai wrote before his death that same year. We also know that Daoqian sent these two rhyming poems, his own and Biancai's, to their mutual friend Qin Guan 秦觀 (1049–1100).[35] Himself a poet, Qin Guan composed a poem in response, again using the same rhymes, only after he learned of Biancai's death.[36] All three poems survive and all conclude with the same word, *chan*.

The word *chan* in Daoqian's poem sent to Biancai concerns extracting himself from the commotion of the world. His poem ends with a wish to return to the internal illumination he experiences during "evening meditation" (*ye chan* 夜禪). The poem is nostalgic and refers to the long personal history that Daoqian shared with the elderly Tiantai master Biancai. The two men, Daoqian and Biancai, both hailed from Yuqian County 於潛縣 outside Hangzhou, where they had lived together decades earlier.[37] Toward the end of his life, Daoqian retired to Yuqian, where a tomb marker was visible by a small

---

33. Zhou, in *Wenzi chan yu Songdai shixue*, 44, discusses Biancai. Biancai's poem is given in Grant, *Mount Lu Revisited*, 137–138. Additional works attributed to Biancai are preserved in the Qing-era *Longjing jianwen lu* 龍井見聞錄.

34. "Writing out Biancai's matching rhyme to Canliao's poem" 書辯才次韻參寥詩, *Su Shi wenji*, 68/2144. The poem often was erroneously attributed to Su, such as in *Su Shi shiji*, 50/2755–2756.

35. The original poem by Daoqian entitled "At Luminous Pavilion Accompanying Venerable Biancai, during Evening Sitting I Thought of Scholar [Qin] Shaoyou" 照閣奉陪辯才老師夜坐懷少游學士, *Canliaozi shiji*, 7.1b; 232.

36. See *Qin Guan ji biannian jiaozhu*, 227–228. That poem explicitly identifies the original author by name as Biancai and intentionally matches the same end-rhyme words as in both Daoqian's and Biancai's poems. Qin uses the final rhyme *chan* to describe Biancai's passing as his entering various *dhyāna*, like the Buddha in the moments before *parinirvāṇa*.

37. To my knowledge, no writing by Daoqian or Biancai survives from this period at Mingzhi Temple 明智寺 on Mount Xipu 西菩山. Su Shi traveled to the temple in 1074 (*Su Shi shiji*, 12/584–585) and is said to have met the two monks, *Xianchun Lin'an zhi*, 84/4135. Further stories about the meeting preserved in later gazetteers for Yuqian County 於潛縣 may be a topic of further research.

stream.[38] Biancai countered Daoqian's poem with a declaration that if the dharma is ultimately without distinguishing marks, then "scholarly pavilions and mountain temples fundamentally are without difference, / and so it is that *wenzi* is not separate from *chan*" 臺閣山林本無異，故應文字未離禪. By writing this line directly to Daoqian, Biancai suggests he believes Daoqian holds the opposite view: that somehow poetic activity was fundamentally distinct from the stillness of evening meditation. The argument that fundamentally there is no difference is itself inherently a Buddhist one. Biancai's poem is not an argument that Confucianism and Buddhism are the same in practice or in history, or that a person can or should use poetry as a Buddhist pathway. Rather, the two men are exploring how they, as practicing monks, can engage in a worldly activity such as poetry in a way that respects the integrity of their Buddhist commitments. Both views are largely consonant with what we have already seen in previous chapters. Daoqian here expresses his view that poetry is something outside the Buddhist path, possibly even an obstacle. Biancai's response encourages Daoqian to realize that an awakening to the universal Buddhist truth will inevitably also encompass one's behavior in the world.

Huihong was a student of the writings of both Su Shi and Huang Tingjian. It is therefore possible that he was aware of one or both of the antecedents described above. If so, Huihong's ideas about *wenzi chan* were not limited to debates among Chan monks but also included literati and Tiantai monks. Further, the idea that awakening ultimately is "not separate from the written word" (*bu li wenzi* 不離文字) can be traced back to Chinese scriptures, including the *Scripture for Humane Kings*.[39] A similar idea is also found in the early Song Chan text *Jingde chuandenglu*, though there it is said to get only the flesh of the master and not his bones or marrow.[40] For Huihong himself, Buddhist scriptures were very important, perhaps especially the *Shoulengyan jing* 首楞嚴經 (*Śūraṃgamasūtra*), for which he composed an exegetical commentary.[41]

While there may have been earlier uses, the term *wenzi chan* has, throughout the history of Chinese Buddhism subsequent to Huihong, been most strongly associated with him. He is the earliest person in the written record to use the term repeatedly. It is, moreover, part of the title of his collected works, *Shimen wenzi chan,* wherein the term appears eight times. There are other, more-and-less related phrases, like "using brush and ink to do the deeds of a buddha" 以筆墨為佛事, which I believe Huihong regarded as proper pious writing and distinct from *wenzi chan*. The former was the use of writing or language by an awakened being to liberate others, whereas the latter re-

---

38. Daoqian spent his final days west of Hangzhou, where he wrote several poems about life at "Twin Brooks" 雙溪 of Changhua 昌化 (*Canliaozi shiji*, 12.6a-b). According to my research, early Ming-era gazetteers record that Daoqian's tomb (*Canliao mu* 參寥墓) was placed just north of another stream nearby, "Intersecting Brooks" 交溪. *Chenghua Hangzhou fu zhi*, 12.19b-20a.

39. *Renwang huguo bore boluomiduo jing* (T8.839b9–23).

40. *Jingde chuandenglu* (T51.219b29-c1).

41. The *Śūraṃgamasūtra* is widely regarded as an indigenous Chinese sūtra, or apocryphon; see Benn, "Pseudo-Śūraṃgama sūtra."

ferred to writing still laden with worldly thoughts and sentiments. To illustrate the difference, I next provide an analysis of all eight examples from Huihong's book *Shimen wenzi chan* in which Huihong himself employed the term *wenzi chan* in his poetry and prose.

Huihong's Uses of *Wenzi Chan*

Huihong's own use of the term *wenzi chan* varied somewhat in his writings but never did it describe a path to liberation or a movement within monastic institutions. On the contrary, he used *wenzi chan* to refer to worldly writing by monastics, to creative absorption in literary pursuits by members of the literati, and to his own poetry as emotion-laden word craft.

I begin with a mildly humorous example. In an eight-line regulated poem entitled "Venerable Xian Sought a *Gāthā* [*ji*]" 賢上人覓偈, Huihong, rebuking a nun, writes,[42]

	You are lazy when it comes to contemplating bones,	懶修枯骨觀
2	but cherish studying *wenzi chan*.	愛學文字禪
	Rivers and peaks encourage your refined inspirations,	江山助佳興
4	and you sometimes make banquet poetry collections.	時有題葉篇
	When we met, we did not have leisure to speak [them out],	相逢未暇語
6	They will nonetheless all become brilliantly clear.	輒復一粲然
	Why must you exhaust that which you study [i.e. *wenzi chan*]?	豈須究所學
8	Seeking a *gāthā* is indeed worthy in itself.	覓偈亦自賢

The first line refers to the ascetic practice of contemplation, called "white-bones contemplation" 白骨觀, that inculcates a profound realization of impermanence. Such ascetic practice and *wenzi chan* are crafted as opposing concepts in this couplet. A "passion" (*ai* 愛) for the written word outstrips Venerable Xian's willingness to cultivate detachment from sensuous desire. The poem closes by noting that it would be better to have a *gāthā* than to pursue *wenzi chan*. Here, *wenzi chan* is a name for poetry, especially that based on a misunderstanding about the correct relationship between poetry and the Buddhist path.

Huihong uses *wenzi chan* several more times to refer to worldly poetry written by a monastic. The first of three additional examples of such references concerns Huihong himself. He refers to his own poetry as *wenzi chan* in the seven-character regulated quatrain "Given to Chan Student Fahu" 與 法護禪者, which includes the couplet "Hand copying *Chanlin sengbao zhuan* / and quietly intoning the *wenzi chan* of Shimen" 手抄禪林僧寶傳，暗誦石 門文字禪. Zhou Yukai reads the latter line as a reference to Huihong's working title for his then-current collected works and argues that the poem is evidence

---

42. *Shimen wenzi chan*, fasc. 9, 1:646. Kakumon Kantetsu suggests this poem is to a nun, about which see also *Zhu Shimen wenzi chan* 1:642n2.

that Huihong's poems were circulating under this title by no later than 1124.[43]
As the five-character phrase is parallel to *Chanlin sengbao zhuan,* the title of
another of Huihong's works, this is a reasonable conclusion. We might add
that the verb "intone" (*song*) suggests that *wenzi chan* was primarily a reference
to Huihong's poetry and not to the other writing also found in *textus receptus*
of his collected works.

Second, Huihong used *wenzi chan* to describe mainstream *shi* written by
other monks. This is the case for the title appended to a set of three poems,
"For a Monk Occupied with *Wenzi Chan*" 僧從事文字禪.[44] These three poems
offer generic praise for Wang Wei's "pure" lines;[45] they also advise the monk
to follow the "three more's" 三多, a reference to the Northern Song dictum
attributed to the Confucian Ouyang Xiu that one can improve as a writer if
one would "read more, write more, and discuss more" 看多，做多，商量多.[46]
In other words, when it came to writing poetry, Huihong offered conventional
poetic advice in the vein of a Confucian scholar.

Third, it is possible that monks' poetry could serve some religious purpose
qua "outer learning" (*waixue*), that is, non-Buddhist learning to be used for
proselytization. Such views on poetry were frequently advocated elsewhere
in the Song, but no mention of that use is made in the above texts. Such mis-
sionary uses of poetry are hinted at in two further examples in which Huihong
used *wenzi chan* to praise laypeople for their ability to understand Buddhism,
though there, too, it is not explicit.[47] In these two cases, *wenzi chan* refers to
monks' poetry encountered and appreciated by lay people. In this way, *wenzi
chan* as poetry is not beyond appreciation, but *wenzi chan* is not itself a monas-
tic path to liberation.

I will next illustrate how Huihong explicitly used *wenzi chan* as part of a
rhetoric of humility. In the following two examples, *wenzi chan* refers not to
awakened speech but rather its opposite. Here, *wenzi chan* is a name for
monks' poetry that is not in accord with the deportment of an awakened
teacher. I begin with a colophon Huihong inscribed on his own youthful
poetry, which had been collected by another monk, entitled "Inscribed after

---

43. Zhou, *Songseng Huihong xinglü,* 307–308.

44. Zhou, *Songseng Huihong xinglü,* 302, where Zhou interprets these poems to be critical
of the monk.

45. Huihong refers to Wang Wei as Wang Youxia 王右轄. The same naming convention
appears in Huang Tingjian's poem on "A Painting by Wang Wei" 摩詰畫, *Huang Tingjian shi ji
zhu,* 1249.

46. Found in *Houshan shihua,* 1.5a, attributed to Chen Shidao.

47. One example is the fourth poem of five, entitled "I Was About to Set Out to Another
Mountain..." 余將經行他山...discussed below. A second example is a praise poem (*zan*) for the
late distinguished layman Pan Xingsi 潘興嗣 (n.d.), cognomen Yanzhi 延之, stating, "his repar-
tee was not less than Layman Pang, thus he understood *wenzi chan* [i.e., monks' writing]" 機鋒
不減龐蘊而解文字禪. *Shimen wenzi chan,* fasc. 19, 2:1230. Pan was a lay student of Huanglong
Huinan and later wrote a preface for the *Mingshu huiyao* 冥樞會要 three-fascicle digest of *Zongjing
lu* arranged by Huanglong lineage monks.

Fojian Collected My *Wenzi Chan*" 題佛鑑蓄文字禪. Thinking about his juve-nilia in dismissive terms, Huihong disclosed other thoughts about religion and writing.[48]

> When I was young, I only knew how to read for pleasure, but didn't yet grasp what was essential. I would pick up a brush to write like someone was pushing on my elbow. I felt like a mute person who longed to speak but whose meaning was lost with his heavy tongue. I was laughed at by many. However, when I was about sixteen or seventeen years old, I became the attendant to Dongshan Yun'an and studied the dharma that transcends the world.[49] Suddenly, I was filled with self-confidence and was without doubts. When I read seven thousand [lines] by Su Shi, I wrote a thousand of my own. I could make progress with regular small steps. Indeed, the benefits for a person who studies the Way are not only for the moment between life and death, but also profit that person's literary language. Just so, my self-confidence increased. Now, thirty-eight years later, I visit here in Xiang[50] the master Fojian Jingyin, who was always beloved by teacher Yun'an. We have both become quite old; however, our friendship does not feel old. He brought out some lines of poetry I wrote when I was young and we read them together. In my mind I could see that old mountain forest spot we would travel to, and so intone the couplet by Bai Juyi: "Willow branch in hand, I sit and face the water / idly recalling past affairs—as though in a previous life."[51]

> 余幼孤知讀書為樂而不得其要，落筆嘗如人掣其肘，又如瘖者之欲語而意窒舌大，而濃笑者數數。然年十六七從洞山雲庵學出世法，忽自信而不疑。誦生書七千，下筆千言，踥步可待也。嗚呼，學道之益人，未論其死生之際，益其文字語言，如此益可自信也。今三十八年矣，而見雲庵平時親愛之人，佛鑑大師淨因於湘中，頹然相向俱老矣，而故意特未老，又出余少時詩句讀之，想見山林之舊游處。誦白公詩曰：「手把楊枝臨水坐，閑思往事似前身。」

In this case, *wenzi chan* as used in the printed title refers to a few of Huihong's earlier poetic works held by Fojian for about thirty-eight years. Zhou Yukai cites the reference to "thirty-eight years later" as reason to think that this text was written in 1124.[52] Zhou adds that this reference corroborates his earlier observation that the poems began to circulate under the name [*Shimen*] *Wenzi chan* in that year. I do not follow Zhou's contention that *wenzi chan* in this text refers to an early draft of what later became the complete published collection. The inscription itself clearly suggests that Huihong's response here is

---

48. *Shimen wenzi chan*, fasc. 26, 2:1517.

49. Alternatively, *chushi* 出世 could refer to "coming out" as an abbot at one's first appoint-ment, in which case this phrase would denote the "way of an abbot."

50. Xiang is the name of a river in Hunan and was by extension an old name for Hunan.

51. From "Seated Facing Water" 臨水坐, *Bai Jiyu ji*, 16/2/343. Adapted from the transla-tion in Watson, *Po Chü-i*, 85.

52. Zhou, *Songseng Huihong xinglü*, 310.

about some of his juvenilia, probably in his own calligraphy, that Fojian had in his personal collection and retrieved to share.[53]

Moreover, in light of the involvement of Huihong's close disciple Jueci 覺慈 (n.d.) in compiling and publishing the *Shimen wenzi chan* collection, it is not clear when the term *wenzi chan* became the title of the entire belletristic collection. Jueci had begun as a boy of about eleven to follow Huihong and later served as the amanuensis for Huihong's commentary on the *Lotus Sūtra* when Huihong became too ill to write.[54] In addition to his role in creating the published *Shimen wenzi chan,* Jueci was entrusted with the task of compiling and posthumously publishing Huihong's *Commentary on Wisdom and Realization* 智證傳. Jueci fulfilled his charge with the publication of the latter book in 1134.[55] If the title *Shimen wenzi chan* was not appended by Huihong himself, we should suspect it was Jueci, who either condensed a longer title or knew his teacher's rhetoric well enough to set the text correctly.

With these assumptions, we may tentatively remark that Huihong looked on the poetry of his youth with nostalgia but a clear, critical eye. As he grew older, he likely thought of these earlier literary attempts as *wenzi chan,* the writings of a not-yet-liberated young man. The term *wenzi chan* here probably provided Huihong a way to narrativize the literary output of his youth. This idea is reinforced by Huihong's quotation of a well-known *jueju* poem by Bai Juyi. Huihong could expect that his audience would know, or could look up, the other couplet from that poem wherein Bai contrasts his youthful life in the capital with his present dedication to a Pure Land confraternity. Huihong's situation echoed this clever allusion. Looking at his youthful *wenzi chan,* Huihong, too, was confronted by something that seemed to be from another lifetime. In this recounting, Huihong's writing gradually improved once he gained some religious insight. Huihong states that it was his religious life that furthered his literary activities, his literary productivity being a welcome side effect of a religious practice. Nowhere in this inscription about his own *wenzi chan* does Huihong describe his poetry or literary practices as activity that led to an awakening or spiritual achievement. Literature is subordinated to and benefited by the soteriological goal of liberation from the cycle of birth and death.

The second example in which Huihong used the phrase *wenzi chan* as a humble reference to his own worldly speech is in the preface to a commemorative "Inscription for a Lazy Hermitage" 懶庵銘 for one Venerable Ren of Nanzhou 南州仁.[56] Well-known poets like Huihong frequently received requests to compose such "studio poems" to christen new intellectual spaces

---

53. On the Song-era cultural norm of showing a guest calligraphy and the asking for a colophon, see Ebrey, "Zhu Xi's Colophons," 226–227.

54. See Zhou, *Songseng Huihong xinglü,* 249, 298, 299.

55. See Zhou, *Songseng Huihong xinglü,* 337–338.

56. *Shimen wenzi chan,* fasc. 20, 2:1241–1242. See also Zhou, *Wenzi chan yu Songdai shixue,* 44–45.

with new studio names.[57] These poems generally were opportunities to explore the virtues of the chosen name. In the preface to this inscription, Huihong discusses kinds of stainless laziness, embodied by "three lazy [masters] of Chan."[58] He follows with the assertion that Ren of Nanzhou "climbs up to heights to gaze out over the distance, and takes the language of feelings not-yet-forgotten to be *wenzi chan*" 以臨高眺遠、未忘情之語為文字禪. Zhou Yukai has pointed to this statement as the demonstration of Huihong's own definition of *wenzi chan*.[59] To understand this definition of *wenzi chan*, I will examine how Huihong elsewhere uses these two phrases, "feelings not yet forgotten" and "climbing up to heights to gaze out over the distance." In brief, the former is an allusion that describes worldly speech laden with feelings of a not-yet-awakened being. The latter refers to an established trope in which a poet would be overcome by sentiments and inspiration.

Huihong used similar rhetoric to effect humility in a colophon, "Inscribed after Poems Gathered by Venerable Bi" 題弼上人所蓄詩. This inscription on a monk's poetry does not include the words *wenzi chan;* however, Huihong does discuss his own poetic creativity as "residual karma" (*xiqi* 習氣) and the result of worldly feelings. The text introduces several other common features of Huihong's rhetoric of humility.[60]

> In Chan temples long ago, the elders regarded the oral explanation of principles as the core and would berate monks who dedicated themselves to brush and ink. When I was an itinerant monk, I would stay in different communities. As I have much residual karma that I cannot rub away, from time to time I would produce that language of not-yet-forgotten feelings. As soon as I created it, I tossed it away. If people were going to laugh at it, then better they don't hear it. When passing by Mount Lu, I was shown a large scroll of poetry by Venerable Bi. After reading it, I felt a sense of expansiveness. One could not admonish him for unnecessary speech.
>
> 往時叢林老衲多以講宗為心，呵衲子從事筆硯。予游方時，省息眾中，多習氣抉磨不去，時時作未忘情之語，隨作隨棄，如人高笑，幸其不聞。過廬山，見弼上人出一巨軸。讀之茫然，不可諱為多言之戒。

In the above colophon, Huihong uses the rhetoric of "not-yet-forgotten feelings" to humble himself. He has presented himself as someone who is unaccountably moved by beautiful vistas. This sudden rise of feeling marks a loss of self-control, which he states is surely the karmic remainder of his worldly

---

57. On the Song-era practices of naming of a studio and the invitation of poems, see Zhang Yunshuang, "Porous Privacy," 134–166.

58. An explanation of the "three lazy [masters] of Chan" is given in *Zuting shiyuan*, (ZZ64.325b21-c2; *Gozan-ban*, 196b).

59. Zhou, *Wenzi chan yu Songdai shixue*, 46.

60. *Shimen wenzi chan*, fasc. 26, 2:1518.

being. In other words, the basis of his poems is ordinary human emotion, not the kind of language charged with salvific power.

When Huihong writes "feelings not yet forgotten," he probably had in mind the following well-known story from the chapter "Grieving for the Departed" found in *New Account of Tales of the World,* or *Shishuo xinyu* 世說新語, a text that circulated widely in the Song.[61]

> When Wang Rong lost his son [Wang Sui, d. ca. 275], Shan Jian went to visit him. Wang's grief was such that he could not control himself. Jian said, "For a child that was just a 'critter at the bosom,' why should you come to this?" Wang said, "A sage may forget his feelings, and the basest people cannot attain feelings. Where feelings gather is precisely among people like us." Jian was persuaded by his words and grieved on his behalf all the more.

> 王戎喪兒萬子，山簡往省之，王悲不自勝。簡曰：「孩抱中物，何至於此！」王曰：「聖人忘情，最下不及情。情之所鍾，正在我輩。」簡服其言，更為之慟。

This early medieval story revolves around the strict emotional stoicism one might expect of a cultivated gentleman. But what to do when the situation is the death of a young child? One would imagine that such deaths were to be expected in medieval time, when infant mortality was a common concern. The text suggests that for a gentleman, therefore, a young child's death was not grounds for "losing self-control" 不自勝. Think of Zhuangzi's iconoclastic mourning for his late wife. Wang's timeless response over the loss of a child asserts that ideals such as "forgetting one's feelings" may be well and good for sages or saints, yet sentiments still "gather" and coalesce in "people like us."[62] If a sage forgets his feelings, then to have *not-yet*-forgotten feelings and therefore to lose self-control signify that one is not yet liberated as were the sages of antiquity.

A rich and complex relationship to feelings exists in the middle of the

---

61. *Shishuo xinyu jiao jian,* 349; "Shangshi" 傷逝, no. 17. Translation adapted from Chen, "On Mourning and Sincerity," 76, and Mather, *Shih-Shuo Hsin-Yü,* 347. Prior to the Huang Bosi 黄伯思 recension completed around 1109 (extant in a 1210 ed.), and before the widely circulated Southern Song 1138 recension (extant in Japan), at least twenty-three different manuscript copies of *Shishuo xinyu* are known to have been in private collections. Among them, for example, was a copy in possession of Huang Tingjian, who made numerous allusions to the text in his poetry. Pan Jianguo, "*Shishuo xinyu* zai Songdai," 168.

62. The spiritual ideal of "forgetting," *wang,* can be traced back to the Zhuangzi. The modern use of *zhongqing* 鍾情 for romantic passion follows from the so-called cult of *qing* from the late Ming on. Earlier, *zhong* would also describe the gathering of sad or troubled sentiments, as in the opening line of *Ouxing* 寓興 by Quan Deyu 權德輿 (759–818). Tang dictionary *Yiqie jing yinyi* (T54.367b1) uses the verb to describe the gathering of fluids: "where water gathers is called a marsh" 水鍾曰澤. In classical texts, consider *Huainanzi* 淮南子, sec. 3.16 (*Tianwen xun* 天文訓), wherein *zhong* is the manner in which *qi* coalesces. *Qi* here has the quality of a fluid. My thanks to Harold Roth for discussing this passage with me.

range of human experience, but not among sages or coarse people. When Shan Jian heard this explanation, he was more deeply moved than before. That Shan Jian was moved is because he, too, belongs to the category of "people like us," that is, someone refined enough to notice and articulate feelings but still subject to the passions. He is not a sage who has mastered such feelings and no longer loses self-control. Though during the time of the *Shishuo xinyu* such people mostly belonged to the aristocracy, when Song writers referred to this passage, the "people like ourselves" were understood to be members of the literati. This passage was important to Su Shi and Daoqian, both of whom cited it when confronting grief, a topic I address in Chapter 6.

Had Huihong taken recourse to this conventional language only once or twice, it would be difficult to reach a strong conclusion. He however repeatedly deployed this allusion. He wrote a colophon known as "Inscribed after My Own Poems" 題自詩 on an unauthorized collection of his poetry. Looking at this collection of his works, Huihong uses the convention of "feelings not yet forgotten" to describe his karmic tendency to lose self-control at the sight of beauty.[63]

> I did not at first intend to become skilled at crafting poems and belles lettres, but my karma from previous lives would not be washed away; and so, when I climb up to heights and gaze out over the distance, I am unable to forget my feelings. From time to time I play with language,[64] but as soon as I create it, I toss it away. Now, some devotees of such things have, unknown to me, been able to copy down my poems, and at Venerable Qi's place in Nanzhou I saw an especially large arrangement [of my poems]. Upon reading it, my face turned red with shame and I began to sweat. I think highly of Qi's love of learning, however, for even in this case of such coarse language as mine, he still was unwilling to discard [them]— how much more so must it be for those talented at poetry! Because it was presented to me, I inscribed this at its end.

> 予始非有意於工詩文，夙習洗濯不去，臨高望遠，未能忘情，時時戲為語言，隨作隨毀。不知好事者，皆能錄之，南州琦上人處見巨編，讀之面熱汗下。然佳琦之好學，雖語言之陋如僕者，亦不肯遺，況工於詩者乎。因出示輒題其末。

It is difficult to know to what extent Huihong meant for any of these sentiments to be taken at face value. It would have been arrogant to write anything other than humble remarks on a copy of one's own poetry. But we see that Huihong continuously uses the convention of not-yet-forgotten feelings, which he elsewhere associates with *wenzi chan*. Huihong wonders here if the reason he is unable to forget his feelings is because of lingering karma from

---

63. *Shimen wenzi chan,* fasc. 26, 2:1520. Punctuation slightly departs from *Zhu Shimen wenzi chan.*

64. On "playfulness" in the poetry of Su Shi and Huang Tingjian, see Zhou, "Youxi sanmei."

a previous life. If he could wash himself of this karma, perhaps he would not feel called to sing in verse when encountering beauty. At being shown his own love of beauty, however, he purports to have felt ashamed to the point of a physical reaction. These themes allow Huihong to discuss his engagement with poetry and high literature as a narrative of not yet being liberated. Not-yet-forgotten feelings describe a quality of worldly literature, the opposite of expressions of liberation and wisdom.

In yet another colophon, "Inscription for a Collection of Poems by Venerable Yan" 題言上人所蓄詩, Huihong describes a similar affect and physiological response to sentiments that should be forgotten. The colophon begins with this excerpt.[65]

> I, in this illusion and dream of living among men, at play with brush and ink, climb up to heights and gaze into the distance, and then compose words of a feeling not yet forgotten. I will suddenly break out ashamed with sweat when I realize: "This is like the seasonal cicada or bird who naturally sings and naturally ceases. Who would collect or record [such natural chirping]?"[66] Now, Venerable Yan of Baoshan edited his work and compiled a scroll, and I was astonished when I read it. I will not again assess whether [the texts of his poems] are errant or correct, but can this not be taken as a warning against superfluous speech?

> 予，幻夢人間，游戲筆硯，登高臨遠，時時為未忘情之語。旋踵羞悔汗下，又自覺曰：「譬如候蟲時鳥，自鳴自已，誰復收錄？」寶山言上人乃編而為帙，讀之大驚。不復料理其訛正，可為多言之戒？

This sort of rhetoric allowed Huihong to create the persona of someone transgressing the norms of deportment for a monk, thus affording him a dual authority: he was an experienced poet who could pronounce on belletristic matters as well as a righteous monk who regretted his deviations from the monastic way.

A related early example comes from a suite of five poems. These poems share the extraordinarily long title "I Was About to Set Out to Another Mountain When an Urgent Message Arrived from Town with a Poem by [Gong] Dezhuang Seeking To Delay Me. That Night, Hu Yantong Also Joined Us, and with Those Two Gentlemen I Stayed Awake until Dawn Conversing. The Next

---

65. *Shimen wenzi chan,* fasc. 26, 2:518–519. In the end, Huihong redeems Ven. Yan's collection of poems for being *bi* 鄙, "ugly" or "coarse." This is an interesting tactic often adopted by Huihong but beyond the purview of this chapter.

66. This line seems to be a rehash of comments made in two letters written by Su Shi. *Zhu Shimen wenzi chan* suggests the epistle "To Cheng Zhengfu" 與程正輔: "This is like the seasonal songs of the cicada; naturally it sings and then ceases. What was gained or lost? There is no need to write, and no need not to write" 如此候蟲時鳴，自鳴而已，何所損益？不必作，不必不作也. *Su Shi wenji,* 54/1614. Consider also Su's "Letter in response to Li Duanfu" 答李端叔書: "It is like the seasonal songs of the cicada, which naturally sings and then ceases. Can we say something was gained or lost?" 譬之候蟲時鳥，自鳴自已，何足為損益. *Su Shi wenji,* 49/1432–33.

Day the Frost Was Heavy, and Together We Read Poems Sent by Cai Defu and His Brother; and Thinking of Them, I Wrote These Five Poems" 余將經行他山，德莊自邑中馳書作詩見留。是夕，胡彥通亦會二君于談，達旦不寐。明日霜重，共讀蔡德符兄弟所寄詩，有懷其人五首. The man Gong is Gong Duan 龔端 (1075–1127), an official from Huihong's hometown.[67] Hu Yantong remains unidentified. The identity of Cai Defu is uncertain; however, in the poem below, the Cai family are referred to as "neighbors." So this person is likely related to Huihong's childhood friend Cai Jingguo 蔡康國 (1072–1119), also known as Ruxiao 儒效, with whom he studied Confucian classics.[68] The title indicates that this set of poems was composed during a period of itinerant wandering, which was likely either the period in 1098 before Huihong returned to study in Baofeng Cloister 寶峰院 or late autumn 1099 after he was thrown out and was staying with his childhood friends in Junzhou 筠州.[69] I have translated the fourth of the five poems Huihong wrote about having stayed awake the whole night, talking until dawn.

	My eremitic neighbor for over ten years,	旁舍潛夫十年舊
2	Time and again we sat over tea on my monk's wool [mat].	會茶時復坐僧氈
	With our Yifu-like ochre mouths, we are overly fond	愛將夷甫雌黃口
4	of explaining the *wenzi chan* of Concentration Grove.[70]	解說定林文字禪

Line 3 alludes to a tale concerning Wang Yan 王衍 (256–311), courtesy name Yifu, who was born an aristocrat and rose steadily through the ranks at the Western Jin court. He gained a reputation for inconsistency and speaking before thinking, and it was therefore said he had "ochre in his mouth." Ochre was used as a kind of eraser to blot out mistakes and allow one to rewrite a text. "Having ochre in the mouth" became an idiom to describe someone who speaks brashly, is often self-contradictory, and who is quick to shift positions to suit short-sighted needs. Though still rather young at the time of writing this poem, Huihong was already reflecting on his education. He notes that he and his compatriots were fond of learning and debate, quick to take up one pedantic position and then another. When these late-night ochre-mouthed exchanges came to the literary works from Meditation Grove, likely

---

67. Zhou, *Songseng Huihong xinglü*, 19–20.
68. Cai Jingguo successfully entered government service, according to his *muzhiming* authored by Gong Duan. An excerpt of this *muzhiming* and evidence of Huihong's childhood study of the classics is given in *Songseng Huihong xinglü*, 9.
69. *Shimen wenzi chan*, fasc. 15, 2:974. Zhou, *Songseng Huihong xinglü*, 36, argues that these poems were written in 1098 in late autumn or after, in Jiangxi, near Huihong's hometown, not long before returning to see Zhenjing Kewen at Baofeng Cloister in Jing'an 靖安. *Shimen wenzi chan*, fasc. 15, 2:42–43. More details on this episode in the next section of this chapter.
70. Commentaries are silent on the referent of *dinglin* here. I have rendered *dinglin* as the name of a place (perhaps the distant Dinglin Temple of Nanjing mentioned elsewhere by Huihong) rather than as a synonym for the common phrase "Chan forests" (*chanlin* 禪林), meaning Chan temples.

the work of one or more unnamed monks,[71] he refers to the poems as *wenzi chan*. This *wenzi chan* was a topic for discussants with "ochre in the mouth," not a term for a path to awakening.

The penultimate case in which Huihong used the phrase *wenzi chan* brings together many of these themes. It is a lengthy colophon appended to some of Huihong's own poems, calligraphed and presented to the monk Daolong 道隆 (n.d.). In the first section of the colophon, we return to Huihong's reflections on his juvenilia, as he distances himself from his youthful literary work then jests about lethargy in old age. The second section of the colophon names the recipient and explains the circumstances of this gift of poems, the titles of which are not recorded. The third section appears to record a conversation between Huihong and Daolong that had just taken place. I have translated the entire colophon, entitled "Inscription on My Own Poems Given to Venerable Long" 題自詩與隆上人.[72]

> When I was young, I was crazy for the ornate and beautiful language of feelings not forgotten, but in my dotage I laugh at myself and do not make [such poems] anymore. Since I returned from Changsha I have lived in the mountains at Long'an, where there is nothing to do, so I study the method of sleeping while seated: I eat my fill, lean back in my chair, and saliva flows from the corner of my mouth. I am rather content to think I have attained its mysteries! My neighbor is the monk Long, who delights in my former affliction [of poetry] and visits me frequently—even on winter days—without tiring. He has asked me if I can still remember my compositions of old. Now, as I was taking up paper to write several poems to leave with Long, I teased him and said, "When Chan master Daguan lived in the capital, his literati interlocutors mostly interacted with him because of his talent for composing poems as spoken responses.[73] Daguan would laugh and say,
>
> > To explain and reply in the speech of any locale,
> > Or being able to recite pentametric verse,
> > These two are both fine arts,
> > It's just that the money is slow to arrive.[74]

---

71. If *dinglin* is the name of a place, the line is likely referring to a single person and his *wenzi chan*. If *dinglin* is the common phrase meaning Chan temples, then the line surely refers to poetry by multiple monks. Whether the poems of a single monk or multiple monks, line 4 alludes to an all-night discussion about someone else's *wenzi chan*, after which Huihong recorded the poem.

72. *Shimen wenzi chan*, fasc. 26, 2:1521–1522. For more on Huayan Daolong 華嚴道隆, see his biography in *Chanlin sengbao zhuan* (ZZ79.531a19–532b3). My thanks to George Keyworth for spotting an earlier error here.

73. For more on Daguan Tanying 達觀曇穎 (989–1060), see Huihong's *Chanlin sengbao zhuan* (ZZ79.545c16–546b20). Daguan was the author of the *Wujia zongpai* 五家宗派, now lost.

74. Elsewhere, the second line has *yin* 吟 instead of *yan* 言. *Chanlin sengbao zhuan* (ZZ79.532a9–10), along with a lengthier response attributed to Daolong.

To this Long said, "That was expected. I won't respond." Everyone seated nearby laughed at that. Long has the style name "Old Man Silence" and is one of Xiang area's superlative pure ones.[75]

余少狂為綺美不忘情之語，年大來輒自鄙笑，因不復作。自長沙來歸，舍龍安山中，無可作做，學坐睡法，飽飯靠椅，口角流涎，自喜以謂得其妙。旁舍有道人隆公，雅好予昔所病者，時時過予，終日而未嘗倦。問予昔所作尚能尋繹乎。予引紙為錄此數篇以遺之，而戲之曰：「昔達觀禪師居京師，士大夫相從者，皆以能詩答話多之。觀笑曰，『解答諸方話，能言五字詩，二般俱好藝，只是見錢遲。』」隆公曰，「果爾，吾不復耳。」坐客皆笑之。隆字默翁，湘中清勝者也。

Even as Huihong made copies of his poems to offer as a gift to another monk, he is far from an outspoken advocate for *wenzi chan* as a path to awakening. The colophon appears to reflect a conversation that had taken place as Huihong was completing the calligraphy to which the colophon was attached. The tale about the monk Daguan in Kaifeng was a clever reference to Huihong's own making of this gift of brushwork. With the punch line to this story, Huihong is implying that Daolong might be planning to sell the calligraphy, which, unlike the recitation of poetry, was fungible.[76] At the same time, although he has written out some poems, Huihong insists that he would no longer write verse as effusive as his juvenilia (like the very verses he selected to copy out). Instead, he declares he has mastered the art of napping, and drooling, while seated. This humorously humble rhetoric allows him to declare that his earlier poetry was passionate and well-crafted. Huihong placed this particular message as a paratext to frame the reader's encounter with his verse (his *wenzi chan*, perhaps) in order to undermine the text's authority as a monk's awakened words and to elevate its artfulness. The witty and ironic Huihong even included that quatrain attributed to Daguan to critique the special status of poetry. Huihong's willingness to inscribe this entire episode on a copy of his own poetry displays his good humor and ability to use humility as a way to boast.

The above analyses do not imply that Huihong did not excel at poetry or at literary criticism, as he clearly did, but rather that the term *wenzi chan* was not a spiritual path and certainly not a movement advocated (or founded) by Huihong. In Huihong's writings, he may refer to poetry written by one not yet liberated as *wenzi chan*, which is also the term he used to refer to his

---

75. The Xiang area corresponds to modern-day Hunan.

76. Ronald Egan, "Su Shi's Informal Letters," 485–486, gives several examples of Su Shi presenting calligraphy as currency to pay for services and gifting a work to an impoverished friend to sell. Egan also cites a case in which Daoqian received medical treatment from a Jiujiang-area Daoist who was talented in healing arts. Having no money, Daoqian then asked Su Shi for calligraphy with which he intended to remunerate the Daoist doctor. Su responded by teasing the monk that he should present his own calligraphy of Chan "turning words" 轉語 as currency. "[Letter] to the Daoist Hu" 與胡道士, *Su Shi wenji*, 60/1852.

juvenilia. Huihong used *wenzi chan* and "not-yet-forgotten feelings" to refer to poetry that expressed unceasing emotion. In other words, *wenzi chan* as used by Huihong denotes the exact opposite of how the term has been understood by most modern scholars.

This curious discrepancy was noted by Zhou Yukai in the 1990s, but he nonetheless suggested that scholars continue to use *wenzi chan* in "a broad sense" to refer to all Chan texts because they all use language, including *gong'an* and *yulu*.[77] To Zhou's way of thinking, nearly all Song-era Chan texts can be fruitfully understood through the lens of *wenzi chan*. To make the term *wenzi chan* into a capacious heuristic, however, deviates from the way it was used by monastic writers of the Song. The term *wenzi chan*, as I have just demonstrated, signals uneasiness with the relationship between Buddhism and poetry rather than their harmony. To conflate *gong'an* with *wenzi chan* introduces ambiguity and imprecision into our historiography, and effaces the meaningful distinctions between worldly and religious literature made by Song-era monks themselves.

Huihong wrote a tremendous quantity of poetry, two works of poetic criticism, and several scriptural commentaries (two of which are extant). Even in his own day, he courted controversy through his profuse writing. His literary activity and outspoken remarks attracted attention from senior figures in his own Chan lineage. It was widely known that the universally respected teacher Lingyuan Weiqing had chastised Huihong in a public letter. I believe this little-studied epistle, the focus of the next section, sheds light on Huihong's reputation as well as on his own understanding of the role of written words in Buddhist spiritual life.

Lingyuan Weiqing's Epistle to Huihong

Lingyuan Weiqing 靈源惟清 (d. 1117), the author of the once-infamous epistle, was one of Huihong's most esteemed avuncular instructors. Weiqing died shortly after writing his censorious letter, leaving Huihong no opportunity to respond directly. Huihong instead delivered his written response to Weiqing's memorial shrine. I argue that Weiqing's letter and Huihong's response, in which he justified creating sūtra commentaries, reveal Huihong's mature attitude toward the role of language in Buddhist teachings, an attitude that differs from how Huihong used *wenzi chan* in the examples given above. Because Weiqing's letter played a critical role in the later reception and controversial Ming-era rehabilitation of Huihong, I will analyze their personal relationship and the letter in detail.

Lingyuan Weiqing was a well-regarded teacher of the Huanglong branch

---

77. Zhou, *Wenzi chan yu Songdai shixue*, 46. I have found no evidence that Huihong himself used *wenzi chan* in this "broad sense" and therefore cannot agree with Zhou's suggestion that the entirety of the thirty fascicles of *Shimen wenzi chan* was intended as an exercise in (religious) *wenzi chan*.

of the Linji lineage, which dominated Chan monasteries in Jiangxi during the latter half of the Northern Song. Huihong and his beloved teacher Zhenjing Kewen 眞淨克文 (1025–1102) belonged to this same branch of Linji. Kewen was a direct disciple of Huanglong Huinan; Weiqing was a second-generation disciple of Huinan via Huitang Zuxin 晦堂祖心 (1025–1100). Weiqing and Huihong thus appear to be of the same generation in the family tree of the Huanglong lineage. Weiqing was the senior of the two men and had quickly risen to become a standard-bearer of the tradition and abbot of an important monastery on Mount Huanglong. Huihong, on the other hand, spent less than one full year, from 1107 to 1108, as the abbot of a small Chan monastery in Linchuan near his old hometown, leaving his post to wander Jiangxi area monasteries, before agreeing to serve as abbot of another monastery, a position he lost, after encountering legal trouble, within a single month.[78] Only during these brief periods of his early career did Huihong deliver Chan-style sermons and dialogue.[79] Modern Chinese scholars, led by Zhou Yukai, have compiled the abundant evidence available for chronicling Huihong's life.[80] I draw out only a few events to illuminate Huihong's relationship with Lingyuan Weiqing.

Huihong was born in 1071 south of Mount Lu in Xinchang 新昌 County outside Junzhou 筠州 (near the modern city of Gao'an in Jiangxi). He spent his formative years at monasteries in the area and returned to Jiangxi shortly before his death. In 1082, he became an acolyte, and when he was orphaned in 1084, he came to reside in a local monastery. He studied with Kewen from 1088 to 1090, receiving his ordination certificate in 1090. He later served as Kewen's attendant from 1094 to 1098, during which time Kewen became the abbot of Baofeng Cloister at Mount Shimen in northern Jiangxi.[81] After a year of itinerant wandering, Huihong returned to study with Kewen at Shimen. In 1099, Huihong purportedly had some kind of insight that prompted an outburst of antinomian behavior, after which, "because he violated the Chan rules, he was expelled" from Kewen's community 因違禪規遭刑去.[82] Years later, Dahui Zonggao, who had met Huihong, famously warned his own students that "Juefan also thought to himself that he had an awakening, but he left his master too early. One day when he was studying with Zhenjing Kewen, Kewen said to him, 'Huihong, sometimes there are things you get, and sometimes

78. Zhou, *Songseng Huihong xinglü*, 115–124, 143–145. The first abbotship was at Bei Jingde Monastery 北景德寺 of Linchuan 臨川, the second, Qingliang Monastery 清涼寺 outside of Nanjing.

79. *Jiatai pudenglu* (ZZ79.333a22-b17). Zhou, *Songseng Huihong xinglü*, 120, 143.

80. Note that Zhou, *Songseng Huihong xinglü*, draws on and largely supersedes earlier work by Yanagida Seizan, Huang Ch'i-chiang, Huang Qifang 黃啓方, Wu Ching-yi 吳靜宜, Chen Zili 陳自力, and Li Gui 李貴.

81. This timeline is based on Zhou, *Songseng Huihong xinglü*, 6–48, 327–337.

82. This recorded in *Luohu yelu* (ZZ83.383b9), preface dated 1155. "Chan rules" probably refers to the "rules of purity" (*qinggui*) observed at this monastery. For more on this incident, see Zhou, *Songseng Huihong xinglü*, 41–42.

there are things you don't get.'" 覺範亦自有悟處，却是離師太早。他參真
淨，淨一日謂之曰：「惠洪有時也有到處，有時也有不到處。」[83] In the
conversation that followed, Huihong had a new insight, according to Dahui.
Dahui also notes that Huihong unfortunately left the monastery the next day
owing to some incident. The incident surely is the violation of rules mentioned
above, for in another sermon on the topic, Dahui wrote that "following an
insight in the morning, by evening [Huihong] was thrown out of the monas-
tery" 早上有見處，晚下被趕出院.[84] In both sermons, Dahui concluded that
Huihong's Chan writings reveal his insight was only partial.[85] Huihong, after
leaving Shimen in 1099, had several more experiences that he described in
correspondence to Kewen, seeking his guidance. But Huihong would not see
his master again before the latter's death in 1102, which may be why Dahui
remarked that "he [Huihong] did not receive his teacher's transmission" 他無
師承.[86] Huihong nonetheless continued to honor Kewen throughout his life,
and would refer to himself with the toponym Shimen.

Following the loss of his master, Huihong venerated Weiqing as one of
his instructors.[87] He observed the three-month summer retreat with Weiqing
in 1106.[88] Weiqing, in addition to his stature as a leading abbot with numer-
ous disciples, was talented with a brush. He regularly corresponded with the
illustrious Huang Tingjian, who venerated Weiqing's own teacher Huitang
Zuxin. This association with Huang Tingjian surely enhanced the stature of
Weiqing in the mind of Huihong, who himself was a consummate student of
the writings of Su Shi and Huang Tingjian.[89] Weiqing, too, appears to have
been fond of Huihong and maintained correspondence even when Huihong
was imprisoned from 1109 to 1110 and sent into exile in Hainan from 1111
to 1114.[90] Of the four extant letters addressed to Huihong, only the final one
was of historical significance. In this epistle Weiqing notes that Huihong was
released from exile, and encourages Huihong to visit.[91] The substance of the

---

83. *Dahui Pujue chanshi pushuo* (949a3–950a8). On Dahui's criticisms, see Yanagida, *Zen no bunka*, 54–55; Levering, "Monk's Literary Education," 378–379, translates a portion of Dahui's text; and Keyworth, "Transmitting the Lamp," 250.

84. *Dahui Pujue chanshi pushuo* (928b17–20).

85. Dahui singles out sections of the *Chanlin sengbaozhuan* for including "places where he fabricated things" 杜撰處. In a perhaps analogous way, Tsuchiya, "Xuansha Shibei sanju," pro-
vides a careful critique of Huihong's writing about Jianfu Chenggu 薦福承古 (970–1045) and concludes it is only partly correct.

86. *Dahui Pujue chanshi pushuo* (928b19).

87. The relationship noted by Yanagida, *Zen no bunka*, 30–33, 41, 47.

88. Zhou, *Songseng Huihong xinglü*, 109–111.

89. Huihong wrote several poems in appreciation of the poetic correspondence between Weiqing and Huang. Zhou, *Songseng Huihong xinglü*, 104, notes that Huihong read the poetry in Huang's own hand while visiting Weiqing's monastery on Mount Huanglong in 1105.

90. On the dates and sequence of Huihong's exile, see Keyworth, "Transmitting the Lamp," 210–217. Huihong's several rounds of imprisonment and exile are discussed in Keyworth, 242, 246–248. For correspondence, see Weiqing's four epistles cited below and additional sources listed in Zhou, *Songseng Huihong xinglü*, 166, 169.

91. In 1114, the year of his release, Huihong corresponded with Weiqing, sending a set of

letter is a response to Huihong's composition of a traditional commentary on the *Śūraṃgamasūtra, extant today as part of *Lengyan jing helun* 楞嚴經合論. According to Huihong's preface, he wrote this commentary between 1112 and 1116, although he did not finalize it until 1118.[92] It seems likely that Wei-qing's letter was written after seeing the commentary in 1116 or perhaps later in 1117, shortly before his own death.[93]

At least three recensions of this letter survive. The full letter is preserved in the Gozan reproduction of a Song collection entitled *Venerable Lingyuan's Brush Talk* 靈源和尚筆語. This Gozan recension was based on a Southern Song reproduction of an earlier text.[94] A smaller fragment was anthologized in the Southern Song reader *Treasured Instructions from the Forests of Chan* 禪林寶訓, which enjoyed frequent reprinting in the late-imperial period.[95] A larger fragment was quoted by Yongjue Yuanxian 永覺元賢 (1578–1657), to which he added critical comments.[96] Despite variations among these recensions, significant portions of Weiqing's letter are consistent and provide a substantial foundation for analysis. The following translation omits the initial pleasantries of the epistle.[97]

> [Anyway,] I understand that while [exiled] in the south you would from time to time investigate the *Śūraṃgama*, and that you added a commentarial explanation. [If this is so, then] this is not what I would expect! By means of such studying of written words you will not be able to penetrate to the source of human nature, and you obstruct from future generations the wisdom eye of earlier buddhas. Your error is precisely in relying on the explanations written by others, and thereby you block the gate to understanding the self. If you fill your mouth [with the words of others] is this really better than shallow learning? Even if you make

six poems, "Encomia upon Portraits of the Six Ancestors (with preface)" 六世祖師畫像贊(并序). *Shimen wenzi chan,* fasc. 18, 2:1156–1160; Keyworth, "Transmitting the Lamp," 271; Zhou, *Song-seng Huihong xinglü,* 187.

92. *Lengyan jing helun* (ZZ12.94c19–95b5).

93. Zhou, *Songseng Huihong xinglü,* 224.

94. Kawase, *Gozan ban no kenkyū,* 2:62–63, nos. 132, 133. On various Gozan editions of *Lingyuan heshang biyu,* see Huang Ch'i-chiang, *Bei Song Huanglong Huinan chan shi san yao,* v–viii.

95. *Chanlin baoxun* cites *Zhangjiang ji* 章江集, another lost collection, as its source. *Chanlin baoxun* preserves textual variations as well as additional epistolary material not in *Lingyuan heshang biyu.* Cf. Keyworth, "Transmitting the Lamp," 426–427, which translates the epistle from *Chanlin baoxun.*

96. *Yongjue Yuanxian chanshi guanglu* (ZZ72.572b24–c12). The text quoted by Yuanxian includes a passage *not* found in *Chanlin baoxun.* Therefore, Yuanxian preserves a third textual stemma closer to the *Chanlin baoxun* than the Gozan edition.

97. This diplomatic text notes differences between the Gozan edition of *Lingyuan heshang biyu* and the text in *Yongjue yuanxian chanshi guanglu* (ZZ72.572b24–c12). The latter is the base, and the symbols 【-】【+】【/】 signal where the Gozan edition respectively "lacks," "adds," or "varies" text. In preparing my translation I consulted the historical lexicons and annotated reading guides compiled in Japan, including two undated Edo-period manuscripts both entitled *Reigen Hitsugo bekkou* held at Komazawa University as well as *Kokuyaku Reigen Oshō Hitsugo.*

your spirit perspicacious, in the end it will still be difficult to reach that wondrous experience. This is the reason your actions and understanding are mostly mis-aligned.[98] [Your learning and study each day further increase your ignorance.][99] Now,[100] because I am fond of you, Juefan, and your wit and mind are radiant and sharp, this is why I reflect this back to you. If you "diminish it and again diminish it" [per *Dao de jing*],[101] when we meet sometime in the future, you certainly and distinctly will have a wondrous insight!

【+或】聞在南中時究楞嚴，特【/而】加箋釋。【+若爾則】非不肖所望【+者也】！【-蓋】文字之學，【+所以】不能洞當人之性源，【-徒】與後學【+所以】障先佛之智眼。【+其】病【+正】在依他作解，塞自悟門。資口舌則可勝淺聞？廓神機終難極妙證，故於行解多致參差【+由此也】。【-而日用見聞尤增隱昧也。】予善覺範，慧識英利，足以鑑此。倘【/儻】損之又損，他時相見，定別有妙【/好】處耳。

Weiqing reproached Huihong for his foolishness. How could someone who was not yet awakened hope to liberate others through language he had not realized himself. Weiqing encouraged the younger monk to come visit and promised to offer guidance toward liberation. But Weiqing died in the autumn of 1117, before the two men could meet again. As a result, this asser-tion that Huihong was not yet awakened became the final statement from this important avuncular figure.

A similar reputation continued to shape the Southern Song reception of Huihong. Dahui's views were mentioned above. Xutang Zhiyu also criticized Huihong, announcing in a public sermon that as he was reading Huihong's *Chanlin sengbao zhuan,* he began to question Huihong's own reliability as a ra-conteur of awakened dialogue.[102] Then, after noting that Huihong had written a commentary on the *Śūraṃgama,* in his sermon Xutang publicly wondered, "Why would he take words with no benefit and pull the wool over the eyes of future students?" 豈肯以無益之詞瞎後世學者眼. This statement echoes the rhetoric found in Weiqing's letter. In the end, Xutang would concur with Dahui that Huihong had only partial insight because he left Kewen's monas-tery too soon. Even during the late-Ming rehabilitation of Huihong's reputa-tion, Weiqing's letter and similar criticisms would resurface.

---

98. Practice and understanding misaligned, or off-the-mark, is the opposite of the ideal state described as "practice and understanding match one another" 行解相應.

99. The sentence marked off by brackets is not in the Gozan edition.

100. The portion of the epistle starting here does not appear in *Chanlin baoxun.*

101. This "doing less" is an allusion to chap. 48 of *Laozi Dao de jing,* 2.5b-6a, which compares ordinary learning with acquiring the *dao.* "In pursuit of learning, every day there is gain; in pursuit of the Dao, every day there is diminishing. Diminish it and again diminish it, in this way arrive at non-action. When nothing is done, nothing will be left undone" 為學日益，為道日損。損之又損，以至於無為。無為而無不為.

102. All references here to "General Sermon after Being Beseeched with Incense before Summer Retreat at Shuanglin" 雙林夏前告香普說, *Xutang heshang yulu* (T47.1013c22–1015a27; Gozan ed., 57b-60a).

Huihong himself responded almost immediately to Weiqing's missive, a letter that was surely among the final correspondence between Huihong and Weiqing. The unambiguous message in Weiqing's letter weighed on Huihong when, several months later on the sixth day of the second month in 1118, he composed a formal memorial offering, a "prayer text" (*jiwen* 祭文) to recite at Weiqing's funereal stupa. In it, he lodged a protest against the verdict of the late master. With formal language and four-character lines set into rhyming couplets, Huihong suggests the possibility that both men had been right all along. I translate here an excerpt from the lengthy text titled "Prayer Text for Chan Master Zhaomo" 祭昭默禪師文.[103]

> Though I have been partial to Chan learning, and in the end abandoned the nets of the teachings, I made a commentary to guide others to reject [dualistic] judgments of good and evil.[104] When you, Lingyuan, heard about it you said, "[as the *Vimalakirti* says] '[do not inflict injury] on those who are without wounds,'"[105] and with an epistle admonished me for my numerous crooked ways. But, with perfect speech, phoenixes fly from the mouth and compositions write themselves. Aśvaghoṣa and Nāgārjuna argued and wrote with eloquence and care. Perhaps written words do not obstruct the Way; like searching for a pearl in the ocean depths or snatching jade from lofty peaks.[106] Each person has their own will, just as salty and sour taste different. In vain there lingers this thought, but I prostrate and do not dare assume this. Alas! What a terrible pity!

> 我憂禪學，終背教綱。造論導之，排斥否臧。公聞乃曰：彼自無瘡。以書教誡，欹傾數行。至言吐鳳，自然文章。馬鳴龍勝，論著精詳。文字於道，疑不相妨。索珠層淵，採玉崇岡。人各有志，鹹酸異嘗。但餘此意，拜未敢當。嗟吁惜哉，巍巍堂堂。

Huihong's self-defense seems to misunderstand Weiqing's criticism. Weiqing was not suggesting that everyone should abandon words or language altogether. What Weiqing was saying was that Huihong would not achieve an awakening through book learning. One can imagine how Weiqing would respond to the above plaint: whereas Aśvaghoṣa and Nāgārjuna were awakened and could use language to awaken others, the final gate to awakening would not be found outside of one's own mind. We know that Weiqing was not ideologically opposed to the use of language for the sake of awakening others. Huihong knew this when he wrote "ever since Weiqing laid down and quickly passed, no one has delighted in using brush and ink to carry out deeds of a buddha"

---

103. *Shimen wenzi chan*, fasc. 30, 2:1706–1708.

104. Huihong later used similar language to explain his intentions in his preface to the commentary, written a few months later in 1118.5.1. See *Lengyan jing helun* (ZZ12.95a4–6).

105. Watson, *Vimalakirti Sutra*, 43–44. *Weimojie suoshuo jing* (T14.540c29–541a1).

106. Two idioms for intense literary efforts aligned with traditional literary creation of crafted, beautiful texts; the first derived from the "Liu Yukou" chapter of *Zhuangzi*, as in the expression "searching the black sea-depths to get a pearl" 探驪得珠.

昭默自臥疾後，無他嗜好以翰墨為佛事。[107] This seems to be the ideal to which
Huihong aspired. Huihong therefore appears to be sidestepping the main
thrust of Weiqing's letter. The explicit rhetorical purpose of Weiqing's epistle
was to encourage Huihong to achieve awakening, thereby implying that
Huihong was not yet awake. At the same time, Weiqing had not seen Huihong
in some years, and it is possible that the young man he was remembering had
in the intervening time come to a great realization. Huihong himself would
later point at the insights he had gained in deep exile.[108] If so, Weiqing's passing
before the men had a chance to meet again was the unfortunate situation that
seems to be the referent of the final lines in Huihong's memorial.

Almost three months after writing the memorial, Huihong added to his
*Śūraṃgama commentary a preface dated the first day of the fifth month in
1118 in which he defended the compatibility of Chan and the sūtra exege-
sis.[109] Shortly before, Huihong wrote a poem about a dream in which he visited
the pagoda of his old teacher Zhenjing Kewen, with whom he discoursed on
the dharma. That poem uses scriptural language to describe an experience
of unfettered wisdom: "In the eighth year of Zhenghe, when I was forty-eight,
/ in a single moment of consciousness, I comprehended all dharmas. / The
impurity of upside-down deluded thinking was eliminated / by the light pen-
etrating from gnosis of universally equal nature" 政和八年四十八，一念了
知一切法，顛倒妄想垢消滅，平等性智光通達。[110] Huihong talks about his
insights in other writing as well. In "Autobiography of the Sound of Silence"
寂音自序 composed in 1123, Huihong concludes that "as a result of my mis-
fortunates, I obtained a complete view of the intentions of the buddhas and
ancestors, that which cannot be expressed through writing" 因禍以得盡窺佛
祖之意，不能文以達意。[111] Weiqing's opinion to the contrary, Huihong was
confident of his insights.

There is evidence to suggest that Huihong did not break away from Weiqing
either before or after Weiqing's critical letter. He continued to revere and honor
Weiqing and did not publicly break from their shared lineage. Huihong had,
throughout his life, sent young men to study with Weiqing, once telling a
student, "When the old man speaks or laughs there is fragrant perfume; / he
is the bones and marrow of the dharma, king of the sangha." 此老唾笑生馨
香，法中骨髓僧中王。[112] After Weiqing's death, Huihong included a lengthy
and flattering biographical entry for Weiqing in *Chanlin sengbao zhuan*, even

---

107. *Shimen wenzi chan,* fasc. 26, 2:1500.

108. Huihong wrote a colophon to explain his inability at age 16 *sui* to understand a verse
spoken by his first teacher, a verse that he came to deeply grasp while reading a passage from the
Vimalakīrtinirdeśa. See "Inscription on a saying by Chan master Qing of Xiangshan" 題香山艤禪
師語, in *Shimen wenzi chan,* fasc. 25, 2:1476–77.

109. *Lengyan jing helun* (ZZ12.94c19–95b5).

110. *Shimen wenzi chan,* fasc. 17, 2:1090. I've translated the phrase *pingdeng xing zhi* bearing
in mind a then-popular passage from *Yuanjue jing,* following the foundational exegesis by Zongmi,
Yuanjue jing da shu (ZZ9.413a23-b1).

111. "Sound of Silence" 寂音 was one of Huihong's monikers. *Shimen wenzi chan,* fasc. 24,
2:1440. See also Zhou, *Songseng Huihong xinglü,* 301.

112. *Shimen wenzi chan,* fasc. 8, 1:533–534.

giving it a privileged position as the final entry. Huihong also viewed and wrote inscriptions of appreciation for seven specimens of Weiqing's calligraphy, noting at least once that he cried uncontrollably on seeing it.[113]

Huihong did not reject Weiqing as an authority, but absent Weiqing's imprimatur, Huihong asserted his own authority to create language with salvific power. We see this, for example, in some of the seventy-two verses under the header "*jisong*" 偈頌 gathered into a single fascicle separate from his prolific output of poetry in sixteen fascicles of *shi*, at least in the extant Ming edition of *Shimen wenzi chan*. Judging from their titles, a few of these verses were written in response to students "seeking a *gāthā*" (*qiu ji* 求偈 or *qi ji* 乞偈). Huihong also wrote several liturgical hymns, such as a verse in four-character lines to benefit hungry ghosts.[114] While in exile in 1112, he wrote eight "*Gāthā* for Daily Use" 日用偈 in rhyming couplets of four-character lines.[115] One unusual and creative experiment was to compose a suite of eight verses, each rhymed to one of eight words from a line in an influential commentary on the *Avataṃsakasūtra* by Li Tongxuan 李通玄 (635–730; alternatively, 646–740).[116] Huihong wrote that he "made these eight *gāthā* to venerate him [Li], during the period when I was imprisoned in Jiankang [Nanjing]" 作八偈供之時在建康獄中. All of these verses from the "*jisong*" fascicle of his collected works might be examples of Huihong's own "using brush and ink to carry out deeds of a buddha." Huihong sometimes used a Chinese word for *gāthā* within his own poetry. We however do not have among his extant writings his explanation for a generic difference between *jisong* and *shi*, as far as I am aware.[117] Be that as it may, his references to *jisong* are the rhetorical opposite of his use of *wenzi chan* to refer to his poetic juvenilia of worldly writing.

When Huihong refers to his passionate juvenilia, it is possible that he has in mind poems such as "The Swing" 鞦韆, in which he depicts the beauty of a young woman swaying back and forth on an ornate wooden slat suspended from colorful cords. Playing on a swing is associated with the Qingming festival in spring, hence the reference to numerous blossoms.[118]

---

113. *Shimen wenzi chan,* fasc. 26, 2:1497–1502. See also Zhou, *Songseng Huihong xinglü,* 250, 255.

114. "*Gāthā* to End Hunger" 食不繼偈, *Shimen wenzi chan,* fasc. 17, 2:1084.

115. Correspondences exist with Huihong's 1122 compilation *Zhizheng zhuan* (ZZ63.178b8), as noted in *Zhu Shimen wenzi chan,* 2:1115–1116.

116. *Shimen wenzi chan,* fasc. 17, 2:1110–1112, each verse rhymes one of the eight words *da ben qing wang zhi xin ti he* 達本情忘知心體合. *Xin Huayan jing lun* (T36.721a7–8) gives 亡 for 忘. The verses were written on the twenty-eighth day of the third month, the traditional memorial date for venerating Li Tongxuan.

117. Huihong defines *ji* in his *Śūraṃgama commentary, Lengyan jing helun* (ZZ12.43b11–12), and in his *Lotus Sūtra* commentary, *Fahua jing helun* (ZZ30.374a14–16). These definitions echo other exegetes discussed in Chap. 1 above.

118. *Shimen wenzi chan,* fasc. 11, 1:769–770. I have borrowed parts of Porter's felicitous phrasing in his translation; Red Pine, *Poems of the Masters,* 398–399. I thank Rafal Felbur for sharing and discussing his unpublished translation of this poem. Chen, *Shi Huihong yanjiu,* 297–308, citing this poem on p. 300, offers strained interpretations to reconcile the obvious conflicts between monasticism and sensuality.

From an ornate double frame the halcyon ropes sway,　　　　畫架雙裁翠絡偏

2　Fair lady in springtime plays before the small pavilion,　　佳人春戲小樓前

　　Fluttering by, her blood red gown brushes the floor,　　　飄揚血色裙拖地

4　In a trice, her jade-white face rises off to heaven.　　　　斷送玉容人上天

　　The adorned platform [on which she stands] glistens,　　　花板潤霑紅杏雨
　　　　soaked with red apricot-blossoms,

6　The colored ropes jauntily descend from green poplar mists.　彩繩斜挂綠楊煙

　　She swoops down to a quiet place, and stands in repose,　　下來閑處從容立

8　As an immortal banished from the palace on the moon.　　　疑是蟾宮謫降僊

The poem is full of sexual images, beginning with springtime playfulness and the rocking motion of the swing. The poet fixates on the maiden's changing complexion, juxtaposing her red clothing and her jade-white skin. The sexuality is ornamented by wind and rain as well as falling apricot blossoms. The poem's sensuousness resolves into a quiet stillness and finally declares the young woman an exiled maiden of the moon. The passions described here are not subtle. The poem circulated widely, especially after it was anthologized in *Poems of a Thousand Poets* 千家詩, compiled by Liu Kezhuang 劉克莊 (1187–1269). The poem's lowbrow nature, especially inappropriate coming from the brush of a monk, was the subject of comment in succeeding centuries.[119] This was not the only sensuous poem by Huihong to cause a stir among his contemporaries and historical critics. In "Spending the Night of the First Full Moon at Mount Baizhang" 上元宿百丈, Huihong describes intense homesickness while traveling around the New Year of 1106 and expresses a desire to return to the urban pleasures of youth and "fragrant mists amid tender red-[dust]" 軟紅香霧, a reference to beautiful women.[120] When encountering this poem, the daughter of Wang Anshi 王安石 (1021–1086), wife of Cai Bian 蔡卞 (1048–1117), colloquially declared Huihong a "rakish monk" 浪子和尚 for indulging in such sensual feelings.[121] Nine years later, Huihong himself noted that the poem still circulated orally among Buddhist monks of the capital, Kaifeng.[122] Can we, then, understand the significance

---

119. See comments by Fang Hui 方回 (1227–1307) in *Yingkui lüsui,* 27/29a.

120. *Shimen wenzi chan,* fasc. 10, 1:709. Hsiao, "*Wenzi chan,*"232–233, 257–258, reviews historical criticisms, and convincingly reads the poem as a metaphor for yearning for Buddhist liberation. However, in her efforts to rehabilitate Huihong's reputation, she excludes the poem's final couplet and Huihong's frank acknowledgement of the existence of sexual desire. Huihong similarly addresses a mountain monk's unbearable springtime lust for women in a set of two poems entitled "Presented to Xiang, the Scribe at Weishan" 贈溈山湘書記, *Shimen wenzi chan,* fasc. 14, 2:940.

121. *Nenggai zhai manlu,* 11.17a-b. Zhou, *Songseng Huihong xinglü,* 108, states that this poem was written at the beginning of 1106. The derogatory moniker *langzi heshang* implies a monk derelict in his duties while pursuing his own amusement. For centuries, the term was reiterated by critics regarding Huihong, including Chen Yuan 陳垣 (1880-1971) and Qian Zhongshu, *Tanyi lu,* 1:204.

122. Huihong, *Lengzhai yehua,* 5/52, writes that a monk at Xiangguo Monastery 相國寺 recited the poem (with variants) and teased that Huihong had returned to the city of his memo-

of the rhetoric of *wenzi chan* as a way to create its opposite? Only by marking off his worldly poetry (like his sensuous poems about young women swaying on swings) as youthful displays of ornamental language bereft of religious efficacy, that is, as *wenzi chan*, was Huihong able to assert his authority as one who could discern and write awakened words. *Wenzi chan*, therefore, does not refer to a monastic path to awakening, the practices of *gong'an*, or the compilation of *yulu*.

In light of the examples just given of Huihong's use of the term *wenzi chan*, it is puzzling that so many modern scholars came to misunderstand the nature of *wenzi chan* in the Song. If our modern ideas have a source in the premodern record, I think the most likely candidate can be found among Ming texts. It was in the late Ming that some Buddhist monastic writers used *wenzi chan* to refer to literature that expressed awakening. Though more research may uncover some intermediate steps in the Southern Song or Yuan, at present it seems that our modern understanding derives directly from the new exegesis by Zibo Zhenke that accompanied the reprinting of Huihong's works in the late Ming.

Ming Re-publication and a New Exegesis of *Shimen Wenzi Chan*

Zibo Zhenke's influence on Ming and Qing—and possibly our modern—ideas about the relationship between Chan and poetry is the focus of this section. Zhenke's major contribution to the interpretation of *wenzi chan* is conveyed in his preface to *Shimen wenzi chan*. I believe this eloquent and oft-referenced section has been fundamental to the modern understanding of *wenzi chan* as a path to enlightenment.[123]

> If Chan is like spring, then *wenzi* are the flowers. Spring appears in blossoms, and blossoms in their entirety are spring; blossoms appear in spring, and spring entirely is blossoms. Likewise, how could Chan and *wenzi* be two separate things?

> 蓋禪如春也，文字則花也。春在於花，全花是春，花在於春，全春是花。而曰禪與文字有二乎哉？

Beautiful and compelling as this portion of the preface may be, it represents a late-Ming vision of Huihong. Zhenke's preface, dated 1597, adorned the newly printed edition of *Shimen wenzi chan* that he sponsored, the production and dissemination of which were part of Zhenke's revival of Huihong's ouevre. Zhenke was also instrumental in the re-publication of Huihong's

---

ries. Huihong played along by writing a new poem about yearning for mountains. Zhou, *Songseng Huihong xinglü*, 198, shows that this event took place in 1115.

123. *Shimen wenzi chan*, front matter, 1:1–2.

commentary on the *Lotus Sūtra* as well as his *Commentary on Wisdom and Realization* 智證傳.[124]

During a visit to the historic temple on the eastern slopes of Mount Shimen to pay homage to Huihong, Zhenke composed a memorial essay, entitled "Text to Venerate the Chan Master Yuanming of Shimen" 禮石門圓明禪師文. Writing in 1598, one year after his, Zhenke's, composition of the *Shimen wenzi chan* preface, Zhenke climbed to the namesake peak and lamented the manner in which Huihong's insights had long been misunderstood by Chan teachers. The memorial offers the relationship between water and waves as another metaphor for thinking about *wenzi chan*.[125]

> Thus, [Huihong] Shimen used *Wenzi Chan* as the title of his work. *Wenzi* are the waves, and *Chan* is the water. If it were necessary to abandon *wenzi* in order to seek Chan, this is like being thirsty but refusing to drink waves and pushing waves aside to seek water.

> 故石門以文字禪名其書。文字波也。禪水也。如必欲離文字而求禪。渴不飲波。必欲撥波而覓水。

If Zhenke often held up Huihong as an early pioneer of a correct understanding of the profound compatibility of Chan and language, I would argue that we should interpret these Ming texts as telling us more about Zhenke's doctrinal and practical positions than about Huihong's. Zhenke may have tipped his hand in a poem he wrote about the temple at Mount Shimen, the namesake of *Shimen wenzi chan*, that mentions in its opening line, "I am fond of Shimen Temple" 我愛石門寺.[126] To be "fond of" (*ai* 愛) suggests to be "partial to" or "overly fond of." However inaccurate with respect to Huihong's own uses of the term, the Ming interpretation of *wenzi chan* is important not least because it has influenced the history of the study of Chinese Buddhism down to today.

A similar memorial text for Huihong was composed sixty-five years after Zhenke's by Daomin 道忞 (1596–1674), a Ming loyalist who in the early Qing took refuge as a monk. This memorial, dated 1663, includes Daomin's assertion that he spoke these very words directly to the spirit tablet of Huihong.[127]

---

124. Liao, *Zhong-bian, shi-chan, meng-xi*, 110–115, details Zhenke's project. On Zhenke's role in reproducing Huihong's *Lotus Sūtra* commentary, see the colophon by Feng Mengzhen 馮夢禎 (1548–1605) appended to *Fahua jing helun* (ZZ30.429a15); for his role in reproducing *Zhizheng zhuan,* see the preface in *Zibo sunzhe quanji* (ZZ73.262c12).

125. *Zibo zunshe quanji* (ZZ73.269b18-c1). Liao, *Zhong-bian, shi-chan, meng-xi,* 137–143, offers an erudite analysis of Zibo's doctrinal position. Note that Huihong's memorial pagoda was located elsewhere, at Tong'an Monastery 同安寺 on another, nearby mountain.

126. *Zibo zunzhe quanji* (ZZ73.358c3–5).

127. "Prayer text for the spirit of the Baojue Yuanming Chan master [Hui]hong" 祭于圓明寶覺洪公禪師之靈. *Bushui tai ji,* fasc. 25, 406c22–407b14. For further analysis, see Liao, *Zhongbian, shi-chan, Meng-xi,* 145–148.

In the case of both Zhenke and Daomin, we have, respectively, a late-Ming and early Qing writer asserting that Huihong would have understood their various doctrinal positions. Furthermore, they contend, were he alive, Huihong would agree that certain unnamed contemporaries (of Daomin and Zhenke) are misguided. In other words, these learned men made an ally of Huihong in their disagreements with other Ming and Qing monks.

The historical record corroborates that Zibo Zhenke's near contemporaries were not united in support of reviving Huihong's writings.[128] Liao Chaoheng and Jiang Wu each recently analyzed the place of Huihong in debates between Miyun Yuanwu 密雲圓悟 (1566–1642) and Hanyue Fazang 漢月法藏 (1576–1635), the latter of whom regarded Huihong as a model.[129] To this debate we can add the voice of Yongjue Yuanxian 永覺元賢 (1578–1657), an important figure in the Caodong revival of the late Ming. Yuanxian's response to the reprinted editions of Huihong's works made recourse to the infamous epistle sent by Lingyuan Weiqing. Yuanxian interpreted Weiqing's letter as an assertion that this Song master knew that Huihong had not yet realized awakening. The gist of Yuanxian's position as a reader, therefore, was that while Huihong was surely a talented stylist and gifted literary writer, his religious works should not be treated as those of an awakened teacher. I translate the passage in full.[130]

> Huihong Juefan had six types of writing, and Elder Daguan [Zhenke] had a deep appreciation for them and so printed them into circulation. The only one I delight in is [Shimen] Wenzi chan. This old writer was truly a famous man, the likes of which the sangha seldom sees. However, when it comes to his expositions of Buddhist teachings, then what is pure [i.e., correct] and what flawed are about evenly mixed. People in our generation cherish his belles lettres and likewise value his Buddhist teaching, but this is not something I dare to understand. In his own time, Juefan was a talented and renowned writer who could freely belittle and insult men and as such was feared throughout the world. Only Lingyuan [Weiqing] had the profound knowledge that Huihong was not awakened. He once wrote a letter to admonish him: [Weiqing's epistle, not replicated here, is translated in full above.—Trans.] Lingyuan wrote this letter surely as medicine for Huihong. However, that chronic condition of his did not get better! What can be done about it?

---

128. Liao, *Zhong-bian, shi-chan, meng-xi,* 28–36, gives a *dramatis personae* of major literary monks from this period; and Liao, 36–46, describes their reception of Huihong. See also Liao, 121–127, for Hanyue Fazang 漢月法藏 (1576–1635) and the making of Huihong into an orthodox Linji figure. Similar issues are discussed with clarity in Grant, "Through the Empty Gate," 95–96.

129. Jiang Wu, *Enlightenment in Dispute,* 137, 142, 154; Liao, *Zhong-bian, shi-chan, meng-xi,* 135–137.

130. One of many untitled entries in a subsection entitled "Somniloquies" 寱言, *Yongjue Yuanxian chanshi guanglu* (ZZ72.572b24-c12).

洪覺範書有六種，達觀老人深喜而刻行之。余所喜者，文字禪而已。此老文字，的是名家，僧中希有。若論佛法，則醇疵相半。世人愛其文字，併重其佛法，非余所敢知也。當其時，覺範才名大著，任意貶叱諸方，諸方多憚之，唯靈源深知其未悟，嘗有書誠之曰：[...]。靈源此書，大為覺範藥石，然其痼疾弗瘳，亦且奈之何哉。

Since Yuanxian concluded that Huihong was worth reading as a literary figure but not as an awakened Chan teacher based on the well-respected Weiqing's public epistle to Huihong, we can interpret Yuanxian's text as one of resistance to the revival by Zibo Zhenke of Huihong and his writings.

The fact that Zhenke was a principal cause of renewed interest in Huihong was known at the time. Zhenke's near contemporary Zhuanyu Guanheng 顓愚觀衡 (1579–1646) wrote the following in an epistle to a local scholar, Che Yizun 車以遵 (1598–1680).[131]

> The many writings of Juefan Huihong, including [*Chanlin*] *Sengbao zhuan, Commentary on Wisdom and Realization,* and *Shimen wenzi chan,* had disappeared by the time of the Ming Jiajing emperor [r. 1521–1567], and few had even heard his name. Master Daguan [Zhenke] long sought out [Huihong's] works, and one by one obtained them all, and having obtained them then printed them, and so they circulate throughout the world. Now, people have recently begun saying that Daguan [Zhenke] was a reincarnation of Huihong come to revitalize these old books, and if you look at his behavior, it would seem that this is exactly so!

> 洪覺範禪師所著僧寶智、證等傳、及石門文字禪諸書至我朝世宗年間埋沒，多不聞其名者。達觀禪師一出策杖寰海遍搜尋之，一一皆得，隨得隨梓，海內遍傳。若今日始出入，謂達觀大師乃覺範後身，重來翻騰故書，觀其所行若實然。

This letter attests to the state of knowledge in the early Qing, in which Huihong had become so associated with Zibo Zhenke that the latter was rumored to be a reincarnation of the former. Zibo Zhenke's misprision, or creative mis-reading, had in effect become an authoritative interpretation of *wenzi chan*.[132] After the memory of Huihong had all but disappeared from Chinese Buddhism, Zhenke stepped into the vacuum to refurbish Huihong as the paragon of a Ming ideal of literary Buddhism.

Zhenke's idea of the perfect correspondence of Chan and poetry also provided the foundation for a famous dictum of the early Qing dynasty. Mid-twentieth-century Japanese sinologist Kaji Tetsujō 加地哲定 (1890–1972) made clear in his history of Chinese Buddhist literature that the well-known phrase "complete unity of poetry and Chan" 詩禪一致 was first used by Wang

---

131. *Zizhu lin Zhuanyu Heng heshang yulu* (681b23–28).
132. Liao, *Zhong-bian, shi-chan, meng-xi,* 113, positively frames Zhenke's work as a "creative interpretation."

Shizhen 王士禎 (1634–1711) to dispute earlier Song-era statements.[133] I affirm Kaji's warning against adopting this Ming ideal as an anachronistic frame for the earlier history of Chinese Buddhist literature. I think it significant that Wang Shizhen rested his assertions on citations to Zibo Zhenke's preface to *Shimen wenzi chan*. According to Kaji, Wang Shizhen posited an absolute equivalence between poetry and Chan by explicitly arguing that Song-era comparisons between poetry and Chan were merely metaphoric and hence insufficient. Prior to Wang's "complete unity of poetry and Chan," the phrase "take Chan as a metaphor for poetry" 以禪喻詩 had been popular. The locus classicus for the phrase "take Chan as a metaphor for poetry" is in a published letter by Yan Yu 嚴羽 (fl. S. Song).[134] In the letter, Yan Yu cites Dahui Zonggao as the authority for the claim of equivalency of Chan and poetry. Yan Yu's sense of *chan*, however, is metaphoric and non-technical. Similarly, the term *sanmei* 三昧 (Skt. *samādhi*) was appropriated for vernacular and non-technical uses by literati to describe "a wonderful ability."[135] We can see that these texts and ideas emerged from what Jiang Wu aptly termed "literati textual spirituality," or what Mark Halperin once called the "worldly devotion" of the Song intelligentsia.[136]

This literati veneration of text provides the context for my last example in which Huihong used the phrase *wenzi chan*, his poem "Sent to Venerable Yong as well as Elder Ren" 贈湧上人乃仁老子也. Here, Huihong compares his rapt viewing of an autumn mountain landscape painting with the kind of literary absorption that can emerge from pouring oneself into the study of poetry, an immersive state that he calls *wenzi chan*. Huihong describes his ability to study poetry by candlelight until dawn, a remarkable concentration that he likens to the meditative powers of a hundred monks. Huihong addressed this poem to Yong (n.d.), the orphaned disciple of the late painter-monk Huaguang Zhongren 華光仲仁 (d. 1119?).[137] Zhongren famously was enamored with, and often painted, plum blossoms. He had befriended Su Shi, Huang Tingjian, and others who suffered in the divisive political battles and dangerous exiles of the Northern Song.[138] For these men, the plum blossom was not a sign of beauty but rather an image pointing to the protection to be found in friendship and wine, especially during political crisis.

---

133. Kaji, *Chūgoku Bukkyō bungaku kenkyū*, 261–278.

134. "A reply to my uncle Wu Jingxian of Lin'an" 答出繼叔臨安吳景仙書, *Canglang shihua jiao shi*, 251–258.

135. Benn, *Tea in China*, 129–130, concludes that "no doubt for some writers there is nothing especially profound lurking behind this phrase." I think much the same can often be said for the use of *chan* in metaphors for poetry.

136. In his *Enlightenment in Dispute*, 53–64, Jiang Wu also cites Halperin, *Out of the Cloister*, 4.

137. "Sent to Venerable Yong as well as Elder Ren" 贈湧上人乃仁老子也, *Shimen wenzi chan*, fasc. 11, 1:730–731. Master Zhongren was a painter and Yong his disciple. Zhou, *Songseng Huihong xinglü*, 269; Zhou, 250–251, dates this poem to 1120, likely after Zhongren's death. Huihong also composed a prayer text for Zhongren, see *Shimen wenzi chan*, fasc. 30, 2:708–710.

138. On the political significance of the plum blossom and a full translation of Huang's poem on Zhongren's plum blossom painting, see Murck, *Poetry and Painting*, 179–188.

Huihong met Zhongren late in life, after Huang and the others were dead. In "Sent to Venerable Yong," written shortly after Zhongren's death, Huihong uses the rhetoric of synesthesia to praise the visual arts. Just as one knows a literati painting has succeeded when one can hear poetic lines among the brushstrokes, so, too, one knows a poem has succeeded when one senses the concentration behind it. Here, *wenzi chan* refers to the kinds of contemplation associated with the arts. It was, notably, not loaded with the weight of Chan soteriology, nor was it grounds for a new social institution. It echoes how Huang Tingjian had earlier used the term, described above. Either this poem addressed to Venerable Yong is an exception to the other ways Huihong used *wenzi chan*, or here he deployed the term to mean literary insight and concentration.

As Richard Lynn has shown, the Chan-poetry analogy of the Song was one in which poetry is said to be *like* Chan, not to *be* Chan.[139] In this view, poetic language and religious language have an analogic relationship or family resemblance.[140] Though both poetry and Chan are known for heightened uses of language, it is heightened language of two distinct kinds. Metaphoric likeness is different from literal equivalency. Metaphors subordinate one of the two clauses to the other. By contrast, Ming writers like Wang asserted that poetry is a means to a religious achievement, that the path of poetry is the equal of the monastic path.

Zibo Zhenke's newly issued edition, together with its novel exegesis in his preface, were also influential in Japan. It is the Ming edition by Zhenke—preface included—that circulated to Japan and served as the basis for the only premodern commentary, *Sekimon Mojizen Chū* 石門文字禪註, by Sōtō monk Kakumon Kantetsu 廓門貫徹 (d. 1730). The preface by Zhenke together with the learned commentary by Kakumon Kantetsu were well-received, though not universally.[141] There is also earlier evidence from Japan that Gozan monks had interpreted Huihong's poetic works and the term *wenzi chan* in this positive manner. Sometimes, the presence of ideas in Gozan writing are suggestive of similar ideas circulating on the Chinese continent during the late Song or Yuan. The history of the relationship between Buddhism and literature in Japan is, however, markedly different from that in China, where the Confucian tradition was a bulwark against Buddhist learning. In pre-Edo Japan, there was no Confucian social institution invested in

---

139. This material has been turned over, focused on Ming interpretations, by Lynn, "Orthodoxy and Enlightenment," and includes further evidence of Wang's complicated relationship with Yan Yu. Also Lynn, "Sudden and the Gradual in Chinese Poetry Criticism," focuses on sources from the two Song dynasties. Lynn is careful to discuss "the Chan-poetry analogy" as a metaphor among critics.

140. Qian Zhongshu in his essay "Yi chan yu shi" 以禪喻詩, *Tanyi lu*, 2:745, discusses what is and is not denoted by this metaphoric relationship.

141. See Sawada, *Practical Pursuits*, 127–129, 295n48, on "literary Zen" as among the terms of disparagement in the Edo period. On the broadly positive reception of the Kakumon Kantetsu commentary, see Keyworth, " 'Study Effortless-Action.' "

anti-Buddhist polemics. Moreover, Japanese monks from the eighth to six-teenth centuries were frequently the keepers of learned continental tradi-tions, including so-called Confucian literature. For this reason, I do not think Gozan writing alone sufficient evidence of a positive interpretation of *wenzi chan* in China earlier than the Ming. Nonetheless, Zibo Zhenke's exegesis that accompanied his publication efforts has had a widely felt impact across the world of Chan and Zen down to today. This creative interpretation of *wenzi chan* as a term, however, would be anachronistic for understanding Song-era Chan literature.

Coda

I have focused in this chapter on how Huihong himself used the term *wenzi chan,* with the connotations of "feelings not yet forgotten," as a self-deprecatory reference to his poetry and the worldly poetry of other monks, not as a path that he advocated as a means to liberation. This undermines the idea that a movement started with Huihong under such a banner. Looking after Huihong to the Southern Song, one sees a profusion of literature and other writing by monks. Possible causes for this apparent quantitative amplification include demographic transformations, economic and commercial development, changes in education, and shifts in patterns of religious patronage. It is not clear that this increase in monks' poetic output in the Southern Song resulted in an increase of monks' poetry as a percentage of all poetry written. More-over, despite there being *more* writing during the Southern Song, there does not appear to be a monastic or institutional movement under the banner of *wenzi chan;* this writing (including petitions and other public notices) was part of the growth of monasteries and their reliance on patronage networks. The normative distinctions between inner and outer forms of learning remained in place, even as practices began to change. Though more work is needed to better understand these changes in the Southern Song, the term *wenzi chan* during the Southern Song was rarely used and then generally only to refer to the title of a book by Huihong. It is for these reasons that I propose that we refrain in our study of Song-dynasty monastic Buddhism from using the term *wenzi chan* as a historical category with either institutional or positive doctri-nal connotations.

4

Poetry as Outer Learning: The Poetry Demon

THE POET Li Zhong 李中 (fl. mid-10th c.) was a prominent figure in the briefly independent Southern Tang kingdom 南唐 (937–975) between the Tang and Song dynasties. He frequented Mount Lu, a haven of monastic centers and learning during the tumultuous tenth century.[1] There, he wrote the poem "Presented to the Great Master Bai of Donglin [Temple]" 贈東林白大師, likely after the monk's retirement.[2]

	You've long stopped among sacred traces at Tiger Stream;	虎溪久駐靈蹤
2	When you're not engaged in *chan*, the poetry demon is still strong.	禪外詩魔尚濃
	You roll up your bedding and intone [poetry] all day,	卷宿吟銷永日
4	Arrange your chair and sit facing the thousand peaks.	移牀坐對千峰
	The dark mosses coolly enclose the secluded paths,	蒼苔冷鏁幽徑
6	While you sit idly in gentle breezes by that old pine.	微風閒坐古松
	You yourself noted lately you feel older and ill,	自說年來老病
8	But if you step out of the [temple] gates, gradually you will lessen this lethargy.	出門漸覺踈慵

The poem's first line evokes the image of the eminent Lushan Huiyuan, who repaired to Mount Lu, never again to emerge, forever remaining on the other side of Tiger Stream. Huiyuan was often remembered by later Chinese Buddhists for his involvement with the poetry of elite visitors to Mount Lu, as discussed in Chapter 3. Here in Li Zhong's poem, however, religion and poetry are in conflict. The poetry demon is always lurking, he writes, and though one might repel the demon while in meditation or religious activity, the demon is waiting, and Master Bai, now in his idle dotage, has grown all the more fond of composing poetry.

---

1. On Buddhism in the Southern Tang, see Brose, *Patrons and Patriarchs*, 71–88.

2. *Quan Tang shi,* 747/8508–8509. Owen translates the first couplet in "How Did Buddhism Matter," 398. Li Zhong wrote a related poem, "Sent to Great Master Bai of Lushan" 寄廬山白大師. *Quan Tang shi,* 747/8503–04.

The potential problems of monastic poetry in China were Buddhist broadly defined, that is, not limited to any one sect, style, or lineage. Ideally, the ascetic rigors of the monastic order entailed a conscious rejection of the profane and worldly. The apparent conflict between literature and monasticism was pervasive, and evidence of it runs through many different types of monastic writing. In this chapter I aim to demonstrate the widespread concern about the place of poetry in the lives of monks by foregrounding prescriptions and admonitions in generally non-sectarian writing shared by all Chinese monks. I will also draw connections from these non-sectarian texts to the specialized texts of Chan and Tiantai, thereby illustrating the ubiquity of the discourse of "outer learning" among elite monks of the Song.

Ultimately, I aim to interpret monks' poems against monastic prescriptive texts known in the Song, including biographies of eminent monks, translated Indic Vinaya, Mahāyāna precept texts, sūtra commentaries, primers, meditation instructions, and domestically produced "rules of purity" (*qinggui* 清規). By following an archaeology of Song knowledge, we will see the variegated ways in which elite monks of the period reiterated these precedents and inscribed a ubiquitous concern for the propriety of poetry. In the latter part of this chapter, I analyze poems that thematize these prescriptive legal ideas. I argue that prohibitions against poetic writing transformed the forbidden practice into poetic topoi, and that these topoi demonstrate that Song writers were aware of the prohibitions. Monastic rules circumscribed literary composition by aspiring monks and situated poetry as one of the forms of so-called outer learning. The very idea that outer learning should be pursued only during breaks in the monastic schedule was then inscribed as a conceit within monks' poems. This chapter concludes with poems that depict the forbidden delight of versifying with the poetry demon. It should be clear by then that poems themselves were not the problem; it was, rather, that the habitual pleasures of poetry were a possible distraction from focused monastic regimens.

The Propriety of Poetry in the Lives of Monks

Traces of monastic anxiety over poetry are present in the poetry itself as well as across other kinds of Buddhist texts. This anxiety reflects, and is reflected in, the discourse of *waixue* 外學, "outer learning," or "the study of things outside [the Buddhist tradition]." Cao Shibang has documented *waixue* in early Chinese texts, which granted allowances for studying the non-Buddhist arts as instruments for liberating others.[3] On the one hand, worldly learning

---

3. Cao, *Zhongguo shamen waixue de yanjiu*, surveyed *waixue* in early Chinese Buddhist sources. The Chinese idealized pictures based on prescriptive sources contrasts with known practices of how non-Buddhist books were handled by early Indian monastic communities. For example, books were stores of value and could be bequeathed by "shaven-headed householders" in return for elder care, discussed by Schopen, *Buddhist Monks and Business Matters*, 11, 50, 104, 119.

could be used by awakened teachers as "skillful means," *upāya-kauśalya* in Sanskrit (Ch. *shanqiao fangbian* 善巧方便, more often *fangbian*; hereafter *upāya*). This understanding of worldly learning based on the concept of *upāya* limited to proselytization a monk's participation in public letters and verse. Poetry at the same time was understood to be a potential obstacle, or *kleśa* (Ch. *fannao* 煩惱), that could prohibit progress on the path. This dual quality of poetry—both as medicine and poison—is found throughout the *waixue* discourse.

Song writers thinking about the Chinese term *waixue* found authoritative glosses in the Chinese translations of Vinaya texts. Monastic codes and rule books across Buddhist languages enumerate the activities that are proscribed or restricted. In addition to poetry, other regulated activities include spell-craft and medicine. The *Brahmajālasutta* legislates medical arts out of concern that a monk will be consumed by the desire for profiting from a worldly livelihood.[4] In later Tibetan Buddhist curricula, medical knowledge was situated as a form of outer, or "worldly" (*laukika*), learning, which Janet Gyatso has described as its being placed "along with—but different from—the *summum bonum*."[5] The ultimate good that goes "beyond the world" (*lokottara*) and leads to liberation, she asserts, is often what we today mean when we refer to something as "Buddhist." Medical knowledge in Tibet offered a way of understanding the world that was overlapping but not entirely compatible with the dominant Buddhist episteme. The case of poetry and Buddhist soteriology in China similarly necessitated hermeneutics to reconcile partially incompatible ways of knowing the world.

The operant metaphors of "worldly" 世間 and "beyond the world" 出世間 appear in Chinese Buddhist discourses; however, the hermeneutical strategy of arranging things as "inner" 內 and "outer" 外 dominated Chinese discussion of monkish literary creativity. There are examples of other Buddhist cultures arranging knowledge as outer and inner based on the Indic conception of "five fields of learning" 五明 (Skt. *pañcavidyā*). This broader Buddhist phenomenon was also known in Song-era China, for example through Fayun's 法雲 (1088–1158) lexicon *Meaning of Terms from Translations* 翻譯名義集 (preface dated 1143). Here as elsewhere, the first four practical types of knowledge may be used in the service of a profane livelihood, including "skill in arts" 工巧[明] (Skt. *śilpa[vidyā]*),[6] which were all said to be "outer" (Ch. *wai*; Skt. *bāhyaka*). When poetry came up, it was discussed as a form of worldly

---

4. *Brahmajālasutta* in Walshe, *Long Discourses of the Buddha*, 72, and discussed by Birnbaum, *Healing Buddha*, 5–6.

5. Gyatso, *Being Human in a Buddhist World*, 102.

6. I have rendered the compound *gongqiao* as "skill in arts." In numerous Chinese receptions, however, the phrase is a single thing parallel to "techniques of art" 工巧技術, and the emphasis falls on literary and performing arts. The Chinese understanding of *gongqiao* 工巧 is sometimes rendered as two nouns, "arts and technology," which harkens back to an interpretation that more closely adheres to the variegated nature of the Indic category that encompasses arts as well as various mathematical, natural, and astral sciences.

knowledge. The fifth field, an exclusively Buddhist one directly related to liberation alone, was "inner learning" 內明 (Skt. *adhyātma-vidyā*).[7] For most Chinese writers, however, this canonical perspective on fields of learning seems to have been less important in discussions of poetry and literary creation than was the broader Chinese understanding of the inner-outer dyad.

The conceptual dyad of inner and outer, as Robert Campany has observed, is one of several Chinese strategies for conceptualizing the relationships between the plurality of " 'religion'-like entities" that existed in China, such as what we conveniently refer to as Buddhist and Confucian traditions. In addition to inner and outer, other strategies include, for example, organic metaphors of roots and branches that appear to assert that "the two (or more) things in question are in some ultimate sense really the same."[8] Such depictions of an imagined organic whole, such as might pertain to Buddhist knowledge and Chinese poetry, nonetheless involved assertions of hierarchical positions. In the inner-outer dyad, inner is usually superior to outer phenomena.[9] In Chinese Buddhist discourse, the "inner" often corresponds to what we today would call "Buddhist," whereas those things deemed "outer" were understood to be somehow not essentially Buddhist. These outer, non-Buddhist arts or activities, however, could be adapted and used for Buddhist purposes or revealed as Buddhist through hermeneutics. When monks engaged in worldly arts as such, they frequently transformed received artistic genres in response to these tensions or created new modes particular to Buddhist culture and learning.

Buddhist outer learning in China is distinct from other Buddhist traditions of worldly learning because it is defined in relation to the dominant fields of learning in China: the Confucian classics, literature, and histories. The Buddhist relationship to so-called Confucian learning was ambiguous, creating things that were imagined to be "along with—but different from— the *summum bonum*." This was observed historically when eminent monks were praised for having thoroughly "penetrated both inner and outer" 通內外, which generally meant both Buddhist and Ruist, or Confucian, learning.[10]

---

7. *Fanyi mingyi ji* (T54.1144c14–21). This is the same distinction discussed in other contexts by Ruegg, *Ordre spirituel*, 100–104; on "fields of learning" and the reception of these Indic divisions in later Tibet, see Lin, "Adapting the Buddha's Biographies," 19–21.

8. Campany, "On the Very Idea of Religions," 307–309. My reference to "religion"-like entities alludes to one of several laudable goals in Campany's study of early medieval Chinese discourse. Campany, 290, observes that, although the Western term "religion" does not demarcate some universally recognized category, the study of analogous "religion"-like discourses can clarify "certain aspects of both members of the comparison and the nature of the differences between them."

9. Campany, "On the Very Idea of Religions," provides the exceptional example of *fangwai* 方外 and *fangnei* 方內, in which *fangwai* indicates transcendence of the mundane world.

10. For example, the biography of Dao'an in *Xu gaoseng zhuan* (T50.628c26–27) states that "the teachings of Śākyamuni are inner, and the teachings of the Ruists are outer" 釋教為 內儒教為外.

Even when so praised, the aims of poetry *per se* were depicted as subordinate to the inner Buddhist soteriological goals.

Already in the Tang, Bai Juyi judged one monk's poetry to be *upāya*. "Ten Rhymes Inscribed for the Venerable Daozong" 題道宗上人十韻 articulates this instrumental attitude toward poetry for the sake of proselytism. Daozong "uses poetry to do deeds of a buddha" 以詩為佛事, in which his verses "first draw you in with poetic lines, / then bring you to Buddhist wisdom" 先以詩句牽，後令入佛智.[11] Bai here, and again in the preface to the poem, praises Daozong for the subordination of literary arts to the didactic strategies of a Buddhist teacher. Bai at the same time regarded the compositions of contemporary Jiangnan poet-monks as merely poetic and not soteriologically efficacious. In this same text, Bai also disparages the early versifying monk Tang Huixiu 湯惠休 (5th c.), to whom he mis-attributes the poem "Sorrows of Parting," a work of deep, unfulfilled longing.[12] Tang Huixiu, who laicized later in life, was one example of a monk who spent too much time poeticizing and not enough time dedicated to Buddhist learning. Bai elevated Daozong's work not because it proved to be better poetry than that of the Jiangnan poet-monks, but because his words were alive with soteriological possibility. This was one aspect of the outer-learning discourse.

The pertinence of outer learning for the relationship between Song monks and poetry can be illustrated with didactic anecdotes from *The Song-Era Biographies of Eminent Monks* 宋高僧傳 (hereafter *Song gaoseng zhuan*), compiled by Zanning.[13] Outer learning and monastic law were used by Song Buddhist biographers, including Zanning, to situate poetic compositions within the lives of eminent monks. As a genre, biographies of eminent monks were a vehicle for conveying Buddhist ideals.[14] These narrative representations "of what monks were *supposed* to be," as Kieschnick writes, were intended by Zanning to offer inspirational models for ordinary monks.[15]

Zanning included a biography for the now relatively obscure monk Zhihui 智暉 (873–956), who in the *Jingde chuandenglu* was portrayed as a bare branch on the Chan family tree. A rather different picture emerges from the *Song gaoseng zhuan*, where he is categorized as a talented "merit rouser"

---

11. *Bai Juyi ji*, 21/470–471. Adapted from the full translation and discussion in Mazanec, "Invention of Chinese Buddhist Poetry," 53–54.

12. The poem preserved in *Wenxuan* is by Jiang Yan 江淹 (444–505) in imitation of Tang Huixiu. See Williams, *Imitations of the Self*, 208. The historical confusion about attribution was noted in the Song-era Chan dictionary *Zuting shiyuan* (ZZ64.356b21–c1).

13. Zanning created a pastiche as he worked from numerous earlier texts to construct this collection. On the sources used by Zanning, see Yang Zhifei, "Zanning *Gaoseng zhuan* yanjiu," 187–255, and Jin Jianfeng, "Shi Zanning *Song gaoseng zhuan* yanjiu," 135–151. Zanning incorporates additional inscriptions by Jiaoran. Though many scholars regard Zanning as a faithful transmitter of text, note that Barrett decried "the utterly untrustworthy Zanning" in *Li Ao*, 57. Regardless, his text was authoritative for Song readers.

14. For the history of numerous printed editions and the canonization of the *Song gaoseng zhuan*, see Yang Zhifei, "Zanning *Gaoseng zhuan* yanjiu," 63–95.

15. Kieschnick, *Eminent Monk*, 1–8.

興福.[16] Zanning explicates how Zhihui encountered the religious dispensation that sanctioned his writing of poetry.[17]

> Zhihui lived quietly in the mountains, doing nothing but intensely searching through the teachings of the canon and gaining a thorough mastery of meditation and Vinaya. Every day he intoned a hundred thousand words and carefully chewed over their meaning. When he learned that the Buddha permitted one period of non-Buddhist study [per day], Zhihui became rather good at poetic composition and accomplished in the style of [*Li*]*sao* and the *elegantiae* [of the *Classic of Poetry*] [i.e., mainstream *shi*]. In addition to calligraphy, he excelled at fine brushwork. The sight of a white wall would generate clouds and mountains in the palms of his hands. He often remarked, "I admire the six techniques of painting of [the monks] Sengzhen and Daofen.[18] A pity we are not contemporaries! Painting on walls one after another, their creations seem alive."

> 山中闃然，曾無他事，唯鉤索藏教，禪律亙通，日誦百千言義味隨嚼。聞佛許一時外學，頗精吟詠得騷雅之體。翰墨工外小筆尤嘉。粉壁興酣雲山在掌。恒言，「吾慕僧珍、道芬之六法，恨不與同時。對壁連圖各成物象之生動也。」

Zanning's portrait of Zhihui is an illustration of a learned monk taking great joy in the arts of poetry, calligraphy, and painting. These arts are not practices for a beginner, however, nor are they the means for advancing along the Buddhist path. A reader of this eminent monk's biography is instructed that these worldly arts are outer learning and only became possible for Zhihui after he had already devoted himself to mastery of the inner arts of the Buddhist path. Zhihui's joy and freedom, in other words, are consequences of his dedication to monastic rigors and long abstinence from the arts. The remainder of this biography describes the wandering Zhihui tirelessly performing good deeds and engaging in literary arts only in his spare time. If the life of an eminent monk was meant to be a model to others, the biography of Zhihui recommends that literary talent should be incidental to "entirely caring about benefitting others, his heart having no other concern" 惟切利他，心無別務.[19]

The biography of monk Xuanyan 玄晏 (743–800), son of the calligrapher Li Yong 李邕 (678–747), is another example of the convergence of poetry with

---

16. On the typologies of the *Gaoseng zhuan* tradition of hagiographies, see Kieschnick, *Eminent Monk*, 8–9. For a brief note on Zhihui, see Demiéville, *Poèmes chinois d'avant la mort*, 53–54.

17. *Song gaoseng zhuan* (T50.883c22–27). I follow the Song and Yuan variant of *ya* 雅 for *tui* 推.

18. Sengzhen is listed in fasc. 7 of the Tang *Lidai minghua ji* by Zhang Yanyuan 張彥遠 (9th c.). I have not located biographical information for Daofen. From the context here, we may judge that he was also a monk skilled at painting. "Six techniques," or *liufa* 六法, is a term referring to the six skills found in the *Gu hua pin lu* 古畫品錄 by Xie He 謝赫. In that text, the six techniques serve as an organizational scheme for pithy statements attributed to venerable practitioners. When Zhihui speaks about *wuxiang* 物象 and *shengdong* 生動, he is referring to two of the six skills in Xie's preface.

19. *Song gaoseng zhuan* (T50.884a3).

Buddhist practice. His biography is found among the section on "Miscella-
neous Sermonists" 雜科聲德, which includes those eminent monks who did
not fit easily into another category. Xuanyan received the tonsure in 756 and
full ordination in 768, a period in which he practiced his rigid interpretation
of Buddhist monastic deportment. It was said, for instance, that if he had to
dwell with poorly behaved monks, he would "become nervous and uncomfort-
able, as though he had bathed his body in *khadira* lye."[20] And yet, Xuanyan's
strict adherence to Vinaya included his discovery of an allowance for poetry.[21]

> Later in life, after he learned that the *vinayapiṭaka* includes "one period of non-
> Buddhist study [per day]," he then on occasion wrote a poem in which he gave
> free reign to his thoughts as though he were wandering alone beyond the world.
> Liu Changqing,[22] who himself was celebrated for his five-character poems, sighed
> in appreciation at Xuanyan's work. After this, whenever [Xuanyan] wrote in verse
> about the wind and clouds, or grass and trees, these poems were chanted and
> recited by those skilled at literary writing.

> 而聞律藏有一時外學之說，或賦詩一章，運思標拔孤遊境外。彭城劉長卿名重
> 五言，大嗟賞之。由是風雲草木每有賦詠，輒為工文者之所吟諷也。

Zanning makes Xuanyan an exemplar by praising this son of a famous cal-
ligrapher for his strict adherence to the Buddhist code of conduct. The tale
of Xuanyan's pious literalism, however, also makes for a rather humorous
story. Though belonging to a family of erudite men, Xuanyan had avoided
writing poetry because he thought it was forbidden. But when he discovered
an exemption in the code allowing one period of the day for practice of the
outer arts, his poems quickly became popular among discerning contempo-
raries. A closer look at the language concerning outer arts, however, would
reveal that their study was for the purposes of proselytization, as will be dis-
cussed below. Xuanyan's confusion on that score notwithstanding, Zanning
portrayed Xuanyan as virtuous for his strict adherence to the letter of the law.

The "Miscellaneous Sermonists" category of *Song gaoseng zhuan* also con-
tains biographies of poet-monks from the late Tang, including Guanxiu and
Qiji. No explicit reference to outer or inner learning is mentioned in either

---

20. *Song gaoseng zhuan* (T50.893a28–29). Dharmakṣema's translation of *Da banniepan jing*
(T12.459b28–29) provides this idiom, that bathing in *khadira* lye is as dangerous as living with
vipers, hence Xuanyan's discomfort with living among sinners. See the Tang lexicon *Yiqie jing
yinyi* (T54.474c8) on the Indic practice of washing the body with this astringent. The Chinese
qutuoluo 佉陀羅 is a transliteration of the Sanskrit *khadira*, a tree valued for producing therapeu-
tics as well as the astringent catechu ash.

21. *Song gaoseng zhuan* (T50.893b3–7).

22. Quan Deyu recorded in the preface to a collection of matched poetry involving Liu
Changqing (*jinshi* 733) that Liu regarded himself as especially skillful at pentasyllabic verse.
See *Wenyuan yinghua*, 716/3702–3703. On reading *huo* 或 as "all at once," see *Tang Wudai yuyan
cidian*, 171.

biography. Guanxiu and Qiji alike are depicted as having from childhood a natural inclination toward both Buddhist learning and poetry. In the case of the two men, Zanning does not explicitly narrate a tension between poetry and monasticism, perhaps because poetry was a quintessential part of the careers of these Buddhist monks. In their biographies, Guanxiu and Qiji are said to have made time for poetry in between periods of practice of monastic rigors. Gleaned from a colophon written by Guanxiu's disciple Tanyu 曇域 (n.d.), Zanning relates how the young Guanxiu went to the neighboring temple to discuss poetry and find matching couplets at every break in his monastic schedule.[23] Similarly, Qiji received in mid-career the administrative position of "clerical rector" 僧正 that kept him occupied, and therefore "he frequently used his free time at dawn or in the stillness of night to work on his own compositions" 其如閑辰靜夜多事篇章.[24] At least as depicted by Zanning in *Song gaoseng zhuan*, Guanxiu and Qiji practiced poetry at the margins of monastic training. Even so, their biographies do not present poetry as an explicit obstacle on the path.

From these examples, we can see that poetry was ambiguously valorized in the *Song gaoseng zhuan*. In each of the two biographies, Zanning praised the two eminent monks for their literary accomplishments. But at the same time Zanning ensured his readers would regard poetry as outer learning, a partially sanctioned but nonessential activity. He created narratives that literally embodied the postponement of creative arts until after the mastery of Buddhist teachings, or during periods of free time in the monastic schedule. This orthodox representation accords with what we know from his other writings, for example, the entry for "outer learning"—translated later in this chapter—in his *Great Song Historical Digest of the Buddhist Order*.[25]

Biographies of monks could also portray poetry as a religious obstruction, or *kleśa*, as in the following examples of poet-monks quitting poetry to focus on Buddhist learning. The *Song gaoseng zhuan* biography of Jiaoran 皎然 (720–ca. 795) indicates that even this exemplar among poet-monks quit writing for a period shortly after completing a draft of *Exempla of Poetry* 詩式, likely in 786.[26] According to Zanning, Jiaoran "wished to stop following the way of poetry because it was adverse to the purpose of Chan" 欲屏息詩道非禪者之意.[27] This narrative includes Jiaoran's well-known address to his brush and

---

23. The section from Yanyu's preface is translated in Mazanec, "Invention of Chinese Buddhist Poetry," 112–113. *Song gaoseng zhuan* (T50.897a15–16).

24. *Song gaoseng zhuan* (T50.897c25–26).

25. *Seng shi lüe* (T54.240c19–241a5).

26. See Jia, *Jiaoran nianpu*, 128.

27. *Song gaoseng zhuan* (T50.892a5–15). Zanning derived the details for the above story from Jiaoran's colophon known as the "middle preface" 中序 to the very *Exempla of Poetry* that had supposedly been at hand during this crisis. The "intermediate preface" includes the story of forsaking brush and ink as well as the encounter with Li Hong. See Williams, "Taste of the Ocean," 3–4, on the complex history of editions of *Shi shi*. For this passage, see *Shi shi*, 3.b and *Shi shi jiaozhu*, 1–10. *Quan Tang wen*, 917/9554a-b, includes the sexagenary date for 792, not 789 as found elsewhere.

inkstone: "I am tired of being your servant, and you are wearied of my fool-ishness!" 顧筆硯曰：我疲爾役，爾困我愚.[28] In this way, the *Song gaoseng zhuan* portrays even the great monkish writer Jiaoran struggling to reconcile a relentless writerly impulse with his goal of religious liberation. This account concludes with senior official Li Hong 李洪 responding to Jiaoran's unease with praise for the monk's *Exempla of Poetry*. Li proposed that a vow of abstinence would be "but the partial views of the lesser vehicle" 小乘褊見, alluding to an unnamed Mahāyāna perspective on the matter, reflecting perhaps a flexible understanding of *upāya* that would give license to antinomian behavior.[29] This story turns on an interesting reversal of positions. The monk has written a peerless tract on poetry, and the government official instructs that monk on interpretation of Buddhist doctrine. Zanning ultimately praised Jiaoran for participating in social literary activities solely with men who could "share in delighting in the Way."[30] The monastic regulations prohibiting excessive study or composition of poetry are integrated within this biography of an eminent poet-monk.

The conception of poetry as spiritual obstruction was not limited to hagiography. Jiaoran elsewhere expressed similar sentiments in his reply to an epistle from Quan Deyu 權德輿 (759–818).[31] Therein, Jiaoran wondered at his own lingering commitment to the ways of poetry despite his other renunciations and attributed this penchant to "remnant afflictions not yet eliminated" 餘塵未泯 that signaled the certainty that "there are powerful desires therein" 豈有健羨於其間哉.[32] In his choice of the words "powerful desires" 健羨, Jiaoran drew on classical Confucian diction for a term seldom used in the Buddhist canon, recasting a passage from Sima Tan's 司馬談 (ca. 190–110 BCE) discussion of philosophical schools into a witty comment about Buddhist deportment.[33] His response to Quan Deyu might have been in part a rhetorical flourish, but it is nonetheless striking how Jiaoran humbled himself in a manner specific to his station as a monk by casting his worldly literary activity as the fruit of remnant worldly karma. Jiaoran closed the letter by noting the numerous interlocutors with whom he had recently corresponded and inserted his desire to retreat into mountains "to aid my study of *chan* and doctrines" 助禪教. In *Exempla of Poetry*, Jiaoran used the same verb, "to aid,"

28. *Song gaoseng zhuan* (T50.892a11). This is recounted in Watson, "Zen Poetry," 113–114, and handled with some skepticism in Owen, *The Great Age*, 287–288.

29. *Song gaoseng zhuan* (T50.892a22).

30. *Song gaoseng zhuan* (T50.892b15–16).

31. On Quan Deyu's personal and familial ties to Buddhism, see Jinhua Chen, "Family Ties and Buddhist Nuns in Tang China." Jia, *Jiaoran nianpu*, 138, estimates the reply was likely composed in 790.

32. Jiaoran, "Letter in response to Quan Deyu" 答權從事德輿書, now in *Quan Tang wen*, 917/9551–9552. The letter is translated in Yang Jingqing, *Chan Interpretations*, 179.

33. This comment comes toward the end of Sima Tan's lecture in *Lun liujia yaozhi* 論六家要旨, recorded in his son Sima Qian's *Shiji* 史記. See Knechtges and Chang, *Ancient and Early Medieval Chinese Literature*, 2:967–969. Translated by Harold Roth and Sarah Queen, in de Bary and Bloom, *Sources of Chinese Tradition*, 278–282.

to argue that the study of Buddhism had nurtured the literary capacities of Xie Lingyun.[34] Although Jiaoran advocated for Buddhism as an aid to poets, poetry was not an aid to Buddhist monastics.

In the Song as well, monks abandoned their literary endeavors to single-mindedly pursue religious goals. Daoqian earned a literary reputation after he spontaneously composed a witty response poem at a banquet with Su Shi in the autumn of 1078.[35] But he was soon censured due to his involvement in the "Poetry Trial at Raven Terrace" in 1079.[36] By 1081, Daoqian had retreated to Mount Ayuwang, where he lived with the notoriously strict Chan master Dajue Huailian 大覺懷璉 (1010–1090), and there swore off poetry. A letter from Qin Guan to Su Shi relates the following news.[37]

> Daoqian went to live with Huailian on Mount Ayuwang, the place is most ideal for him. More recently a letter arrived, and though he previously said that he "completely stopped [orally] composing poetry," now I learn that since then he has already broken his vow [to stop poetry]!

> 參寥在阿育王山璉老處，極得所。比亦有書來，昨云已斷吟詩，聞說後來已復破戒矣。

Around the same time Qin Guan sent an epistle to Daoqian.[38]

> Recently I heard that you were not writing poetry, and I had a short poem I was going to send to tease you. Now you've already broken your promise! It seems [karma] that has ripened is difficult to disregard.

> 頃聞公不作詩，有一小詩奉戲，又已復破戒矣。可謂熟處難忘也。

The phrase "that [which] has ripened is difficult to disregard" 熟處難忘 appears in many Buddhist texts from the Song on as a reference to literary inclinations as karmic habits. This brief period of literary abstinence in

---

34. Entry titled *Wen zhang zong zhi* 文章宗旨, in *Shi shi*, 1.c; *Shi shi jiaozhu*, 118–120; translation in Williams, "Taste of the Ocean," 23.

35. In 1078, at a banquet in the Xuzhou governor's house, Daoqian wrote a poem titled "Su Shi from the Head Seat Sent a Singing-Dancing Girl to Seek a Poem of Me, and I Offered This Poem to Play Along" 子瞻席上令歌舞者求詩，戲以此贈 in which the third and fourth lines rebuff the young woman:, "My *chan* mind is now like a mud-soaked willow-catkin, / how could it chase the spring wind [moving] wildly up and down?" 禪心已作沾泥絮,肯逐春風上下狂。*Canliaozi shiji*, 3.4a; 64. This incident was widely recorded, and the many variants of Daoqian's poem attest to its wide circulation across East Asia. This verse appears also in Chan literature, such as *Chanzong zaduhai* (ZZ65.58b19–20), and quoted by later Chan masters.

36. Daoqian was among the associates named and fined (*Dongpo wutai shi'an*, 288–289) and his poem written for Su Shi entitled "Studio of Lucid Clarity" 虛白齋 (*Canliaozi shiji*, 3.4a; 62–63) is included in the legal case documents.

37. "Missive to Su [Shi]" 與蘇公先生簡, *Huaihai ji jian zhu*, 30/992.

38. "Missive to Master Canliao" 與參寥大師簡, in *Huaihai ji jian zhu*, 30/1012.

Daoqian's life coincided with his only training under a Chan master. Writing about this centuries later, Yuejiang Zhengyin 月江正印 (1267–after 1350) remarked that "Huailian made broken bowstrings taut again, / else there would not have been Foguo [Weibai] or Daoqian!" 大覺斷絃今復續，可無佛國與參寥.[39] With Huailian's support, it was said, Daoqian was "brought back to life" 復生 and once again began traveling and writing freely.[40] Though both Jiaoran and Daoqian made a public show of forsaking poetry, neither monk could give it up for long.

Records of the lives of monks were important sites at which poetry was explicitly connected to the discourse around outer learning. The urge to write poetry could be a karmic obstacle, though poetic learning could be used instrumentally to proselytize. Whether *kleśa* or *upāya*, poetry itself fundamentally was not the Buddhist path. To underscore this, the several biographies cited above also referenced a separate period in the monastic schedule for literary learning. The scriptural origins of this practice were propagated during the Song in legal codes and sūtra commentaries, the topics to which we now turn.

Outer Learning in Vinaya and Tang and Song Exegeses

Song exegetes drew on scriptural authority to explain outer learning. But several different attitudes are found across monastic legal codes as well as in influential Tang commentaries, necessitating thoughtful hermeneutics by Song monks. Several key ideas emerged from these earlier texts. First, the concept of a dedicated period of outer learning separate from Buddhistic study was grounded in Vinaya texts. Second, the goal of using literary learning to convert educated elites also emerged from such early Buddhist texts. Third, although some Mahāyāna bodhisattva precept texts offered similar exhortations, stricter prohibitions also appeared in Mahāyāna writing. These canonical sources were taken up by Tang and Song exegetes. I begin with the primary sources and then turn to how Tang and Song commentaries developed the discourse of outer learning.

Vinaya (Ch. *lü* 律) texts are collections of Buddhist monastic law.[41] As early Buddhism developed, varying interpretations of discipline were codified in different communities. Five Vinaya were translated into Chinese; however, only that of the Dharmaguptaka, known as the *Sifen lü* 四分律, was upheld by monks in China beginning with an edict from Emperor Zhongzong 中宗 (r. 705–710).[42] The *Sifen lü* includes regulations concerning the study

---

39. This poem about the *mengtang* is recorded in *Yuejiang Zhengyin chanshi yulu* (ZZ71.148c9–11).

40. As found in "Inscription on the *Mengtang* at Mount Ayuwang" 阿育王山下蒙堂記 by Yuanji Juding 圓極居頂 (d. 1404), an early Ming inscription about Daoqian's living in a *mengtang* 蒙堂 together with Huailian, preserved in *Zenrin shōkisen*, 46a11-b16, as well as in a Yuan-era inscription on "Record of the Fourth Dhyāna Dwelling" 四禪寮記 in *Yuting ji*, 6.24a-26a.

41. My discussion of Vinaya in China enriched by Heirman, "*Vinaya*: From India to China."

42. The Vinaya of *Tanwude* 曇無德 (Skt. *Dharmagupta*) is better known in Chinese as *Sifen*

of writing as one of several worldly arts that are prohibited, the single excep-
tion being if one needs to "subdue" non-Buddhists.[43] The *Sifen lü* does not
specifically stipulate poetry or *waixue*.[44] As a result, the Chinese translations
of other Vinaya texts served as authoritative sources for the Chinese concept
of outer learning.

One of the *Mūlasarvāstivāda Vinaya texts translated by Yijing 義淨 (635–
713), known in Chinese as the *Pinaiye zashi*, was the *locus classicus* for Song-
dynasty discussions of "one period of outer learning" 一時外學. The set of
translations by Yijing has often been thought to have been of little historical
consequence, however, it was still read and quoted by exegetes, as illustrated
below.[45] According to *Pinaiye zashi*, each day should be divided into three
periods, with outer learning restricted to only the final division of any given
day.[46] The relevant passage in *Pinaiye zashi* details other qualifications for en-
gaging in outer literary arts. According to the *Pinaiye zashi*, the Buddha himself
said that "it is not appropriate for undiscerning dullards with little wisdom to
study non-Buddhist writing. Only those with self-knowledge, luminous
wisdom, broad learning, and excellent memory who are able to rebuff non-
Buddhists are permitted such study" 不應愚癡少慧不分明者令學外書；自知
明慧多聞強識能摧外道者，方可學習.[47] In addition to restricting time each
day, this juridical opinion from *Pinaiye zashi* limited the study of non-Buddhist
texts to especially gifted and wise monks.

In addition to the disciplinary codes for Buddhist monks and nuns,
Mahāyāna precept texts provided fundamental models for the appropriate
relationship between worldly literature and the bodhisattva path. The
Mahāyāna precept texts, sometimes called bodhisattva precepts, are not con-
sistent with one another. The important Chinese indigenous scripture *Fanwang
jing* 梵網經, likely composed in the fifth century, adopted a hardline view of
non-Mahāyāna texts and absolutely prohibited them.[48] A passage in the *Lotus
Sūtra* followed a different tack, though similarly extreme, and forbid a bod-
hisattva from overly close associations with people who compose literature,

---

lü 四分律 (Skt. *Cāturvargīya-vinaya*). Heirman, *"Vinaya,"* 192–195, argues that exclusive impe-
rial recognition of the *Sifen lü* as championed by Dao'an 道岸 (654–717) was the culmination of
criticisms against the previously eclectic and selective application of Vinaya codes in China.

43. *Sifen lü* (T22.754b6–9 and 775a11–13).

44. The curious case of the absence of *waixue* from *Sifen lü* was noted by Cao, *Zhongguo
shamen waixue de yanjiu*, 1–13. He argues that this is evidence for the influence of the *Shisong lü*
(*Sarvāstivāda-vinaya*) based on the popularity of *waixue* among scholars of non-Sarvāstivāda
Vinaya and concludes that this influence occurred in the period before the sangha was united
under Dharmaguptaka hegemony. However, the *Shisong lü* (T23.274a24–b10) does not specify
how many periods in each day are permitted.

45. On the origins and historical irrelevance of Yijing's text, see Heirman, *"Vinaya,"*
177–179.

46. *Pinaiye zashi* (T24.232b3–15). For an updated survey of Yijing's Vinaya translations, see
Kishino, "Study of the Nidāna," 13–19.

47. *Pinaiye zashi* (T24.232b4–6).

48. *Fanwang jing* (Funayama 164–165, 384–385; T24.1006c19–23). The *Fanwang jing* (Fu-
nayama 148–149; T24.1006b1–5) does divide the day into six periods, but all periods are for
constant practice.

later interpreted in some Song commentaries to mean poetry in particular.[49] By contrast, two translated Mahāyāna precept texts, *Sūtra on the Wholesome Precepts of the Bodhisattva* 菩薩善戒經 and *Sūtra on the Bodhisattva Stages* 菩薩地持經, both permitted one period of *waixue* (out of three periods in a day), a similar limitation to that stated in *Pinaiye zashi*.[50] Of these two Mahāyāna precept texts, the first permitted *waixue* for the purpose of subduing non-Buddhists, the same rationale found in all mainstream Vinaya. The second restricted outer learning to those who were intelligent and possessing of an excellent memory as well as those who had already thoroughly penetrated the buddhadharma and obtained "unshakable wisdom" 不動智, a quality that in another bodhisattva *bhūmi* text was associated with the profoundly advanced eighth of ten stages on the bodhisattva path to liberation.[51] Presumably, this wisdom made it possible to employ non-Buddhist learning to liberate others without generating karma that might cause one to backslide.[52]

Additional explicit Mahāyāna allowances for poetry are found in writings by the influential mid-Tang Tiantai luminary Jingxi Zhanran 荆溪湛然 (711–782).[53] Zhanran's *Personal Notes on the Commentary to the "Vimalakīrtinirdeśa"* 維摩經疏記 provided a stipulation restricting outer learning to bodhisattvas of the fifth *bhūmi*.[54] This he derived from his reading of the eighty-fascicle *Huayan jing* 華嚴經 (Skt. *Avataṃsakasūtra*).[55] There, it is an imperative for bodhisattvas to master outer learning in order to benefit sentient beings. Zhanran in this passage is contrasting the teachings found in the Vinaya with what he regarded as a Mahāyāna view.[56]

---

49. *Miaofa lianhua jing* (T9.37a21–24). The Northern Song Tiantai monk Shenzhi Congyi 神智從義 (1042–1091) explicitly offers "songs, poetry and the like" 歌詩之流 as the substance of the prohibition in his *Fahua jing sandabu buzhu* (ZZ28.304c13–14). Another Song commentary interpreted this passage to mean that it is bodhisattvas who should not compose worldly literature. See Jiehuan's 戒環 (fl. 1120s) *Fahua jing yaojie* (ZZ30.329b13–14).

50. Guṇabhadra's nine-fascicle *Pusa Shanjie jing* (T30.1016c24–1017a1) and Dharmakṣema's *Pusa dichi jing* (T30.915b29-c5).

51. *Shidi jing* (T10.562a15). The Sanskrit *bhūmi* and Chinese translation *di* 地 refer to the stages, or literally "ground," of the bodhisattva path. The concept of *bhūmi* was used across texts to present different models of the path, varying both the qualities and total number of individual stages. Ten-stage models were standard in East Asia. For a convenient overview of the most influential models, see Hirakawa, *A History of Indian Buddhism*, 303–308.

52. Parallel passage in Xuanzang's translation of *Yuqie shidi lun* (T30.519b2–3).

53. Zhanran is the putative ninth patriarch of Tiantai, renowned for revitalizing the lineage. Among his innovative propositions, his controversial assertions about the buddha-nature of insentient things led to considerable discord in later times. On this point, see Sharf, "How to Think with Chan *Gong'an*," as well as the extensive work of Linda Penkower.

54. The *Weimojing shuji* was based on Zhanran's notes from the period when he was compiling the ten-fascicle *Weimojing lüeshu*, which was a distillation of the twenty-eight fascicle commentary by Zhiyi 智顗 (538–597) titled *Weimojing wenshu* 維摩經文疏. For more on the relationship between Zhanran's texts, see *Bussho kaisetsu daijiten*, 11:127d-128a.

55. Corresponding to *Huayan jing* (T10.192b8–13).

56. *Weimojing shuji* (ZZ18.892a1–7); cf. *Weimojing lüeshu* (T38.600c4–9).

As for the idea that if one wishes to subdue others, one first must become learned, it is in [Vinaya of] the lesser vehicle that for the sake of subduing non-Buddhists "one period" only is acceptable. The highest teachings of the Mahāyāna make clear regulations for beginners: [outer learning] impedes progress on the wondrous path, so it is not permitted. Only a bodhisattva of the fifth stage can practice such mundane activities. [The *Fanwang jing* states,] "These [outer texts] cut off the seeds of buddhahood and obstruct the causes of awakening."[57] Men of the cloth today do not cultivate whatsoever morality, meditation, or wisdom, and merely mouth that they will subdue non-Buddhists [as an excuse to pursue outer learning]. This is just like [trying to wear one's] clothes upside down.[58] Dye may spread easily, but the methods of the correct path are difficult to instill. A habitual pride festers in one who opposes and belittles study of the fundamentals. A terrible pity! Such men are truly mistaken. While they sit in cloisters of permanence,[59] wear donated robes, eat from the table of the pure assembly, and tread upon invaluable land [of the temple], at the same time they behave profanely in body, speech, and mind. Their fourfold deportment cleaves to delusion![60] If they want to regard such [worldly behavior] as a model, then they [at least] ought to aspire to the ten virtues [of a Confucian gentleman]!

為欲伏彼初應受學者，小乘破外，稍通一時。大乘標宗，初心明制，妨入妙道，故不令為。五地菩薩方修世業，「是斷佛種障道因緣」。今出家人，戒定慧心一無所修，而云伏外，義等倒裝；散染易流，道法難寄，增長慢習，[61]反輕學宗，深可悲也。甚為謬也。況坐常住院，著信施衣，飡淨眾厨，踐無價地，而三業從俗，四儀拘迷。若欲傚之當思十德。

In addition to reiterating the Vinaya and Mahāyāna precept texts, Zhanran adds that outer learning should only be engaged in by a practitioner who has attained at least the fifth of the ten *bhūmi*, a significant level of attainment. Other commentaries expressed a similar conceit regarding the fifth *bhūmi* as a prerequisite for participation in worldly fields of learning.[62] This is similar in kind to some of the Mahāyāna precept texts. Here, however, Zhanran's stipulation does not seem to emerge from his concern over an individual's

---

57. *Fanwang jing* (Funayama 164–165, 384–385; T24.1006c19–23).

58. I read this similar to the phrase "looking for your collar by lifting your skirt" 倒裳索領, a foolish activity contrary to one's goals, as used, for example, in Zhiyi's admonition. *Mohe zhiguan* (T46.42c27), translated by Swanson in *Clear Serenity*, 1:649.

59. Synecdoche for a monastery. These administrative wings of a monastery are so-called because they control the items that are not the personal possessions of an abbot or officer and that remain permanently with the monastery.

60. Deportment in the four activities of walking 行, standing 住, sitting 坐, and lying down 臥, that is, all human activity.

61. I have emended *manxi* 慢習 for *manji* 慢集 on the basis of the *Chuiyuji* quotation.

62. See the earlier *Fahua jing yiji* (T33.672b1–3) by Guangzhai Fayun 光宅法雲 (467–529), as well as Chengguan's *Da fangguang Fo Huayan jing shu* (T35.799c2–27). The latter was quoted by Song writers, such as Huayan exegete Xiao'an Guanfu 笑庵觀復 (fl. 1141–1152) in his *Yijiao jing lunji* (ZZ53.638b2).

progress on the path but rather is out of his interest in making monks into suitable vessels for communicating the dharma. Hence, he complains that too many monks will say that they are studying outer learning but do not pursue the Buddhistic disciplines that are supposed to constitute the inner studies. This passage in its entirety would later be reproduced by Zhiyuan in his sub-commentary to Zhanran's exegesis of the *Vimalakīrtinirdeśa*.[63]

The talented early Song versifier Gushan Zhiyuan wrote an erudite exposition of the history behind "one period of outer studies" in his *Record of the Abundance Descended from the Abbreviated Commentary on the "Vimalakīrtinirdeśa"* 維摩經略疏垂裕記 (hereafter *Chuiyuji*). He called upon most of the same major scriptural sources as other Song-era thinkers used to understand *waixue*, including those introduced above.[64] In *Chuiyuji*, Zhiyuan asserted that a monk's pursuit of outer learning must be for the sake of subduing non-Buddhists. The *Vimalakīrtinirdeśa* valorizes a secular figure, the layman Vimalakīrti, as an eminent authority on Buddhist salvation. One of Zhiyuan's concerns in his commentary was to defend monasticism as a religious practice. If Vimalakīrti was able to marry and live as a householder and still achieve perfect awakening, then why should people of the Song dynasty continue to pursue ascetic monasticism? Zhiyuan argued that readers should not overemphasize Vimalakīrti's secular behavior, nor should they disregard Vimalakīrti's underlying perfect intention to benefit sentient beings. Though, for example, Vimalakīrti wears the clothes of a layperson, he upholds the pure conduct of a monk.

It is in this context of appropriate deportment for monks that Zhiyuan discussed outer learning.[65] The relevant portion of Kumārajīva's translation of the skillful means deployed by Vimalakīrti reads, "He studied the many errant ways [of non-Buddhist teachings], but this could not corrupt his right faith" 受諸異道，不毀正信.[66] Zhiyuan added that "in our country the mundane classics are the [Confucian] Five Classics and so on" 此方世典即五經等 and explicitly included *The Classic of Poetry*.[67] In a pertinent passage, Zhiyuan notes, before quoting Zhanran, the various dispensations for proselytization.[68]

> It is for the sake of subduing others that the Dharmaguptaka school's [Vinaya] permits *bhikṣu*s one of the twelve periods of the day for outer learning.[69] And it is

63. Note that the *Chuiyuji* (T38.761a25-b9) quotation of *Weimojing shuji* is not identical to the received *Weimojing shuji*.

64. The *Chuiyuji* has been little studied in English. See *Bussho kaisetsu daijiten* 11:133a-b for a helpful overview of the text.

65. Zhiyuan's broader discussion of *waixue* runs across the eighth item, entitled "manifesting affinities with errant ways" 示同異道, and ninth item "studying worldly classics" 受世典, *Chuiyuji* (T38.761a26–27 and 761b11).

66. *Weimojie suoshuo jing* (T14.539a23); adapted from Watson, *Vimalakirti Sutra*, 33, and McRae, *Vimalakīrti Sutra*, 82. See also a translation of the parallel passage from the Tibetan in Thurman, *Holy Teaching of Vimalakīrti*, 20–21.

67. *Chuiyuji* (T38.761b11–18).

68. *Chuiyuji* (T38.761a25–b9).

69. Zhiyuan is in error. This is not in the *Sifen lü* Vinaya, despite such assertions in several

for the sake of vanquishing non-Buddhists that the *Pinaiye zashi* [of *Mūlasarvāsti-vāda*] divides each day into three and allows the latter part of a day for such study. While laypersons [rightfully] have their roots in the home, monks today have forgotten their [appropriate] roots and chase only the branches; though they look like ascetics, they have turned their backs on Buddhist learning.

為伏物故者,曇無德部比丘於十二時開一時外學。為降伏外道故,鼻奈耶明日分三時許日後分學。況今居士本在家眾,今世比丘忘本逐末,形似沙門,心背佛學。

The verbs "subdue" 伏 and "vanquish" 降伏, as well as "smash" 破, which is frequently seen elsewhere, suggest more annihilating other paths than turning someone toward the light.[70] Zhiyuan strongly critiques monks who study poetry without a correct understanding of its proper function for monks. Such people are monks only in outer appearance; within their hearts they betray the Buddhist teachings. To bolster this point, Zhiyuan references two Vinaya texts. The next portion of his commentary reproduces the exact passage by Zhanran already translated above. Clearly, Zhiyuan, who wrote hundreds of poems, including one entitled "The Poetry Demon" (translated in my introduction), was familiar with minutiae from the various monastic legal codes and exegetical tradition regarding literary activity. This same writer also composed parting poetry and lamentations, analyzed in Chapters 5 and 6, many of which illustrate his awareness of a tension between literary pursuits and the Buddhist path.

The concept of outer learning allowed multiple hermeneutic resolutions to adjudicate competing scriptural and commentarial authorities. Classical Vinaya texts restricted the study and practice of *waixue* with the justification that monks, especially the young and inexperienced, might be tempted to abandon Buddhist teachings. Exceptions are made for talented monks who could become adept at debate. Mahāyāna precept texts are divided on the matter. The *Fanwang jing* prohibits non-Buddhist learning altogether. The *Pusa dichi jing*, on the other hand, permits such learning for advanced practitioners who already possess an unshakably firm grasp of Buddhist teachings. Similarly, Zhanran offers an interpretation that only bodhisattvas with relatively high attainment can use worldly learning as *upāya*, otherwise poetry could be an obstacle. He elaborates on this in another commentary.[71]

Tang texts. The mistake probably arose from a passage known to Zhiyuan in Zhanran's *Fuxing* (T46.266a20–24), a commentary on the monumental meditation manual *Mohe zhiguan* 摩訶止觀; corresponding to "Putting an End to All Mundane Responsibilities," in Swanson, *Clear Serenity*, 1:649–652.

70. Some common variations are *po waidao* 破外道, *po waidao eyalun* 破外道惡邪論, *po wailunshi* 破外論師, and *xiangfu mojun* 降伏魔軍.

71. *Fuxing* (T46.266a20–24). See the corresponding passage in the *Weimojie suoshuo jing* (T14.557a16–22), as well as Thurman, *Holy Teaching of Vimalakīrti*, 101. "Motley phrases," *zaju* 雜句, probably means inappropriate use of impure worldly speech.

The *Vimalakīrti* says, "Those fond of motley phrases and rhetorical flourishes most often are bodhisattvas that have only recently given rise to *bodhicitta*." This censure does not make an allowance for outer studies; however, once one advances on the path and reaches a station where all six faculties are purified, then [outer] learning should not pose any problems."

淨名云：「若好雜句文飾者，多是新發意菩薩。」此斥不許習外，且令進行至六根淨位，學應不難。

The multiple positions in these traditional texts were known to some Song exegetes; they reiterated these positions in their own writing and, like Zhiyuan, were also writers of poetry and verse. The basic contours of these positions within the discourse of outer learning were known more broadly among the monastic community of the Song, including within Chan monasteries, through the explanations found in digests and primers. The traditional regulations and justifications outlined above were in the Song more likely known through educational kinds of texts.

Song Monastic Education and Outer Learning

Song-era "rules of purity," or *qinggui* rule books, supported a tradition of norms regarding the monastic uses of literary learning. By the late twelfth century, in public monasteries these *qinggui* had gained an authoritative status "equal to that of the Vinaya," as Foulk writes.[72] The foundational *Rules of Purity for Chan Monasteries* 禪苑清規 (preface dated 1103; hereafter *Chanyuan qinggui*) is the earliest of these standardized rule books for a public monastery.[73] The text was compiled by Chan master Changlu Zongze 長蘆宗賾 (d. 1106).[74] Zongze's initial compilation was completed in 1103, and new editions of the text were printed in 1111 and 1202. A preface to the 1202 edition notes that previous woodblocks had been rubbed so often that the carvings had worn away. The text consists of rules of etiquette for individual monks, procedures for communal rituals, guidelines for transitions in the monastic bureaucracy, rules governing social interactions within the monastery, and sections on relations with the outside world.[75] More than simply prohibitions, a *qinggui* was a "liturgical handbook or ritual manual."[76] Zongze's rule book reflected widespread protocols and then, in turn, became the means by which procedures at public monasteries were further standardized.

72. Foulk, "*Chanyuan qinggui*," 297, where he limits his claim to the Zhejiang area. Foulk, 275–276, notes that the *Chanyuan qinggui* is attested in Japan and Korea by the 13th century.

73. Foulk, "*Chanyuan qinggui*," 284–286, translates the preface and thoughtfully situates it among competing voices of monastic orthopraxy and patronage.

74. For a chronology of Zongze's career, a useful attempt to reconcile the newly available sources is Yang Jun, "Songseng Cijue Zongze xinyan."

75. These categories based on Foulk, "*Chanyuan qinggui*" 289–295.

76. Foulk, *Standard Observances*, 2:23.

The place of verse in Song-era Chan monasticism is visible from this and later *qinggui*. Additional rule books were compiled over the succeeding centuries and evince an ongoing intertextuality.[77] Three more types of *qinggui* texts reveal the strata of monastic society, which was relevant to the role of poetry across these classes of people. *Master Wuliang [Zong]shou's Smaller Rules of Purity for Daily Use* 無量壽禪師日用小清規 (colophon dated 1209), also known as *For the Daily Use of Those Entering the Assembly* 入眾日用, focused on daily life in the general assembly and was addressed to newcomers.[78] Similarly, the *Guidebook for Entering the Assembly* 入眾須知 (dated ca.1263) described numerous daily procedures in a manner that assumes familiarity with the *Chanyuan qinggui*, or ready access to it. A second type of rule book was addressed primarily to monastic officers. Chronologically, the first extant book of this type is *Essentials of the Revised Rules of Purity for Major Monasteries* 叢林校定清規總要 (preface 1274; hereafter *Jiaoding qinggui*) by Jinhua Weimian 金華惟勉 (n.d.). The two-fascicle rule book included model texts one could copy out for rituals and bureaucratic procedures. New editions were produced in 1284 and 1293, suggesting that there was a demand for such a manual.[79] In a similar vein, the ten-fascicle text *Auxiliary Rules of Purity for Chan Monasteries* 禪林備用清規 (completed 1286, published 1311; hereafter *Beiyong qinggui*) by Zeshan Yixian 澤山一式咸 (n.d.) included detailed instructions for the leaders of the monastic bureaucracy.[80] This text, though relatively late, provides detailed explanations of procedures that mirror textual fragments from the Northern Song. A third type of *qinggui* consisted of those supplements for a single monastic community, such as the *Rules of Purity of Huanzhu Hermitage* 幻住庵清規, written by Zhongfeng Mingben in 1317. These later texts borrowed from or directly referenced the *Chanyuan qinggui*. All three types of *qinggui* were interrelated and show the ongoing and widespread influence of this type of prescriptive text across public monasteries from the eleventh to fourteenth centuries.

Within a Song public monastery, three classes of people could have a range of educational needs. Children who lived and worked in a monastery were called *tongxing* 童行 or *tongzi* 童子; I refer to them interchangeably as "acolytes" and "postulants." They might live in a monastery, but postulants were not yet ordained into the novitiate.[81] Though they were forbidden from ordaining before the age of nineteen, we know from life stories of eminent monks that

77. An overview of the extant *qinggui* texts and their position with the genre can be found in Foulk, "*Chanyuan qinggui*," 298–306.

78. *Ruzhong riyong* (ZZ63.556b7) gives the alternate titles and (558c17) has the dated colophon by Zongshou.

79. *Conglin jiaoding qinggui zongyao, Gozan-ban*, 539–540. For more on the relationship between this and other Song and Yuan *qinggui*, see Foulk, "*Chanyuan qinggui*," 302.

80. Foulk, "*Chanyuan qinggui*," 303.

81. On the ambiguity of these terms at this time, see Yifa, *Buddhist Monastic Codes*, 267n9.

this prohibition was not always observed.[82] There were also adult postulants who lived semi-monastic lives and might have become candidates for ordination; they could be called *xingzhe* 行者 or *daozhe* 道者. In practice, these naming conventions varied greatly. In some temples, acolytes lived in a separate "acolyte's hall" 童行堂, where they received instruction appropriate for beginners.[83] These acolytes are distinct from the *shami* 沙彌 (Skt. *śrāmaṇera*), also known as "junior monks" 小僧, which I refer to as "novices." A novice is one who has taken the tonsure and entered the novitiate but has not yet received the complete set of Vinaya precepts. An ordained novice enjoyed the rights and privileges of a member of the Buddhist order, including exemption from taxes and corvée labor. In the Song, another form of address for a novice was "monk" (*seng* 僧), though they had not yet taken the vows of a full ordinant. Full-fledged monks, known as *biqiu* 比丘 (Skt. *bhikṣu*), "senior monk" 大僧 or simply "monk" 僧, were qualified to serve as monastic officers and abbots. Whereas young acolytes might need training in literacy and basic social etiquette, the relatively older novice monks might continue in-depth study, specialized sectarian training, or advanced monastic protocols.

The *Chanyuan qinggui* assumed there were different levels of literacy within the sangha. It provided instructions to the erudite scribe (to which we return later in this chapter), daily rituals to ensure that illiterate newcomers could recite the *Heart Sūtra*,[84] and instructions for students to use a dictionary when they encountered unfamiliar words while in the library reading sūtras.[85] Rules for using the monastery library, per *Chanyuan qinggui*, forbid "placing on [desks] brushes and ink, other miscellaneous objects, as well as Chan texts" 安置筆硯雜物及禪策文字. Such prohibitions might lead us to speculate that students had been bringing Chan texts as well as writing implements into the monastery library. *Chanyuan qinggui* says, "In the dormitory halls you must not recite scripture with a loud voice, nor mixed writings of idleness; at your personal desk space, Chan texts should always be covered and kept neat" 諸寮舍不得高聲讀誦經典並閑雜文字，自己案分禪策文字常蓋齊整.[86] From this we know that young monks could have personal study spaces within a dormitory, and in that personal space they were encouraged to study Chan texts and allowed some unnamed kinds of worldly writing.[87]

---

82. Yü Chün-fang, "Ch'an Education," 80–81. She also offers interesting examples of the diverse educational backgrounds of famous Buddhist monks. Hongzhi was a wunderkind who excelled at Confucian learning and the memorization of poetry. By contrast, Dahui did not begin his formal education until he was thirteen and is said to have thrown an inkwell before leaving the school to join the sangha.

83. An abbot should provide instruction in the Acolyte's Hall after the lecture, per *Chanlin beiyong qinggui* (ZZ63.665c18).

84. *Chanyuan qinggui* (ZZ63.548c15).

85. *Chanyuan qinggui* (ZZ63.532b7); Yifa, *Buddhist Monastic Codes*, 160.

86. *Chanyuan qinggui* (ZZ63.552b11–12); Kagamishima, *Yakuchū Zen'en shingi*, 373–375.

87. *Xianza* 閑雜 often refers to idle gossip, but in *Chanyuan qinggui* it refers to worldly phenomena, such as prohibited sundry goods of a merchant (who is forbidden from entering the dormitory). Zongze's idiosyncratic use of the phrase *xianza wenzi* 閑雜文字 appeared once more

We have few concrete details concerning basic literacy of monks in the Song dynasty.[88] In comparison, Erik Zürcher, having examined Tang manuscript evidence from Dunhuang, concluded that the acquisition of basic literacy relied on repeatedly writing secular primers as well as difficult Buddhist technical terms.[89] It is unclear, however, to what extent these practices in the late-Tang Dunhuang area might have been shared by monks in other regions and during the Song. Yü Chün-fang has translated a surviving fragment from the Yuan-era Chan rule book *Rules of Purity for the Village Temple* 村寺清規 (comp. 1341), which recommended that young monks study the "*jisong* of ancestral teachers" 祖師偈頌.[90] This may have been the purpose of earlier collections such as the Southern Song anthology *Gāthā of Various Patriarchs of the Chan Schools* 禪門諸祖師偈頌.[91] Earlier monastic rule books, for example *For the Daily Use of Those Entering the Assembly* 入眾日用 (colophon dated 1209), are silent on the matter of literary education.[92] To my knowledge, the detailed monastic curricula of Chan monks in the Northern or Southern Song is unknown today.[93]

Indirect evidence of the literary education for acolytes includes the verses generally known as "Admonitions for Young Acolytes" 訓童行.[94] These verses may be found in *yulu* or *qinggui* or survive in later collections. The verses to

---

in a prohibition for newcomers in the dormitory: "You may not hang up painted scrolls, nor display written words of idle impurity" 不得懸掛書畫圖幀及牓貼閑雜文字, *Chanyuan qinggui* (ZZ63.549a8–9); following the variant 幀 for 慎 attested in early medieval editions, per Kagamishima, *Yakuchū Zen'en shingi*, 328–329.

88. I am building on the excellent essay by Yü Chün-fang, "Ch'an Education." Levering, "Dahui Zonggao and Zhang Shangying," 135–139, also expanded on Yü's work and hypothesized about basic literacy and sūtras known by monks and nuns.

89. Zürcher, "Buddhism and Education," 318–330, argues that Buddhist monasteries played a critical role in broader secular education. Local education (*xiangxue*)—before the possibility of moving up to prefectural or county schools—took place at the monastery. He lists primers found in the Dunhuang cache. *Leishu* are the third most numerous kind of text, above *Qianzi wen* and behind only *Lunyu* and *Chunqiu zuo zhuan*. Zürcher, "Buddhism and Education," 328, shows that *Wenxuan* was the only "higher literature" to be used commonly as a primer.

90. Yü Chün-fang, "Ch'an Education," 97–98.

91. On the textual history of editions of this text, see Shiina, "*Zenmon shososhi geju* no bunken-teki kōsatsu."

92. *Ruzhong riyong* (ZZ63.558c14–16).

93. In the early Yuan, per a colophon dated 1286, Chan monasteries were said to teach the "Three Classics of Buddhas and Ancestors" 佛祖三經, consisting of the *Sūtra in Forty-Two Sections* 四十二章經, the *Deathbed Injunction Sūtra* 遺教經, and *Guishan's Admonitions* 溈山警策, each with a commentary by Chan Master Shousui 守遂 (1072–1147). *Guishan jingce zhu* (ZZ.231a15). The 1286 colophon suggests the three texts were used in earlier curricula, but Shiina, "*Busso sangyō chū*," 29, shows that Shousui had promoted sūtra learning in general, and only in 1286 were these three texts singled out and given the moniker "Three Classics." Dan Stevenson communicated to me his knowledge of an extant Southern Song Tiantai curriculum, which I have not been able to access.

94. E.g., *Chanyuan qinggui* (ZZ63.548b4). This fascicle is not included in Yifa, *Buddhist Monastic Codes*. Several additional songs in this genre written during the Song and Yuan are listed in *Zenrin Shōkisen*, fasc. 11.

train acolytes are written in simple and direct language, unlike that in other Chan texts. The following is one example from among the twenty verses collectively titled "Zifu Hymns of Admonition for Young Acolytes" 資福訓童行頌, written by Cishou Huaishen during his first abbatial appointment at Zifu Monastery.[95]

	For a renunciant, words and deeds must be appropriate,	出家言行要相應
2	With constant[96] vigilance, as though walking on thin ice.	戰戰常如履薄冰
	Though you have not yet shaved your face or hair,	雖是未除鬚與髮
4	Straightaway you ought to imitate a monk.	直教去就便如僧

This verse exhorts the young acolyte to begin to talk and act like a monk, exercising caution with every word and deed. Another of Cishou's verses to train young acolytes extols the importance of learning.

	It is essential to study writings as well as to recite sūtras,	也要學書也念經
2	You must clearly discern the mind-ground of a renunciant.	出家心地要分明
	One day you will have a gleaming head and a square robe,	他年圓頂方袍日
4	Every action from moment to moment all self-evident!	事事臨時總現成

Cishou's verses to train acolytes are typical of the genre. The diction is simple, the grammar is straightforward, and the intention is didactic. This sort of churchy children's songs would never have circulated among lettered men. Also for acolytes, Cishou created mnemonics by lodging instructions for etiquette within the honeyed form of rhyming seven-character verse. The rhyme and meter would not only aid memorization but also hopefully shape appropriate deportment and instill values. The ideas in these verses represent the master's ideals for the next generation of young monks. In contrast to those hymns that constituted the daily liturgy, the verses to train acolytes more closely mimicked the quatrains of mainstream poetry. If such verses were in fact used to train acolytes, then these songs may have been among the first Buddhist hymns encountered by some young men in the Song.

Another kind of rhyming primer, extant from the thirteenth century, is represented by the Jin-dynasty *Jade Forest Primer from Chan Gardens* 禪苑蒙求瑤林, a lengthy set of rhyming four-character phrases by Zhiming 志明 (n.d.).[97] Each phrase alludes to one edifying story.[98] A preface written by a scholar in

---

95. Zifu was near the river between modern Yangzhou and Nanjing. The same verses, entitled "Chan Master Cishou's Admonitions for Young Acolytes" 慈受禪師訓童行, later appeared in Ming-era *Zimen jingxun* (T48.1080c18) but in a different sequence.

96. Emending 長如 in the *Taishō* edition with 常如 per *Zimen jingxun* (T48.1081a28).

97. Of the four prefaces in *Chanyuan mengqiu yaolin* (ZZ87.48c9–49a23), the earliest is dated 1225. The extant copy is from a later edition by a disciple of Wansong Xingxiu 萬松行秀 (1166–1246), the Yuan monk Xuetang Delian 雪堂德諫 (n.d.) dated 1255.

98. Later Xuetan Delian added a commentarial apparatus that includes the main text of the tales and a citation to his sources. He cites Song Chan texts including lamp record antholo-

1226 records a conversation with Zhiming in which the former accuses the latter of recording the obvious. The latter responds, "Young children not knowing anything are unable to go on itinerant wanderings; if they can mouth this [primer] from memory, they'll roughly know how to ask for guidance; if so, wouldn't this book be of some aid?" 童稚無識未能參叩，使成誦在口粗知問津，則吾此書不為助.[99] The style of rhyming four-character phrases is in imitation of the Tang *Mengqiu* 蒙求, by Li Han 李瀚 (n.d.).[100] Similar four-character rhyming primers were used in later dynasties, including the undated *Shishi mengqiu* 釋氏蒙求, in which the author's preface suggests that the four-character phrases—each referencing a different story—be chanted and committed to memory.[101]

In practice, these primers were likely adapted and used in various ways. If evidence of such variations at the level of local practice emerge, they may corroborate my argument about monastic literary cultures in the Song. In contrast to these primers for postulants, other works for monastic education address the ordained novice. One such text for novices is *Essential Reading for Buddhist Monks* 釋氏要覽 (hereafter *Shishi yaolan*), an encyclopedic primer compiled during the early Song by the monk Daocheng 道誠 (fl. 1009–1019). Little is known about Daocheng's life and career beyond what can be gleaned from colophons to this text.[102] We know that he had been a sūtra lecturer in the capital, where the court bestowed on him a purple robe, before retreating to Hangzhou. After ten years of reclusion and study, Daocheng finished his primer. Its completion in 1019 coincided with a sudden expansion of the sangha, as Daocheng notes in his preface, because that same year Emperor Zhenzong 真宗 (r. 997–1022) permitted hundreds of thousands of men and women to join Buddhist orders.[103] His *Shishi yaolan* received at least nominal support from Wang Sui 王隨 (973–1039), who added a colophon dated 1024 to accompany a woodblock-print edition.[104]

In his forward to *Shishi yaolan*, Daocheng indicates that he intends the three volumes to serve as a guidebook especially for acolytes (*tongxing*).[105] The text includes definitions for technical terms with numerous classical quotations, excerpts from commentaries, as well as original exposition. Though it was not admitted into the Song canon, the *Shishi yaolan* seems to

---

gies, *Rentian yanmu* 人天眼目, *Chanlin sengbaozhuan*, *Linjian lu*, and *Biyanlu*, giving us a glimpse of what Chan materials circulated in north China under the Jin and Yuan.

99. *Chanyuan mengqiu yaolin* (ZZ87.49a19–20).

100. On the *mengqiu*, see Galambos, "Confucian Education in a Buddhist Environment."

101. *Shishi mengqiu* (ZZ87.227b9–15), based on an Edo-period redaction.

102. Other extant biographic materials are discussed by Fu Shiping in the introduction to *Shishi yaolan jiaozhu*, 1–3, 7–9. See also details in early catalogue entries, *Shishi yaolan jiaozhu*, 591.

103. *Shishi yaolan* (T54.0257c26). *Fozu tongji* (T49.406a26–28) gives precise numbers for this event, recording that 230,127 men and 15,643 women received Buddhist ordination; in addition, 7,811 men and 89 women joined the Daoist order. For more context, see also Ebrey, "Song Government Policy," 84.

104. "Afterword" 後序, *Shishi yaolan* (T54.310b2–17).

105. *Shishi yaolan* (T54.257c20–258a2).

have enjoyed a readership, judging by widespread citations in Chan, Tiantai, and other Song texts.[106] The Southern Song *Jiaoding qinggui* rule book for Chan monastic officers instructed its readers to consult the *Shishi yaolan* for more details on certain matters.[107] Such references indicate that readers were expected to be familiar with the text or that a copy of *Shishi yaolan* was expected to be close at hand.

In addition to the author's stated intention that the book be used for acolytes, there is some evidence that the use of *Shishi yaolan* as an introduction to well-educated monastic life had a long history in monastic education from the Song onward. The Southern Song Tiantai sectarian history *Chronicle of the Buddhas and Ancestors* 佛祖統紀 described the text, then still in notable circulation, as "a guidebook to the rules of the assembly for the benefit of those who would leave home [and join the novitiate]" 為出家者眾法之須知.[108] Over subsequent centuries, the *Shishi yaolan* continued to be used as a primer according to a colophon appended to a new early-Ming edition of the *Shishi yaolan* held in Harvard-Yenching Library. In that colophon, dated 1433, Baocheng 寶誠 (n.d.) writes that "since I received this book as a youth, I have carried it with me for forty years" 自幼得此集，嘗隨身四十年矣. He had begun reading it when a mere acolyte. Colophons to additional reprints indicate *Shishi yaolan*'s ongoing value for the education of novices.[109] Present-day Chinese scholars have documented numerous early modern and modern editions from China and Japan.[110]

Though certainly not a direct reflection of the thinking of every Buddhist monk, the lexical glosses in *Shishi yaolan* would have been widely recognized in the early Song dynasty. Because of its role in the education of future monks, *Shishi yaolan* is a useful place for us to glean a normative view of poetry in the life of a monk. All extant versions of *Shishi yaolan* include a section entitled "Intent on Learning" 志學, which explicitly discusses the matter of monastic education and curriculum.[111] One entry in this section

---

106. For example, *Lebang yigao* (T47.235b26-c5), the Tiantai-inspired Pure Land collection by Zongxiao 宗曉 (1151–1214), defers to the authority of quotations from the *Shishi yaolan*. On Zongxiao and his place in the Song Tiantai and Pure Land projects, see Getz, "Rebirth in the Lotus."

107. *Conglin jiaoding qinggui zongyao* (ZZ63.602a6–8).

108. *Fozu tongji* (T49.406b2–4).

109. The larger volume that includes the early Ming *Shishi yaolan* bears a preface dated 1529 by monk Zonglin 宗林 (n.d.). The 1529 volume reproduces two earlier texts for novices, both sponsored by a monk named Baocheng 寶誠 (fl. 1433). The first text is the *Shishi yaolan*. The second text is a classic primer by Daoxuan entitled *Exhortation on Manners and Etiquette for Novices in Training* 教誡新學比丘行護律儀. Heirman, *Pure Mind in a Clean Body*, 13, 40, 76–78, discusses the contents of Daoxuan's manual. See also Yifa, *Buddhist Monastic Codes*, 26–28, 226n103.

110. See the introduction to *Shishi yaolan jiaozhu*, 3–5, as well as the important book review by Yang Zhifei, "Zhonghua shuju ben *Shishi yaolan jiaozhu* de banben wenti."

111. *Shishi yaolan* (T54.292c24–293a2). The term *zhixue* itself emerges from the *Analects* (*Lunyu* 論語) and is what Confucius did when he was fifteen years of age (吾十有五而志於學).

addresses "the pursuit of outer learning" 開外學.[112] Here, Daocheng quotes the above-discussed passages from *Pinaiye zashi* and *Pusa dichi jing* that portray outer learning as the prerogative of exceptionally intelligent individuals. In this regard, the *Shishi yaolan* must have seemed to Song readers to be conservative in its perspective. Daocheng brought together classical Vinaya and historical examples to exhort young monks of the Song to study literature in the context of their monastic commitments. The *Shishi yaolan* was one vector for the circulation of conservative ideas about the place of literature in monastic education.

Zanning, in his *Great Song Historical Digest of the Buddhist Order* (hereafter *Seng shi lüe*), directly expounded on outer learning. This similarly early Song text offered historical background for contemporary practices. Extant citations to the *Seng shi lüe*—including in Tiantai Zhiyuan's *Chuiyuji* of 1015, *Shishi yaolan* of 1019, and the *Meaning of Terms from Translations* of 1143 mentioned above—attest to the fact that it quickly attracted and maintained a readership. The colophons appended to the extant *Seng shi lüe* demonstrate that the text was well enough regarded to be reprinted in the early Southern Song. The text was also cited as an authority in the Yuan expanded edition of the Chan rule book *Chixiu Chanyuan qinggui*.[113] Perhaps one reason for the popularity of this text is that Zanning wove new ideas together with references to the authoritative texts discussed above. Whatever the reason, the *Seng shi lüe* was an important link in the transmission of ideals of outer learning to Song readers. The passage in *Seng shi lüe*, translated in full below, makes reference early on to the Chinese (Confucian) classics but proceeds by hewing to many kinds of Buddhist literature.[114]

> Our tradition traversed great distances to convey the dharma of three vehicles. Along the way, it has occasionally clashed with demonic obstacles and needed to defend itself. In the arts of defense, nothing is as important as knowing one's enemy. That enemy in the Indic West was [the Brahmanic] Vedas, whereas in the Sinitic East it is the Confucian classics. For this reason, there was a four-Veda cloister within Jetavana monastery[115] [for students] to plumb the principles of the outer paths. Also there [was] a scriptorium collection of texts in all languages of the world, and though the Buddha completely permitted reading these texts

---

This allusion implies only rudimentary literacy in Confucian classics. The contents of this section—with one other exception—cite only Buddhist texts.

112. In his admonishments for *waixue*, and in addition to emphasizing the need for above-average intelligence, Daocheng reiterates that *waixue* is to be limited to "one period" each day. He also paraphrases a passage from Daoxuan's *Zhong Tianzhu Sheweiguo Qihuansi tujing* discussed immediately below as proof of the presence of *waixue* in ancient India.

113. *Chixiu Baizhang qinggui* (T48.1139c29–1140a1).

114. *Seng shi lüe* (T54.240c19–241a5).

115. The fourfold division of the Vedas represents the canon of Brahmanism and here is metonymy for non-Buddhist knowledge. The four divisions are the Ṛg-veda, the Yajur-veda, the Sāma-veda, and the Atharva-veda.

in order to subdue non-Buddhists, he forbade adopting their views.[116] In our country, when virtuous and eminent monks were able to defeat non-Buddhists, it was usually due to vast erudition. Think about the people from [the ancient tribes of] Yi and Di, who did not speak a shared language and did not share customs of food and drink. How could intentions or desires be communicated? By contrast, what about one who knows even some of a foreign language? Immediately he is well understood. That is why monk Dao'an was able to convert Xi Zuochi when using his wit.[117] Huiyuan charmed the likes of Zong Bing 宗炳 and Lei Cizong 雷次宗 using [*The Classic of*] *Poetry* and *Rites*.[118] Fuli softened Quan Wu'er (fl. 681) with the [*Treatise on*] *Resolving Doubts*.[119] And Jiaoran befriended Lu Yu 陸羽 with the *Exempla of Poetry*.[120] The only technique deployed in each of these examples was outer learning.

夫學不厭博，有所不知蓋闕如也。吾宗致遠，以三乘法而運載焉。然或魔障相陵，必須禦侮。禦侮之術，莫若知彼敵情。敵情者，西竺則韋陀，東夏則經籍矣，故祇洹寺中有四韋陀院，外道以為宗極。又有書院，大千界內所有不同文書並集其中，佛俱許讀之，為伏外道，而不許依其見也。此土古德高僧能攝伏異宗者，率由博學之故。譬如夷狄之人，言語不通，飲食不同，孰能達其志通其欲，其或微解胡語，立便馴知矣。是以習鑿齒道安以詼諧而伏之，宗雷之輩慧遠以詩禮而誘之，權無二復禮以辨惑而柔之，陸鴻漸皎然以詩式而友之。此皆不施他術，唯通外學耳。

Zanning reviews the received discourse on outer learning and reimagines authoritative sources. Daoxuan in his *Illustrated Sūtra of the Jetavana Monastery in Śrāvastī, Central India* 中天竺舍衞國祇洹寺圖經 revealed the original Buddhist community at Jetavana to have had a scriptorium for outer learning. Zanning interprets this as justification for situating the Confucian classics as outer learning. He articulates the logic by which outer learning referred to Chinese learning and not non-Buddhist Indian learning. In this passage, Zanning appears unconflicted in his support of outer learning in monastic education, as did Daocheng above. Nonetheless, Zanning's rhetorical posture is defensive, offering justifications and exemptions for generally restricted behavior. Though the subject of outer learning had been updated to suit the

---

116. Zanning likely received this idea from Daoxuan's *Zhong Tianzhu Sheweiguo Qihuansi tujing*; Daoxuan also appended a note to his description of the scriptorium to inform his readers that "the Buddha permitted *bhikṣu*s one period of reading for the sake of subduing non-Buddhists." *Zhong Tianzhu Sheweiguo Qihuansi tujing* (T45.893a29-b2). On the scriptorium, see Zhihui Tan, "Daoxuan's vision," 333–334.

117. This story is in Dao'an's biography in *Gaoseng zhuan* (T50.352b22). For more on Xi Zuochi, see Knechtges and Chang, *Ancient and Early Medieval Chinese Literature*, 2:1428–1432.

118. This story in Huiyuan's biography in *Gaoseng zhuan* (T50.358c18).

119. This story appears in Fuli's biography in *Song gaoseng zhuan* (T50.812c3).

120. This well-known story also appears in Jiaoran's biography in *Song gaoseng zhuan* (T50.892a24).

needs of the early Song, the very idea of outer learning itself perpetuated the spirit of the law from the Vinaya passages above.

One striking quality of the above passage from *Seng shi lüe* is how Zanning discusses *upāya*. While *upāya* is often imagined in terms of a good doctor prescribing proper medicine, Zanning uses martial metaphors of combat. Such confrontational language also appears in Zhiyuan's *Chuiyuji* above as well as in certain Vinaya, leading us to conclude that this sense of *upāya* was generally associated with outer learning in China, at least until the late Ming.[121] Zanning connects this aggressive logic of *upāya* to several examples of famous Chinese monks who expertly deployed humor, Chinese classics, rhetoric, and poetics in order to convert Chinese peers to the Buddhist path.

The unambiguous hierarchical arrangement of Buddhism over Confucian learning promulgated by Zanning here does not easily square with generalizations by modern scholars focused on Zanning's other writings. Albert Welter has written that "appeals for harmony appear in several contexts in Zanning's writings and must be counted as one of the leading characteristics of this thought." Welter has also considered Zanning as one of the so-called Confucian Monks dedicated to Ruist learning who "believed that the complex issues involved in wedding the Buddhist and Confucian traditions could be overcome."[122] Some of Zanning's writings are dense with allusions and Confucian erudition, and these texts support such an interpretation. At the same time, however, the above passage on outer learning suggests that this does not adequately account for Zanning's total oeuvre. We as modern readers may pursue several possible routes to resolve the apparent tension within Zanning's corpus. An argument by biography would suggest that Zanning held different views at different stages of his life; but even within the single text of *Seng shi lüe* we see these conflicting statements. I would suggest that we instead understand the text to be polyvocal, simultaneously addressing multiple rhetorical situations. Zanning received an imperial commission to compile the *Seng shi lüe* shortly after completing the *Song gaoseng zhuan*. He would have known at the time of composition that the text was likely to enjoy a readership among elites of the imperium. Welter has aptly described this aspect of Zanning's work—which we might call apologetics—and thus has focused his analysis on demonstrating that the text "is based on the aim of assuring a role for Buddhism in China."[123] In other words, Zanning's address to the imperial bureaucracy, which might have been heartfelt and sincere, was nevertheless instrumental.[124] On the other hand, if Zanning's project to shape and revitalize Buddhist monasticism at the beginning of the new dynasty

---

121. Bell, "Genuine Anguish," 19–23, 204–213, discusses the late Ming and early Qing transformations away from a focus on expedient means in the discourse of Buddhism and poetry.

122. Welter, "Buddhist Response," 29, 36, based on his reading of Makita, "Sannei to sono jidai," 105.

123. Welter, "Buddhist Response," 36–47.

124. Welter, "Buddhist Ritual and the State," 390–392, offers a thoughtful analysis of how the *Seng shi lüe* is addressed to imperial bureaucracy.

were to be successful, then his audience also needed to include a Buddhist monastic readership. Zanning's passage on outer learning is one such way to address fellow monks.

The above-referenced primers were cited by monks across sectarian identities and were reprinted frequently with colophons attesting to their usefulness. Although more direct evidence of their use in monastic education is limited, these primers appear to have been part of the creation of a broadly shared monastic culture in the Song dynasty. Primers provided clear definitions of outer learning to aspiring students and transmitted the idea that a division separated inner Buddhistic learning from the worldly learning related to literary activities, including poetry.

In addition to encyclopedias and primers, Chan "rules of purity" texts constituted another set of routes for the circulation of the discourse of outer learning within the Chan monastic community. The production of new prescriptive texts demonstrates that Song writers continued to legislate outer learning and that juridical authority referenced but was not limited to classical Vinaya. The *Chanyuan qinggui*, among its rules and procedures, includes instructions for the "temple scribe" 書狀, a monastic officer.[125] The scribe drafted various official and religious documents and composed and calligraphed petitions as well as epistolary correspondence with imperial officials. He was accountable for all aspects of literary composition, including the presentation on paper and the folding of an envelope.[126]

> In addition, he must recognize what [language] is appropriate for superiors as opposed to inferiors, for the pure versus the defiled, for monks as opposed to lay people. He must not wantonly issue a letter, especially if corresponding with a government official.

> 及識尊卑觸淨[127]僧俗所宜。如與官員書信，尤不得妄發。

After many such admonitions, Zongze goes on to describe the virtues of an excellent scribe.

> He should read widely—through ancient and modern correspondence and petitions—so as to be more knowledgeable. If the scribe uses refined and solemn language and follows appropriate forms, then when sent a thousand miles away [his letter] will be radiant to every one of the most erudite of men.[128] He must never

---

125. Also referred to as *shuji* 書記 or *neiji* 內記 in *Chixiu Baizhang qinggui* (T48.1131a12–23). The title "scribal assistant" (*shuzhuang shizhe* 書狀侍者) is used ambiguously, sometimes to refer to the scribe himself and sometimes to an assistant.

126. *Chanyuan qinggui* (ZZ63.532a2–3). Cf. translation in Yifa, *Buddhist Monastic Codes*, 158.

127. Reading *zhuo* 濁 for *chu* 觸, a common substitution in Song texts. See also *Zengaku daijiten*, 763.d. In this context, I think the pair of terms may refer to laypersons who either do or do not keep faith in Buddhism and observe lay practices.

128. *Meimu* 眉目 is a synecdoche for learned men of exceptionally great talent. Translation

intend to wield brush and ink to slight or bully his brothers, however, or otherwise engage in activities not for the buddhadharma. As for Guanxiu and Qiji, they were known merely as poet-monks, while Jia Dao and Tang Huixiu[129] drifted off to become secular officials. How could this be the purpose of "leaving home"?

古今書啟疏詞文字，應須遍覽，以益多聞。若語言典重式度如法，千里眉目一眾光彩。然不得一向事持筆硯輕侮同袍，不將佛法為事。禪月齊已止號詩僧，賈島慧休流離俗窟，豈出家之本意也。

The scribe must learn the literary conventions that allow his epistles to impress learned men. Zongze immediately adds an exhortation to avoid the misuse of these talents and resources. The overall tenor of this Song-dynasty monastic code is similar to the tension animating the legal case found in the classic *Shisong lü* (*Sarvāstivāda-vinaya*) dispensation for outer learning.[130] Both *Chanyuan qinggui* and *Shisong lü* acknowledge that the missionary activity of Buddhist monks is hampered by an absolute prohibition on outer learning. Zongze's emphasis on proselytization is far from the radical attitude toward the inadequacies of language found in some Chan texts.

Still, the above passage by Zongze explicitly names monks famous for their poetry as a matter of opprobrium. Guanxiu and Qiji are imagined as having focused exclusively on poeticizing, while Jia Dao and Tang Huixiu, both monks as young men, renounced their vows and laicized. With these examples Zongze appears concerned that monks who study the literary arts may be tempted to abandon the monastic path. Zongze's own terms question whether such monks understand the meaning of "leaving home" 出家, or ordination, as a monk. Zongze had in mind some religious purpose to ordination that could not be fulfilled by monks who dedicated themselves to poetry.

Finally, prohibitions on poetry were also found in early Chinese meditation texts. Meditation manuals stated that creative writing hindered progress on the spiritual path because an obsession with creativity could be a distraction. One such admonition against creative writing occurs in Zhiyi's abbreviated meditation manual known as the *Xiao zhiguan* 小止觀. Zhiyi enumerates obstruction of three types, body, speech, and thought.[131] Among the dangers

---

modified from Yifa, *Buddhist Monastic Codes*, 158–159. Her notes make several improvements upon Kagamishima, *Zen'on shingi*, 127–129.

129. Kagamishima, *Zen'on shingi*, 127–129, misidentifies Huixiu as the Tang Vinaya specialist Huixiu 慧休. Yifa, *Buddhist Monastic Codes*, 284n78, notes that Huixiu is unlikely to refer to the Vinaya specialist Huixiu, but she does not offer an alternative. Huixiu surely is none other than the early medieval and erstwhile monk Huixiu 惠休, better known as Tang Huixiu 湯惠休 or Tang Xiu 湯休. Tang Huixiu was defrocked and had a lackluster bureaucratic career during the Liu Song dynasty. His love of poetry was often cited as one of the symptoms of his dissatisfaction with cloistered life. At least eleven of his poems survive.

130. *Shisong lü* (T23.274a24-b10).

131. The following translations are based on *Xiuxi zhiguan zuochan fayao* (T46.464b29-c9).

of speech and thought, Zhiyi includes "fondness for [poetic] intoning" 好喜吟咏, "worldly language" 世間語言, "allowing one's feelings to be unrestrained" 心情放逸, and "ruminating on the literary arts" 思惟文藝, all activities that "smash the heart of a monastic" 破出家人心 such that "he is unable to concentrate" 不能定. Without the ability to concentrate, a practitioner will at times behave "like an elephant out of control and drunk [with lust]" 如無鉤醉象. Such is the power of poetry and song. Not only would such practitioners be unable to meditate and make progress on the path, they would be a dangerous nuisance to themselves and others. Perhaps as a performative flourish, Zhiyi illustrated his point with an original Chinese *jisong* that was didactic and notably unpoetic.

Another early Chinese meditation text, *Essential Methods for Curing Chan Sickness* 治禪病祕要法, makes more explicit this same concern over poiesis. This text specifies that it is the pride that comes from creating beautiful sounds that is an impediment to concentration and the important monastic business of meditation.[132] *Essential Methods for Curing Chan Sickness* prescribes a series of macabre and gruesome visualizations as the remedy for overly active literary creativity. In each of the two above meditation manuals, the practice of poetry becomes a deeply ingrained habit that emerges unbidden during inopportune moments of religious practice.

When we consider the above examples, despite some differences among them, we find that all discuss a tension between outer learning and ascetic monastic commitments. Literary activity, including poetry, is understood to be a form of outer learning. In some texts, including Vinaya and *qinggui*, the tension is productive and empowers monks to proselytize. In *Fanwang jing* and Zhanran's commentaries, literary endeavors are an obstacle to be avoided until an advanced stage along the bodhisattva path. Meditation texts likewise describe the troubles of being overly fond of poetry and literary creation. These ideas and phrases found in classical texts reappear in the biographies in *Song gaoseng zhuan* compilation as well as in early Song encyclopedic primers. In these Song examples, we see how scriptural prohibitions and admonishments were reimagined and thus continued to shape how monks in Song China conceived of the relationship between poetry and monasticism. The problem of monastic poetry was not limited to any one sect, style, or lineage, and evidence can be found in formative Chan monastic codes as well as in Tiantai sūtra commentaries.

This tension found in the outer-learning discourse, I believe, was a fundamental substratum for much of the poetry of Song monks. And it may be one reason that Chan monks and their disciples so often insisted that the verses they wrote were *jisong*, especially when writing in *shi* forms, as seen in previous chapters. The next section demonstrates some explicit ways this tension was expressed in poetry.

---

132. For an extended discussion and translation of *Methods for Curing*, see Greene, "Meditation, Repentance, and Visionary Experience," 77, 581–584.

Outer Learning as Poetic Topoi

The poems translated in the rest of this chapter demonstrate that the concept of outer learning was widely known by monks of the Song and its preceding decades and could be an explicit influence on monks' poems. Some of these poems have been studied by scholars of Chinese literature, who have regarded them as evidence of the influence of Buddhism within mainstream literary history. These same poems can also be understood in the context of Buddhist history, such as that outlined above. My goal here is to illustrate interpretations of two topoi grounded in the history of Buddhist monastic education and ascetic values.

The first set of examples of monks' poetry refers to two phrases, "the surplus of *chan*" (*chanyu* 禪餘) and "outside of *chan*" (*chanwai* 禪外). I take these as near synonyms connoting "when not engaged in *chan*." My interpretation is similar to glosses in modern Japanese Buddhist dictionaries, which give *chanyu* as "spare time away from being a monk"[133] and *chanwai* as "one's spare time when not practicing *zen*."[134] These phrases are related to the traditional regulations of outer learning that may occur during the time between monastic activities. Such gaps in the monastic schedule were sometimes referred to as *xianxi* 閑隙 or *xi* 隙.[135] Sengyou 僧祐 (445–518), for example, worked on his catalogue "in gaps between the six periods [of the day]" 六時之隙.[136] The *Song gaoseng zhuan* biography for poet-monk Lingyi 靈一 (727–762), drawing on his funerary inscription, likewise noted that he "at every break from meditation or [sūtra] chanting, immediately would compose poems and songs" 每禪誦之隙，輒賦詩歌.[137] Similarly, the biographies of the poet-monks Guanxiu and Qiji, discussed above, described them turning to poetry during breaks from their monastic occupations. Another term to denote periods of break time was *xia* 暇, as when the *Rules of Purity of Huanzhu Hermitage* refers to "break time between seated meditation and sūtra recitation" 坐禪諷經之暇.[138] Such breaks were another time when poetry was composed. Chan monk Yayu Shaosong, creator of 376 "poems of gathered lines" 集句詩, noted in his preface that "during the break time between *chan* and chanting, for expressing thoughts and feelings, nothing surpasses poetry" 余以禪誦之暇，暢其性情，無出於詩.[139] That so many terms refer to the same concept, a period of free time between monastic activities in which one can pursue additional studies, suggests that it was a common experience in the

---

133. *Bukkyō daijiten*, 1069.

134. *Zengaku daijiten*, 706d.

135. For example, *Fayuan zhulin* (T53.911a17–19).

136. *Chu sanzang jiji* (T55.90b11).

137. *Song gaoseng zhuan* (T50.799b18), and "Inscription for the Pagoda of Vinaya Master Yi at the Yangzhou Qingyun Temple" 唐故揚州慶雲寺律師一公塔銘 by Dugu Ji 獨孤及 (725–777). *Quan Tang wen*, 390/3963.

138. *Huanzhu'an qinggui* (ZZ63.584b13).

139. *Yayu Jiang Zhe jixing jiju shi*, 1a/481.

daily lives of monastics. The terms *chanyu* and *chanwai* appear in texts from
the late Tang and Song but were not especially common;[140] Song lexicons,
such as the *Zuting shiyuan*, did not provide glosses. This relative dearth sug-
gests that *chanyu* and *chanwai* were primarily poetic topoi and not commonly
used in other monastic literature or that the phrases were vernacular terms
well understood and not in need of written exposition.

I do not translate the word *chan* in the following poems because of the
wide-ranging valences used by different writers. The Tiantai monk Zhiyuan
wrote poems in which *chan* clearly refers to meditation and not to the Chan
school. At the same time, as Griffith Foulk has clarified, late Tang and Song
proponents of the Chan lineage often used the word *chan* as a synonym for
Buddha mind or awakening and distinguished this from meditation *per se*.[141]
Chan also sometimes referred to the records of the language used by awak-
ened masters, words with salvific power. In a few cases, references to architec-
ture or material culture provide context that make clear when *chan* explicitly
denoted seated meditation.

In some poems the emphasis is on breaks from *chan* and likely refers by
metonymy to the professional commitments of a monk. This interpretation
is based on the widespread normative depictions of poet-monks composing
poetry in the spare time away from their duties and monastic schedule, as
noted above. Although both *chanyu* and *chanwai* could refer to a time-based
distinction, a more literal gloss of *chanyu* as "the surplus of *chan*" conveys the
sense that poetry is an ancillary activity to the primary claims on a monk's at-
tention.[142] Similarly, a literal gloss on *chanwai* as "outside of *chan*" echoes the
discourse of outer learning. The connotation of both *chanyu* and *chanwai* as
found in poems more often refers to a temporal distinction: those times when
one is not engaged in *chan*. Therefore, the image of *chanwai*/*chanyu* illus-
trated in the poems translated below is homologous to the "one period of
outer learning" found in *Song gaoseng zhuan* biographies, Vinaya, and the ex-
egeses already discussed. Poetry, in other words, is relegated to the gaps
between the rigors of a monastic life.

An example of the place of poetry in a monastic's daily life can be found
in some poems about or addressed to monks by the tenth-century poet-monk
Qiji. In these poems Qiji acknowledges that composing poetry and engaging
in *chan* are distinct occupations that are only occasionally complementary.
In his poem "Thanking Venerable Kezhun of Xichuan for Sending from Afar
His Collected Poems" 謝西川可準上人遠寄詩集, Qiji offers praise with a
couplet alluding to the iconic poetry of the monks Lushan Huiyuan and Zhi
Dun. "That which was outside of walking meditation at the Mount Lu Society,

140. E.g., Hsiao, *Tangdai Shige yu Chanxue*, 192, conveniently lists the numerous Qiji poems
that include *chanyu* or *chanwai*.

141. Foulk, *Histories of Chan*, 94. On the wide-ranging lexical uses of *chan* in the Song, in-
cluding meditation, *prajñā*, the Chan lineage, and bodhi, see Foulk, 5–7 and 93–100.

142. See a similar Song explanation of *ci* as the "surplus of classical poetry" 詩餘 in Owen,
Just a Song, 2.

/ and in the surplus time after meditating at Wozhou [Monastery]" 匡社經
行外，沃洲禪宴餘.[143] Qiji uses "outside" and "surplus" as synonyms to refer
to monks' writing poetry when not engaged with their primary religious oc-
cupations. When writing to Huixian 惠暹 (n.d.), Qiji praises the monk, stating
that "with the surplus after your efforts with sūtras and treatises, then you
endeavor at poetry" 經論功餘更業詩.[144] Qiji echoed the mainstream Buddhist
discourse that relegated poetry to the margins of proper monastic life. Simi-
larly, in an autobiographical poem, Qiji noted that in his life "outside of *chan*,
I searched for poetry's wonders" 禪外求詩妙, suggesting that his primary ac-
tivity was *chan* and poetry a close ancillary.[145] In another poem, Qiji describes
his grief for a fellow monk: "In the surplus [time] after *chan*, I head out to the
Stone Bridge, / my wooden clogs leave traces in [fallen] pine flowers" 禪餘
石橋去，屐齒印松花.[146] As exemplified in these lines, the creation of poetry
during breaks in monastic duties was itself a poetic theme for Qiji.

The above set of poems by Qiji offers an example of how the broader
monastic discourse regarding poetry as an "outer" pursuit influenced an in-
dividual's poetic practice. That poems may be written at the margins of mo-
nastic life was only one of several viewpoints regarding poetry found in Qiji's
works, however. He altered his message depending on his audience and
context. He wrote, for example, to a poet-monk that "the mysteries of *chan*
are without peer; / the wonders of poetry are beyond critique" 禪玄無可並，
詩妙有何評;[147] and to a Chan monk, "after awakening at the Chan barrier,
what is there to doubt? / Since [realizing] the profundity of the *Poetry Stan-
dards*, I no longer rely on others" 禪關悟後寧疑物，詩格玄來不傍人. In both
cases, Qiji suggests that poetry is not an obstacle for the monk who is already
awakened. In works addressed to scholar officials, Qiji asserted a strong
analogy between *chan* and poetry.[148] Many of these statements were addressed
to Zheng Gu 鄭谷 (851?–910?), whom Qiji held in especially high esteem,
and it seems possible that this literary friendship was the primary crucible for
Qiji's novel poetic theory. As several scholars have demonstrated, Qiji's use
of *chan* rhetoric to imagine poetic practices was an original and significant
contribution to mainstream Chinese literature and poetic theory.[149] Similar
analogies between poetry and *chan* continued to enjoy popularity among the
literati of the Song. Such a stance, however, was negated by the writers of

---

143. *Qiji shiji jiaozhu*, 6/323.

144. "Presented to Venerable Huixian" 貽惠暹上人, *Qiji shiji jiaozhu*, 7/397.

145. "On Myself" 自題, *Qiji shiji jiaozhu*, 6/318–19, here in close agreement with Mazanec,
"How Poetry Became Meditation," 138.

146. "Recalling the Monk Huading" 懷華頂道人, *Qiji shiji jiaozhu*, 3/168. A variant reads
"With the surplus after *chan*, I go out onto the bridge" 禪餘橋上去, which does not alter my
argument.

147. "On encountering a poet-monk" 逢詩僧, *Qiji shiji jiaozhu*, 5/242.

148. Here, I depart from Hsiao, *Wenzi Chan*, and Mazanec, "How Poetry Became Medita-
tion," who both commit to Qiji's assertions as affirming a profound unity of poetry and *chan*,
and not a mere analogy.

149. In addition to Hsiao and Mazanec, see Owen, "How Did Buddhism Matter?"

Buddhist monastic normative texts, as when Zongze in *Chanyuan qinggui* singled out and censured Qiji for being "merely a poet-monk."

Moving to Song examples of literary exchanges between another set of monks, we find that poetry was depicted as actively antagonistic to the ideals of monastic serenity, not just temporally separate. The following poem by Baoxian 保暹 (late tenth to early eleventh centuries) makes this division explicit. The poem is entitled "Early Autumn Idle, Sent to Monk Yuzhao" 早秋閒寄宇昭.[150]

	Beneath the open window, my bedding illumined,	窗虛枕簟明
2	I faintly sense that the morning chill broadens.[151]	微覺早涼生
	Deep in the temple no one speaks,	深院無人語
4	But the sound of rain dropping from tall pines.	長松滴雨聲
	Poetry comes, and when I am outside of *chan* I catch it;	詩來禪外得
6	Melancholy intrudes, but in stillness abates.	愁入靜中平
	Afar I recall Xilin [Temple],	遠念西林下
8	Longing mixes with comfort.[152]	相思合慰情

Both Baoxian and Jiangnan Yuzhao 江南宇昭 were among the so-called nine monks of the early Song. The nine monks, who lived in the Jiangnan region, were a motley and loosely confederated group who corresponded frequently and are thought to represent the range of Buddhist identities, including Chan and Tiantai. The poem translated just above is about solitude in early morning. The poet wakes to silence punctuated by the sound of dripping water. The scene is austere. During a morning's first moments, when the author is not engaged in *chan* he finds his mind occupied with poetry that seems to come from outside. When not actively engaged in monastic practice, he can capture some of this language in composition. As he composes, he is filled with sadness, and these feelings then dissipate in the quietude of the monastery. In the final couplet, the poet reveals the source of his poetic urge. He has been thinking of Yuzhao, and memories of his old friend are a source both of pain and of comfort in the quietest hours of the morning. It is nonetheless explicit in Baoxian's poem that poetry is not a part of the monk's professional monasticism; it is literally outside of *chan* that he contemplates and composes poetry. Baoxian further links this poetic inspiration with a sorrow that rises and falls amid his monastic equanimity.

The Northern Song monk Daoqian, who briefly renounced *poiesis* to focus

---

150. *Quan Song shi*, 3:1449. Shaku Seitan, *Hochū Wa-Kan kōsō meishi shinshaku*, 99–111, annotated translations of four *jueju* poems by Baoxian.

151. This couplet echoes the opening of "Traveler's Sentiments" 旅情 by Du Mu 杜牧 (803–852): "Beneath the open window, my bedding covered in rime, / I lay weary and recall Xiaoxiang" 窗虛枕簟涼，寢倦憶瀟湘. *Quan Tang shi*, 525/6015.

152. Xilin Temple presumably is where Yuzhao and Baoxian last met. Biographical information about Yuzhao places him in Jiangnan. I am not aware of evidence to suggest that this Xilin is either of the well-known temples of the same name on Mount Lu or Nanyue.

on monastic training, composed several poems about *chanyu* and *chanwai*. In the second of ten "Poems Matched to the Rhymes of Wenfu's 'Autumn Day on the Lake,' in Six-Word Lines" 次韻聞復湖上秋日六言, Daoqian writes about going for a hike during his breaktime.[153]

	Sometimes, in the surplus after *chan*, I climb up to the top of a peak,	禪餘偶登絶巘
2	Then settle on a rock to rest, yawn, and stretch.	據石聊為欠申
	Tracks and bypaths cannot divide my field of vision;	眼界謾分畦畛
4	Everyone knows the Great Way has no partitions!	誰知大道無鄰

Here, the word *chan* is indeterminate, and it is possible Daoqian used *chan* to refer to daily monastic regimens. Hiking frequently appears in poems about *chanyu* or *chanwai* and sets the scene for a poem amid a natural setting. Daoqian describes a feeling of ease that comes from climbing to a height. Here, he is drawing on a conceit attributed to Confucius, who on Mount Jing with his disciples remarked, "A gentleman without fail will give a recitation when he climbs to a height" 君子登高必賦.[154] Daoqian situates this classically Confucian activity of climbing to a height and poeticizing as a form of outer learning that he pursues when not engaged in Buddhist activities such as *chan*. The second couplet expands the poet's focus to the sprawling countryside below, crisscrossed by roads, paths, and fences. Daoqian takes this patchwork landscape as a metaphor that he then uses to offer instruction to the younger monk, Wenfu. Though the roads below that lead up to the peak are variegated, at the top, one should not focus on the differences between those paths. Daoqian suggests that even when pursuing poetic explorations during one's outer learning, a monk should still bear in mind Buddhist principles. This overcoming of the first couplet's division between *chan* and poetry nonetheless makes poetry subordinate to Buddhist ways of ordering the world.

Daoqian played with similar images in a longer ancient-style poem of nine rhyming couplets entitled "The Far-Reaching Studio (Written for Venerable Yu)" 遠齋為玉上人作.[155] Considering the context, "Far-Reaching Studio" was likely a new studio name that Yu planned to take as a pseudonym. Perhaps a copy of this poem in Daoqian's own hand was intended to be displayed in the studio.[156] Befitting such a text, the poem by Daoqian explores the virtues of this newly selected name (line 11) and praises its suitability for Yu, who embodied "far-reaching visions that stretch from the top of Kunlun to the

---

153. *Canliaozi shiji*, 10.1a; 309–310.

154. A passage from *Han's Outer Commentary on the Odes* 韓詩外傳, ca. mid-2nd c. BCE.

155. *Canliaozi shiji*, 8.3a; 467–468; in two close rhymes, *tuwng* 東 and *tsyowng* 鍾. The subtitle printed in half-sized characters in Song editions.

156. Daoqian was a sought-after calligrapher. Extant examples are discussed in Chap. 2, n. 14 above. Additionally, records of his brushwork done in 1101 and carved near Shaolin Temple include *Luoyang shike ji ji*, 2.45b. On the solicitation of literary interpretations for a studio name, see Yunshuang Zhang, "Porous Privacy," 148.

bottom of the eastern seas." Daoqian did not offer such praise of literary activity without caution, however, and the concluding three couplets of the poem offer the following admonitions.

	Five-thousand scrolls of Indic books came from the west,[157]	西來竺書五千軸
14	I reckon you will spend months and years grinding away [at those books].	期子歲月加磨礱
	[And you can] read *Lisao* or *Chu ci* in a desultory manner,	離騷楚詞亦謾讀
16	Why do diction and decoration need to be well-crafted?	言語糟粕何必工
	Yet, if in the surplus of *chan* you still have karmic habits,	禪餘習氣如未盡
18	From time to time, go lean on a gully rock intoning of wind in the pines.[158]	時倚澗石吟松風

The first of these couplets concerns the reading of Buddhist canonical texts, one possible activity in a writing studio. A pious Buddhist could spend an entire lifetime—perhaps several lifetimes—trying to understand the vast canon. By contrast, the second couplet is about *not* reading literary works. In his Far-Reaching Studio, Yu surely had literary works at hand. Daoqian, however, suggests that the refinement of literary learning, if not understood as an outer pursuit, may be of little use to a monk. This sets up the conclusion in the final couplet, in which Daoqian prods Venerable Yu by referring to the writing of poetry as the result of residual karma.[159] Yu perhaps placed this calligraphy so that he could view it from his reading and writing desk, where he might craft his own lines of poetry. Daoqian's lines would invite the viewer in the studio to consider whether his poetic intoning was an indulgence in what Buddhists considered worldly activity: climbing to heights, leaning against rocks, and singing of wind and pine. The alternative, poetry that participates in the discourse of outer learning, is hinted at as well.

A similar distinction between monasticism and poetry is found in a poem addressed to a monk from a layperson, Gu Feng 顧逢 (fl. late S. Song and

---

157. This number used as a synecdoche for the Buddhist canon. The number derives from a colophon by Zhisheng 智昇 (fl. 730) in *Kaiyuan shi jiao lu* (T55.680b1) indicating that the total number of works in translation to be entered into the Kaiyuan Chinese canon constituted 5,048 scrolls.

158. The soughing or whistling sound of wind among pines was sometimes compared to human whistling and voices. The zither tune "Wind in the Pines" 風入松 was a classic by the time of the Song dynasty. However, the verb "intone [poetry]" (yin) here suggests Daoqian is not directly referring to a zither.

159. Karmic habits (*xiqi* 習氣), or residual karma (*canxi* 殘習), are the present results of previous delusion. Residual karma remains after the affliction itself has ended and is thus distinct from the present active affliction. Residual karma is sometimes used to explain why bad things happen to good people. Here, it is a response to how a monk who has renounced the world would still be attached to poetry. Daoqian, at least, is teasing Yu that as a monk this should be the case.

early Yuan), in the second of two "Poems Presented to the Tattered-Robed Guangchun" 贈廣淳破衣其二.[160]

	Outside of *chan*, you are fond of writing and the brush;	禪外親文墨
2	In recent years you are yet more sentimental.	年來更用情
	After sitting cross-legged beneath three rafters,[161]	三椽趺坐後
4	You spend all morning reading texts aloud.	徹曉讀書聲
	Your broken inkstone is moist by the rain-blown window,	破硯兩窗潤
6	Your solitary lamp is bright under a snow-filled roof.	孤燈雪屋明
	And wishing to visit eminent elders,	更參諸大老
8	You have no need to plan a myriad mountain journeys.	莫計萬山程

Several markers of place and time are given, and the action of the poem occurs at liminal periods in monastic life. The addressee, Guangchun, is envisioned as already done with his perfunctory morning routine of sitting in a meditation hall before he turns to reading secular books (not sūtras). The poet draws a distinction between poetry and *chan*, and this underlies the force of line 2. Guangchun has tended to write poetry with more sentimental lines, and Gu Feng teases him for his devotion to literary writing, which is so intense that he can travel through his books.

Finally, let me return to a tenth-century poem that connected *chanwai* with "poetry demon" that I introduced at the beginning of this chapter. The poem, by Li Zhong, includes the line, "Outside of *chan*, the poetry demon is still strong."[162] In Li Zhong's poem, the Buddhist monk's regular occupation and his fondness for poetry are in a tension. The poetry demon is always lurking, he wrote, and would emerge whenever he took a break from the rigors of daily life.

The Poetry Demon

The poetry demon, or "the Māra of poetry," may be the most evocative expression of the tension between *poiesis* and Buddhist salvation and conveys the sense that poetry firmly belongs to the realm of delusion. *Mo* may be the Chinese word for demon, but it is also the Chinese name of Māra, the tempter, wielder of illusions, and knower of desire.[163] Māra is the antagonist to progress on the Buddhist path. As others have noted, the phrase "poetry demon"

---

160. *Quan Song shi,* 64:40000. There are no biographical records for a monk named Guangchun. Four additional poems by Wu Weixin 吳惟信 (fl. late S. Song), entitled "Presented to Tattered-Robe Guangchun" 贈廣淳破衣 (*Quan Song shi* 59:37066–67), depict a wild and iconoclastic recluse.

161. Taking *san chuan* 三椽 as short for the well-known regulation stipulating the size of a monk's space in the meditation hall, *santiao chuan xia* [*qichi dan qian*] 三條椽下[□□單前].

162. *Quan Tang shi,* 747/8508–8509.

163. On the Chinese character *mo* in early Buddhist texts, see Funayama, *Butten wa dō kanyaku sareta no ka,* 185.

was first used by Tang poets to refer to an intense urge to write poetry.[164] This denotation of a kind of muse continued into the Song among mainstream poets. From its beginnings in mainstream literature, the term "poetry demon" was often associated with natural imagery. I here add a new emphasis on a distinctive additional connotation when monks depicted the poetry demon in their own writing. For Buddhist monks, the poetry demon was an urge to write that obstructed religious pursuits. This was also evident in poems about the poetry demon as an impediment to Daoist religious commitments.[165] The term "poetry demon" was seldom used by Chan monks in the Song, perhaps because they sought to portray themselves as writers of *jisong* and not *shi*. To illustrate how the term intersected with the discourse of outer learning, this section focuses on poems by the aforementioned Qiji, a pre-Song poet-monk (who studied Chan as a young monk),[166] and the early Song Tiantai master Zhiyuan.

The demon of poetry was a Chinese creation, not a canonical demon derived from translated Indic scripture. Writing in the late Ming, Yunqi Zhuhong proposed that the obsession with poetry belonged to the class of "demons of the mind" 心魔, to be distinguished from the "Celestial Lord Māra" 天魔 and his minions, in other words, metaphors for mental processes as opposed to malevolent, independent beings.[167] Earlier discussions of "demons of the mind" developed in Tang exegesis of the ten types of *māra* found in the *Avataṃsakasūtra*. Zhanran, for example, equated "demons of the mind" with "demons of the afflictions" 煩惱魔 (Skt. *kleśa-māra*), one of the classical "four types of *māra*" 四魔 that are ubiquitous across Buddhist traditions.[168] Later, "demons of the mind" were included among the fifty-three types of *māra* in the indigenous Chinese **Śūraṃgamasūtra*.[169] Hsiao Li-hua recently published a convenient survey of references in early Chinese translations of scripture to literary creation as deluded activity, in some texts literally, "the work of Māra" 魔事, and the opposite of "the deeds of a buddha"

---

164. Owen, *End of the Chinese "Middle Ages,"* 118, discusses the "poetry imp." Mazanec, "How Poetry Became Meditation," 130, argues this was part of the *kuyin* discourse of one-upmanship, and not a Buddhist discourse.

165. Poems referencing Daoist religion include "Sending Off a Person Abandoning Office to Enter the Way" 送人棄官入道 by Han Wo 韓偓 (844–923) (*Quan Tang shi*, 680/7797), and "On the Road to Jade Immortal [Abbey]" 玉仙道中 by Yin Wengui 殷文圭 (d. 920?) (*Quan Tang shi*, 707/8135). Thanks to Tom Mazanec for suggesting these references.

166. For a brief biography of Qiji in English, see Mazanec, "Invention of Chinese Buddhist Poetry," 384–387.

167. John Kieschnick, "Literal and Metaphoric Demons in Chinese Buddhism," unpublished paper analyzing a passage from *Yunqi fahui*, fasc. 13 (43.a15–23).

168. *Fuxing* (T46.406c27–407a13). The *simo* 四魔 are *kleśa-māra* of the mind and emotions; the *skandha-māra* of conditioned selfhood and embodiment; the *māra* that is death; and *deva-putra-māra* (*tianzi mo* 天子魔), the lord of the sixth heaven of desire often taken as an objectively existent being and not a metaphor. A *locus classicus* among Chinese sources might be *Da fangdeng daji jing* (T13.105c11–17) or *Dazhi dulun* (T25.458c3–6). Thanks to Dan Stevenson for suggesting these references.

169. *Shoulengyan jing* (T19.151c28–153b3).

佛事 that lead to liberation.[170] She concluded that this attitude toward literary activity found in scripture, especially in *prajñāpāramitā* texts, can also be found in early Chan texts.

In contrast to these canonical exegeses of *māra*, the cultural history of the "poetry demon" developed outside scripture. The vices were nonetheless real, however. When the poetry demon is mentioned together with other impediments, the reference most often is to the "demons of sleep" 睡魔 and "demons of drink" 酒魔. The "demons of sleep," or drowsiness, are most often referenced together with tea, its medicinal cure. In a light-hearted poem "Thanking Venerable Ren for the Gift of Tea" 謝仁上人惠茶, Zhiyuan suggests that "although [this gift of tea] may have some effect to dispel the demon of drowsiness, / contrarily it may invite the poetry demon right before my eyes" 睡魔遣得雖相感，翻引詩魔來眼前.[171] Such an ambiguous attitude toward this demon is reflected in the poems of many who took pleasure in poetry.

The earliest explicit reference to a poetry demon is probably in the writing of Bai Juyi, where it seems to be a source of pride for the poet.[172] In later dynasties, Bai's demons were surely the best known, and none better than the demon of "Idle Intoning" 閒吟.[173]

	As I diligently studied teachings from the gates of emptiness,	自從苦學空門法
2	I dispelled lifelong [habits of] thought of many kinds.	銷盡平生種種心
	Only the demon of poetry is not yet vanquished,	唯有詩魔降未得
4	Every encounter with wind or moon leads to idle intoning.	每逢風月一閒吟

In this poem about poetry, Bai Juyi savors his love of verse. He cannot help himself when he happens upon a poetic scene. This deeply rooted habit seems to be indomitable, but the poet is describing a pleasurable inspiration. Bai compares this "demon of poetry" with other states of mind. He knew that "thoughts of many kinds," a common term with a Buddhist tenor, could succumb to the wisdom of the teachings of emptiness, but he is not to my knowledge alluding in this poem to a particular scripture. Instead, Bai weaves this novel Chinese demon together with generic Buddhist language.

Bai elaborated on the demonic aspect of literature in other writings. In a late poem he explicitly compares his ability to successfully quit drinking with his inability to stop composing poetry. Entitled "Sending a Poem To Be Inscribed on a Wall of My Old Cottage on Mount Lu, and To Be Shown to the Monks of the Two [East and West] Forest Temples" 寄題廬山舊草堂，兼呈二林寺道侶, the poem is thought to have been written in 841, after Bai took

---

170. Hsiao, *Wenzi chan*, 17–21 and 26–28.

171. *Xianju bian* (ZZ56.934b21–24).

172. The same demon of poetry also appears in works by Bai's near contemporaries, Liu Yuxi 劉禹錫 (772–842) and Yao He 姚合 (ca. 779–ca. 849). Owen, *End of the Chinese "Middle Ages,"* 118, discusses possession by the "poetry imp" as a source of pride.

173. Modified from Watson, *Life and Times of Po Chü-i*, 88; see also Yang, *Chan Interpretations*, 179–180.

ill. In it, he contemplates the passage of time since he last lived in his cottage, thirty years prior, with this significant couplet.[174]

I have gradually vanquished the demon of wine, and do not get wildly drunk;	漸伏酒魔休放醉
2　But the karma of words remains; I have not abandoned verse.	猶殘口業未拋詩

Bai Juyi also developed this idea in a lengthy and well-studied epistle known as "A letter to Yuan Zhen" 與元九書.[175] Some medieval Japanese readers reinterpreted Bai's works as establishing a resolution of the tension between poetry and Buddhism; however, there is no evidence that historical Chinese writers read it this way. I would argue that Bai was writing directly along the fault lines, giving poetic names to the unresolved tension between the profane urge to make beautiful language and ineffable liberation.

From the late Tang into the tenth century, the notion of the demon of poetry continued to circulate among poets. It is perhaps not surprising that the most interesting depictions of the poetry demon are in poems by the two poet-monks Guanxiu and Qiji.[176] Of the two, Qiji seems to have developed the idea more richly.[177] In the poem "Fondness for Intoning" 愛吟, for example, Qiji uses poetry demon to refer playfully to poetic rumination.[178]

Just as I am about to still my thoughts and retreat within the gates of *chan*,	正堪凝思掩禪扃
2　Once again the demon of poetry afflicts this monk.[179]	又被詩魔惱竺卿
I lean by the window to chase the evening light,	偶憑窗扉從落照
4　Unable to sleep through snowy gusts until the hour before dawn.	不眠風雪到殘更
Jiaoran was not necessarily deluded by his residual karma;	皎然未必迷前習
6　Zhi Dun, how could he not have known his future births?	支遁寧非悟後生

---

174. *Bai Juyi ji* 35/804. Adapted from Waley, *Life and Times of Po Chu-i*, 207, and LaFleur, *Karma of Words*, viii.

175. See Waley, *Life and Times of Po Chu-i*, 107.

176. For an example by Guanxiu, see *Guanxiu geshi xinian jianzhu*, 2.524–525. A Japanese translation in Kobayashi, *Zengetsu Daishi*, 54–55.

177. Hsiao, *Tangdai Shige yu Chanxue*, 86–92, assumes that Qiji had a monolithic artistic vision in which he resolved any contradictions between poetry and Chan. In contrast, I think Qiji sometimes wrote poems about the conflict between poetry and Chan.

178. *Qiji shiji jiaozhu*, 7/385–386. My interpretation responds to how this poem is treated by literary scholars. Cf. Mazanec, "Invention of Chinese Buddhist Poetry," 297–298, and Mazanec, "How Poetry Became Meditation," 129–130.

179. The phrase *zhu qing* 竺卿 is an eloquent reference to "a monastic official." Following *Qiji shiji jiaozhu*, the line refers to Qiji himself. For a similar example by Guanxiu, see *Guanxiu geshi xinian jianzhu*, 497n2.

As I copy out their writing, they meet a fine mirror   傳寫會逢精鑒者
8   Who ought to know these are [just] songs of idle   也應知是詠閒情
    sentiments.

This poem depicts poetry as a disturbance to the monk's serenity, even though
he ultimately finds it to be a worthwhile worldly pursuit. This is reflected in
the poem's title, where "fondness," *ai* 愛, could also be read as "desire" and
a cause of suffering. Elsewhere, Qiji used the same word, *ai,* to refer to finding
intense pleasure in poetry.[180] Though the term is multivalent, his fondness in
this poem becomes a demon that "afflicts" him with *nao* 惱, a common Bud-
dhist term for karmic vexation. Unlike poems that depict composition during
a monk's free time "outside of *chan*," this poem is on the cusp of concentra-
tion. Qiji was about to meditate when he was struck by a poetry demon. As he
grew restless and bothered, he spent the night gazing at poetic scenes outside.
Unable to sleep, he wondered about famous monks from history. Qiji knew
of the reputation of Jiaoran and Zhi Dun as exemplary poet-monks, but he
here seems to be anticipating or responding to a common critique that these
monks were too interested in poetry and not sufficiently focused on Buddhist
learning. As seen above, such critiques could be deflected by alluding to outer
learning. If we take seriously Qiji's Buddhist learning, which I think we should,
this poem clearly states a tension. Qiji at first describes feeling afflicted by an
incessant urge to write poetry that interrupts his monastic routine. In the end,
he concludes that he, and perhaps any critics, ought to know that great Bud-
dhist monks have often delighted in the pleasures of idleness with a song.

In the mainstream poetic tradition, "idleness" was associated positively
with reclusion and conveyed an ideal disengagement from duties of the world.
This is likely how Qiji used the word in his poem "Fondness for Intoning,"
which I translated above. In Song writing by Chan monks, idleness had an
ambiguous status, however. In some Song texts, "idle sentiments" could have
an additional connotation similar to the "feelings not yet forgotten" discussed
in the previous chapter and could be regarded with suspicion.[181] This ambi-
guity is seen, for example, within the works of Chan monk Wuwen Daocan
無文道璨 (1213–1271), who wrote of the pleasures of idle periods in a mon-
astery when he could read poetic classics like *Songs of Chu* and compose
poems.[182] In other poems, however, Daocan still aspired to "completely sweep
away my lust for the written word, / so the clouds may part and I can behold
the azure sky" 盡掃文字淫，披雲覩青天.[183] Idleness was a difficult practice,

---

180. E.g., "Listening to Snow during Evening Sitting, Sent to Someone Who Understands"
夜坐聞雪寄所知. *Qiji shiji jiaozhu,* 5/274.

181. For two late Northern Song examples, see the didactic verse in *Chanmen zhu zushi
jisong* (ZZ66.733c4) and the more playful verse in *Yuanwu Foguo chanshi yulu* (T47.805c5–7).

182. Huang Ch'i-chiang, *Wuwen Yin,* 53–61, discusses Daocan's poems of idleness as well as
the fascinating topic of Daocan's complex sense of longing and nostalgia for his childhood home.

183. "Responding to Tang Bojin" 和湯提幹(伯晉), *Wuwen Yin,* 1.10a; following analysis in
Huang Ch'i-chiang, *Wuwen Yin,* 95–97.

and the habits of a literary mind could readily become an impediment to liberation. The phrase "a lust for written words" (*wenzi yin* 文字淫) was coined by literary monk Juzhou Baotan 橘洲寶曇 (1129–1197). He once wrote to a layman that "whether rising or falling, your thoughts are of the Way; / you've cleansed away your lust for the written word" 俯仰道德意，祓除文字淫.[184] Poetry need not ultimately be abandoned, but to be overly fond of making or consuming poetry could be an obstacle on the path.

Like Qiji, the monk Zhiyuan—whose poem provided the inspiration for this book's title—wrote of a similar disruption to meditation in the "Poetry Demon," a translation of which appears at the beginning of this book's introduction.[185] Zhiyuan offers the poetry demon as a metaphor for an obsessive tendency toward poetic thoughts that afflicts the monk who is so enamored with his ruminating mind that he is unable to remain in meditative concentration. Lines of poetry and fragments of phrases are as demonic minions that will not leave the monk in peace. There is no doubt that Zhiyuan was well aware of the appropriate and inappropriate uses of outer learning, as he himself wrote in his *Vimalakīrtinirdeśa* commentary. "Monks today have forgotten their [appropriate] roots and chase only the branches; though they look like ascetics, they have turned their backs on studying Buddhism."[186] Although the poem itself may be a playful description of Zhiyuan's own fondness for poetry, it also clearly states a perceived tension between aesthetic pursuits and ascetic practices.

Qiji elsewhere uses the image of the poetry demon to refer to literary inspiration without religious value. The unending turnings of the mind are subtle vexations. In the poem "Quiet Sitting" 靜坐, he asserts that he would use meditation to render them silent.[187]

	Day after day I just laze about,	日日只騰騰
2	So what is it that stimulates the machinery of thought?	心機何以興
	The poetry demon causes suffering with no profit,	詩魔苦不利
4	Then the silence of meditation is fit to respond.	禪寂頗相應
	My inkstone completely speckled with dust,	硯滿塵埃點
6	My robes wrinkled from sitting and reclining;	衣多坐臥稜
	In this way, I refresh myself	如斯自消息
8	As befits a monk of idleness.	合是箇閑僧

An obsession with poetry leads to an unending procession of thoughts that have no religious benefit. Qiji's first couplet plays with a poem by Sikong Tu

---

184. *Juzhou wenji*, 3.13b-14a; and once more when referring to Su Shi's dream of a poem by Daoqian, *Juzhou wenji* 1.6a-b; analyzed in Huang Ch'i-chiang, *Yiwei Chan*, 128–130.

185. *Xianju bian* (ZZ56.934a24-b2).

186. *Chuiyuji* (T38.761a25-b9).

187. *Qiji shiji jiaozhu*, 3/169. Taking in line 8 the variant 僧 in lieu of 生.

司空圖 (837–908) that depicts a monk sauntering about lost in thought.[188] The poem is about a contrast between seated contemplation and poetry.[189] The silence of meditative practice is juxtaposed to the noise of poetry (recall that poems were intoned and recited). A step further would propose poetic thought as deluded mental activity, which the monk's practice of nonactivity can quell. The quiet mind is a respite from poetic obsession. Qiji elaborates on this theme at the end of another poem, "Sent to Minister Zheng Gu" 寄鄭谷郎中.[190]

	You still must laugh at me, for when not taming my heart	還應笑我降心外
8	I provoke the poetry demon who aids the false Buddha-Māra.[191]	惹得詩魔助佛魔

Qiji insists that we, like Zheng Gu, laugh at him. Even though he knows better, he cannot help but provoke the demon. He simply must write poetry.

In the above examples, Qiji invokes the poetry demon to describe a rift between Buddhist piety and the inner mechanisms of literary creativity. Elsewhere, he explores different views on the relationship between Buddhism and poetry. For example, he writes, "If the nature of the Way is accommodating like water, / then poetic feelings coalesce like ice" 道性宜如水，詩情合似冰.[192] This nicely depicts the relationship between religion and poetry as like a state of transformation from liquid to crystal. In another poem, Qiji suggests a more non-dualistic understanding: "Sitting, lying, walking, and standing, / I enter meditation, still intoning" 坐臥與行住，入禪還出吟.[193] In his voluminous writings, Qiji explored manifold relationships between poetry and Buddhism, including the fundamental tension between literary inspiration and monastic occupation.

Qiji's standing as a poet suffered during the Song dynasty. Ye Mengde, for example, wrote that a "monastic style" 僧體 of poetry reached its apogee with earlier Tang-era poet-monks and "deteriorated unto the likes of Guanxiu

---

188. *Bodong* 柏東. *Sikong Biaosheng shi wen ji jian jiao*, 115.

189. The phrase "silence of *chan*" (with a lower case 'c') refers to meditation, not the Chan school.

190. *Qiji shiji jiaozhu*, 8/415. Mazanec, "Invention of Chinese Buddhist Poetry," 329, followed by Owen, "How Did Buddhism Matter?" 402, each translated another poem Qiji sent to Zheng Gu.

191. In canonical literature, *fo mo* often is two nouns, "buddha" and "māra," frequently meaning awakening and delusion. Reading *fo mo* as a single noun "Buddha-Māra," or "regarding Māra as the Buddha," is also widely attested in medieval Buddhist literature. Expanding on this connotation, *Bukkyō go daijiten*, 1198c, glosses *fo mo* as 'seeking the Buddha outside oneself.' See also *Zengaku daijiten*, 1093.

192. "Encouragement for a poet-monk" 勉詩僧. Owen, "How Did Buddhism Matter?" 401, analyzes how the imagery here is "both contrastive yet asserting an identity underneath." This and additional texts were earlier foregrounded by Hsiao, *Tangdai Shige yu Chanxue*, 182–196, and Sun, *Chansi yu shiqing*, 324–328.

193. "Sitting in Stillness" 靜坐, *Qiji shiji jiao zhu*, 3/143. Translation follows Mazanec, "How Poetry Became Meditation," 144.

and Qiji, whose poems are extant but not worth talking about" 陵遲至貫休、齊已之徒，其詩雖存，然無足言矣.[194] Even though the reputation of Qiji's poetry was rehabilitated some centuries later in the early Qing dynasty, a period of shifting attitudes toward poet-monks,[195] his writing and innovations with regard to Chinese Buddhist poetry seem to have had little impact on Song-era Buddhist monasticism. Although largely an argument *ex silencio*, it is significant that the poetry of Qiji and Guanxiu was criticized in prescriptive writing by Song Buddhist monks. As shown above, Zongze chastened monastic scribes against poeticizing with the warning that "Guanxiu and Qiji were known merely as poet-monks, while Jia Dao and Tang Huixiu drifted off to become secular officials." A similar judgment was conveyed by Wansong Xingxiu 萬松行秀 (1166–1246) based on the legendary understanding that the two monks studied with the late-Tang Chan master Shishuang Qingzhu 石霜慶諸 (d. 888). Wansong wrote that "at that time, Qiji, Guanxiu, and Xuantai all used poetic writing to do Buddhist deeds, but only Xuantai had awakened to [Buddha] mind and was entered into the chart of ancestral masters" 時齊己、貫休、泰布衲等以詩筆為佛事，唯泰布衲悟心，入祖師圖.[196] From this, it appears that Guanxiu and Qiji were not regarded as awakened Chan teachers, and so their writing was merely poetry. It is ironic, then, that Song Buddhist monks cited Qiji as correct when distinguishing Chinese *jisong:* "Although the form may be the same as poetry, the aim is not that of poetry" 雖體同於詩，厥旨非詩也.[197]

The poetry demon first appeared in the writings of mainstream poets to depict a sudden and intense inspiration. Late-Tang monks then wrote of their obsession with poetry in the context of Buddhist monasticism; they depicted a tension between poetry and monkhood. Among monks of the early Song, too, the poetry demon would interrupt daily practices and meditation. Soon after the advent of the Song, the phrase "poetry demon" fell out of use among monks. Productive tensions between monastic norms regulating literary learning and the poetic practices of individual monks nonetheless continued to shape Song monastic literary cultures.

Coda

Discussions in prescriptive Buddhist literature about the place of mainstream poetry in the lives of monks—distinct from religious verse—presented poetry

---

194. *Shilin shihua*, 1.31a-b. A complete translation in Protass, "Buddhist Monks and Chinese Poetry," 136–138.

195. The literary reception of Qiji described in Mazanec, "Invention of Chinese Buddhist Poetry," 360–361.

196. *Wansong laoren pingchang Tiantong Jue heshang niangu qingyi lu* (ZZ67.467c11–12). For more about the historical veracity of this tale, see Protass, "Buddhist Monks and Chinese Poetry," 42–43n93, and Mazanec, "Invention of Chinese Buddhist Poetry," 353–354.

197. *Chanmen zhu zushi jisong* (ZZ66.726c9), the previously discussed preface to Longya's verses.

as both *kleśa* and *upāya*. When poetry is thought of as *upāya*, it represents a dispensation for the purposes of proselytization; when poetry is thought of as *kleśa*, it is an exhortation to ascetic practice. In either formulation, poetry is subsumed within a Buddhist worldview and situated as outer learning. Note that its status as outer learning does not mean that monks could not or did not write poetry. Rather, monks were admonished against composing poetry if they did not possess sharp intelligence, a good memory, and a capacity to resist the pleasures of writing. The obsession over clever couplets and rhymes was depicted as residual karma, or a lingering literary habit.

Although writers in the Song regarded as "classical" or "ancient" scriptural references that relegated outer learning to a portion of the daily monastic regimen, outer learning was nevertheless embedded in numerous normative texts and across sects and schools of Song-dynasty Buddhism. These newly composed texts renewed the discourse in which Chinese mainstream poetry was adventitious to the Buddhist monastic path of liberation. Monkish poets responded to this canonical idea by inscribing their spare time within their verse. They could thereby also describe poetry as a forbidden pleasure and refer to visits from the muse in terms of vexations caused by Māra.

This chapter has moved from canonical Buddhist ideas about the dangers of poetry to individual monks' poems that deliberately tested the boundary between worldly arts and Buddhist principles. I hope, by gradually shifting across these registers of discourse, to have surveyed the contours of monastic literary culture and illuminated some points of contact between Buddhist normative literature and individually authored works of Buddhist verse. By understanding the religious and literary norms that shaped monastic verse culture, we can find meaningful ways to study this relatively unexplored body of sources. The connections between normative literature and individual poems will continue to occupy us in the coming chapters.

PART THREE

Monks and Literary Sociality

5

Parting Poetry

THIS BOOK'S third part explores monks' participation in two prominent modes of poetry found in extant Song collections. Poems of parting, discussed in this chapter, and elegiac lamentations (in Chapter 6) are among the most conservative and venerated types of occasional verse in the Chinese literary tradition. They both played major roles in literary exchange and poetic affirmations of sociality. The poems in these two chapters closely resemble mainstream poetry. By composing poems such as these, monks more directly took part in the literary tradition than they did in their didactic verse such as encomia on paintings or "eulogizing the old [precedents]" (*songgu*). Poems of parting and lamentation are therefore useful for revealing how ideas in Buddhist normative texts, discussed in previous chapters, formed a productive tension when put into practice.

As will be explored in this and the following chapter, poems of departure and mourning raise questions about *qing* 情, "emotion," especially the emotion of sorrow. The early history of the term *qing* remains the subject of a debate that dates back to classical times. Already in several classical texts it is referred to as a personal or internal response to a situation and is associated with concepts like "aversion and desire, joy and anger, sorrow and delight" 惡欲喜怒哀樂.[1] Chinese theories of poetry found in texts from classical to medieval times debate the nature of these affective responses to the world and their relationship to the composition of poetry.[2] By the Song dynasty, all of the mainstream traditions of poetics shared a focus on the pivotal role of *qing*. Writing about Su Shi, Ronald Egan has noted that "the belief that the emotions (*qing*) are fundamental and intrinsic to poetry was too well established for the question [of their role in Su Shi's poems] to go unasked [by contemporary Song-era critics]."[3] *Qing* are elemental to Chinese poetry.

In contrast to its pre-Buddhist meanings and poetic uses, this same word, *qing,* in Buddhist texts generally refers to mental activities of the ordinary

---

1. Eifring, "Emotions and Conceptual History," 29, compares this list from Zhuangzi with other similar classical texts. The essays in this volume are a good starting point for the voluminous writing about *qing.*

2. On shifts in early medieval theory, illustrated by Lu Ji, see Owen, *Readings in Chinese Literary Thought,* 73-181 passim.

3. Ronald Egan, *Word, Image, and Deed,* 197, with reference to the earlier discussion on 179n31.

deluded mind, or deluded feelings.[4] In Chinese Buddhist usage, the word *qing* most often appears in a compound meaning literally "[those] possessing *qing*" 有情, that is, "sentient (i.e., feeling) beings," a term that does not refer directly to the emotions *per se*. But as Christoph Anderl has observed in his study of the Chan text *Zutangji* that "very rarely [the Buddhist word] *qing* is modified in a way that makes it into a positive concept." Affective responses, whether pleasant or painful, are generally regarded as hindrances to Buddhist liberation. *Qing* from this perspective distorts one's view of the world and often leads to further suffering. Emotions are not to be celebrated. If *qing* are fundamental to Chinese poetry, then what did Buddhist monks do with their poems of parting?

When considering emotions in the poetry of Chinese Buddhist monks, the distinctions drawn by Philip Fisher between "occasioned" and "dispositional passions" in Western traditions may serve as useful comparisons. Emotional responses to events, that is, occasioned responses, are different from character traits, which are dispositional. The former, according to Fisher, are "strong, coarse, or violent states," while the latter are "settled, persistent, and temperamental facts."[5] One-time events, like grief at an unexpected death, differ from underlying inclinations such as ambition or avarice. To generalize, Buddhist tradition understands eruptive emotions like anger to arise from dispositions such as hatred; each eruption further re-inscribes those deep-rooted ways of being, making them more likely to reoccur in the future. Buddhist texts do promote particular affective states for enabling restraint or inspiring devotion, but Buddhist monastic literature generally is skeptical of ordinary emotions, regarding them as unwholesome.[6] Releasing the grip of the passions is part of progress toward liberation. Poetry gives voice to *qing* and makes more likely a passionate response again in the future. We have already seen how Song monks expressed this idea in terms of karma: the writing of poetry is the result of residual karma; karmic habits are hard to forget.

The poems we will look at in this chapter were written by monks and addressed to fellow monks. From these examples we see practices by which the monastic community addressed itself in verse form, partly in response to the ritual contexts of monastic parting. One of my primary goals in this chapter is to read monks' parting poems for the way they subvert the conventions of the broad genre of Chinese parting poetry. One could go so far as to assert that "Buddhist parting poetry" constitutes its own subgenre. I am not, however, proposing genre analysis as a matter of mere classification or of a clarification of affinities.[7] My analysis is not about pigeonholes as much as about pigeons.[8]

---

4. Anderl, "Semantics of *Qing*," 149–150, hereafter also drawing on 152–157 and 163–166; with reference to Harbsmeier, "Semantics of *Qing*."

5. Fisher, *Vehement Passions,* 18–27.

6. Scheible, *Reading the Mahāvamsa,* 3–6, discusses wholesome affective states as "highly prized Buddhist emotions" that transform the hearer-reader.

7. As suggested in Frye, *Anatomy of Criticism,* 247–248.

8. The indelible metaphor of pigeons and pigeonholes from Fowler, *Kinds of Literature,* 37.

To this end, Carol Newsom has observed that "texts do not 'belong' to genres so much as participate in them, invoke them, gesture to them, play in and out of them, and in so doing continually change them." Newsom concludes that "the point is not simply to identify a genre in which a text participates, but to analyze that participation in terms of the rhetorical strategies of the text."[9] This way of reading emphasizes differences as deliberate decisions. To approach monastic parting poetry in this way means analyzing individual works as the product of a negotiation of literary, social, historical, and Buddhological contexts. In that case, I begin with the literary contexts in which monks wrote their parting poetry and then move on to the ritual contexts particular to monks. I conclude this chapter with close readings of individual parting poems.

Parting Poems in Song Literature

Parting poetry was a well-established social and literary phenomenon in China throughout imperial times.[10] Often known as *songbie shi* 送別詩, *songxing shi* 送行詩, or *zengbie shi* 贈別詩, these poems were frequently written on occasions of parting from friends, close associates, and family.[11] Like the *propemptikon*, Chinese parting poems offer benedictions for safe and successful travel. They also usually express melancholy.

Some of the earliest Chinese poetry is about separation. In the anonymous collection of lyrics known as *Nineteen Old Poems* 古詩十九首, the first verse, often taken to be in the voice of a woman longing for her husband traveling far from home, begins, "Wandering and wandering, again wandering and wandering" 行行重行行.[12] The anthologized "parting banquet" 祖餞 poetry of the Six Dynasties may have offered important precedents for the exchange of farewell poetry. Zeb Raft has thoughtfully written on the latter as a kind of functional verse, stating that "the banquet is not itself a point of focus in such banquet poems. Rather, the parting scene is present as a fulcrum for the elevation of a few carefully chosen words . . . that may shape memories of the past and influence relationships of the future. The poem, presumably presented in its author's calligraphy, becomes a talisman consecrated at the parting ceremony."[13] These aspects of parting poetry visible already in the Six Dynasties are similar to the culture of parting poetry of the Song.

I turn now to prescriptive texts by preeminent and aspiring literati intended to instruct their contemporary readers on the contours of genres and

9. Newsom, *Book of Job,* 12.

10. Matsubara, *Chūgoku ribetsu shi no seiritsu,* surveys the origins of parting poetry from the Six Dynasties to the High Tang.

11. Cai Lingwan, "Sheng Tang songbie shi de shenmei neihan," 27–32.

12. A comprehensive bibliography of translations and scholarly studies of *Nineteen Old Poems* in Knechtges and Chang, *Ancient and Early Medieval Chinese Literature,* 1:289–292.

13. Raft, "The Space of Separation," 278–279, discusses *zujian* poems in the context of "letter poems," or poems sent from afar.

norms. A kind of Song-era literary criticism known collectively as *shihua* 詩話, "remarks on poetry," became increasingly popular after Ouyang Xiu composed *Remarks on Poetry from the Retired Scholar with Six Single Things* 六一詩話.[14] In this foundational work, rather than propose general theories of literature, Ouyang crafted seemingly desultory comments on topics once regarded as banal. Within only a few generations, *shihua* developed, as Ronald Egan writes, into "the principal vehicle for the adjudication of literary standards and taste, to which scores of critics avidly devoted themselves."[15] *Shihua* of the Song dynasty reveal the contemporary expectations against which monks' parting poems were written.

Shihua do not only describe exemplary poems, they also prescribe models for how poetry ought to be written. Later *shihua* often were organized by topic. Several dedicate entire sections to parting poetry. For example, in *Jade Chips of the Poets* 詩人玉屑, Wei Qingzhi 魏慶之 (fl. 1240–1244) used the header *songbie* 送別, "sending off," to enumerate ten exemplary couplets from the Tang dynasty. *Songbie* poems are not distinguished by literary form. They are, rather, a mode recognized by topic as well as the circumstance of production, often noted in a title or prefatory note. *Jade Chips* includes a couplet from a poem by Han Yu addressed to Wang Zhongshu 王仲舒 (762–823).[16]

A man sobs as he recalls your favor;	人由戀德泣
4 A horse, too, whinnies when leaving the herd.	馬亦別羣鳴

Sadness in this couplet is emphasized as the natural response to parting. Though *Jade Chips* only gives these two lines, any learned person would know, or could easily look up, that the poem concludes as follows:

The cold sun at twilight has begun to glow,	寒日夕始照
6 The squally river in the distance grows gradually peaceful.	風江遠漸平
Quiet, none say a word,	默然都不語
8 I reckon they know the feelings of this moment.	應識此時情

The poet is surrounded by transient phenomena of the natural world moving away from him in near silence. Han's poem projects on the physical topography his inner world of melancholy.

The following couplet by Chen Tao 陳陶 (9th c.), from his poem "Pre-

---

14. Five single things are his books, his collection of inscriptions, and his zither, chess set, and wine jug. These five plus one old drunkard (himself) made six single things. For an introduction to the abundant recent scholarship on the *shihua* genre, one may read Ronald Egan's *Problem of Beauty*, chap. 2.

15. Egan, *Problem of Beauty*, 62.

16. *Shiren yuxie*, 75–76; "Arriving at Shitou Station, a poem sent to the elder vice censor-in-chief Wang Ten [Zhongshu] of West Jiang[nan] Circuit" 次石頭驛寄江西王十中丞閣老, *Han Changli shi xinian jishi*, 12/1187–1188. Written in 820 when Han Yu was returning to the capital after a period of exile, the poem itself references recently passing Nanchang.

sented When Parting at the City on the Pen [River]" 湓城贈別, was also se-lected as an exemplar in *Jade Chips*. "City on the Pen" refers to where the Pen River meets the Yangzi, the location of the city of Jiujiang 九江, or Nine Rivers.[17]

> The spring waters are wide at Nine Rivers,   九江春水闊
> 4   And the evening clouds thick at Three Gorges.   三峽暮雲深

This couplet, from a parting poem, emphasizes the insurmountable obstacles and distances that will soon separate the author from the poem's recipient and prevent their reunion. This is a common theme wherein distance readily serves as a symbol for the longing to be together. It is a topos often inverted in Buddhist parting poems such as those below.

The volume known as *Canglang's Remarks on Poetry* 滄浪詩話, attributed to Yan Yu 嚴羽 (1191–1241?), was especially well received by later generations in the Ming dynasty and on.[18] An entry concerning parting poetry reads, "As for the best poems of the Tang, many were written when heading off to serve in border garrisons, being sent into exile, setting off on leisurely travel, or at another such moment of parting; time and again they move and reveal a man's intentions" 唐人好詩，多是征戍、遷謫、行旅、離別之作，往往能感動激發人意。[19] According to this text, excellent poems were written when poets were about to part from friends and deeply felt sentiments were stirred.

In addition to *shihua*, exemplary Tang parting poems were anthologized in the Song. The following by Meng Haoran 孟浩然 (689–740) was written to say farewell to his friend Du Huang 杜晃.[20]

> The lands of Jing and Wu link together where water serves as   荊吳相接水為鄉
>   home;
> 2   Now you set out as the spring river boundlessly flows.   君去春江正淼茫
>   Where will you moor this solitary skiff tonight?   日暮孤舟何處泊
> 4   Then even a glance at the horizon will break my heart.   天涯一望斷人腸

Meng Haoran imagines Du Huang as a traveler in a vast landscape. The trav-eler leaves in spring when snowmelt amplifies the big river. By sundown, Meng

---

17. *Quan Tang shi*, 745/8478.

18. Amid ongoing debate about the nature and history of *Canglang shihua*, Chen Fang, "*Canglang shihua* Mingdai jieshou yanjiu," convincingly argues that although the received book was created no earlier than the Ming, the five sections were likely authored by Yan Yu and may have formed a coherent whole as a reactionary Song text. Regardless, the text was of increased importance from the Ming on.

19. *Canglang shihua jiao shi*, 198.

20. "Sending Off Du Fourteen to Jiangnan" 送杜十四之江南, *Meng Haoran shiji jianzhu*, 266–267; accepting variants in lines 2 and 3. This poem in the *songxing* section of the Song an-thology *Wenyuan yinghua*, 268/1356. My understanding is enriched by Kroll, *Meng Hao-jan*, 72–77, on other poems written in the region of Lake Dongting.

will wonder how far his friend has traveled since departing earlier in the day. He believes that, were he to look off in the direction of his friend, he would suffer wrenching pangs of separation. This oft-anthologized quatrain deploys local geography, transient natural phenomena, metaphors of distance, and sorrow appropriate to the occasion.

In addition to *shihua* and anthologies, newly written Song parting poetry abounds. Su Shi wrote the following, a couplet from the second of two poems, when taking leave of his beloved brother Su Che 蘇轍 (1039–1112), not knowing when they would meet again.[21]

	If in life there were no partings,	人生無離別
6	Who would know the gravity of love and kindness?	誰知恩愛重

Su's poem voices the tender sadness of leaving a loved one. Nostalgia, longing, and sorrow are characteristic of parting poetry, including that celebrated in *shihua*. Each of the above elements and poetic strategies typical of parting poems also appeared in monastic parting poetry, although in ways contrary to what was expected, a structural tension illustrated in the next section.

The Structural Tension of Buddhist Parting Poems

Many events in the lives of Buddhist monks might occasion a parting poem. Monks composed verses to send off students, visitors, and friends, as well as to bid farewell when taking leave of a sangha. *Songbie* 送別 (sending off) and *libie* 離別 (leave taking) poems serve complementary functions and have similar themes. The emotional timbre of parting poems by Chan monks, however, departed from the norms established by *shihua* discussed above.

The following leave-taking poem expresses sentiments that are the opposite of normative expectations. Huanglong Huinan composed the verse "Retiring from the Cloister and Leaving Mount Lu" 退院別廬山 to mark his departure for a new abbatial position.[22]

	After ten years of being a mountain monk of Lu,	十年廬嶽僧
2	It takes just one day to emerge from the peaks.	一旦出巖層

---

21. "On Taking Leave of Ziyou at Yingzhou" 潁州初別子由, *Su Shi shiji*, 6/278–281. This poem analyzed in Yoshikawa, *Sōshi gaisetsu*, 165–166. My translation adapted from that of Burton Watson in Yoshikawa, *Introduction to Sung Poetry*, 107.

22. *Huanglong Huinan Chanshi yulu* (T47.635c13–16). Cf. translation in Charles Egan, *Clouds Thick, Whereabouts Unknown*, 114. Huinan had been the abbot of Tong'an Chongsheng Chan Cloister 同安崇勝禪院 and then Guizong Temple 歸宗寺, both on Mount Lu, before moving to the newly renamed Jicui 積翠 on Mount Huangbo 黃檗山 (in Yifeng County 宜豐縣 near Nanchang 南昌).

My old friends come to the river to bid farewell,	舊友臨江別
4 As this lone skiff marked with a crane sets out.[23]	孤舟帶鶴登
Water flows following twisting banks,	水流隨岸曲
6 My sail swells as the wind soars.	帆勢任風騰
Whether leaving or staying, fundamentally without attachments,	去住本無著
8 A master of Chan severs all love and hate.[24]	禪家絕愛憎

The clash between Buddhist ideals of nonattachment and the expected emotional response to parting is one theme of this poem. The final couplet addresses the generic expectation that one should have certain emotions when saying farewell even as it challenges the normative expression of such sentiment. In contrast to the mainstream poems discussed above, Huinan states that neither leaving nor staying is an inherently maudlin situation. Nostalgia is not located in the act of parting itself; rather, it is the minds of those who face separation that create such sentiments. The message of the final couplet may be addressed to Huinan himself as he departs as well as to those with whom he leaves the poem.

The literary themes and performative functions of Huinan's poem together create a poetics of circumstance. Huinan uses the riverside leave-taking scene as a token for a proper Buddhist response to separation. The downriver journey becomes a metaphor for serenity in the face of change, as Huinan leaves one community for a new abbotship. Per Huinan, a true master should be without personal preference and so should face the feelings of departure with equanimity. He uses the occasion of farewell as an example of impermanence. This parting message therefore functions as a Buddhist teaching. It is a nice orchestration of themes and functions to express a Buddhist principle pertinent to the occasion through direct subversion of literary convention.

Another Northern Song poem that incorporates themes and functions, albeit through a different strategy, is poet-monk Daoqian's "Seeing Off Venerable Ding on His Return to Kuaiji" 送定上人還會稽. The five-character regulated poem begins with a conventional autumn scene, then addresses Ding's remarkable sentiments.[25]

Westerly wind rattles a stand of trees,	西風警群木
2 Whistling and rustling forth autumn sounds.	蕭瑟散秋聲
Though a feeble wanderer has thoughts of home,	病客有歸思
4 This lone cloud has no feelings of attachment.	孤雲無戀情

---

23. I have taken this phrase to be related to *hezhou* 鶴舟, found in Tang and Song poetry, to refer to a craft adorned with cranes. Imagery associated with cranes is rich and variegated, but the image of the crane as a solitary and aloof individual (*guhe* 孤鶴) may be pertinent here as the author boards the lone skiff (*guzhou*).

24. Modified from my earlier translation, "Returning Empty-Handed," 389.

25. *Canliaozi shiji*, 8.5a; 269–270.

> Though the moon will unite us when we are a thousand miles apart, 　　　月當千里共
>
> 6 Men resent how hard it is for "all four" to coincide.[26] 　　　人恨四難并
>
> When it comes to hard work and study, who is like you? 　　　苦學誰如子
>
> 8 At some future time we will be joined in song! 　　　它年在一鳴

A "feeble wanderer" is one physically ill while far from home, but here it refers to homesickness. Daoqian contrasts such a pitiable traveler with the "lone cloud" in the next line. A cloud frequently referred to an itinerant monk, in this poem, Venerable Ding.[27] When read together, the lines of the couplet suggest that Ding is a true ascetic who has transcended the longing for home common to wanderers. Daoqian has explicitly juxtaposed conventional sentiments with the appropriate monastic stoicism. The third couplet is about distance and offers a similar juxtaposition. At first, Daoqian suggests that the moon visible in the sky will unite the two men across distance; however, he turns to an allusion that suggests that Ding consider the substantive difference between being together and being apart. The final couplet offers conventional praise and hopeful valediction. Daoqian's poem veers away from mainstream Chinese poetry to Buddhist asceticism, then back toward literary norms.

Xuedou Chongxian, the highly esteemed Chan abbot of the early Northern Song, wrote five parting poems collectively titled "Sending Off Venerable Baoxiang [Yunhuan]" with a headnote. Additional details about this text are in Chapter 2. I reproduce my translation of Chongxian's headnote here by way of explaining the purpose of presenting parting poems to a fellow monk.[28]

> Great Master [Yun]huan, a Chan worthy, is about to head to Cinnabar Hill[29] for an appointment that will make resplendent the cardinal tenets. When the time arrives for him to leave, we must not urge him to tarry or stay, but rather [give him] an appropriate composition to mark the beginning of a distant journey. Though one remains and one goes; one will be there, and one here; still, what space is between us? I hurriedly stitched together some uncultivated words to use as a token to bid farewell.

> 大師歡禪德，將赴丹丘辟命光闡宗乘，蓋時應必行，固不可抑留者也。且撫會之作肇曠絕之道，雖一凝一流一彼一此又何間然。率織蕪辭以代驪別。

---

26. Xie Lingyun 謝靈運 wrote, in the voice of Cao Pi, about the difficulty of the coincidence of four, that is, a pleasant time of day, lovely scenery, an appreciative mind, and a cheerful event. This text discussed in Williams, "Brocade of Words," 179–180, and Harrison Huang, "Excursion, Estates, and the Kingly Gaze," 48.

27. On the imagery of clouds in monks' poetry, see Ge, *Zhongguo zongjiao yu wenxue lunji*, 93–109.

28. *Zuying ji*, 1.1b; *Mingjue chanshi yulu* (Gozan ed., 75; T47.698a13-b9).

29. Several locations named "Cinnabar Hill" existed in the Song. Internal references in the poems suggest its probable location to be outside Taizhou, near Tiantai.

First, Chongxian asserts that his parting poems are for the benefit of Yinhuan and to encourage him in his endeavors to propagate the dharma. When Chongxian exhorts his community against pressuring Yinhuan to dawdle, he surely has in mind the natural tendency to put off the moment of departure, grasping for more time with the one who is leaving. It is precisely for this reason that the preface and accompanying poems do not directly express the nostalgia one might expect in a parting poem.

One further example by Xuedou Chongxian was written to mark his departure from the community at the large Lingyin Monastery 靈隱寺 in Hangzhou. After three years as an officer, Chongxian was about to take up his first abbatial position at Cuifeng Temple 翠峯寺 in Suzhou. Entitled "Taking Leave of the Chan Masters at Lingyin to Comply with the Invitation at Cuifeng" 赴翠峯請別靈隱禪師, Chongxian's parting verse explores the nature of monks' parting poetry.[30]

	Of my feelings when about to depart, I'm too lazy to speak–	臨行情緒懶開言
2	Propagating cardinal tenets is also so much idleness.	提唱宗乘亦是閑
	For such venerable guiding masters and a sea of worthy monks	珍重導師并海眾
4	I could not exhaust thoughts that linger and bend toward this temple.	不勝依戀向靈山

Chongxian marks his leaving with a poetic inquiry. His first premise is that most parting poems merely mouth platitudes and idle sentimentality. Chongxian also critiques the kind of parting poetry that must have been in vogue among monks, which was a tendency to replace sentimental truisms with Buddhist dogma. Such obvious philosophical posturing is also in vain, according to Chongxian. Perhaps like "emptiness sickness," an overly philosophical poem occludes the conventional reality of parting too completely.[31] The second couplet turns from abstractions to the present moment of the poem. Here, Chongxian extols the monks at Lingyin Monastery and confesses a sentimental attachment to this community that could not adequately be put into words. Chongxian thus uses a poem to creatively respond to the situation at hand. His orchestration of themes, techniques, and the function of the poem is particularly skillful. He is able to successfully participate in the mode (or genre) of parting poetry and still maintain his ascetic deportment. A similar tension between monastic aspirations to equanimity and the poetic emotion of longing for home can be seen in the poetry of Daocan 道璨 (1213–1271), aptly analyzed elsewhere by Huang Ch'i-chiang.[32] Many monks'

---

30. *Mingjue chanshi yulu* (Gozan ed., 89–90; T47.706b18–20). The Taishō punctuation is misleading. The theme of *fuqing* 赴請 is well-established in monks' poetry. One should not read this as *qingbie* 請別 (asking leave), which also would not make sense of the sequence of Chongxian's career; on which, see Huang Yi-hsun, *Xuedou qiji*, 18–33.

31. See Ahn, "Malady of Meditation," 33–71, on the dynamics of "emptiness sickness."

32. Huang Ch'i-chiang, *Wuwen yin de misi yu jiedu*, 56–64.

poems likewise use sets of themes and literary techniques to respond to the problem of emotions in parting poetry.

Ritual Contexts of Parting

Judging by the surviving corpus of monks' verse, parting poetry was one of the most common literary modes for elite Buddhist monks. Parting poems in the modern Buddhist canon are numerous, appearing in almost every *yulu* from the Northern and Southern Song dynasties on. The ubiquity of parting poetry circulating among Song and Yuan monks is conveyed by the *Jōwa-shū*, that compilation by the Japanese monk Gidō Shūshin based on Song and Yuan books circulating in fourteenth-century Japan. Gidō organized the nearly 3,000 Chinese monks' poems into sixty-five sections. The "sending off wandering" 送行 section has 204 poems, second only to the 262 encomia. This high proportion of parting poems is roughly in keeping with the practices of mainstream poets. The collected poems of such a figure as Su Shi likewise have a large proportion of occasional writings, though the occasions of composition often differ from those within a Buddhist monastery.

Song monks were not the first in China to write such parting poetry. The Song, however, witnessed the production of social poems by more monks on a greater scale and with seemingly more frequency. The ritual and rhetorical modes in which poetry was written in monasteries of the Song, moreover, came to serve as models for later dynasties and in Japanese Zen.[33] In the course of a Song Buddhist monk's life, there were many occasions when a parting poem might be written. I will discuss below three prominent circumstances that appear throughout Chan literature, which are: poems for a monk about to depart for a period of mendicancy; poems for a monastic officer leaving to accept an abbatial appointment; and poems addressing the itinerant wandering of Chan students, who moved from teacher to teacher. I have devised these categories from my extensive reading through the parting poems in *yulu* as well as a survey of the corresponding rituals of farewell encoded in the "rules of purity" monastic codes.

The foundational *Chanyuan qinggui,* completed in 1103 by Chan master Changlu Zongze, details a ritual for seeing off a monk who is about to go out to beg alms and who will, until his return, manage the yield of donations. The monastic position of the alms-begging monk is known as "head of transformations" 化主, a title likely derived from a euphemism for the sangha's fruitfulness as a field of merit wherein donations are subject to "transformations

---

33. On later Japanese imitations of Song parting poetry, see, for example, the mid-twentieth-century sectarian Zen scholarly manual. Hata, *Shige sakuhō,* 69–71. Hata includes a section on *sōan* 送行, a type of poem to be written after the completion of the ninety-day summer retreat or whenever a student graduates or leaves. He illustrates the mode with two examples for Japanese monks headed off to Yuan China, written by Daichi Sokei 大智祖継 (1290–1367), who himself had spent ten years in China.

of karmic conditions" 化緣.[34] The temple's fiscal well-being and relationships with patrons were serious matters, and receiving a donation was an important opportunity to teach the dharma. The *Chanyuan qinggui* includes several days' worth of protocol to fortify the monk who is about to leave the community and wander among the temptations of the secular world. These rituals include a tea ceremony and a feast the day before the monk's departure. Then, "when the day [of departure] arrives, the abbot ascends the high seat [to lecture], seeing [the monk] off and additionally encouraging thoughts of enlightenment with a *jisong*, [the abbot] then escorts him to the monastery gate" 至日，住持人陞座餞送兼以偈頌激發道心，送至門.[35] This prescriptive text depicts the likely ritual contexts for parting poems that encourage an individual embarking on mendicant practice.

One finds within Song *yulu* sermons along with parting poems addressed to fundraising monks that roughly match the above description from *Chanyuan qinggui*. For example, Yuanwu Keqin, while abbot of the Zhenru Chan Cloister 真如禪院 on Mount Yunju 雲居山, is said to have "ascended the hall [for a sermon] to see off heads of transformation" 送化主上堂.[36] Having completed the sermon, Keqin added this verse.

	Thirty-some itinerant monks,	三十餘員雲水客
2	As you go in various directions to spread the teachings, vigorously practice and uphold [the precepts].	諸方分化力行持
	Our various temple-gate rituals all can be relied upon;	山門庶事渾依賴
4	This very moment the golden hairs [of Mañjuśrī] take flight!	正是金毛奮迅時

This verse references a farewell ceremony similar to that described in the *Chanyuan qinggui*. Verses structured with rhyme and tonal prosody were sometimes mnemonics. Perhaps this verse describing a farewell ceremony at a temple gate served just such a purpose for some of the monks as they wandered.[37] Rhyming lines when recalled by a solitary traveler could transport his thoughts back to the rigors of communal monasticism. Keqin crafted these parting words specifically for the occasion of sending off fundraising monks. The result was a didactic verse, part of a public ritual rather than a personal poem of parting.

In addition to verses addressed to fundraising monks, Song-era *yulu* include sermons and parting poetry to celebrate a senior monk's departure for a new abbatial appointment. Changlu Zongze, the very compiler of the

---

34. The phrase *huayuan* appears in the *Chanyuan qinggui;* however, this gloss comes from *Shui hu zhuan* 水滸傳, as quoted in *Zenrin shōkisen*, 211a2–3.

35. *Chanyuan qinggui* (ZZ63.535b6–7). Translation adapted from Yifa, *Buddhist Monastic Codes*, 176.

36. *Yuanwu Foguo chanshi yulu* (T47.748c9–17).

37. For relationships between memory and Chinese poetry, including emic discussions, see Nugent, *Manifest in Words*, 72–125.

Chanyuan qinggui, composed such sermons and verses.[38] His sermons and poems found in *Recorded Sayings of Chan Master Cijue* 慈覺禪師語錄 closely correspond to the ritual protocols he laid out in his monastic rule book.[39] For example, while abbot at Mount Changlu, Zongze "ascended the high seat to see off Venerable Min, who was going to Chongning [Temple] in Chuzhou" 送珉長老赴滁州崇寧上堂. Immediately following the record of the short sermon, the *yulu* adds that the master "also had some verses" 復有頌, after which come two parting poems.[40] Similarly, Zongze delivered a farewell sermon followed by a five-character quatrain while he was abbot of Hongji Cloister, the same place where he wrote the *Chanyuan qinggui* that describes this ritual.[41] The ritual protocols for sending off a new abbot, described in Zongze's rules of purity, were put into practice in Zongze's monastic communities.

Records from other monastic communities show that a parting verse was sometimes recited in the Dharma Hall as part of the farewell sermon. New rules included in purity texts written in the Southern Song elaborated on the procedures for sending off a monastic officer to his first abbatial appointment.[42] These procedures are reflected in the *yulu* of Cishou Huaishen. When he was abbot of Huilin Chan Cloister in Kaifeng, a monk named Qin 親 (n.d.) received an invitation to become abbot of the Chan temple at Mount Jiuxian 九仙山 west of Hongzhou. The day before his departure, the monk was honored with a sermon and that evening attended a "small convocation" (*xiaocan* 小參) in the abbot's quarters.[43] Finally, on the day of Qin's departure, Huaishen "ascended to the hall to send off the elder to Jiuxian" 送九仙長老上堂. He began his sermon by reciting a seven-character regulated quatrain. The verse directly addresses the rhetorical situation of parting, noting both the time two people have spent together as well as the present moment in

---

38. The extant *Cijue chanshi yulu* 慈覺禪師語錄, reproduced in Shiina, "*Jikaku zenji goroku honkoku,*" has an unusual textual history. A medieval Korean woodblock reproduction of a Song ancestral redaction was still known in the early twentieth century but is now lost. However, an early twentieth-century transcription by a Japanese colonial scholar was completed based on this high-quality medieval Korean edition. That transcription then sat uncatalogued in the Komazawa University Library, per Shiina, "Chōro Sōseku sen *Jikaku zenji goroku* no shutsugen to sono yigi."

39. On a monastic officer receiving an appointment, see *Chanyuan qinggui* (ZZ63.542b3–13), translated in Yifa, *Buddhist Monastic Codes,* 213–214.

40. See Shiina, "*Jikaku zenji goroku* honkoku," 220, no. 46. Two quatrains follow, one pentasyllabic, one heptasyllabic, with different end rhymes. The title "venerable" 長老 in this and the next examples likely refers to a monk of a certain seniority. In Zongze's *Chanyuan qinggui* (ZZ63.529a16-b1) the title refers to someone who reached the rank of abbot. For translation, see Yifa, *Buddhist Monastic Codes,* 145–149.

41. Shiina, "*Jikaku zenji goroku,*" 191, no. 90.

42. *Conglin jiaoding qinggui zongyao* (ZZ63.596c10–17) as well as *Chanlin beiyong qinggui* (ZZ63.636c17–24) describe ceremonies in which the departing officer "borrows the dharma seat" 稟借法座 and is allowed to "ascend the high seat to [give a sermon in which he] takes leave from the assembly" 上堂辭眾. Afterward, the monastery bell is rung as the monk departs the monastery gate.

43. *Cishou huaishen chanshi guanglu* (ZZ73.102b16-c7).

which one of them will leave for mountainous Hongzhou and one will remain in the capital metropolis of Kaifeng.[44]

	Here in Huilin we age amid ruddy dust,	慧林投老入紅塵
2	At a turn of the head, three years become a tap of the foot.	俯仰三年成蹉跟
	I laugh at myself for wanting to return [to mountains] when I cannot yet return,	自笑欲歸歸未得
4	And time after time [I] send guests out from the capital city.	時時送客出都城

As found in this *yulu*, when the parting poem ends, Cishou begins his sermon to explain the meaning of the verse and offer a kind of auto-commentary.[45] His poem describes the bustling city of Kaifeng as filled with the "adventitious dust of defilements" (*kechen fannao* 客塵煩惱; Skt. *āgantukakleśa*). (As he has elsewhere described Kaifeng, "This bustling city of ruddy dust is the tiger's cave, the palace of Māra" 紅塵閙市虎穴魔宮.)[46] Cishou encourages the departing monk to abandon any attachments to the city. The imperial capital teems with fleeting pleasures, human suffering, and political intrigue, yet although these are dangerous temptations and delusions, the monk knows them to be ultimately empty, for they pass into nothingness at the snap of a finger. We might expect a monk to declare no preference between being in or out of the world, and yet Cishou expresses a longing for a monastic life away from the capital. Cishou writes that he laughs at his own desire to leave the city. He would not be granted permission to retire from the abbotship of Huilin Cloister until 1126.[47] His final sermon was given only weeks before the start of the fatal Jin attacks on Kaifeng in late autumn. Amid the destruction of Kaifeng in the Song-Jin wars, Cishou repaired south to Suzhou and after a few years settled in a war-ruined temple at Baoshan 包山, outside the city, where his quiet residence in the dilapidated cloister inspired donors to sponsor repairs.[48]

Before Cishou was permitted to leave Kaifeng, he would continue to properly bid farewell to monks departing from the popular Huilin Cloister. He opines in "Sending Off Chan Student Xian as He Leaves the Capital" 送暹禪者出京, another farewell poem written at Huilin Cloister, "in the end returning to mountains is most splendid wandering, / because when a man of the Way examines the world, he fundamentally is without seeking" 畢竟歸山

---

44. *Cishou huaishen chanshi guanglu* (ZZ73.102c8–13), part of the initial 1133 collection. A regulated sequence with first-line end rhyme and a single tonal violation in the fifth position of line 2.

45. Cishou used a similar structure in his earlier farewell at Zifu Cloister 資福院 of Zhenzhou, first reciting a verse and then the sermon. *Cishou huaishen chanshi guanglu* (ZZ73.96a14–21).

46. *Cishou huaishen chanshi guanglu* (ZZ73.93a13).

47. *Cishou huaishen chanshi guanglu* (ZZ73.107c16–108a6).

48. *Zhongwu jiwen*, 6.5b-6a; *Wujun zhi*, 950–951; *Jiatai pudenglu* (ZZ79.342a2-b21). Baoshan of Suzhou was soon renamed Xianqing Monastery 顯慶寺.

是勝游，道人閱世本無求.[49] Perhaps the primary audience for these poems and sermons was solely the community in attendance at the ritual, with Cishou encouraging the Kaifeng City monks to discover the benefits of rustic simplicity. It is also possible that Cishou intended these verses to reach the imperial court in the hope that the court might grant him leave.

Several of the above examples make explicit that the parting poems were, at least in these cases, intoned aloud in public settings. Orality was important to the presentation of a parting poem. At the same time, it is likely that these verses were calligraphed and presented to the departing monk, like the manuscripts discussed in Chapter 2, each of which had a single poem and a colophon that might indicate the place, time, recipient, and occasion of the gift. When a manuscript was presented, the fundraiser or incumbent abbot was given an autographed physical text that he could take along as he traveled and display to donors to inspire their piety and generosity. The traces from the master's brush would buttress the monk's status and tacit relationship with the departed monastery.

In addition to the above occasions of parting, the most common event for which a poem of parting would be composed was *xingjiao* 行腳, or "itinerant practice," often depicted as "wandering the realm" (*youfang* 游/遊方). *Xingjiao* was a significant component in the training and development of Chan monks. During this period of itinerancy, a monk traveled long distances to study with a renowned teacher. He might settle down under the tutelage of one teacher for several years and work as a monastic officer while receiving specialized instruction. There are other occasions and circumstances in which a parting poem would be composed, among them were poems written in response to a request, often marked by *qiu* 求, or a synonym such as *qing* 請, in the poem's title. Given the large number of itinerant monks, I suspect many departures that garnered a poem did not warrant a formal sermon or complex farewell ritual.

In addition to parting poems from the abbot, the officers of a monastery could compose farewell verses addressed to a departing colleague. It is unclear where and when the community of monastic officers began composing such poetry. To my knowledge, the earliest textual evidence of a community of monks composing parting poetry for another monk is in the Southern Song miscellany *Glorious Matters from Monasteries* 叢林盛事 (preface dated 1197; printer's colophon dated 1199). It records a farewell event at which all the dharma brothers at the monastery wrote parting verses, among which a quatrain by Yunju Dehui 雲居德會 (n.d.) was especially beloved.[50] Orphaned colophons attesting to lost scrolls of poetry are preserved in *yulu* dating from the late Southern Song on.[51] One example is a colophon dated 1245 by

---

49. *Cishou Huaishen chanshi guanglu* (ZZ73.114b10–12).

50. The quatrain is preserved with the story in *Conglin shengshi* (ZZ86.695b20–24).

51. It seems likely that colophons were created by monks before the Southern Song but that the compilers of Chan *yulu* did not include prefaces and colophons composed by Chan masters until relatively late in the Song. I would argue that we have a lack of evidence rather than evidence of lack.

Wuzhun Shifan 無準師範 (1178–1249) that was added to a "scroll of verses" 頌軸 on which numerous members of the community had written encouragement for the departing monk.[52] Only Wuzhun's colophon is extant.

Such scrolls of poetry contained calligraphic traces that made them valuable objects. Yuansou Xingduan 元叟行端 (1255–1341) wrote a colophon after viewing a scroll of parting poems written for a monk named Haiweng 海翁 (n.d.) during the Xianchun regnal period 咸淳 (1265–1274) of the late Southern Song. After Haiweng died, the scroll passed to another monk. Xingduan remarked that the younger monk was right to cherish the scroll, which bore calligraphy by late masters, because "thereby you certainly will raise up this Way that will brilliantly illumine those in our generation" 固將揭斯道焜耀當世.[53] Similar practices of writing colophons of appreciation for calligraphy by individual Chan masters began at least by the Northern Song, at which time Huihong wrote about viewing calligraphy from monks' private collections.[54] We see that monks themselves collected and circulated the written traces of collections of parting poetry.

In a few cases, a colophon explicitly notes that a departing monk had circulated a scroll and requested verses. Wuchu Daguan wrote in response to one such request, "About to return east, you took this scroll to various dignitaries at Nanjian [Temple] to seek their literary compositions in their calligraphic traces—to comfort your thoughts about parting—and now you've compelled me to write upon it my own humble composition. Alas!" 將東歸以此軸求南礀諸公逸跡藻製，慰別後之思，且俾余書拙作其上。噫![55] Many masters, like Wuchu, were concerned about the intentions of itinerant monks who sought verses. In this spirit, the Yuan monk Tianru Weize 天如惟則 (1286–1354), a disciple of Zhongfeng Mingben, wrote "Colophon on a Scroll of Parting Poems for Venerable Xian" 跋賢上人送行詩軸.[56]

The venerable Xian from Sichuan took a southerly pilgrimage and now is about to head home. About thirty-five people presented parting poems, forming a big scroll. Humph, when you set out to travel ten thousand miles from Sichuan to

---

52. One of twenty-six "prefaces and colophons" 序跋 in *Fojian chanshi yulu*, 3.5b–6a; *Wuzhun Shifan chanshi yulu* (ZZ70.274b14–18).

53. "Inscribed after a Scroll of Parting Poems by Various Associates for the Scribe Haiweng" 書海翁書記諸友贈行頌軸後, *Yuansou Xingduan chanshi yulu* (ZZ71.545c18–19). Yuansou noted that he had not seen his friend Haiweng in thirty-four years. A "distant dharma descendent" named Venerable Jian 鑑 (n.d.) now possessed the scroll and showing it to Yuansou also informed him of Haiweng's death.

54. Fasc. 26 of *Shimen wenzi chan* includes numerous inscriptions, such as "Inscribed after the copy of Lingyuan Weiqing's [calligraphy] in the collection of Venerable Cai" 題才上人所藏昭默帖 and "Inscribed on a small convocation in Lingyuan Weiqing's own writing" 題昭默自筆小參. (N.b., Zhaomo was a sobriquet of Lingyuan Weiqing, who retreated to convalesce at Zhaomo Hall 昭默堂 on Mount Huanglong ca. 1101.)

55. "Inscribed on a scroll of poetry to see off [lacuna]" 題送□□詩軸. Xu, *Zhenben Song ji wu zhong*, 2:828.

56. *Tianru Weize Chanshi yulu* (ZZ70.813b16–22).

Zhejiang in search of something, was it for this [scroll of poems]? Is it this [scroll of poems] that you obtained and take home?

蜀中賢上人南詢將歸，詩以贐者凡三十五人，成大軸。噫！蜀至浙萬里出而求者此歟？得而歸者此耶？

Weize has here added a touch of Chan humor. Venerable Xian surely did not travel the length of the Yangzi River just to acquire some poems. The proper motive for the pilgrim to have set out on his itinerant voyage was to seek the dharma. If he is returning, does that mean that he obtained what he sought? The gravity of itinerant study is underscored by an allusion to the "southerly pilgrimage" (*nan xun* 南詢) in which the young boy Sudhana visited fifty-three teachers, as told in the *Gaṇḍavyūha*. Because references to this spiritual journey are ubiquitous in Song Chan literature as a symbol for Chan itinerant practice, I will focus on the symbolism of Sudhana's pilgrimage before turning to an intact example of a parting poetry collection authored by a community of monks.

The *Gaṇḍavyūha* and a Poetics of Itinerant Wandering

The symbolism of itinerant wandering in Chan training was explicated in the Song-dynasty Chan lexicon *Zuting shifan*, which includes a gloss for the term *xingjiao*.[57]

Xingjiao is to go a great distance from one's home, to walk through the world, to slough off sentiments and burdens, to search for a masterful benefactor, and to seek the dharma and confirm one's awakening. Best is that thereby one learns from extensive wandering without a constant teacher, as with Sudhana's southern pilgrimage and Sadāprarudita's eastward pilgrimage.[58] Without doubt, sages of the past sought out the dharma. What Yongjia described [in *Zhengdao ge*] as "wandering among rivers and oceans, wading through mountain streams, / seeking teachers to inquire of the Way is the practice of Chan," how could it not be so?

行脚者，謂遠離鄉曲，脚行天下，脫情捐累，尋訪師友，求法證悟也。所以學無常師徧歷為尚，善財南求、常啼東請，蓋先聖之求法也。永嘉所謂：「游江海，涉山川，尋師訪道為參禪。」豈不然邪？

Many poems in *yulu* were presented to students on the occasion of their leaving for a period of *xingjiao* practice. The poems often addressed the simple facts of the student leaving: how long the student had stayed at the monastery to study and where he might go next; or there might be a few words about his spiritual insights (or lack thereof). Like other parting poems, Buddhist occasional verses invoked the context in which they were written. In parting

---

57. *Zuting shiyuan* (ZZ64.432c19–22).
58. On Sadāprarudita's eastward pilgrimage, see Conze, *Perfection of Wisdom*, 277–290.

poems for *xingjiao* students, the coming and going of a student could serve as a metaphor for the student's understanding of the dharma. *Xingjiao* was an arduous physical practice that could double as an allegory for the spiritual journey a student underwent before awakening.

The symbolism of *xingjiao* practice resonated with the imagery of the *Gaṇḍavyūha*, known in Chinese as the *Ru fajie pin* 入法界品. Robust art-historical evidence illustrates the widespread popularity of the *Gaṇḍavyūha* among monks during the Song.[59] Found in the *Huayan jing* (Skt. *Avataṃsakasūtra*), the *Gaṇḍavyūha* concerns the journey of a merchant-banker's young son named Sudhana 善財童子 who, listening to a sermon by the great bodhisattva Mañjuśrī 文殊, generates "the aspiration to awakening" (*puti xin* 菩提心; Skt. *bodhicitta*). On the advice of Mañjuśrī, Sudhana begins a southerly pilgrimage to find "wholesome companions" (*shanzhishi* 善知識; Skt. *kalyāṇamitra*), an epithet for Buddhist teachers. Sudhana endures an epic journey, traveling to 110 cities and encountering fifty-three teachers. His journey culminates when he meets the future Buddha Maitreya 彌勒, who shows Sudhana the pure dharma realm (*fajie* 法界). He thus reveals that Sudhana's entire journey was made manifest by the power of Mañjuśrī.[60]

This pilgrimage was generally understood as an allegory of progress along the bodhisattva path. Awakening is extremely difficult and rarefied, though entirely possible given enough lifetimes of focused training and dedication. Sudhana is the model practitioner. As the *Gaṇḍavyūha* ends, Sudhana has a visionary experience wherein the bodhisattva Samantabhadra 普賢 awakens sentient beings. Sudhana will now live in the world embodying this wisdom. His identification with Samantabhadra at the conclusion of the text reaffirms Sudhana's role as the model practitioner and Samantabhadra as the bodhisattva of the path of practice. In some iconic Chan texts, including the *Record of Linji* 臨濟錄, references to Sudhana's pilgrimage are employed in the context of urging students to seek truth with great sincerity and effort.[61]

An additional and radical interpretation of this narrative appeared in Chan texts beginning in the early Song dynasty and emerges from the development of Chan subitism.[62] In this new reading, emphasis is placed on the significance of Maitreya sending Sudhana back to Mañjuśrī. Sudhana cycles

---

59. Fontein, *Pilgrimage of Sudhana*, discusses Song-era printed illustrations and verse celebrating each step of Sudhana's pilgrimage. Wong, "Huayan/ Kegon/ Hwaŏm Paintings," surveys an even broader geographic area.

60. For example, from the 80-fascicle *Huayan jing* (T10.439a22–23), Maitreya reveals to Sudhana that "all the wholesome companions you have seen, all the bodhisattva practices you have heard, all the modes of liberation you have entered, all the vows you have fulfilled, all are the magnificent numinous powers of Mañjuśrī" 汝先所見諸善知識聞菩薩行、入解脫門、滿足大願，皆是文殊威神之力.

61. Kirchner, *Record of Linji*, 195–196, 285–286.

62. Paul Demiéville in "The Mirror of the Mind" introduced the term "subitism" into Chan studies as a reference for sudden awakening. The sudden-gradual polarity had precedent elsewhere but assumed its greatest significance within China. Pre-Chan, the terms "sudden" 頓 and "gradual" 漸 described the nature of awakening and were used in *panjiao* hermeneutic systems to rank the teachings of the Buddha.

back to the beginning of his journey, encountering Mañjuśrī once more. The result is the same as the cause. Sudhana is never separate from the wisdom of Mañjuśrī, an interpretation that rebukes Sudhana's path as a gradual progression. The tenth-century polymath Yongming Yanshou 永明延壽 (904–976), for example, writes,[63]

> The boy Sudhana journeyed south, throughout the dharma realm to visit fifty-three wholesome companions, and grasped the dharma gates [i.e., teachings] to 110 cities. He began with a visit to his very first teacher, Mañjuśrī. At that time he was already awakened to his own mind. Afterward, he step-by-step visited many different wholesome companions. He said to each of them, "I have already given rise to the mind of awakening, but I am searching for the bodhisattva's graduated path of wisdom that leads to Maitreya and the attainment of buddhahood in my next lifetime." Later, Maitreya instead instructed him to go back and revisit his initial teacher, Mañjuśrī. This signifies that the prior mind and latter mind are the same, without any difference whatsoever. From beginning to end, he never parted from the one mind. This is most extraordinary.

> 善財童子南行，遍法界參五十三員善知識，得一百十城法門。為求菩薩之道，最先參見文殊初友，已悟自心。後漸至諸善知識，皆云「我已先發菩提心，但求菩薩差別智道，及至彌勒，證一生成佛之果。」後彌勒却指歸再見初友文殊。以表前心後心一等，更無差別，始終不出一心。離此別無奇特矣。

There is a structural parallel between this way of seeing Sudhana's pilgrimage and certain Chan models of awakening. Sudhana began his journey to the south with Mañjuśrī and in the end returned to Mañjuśrī. Although back where he began, Sudhana now envisions fulfilling the vows of Samantabhadra. The importance of this ultimate return to the source may be understood in light of the oft-quoted parable from a sermon by Qingyuan Weixin 青原惟信 (fl. Northern Song).[64]

> The Master ascended the hall and said, "Thirty years ago, before this old monk had studied Chan, when I looked at mountains they were mountains, and when I looked at water it was water. Then, sometime later with my own eyes I saw a wholesome companion, and there was a point of entry: when I looked at mountains they were not mountains, and when I looked at water it was not water. But now I have attained great ease, and, like before, when I look at mountains they are just mountains, and when I look at water it is just water. Great assembly! These three ways of seeing things, are they the same? Are they different? If there is a

---

63. *Zhu Xinfu* 註心賦 (ZZ63.152a23-b4), a widely circulated prose poem with auto-commentary. This text survives only in a relatively late edition, and Yanshou's authorship has been regarded with suspicion. Yanagi, *Eimei Enju*, 46–47n17, with a recently recovered Northern Song biography, demonstrated Yanshou's authorship of the *Xinfu* and auto-commentary.

64. *Jiatai pudenglu* (ZZ79.327a24-b4).

monk or layperson who can get this, then you could say you had seen this old monk with your own eyes."

上堂曰："老僧三十年前，未參禪時，見山是山，見水是水。及至後來親見知識，有箇入處，見山不是山，見水不是水。而今得箇休歇處，依前見山只是山，見水只是水。大衆，這三般見解，是同是別？有人緇素得出，許汝親見老僧。

Qingyuan Weixin's sermon describes the spiritual path in three phases. First, there is the ordinary way of seeing things wherein things appear to be what the seer is conditioned to see. In terms of Sudhana's pilgrimage, this first stage may refer to Sudhana before encountering Mañjuśrī. Second, there is an encounter with a teacher and a recognition of the nature of emptiness. Things are not what they appear to be. For Sudhana, this represents almost the entirety of his epic pilgrimage after encountering Mañjuśrī and giving rise to *bodhicitta*. In other Chan materials, this part of the spiritual path often appears as a restless spiritual urgency that drives itinerant practice. Finally, there is a return to the mundane world with the wisdom to understand the mechanisms of karma and liberation. Sudhana's pilgrimage concludes with his return to Mañjuśrī and visionary enactment of Samantabhadra awakening beings. Qingyuan Weixin's sermon provides a model for understanding how Sudhana's pilgrimage may be used as an allegory of Chan *xingjiao*.

Buddha-Nature, Emptiness, and Humor in *A Sail Full of Wind*

An especially fruitful object of study for understanding the practices of monastic parting verse is the collection known as *Yifanfeng* 一帆風, literally, "a sail full of wind." *Yifanfeng* is one of the only intact examples of a body of parting poetry written by a community to see off a single individual.[65] It is a compilation of forty-four poems (or sixty-nine poems in one expanded edition) attributed to forty-four (or sixty-nine) Chinese monks. The authors include Chan master Xutang Zhiyu and several of his disciples. The poems were written to send home the Japanese pilgrim-monk Nanpo Jōmin 南浦紹明 (1235–1309).[66] As I have written elsewhere, the various editions and manuscripts of *Yifanfeng* have been the subject of debate in Chinese and Japanese scholarship.[67] My interest here is in the two-fold function of the parting

---

65. On the broader Song-era practices of collecting parting poems for a traveler, see Cong Ellen Zhang, *Transformative Journeys*, 113–116.

66. Nanpo is also known as Daiō Kokushi 大應国師 (National Instructor Daiō). The later Rinzai Zen tradition celebrated Nanpo as the founder of the prominent *Ō–Tō–Kan* lineage. Among the enormous body of Japanese-language scholarship, I have found especially useful the materials in Fukuoka-shi Bijutsukan, *Daiō kokushi to Sōfukuji*.

67. My views on the textual history are unchanged from those expressed in Protass, "Returning Empty-Handed." Based on recent manuscript findings in Japan, I regard the twenty-five supplemental poems together with the original forty-four poems as a single corpus given to Nanpo by Chinese monks. I have made improvements to my translations and clarified points of argument.

poems. I first examine the way that the *Yifanfeng* poems apply Buddhist themes and Chan humor to the mode of parting poetry; next, I look at how these poems deploy poetic forms to express religious ideals.

The *Yifanfeng* collection of parting poems is a valuable text in that it represents a community of authors writing on a single occasion. The event of Nanpo's leave-taking stretched out over many months, as he first took leave of Xutang at Jingshan in autumn of 1267 and finally boarded a ship from Ningbo in late spring 1268.[68] The original format of the poems in *Yifanfeng* is lost to us, but it likely consisted of separate sheets of paper, each bearing one to two poems.[69] Whereas *Yifanfeng* collects farewell poems addressed to a single recipient by many different authors, *yulu* collect poems that are, inversely, by a single author addressed to many recipients. The multiple strategies and poetics that appear in the *Yifanfeng* poems are nonetheless representative of similar dynamics found in many Chan parting poems. Each poem in *Yifanfeng* is attributed to a different monk, many of them disciples of Xutang, though nothing is now known about most of the authors.[70] Nonetheless, these authors were part of a loose confederation of monks. Moreover, the internal coherence and shared allusions across many of the *Yifanfeng* poems suggest a community of writers.

Among the *Yifanfeng* parting poems are allusions to Sudhana's pilgrimage. Nanpo was returning to Japan after his study in China, a situation analogous to the climax of Sudhana's pilgrimage. We can see some of this imagery in the following *Yifanfeng* parting poem written by Chicheng Xinghong 赤城行弘 (n.d.).[71]

	Seeking the ultimate truth in the south, you knew when to stop;	南詢端的便知休
2	There never were two suns in the sky above.	天上原無兩日頭
	Could it be this that you understood so clearly, clearly?	可是明明窮得到
4	Now a sail full of wind urges you across autumn white waves.	一帆風急鷺濤秋

---

68. Following Kinugawa, "Sōbetsu shishū *Yippanfū* no seiritsu katei."

69. For details about the significance of the early manuscript editions and their unique sequence of poems, see Kinugawa, "Sōbetsu shishū *Yippanfū* no seiritsu katei."

70. Xu, "Ri cang Songseng shiji *Yifanfeng*," 154–164, gives biographical information about seventeen monks who authored poems in the *Yifanfeng* collection. In addition to relationships with Xutang, several monks were later known to be associated with Wuzhun Shifan, and one with a Caodong lineage. Biographic information does not survive for the other authors.

71. *Yifanfeng*, Chicheng Xinghong 赤城行弘 / poem no. 5. Citations to *Yifanfeng* include the name of the author and a poem number. Poem numbers follow the sequence in the Edo woodblock editions and are written "poem no." for the first forty-four beginning with Xutang's verse as "poem no. 1," and then "suppl. no." for the latter twenty-five supplemental poems. The Chinese text here is based on a comparison of two Edo woodblock editions and three large fragments of a manuscript edition by Shūhō Myōchō 宗峰妙超 (1282–1337). Shūhō Myōchō, also known as Daitō, was a direct disciple of Nanpo. For more on the textual history of *Yifanfeng*, see Protass, "Returning Empty-Handed," 390–396.

This poem thematizes Nanpo's spiritual quest. Presented to him shortly before his return home, Nanpo is depicted as having had a penetrating insight into the universal buddha-nature (*foxing* 佛性) that inheres in all beings. At this insight he stopped seeking for the truth outside himself and thus "knew when to stop" pilgrimaging in the mode of Sudhana. In terms of Qingyuan Weixin's sermon, Nanpo surpassed seeing mountains as not mountains. The final line echoes the early Song poem "An Impromptu Send-Off for the Talented [Huang] Jiangxia" 即席送江夏茂才, by Lin Bu 林逋 (967–1028), which concludes with the couplet, "how can I bear to watch your sail full of wind become a small speck / on autumn white waves of the vast sea" 一點風帆若為望，海門平闊鷺濤秋.[72] In Chicheng Xinghong's farewell poem, however, the emotional timbre has been inverted, and Nanpo's departure marks a triumphant conclusion to his pilgrimage.

References to Sudhana and the *Gaṇḍavyūha* appear throughout *Yifanfeng*. As noted by Kenji Kinugawa, Xutang himself used similar imagery in an encomium entitled "Sudhana" 善財.[73]

	A tour of the southern lands ends in a moment;	歷盡南方只片時
2	After the winds of karma blew fog through one hundred cities.[74]	百城烟水業風吹
	Even here at the end there is no wholesome companion;	如今到處無知識
4	Who do you need to see when you let go your grip of the precipice edge?	撒手懸崖要見誰

The phrase "hundred cities" is explained in *Zuting shiyuan* as an abbreviation of Sudhana's "gradual southerly travels to 110 cities and visits to fifty-two wholesome companions after giving rise to the aspiration for awakening" 發菩提心已，漸次南行，歷一百一十城，見五十二善知識.[75] It was a metonymy for Sudhana's entire pilgrimage. The image of fog does not appear in the *Gaṇḍavyūha*. In Tang poetry, the phrase "foggy waters" 烟水 can evoke a seemingly impassible wall or distance. In Song Buddhist writing, including other poems about Sudhana, fog becomes a metaphor for the bumbling world not-yet-awakened. Sometimes written out as "foggy waters vast, vast" 烟水茫茫, this imagery of fog leaves the impression that ignorance is both thick and vast. The second couplet's iconoclasm transforms this poem from mere praise of Sudhana's achievement to an inquiry into the meaning of a journey. Similar

---

72. *Lin Hejing shiji*, 163.

73. The poem not in *Xutang heshang yulu* is preserved in *Jōwa-shū*.

74. Amending "winds of karma" 業風 (*Jōwa-shū*, 2.3a) for "leafy wind" 葉風 (*Dai Nihon Bukkyō zensho*, 143:31). On the prevalence of this error across editions of the anthology, see Asakura, "Gozan-ban *Shinsen Jōwa bunrui kokon sonshuku geshu* shū kō," 235.

75. *Zuting shiyuan* (ZZ64.349b13–17). The number of teachers is either given as fifty-two or fifty-three, depending on whether one includes Samantabhadra after the second visit to Mañjuśrī. Huang Yi-hsun, *Songdai Chanzong cishu*, 135–136 and 253, offers insightful comments pertinent to interpreting Sudhana's pilgrimage.

ironic images of Sudhana's journey recur throughout *Yifanfeng*, which will be analyzed later in this chapter. The repetition of images and rhetorical strategies connects these poems to a community of authors based around Xutang.

Another parting poem in *Yifanfeng* is by the monk Dewei, a close disciple of Xutang, who was introduced in Chapter 2 as the recipient of a poem in Xutang's own calligraphy.[76]

	Casting off, the ship's bow spins north,	撥轉船頭向北看
2	Boundless high tide dashes against the coast.	全潮拍岸正漫漫
	The pilgrim Sudhana did not know he had it,	咨詢童子不知有
4	And walked in vain to a hundred cities through fog and cold.	空走百城烟水寒

This poem depicts the scene in Ningbo where Nanpo's boat would set sail. It is an example that explicitly links Sudhana's pilgrimage to the image of Nanpo's home-bound vessel. Because the harbor of Ningbo opens to the north, from the vantage of the poet a traveler from Japan would alight at Ningbo traveling south and depart for home to the north. Many parting poems to Japanese monks identify Sudhana's southern pilgrimage with this aspect of Ningbo's topography. The first two lines of Dewei's poem adhere to the conventional expectations for a parting poem. These lines describe the local scene of the port where Nanpo will depart and the enormous landscape into which he will disappear. The couplet is at once general and specific. The images of ocean, coast, and boats are not exclusive to Buddhism, but some readers could interpret these lines as expressing a subtle Buddhist truth. The poem's last two lines use the imagery of Sudhana's arduous pilgrimage to describe Nanpo's period of study and the narrative of the *Gaṇḍavyūha* as an allegory for Nanpo's journey through China.

There is a shift in the second half of the poem, where Dewei seizes the moment of farewell to describe Nanpo's departure in terms of Buddhist principles. This couplet evidently left an impression on Nanpo, for after returning to Japan, he wrote an encomium "In Praise of Kannon" 観音.[77]

	Clouds undulating, water boundless;	雲淡淡，水漫漫
2	The universal gate appears, do not slight it.	普門現，不相謾
	The pilgrim Sudhana did not yet know he had it,	咨詢童子未知有
4	Walked in vain to a hundred cities through fog and cold.	空走百城烟浪寒

The final couplet is borrowed directly from Dewei's parting poem. His curious remark, "The pilgrim Sudhana did not know he had it," refers to buddha-

---

76. *Yifanfeng,* Dewei / suppl. no. 8.
77. *Entsū Daiō Kokushi Goroku* (T80.123c18–19). Where the *Taishō* canon has *chuixun* 吹詢, I have emended the text to read *zixun* 咨詢 on the basis of the 1372 edition of *Entsū Daiō Kokushi Goroku,* 2:101.a.

nature. As buddha-nature is universal, it follows that all beings in Japan also must be imbued with it. By this reasoning, a person wishing to seek their buddha-nature has no reason to leave Japan and go to China. Nanpo traveled to China to discover that he had possessed buddha-nature all along. Recall that in Sudhana's pilgrimage the ultimate goal was not really in the south, even though he discovered it while journeying there. Both Sudhana and Nanpo traveled great distances to discover that what they sought did not require them to go anywhere at all.

This next poem, by Xiangshan Keguan 象山可觀 (n.d.), a disciple of Xu-tang, bids farewell to Nanpo with reference to the universality of buddha-nature.[78]

	At the end of foggy waves you'll see green hills,	烟波盡處見青山
2	Clearly here in the south is a road to take back home.	的的南方有路還
	As for buddhadharma, we know for certain there is neither there nor here;	佛法固知無彼此
4	Everywhere under heaven the wind and snow feel cold.	普天風雪一般寒

In the *Platform Sūtra,* Huineng defends his capacity to grasp the truth, declaring "there is no north and south in buddha-nature."[79] Here instead it is the host, a Chinese monk, who conveys to his Japanese friend that there is no Japan or China.

In the poem by Chicheng Xinghong, already given above, Sudhana's pilgrimage to the south conveys that Nanpo stopped seeking truth outside himself.[80]

	Seeking the ultimate truth in the south, you knew when to stop;	南詢端的便知休
2	There never were two suns in the sky above.	天上原無兩日頭

Our one sun shines the same everywhere, which is a metaphor for buddha-nature. This next couplet from a poem by Jiangnan Cirong 江南慈容 similarly stresses the omnipresence of Buddhist truth. A conventional parting poem might emphasize the distance between friends as a reason for sorrow, or contrariwise, express a hope that such distances could somehow be diminished. This poem instead rejects such ordinary conceptions of distance.[81]

	Light in the daytime, dark at night—same throughout the world;	晝明夜暗一寰宇
4	Who says our ancestral homes are separated by ocean cliffs?	誰道家山隔海涯

78. *Yifanfeng,* Xiangshan Keguan 象山可觀 / poem no. 28.
79. Yampolsky, *Platform Sutra,* 127–128.
80. *Yifanfeng,* Chicheng Xinghong 赤城行弘 / poem no. 5.
81. *Yifanfeng,* Jiangnan Cirong 江南慈容 / poem no. 11.

The initial image "light in the daytime, dark at night" invokes the third stage of Qingyuan Weixin's sermon. "Mountains are just mountains," phenomena of the world are impermanent and yet imbued with buddha-nature. The next line disrupts the expected expression of nostalgia associated with distance. In the Chan practice of Xutang's community in the late Southern Song, the point when one knows for oneself the immediacy of buddha-nature marks a dramatic turning point in one's spiritual journey. And, according to the community's poetic practices, the sentiments associated with farewell and distance no longer hold sway for one who has realized this truth.

Other *Yifanfeng* poems explore the parallel poetic logic of emptiness.[82] Several *Yifanfeng* parting poems use themes of emptiness to address Nanpo's itinerant study. For example, Jiangxi Daodong 江西道東 (n.d.) wrote the following poem about the emptiness of coming and going.[83]

	Ten meters tall, woven-grass sails! A ten-thousand *li* wind!	十幅蒲帆萬里風
2	Coming, he was without traces, and going he is the same;	來無蹤跡去還同
	I raise my eyes [to the sea], and mistake a cloud-mountain dwelling	擡眸錯認雲山處
4	Where a man exists between the color of sky and seas.	人在水天一色中

The theme of this passage is the emptiness of mover and movement, as in Nagarjuna's verses on *Gatāgataparīkṣā* in the *Mūlamadhyamakakārikā*. Song-dynasty authors were more likely to recognize such ideas as being from the *Vimalakīrtinirdeśa* or **Śūraṃgamasūtra*.[84] In the latter, the Buddha describes a profound *samādhi* in which one responds to the world "coming without attachments and passing without any trace" 來無所粘過無蹤跡.[85] The writer of the poem quoted just above has applied the pith of the sūtra's passage about the emptiness of movement to the event of Nanpo's taking leave.

---

82. The term "emptiness" refers to the Buddhist understanding that all phenomena are empty of self-existence and arise in dependence on each other. The fundamental impermanence of all things is not the same as nonexistence or nihilism. This is a basic teaching of the *prajñāpāramitā* family of sūtras. It is also a fundamental idea in the *Avataṃsakasūtra*, the scriptural source of the Sudhana pilgrimage story.

83. *Yifanfeng*, Jiangxi Daodong 江西道東 / poem no.3.

84. Well-known to Song readers, in the debate between Mañjuśrī and Vimalakīrti, the layman declares that Mañjuśrī has come without coming, to which Mañjuśrī affirms the emptiness of movement, "If one has come, one cannot further come; if one already departed, one cannot further depart. Why is that? When coming there is nowhere to come from, when departing nowhere to go" 若來已，更不來；若去已，更不去。所以者何？來者無所從來，去者無所至. *Weimojie jing* (T14.544b16–17); translation adapted from Watson, *Vimalakirti Sutra*, 65.

85. *Shoulengyan jing* (T19.151b29-c4). This section of the sūtra details deluded mental states and an extended discussion of demons. The Buddha teaches Ānanda a set of meditative *samādhi* that reveal ever more subtle strata of awareness. This passage corresponds to a pivotal stage in the text's conception of awakening.

Additional poems similarly affirmed Nanpo's practice of itinerant wandering with reference to emptiness. The following is by Siming Zhiping 四明志平 (n.d.).[86]

	You wandered throughout mountains and rivers with your eyes empty,[87]	江山歷盡眼頭空
2	The frost is severe in the cold grove: tree after tree is red.	霜肅寒林樹樹紅
	Today as you return from China to your country of origin,[88]	今日大唐還本國
4	May a single sail of wind [carry you] ten-thousand miles across misty waters!	萬程煙水一帆風

The first line describes the eye itself as empty, an idea found in other texts from this community, in numerous other Song-era Chan texts, as well as in scriptures.[89] The faculties of perception are distinguished from perceptions themselves as well as from their objects; the eye is different from vision, which is different from what is seen. Because these three—form, eye, sight—arise together and none has an independent existence, it is said there is no form, no eye, and no sight. The six senses, each thus divided into three aspects of sense for a total of eighteen, are all empty. Often, the faculty of sight is listed first and when mentioned alone may refer to the complete list of six senses. This poetic line depicts Nanpo completing his itinerant wandering among mountains and rivers with an understanding that all of his sense faculties are ultimately empty of self-existence.

Poems of parting such as those translated above perform the ordinary social custom of presenting a poem to see off a guest. The difference is that the monk-poets convey a proper Buddhist response where one would expect nostalgia or longing. Though the form appears similar to normative parting poems, the purpose of these monastic parting poems is to offer a religious benediction specifically within the context of Chan itinerant wandering. Moreover, a kind of subversive Chan humor, based on the principles of buddha-nature and emptiness, has been injected into Chan parting poems and in *Yifanfeng*.

---

86. *Yifanfeng*, Siming Zhiping 四明志平 / poem no. 39.

87. The two-character phrase *yantou* 眼頭 is a colloquial way to speak of the *yan* 眼 (eye). Lei, *Chanji fangsu ci yanjiu*, 356–358, illustrates similar vernacular uses of the suffix *tou* for words related to the body, including *bitou* 鼻頭 (nose) and *shetou* 舌頭 (tongue). Here, the extra character helps to fill out the line. The phrase 眼頭空 may be taken as equivalent to 眼空, both meaning "the eye is empty." The latter, 眼空, is common in Buddhist sources, especially *prajñāpāramitā* texts.

88. The phrase *Tang chao* 唐朝, literally, "Tang dynasty," refers to China (then under Song dynastic rule) and not to the Tang era *per se*. Use of *Tō* 唐 to refer to Song China was widespread among Japanese pilgrims and frequently appeared in medieval Sino-Japanese correspondence.

89. See *Yifanfeng*, Maoshan Qihe 鄚山契和 / poem no. 31, as well as *Xutang heshang yulu* (T47.1037a3–5).

Chan humor is funny with a purpose.[90] Chan tales often depict incongruities: iconoclastic behavior, seemingly contradictory statements, and even flat-out heresies. A good Chan master usually has a sharp wit. Witty repartees are not just for amusement, however, and the subversion of norms is to point to Buddhist principles.[91] The humor of Chan parting poetry is often like that found in *Yifanfeng* parting poems. For example, the line "Sudhana did not know he had it" alludes to the scriptural imagery of Sudhana's pilgrimage. But any sense of reverence is quickly disrupted, "and he walked to a hundred cities in vain!" Such iconoclasm is a joke on Nanpo. If Nanpo understands the joke, then he is part of the inside group that grasps the Buddhist principles and perspective that reveal the truth of this iconoclasm.

Many of these parting poems suggest, tongue in cheek, that Nanpo, like Sudhana, had made his trip in vain. Several *Yifanfeng* poems tease Nanpo for exactly this. Xishu Zhengyin 西蜀正因 (n.d.) writes,[92]

	The moon rises in the east, the sun sets in the west;	月從東上日西沈
2	You mistakenly came to China in bitter pursuit of an answer.	錯向中華苦訪尋

Nankang Yongxiu 南康永秀 (n.d.) writes,[93]

	Driven to the point where dust is airborne at the bottom of the sea,	拶到塵飛水底時
2	At that time, your mouth was the same as your nostrils, your eyes just like your brows![94]	口如鼻孔眼如眉

---

90. On the ubiquity and diversity of interpretations, see, for example, the following sources: Faure, *Rhetoric of Immediacy*, chap. 6, gives a historical and cultural criticism of the trickster figure in order to reveal the serious nature of humor in Chan; Wright, *Six Perfections*, 258–262, focuses on Buddhist ethics in a discussion of Buddhist wisdom and laughter (what he calls "comic wisdom"); Hyers, "Humor in Zen: Comic Midwifery," is a theological survey of Chan humor and remains insightful, if retrograde in certain regards.

91. Wit in Chinese history often had layers of purpose, and Knechtges, "Wit, Humor, and Satire," skillfully applies the Freudian distinction between wit and humor to illustrate this. More on humor and wit in Chinese culture (excluding Buddhist aspects) is introduced in Myrhe, "Wit and Humor." Further, Chey, "*Youmo* and the Chinese Sense of Humour," has examined the many classical terms displaced by modern *youmo* 幽默.

92. *Yifanfeng*, Xishu Zhengyin 西蜀正因 / poem no. 20. Xishu Zhengyin was a disciple of Huaihai Yuanzhao 淮海元肇 (1189–1265). Xu, "Ri cang Songseng shiji," 160–161.

93. *Yifanfeng*, Nankang Yongxiu 南康永秀 / poem no. 35. He was an heir in the lineage of Wuzhun Shifan. Xu, "Ri cang Songseng shiji," 162.

94. Such synesthesia appears in both classical Chinese and Buddhist texts. In *Liezi* 列子, synesthesia depicts freedom from ordinary limits of knowing. In *Shoulengyan jing* (T19.153b11–12), synesthesia refers to a profound meditative state.

That mistake before lifting a foot aboard the ship,[95]	脚頭未跨舩舷錯
4 No one can be told the breadth of the sea or the vastness of the mountains.[96]	海濶山遥舉似誰

Read literally, these verses appear to claim Nanpo made his trip in error. Yet it is almost impossible to imagine that such sentiments would be addressed in earnest to a distinguished departing monk. Nanpo lived in Xutang's community for ten years, served as a monastic officer, and was in daily proximity to these monks. The poems' directness of expression signals this intimacy. The poems are particularly funny in light of Nanpo's position as a respected member of Xutang's community, where he had served as the "guest hall officer" (*zhike* 知客).[97] When Xutang died a few years later, a messenger was sent to Kyoto to inform Nanpo, yet another sign of his stature in the community. The directness of the poems can therefore be read as a form of affectionate play. It is also possible to read these passages as a mark of respect for their recipient, or even confirmation of Nanpo's spiritual attainment. Only one possessing a certain understanding of Buddhist principles would get such a rough joke. Many poems in *Yifanfeng* crack the same joke, among them the following couplets and poems:

Qingzhang Benyin 清漳本因 (poem no. 10)

In the Great Kingdom of the Tang, originally there was no Chan;	大唐國裡本無禪
2 Nonetheless, you came southward, resolutely, to seek it.	剛要南來探一回

Lize Qingda 笠澤清達 (poem no. 15)

Your home is in Japan—what was there to search for?	家在扶桑何所求
2 Now, about to scale mountains and brave the seas, we present gifts to send you off to rest.	梯山航海賦歸休

95. An allusion to a sermon attributed to Deshan Xuanjin 德山宣鑒 (782–865), in *Jingde chuandenglu* (T51.317c15–20). "'Tonight you may not ask any questions. Anyone who asks a question will get thirty blows of my cane!' After some time, a monk stepped up and made a bow. The master struck him. The monk said, 'I did not even speak to ask something! Why did the master hit me?' The master said, 'Where are you from?' The monk said, 'I am from Silla.' The master said, 'It would have been better to strike you thirty blows before you ever stepped aboard the ship!'" 師上堂曰：「今夜不得問話。問話者三十拄杖。」時有僧出方禮拜。師乃打之。僧曰：「某甲話也未問。和尚因什麼打某甲。」師曰。「汝是什麼處人。」曰「新羅人。」師曰。「汝未跨船舷時便好與三十拄杖。」

96. A similar sentiment is found in *Mi'an chanshi yulu* (T47.976c21–23): "The height of mountains and thickness of earth are difficult for a person to see; / the breadth of the sea and the vastness of the mountains, must be known oneself" 天高地厚人難見，海闊山遙只自知.

97. In Huiming's preface found in the woodblock edition, Nanpo is described as "tending guests" 典賓, and in the preface to the verse attributed to Xutang, Nanpo is referred to as "Guest Hall Officer [Jō]min" 明知客.

Lu'nan Deyuan 瀘南德源 (poem no. 18)

    Several years you passed in this southern kingdom,   幾年經歷在南朝

2 How could it be necessary to look outside yourself to find   大道何須苦外求
    the great Way?

Guhong Jingxi 古洪淨喜 (poem no. 21)[98]

    Standing in the wind you laugh at your mistaken search   風前冷笑錯參方
    through this realm,

2 When were wholesome companions ever in China?   知識何曾在大唐

Siming Zuying 四明祖英 (poem no. 34)

    Shimmering sunlight floats atop the ocean,   日光浮動海光搖

2 And blue mists gust the whole route [home].   濕碧吹青路一條

    This southern country never had buddhadharma;   南國自來無佛法

4 Don't bother to say you spent the summer in residence on 莫言今夏在凌霄
    Mount Jing.[99]

Dongjia Congyi 東嘉從逸 (poem no. 42)[100]

    Dear Penglai guest from Fusang country [of Japan],   扶桑國裡蓬莱客

2 You crossed ten thousand *li* to our master's seat,   萬里迢 扣師席

    Even though the Great Tang was always right next to your 太唐元在脚頭邊
    feet,

4 So soon you followed others along traces of old routes.   早是循人舊途跡

The writer of each of these farewell poems implies that Nanpo's leaving Japan to seek the dharma in China was the result of an earlier misunderstanding. The ultimate principle is everywhere. These verses appear to be overly direct in expressing to Nanpo that had he understood buddhadharma before he left Japan, he would have had no need to journey to China. The humor is to be found in the poems' unexpected bluntness and apparent incongruity with the otherwise rule-bound asceticism of this community.

    Several interpretations are possible. These poems perhaps were intended to instruct Nanpo, to point to the principles of buddha-nature and emptiness. But the *Yifanfeng* preface by Huiming suggests that they might be in jest, with Nanpo in on the joke, and therefore affirm Nanpo's success in gaining insight after coming to China. The humorous manner in which Nanpo's Chinese dharma brothers presented these passages, the extra-textual action itself, could suggest that the brothers believed Nanpo had reached the end of his itinerant studies able to grasp the meaning of the poems. If so, then the

---

    98. Guhong Jingxi was Xutang's disciple. Xu, "Ri cang Songseng shiji," 161.

    99. "Frozen Mist Peak" 凌霄峰 is the main peak of Mount Jing. It is used here as metonymy for the monastery. To "spend summer" on the mountain refers to the three-month retreat of intensive practice from the fourth through sixth months of the year, known as *anju* 安居.

    100. Poem no. 42 by Dongjia Congyi has a total of sixteen lines with three end rhymes.

parting verses suggest that Nanpo on the eve of his return to his origins, like Sudhana reaching the end of his pilgrimage, now had the insight that he formerly lacked and that had brought him to China in the first place. This interpretation would best explain how a single collection of parting poems appears to include poems both valedictory and tongue in cheek. These jokes at the expense of the conventions of the *songbie* tradition allowed both the authors and the recipient to enact the Chan monk's conquest of the emotions.

Such an interpretation seems possible with many of the poems, including the following one by Chicheng Yiwei 赤城義爲 (n.d.).[101]

	In the words between host and guest, fundamentally are no words.[102]	主賓句裡元無句
2	A mistake to come to China, a mistake to seek a teacher.	錯入唐朝錯見人
	The misty waters are vast and boundless as always before;	烟水茫茫一仍舊
4	Laugh at that "ruddy dust rising at the bottom of the sea!"[103]	咲他海底起紅塵

This poem may be understood in light of Qingyuan Weixin's sermon about mountains and waters translated above. At first, Nanpo thought he could find an awakened teacher in China and traveled there in accordance with ordinary thoughts akin to Qingyuan's first stage where "mountains are mountains." Later, Nanpo saw the landscape is as "boundless as always before," comparable to the third stage when "mountains are just mountains." The final line of Yiwei's poem alludes to something seemingly impossible, which now Nanpo, too, finds humorous. This is the second stage, when "mountains are not mountains." Seen from the end point of the journey, the apparent contradictions that arise when trying to describe emptiness are laughable.

The subversion of mainstream expectations for parting poetry is visible in the first poem in *Yifanfeng* after that of Xutang. Tiantai Weijun 天台惟俊 (fl. 1245–1269) was a prominent officer in the community of Xutang Zhiyu, serving as the master's assistant for many years.[104] Weijun was technically

---

101. *Yifanfeng,* Chicheng Yiwei 赤城義爲 / poem no. 29.

102. The fourfold relations between host and guest were attributed to Linji by this time in the Song. They were used to explain encounters between good or bad teachers and good or bad students.

103. This popular Chan saying is derived from *Jingde chuandenglu* (T51.421b29-c2). "A monk asked, 'What is a saying of yours, Master Dayang, that reveals the *dharmakāya*?' The master said, 'ruddy dust rising at the bottom of the sea; laterally flowing water atop Mount Sumeru.'" 問：「如何是大陽透法身底句？」師曰：「大洋海底紅塵起，須彌頂上水橫流。」

104. Weijun's poem comes after Xutang's verse in the Edo woodblock edition, but Xutang's verse is appended to the end of the early manuscript edition. Protass, "Returning Empty-Handed," 395–396. For more on Weijun, see Satō, "Kidō Chigu no Shihō monjin ni tsuite," 65–70. Weijun, also known as Dongzhou Weijun 東州惟俊, was the compiler of *The Recorded Sayings of Baolin Chan Temple at Yunhuang Mountain in Wuzhou* 婺州雲黃山寶林禪寺語錄, a portion of Xutang's *yulu*.

proficient at poetic composition. His *jueju* begins with a first-line rhyme and progresses in observance of regulated prosody.[105]

> Since coming empty-handed from the East, ten winter frosts   空手東來已十霜
> have passed,
> 2 And now still empty-handed you ride a homeward ship.   依然空手趁回檣
> Brightly illumine the one intention of the ancestral teacher,   明明一片祖師意
> 4 Do not act Chinese when you propagate [Chan teachings in   莫作唐朝事舉揚
> Japan].[106]

Though Weijun's poem is free of formal errors, the emotional timbre of this couplet is remarkably cheeky. It would normally seem rude to tell a guest that he came with nothing, stayed a long time, and left empty-handed. The two-character word *kongshou*, "empty-handed," occurs twice in the initial eleven syllables, which might signal a clever play on words. But a reader might also wonder if the repetition was the result of a clumsy or rushed hand. Weijun may have been technically proficient with tonal meter, but his poem seems to break with convention by repeating a phrase and altogether failing to express sadness at parting with his friend. The *Yifanfeng* poems repeatedly use the words "empty-handed" 空手 and "nothing" 空 to simultaneously invoke their conventional meanings of something lacking and their more profound implications of Buddhist emptiness.[107] The same phrase appears in a sermon by Xutang, "Instructions for Head Seat Ruzu" 示如足首座, as a description of the awakened behavior of the Chan ancestors: "as an ancient worthy remarked, 'the great master Bodhidharma came empty-handed and left empty-handed' " 古德道：達磨大師空手來，空手去.[108] This shared knowledge of a dual usage allows the authorial community of the *Yifanfeng*, associated with Xutang, to subvert the conventional norms of a parting poem and re-appropriate its social function in a Buddhist monastic setting. Thus, the *Yifanfeng* poems can be read as insults, teachings, or in-jokes among awakened monks. Throughout *yulu* literature, mutual insults appear as mutual confirmation or as "expedient means" from a Chan master.[109]

The Chan humor found in the *Yifanfeng* parting poems is not merely funny. Chan humor expresses the iconoclastic implications of emptiness and the apparent contradictions of deluded beings possessing buddha-mind.

---

105. *Yifanfeng*, Tiantai Weijun / poem no. 2.

106. Here Nanpo is admonished, when he returns to Japan, that he should not propagate the Chan teachings as though they can only be found in China. The higher intentions of Bodhidharma, the truth of Chan, are universal. The binome *juyang* 舉揚 ("propagate") is a common verb in Chan texts, often used to refer to the didactic behavior of an abbot, and frequently followed by a noun referring to Chan teachings, such as *zongzhi* 宗旨 ("the cardinal meaning").

107. For a similar usage of the term by another Japanese pilgrim, see Kodera, *Dōgen's Formative Years*, 77–78; Heine, "Empty-Handed, but not Empty-Headed," 218.

108. *Xutang heshang yulu* (T47.1012b1–2).

109. Anderl, "Zen in the Art of Insult," 388–389.

Chan uses words in doubled meanings to convey concepts that are unfamiliar, often impenetrable by conventional thinking. At the same time, these poems play with the ordinary expectation that people feel sad when parting. Through the direct subversion of this generic expectation, the *Yifanfeng* writers asserted their shared Chan sociability and performed the proper rituals for when awakened beings say farewell.

A Contrastive Parting Poem

In this section I offer examples of poems about separation by the Tiantai monk Gushan Zhiyuan, the same poet who wrote "The Poetry Demon," the verse that opens this book. The parting poems by Chan monks just discussed in general subverted mainstream genre norms regarding emotions as a means to affirm Buddhist teachings. Unlike these Chan monks, Zhiyuan depicted his sadness. His poem "Seeing Off Xizhong on Travels to Zha" 送希中遊霅 resolves the structural tension of Buddhist parting poetry in an ironic manner.[110] Here, Zhiyuan concludes with acknowledgement that he *should* write a poem expressing non-attachment but that he has been moved, stirred as he puts it, by the sight of the flowing waters that will carry his friend away.[111]

	As the sun sets, the cicada's cry grows urgent.	日暮蟬鳴急
2	Looking over the flowing river stirs this chant of parting.	臨流動別吟
	A single sail rushes into evening radiance.	片帆衝晚照
4	A returning bird enters the distant grove.	歸鳥入遙林
	The appearance of the moon is quiet on the cold creek.	月色寒溪靜
6	A bell sounds deep from a mountaintop temple.	鐘聲岳寺深
	Here, along duckweed banks I meet my old friend	蘋洲逢舊識
8	and ought to be able to speak of no-mind.	應得話無心

The lyric voice of the monk, against expectations apposite to his station, begins to intone the sentiments of separation. Feelings quicken like the sound of crickets that crescendo toward dusk. As soon as Zhiyuan imagines the sail disappearing into the twilight horizon, he immediately turns his poetic attention to images of serenity. The reflection of the moon on water, here a frozen creek, is a common trope for the manifest world that is ultimately empty. This line suggests a philosophical resolution: perhaps the sorrow of parting is as fleeting and unsubstantial as a reflection of silvery moonlight. Feelings will rise and fall. Then, evoking a vast auditory landscape, distant temple bells ring at dusk and are heard but not seen. In that moment, the poet knows that he *should* speak of the emptiness of his sorrow. Zhiyuan's statement that he

---

110. Zhiyuan praised Xizhong as "my friend, whose will is focused on the tenets of [Buddhist] truth, who has tangentially penetrated the Confucian arts, and taken the sobriquet Xizhong" 吾友志慕真宗，旁通儒術，希中為字. *Xianju bian* (ZZ56.905c24–906a1).

111. *Xianju bian* (ZZ56.946c17–20).

"*should* be able" 應得 reveals his knowledge of this moral obligation.[112] The implication is that despite knowing better, the poet feels sadness as he sees off an old friend. This appears to subvert the expectations of monks' parting poetry, akin to the parting poems by Xuedou Chongxian discussed above, thereby at once demonstrating knowledge of appropriate deportment and expressing the natural human response to parting. Regardless, it is further evidence of a monastic literary culture situated at the intersection of mainstream and monastic norms.

Zhiyuan wrote other poems that expressed conventional emotions. On the theme of separation, he composed a quatrain entitled "You Did Not Come" 君不來.

	Last year I sent you off on the empty river,	前年送君空江上
2	The sail swelled and perfectly met the rising west wind.	張帆正值西風起
	Today [also] a west wind, and you still have not returned.	今日西風君未歸
4	Vast, vast, I see only the empty river.	茫茫只見空江水

This is a nice conventional poem. Only in the context of Zhiyuan's other writings and Tiantai studies does it become possible to argue that, although this poem may express emotions, Zhiyuan understood that emotions are not inherently separate from ultimate reality. To prefer either emotions or no emotions would be a misunderstanding. This topic is addressed in the next chapter, where I will read Zhiyuan's mourning poetry together with the section of his *Mahāparinirvāṇasūtra* commentary explicating Ānanda's wails of lamentation for the Buddha.[113]

Coda

Buddhist monks used the standard forms of parting poetry but adapted genre conventions to meet specific Buddhist monastic ideals. This does not, though, require that we define a new genre of "Buddhist parting poetry." If we are more interested in pigeons than in pigeonholes,[114] then our goal will be to make sense of the extant monks' poetry instead of focusing on taxonomies.[115]

---

112. Without the word 得 in this line, I would read it as "and so respond with talk of no-mind." In that case, each line would reflect the mind that is without attachments. The poem would still depict an outer landscape that mirrored the poet's inner feelings, although the poet would then claim to be non-attached to the emotions. This would resonate with Zhiyuan's views on the emotions as not separate from ultimate reality, as he argued in his *Mahāparinirvāṇasūtra* commentary, which is discussed in the next chapter.

113. Aspects of emotions in different *Nirvāṇasūtra* texts and paintings, not included in the next chapter, can be found in Protass, "Buddhist Monks and Chinese Poetry," 245–270.

114. Again from Fowler, *Kinds of Literature*, 37; see n. 8 above.

115. Rather than imagining the *Yifanfeng* poems as belonging to one genre, or hybrid sub-genre, these parting poems should be seen as in a dialogue with genre conventions. This resonates with Newsom, *Book of Job*, 221.

As monastic parting poems are a type of occasional poetry, the circumstances of composition are essential to understanding the corpus. Buddhist prescriptive texts, especially the Chan "rules of purity" and the lexicon *Zuting shiyuan,* illuminate the ritual and symbolic worlds within which these poems were composed and received. Parting poems frequently address the circumstances of itinerant study, a practice woven into the fabric of Song-dynasty monasticism and that generated many occasions of arrival and leave-taking. The *Yifanfeng* parting poems, for example, are situated within the dual occasion of a ritual departure at the end of a visitor's long pilgrimage as well as a personal farewell to a familiar colleague.

These poems use the same literary forms as conventional parting poetry but are distinctly Buddhist in terms of themes and functions. By avoiding expressions of nostalgia or sadness, these monks' poems deviated from mainstream parting poetry and the norms in Song "remarks on poetry" and anthologies. This cool equanimity appears to be characteristic of parting poetry in most Song-dynasty Chan monastic communities. But with cases like Xuedou Chongxian and Gushan Zhiyuan, monks could further invert any such expectations for monks' parting poetry and question whether stoicism was the finest expression of the dharma when bidding farewell. Individual writers regularly composed new parting poetry, and the poetics of parting were not singular. Nonetheless, the general dynamics of Buddhist monks' parting poetry lie at the intersection of Buddhist ideals and Chinese literary traditions. We turn in the next chapter to a consideration of mourning verse composed by monks, including personal expressions of grief and ritual lamentations.

6

Personal Lamentations and Funerary Verse

> Ananda, grieving all night in the square
> gave up & went to bed & just then woke
> —*Gary Snyder,* "Burning" no. 6

MONKS OF the Song dynasty who wrote poetic laments perceived a tension between their grief and the ideal found in Buddhist teachings of nonattachment to emotions. They noted that in Buddhist scriptures Ānanda, because he was not yet awakened, wailed grievously when the Buddha died. Control of vehement feelings was thought to reveal the depth of one's understanding of the dharma. The full significance of monks' laments becomes apparent when we read ritual verses composed for and recited during monastic funerals. This chapter compares two distinct modes of poetic writing in response to grief. In one mode, verse and sermon were woven together for performance at funerals. A consideration of the ritual context and communal setting in which these didactic verses were intoned will aid our interpretations. But monks also wrote to express personal grief in a mode that borrowed directly from the mainstream poetic tradition of lamention. A comparison of these two modes will illustrate the richness of poetic practices among Song Buddhist monks.

The first section of this chapter focuses on funerary verse used in Chan ritual. Prescriptive texts for monastic funerals frequently asserted the inappropriateness of uncontrolled grief for a monk. The admonitions did not mean that one should not mourn, only that sincere grief, whether for a parent or teacher, was to be manifested within ritual forms. According to the manuals, even the wails performed at a Chinese funeral were to reflect the calm dignity of the Buddha's awakened disciples at the *parinirvāṇa*. An indication of the relative importance of ritualizing grief in monks' writing is that the amount of ritual verse crafted for recitation at funerals is slightly more numerous than that of personal lamentations. In this ritual mode, a Chan abbot encouraged his community to take the death of a monk as an opportunity to deepen their understanding of Buddhist teachings. I compare liturgical manuals with literary fragments; by bringing together these two types of source material, we can construct interpretations of funereal verse based on their likely ritual context.

The latter portions of this chapter focus on monks' poems of personal mourning. I will argue that monks used different strategies to respond to a perceived tension between their monastic identity and the expression of grief. I first scrutinize the poetic strategies of Qisong and Daoqian, two literary monks. I then examine the writings of Tiantai monk Zhiyuan, followed by mourning poetry written by abbots of Chan public monasteries. Common among monks' poems of the Song era are those of "mourning" 悼, "lamentation" 哀, "wailing" 哭, and "dirges" 挽/輓; all are poems of personal lamentation. Knowledge of the traditions of these well-established genres was propagated by literary historians of the Song dynasty.[1] Glosses in Song Buddhist encyclopedias also suggest that an educated monk was expected to possess this literary knowledge.[2] The disparate poetic strategies used in personal laments form a clear contrast with the didacticism of ritual funerary verses. The examples that follow may illustrate how monks used poetic spaces to create meaningful responses to the gaps between the norms expressed in prescriptive texts and lived religion.

Ritual Verses in Monastic Funerals

The funerary verses offered by an abbot at the funeral of a fellow monk are pervasive in Chan monastic literature. Often, verses were included together with *jisong* in *yulu*, indicating that textual communities regarded such verses as religious writ rather than poetry *per se*. These funerary verses could also be grouped separately in such texts, most frequently under the term *foshi* 佛事, "buddha rites."[3] As seen in Chapter 4, this same term in scriptural language meant "deeds of a buddha" and was the opposite of "the work of Māra." *Foshi* denotes activity that will lead others to liberation. By the Song, the phrase referred to Buddhist rituals and was a euphemism for the ritual care of dead members of the sangha. "Buddha rites" as a bibliographic category encompasses texts for several steps in a funeral ritual. I use "funerary verse" to refer to these multiple sub-genres in aggregate.

By at least the early 1100s, compositions for monastic funerals constituted

---

1. For example, Ruan Yue 阮閲 (*jinshi* 1085) in his encyclopedic *Shihua zonggui, qianji* 43.1 and *houji* 34.1, under the title *shangdao men* 傷悼門 gathered numerous comments on the history and practice of elegiac writing. *Shihua zonggui* was first completed in 1123. Ruan's last colophon is variously given as 1141 辛酉 or 1161 辛巳. On the influence of *Shihua zonggui* in the Southern Song, see Zhang, *Tiaoxi yuyin conghua*, 185–192.

2. *Zuting shiyuan* (ZZ64.404a13–21); *Shishi liutie*, 39/351b.

3. This phrase continued to be used for rituals throughout the late imperial period, as in *Chanlin shuyu kaozheng*. Welch, *Practice of Chinese Buddhism*, 189, 340–345, describes related funerary and memorial activities among monks during the early Republican period. Song-era funeral texts also were transmitted to Japan and collected in *Zengi gemon shū* 禪儀外文集 by Kokan Shiren 虎関師錬 (1278–1346).

part of the specialized literary knowledge required of an abbot. Public monasteries of the Song housed large communities, and a certain amount of bureaucracy was necessary for the proper functioning of these centers of Buddhist learning. For the funerals of monks, new Song compositions adapted parts of the Chinese elegy tradition to the ritual needs of Buddhist monasteries. In the pre-Song era as well, serious-minded Buddhist monks appropriated various aspects of the Chinese elegy tradition. The "pagoda inscription" 塔銘 displaced the lay "tomb inscription" 墓志銘 and "necrology" 誌. Other genres from the Chinese tradition were used in the Song to commemorate the passing of Chan teachers. For example, both the formal "prayer texts" 祭文 and "obituaries" 狀 for deceased Buddhist teachers can be found appended to the received edition of many *yulu* and in the collected writings of literati.

Not all funeral texts in *yulu* were written in verse; many are in formal parallel prose. Nonetheless, a preponderance of distinctive funereal verses were included in *yulu*. The use of these various verses was not confined to one branch of the Chan family tree or to a single time or place. Examples are the numerous verses in the *yulu* of Yuanwu Keqin,[4] Hongzhi Zhengjue,[5] and Xutang Zhiyu.[6] These verses correspond to funerary ritual sequences outlined in various "rules of purity." Many of them accompanied stages in a cremation rite.[7] The act of cremation itself in Song Buddhist texts continued often to be referred to as *chapi* 茶毗, a transliteration corresponding to the Sanskrit *dhyāpita*.[8] By the early 1100s, dharma words offered at the time of cremation were referred to as writs of "lowering the flames" 下火 and "carrying a torch" 秉炬,[9] terms used both in *yulu* to title verses and formal prose texts composed for funerals.[10] Based on the performance directions incorporated into the texts, "lowering the flames" seems to culminate in "lifting the flame before speaking [a final admonition]" 舉火炬云, and "carrying a torch" culminates in "lighting the pyre as one speaks [a final phrase]" 擲下

---

4. *Yuanwu Foguo chanshi yulu* (T47.810a27-c28) includes verses of "encoffinment" 入龕, "offering lamentation" 舉哀, and "lowering flames [for cremation]" 下火.

5. In *Hongzhi chanshi guanglu* (T48.82b10–83c5), approximately thirty verses for "lowering flames" are followed by several verses of "pagoda interment" 入塔.

6. *Xutang heshang yulu* (T47.1060a18 and 1033c7–1034a25) includes sixteen *bingju* 秉炬 verses, each with the name of a monastic officer, and another dozen *foshi* poems.

7. My understanding here is based in part on the erudite commentary by monk Yirun 儀潤 (19th c.) in *Baizhang qinggui zhengyiji*, under *chapi* 茶毗 (ZZ63.436b23–437b1).

8. The character *tu* 荼 is here read *cha* and often miswritten or misprinted as *cha* 茶. *Zenrin shōkisen*, 19/567b8–11, explains that historical shifts in phonetics led 荼 to be homophonous with 茶, leading to erroneous uses of the latter. *Pi* is also printed 毘.

9. Among the earliest examples of "lowering the flames" are those in the 1135 edition of Cishou's *Huilin lu*, 50b-54a; *Cishou Huaishen chanshi guanglu* (ZZ73.132b15). Additional examples by Yuanwu Keqin are discussed in the main text of this chapter.

10. Mujaku Dōchū, *Zenrin shōkisen*, 19/566b14–567a3, observed that these two are rough synonyms, and "carrying a torch" was a longer rite involving more people than "lowering the flames." I believe there was a minor but significant ritual variation for words expressed before versus during the lighting of a pyre.

火云.[11] The somber setting and ritual drama of igniting a funeral pyre likely prepared an audience of mourners to receive the Buddhist teachings on death and impermanence.

I will focus here on verses associated with cremation; however, additional ritual verses can be found in *yulu*. Several types of verse relate to "encoffining" 龕. From *qinggui* we learn that encoffining referred to the wooden structure used to hold a corpse throughout the performance of cremation rites. Funeral verses were recited during rituals that placed a dead body in a coffin, for the rites performed when raising the coffin for conveyance to the pyre, as well as to accompany rites for "pagoda interment" 入塔.[12] Individual verses in these modes correspond to instructions given in various *qinggui*. Each extant *qinggui* exhibits a distinct sequence as well as numerous other smaller differences, likely reflecting variation among communities.[13] For that reason, we cannot reconstruct the exact ritual performance of any given funeral. Nonetheless, a synoptic review of guidelines in *qinggui* illustrates the approximate settings in which funereal verses were recited in Song monasteries.

Some funerary verses were generic and preserved as models to be studied and imitated. Many extant funerary verses are remnants from one-time liturgies performed for an individual's funeral. Within a *yulu*, the titles of individual funereal verses sometimes include the name of the departed and a brief reference to a particular stage of a funeral that compilers felt was important for readers to know. In like manner, *qinggui* texts indicate when in a funeral procession verses should be intoned. The *Chanyuan qinggui* of 1103, for example, makes clear that "some dharma words" 法語 should be recited after igniting the crematory fire.[14] Extant examples in *yulu* from the Song on show that these "dharma words" often took the form of verse or a mix of verse and formal parallel prose and were mostly categorized as "buddha rites." More detailed directions were compiled in *Essentials of the Revised Rules of Purity for Major Monasteries* 叢林校定清規總要 (preface 1274; hereafter *Jiaoding qinggui*). This is the same two-fascicle manual for monastic officers introduced in Chapter 4.

---

11. Examples are numerous and may be found in *Fojian chanshi yulu* (Kunaichō ed.), section titled *foshi* 佛事, 3.10b and 11b, and in *Wuzhun Shifan chanshi yulu* (ZZ70.272a22, b19, and b23). Additional examples are in *Shixi Xinyue chanshi zalu* (ZZ71.74b19-c2).

12. During the Song, a *kan* 龕 was practically synonymous with a *guan* 棺 (coffin). See, e.g., *Conglin jiaoding qinggui zongyao* (ZZ63.612b13) and the gloss for *kanzi* 龕子 in *Shishi yaolan* (T54.307c2–7). Runyi draws a distinction in his Qing commentary, *Baizhang qinggui zhengyiji* (ZZ63.435c7).

13. See, e.g., the list of seventeen rituals in the Yuan text *Chixiu Baizhang qinggui* (T48.1128a22–26) and the subsequent instructions for each ritual event. The late Southern Song text *Conglin jiaoding qinggui zongyao* (ZZ63.612a18– 613a22) describes a sixteen-step funeral process, accompanied by detailed instructions for events, liturgical texts for recitation, and model petitions. Similar instructions can be found in *Chanyuan qinggui* (ZZ63.541a8–541c20), s.v. *wangseng* 亡僧; translated in Kagamishima, *Zen'en shingi*, 237–248, and Yifa, *Buddhist Monastic Codes,* 206–211.

14. *Chanyuan qinggui* (ZZ63.541b1–2); Kagamishima, *Zen'en shingi*, 239–240; Yifa, *Buddhist Monastic Codes,* 207.

Although I rely on this one particular manual here, similar directions occupy an entire fascicle of the *Auxiliary Rules of Purity for Chan Monasteries* 禪林備用清規 (completed in 1286). *Rules of Purity of Huanzhu Hermitage* 幻住庵清規 (preface 1317) instructs that "the abbot performs buddha rites and lowers the flame" 菴主做佛事下火. This terse allusion seems to assume familiarity with instructions that could be found in larger *qinggui,* and Zhongfeng Mingben himself composed numerous texts later collectively entitled "carrying a torch and interment [writs] for various Chan students" 為諸禪人秉炬入塔.[15]

The *Jiaoding qinggui* manual includes sections that distinguish among funerals performed on the occasion of "the nirvāṇa of the current abbot" 當代住持涅槃, funerals for "honored elders from any mountain [temple]" 諸山尊宿, who were often retired abbots, and funerals for the ordinary "deceased monk" 亡僧. In death, as in life, the abbot was regarded as a buddha;[16] therefore, the funerals for an abbot ritually enacted the *parinirvāṇa* of an enlightened buddha.[17] An ordinary monk would be given a simpler ceremony; many *qinggui* suggest for that purpose the use of the standard "*gāthā* of impermanence" 無常偈, attributed to Śākyamuni Buddha in several *Nirvāṇasūtra* texts.[18] For the funeral of an abbot, per *Jiaoding qinggui,* an eminent monk from a neighboring temple was to be invited to preside, or, alternatively, an honored elder from within the sangha could lead the funeral. For the second and third types, that is, funerals for retired abbots or ordinary monks, the current abbot would preside over the ceremonies. The *Jiaoding qinggui* instructs how and when the sangha should "offer lamentations" as well as when the ritualist should intone "dharma words." The latter could be delivered at any funeral. The "lamentations," by contrast, were adapted from Chinese practices to mourn one's parents and were only offered to abbots or other venerated figures.

The *Jiaoding qinggui,* like other liturgies, was modular, offering options that could be adapted to accommodate each situation. The text includes placeholders where a ritualist might tailor modifications. These modifications

---

15. The former in *Huanzhu'an qinggui* (ZZ63.586b14), section on "Seeing Off the Dead" 津送. On this *qinggui,* see Heller, *Illusory Abiding,* 175–221. The latter is a section title in *Tianmu zhongfeng guanglu,* 7/395–396. Some entries are followed by brief notes, such as "for a Japanese monk" 日本人 and "for one talented at healing and herbs" 能醫藥.

16. Argued by Demiéville in "Langue et littérature chinoises," 280. Sharf, "Idolization of Enlightenment," 16–22, discusses a typical Chan funeral of the Song dynasty.

17. This idea articulated by Bodiford, "Zen in the Art of Funerals," 152. Explicit evidence from the Song is in *Conglin jiaoding qinggui zongyao* (ZZ63.611a23) and later in *Chanlin beiyong qinggui* (ZZ63.652c22–653a9). See also Faure, *Rhetoric,* 191–205.

18. The locus classicus for Song usage of the "*gāthā* of impermanence" likely is *Da banniepan jing* (T12.450a16–451a1), which tells that Śākyamuni in a previous life was a Himalayan ascetic seeking the second *pāda* of a *śloka* from Indra (disguised as a *rākṣa*). *Chanlin beiyong qinggui* (ZZ63.653a14–15) suggests the entire assembly recite the *gāthā* three times before lifting the coffin. *Huanzhu'an qinggui* noted the simplicity of this verse (ZZ63.583b14–16) and proposed writing each of the four lines on a separate large sheet of paper to be placed around the coffin (ZZ63.586a6–7). A diagram of the latter practice as done in Rinzai Zen is in *Shinshū Zenke shokan,* 261.

could be as simple as using the name of the dead or an elaborate series of personalized eulogies. The *Jiaoding qinggui*, for example, instructs an abbot to preside over the funeral of an honored elder and conduct a memorial service as follows:[19]

> The abbot ascends the high seat, where he may recount accomplishments of great virtue and renown from each of the abbatial positions throughout the deceased's lifetime. The abbot steps down and goes before the [tablet] seat of the spirit and stands in respect.[20] Preparations and arrangements should be made ahead of time in the westerly corridor of the Dharma Hall. Perform a memorial ceremony following the procedures. One may offer incense; one may raise a lamentation. (Dharma words here.)

> 住持升座，敘彼平生所歷住持，道德響望事。下座，詣靈位前朝立。預於法堂西間，設位安排，祭禮如法。或拈香，或舉哀 有法語

After the abbot gives a talk from the ritual high seat, he offers some dharma words to the spirit tablet waiting in the western wing outside the Dharma Hall. Two further optional ritual procedures may be followed. The procedures for the assembly to offer incense or perform a formal lament are outlined earlier in the *Jiaoding qinggui*. Regardless of the inclusion of these optional procedures, the ritualist should offer guiding dharma words at this juncture in the memorial service.

By the end of the Song, model funerary verses had been composed for a variety of circumstances. The monk Deyin 德因 (b. 1236)[21] compiled fourteen fascicles of exemplary liturgical verse and formal parallel prose.[22] Many of these compositions were Deyin's own, though he borrowed liberally from earlier texts. The model texts in fascicle 13, entitled "Dharma Words for Nirvāṇa" 涅槃法語門, include those for monastic funerals and cremations.[23] Some of these texts are almost entirely in verse, those accompanying cremation, for example. Fascicle 13 begins with three examples of "lamentations," mostly in verse. One example, from a Northern Song text, is translated shortly below.

---

19. *Conglin jiaoding qinggui zongyao* (ZZ63.613b12–16; *Gozan-ban*, 529).

20. On *chaoli* 朝立 as "standing facing [it] in respect," see *Zenrin shōkisen*, 10/403b9–13.

21. For the date of birth, see the opening lines of Deyin's "Song of Myself" 自陳情詞. *Gaofeng Longquan yuan Yin shi ji xianyu lu* (ZZ65.53a8–9). Deyin gives the sexagenary cycle for the year, month, day, and hour of his birth, and the month of conception, adding that he was born under an ominous sign.

22. Preserving the original preface dated 1287, a Japanese edition of 1634 is the ancestral redaction of the extant *Gaofeng Longquanyuan Yin shi ji xianyu lu*. Shiina, *Sō Gen ban*, 559, notes Yuan-era fragments.

23. In addition to verses for monastic funerals, a section of various writs are for specific use at cremations depending on a person's occupation, or for the notably old or young. There is also a verse to be used at the cremation of "those who drunkenly fell off a bridge and drowned" 因醉渡橋溺死, a separate text for courtesans who drowned, and another text for monks who drowned; *Gaofeng Longquanyuan* (ZZ65.49b19).

The ritual of "offering lamentations" was, among all the kinds of monastic funeral activity, somewhat controversial. There are Buddhist sources in which conspicuous wailing is regarded as inappropriate for a monk. *Chanlin beiyong qinggui* and *Chixiu Baizhang qinggui* insist that only after the completion of "buddha rites" could one give "a reasonable offering of lamentation" 理合舉哀. There was disagreement over whether the *ju'ai* 舉哀, "offering of lamentation," was part of the "buddha rites" proper or was a separate custom.[24]

The term *ju'ai* is ubiquitous in Chinese texts, including those of the Song. It literally denotes a grief-stricken wail and generally connotes formal mourning.[25] As was well-known in the Song, the *Book of Rites* stipulated the appropriate times for public grieving as well as who is to do what type of wailing. The principal mourners should "sob" 啼, the siblings should "wail" 哭, and the women should "wail and stomp" 哭踊.[26] Anne McLaren concludes that men's public performances of grief more often involved physical suffering; "the most histrionic form of mourning was reserved for women.... Wailed performance was an aesthetic as well as a moral experience, and the manner in which ritual wailing was performed was an integral part of its efficacy."[27] Many of these ideals were perpetuated in the Southern Song through *Family Rituals* by Zhu Xi 朱熹 (1130–1200), a manual that detailed the steps of a proper death ritual and the etiquette of requisite wailing.[28]

Given the strong cultural assumptions just mentioned, it is not surprising that prescriptive Buddhist sources from the Song dynasty directly addressed appropriate expressions of grief. The *Shishi yaolan,* completed in 1019, for example, includes a section entitled "Seeing Off the Departed" 送終 that comments on Chinese customs. On "wailing," the compiler cites several scriptural authorities, noting that in a *Nirvāṇasūtra* only those disciples not yet liberated thrashed on the ground, beat their chests, and wailed.[29] Another pithy command conveys the gist of these ideals: "When a monk's teacher dies, he must not raise his voice wailing and should shed only a few tears" 比丘師亡不得舉聲大哭應小小泣淚.[30] Another prescription allows that a monk may mourn his parents and his teacher; "however, he must not wildly shout or appeal to Azure Heaven, all unwholesome speech. He should just one time

---

24. See texts quoted in *Zenrin shōkisen* 19/562b2–563a.

25. For example, see Su Shi's depiction of his formal mourning at news of the death of Emperor Shenzong. Yugen Wang, "Limits of Poetry as Means of Social Criticism," 60.

26. Following McLaren, *Performing Grief,* 84–85. This passage in *Li ji ji jie,* 1135. I follow the distinction between *ku* as formal lament and *qi* as crying found in early Chinese literature described by Harbsmeier, "Weeping and Wailing in Ancient China."

27. McLaren, *Performing Grief,* 85–86.

28. Ebrey, *Chu Hsi's Family Rituals,* 65–152.

29. *Shishi yaolan* (T54.308b7–14). Similar ideas are found in various *Nirvāṇasūtra* texts, analyzed in Protass, "Buddhist Monks and Chinese Poetry," 245–270. The *Shishi yaolan* quotation attributed to the *Nirvāṇasūtra* is not a direct quote, however, and more closely resembles a passage in *Sifen lü* (T22.966b3–24), a text also quoted elsewhere in *Shishi yaolan.*

30. Based on a passage from *Fo shuo Mulian wen jielü zhong wubai qingzhong shi jing* (T24.989c11–12).

call out, *ai ai*" 但不得縱聲委曲并致詞稱蒼天，罪逆之語，唯一往其聲哀哀而已。[31] These kinds of commands also appear in the Yuan imperial rules of purity: for example, after one's master has died "one must not lose control, crying and tearing one's robes" 不得披麻慟哭。[32] Such prescriptive texts posited that Buddhist monks were allowed to grieve, especially for their parents or teachers, but were expected to refrain from excessive emotion.[33]

Formal performances of grief at Chan monastic funerals were common from the early 1100s on, even if still contested and in need of justification. The late Southern Song rule book *Jiaoding qinggui* was decidedly in favor of a lamentation for one's teacher as one's spiritual father. The compiler was concerned: "Some say there is no need to teach the vulgar custom of 'offering lamentation,' and they mourn in their heart only" 或曰不用教俗舉哀，但心喪而已。[34] The practice of "mourning in one's heart" is an adaptation of a Confucian ideal. The *Book of Rites* prescribed that a student "mourn in the heart for three years" 心喪三年 for his teacher, in contrast to the three-year period of formal mourning after the death of a parent.[35] For monks who had left home to join the sangha, one's teacher became a father figure. And so the *Jiaoding qinggui* encouraged disciples, referred to as "filial sons" 孝子, to lead the assembly of monks in a formal wail for their late teacher.[36]

As adapted by Chan monastics, the term "offering lamentations" came to have two meanings.[37] First, it described the assembly repeating the word "*ai*" two or three times— "Sorrow! Sorrow! Sorrow!"—a controlled and formal expression of grief. Second, "offering lamentations" was a bibliographic category. Examples of *ju'ai* texts are found in *yulu* and anthologies. If the funeral was for an abbot, according to the *Jiaoding qinggui,* after arranging the master's portrait near his encoffined body, the ritualist would first intone a lamentation text (here referred to as "dharma words"), after which the assembly would wail several times.[38] Such a scene is depicted explicitly in the *yulu* of Dahui, wherein he stands before the funeral portrait of his teacher Yuanwu Keqin, gestures at the portrait, then vocalizes his lamentation text before lighting the incense offering.[39]

So that the reader may better understand how a Buddhist *ju'ai* of the Song era orchestrated a poetic verse, parallel prose, vernacular sermonizing, and performative gestures, I translate below an example from the oeuvre of

---

31. *Shishi yaolan* (T54.308b12–14). This passage repeated in *Jiaoyuan qinggui* (ZZ57.344a3).

32. *Chixiu baizhang qinggui* (T48.1127b5).

33. Most Song positions echo the sources and arguments first articulated by Daoxuan in *Sifen lü shanfan buque xingshi chao* (T40.145b2–8).

34. *Conglin jiaoding qinggui zongyao* (ZZ63.611b1–4).

35. *Li ji ji jie*, 165.

36. Yifa, *Buddhist Monastic Codes*, 307n66, discusses disciples as "filial sons" in *Chanyuan qinggui*. Later, *Chanlin beiyong qinggui* (ZZ63.654a2) added that disciples could also cry.

37. Following the explanation proffered in *Zenrin shōkisen* 19/562b2–563a2.

38. *Conglin jiaoding qinggui zongyao* (ZZ63.611c11–18 and 612a19).

39. *Dahui pujue chanshi yulu* (T47.844c4–12).

Yuanwu Keqin, the *ju'ai* "Offering a Lamentation for Venerable Foyan" 為佛眼和尚舉哀. It is likely the earliest complete text for "offering a lamentation" and was later anthologized by Deyin and others as a model.[40] The "Lamentation for Venerable Foyan" is one of two texts Keqin wrote for his late dharma brother Foyan Qingyuan 佛眼清遠 (1067–1120). The second of the two texts, "Lowering the Flames for Venerable Foyan" 為佛眼和尚下火, is longer and accompanied the cremation.[41] From these texts we learn that Keqin personally presided over the funeral rites for Foyan. "Lamentation for Venerable Foyan" contains multiple genres, beginning with a five-character quatrain in semi-official language, followed by vernacular speech. Then comes a description of physical action ("he pointed at the coffin and said"), followed by an allusive seven-character couplet, then directions spoken to the audience, concluding with the collective cry, "Sorrow! Sorrow!"[42]

"He tread the way for thirty years,	三十年行道
Foremost man on the ocean [of samsara].	海上第一人
He departed like the wind,	颯然恁麼去
Who sees this is neither sour nor bitter?[43]	誰見不酸辛
"Though this be the case, you all should know that Foyan was never born, and never died. He never departed, and never arrived. What about what's happening right now?"	雖然如是。須知佛眼未曾生未曾死。未曾去未曾來。正與麼時如何。
He then pointed at the coffin and said,	乃指龕云。
"[Yantou remarked:] 'Xuefeng and I were born of the same line,	我與雪峯同條生
Xuefeng and I do not die in the same line!'	不與雪峯同條死
"You must clearly discern these ultimate words. I extend a universal invitation to the great assembly to raise their voices together,"	要知末後句分明 普請大眾齊聲舉
then said, "Sorrow! Sorrow!"	乃云。哀哀。

---

40. This and other verses by Yuanwu Keqin continued to be anthologized and arranged, such as in the Kangxi-era *Liezu tiwang lu* (ZZ64.2b5-c21), according to the ritual protocols in *Chixiu Baizhang qinggui*. The prefaces to that collection suggest the reader consult the exemplars alongside the *qinggui*.

41. *Yuanwu Foguo chanshi yulu* (T47.810b14–25). "Lowering the Flames for Foyan" also in the Southern Song copy of Yuanwu's records in *Xu Gu zunsu yuyao* (ZZ68.424c19–425a4). A sermon delivered by Yuanwu Keqin at the memorial vegetarian feast sponsored in Foyan's honor in *Xu Gu zunsu yuyao* (ZZ68.422a20-b8), and *Yuanwu Foguo chanshi yulu* (T47.729c25–730a23).

42. *Yuanwu Foguo chanshi yulu* (T47.810b8–13). Reproduced in Deyin's anthology, *Longquan yuan Yin shi ji xianyu lu* (ZZ65.47a19–22), where the printed text uses small characters to distinguish performative directions from the spoken words printed in full-sized characters.

43. Emending *wei* 唯 to *shei* 誰.

Based in part on ritual protocols in *qinggui*, "Lamentation for Venerable Foyan," was probably vocalized prior to the cremation, and involved Keqin standing before a portrait of Foyan and the closed coffin of his dharma brother. The *ju'ai* ritual begins with Keqin intoning a *jisong*, followed by vernacular speech. He then gestures at the nearby coffin containing Foyan's body and speaks again. The funeral ritual was addressed to a dual audience of the living and the dead and served two purposes: to awaken the gathered mourners and at the same time to offer dharma-words as ritual care for the dead.

The ritual function of such *ju'ai* funeral liturgies depended in part on the salvific efficacy of their doctrinal content. In the above example, Keqin first uses a *jisong* to laud his dharma brother's achievements in life. He then offers spoken commentary on his own verse and declares that ultimately there is no birth and no death. In this way, Keqin first fulfills mainstream expectations, and then subverts the ordinary way of discerning the situation by referring to the discourse of emptiness. Compare Keqin's language with Su Shi's poem below that declares the loss of an individual as an entirely sour and bitter experience, the opposite of the experience that Keqin expresses. Keqin's verse challenges the mourners to come to terms with their ordinary responses to death and to see how these feelings are not separate from the truth of emptiness. He declares that Foyan has not died. Such doctrinal statements about the emptiness of "birth and death" or "coming and going" are typical of Chan funereal verses.[44] To repeat the imagery from the previous chapter, after realizing that mountains are not mountains, in the end mountains are just mountains again. Keqin does not end with a declaration of emptiness. He gestures toward his dharma brother's encoffined body and alludes to Yantou Quanhuo 巖頭全豁 (828–887) speaking to a Chan student about Xuefeng Yicun 雪峰義存 (822–908), Yantou's dharma brother to whom he was reportedly a mentor, an episode that would become a well-known *gong'an*.[45] Yongjue Yuanxian later explained this couplet, arguing, "Is this not a case of 'the same when awakening to the essence, distinct when put in action'?" 莫是悟體則同，發用則別麼.[46] In other words, conventional and ultimate reality are simultaneous and not separate. All ultimately belongs to fundamental thusness, and yet myriad distinctions are perceived. Here, the allusion is given a novel connotation by being spoken at a funeral by Keqin for his own dharma brother. Keqin encouraged the mourners to grapple with this profound teaching. Although from the enlightened perspective, to speak of Foyan being born or dying is a delusion, the sangha has nonetheless gathered for his funeral and to grieve. With this philosophical reflection on the

---

44. See, for example, *Hongzhi chanshi guanglu* (T48.82c8–11) for a verse by Hongzhi for two anonymous monks, one among many that plays with "coming and going," and (T48.82b28–c2) for another among many that play with "life and death."

45. Brose, *Patrons and Patriarchs*, 51, shows this tale was embellished by Song writers, a process by which it became case 51 in *Blue Cliff Record* and case 50 in *Congrong lu* 從容錄.

46. *Yongjue Yuanxian chanshi guanglu* (ZZ72.414b15).

ultimate emptiness of grieving, the formal lamentation ends and Keqin leads the congregation in sending up a cry of grief.

This example demonstrates that ritual funerary verses were not simply literary texts to be read for their moving expressions of sorrow.[47] They were, rather, an essential part of ritual care for the dead, with additional social functions designed for the living community. Verses at monastic funerals might serve the needs of communal mourning, but, though they addressed the living as much as the deceased, they were not meant as an expression of personal grief. These qualities are revealed by a combination of formal analysis, attention to allusions, and monastic social context. Such ritual and social contexts explain why funeral verses so little resemble the personal lamentations we turn to next.

"Lodging Grief": Qisong's Impropriety

There is a kind of poetry written that expresses the universal feeling of grief at the passing of a friend. We today may imagine our friends as chosen family, a circle with whom we share private experiences. In a not wholly dissimilar manner, the medieval Chinese thought of a friend as "one who knows me" (*zhiwozhe* 知我者, *zhiji* 知己, or *zhiyin* 知音).[48] The death of a friend is unlike other losses. For writers in medieval China, neither inscriptions for parents and teachers nor memorials for imperial officials are therefore suitable models for eulogizing a friend. The *Wenxuan*, for example, includes verse-form elegies under many generic names, one such being the *lei* 誄, which was a public form conventionally reserved for an official function.[49] Formal, official elegies were distinct from the "prayer texts" 祭文 that began as a formal genre for official functions and in the Tang evolved into a medium for performing friendship.[50] Song monks used several genres of lament to express personal grief. In this section, I use two laments from the collected works of the monk Qisong 契嵩 (1007–1072) as points of departure to examine the history of the genre and its contexts in the Song. Qisong has often been read by scholars as a key figure in historical Confucian-Buddhist interactions; the examples here, however, show his fundamental commitment to Buddhism.[51]

In the printed collection of Qisong's works, there are three mourning

---

47. Shields, *One Who Knows Me,* chap. 5, describes the readership of Tang funeral writing.

48. Shields, *One Who Knows Me,* 3–4, 269–270.

49. Hightower, "*Wen Hsüan* and Genre Theory," 522–528, surveys funereal genres in *Wenxuan.* Among them are *lei* 誄 (dirge), *diao* 弔 (also written 吊; condolence), *ji* 祭 (requiem), *bei* 悲 (threnody), *ai* 哀 (lament), *bei* 碑 (epitaph), *jie* 碣 (columnar inscription), *zhi* 誌 (necrology), *zhuang* 狀 (obituary).

50. Following Shields, "Words for the Dead and the Living," who shows how *jiwen* transformed during the Tang to a broader emotional range. Such texts were still composed during the Song.

51. My interpretations of Qisong here build on Elizabeth Morrison, *Power of Patriarchs,* 5–7, 115–120.

poems with titles in modes of lamentation, or "verses of grief" 哀辭, each with a prose headnote by Qisong introducing the "verse" (*ci* 辭) and discussing his feelings of "grief" (*ai* 哀). One poem is an ancient-style poem with a single end rhyme, and two composed with rhyming couplets of three- or four-character lines that repeatedly add the archaic exclamation *xi* 兮. The form and content of Qisong's verses of grief are conservative and conventional, serving to laud the dead. I focus on his headnotes, wherein Qisong inscribed details of personal relationships and reflected on the genre itself.[52] These headnotes allude to the prominent traditions of "burial songs" 挽歌 as well as poetry "mourning the deceased" 悼亡, each of which I briefly survey here.[53]

Song scholars understood that "burial songs" began as anonymous Han-dynasty songs.[54] Although early medieval examples include the well-known "burial songs" by Cao Zhi 曹植 (192–232) and Lu Ji 陸機 (261–303), writers in the Song more often referenced the funeral song that Tao Yuanming 陶淵明 (365?–427) dedicated to himself.[55] Qin Guan, for example, wrote a poem entitled "A Dirge for Myself" 自作挽詞, and some debated whether Qin's poem was an inferior imitation of the work by Tao.[56] This is one example of how literati writers in the Song portrayed their own lives by selectively debating texts from the past. Buddhist encyclopedias indicate that monks, too, were expected to be aware of the origins of the literary tradition of the "burial songs."[57]Additional examples such as the nine quatrains in "Ballad of Beimang" 北邙行 by Fohui Faquan 佛慧法泉 (fl. 11th c.) demonstrate Buddhist monks' familiarity with traditions of Chinese mourning poetry.[58]

The verses of grief by Qisong and other monks alluded to "burial song,"

---

52. My thoughts have been enriched by the argument of Fong, "Private Emotion, Public Commemoration," who has demonstrated how widows transgressed genre norms of *daowang* poetry to insert their autobiographical voice. So, too, could a monk be self-reflective upon following or subverting the conventions of poetic grieving.

53. The term *wange* has also been translated as "Coffin-Pullers' Songs" and "Hearse-Pullers' Songs" based on the early Chinese understanding that these songs were sung by pallbearers as they worked. See Birrell, *Popular Song*, 94–99, and Timothy Chan, *Considering the End*, 106n31.

54. Major examples of Song scholarship on dirges include the entry *wange* 挽歌 in Gao Cheng's 高承 (c. 1078–1085) *Shiwu jiyuan*, 9/481; the entry for *wange* 挽歌 in Zeng Zao's 曾慥 (1091–1155) *Leishuo*, 42/35b; with the explanation for the titles *Xielu* 薤露 and *Haoli* 蒿里 and *wange* 挽歌 in Guo Maoqian's 郭茂倩 (1041–1099) collection *Yuefu shiji*, 27/4b-10b.

55. The context and significance of Tao's original *Ni wange ci* 擬挽歌辭 is still debated. It is unclear if Tao Yuanming was writing in imitation of an existing poem, or if *ni* was being used in a broader sense. For a new, compelling reading of Tao Yuanming's poems on death, see Timothy Chan, *Considering the End*, 100–106, esp. 103n19. Compare this with Davis, *T'ao Yuanming*, 1:165–173.

56. Hu Zi 胡仔 (fl. 1147–1167) imputes this criticism to Su Shi in *Tiaoxi yuyin conghua, houji* 3.6b-7b, though such criticism is not in the extant works of Su Shi.

57. *Shangxie* 傷薤 in *Zuting shiyuan*, (ZZ64.404a13–21), and *Xielu haoli* 薤露蒿里 in *Shishi liu tie*, 39/351b.

58. Preserved in *Yunwo jitan* (ZZ86.680a18-b8). These poems were later erroneously attributed to Yunmen Wenyan, as in *Jiaoshi leilin* 焦氏類林, juan 8, an error repeated in *Quan Tang shi bubian, xushi*, 50/1498–1499.

but in form and style they more closely resemble poetry "mourning the deceased." Pan Yue 潘岳 (247–300) was regarded as a forerunner in this tradition.[59] He wrote verses to mourn his late wife.[60] It may seem normal, even natural, to modern readers for a poet to write about the passing of his wife. However, as C. M. Lai has observed, "the mourning of one's wife, unlike that of one's parents, was not regarded as a virtuous duty. It is therefore exceptional that the majority of Pan's works on mourning concern his wife."[61] Pan was canonized for eloquently inscribing personal feelings of mourning. His poems opened the way for the writing of laments for dear friends in a personal style that departed from official elegies.

The genealogies of these traditions, as they were understood in the Song, further explain Qisong's prefatory prose. For a monk like Qisong, who considered himself an orthodox adherent to Buddhist monastic ideals, there was a conflict between identity as a monk and behavior as a friend. When his friends died, Qisong felt unbearable grief, and yet he believed in Buddhist teachings that cautioned him not to be overcome by such emotions. For someone whose life was committed to Buddhist principles, it seemed inappropriate to Qisong to register his grief in song.

Qisong offered a Buddhist interpretation of filial piety in his *Essays to Reinforce the Teachings* 輔教編. He wrote about the proper way for a monk to mourn and for whom. He concluded that monks should participate in funerals for their parents as well as for teachers. He was conflicted, however, on the issue of grief, arguing that "Buddhist teachings do not include instructions for wailing at funerals but in general seek to dissolve desire and aversion and to move toward [karmic] purity" 然喪制哭泣，雖我教略之，蓋欲其泯愛惡而趨清淨也. This passage suggests that Qisong understood Buddhist teachings, in essence, to discourage performing grief. He noted that the Buddha attended his father's funeral and "mourned in his heart and refrained from wailing and stomping" 以心喪而略其哭踊也.[62] This was a restrained response to the loss of a parent compared with the three years of mourning prescribed in Confucian classics. But Qisong also noted that "Maudgalyāyana [Mulian], although an [awakened] sage, still could not dispel his feelings" 目犍連亦聖人也尚不能泯情. Qisong added that the Vinaya authority Daoxuan 道宣

59. Hu Xu, *Daowang shi shi,* rehearses the traditional genre history of *daowang* poetry dynasty by dynasty from *The Classic of Poetry* to "Rhapsody for Lady Li" 李夫人賦 by Emperor Han Wudi 漢武帝 (r. 141–187 BCE) and the *daowang* by Pan Yue 潘岳 (247–300) for his wife. Williams, "Pan Yue's 'Study,'" 352, argues that the grief-filled genre has its origins in *fu* written in the voice of another's widow.

60. In the Song, Mei Yaochen 梅堯臣 (1002–1060) wrote poems exploring his sorrow after his wife's passing. One particularly influential set of three poems, *Daowang san shou* 悼亡三首, has been translated into English by Ronald Egan, "Shi Poetry," 311–313. For a list of Mei's twenty-one poems mourning his wife, see Hu Xu, *Daowang shi shi,* 111–112.

61. Lai, "Art of Lamentation," 410.

62. All passages in this paragraph are based on the Japanese translation in Araki, *Fukyōhen,* 223–227. The passage is in *Tanjin wenji* (T52.662b10-c3).

(596–667) believed a monk must display grief for his parents and teachers.[63] In the end, Qisong concluded that a monk may grieve for his parents and the teachers who brought him into the novitiate but that in other circumstances he should mourn in his heart.

It may seem natural for anyone, monks included, to grieve the death of a friend. Qisong, though, was aware of his commitment to his religious calling and noted the impropriety of composing elegiac poetry. Once again, he extolled the virtues of the departed in "Verse of Grief for the Retired Vice Minister Zhongshan" 致政侍郎中山公哀辭. In the paratext, however, he pondered the conflict between the outpouring of grief and his identity as a Buddhist monk.[64]

> On the day of the interment of the late Vice Minister Zhongshan, I was moved by his former virtues and wrote this verse of grief to convey my sentiment. However, myself being a Buddhist [monk], I outwardly forsake the appearance of forms and inwardly diffuse the falsity of emotions,[65] and so it is inappropriate to have these feelings and then to bemoan them. But I could not bear to contemplate the death of such a worthy person and the further decline of the Way of gentlemen. I moaned and sighed without end, and so I commit my grief to this verse.

> 故侍郎中山公，其喪下葬日，客有感其舊德而為哀辭，以見意也。然客本佛氏者，外遺形質內融情偽，不宜有所感而哀之也。蓋不忍視其賢人歿而君子之道益寡，嗟嘆之不已，姑託哀而辭之。

Qisong's confession that "it is inappropriate" (buyi 不宜) might also be rendered "I ought not." And yet, he could not help himself, he says. He writes that he "could not bear it" (buren 不忍). Even though ren is a verb here—and was probably only intended in its most literal sense—there is some irony that ren, in addition to its ordinary meanings, denotes one of the well-known Buddhist virtues: the perfection of forbearance. This quality is attributed to advanced bodhisattvas, who must "endure the emptiness of all phenomena" 無生法忍. Qisong, by contrast, is unable to bear the impermanence of something that he treasures.

The final words of this passage are "commit my grief to this verse" 託哀而辭之. His phrase is an allusion to the *locus classicus* for the "burial songs" tradition.[66] Scholars and monks in the Song dynasty traced the origins of dirges through a passage in the fifth-century compilation *New Account of Tales of the World*, or *Shishuo xinyu*.[67] "Zhang Zhan after a few drinks used to sing

---

63. Qisong quotes *Sifen lü shanfan buque xingshi chao* (T40.145b8).

64. *Tanjin wenji* (T52.717c11–718a10).

65. Or, if one assumes he had in mind Xunzi's "Human Nature Is Evil," then "spontaneous feelings and learned habits."

66. On this origin story, see Birrell, *Popular Songs*, 96.

67. This and the next translation adapted from Mather, *Shih-Shuo Hsin-Yü*, 418. Chinese text follows "Rendan" 任誕, no. 45, in *Shishuo xinyu jiao jian*, 407.

pallbearers' songs with great pathos and poignancy. Huan Chong said to him, 'You're not one of Tian Heng's retainers; how have you suddenly reached such perfection?'" 張驎酒後挽歌甚悽苦，桓車騎曰：「卿非田橫門人，何乃頓爾至致？」 Readers in the Song dynasty were expected to understand why Huan Chong 桓沖 (328–384) thought that skill in singing dirges reached its pinnacle with the retainers of Tian Heng. Some five hundred years earlier, Tian Heng 田橫 (d. 202 BCE) had ascended to the throne of the kingdom of Qi 齊. The first emperor of the Han, Liu Bang 劉邦 (d. 195 BCE), known as Gaozu 高祖, conquered the territory of Qi and drove out Tian Heng. As the *Shishuo xinyu* has it, Tian Heng committed suicide en route to the Han capital to answer a summons. The *Shishuo Xinyu* text commentary by Liu Jun 劉峻 (462–521), as well as his note for this section, is the source for Qisong's allusion.

> Tian Heng was summoned by Han Emperor Gao, but as he arrived at Shixiang Pavilion (near Luoyang) he slit his own throat, offering his head. His retainers carried (*wan*) his head to the palace. They dared not weep, yet could not contain their grief, so they committed the sounds of their grief to song.
>
> 葢高帝召齊田橫，至于尸鄉亭自刎奉首，從者挽至於宮，不敢哭而不勝哀，故爲歌以寄哀音。

By the Tang Dynasty, this narrative had been condensed to "they committed their grief to song" 歌以寄哀.[68] The literary poems from the later "burial songs" tradition, however, do not resemble the two earliest burial songs, known as *Xielu* 薤露 and *Haoli* 蒿里. Writers in the Song nevertheless understood that the cultural origins of "burial songs" should be traced to this passage in *Shishuo xinyu* and the commentary by Liu Jun.

Turning to look closely at the words "they committed their grief to song," we might note that Richard Mather in his translation of *Shishuo xinyu* gives "to vent" for *ji* 寄, an expression that conveys the sense quite well. A more literal rendition of *ji*, however, conveys that one "temporarily lodges" or "entrusts" one's feelings to verse. Such translations convey how close in meaning *ji* is to *tuo* 託, also sometimes rendered as "to entrust," Qisong's choice of verb. Qisong alluded to this passage to convey that he, too, sought a sense of cathartic release through literary creation.[69]

It was exactly the building up of grief and its requisite release that ran against Qisong's ideals as a Buddhist monk, one who maintains outward and

---

68. The whole narrative appears in *Wenxuan* under the category *wange*. This phrase appears in the *wange* section of several Tang compilations, including Xu Jian's 徐堅 (659–729) *Chuxue ji* 初學記 and Yu Shinan's 虞世南 (558–638) *Beitang shu chao* 北堂書鈔.

69. Additional evidence that Qisong was aware of the classical tradition behind mourning poetry includes his allusion to Lu Ji's 陸機 (261–303) burial songs, in a piece written for a friend who died young, *Tanjin wenji* (T52.718a27).

inward asceticism.[70] And yet Qisong did write laments to mark the loss of certain friends. Qisong's prefatory prose, longer than the lamentations themselves, provides a glimpse of this monk's emotional life. In his prefatory remarks for "Verse of Grief for Judge Li Huishu" 李晦叔推官哀辭, Qisong finds himself shocked that a man in his prime years, who had seemed so alive only a year ago, could suddenly be irrevocably gone.[71]

> Last year, in the second month of spring, [Li] was about to pardon a criminal. He came to my office to discuss the matter and for an entire day was unable to leave. He said, "Long ago [Sengzhao] was called the He Yan 何晏 of monks,[72] but now as I behold you there is no comparison." At that, I was disappointed in myself for becoming his acquaintance so late, and I sent him an epistle to let him know he had unduly praised me. He replied, "These days, those who recognize the world's worthy men are few!" [...] I looked forward to our lively debate on his next arrival. Although I disagreed with him and wondered at his fondness for me, how could I not say he was one who knows me? He had just reached his robust years[73] when we parted a year ago. How am I to make sense of his unexpected death? The ancients would compare the lives of men to the fleet soaring clouds, which cannot be kept forever.

> 去年仲春將施生，來吾室與吾語，終日不能去。嘗曰：「昔謂方袍平叔，予今顧師不足比也。」巨自慨相知之晚，及蒙移書讓其過稱。復曰：「方今天下賢而有識者，幾其人哉！」[...]期將復來劇論，雖然余非其人酌其意愛，豈不謂之知我乎。別去一年志方壯。豈悟其忽然而已亡邪。古人以人生比之浮雲奄忽不可常保。

This paratext offers insights into the situations in which this monk felt moved to write elegiac poetry. Qisong and Li appear to have relished their disagreements; Qisong calls Li "one who knows me." How to make sense of a friend's untimely death? Qisong offers the metaphor of passing clouds, an image suggesting the effervescent nature of all things. He adopts in this headnote a philosophical posture in response to a tragedy: the death of a relatively young man. In the body of the elegy, he concludes, "Since antiquity, wise men seldom achieve old age; / how is it that the principle of heaven cannot be fathomed?" 哲人自古寡眉壽，天理如何不可量.[74] In other words, in a just world, good men would not die so young.

---

70. This view approximates the frequently discussed assumptions underlying Han Yu's criticism of monk Gaoxian's calligraphy. See Ronald Egan, "Ou-yang Hsiu and Su Shih," 407.

71. *Tanjin wenji* (T52.718a14–15 and a20–22).

72. *Gaoseng zhuan* (T50.365a27) records that Liu Chengzhi said this upon reading the *Zhaolun* 肇論 by Sengzhao 僧肇 (374–414). He Yan (189?–249) was a proponent of *xuanxue*, as summarized in Knechtges and Chang, *Ancient and Early Medieval Chinese Literature*, 1:365–368.

73. *Fangzhuang* 方壯 is a well-known allusion to the *Li ji*, in which at age thirty, one is said to be robust.

74. *Tanjin Wenji* (T52.718b4–5).

Qisong writes in these headnotes about a struggle with the acceptance of death. To do so, he embraced the Chinese literary traditions of lamentation. Even as he turned to elegiac poetry, he knew as a learned monk that elegy was a non-Buddhist tradition. He wrote in his *Essays to Reinforce the Teachings* that Buddhism forbade conspicuous wailing and excessive emotion. But Qisong would not prohibit grief altogether, and he found precedent in scriptural depictions of arhats, disciples of the Buddha like Maudgalyāyana, who grieved at the *parinirvāṇa*. These are the central themes that appear again and again across monks' funeral verses.

"Feelings Will Gather in People Like Us": Daoqian and Su Shi

A set of texts composed by Daoqian demonstrates a different framework for engaging with the problem of the emotions. Daoqian was a celebrated poet-monk and never abbot of a public monastery. He and the polymath Su Shi were close correspondents from their first meeting until Su's death in 1101. Though Su befriended many people, there were few men with whom he interacted more frequently than Daoqian.[75] Daoqian sometimes stayed with Su or traveled with him, occasions yielding numerous poems. The two men also communicated through letters and epistolary poetry. Daoqian's own views and poetic strategies come into sharper focus when we place his writing in the context of his correspondences with Su Shi.

Although Su Shi and Daoqian differed in their poetics of lamentation, both men frequently discussed grief as "feelings that gather" (*qingzhong* 情鍾). This phrase derives from a well-known story found in the *Shishuo xinyu*. It is the same passage that appeared in Chapter 3 as part of Huihong's discourse on "feelings not yet forgotten." When Wang Rong lost his infant son, "his grief was such that he could not control himself." To explain his loss of self-control, Wang said, "A sage may forget his feelings, and the basest people cannot attain feelings. Where feelings gather is precisely among people like us."[76] Jack Chen has argued that Wang, with his uncontrolled wailing for a son, a mere infant, broke with conventional expectations for grief. Such vehement emotions were normally viewed as unseemly, but Wang's assertion that a group of "people like us" would understand led many to consider how this expression of grief revealed his exemplary character and inner nature.[77] "Forgetting one's feelings" may be for sages, but sentiments "gather" and collect in people like ourselves. The full weight of Wang's statement is not only that emotion is strongest in people like him, but also that such people possess a praiseworthy ability to express intense feeling with poetic words. Both Su Shi and

---

75. Su's most frequent correspondent was his brother Su Che. Of the monks Su corresponded with, more epistles and poems were addressed to Daoqian than any other.

76. As above, translation adapted from Jack Chen, "On Mourning and Sincerity," 76, and Mather, *Shih-Shuo Hsin-Yü*, 347. Chinese text in *Shishuo xinyu jiao jian,* 349.

77. Chen, "On Mourning and Sincerity," 76–77.

Daoqian would take up this idea in their writing and identify themselves as "people like us." At the same time, they disagreed on whether such feelings could be reconciled with Buddhist teachings.

Su Shi used the phrase "we in whom feelings gather" 情鍾我輩 in a letter to Daoqian written in response to the recent passing of their mutual friend the Tiantai monk Longjing Biancai (1011–1091).[78] Before Biancai died, he retreated to a quiet room for seated meditation; he, ceased talking, eating, or drinking, and turned away all visitors. Finally, he beckoned Daoqian to his bedside, where he declared that his karmic preparations for birth in the Western Pure Land were complete and correctly predicted his time of death.[79] Afterward, Daoqian corresponded with Su Shi to arrange for an inscription to commemorate Biancai. Su would order his brother Su Che to complete the commemorative "pagoda inscription" text. Su Shi composed a prayer text and sent the following letter to Daoqian.[80]

> Twice, your letters arrived and are in my hands, so I know that you are well. Biancai has followed the transformation of things and departed. Though coming and going are fundamentally nonexistent, feelings will gather in people like us, and we cannot escape sorrow. I am sending a eulogy[81] and two taels of silver to procure tea and fruit for funeral offerings.

> 兩得手書，具審法體佳勝。辯才遂化去，雖來去本無，而情鍾我輩，不免悽愴也。今有奠文一首，并銀二兩，託為致茶果一奠之。

Seeking to comfort Daoqian, Su in his letter affirms their friendship, declaring Daoqian to be one of the "people like us." Su also contrasts the ultimate emptiness of coming and going, a euphemism for birth and death, with the unavoidable reality of feeling grief at the loss of a friend. Such sorrow is inescapable and will be felt despite the fundamental emptiness of things.

Su made similar remarks to other monks; such is his lament for Haiyue Huibian 海月慧辯 (d. 1073).[82] Su would later recall Haiyue's extraordinary

---

78. More on the personal relationship between Daoqian and Biancai can be found in Chapter 3.

79. Described in "Pagoda Inscription for Dharma Master Biancai of Longjing" 龍井辯才法師塔銘, composed by Su Che, *Luancheng ji, houji* 24/1439–1443. See also Su Che's "Record of Patchrobe's Studio at Longjing Cloister of Hangzhou," 杭州龍井院訥齋記 composed at the behest of Daoqian, in *Luancheng ji*, 23/505–506.

80. This is the sixth epistle "To Canliaozi" 與參寥子 in *Su Shi wenji*, 61/1861; the same letter is reproduced elsewhere as "Responding to Canliao" 答參寥. In the second half of the letter, Su discusses Daoqian's disciple Faying and his progress with calligraphy.

81. This probably refers to "Prayer text for Biancai of Longjing" 祭龍井辯才文, *Su Shi wenji*, 63/1961.

82. Haiyue was a Tiantai monk, a student of Zushao 祖韶. Zushao was a disciple of the famous Ciyun Zunshi. See *Fozu tongji* (T49.210b28–211a6). Su Che wrote the pagoda inscription for Haiyue, "Pagoda Stele for Dharma Master Haiyue of Tianzhu" 天竺海月法師塔碑, in *Luancheng ji, houji* 24/1445.

death, following Daoqian's request that Su compose an encomium for a por-
trait of Haiyue.[83] Before his death, the master had instructed his community
to wait until Su arrived before closing the coffin to perform funeral rites, so
when Su arrived four days later, Haiyue's body was still seated in a full lotus,
his head warm, all as though he were alive. Following the wonder of Haiyue's
miraculous passing, Su wrote this, the second of three poems, entitled
"Mourning Master Haiyue Bian of Tianzhu" 弔天竺海月辯師.[84]

	Life and death bend as swiftly as an elbow,	生死猶如臂屈伸
2	Yet feelings gather in people like us—how sour and bitter.	情鍾我輩一酸辛
	Bai Juyi did not become a guest of the Penglai [immortals],[85]	樂天不是蓬萊客
4	and relied on [Shencou] to be his host in the western [paradise].[86]	憑仗西方作主人

Su implies here that Haiyue is in the Pure Land and that they will meet again
there. Perhaps the miraculous signs following Haiyue's death inspired Su to
echo two poems by Bai Juyi, one renouncing Daoism and one redoubling his
commitment to Buddhism. The first couplet cleverly juxtaposes Buddhist and
Chinese literary sentiments. Specifically, line 1 refers to an old Indian meta-
phor known in numerous Chinese translations of sūtras. "The moment it
takes to bend an elbow" 屈伸臂頃 is shorthand for "the moment it takes a
strong man to bend his elbow" 猶如力士屈伸臂頃. This expression connotes
that something happened easily and with great speed, perhaps "in a trice."
In Buddhist scriptures, the metaphor refers to action that quickly follows
thought, to superpowers used to travel great distances, and to the unrelent-
ing swiftness of the cycles of birth and death. It is the last of these associations
that Su is drawing upon. Despite his knowing that existence fluctuates with
such speed, Su rounds out this line with resignation, stating that he has not
yet "forgotten feelings." If flavors—bitter, sour, salty, sweet, spicy, and bland—
convey the full range of human emotion, then here "sour and bitter" denote
that only painful feelings have coalesced.

    As poems composed by Buddhist monks came under scrutiny by
members of elite literary circles, well-read laypeople sometimes savored

---

83. Su recalled these events twenty-one years later in a headnote to "Encomia on Portrait
of Haiyue Bian" 海月辯公真贊. *Su Shi wenji*, 22/638.

84. *Su Shi shiji*, 10/479–480.

85. Thought by later commentaries to be a reference to Bai's poem "In Response to My
Guest's Exposition" 答客說, in which Bai declares, "I study the school of emptiness, not immor-
tality; / I'm afraid what you've posited is false tradition" 吾學空門非學仙，恐君此說是虛傳. *Bai
Juyi ji*, 36/840.

86. Bai Juyi bid a final farewell to his friend Shencou 神湊 (744–817), a member of a Pure
Land society, with a poem that includes the lines: "No need for us in disconsolation to follow you
in departing, / I ask now you be my host in the western [paradise]" 不須惆悵從師去，先請西方
作主人. *Bai Juyi ji*, 17/359. *Song Gaoseng zhuan* (T50.807a23–b17) suggests that the poem was
written after Shencou's death.

poetry through metaphors of flavor and taste. A few critics praised monks' poetry for its subtlety and delicacy. Su, however, imagined that the usual monk's poem had "a whiff of vegetables" 菜氣, "the flavor of cabbage and bamboo" 蔬筍氣, or "the taste of pickled stuffing" 酸餡氣, all criticisms linking the aesthetics of monks' poetry to the vegetarian diet.[87] The discourse around vegetarian flavor reflected the perception that monks' poetry was excessively plain, used language cautiously and with little variation, and concerned a narrow set of themes.[88]

Su's use of flavors to describe feelings resonates with his theory of Buddhist poetry elsewhere addressed to Daoqian. During Daoqian's three-months sojourn at Su Shi's official residence in Xuzhou in autumn of 1078, the two men discussed the relationship between Buddhism and poetry, ultimately arriving at a fundamental disagreement.[89] In one of the final poems of this conversation, Su tried to convince Daoqian that a subtle and ultimate flavor lay beneath the bitter and sweet, that poetry and dharma need not be separate realms. The layman wrote that "poetry and the dharma are not incompatible, / I submit this view again for your consideration" 詩法不相妨, 此語更當請.[90] Su pressed Daoqian to reconsider that Buddhism and poetry might not be incompatible. From this we can infer that Su was responding to Daoqian's expressed view that poetry and Buddhism *were* incompatible. Given this, let us consider how Daoqian wrote in his poetic laments about being the type of person in whom feelings coalesce.

The following mourning poems by Daoqian reveal his strategies for negotiating his religious commitment with his anguish at the finality of death. Like Su's, his poems present contrasting ideas, often within a single couplet, to articulate a tension between understanding the fact of impermanence and feelings of grief. Whereas Su suggested that the two remain in a dynamic equilibrium, Daoqian often declared that feelings were in vain, thereby prioritizing religious truth. For example, the following excerpt is from the second of two "Laments for the Attendant Yu Gongda" 俞公達待制挽辭, written after the death of Yu Chong 俞充 (d. 1081).[91] Records indicate that

---

87. This topic addressed in detail in Protass, "Buddhist Monks and Chinese Poetry," 116–158. For a different treatment of this topic, see Zhiyi Yang, *Dialectics of Spontaneity,* 42–44.

88. Zhou, *Zhongguo Chanzong yu Shige,* 45–53, generates these three main points.

89. Judging from the extant collections for both Su and Daoqian, the two men took several day trips together and wrote numerous poems addressed to one another. Traces of an extended conversation are recorded in this set of poems.

90. "Farewell Master Canliao" 送參寥師, *Su Shi shiji,* 17/905–907. Translation adapted slightly from Ronald Egan, "Shi Poetry," 313–315, consulting the earlier translations in Ronald Egan, *Word, Image, and Deed,* 198–199; Fuller, *Road to East Slope,* 244; and Lynn, "Sudden and the Gradual in Chinese Poetry," 385. Grant, *Mount Lu,* 97–99, assumes Su here has quoted Daoqian; however, this is unlikely because it would contradict the other messages from Su in this very poem.

91. Hucker, *Dictionary of Official Titles,* 475, no. 6129, states that in the Song, a *daizhi* or *daizhiguan,* "edict attendant," was a member of the Hanlin academy who attended imperial meetings with officials and took notes on pronouncements.

Yu was a congenial official and known to study Buddhist principles.[92] After praising Yu's virtues, Daoqian reflects on bereavement.[93]

	In the human realm, his dream has been cut off, the yellow millet cooked;[94]	人間夢斷黃粱熟
6	In heaven above, lofty towers are now complete with white jade anew.[95]	天上樓成白玉新
	Amid deserted mountain tombs, traces of past and present;	零落山丘今古事
8	feelings collect in people like us, wounding our spirits in vain.	情鍾我輩謾傷神

First Daoqian establishes his knowledge that death has always been with us. In lines 5 and 6, he alludes to two legends from the Tang, each replete with auspicious signs. Yu will be appreciated in the netherworld. Daoqian abruptly shifts to a concrete image in line 7. He is not only talking about a particular forlorn cemetery, but the cemetery as a fact, as a synecdoche for death, that has been a part of life since ancient times. Given this knowledge, the death of people we know should not come as a surprise. And yet, "feelings collect in people like us." This is the exact phrase Su used in his letter above. For Daoqian, however, this grief is of no benefit. One's heart is broken in vain. Daoqian may be the kind of person who is a vessel for profound feelings, but this kind of person has not-yet-forgotten feelings. This is the appropriate way for someone who understood the transformations of life and death to frame his grief. The difference between Su and Daoqian on this point is subtle, and we may be tempted to ascribe it to the different commitments of a layman and a monk. It should at least be clear that Daoqian contrasted two ideas: familiarity with death and the distress of mourning.

A similar couplet may be found in a burial song Daoqian wrote following the death of Liaoxing Haishi 了性海石 (d. 1091 or 1092?). It is the second in a set of three poems entitled "Lamentations for Great Master Cihua, Metropolitan Bishop" 都僧正慈化大師挽詞.[96]

---

92. For more on Yu Chong see *Huaihai ji jian zhu*, 40/1289.

93. *Canliaozi shiji*, 3.7b; 107–109. These four lines are at the end of a second regulated *shi*. Both poems follow conventional forms of praise.

94. An allusion to the Tang strange tale of "The Golden Millet Dream," included in *Wenyuan yinghua*, 833/4395–4397. Scholar Lu Sheng, en route to take the civil exams, stops at an inn, meets Lü Dongbin, and falls asleep while waiting for a meal. In his dream, an entire successful lifetime passes. He awakes to discover he has been waiting for a bowl of millet and his worldly success was but a dream. He abandons his journey—and the examination—and instead joins Lü Dongbin.

95. An allusion to the auspicious visions that preceded Li He's death as recorded by Li Shangyin in *Li He xiaozhuan* 李賀小傳, translated in Owen, *Late Tang*, 160–161.

96. *Canliaozi shiji*, 7.2b-3a; 233–235. Xu, *Zhenben Song ji wu zhong*, 1:313, misidentifies Cihua 慈化 as Huailian, misreading a note inserted by Daoqian to explain an allusion. Note that Daoqian later wrote another poem, "Osmanthus Flowers by Chuici Hall" 垂慈堂木栖花, about a flowering tree grown from a sapling planted by Liaoxing. *Canliaozi shiji*, 9.8b; 489. Shi, "Su Shi wenxue

	An entire life forsaking luxuries,	平生輕長物
2	He regarded self and the world as a goose's feather.[97]	身世等鴻毛
	Early on, his renown spread through the southeast,	譽出東南早
4	Men revered his grand integrity.	人驚節義高
	His toys and rare objects were just water and stone;[98]	玩奇唯水石
6	Those he associated with were all outstanding men.	結客盡英豪
	Coming and going are fundamentally without traces;	來往元無迹
8	Yet feelings gather, and in vain we are overcome with grief.[99]	情鍾謾鬱陶

Just as with the poem for Yu Chong above, in this poem, having praised the deceased, the final couplet juxtaposes nonattachment and feelings of grief. Line 7 echoes the *Śūraṃgamasūtra,* in which the Buddha describes a profound *samādhi* whereby one responds to the world "coming without attachments and passing without any trace."[100] To understand the fundamental emptiness of life and death would mean maintaining self-control in grief. But the author in fact does suffer when "feelings gather." Again, there is a contrast between knowledge about the impermanence of things and the personal embodiment of this insight. Similarly, Daoqian's conclusion here is that thoughts and feelings of grief will arise, but one should not indulge in or dwell on them, knowing that this grief is no good. An awakened being would "pass without any trace," having moved through the world without thinking that it is a self that moves, so it would befit Daoqian to declare that his upwelling of grief is based in ordinary ways of thinking, not in service to a greater soteriological purpose.

Elsewhere, Daoqian offers spiritual succor. In his "Lamentation for the Wife of Su Shimei" 蘇世美夫人挽辭 he addresses the widower Su Shimei, encouraging him to remember that his wife had enjoyed blessings in the prime season of her life and given birth to sons. Daoqian adds, "Can you not

---

yu Fo Chan zhi guanxi," 243, gives corroborating outside evidence. "Metropolitan bishop" was responsible for administration of monastic affairs within a prefecture. During the Song it was a position within the imperial bureaucracy at the prefectural level. In a subsequent poem, Daoqian turns down the "metropolitan bishop" administrative position vacated at Cihua's passing. *Canliaozi shiji,* 7.3b; 235–236.

97. Sima Qian in a letter to Ren An wrote that "A man has only one death. That death may be as weighty as Mount Tai, or it may be as light as a goose feather. It all depends on the way he uses it." de Bary and Bloom, *Sources of Chinese Tradition,* 371–372.

98. "Toys and rare objects," likely an allusion to the parable of the burning house in the *Lotus Sūtra* about "the father knowing that each of his children was inclined toward different valuable toys and rare objects" 父知諸子先心各有所好種種珍玩奇異之物 (T9.12c6–7). "Water and stone" is perhaps a pun on the late monk's dharma name, literally, Sea Stones 海石, and emphasized his humble mode of life in contrast to that of his friends and patrons.

99. The phrase *yuyao* 鬱陶 is found in several pre-Han texts to describe a welling of grief. The reading of 陶 as *yao* and citations to *locus classicus* can be found in *Hanyu da cidian,* 3:1141.

100. *Shoulengyan jing* (T19.151b29–c4). More details in Chapter 5 about this and a similar passage in *Vimalakīrtinirdeśa.*

see [in your filial sons] Old Lai's robes and white hair?[101] / How strange that you are startled by funeral songs, the sorrows of old" 不見萊衣華髮事，空驚薤露昔人悲.[102] People have long felt sorrow. Surely ancient funeral songs were composed because all lives end in death. Why is Su Shimei surprised by the fact of aging and death? Daoqian suggests Su Shimei focus on the joy of having good filial sons. His wife's death was an appropriate death that arrived at an appropriate time, and Daoqian expected the bereaved to behave accordingly.

A rather different strategy emerges in other poems. For if a widower is expected to bear the loss of his spouse, a mother can never stop grieving for a son. Turning to "Wailing for Venerable Xiu" 哭休上人, we can see Daoqian foregrounding grief. As the final couplet indicates, this Venerable Xiu died out of turn, at a time when he was young enough to be survived by his mother. The first half of the poem is about the kinds of religious truths that might offer comfort, but they are to no avail. The second half turns back to the mundane world wherein we mourn this loss.[103]

	I have long questioned the Fashioner of Things,[104]	從來疑造物
2	Because nowhere do we recognize what is [wholly] real.	無處識其真
	A comely moon will not last a whole night,	好月難終夕
4	And famous blossoms do not endure the whole spring.	名花不盡春
	Now a bronze lamp illumines your room in vain,	青燈空照室
6	A finely woven white cloth is left behind for no purpose.[105]	白氎謾遺巾
	Poor mother, she weeps tears of blood,	泣血怜慈母
8	Her bitter grief affecting all around.	悲酸動四鄰

---

101. Old Lai was an exemplar of filial piety, serving his parents by continuing to act like a child for his parents' amusement. Daoqian is referring to Su's own filial sons, who are already grown.

102. *Canliaozi shiji*, 8.5b-6a; 470–471. "Funeral songs" translates here *xielu* 薤露 (lit., "onion dew"), the name of one of the songs sung by Tian Heng's retainers; it by extension denotes the *wange* subgenre. When the widower Su Shimei later died, Su Shi wrote an elegy for him (though the two men were apparently not related), entitled "Verse of Grief for Su Shimei" 蘇世美哀詞. *Su Shi wenji* 63/1964–1965.

103. *Canliaozi shiji*, 12.5a; 504. The Song edition shows a carver's error wherein the two characters 室白 appear half-sized and fit within a single space, indicating they might be an annotation. The prosody makes clear that these words are part of the poem, however. The error is repeated in the late Song edition at National Central Library. Editions from the Ming are laid out correctly.

104. Ideas about the Fashioner of Things, sometimes translated as Creator, as well as the "force of transformation" 造化, can be found in *Zhuangzi*, chaps. 6, 7, 32, and 33. The reference is to the creative force that both gives shape to the myriad objects and things in the world and also oversees their transformation.

105. A "cloth" (*jin*) was one of the possessions of a monk. In Song poetry, "finely woven white cloth" was metonymy for a monk. "White weave," also written *baidie* 白氎, also appears in many Buddhist texts as a metaphor for a person's character, woven of fine and pure virtue. Here it refers to the virtuous character of the young Venerable Xiu.

Daoqian in this poem seems to be addressing those who survive and are distressed. We might surmise that these lines were written for the benefit of the grieving mother, but they may well have been written for anyone moved by her pain. The beautiful moon and the famous flowers speak to the virtues of the deceased. But even moons and flowers are inextricable from the transformations of all things. So, too, a young man will sometimes not survive his youth. The poem ends with the mother's inconsolable grief. The author does not return to the religious topic posed in the first half of the poem to offer even a tentative response. Daoqian gestures toward religious truths only to disregard them and acknowledge the gravity of the situation at hand, the anguish of this death. We might compare this poem with Daoqian's lament for his close friend Qin Guan 秦觀 (1049–1100) in a poem that records his florid anguish. After nearly one hundred lines of grief, his poem ends, "In the snap of a finger, we are parted forever" 彈指當永訣.[106] Daoqian does not alloy his grief for his close friend with the comforts of Buddhist teachings.

The strategies in Daoqian's laments generally varied according to the situation. He sometimes wrote poems that would suggest that grief was an appropriate response, for example when a mother of a young monk mourns her dead son. In other laments, Daoqian remarked that his grief was suffered in vain. Feelings may collect in "people like us," but for a monk to indulge in such feelings benefits no one. Emotions in these poems are subordinated to the demands of the Buddhist path. Perhaps Daoqian in such laments was intoning his belonging to the company of "people like us" to affirm his relationships with the dead and the living, to repair the social fabric rent by a death. One strategy notably absent from Daoqian's works is that he would neither reconcile the tension nor imagine a kind of dynamic equilibrium. In this, he differed from his friend Su Shi as well as from some other monks.

Zhiyuan's Lamentations and His *Mahāparinirvāṇasūtra* Commentary

Historically, Chinese exegetes have debated a passage in the Mahāyāna *Mahāparinirvāṇasūtra* where several of the Buddha's great disciples lose self-control at the Buddha's announcement of his coming *parinirvāṇa*. These arhats have extinguished the passions and awakened to the truth of the Buddha's teaching, yet they are anguished and abandon their equanimity, the *sine qua non* of saintliness.[107] Why did these arhats cry?

Zhiyi 智顗 (538–597), the putative founder of the Tiantai tradition, asserted that the *Lotus* and *Mahāparinirvāṇa Sūtras* express the perfect teaching of the Mahāyāna. The *Mahāparinirvāṇasūtra* commentary by his disciple, Guanding 灌頂 (561–632), is the foundational commentary on this sūtra in the Tiantai tradition. With regard to this passage, Guanding proposes three

---

106. "Wailing for Scholar Qin Shaoyou" 哭少游學士. *Canliaozi shiji*, 10.7b-8b; 342–348.

107. A more extensive review of how emotions and wailing appear in different Āgama and Mahāyāna *Nirvāṇasūtra* texts is in Protass, "Buddhist Monks and Chinese Poetry," 245–270.

technical explanations for how it might be that the Buddha's disciples, perfectly awakened beings, could appear to suffer from grief and anguish, and he concludes with an insightful reflection.[108]

> Question: How is it that the arhats, who have completely annihilated all sorrow and anguish, are suddenly brought to this?
>
> Answer: It was a remnant of karmic impressions, not current afflictions.[109] Or, they were acting in order to cause others to grieve in a manner suitable for a king.[110] Or, they had not yet eliminated situational mental disturbances, though these were not universal disturbances.[111] As for sorrow and anguish, this reality of the buddhadharma encompasses each and every dharma, so whether "being sorrowful" or "no sorrow," all are part of the reality of the Tathāgata.[112]

問羅漢憂悲都盡何頓至此？答此是殘習非正使也。又示楷模令物攀慕。又別惑未除非通惑也。憂悲者，是佛法界攝一切法，下文有憂、無憂悉是如來境界。

Guanding here is suggesting three technical doctrines that might explain why the arhats appear to have suffered anguish at the death of the Buddha. The second explanation is similar to the concept of expedient means (*fangbian*). Whether or not these three responses are satisfactory, Guanding adds a note concerning the emotions. From the non-dualistic perspective of Tiantai, how can one prefer either the presence or absence of emotions? All that is, just as it is, must somehow be part of how things truly are.

Unlike other major Tiantai sūtra commentaries, Guanding's commentary on the *Mahāparinirvāṇasūtra* was not the subject of an authoritative subcommentary before the Song.[113] Thus, the early Song Tiantai monk Gushan Zhiyuan composed his subcommentary, *The Principal Aim of the Threefold Virtue of the Mahāparinirvāṇasūtra Commentary* 涅槃經疏三德指歸 (hereafter *Sande zhigui*), wherein he elaborates on this final comment by Guanding.[114]

> As for [when Guanding said] "this reality of the buddhadharma," sorrow and anguish come from the fluctuations of the mind, and as the mind is identical with the three truths [of emptiness, conventional existence, and the middle], then

---

108. *Da banniepan jing shu* (T38.46c8–12).

109. This marks the distinction between present, active afflictions (*zhengshi* 正使) and those that are the fruit of previous afflictions that remain after the cessation of the affliction proper (*canxi* 殘習).

110. Reading *panmu* 攀慕 in the sense of *panran* 攀髯.

111. All awakened beings eliminate universal disturbances 通惑, but elimination of the situationally specific disturbances 別惑 is an accomplishment of the bodhisattva, not an arhat. This would explain why the disciples appear to have suffered a temporary situational delusion, not, however, a more general conceptual or perceptive delusion.

112. Rendering *jie* 界 and *jingjie* 境界 as "reality."

113. Shinohara, "Zhiyuan's Autobiographical Essay," 66n23.

114. *Niepan jing shu sande zhigui* (ZZ37.327c7–9).

[these fluctuations of] sorrow and anguish must also be so. Because the three truths are universally inclusive, they are called "reality of the buddhadharma." The sorrow and suffering of the arhats is not excluded from the reality of dharmas. What is there to marvel at? This is a perfect teaching.

是佛法界者，憂悲由心所變，心即三諦，憂悲亦然，三諦徧收名佛法界，故羅漢憂苦無非法界。何所怪哉？此圓義也。

Zhiyuan admires Guanding's insight. He reiterates the idea that one should not prefer being sorrow-less to sorrowful. A similar attitude toward the emotions seems to inform Zhiyuan's lamentations. I turn next to Zhiyuan's lamentations to understand how emotions appear in his poetic practice. In doing so, I draw attention to an aspect of Zhiyuan's works that complements how they have heretofore been understood within the heated debates of Song Tiantai.

Zhiyuan was a prominent monk of wide-ranging talents as well as one of the architects of the revival of Tiantai Buddhism in the early Northern Song.[115] Zhiyuan lived most of his life in Hangzhou near West Lake. He purchased land and moved in 1016 to Ma'nao Cloister 瑪瑙院, later known as Baosheng Temple 寶勝寺, on Gushan Island 孤山, whence his eponym. He associated with the Hangzhou recluse-poet Lin Bu 林逋 (967–1028). Like other revivalists, Zhiyuan lamented the decline of Tiantai teachings and practice after Zhanran, whose writings Zhiyuan especially revered along with those of Zhiyi. Among Zhiyuan's accomplishments was his controversial renewal of the Tiantai commentarial tradition on the Mahāyāna *Mahāparinirvāṇasūtra*.[116] Though Zhiyuan styled himself as a direct heir to Tang-dynasty Tiantai masters, he was later portrayed as a representative of the heterodox "off mountain" (*shanwai* 山外) faction, a slanderous term established by those who regarded themselves as descendants of Zhili 知禮 (960–1028) and the orthodox "home mountain" (*shanjia* 山家) teachings. Daniel Getz, for example, in his careful exposition of Zhili's philosophical critiques, treats Zhiyuan together with his more vociferous dharma brother Qingzhao 慶昭 (963–1017), as representatives of the *shanwai* position critiqued by Zhili.[117] Because Zhiyuan

---

115. The most sympathetic overview of Zhiyuan's life and works is found in Tam, "Life and Thought of a Chinese Buddhist Monk."

116. Zhiyuan either anticipated or responded to criticism that he had not studied the *Mahāparinirvāṇasūtra* face-to-face with a living Tiantai teacher. Tam, "Life and Thought," 180–185, describes Zhiyuan's defense that included a series of propitious dreams. Skonicki, "Viewing the Two Teachings," 20–21, 25–29, translates and further analyzes the cultural logic of Zhiyuan's justifications.

117. Getz, "Siming Zhili," 108–115, clearly elucidates Zhiyuan's active role in one phase of the debate. Getz also establishes the affinity between Zhiyuan's doctrinal position and that of Qingzhao, as well as differences. Zhiyuan's doctrinal position is clearly articulated by Chi-wah Chan, "Chih-li," 107–110, 193–199. Shinohara, too, emphasizes Zhiyuan as a principal participant with a major role in the debates. Shinohara, "Zhiyuan's Autobiographical Essay," 36, and "Illness and Self," 278–279, 292.

lived with Qingzhao during this period, scholars have speculated whether Zhiyuan played some active role in the simmering "seven-year controversy" between Qingzhao and Zhili.[118] It is clear that Zhiyuan manufactured a temporary truce to the debates in 1007, only to have his own writings critiqued by Zhili a decade later, in 1017.[119] In his autobiography, Zhiyuan denies feeling personally bothered by the ongoing controversy, thereby implying the opposite.[120] Though these debates are no doubt significant, the richness of Zhiyuan's life and works cannot be wholly accounted for by Zhili's critiques.

Modern scholarly focus on Zhiyuan's place in this consequential doctrinal contest—often concurring with the later sectarian consensus that he advocated a heterodox Tiantai teaching— has skewed our appreciation of Zhiyuan's contributions to Song Buddhist learning and culture. For example, Zhiyuan's influential commentarial works on the *Śūraṃgamasūtra were already cited by authors as early as Tiantai monk Jingjue Renyue.[121] Zhiyuan was also an avid student and proponent of the Confucian "ancient-style writing" (*guwen* 古文) and wrote explicitly about the relationship between Buddhist and Confucian learning.[122] Zhiyuan was in addition a prolific poetizer, with over four hundred extant poetic compositions. Some of his poems explicitly take up Confucian themes and rebut anti-Buddhist rhetoric.[123] Because my goal is understanding how Song monks used poetry among themselves, not only when currying favor with patrons, I focus on Zhiyuan's poems of mourning written after the deaths of monks.

Turning to Zhiyuan's laments, we find that the word "wailing" 哭, or alternatively "mourning" 悼, often appears in the title. As we have seen in earlier chapters, Zhiyuan was aware of the possible attachment to poetry embodied

---

118. Getz, "Siming Zhili," 78n18, 81, treats Zhiyuan as the co-author of Qingzhao's works, based on a later historiographic tradition, and may overstate Zhiyuan's active role. Regardless, Zhiyuan was clearly aware of Zhili's positions; Chi-wah Chan, "Chih-li," 107. Tam, "Life and Thought," 30–38, 39n76, 175–179. Note that Tam's conclusion about Zhiyuan's early involvement is ambivalent; however, his own documentation suggests Zhiyuan's limited direct involvement in the debate.

119. Getz, "Siming Zhili," 79, 109.

120. Following the persuasive reading by Shinohara, "Zhiyuan's Autobiographical Essay," 43.

121. Numerous large fragments of Zhiyuan's lost commentaries are preserved in later anthologies. Renyue quotes Zhiyuan extensively in his own *Śūraṃgamasūtra tract, known as *Xun wen ji* 薰聞記. Renyue had been the most eloquent defender of Zhili before the two reached a fundamental disagreement and parted ways. See, for example, Ziporyn, *Evil and/or/as the Good*, 432n61, building on work by Andō Toshio. Getz, "Siming Zhili," 18–28, describes Renyue's influence on the development of Tiantai thinking for the remainder of the eleventh century.

122. For example, Andō in "Kozan Chien to Myōkyō Kaisū" focuses on those texts that suggest Zhiyuan saw harmony between the "three teachings." In her discussion of Qisong 契嵩 (1007–1072), Morrison, *Power of Patriarchs*, 114–120, 226, offers thoughtful reflections on the categories by which we discuss "Ru" (Confucian). Skonicki, "Viewing the Two Teachings," 8–14, ably demonstrates Zhiyuan's embrace of *guwen*. Skonicki also shows that Zhiyuan, in his Buddhist apologetics addressed to Confucians, portrayed Confucianism and Buddhism as compatible teachings. Contra Skonicki, I would contend that Zhiyuan's use of the inner-outer and root-branch dyads inherently position Buddhism as the superior or more fundamental tradition.

123. Skonicki, "Viewing the Two Teachings," 14–18, translates Zhiyuan's poems that defend against the anti-Buddhist rhetoric of the followers of Han Yu.

by the poetry demon as well as of the Buddhist prescriptive texts situating poetry as "outer learning." He elsewhere showed his understanding and appreciation of the mainstream Chinese poetic tradition.[124] He did not necessarily see a conflict between Buddhism and poetry. Rather, he seems to have had high standards for both activities and little tolerance for mediocrity.[125] As a learned Tiantai exegete, and unlike most Chan monks from the period, Zhiyuan wrote sūtra commentaries that can also shed light on his poetry.

Compared with the laments of other monks that we have seen above, Zhiyuan wrote with emotion. An example is this lamentation written for Guangjun Baolong 廣鈞保隆 (n.d.), a Tiantai monk connected to Zhiyuan's own dharma family tree.[126]

	This monk from the north has taught us about extinction;	北僧傳示滅
2	Lofty traces such as his are ever hard to find again.	高跡更難尋
	Back home, his room remains,	故國房空在
4	On fresh tomb, grasses already thick.	新墳草已深
	You have broken your old vow to cloudy springs,	雲泉違舊約
6	Ceased your thoughts of discourse with wind and moon.	風月罷論心
	I sit silently looking at your deathbed *gāthā*,	默坐看遺偈
8	Out my western window the moon sinks again.	西牎月又沈

The poem shows a delicate movement toward the extinction articulated in the first line, ending with silence and darkness. Although the poem seems to be full of feeling, there are no affect words. By the end of the poem, Zhiyuan is reflecting on his own situation as a survivor. He sits alone with the last words written out by his friend, and the final line registers Zhiyuan's solitude. The moon does not stop sinking, even though Guangjun is gone and they cannot together watch it slowly edge out of sight. Guangjun's absence will be felt each day as the moon sets.

---

124. In "Given to Poet-Monk, Master Baoxian" 贈詩僧保暹師, *Xianju bian* (ZZ56.930a10–12), "[The poems in] your latest collection are all refined and true, / no need to wait for Confucius to coming culling [to create the *Classic of Poetry*]" 新編皆雅正，不待仲尼刪. In "Expressing What Is on the Mind" 言志, in *Xianju bian* (ZZ56.940a8–22), the poem's title itself is an allusion to the Mao preface to *The Classic of Poetry*. Herein, Zhiyuan gives his support to the *fugu* 復古 movement but ultimately subordinates all Confucian learning to Buddhist learning.

125. In "Sent to a Like-Minded [Friend]" 寄同志, *Xianju bian* (ZZ56.924b16–19), Zhiyuan complains, "How many times have I sighed at those old-fashioned funerals, / I cannot stand people with such vulgar dispositions. / I have been waiting for a visit from you, / so we can sit face-to-face talking about this culture of ours" 幾歎淳風喪，寧容俗態羣，終期一相訪，對坐議新文.

126. "Lamentation for Master Guangjun" 悼廣鈞師, *Xianju bian* (ZZ56.930b17–20). Guangjun was also mentioned by Zhiyuan in "Prayer Text for My Ancestral Teacher" 祭祖師文, *Xianju bian* (ZZ56.890c11), a memorial for Ciguang Zhiyin 慈光志因 (d. 986), a "great-grandfather" figure through whom Zhiyuan traced his own lineage. Zhiyuan recorded that Ciguang's remains 靈骨 had been placed in a *minshe* 民舍 (communal grave?) for over twenty years. Guangjun recovered the remains and stored them honorably inside Jingzhu Cloister 淨住院 of Qiantang 錢唐. This prayer text written thirty-two years after Ciguang's death marked the construction of a proper memorial pagoda 墳塔.

"Taught us about extinction" (*shi mie* 示滅) is a Buddhist euphemism for the death of a monk. The phrase, synonymous with "taught us about stillness" (*shi ji* 示寂), has echoes of the *Mahāparinirvāṇasūtra* depiction of the Buddha's death as an expedient teaching of impermanence and the revelation of the eternal dharma-body (Skt. *dharmakāya*) of the Buddha. In other words, the Buddha in this scripture uses the death of his human body to teach about the impermanence of things and at the same time to point toward the joyous truth of the eternal dharma. The phrases *shi mie* and *shi ji* enabled one to speak of an eminent monk's death being like the death of a buddha. But Zhiyuan uses this phrase without lingering on Guangjun's accomplishments or virtues. The poem is about Guangjun's absence in the world.

Zhiyuan expresses sorrowful sentiments in a lament entitled "Mourning the Ācārya of Fantian Temple, Matching [the Rhymes of] Venerable Cong" 和聰上人悼梵天闍梨.[127] More than ten years senior to Zhiyuan (b. 976), Fantian Qingzhao 梵天慶昭 (963–1017) was the elder disciple of their teacher Fengxian Yuanqing 奉先源清 (d. 1000). The cloister mentioned in line 1 refers to Fantian Temple, where Qingzhao's funeral took place.[128]

	Grief blows through the lecture cloister and stirs the white curtains;[129]	講院悲風動素帷
2	Among swaying pines, it is impossible to again see our teacher.	搖松難更見吾師
	Dust is gathering on his well-worn mat, he will unroll no more;	塵生舊榻休開卷
4	The moon rises in this autumn veranda, but you've ceased making poems.	月上秋軒罷賦詩
	The true dharma—he himself transmitted it to future students;	真法自將傳後學
6	His pure name—who will inscribe a generous stele for it?	清名誰為勒豐碑
	His disciples will recall his noble manner,	橫經弟子懷高跡
8	While we wait to meet him again at the Dragon Flower Tree.[130]	共指龍華作後期

---

127. Qingzhao 慶昭 had the sobriquet Ziwen 子文. The best source for Qingzhao's life is Zhiyuan's "A Record of Activities by Ācārya Zhao of the Old Fantian Temple" 故梵天寺昭闍梨行業記 *Xianju bian* (ZZ56.887b24–888a9). Qingzhao was honored as a *sheli* 闍梨, a transliteration of the Sanskrit ācārya. Further details on Qingzhao are scattered throughout *Xianju bian*. The rhyme may be set to a poem by the same monk for whom Zhiyuan wrote "Preface for the Collected Poems of Master Wencong of Qiantang" 錢唐聞聰師詩集序, *Xianju bian* (ZZ56.908c15–909a23).

128. *Xianju bian* (ZZ56.924b20–24).

129. Lecture cloister was used in the Northern Song to refer to a monastery for Tiantai or Huayan teachings, where expository lectures on sūtras would occur, as opposed to a Chan monastery. White curtains were used in funerals. A curtained tent could mark a ritual space, per the Southern Song *Conglin jiaoding qinggui zongyao* (ZZ63.611b19–20). Some texts also use this term to describe a shroud draped over the coffin.

130. A Dragon Flower Tree will be the site of the awakening of the future Buddha Maitreya.

This lamentation is somewhat more conventional and incorporates emotional responses. In the second half of the poem, he clearly turns to address Qingzhao's students, Zhiyuan's own dharma nephews. The poem ends with a religious trope. Zhiyuan seamlessly blends grief, hope, and doctrine. On a day like this, when even the wind and trees seem to be complicit in their mourning, Zhiyuan and these disciples look forward to meeting the dead again when they are all born in Maitreya's assembly.

Yet another example of explicit grief, though not for a monk, is in "Wailing for Ye Shou" 哭葉授. Ye Shou 葉授 (n.d.) was a promising young man who died early.[131] He had stayed at Zhiyuan's temple while traveling from his home in the south to the northern capital to sit for the imperial civil service examination. He fell ill and died shortly after failing the exam.[132]

	I heard you failed the exam only this past spring,	今春聞落第
2	And my heart pained for you.	為君心悽然
	Then bundling up your books to return south alone,	束書獨南還
4	Frustration swelled in your breast!	憤氣胸間闐
	Though you lodged temporarily here beside the Zhe River,	跡寄淛河旁
6	Your home long was on the shores of the southern sea.	家延南海邊
	Once you fell ill, you would not recover,	遭疾既彌留
8	And so a life reached its end.	一命成棄捐
	Your sack contained no extra gold,	囊中無餘金
10	Only scattered essays written for naught.	零落空文編
	Tortoises and cranes are auspicious types[133]	龜鶴本微類
12	that enjoy long lives over a thousand years;	享壽皆千年
	How come you, sir, an ideal Confucian,	如何君子儒
14	returned to the layered springs after only thirty?[134]	三十歸重泉
	Heaven is high and cannot be questioned,	天高不可問
16	but for you I force myself to question heaven!	為君強問天

Zhiyuan is full of anguish over the untimely death of a young man, in a manner similar to Daoqian in his poem "Wailing for Venerable Xiu," above. The poem culminates with anguish at the threshold of self-control. Though it was not written using explicit Buddhist language, the discourse from the *Mahāparinirvāṇasūtra* may be relevant here. Awakened beings do not doubt

---

It is a common refrain in monks' lamentations to yearn for meeting again in a future rebirth either in the Western Pure Land or at Maitreya's "Dragon-Flower Convocation" 龍華會.

131. See Zhiyuan's earlier poem to send off the young man titled "Given to Presented Scholar Ye Shou" 贈進士葉授, *Xianju bian* (ZZ56.924c13–17). Ye is a family name most common among southern people. Among sources from the middle period, members of the Ye family often have single-character personal names, and so I tentatively take Shou as his personal name.

132. *Xianju bian* (ZZ56.940c11–17).

133. Emending *zheng* 徵 for *wei* 微. These "auspicious types [of beings]" are explained in the late Southern Song commentary *Lengyan jing jian* (ZZ11.1079a7–8).

134. *Chongquan* 重泉 is a name for the Chinese underworld.

the impermanence of life; only those not yet liberated would want to defy this fact. But Zhiyuan's exegesis, following Guanding, had instead argued that, ultimately, one cannot prefer not-sorrow to sorrow.

In one last example, Zhiyuan wrote a lament for a poet-monk entitled "Wailing for Venerable Bianduan" 哭辯端上人.[135] Rather than foreground the pain of personal loss, Zhiyuan, perhaps echoing the lost poems of Bianduan, observes in the poem the ongoing presence of sadness in the world.

	For a lifetime you suffered from poetry,	平昔於詩苦
2	Keenly searching, thoughts never at rest.	精搜省未閑
	From your ramshackle dwelling beyond birds in the sky	壞房空鳥外
4	Came pellucid phrases to fill the world of men.	清句滿人間
	Frail shadows hang on neighboring walls;	瘦影懸鄰壁
6	Your lone tomb recedes into your former hills.	孤墳接舊山
	In mourning I return beneath the tall trees:	弔迴高樹下
8	The cold waters burble on.	寒水自潺潺

Bianduan's life evoked for Zhiyuan a beautiful and melancholic world. The poem praises the late monk for his success as a restless writer. Zhiyuan's referent is the tradition of "painstaking composition" (kuyin 苦吟) associated with the Late-Tang figure Jia Dao 賈島 (779–843), a tradition that remained popular through the first decades of the Song, the time of this composition.[136] Kuyin had once meant "poetry of suffering" but came to express "painstaking composition," something poets spoke of as a pleasure.[137] The kuyin poet is always revisiting and tinkering with his poetic lines. We may here recall Zhiyuan's "Poetry Demon," which represented the pleasures of composing poetic lines as a kind of karmic obstacle. Just so, Zhiyuan paints the life of the poet-monk Bianduan as one of constant struggle with language. Zhiyuan lauded the poet-monk for composing poetic lines that seemed to come from beyond the world. Line 4 describes them as "pellucid" (qing 清), a delicate aesthetic that Zhiyuan elsewhere connected to the ideal of "even and bland" (pingdan 平淡).[138] A careful reader may notice that this praise is limited to the human realm and does not address a soteriological goal.

Zhiyuan discerned that Bianduan's life was unusual and peripheral to the normative Buddhist monastic path, but Zhiyuan is agnostic as to whether that is a good or a bad thing. He admired Bianduan's eremitic evasion of the world. Zhiyuan's poem mentions only a ramshackle dwelling, and extant

---

135. *Xianju bian* (ZZ56.946b17–20).

136. The poetry of the early Song "Nine Monks" was also associated with *kuyin* in Song literary criticism; see *Quan Min shihua*, 11.23b. On Jia Dao and *kuyin*, see Owen, *Late Tang*, 93–112.

137. This transformation is discussed in Owen, "Spending Time on Poetry." See also Owen, *End of the Chinese Middle Ages*, 24, 119–121.

138. *Xianju bian* (ZZ56.909a24). On the aesthetics of *qing* as a descriptor of monks' poetry in the Song, see Gao, "Shiseng zhi 'shusunqi' yu 'suanxianqi.'" On *pingdan*, see Sturman, *Mi Fu*, 140.

records preserve nothing further about Venerable Bianduan's career—perhaps he had no disciples. In death, Bianduan's poetic lines written on neighboring walls remain and yet are quickly fading. Zhiyuan depicts himself as a solitary mourner and Bianduan as a poet who attempted to capture the songs of the natural world with his pure lines. After his friend's body has been interred, Zhiyuan finds some consolation that the waters of the physical world continue to sing out of their own accord.

Zhiyuan was no stranger to Song-era debates about Buddhism and the arts.[139] He once imagined the human longing for poetry as a kind of demon or karmic obstacle. The poems translated here, however, offer his further responses to the broader possibilities of poetry in religious life. I have suggested that Zhiyuan's distinctive use of mourning poetry parallels his sūtra exegesis. Further research may substantiate the idea that Zhiyuan's poetic practices were part of those of a broader community of Tiantai monks in the Song, or perhaps reflect the intra-Tiantai debates of the early Song. Unfortunately, we have only traces of other Tiantai writers of poetry from the Northern Song.[140] Still, these tantalizing clues suggest that Zhiyuan was representative of this community. For example, Lingzhi Yuanzhao 靈芝元照 (1048–1116) in a biographic note for Yilao Kejiu 佚老可久 (1013–1093) says, "[Kejiu] had studied Tiantai teachings from Renyue. He also delighted in ancient and regulated poetry, mostly composing things that were 'even and bland,' and pure and bitter. If one wanted to compare his work, it was like that of Lingche and Qingsai" 嘗從霅溪法師學天台教。喜為古律詩，大抵造於平淡、清苦。比夫然徹清塞之流.[141] Kejiu did not write *jisong*, as Song Chan monks had done. He wrote *shi* poetry in styles that harked back to the late Tang. The poetry of Tiantai monks for the most part offers a point of comparison with the poetic practices and *jisong* of Chan abbots.

Lamentations by Chan Abbots

Abbots of Chan public monasteries throughout the Northern and Southern Song composed personal lamentations in addition to the ritual verses discussed above. In general, two strategies are evident in these laments. The first strategy is didacticism similar to that of the ritual verses discussed above. I will give one example. The second strategy reflects the tensions seen above in poems by Qisong and Daoqian, but it seeks a kind of dynamic equilibrium. I focus on two poems by Xuedou Chongxian that, unlike the emotional poems by Zhiyuan, acknowledge the rising and passing of sentiments without attachments.

---

139. Recall my mention in Chap. 4 that Zhiyuan wrote on "outer learning"; his commentary on the *Vimalakīrtinirdeśa* contained extensive quotations from a range of Vinaya texts.

140. Zhang Liang, "Songdai Tiantai zong sengshi."

141. *Zhiyuan ji* (ZZ59.655a8–23). I am aware of one extant poem by Kejiu not previously noted by other scholars in the Southern Song collection *Rentian baojian* (ZZ87.15a8–16).

A Chan verse that illustrates this first strategy is by Wuzu Fayan 五祖法演 (1018–1104). "Mourning Venerable [Fa]yan of Mount Sizu" 悼四祖演和尚[142] is an eight-line verse using a single end rhyme; however, the tonal prosody departs from a regulated sequence and the line length changes in the final couplet.[143] This verse expresses non-attachment to life or death.

	Here illness, there full extinction [of *parinirvāṇa*].	此病彼圓寂
2	In our school, what is gained and lost?	吾門何得失
	Birth and death are like flowers in the sky,[144]	生死若空花
4	Coming and going are like footprints of a bird [in flight].	去來如鳥跡
	You spring up in the east, and sink in the west,	東涌忽西沒
6	Your portrait hangs on the wall of this frozen hall.	影掛寒堂壁
	In the *trāyastriṃśa* heaven ring Śakra's bell![145]	三十三天撲帝鐘
8	Everywhere intone *prajñāpārami*[*tā*]!	普念般若波羅蜜

From start to finish, this poem circumscribes death within a religious message. No personal sentiments are present. The transformations wrought by death present yet another occasion for the pealing of the bells of wisdom.[146] This strategy, by now familiar, is probably the more common of the two.

A second, more complex strategy found in laments by Chan abbots is to describe their feelings but remain non-attached. An example is the four poems of "mourning" 悼 by Xuedou Chongxian. As with Qisong's elegies, Chongxian's poems were written for laypersons. Unlike Qisong, however, Chongxian reflected on the nature of poetry within his poems. In the final couplet of "Mourning the Functionary from Wuwei" 悼武威評事, for example, the author wonders about the propriety of a devout monk singing songs of sorrow.[147]

	I am ashamed that, old and ill beneath these pine cliffs,	我慚老病松巖下
8	I turn in vain to the groaning wind to sing of your virtuous house.	空對悲風詠德門

---

142. Sizu Fayan 四祖法演 (n.d.) was a disciple of Huanglong Huinan, as detailed in *Jianzhong jingguo xudenglu* (ZZ78.717a16-b12).

143. As found in the Southern Song collection *Xu Gu zunsu yuyao* (ZZ68.415a5–8). The verse would later be placed in a section entitled "*Jisong*," with minor textual errata, in the Ming edition of *Fayan chanshi yulu* (T47.666c22–25).

144. Like someone with an eye affliction looking at the sky and perceiving flowers, so, too, do we misjudge our ordinary experiences to be substantial. This classical Indian metaphor was perhaps best known in the Song from *Shoulengyan jing* (T19.120b29-c1).

145. The bell of Śakra that peals thunder from the *trāyastriṃśa* heaven is described in Daoxuan's *Zhong Tianzhu Sheweiguo Qihuansi tujing* (T45.886a24–27).

146. Further examples that employ a similar strategy are gathered in a section of the Yuan anthology *Chanzong zaduhai* (ZZ65.72a3-c12).

147. *Zuting shiyuan* (ZZ64.375b21–24). Wuwei 武威 is a name for Fuzhou 福州, according to *Xin Wudai shi*, 60/24b.

Chongxian senses the moral restraint of "shame" (*can* 慚) when, old and ill as he is, he can still be discomposed by another's death. In Mahāyāna literature, this kind of shame is one of a bodhisattva's virtues, which enables him to engage in worldly behavior without attachments.[148] In other words, feeling shame as an inner moral restraint when writing an elegy presents a solution to the problem of the emotions because it is how a bodhisattva would respond. A similar use appears in another poem by Chongxian, "Seeing Off Chan Worthy Yun" 送雲禪德: "When the ancients saw a person off, their words would be a cherished treasure; / I am ashamed that with old age and illness, I am destitute of literary elegance" 古之送人言作懷寶，我慚老病困乏辭藻.[149] Chongxian naturally follows this self-deprecatory rhetoric with a literary offering to the departing monk. Chongxian also makes a clever allusion to "old age, sickness, and death" 老病死, the foundational Buddhist teaching of the three types of suffering, each witnessed by Prince Siddhārtha before his great departure into the renunciant life. Chongxian, despite his awareness of his own embodiment of two of the three types of suffering, somehow is disquieted by the third. He turns toward the wind to sing his song even though he knows that it is done in emptiness (*kong* 空). This action is alloyed by the presence of his shame as inner moral restraint.

Chongxian explores another aspect of the tensions between Buddhist ideals and poetic emotions in the first of a series of three poems, "Mourning the Functionary of Hejian" 悼河間評事.[150]

	At your funeral were hundreds or thousands of people;	隨喪人物百千重
2	But with a snap of the fingers here outside town, the whole affair is already empty.	彈指郊原事已空
	All that's left are the freshly planted pines and cypresses	唯有新栽小松栢
4	That will bend in the grieving wind ever for you.	為君遐古動悲風

Chongxian's entire poem moves across a landscape that mirrors his interior one.[151] First, an impressively large funeral procession marches out to the burial site but soon disperses to become a memory. Chongxian sees the emptiness of all things—a Buddhist ideal. As the poet envisions the myriad details of funerary etiquette, he knows that it is ultimately empty.[152] All has passed "with

---

148. I have tentatively taken *can* here as a Buddhist term. In technical literature, *can*, as a translation of Sanskrit *hrī*, is an inner moral restraint (vs. self-loathing or guilt); *kui* 愧, as a translation of *apatrāpya*, is concern for harm to oneself or others (vs. a fear of social embarrassment or censure). Both are wholesome qualities. Following this train of thought, many Mahāyāna texts insist that bodhisattvas can engage in this-worldly behavior and not accrue karma because they abide in *can* and *kui*, inner moral restraint and moral concern.

149. *Mingjue chanshi yulu* (Gozan ed., 95; T47.709b16).

150. *Zuting shiyuan* (ZZ64.375b24-c1; *Gozan-ban*, 294).

151. The relationship between interiority and landscape is explored in Kao, "Chinese Lyric Aesthetics," 83–84.

152. One wonders if he is playing with the layers of *kong* to also indicate that such behavior is in vain.

a snap of the fingers." Then, in a second vision, Chongxian sees pine and cypress saplings and finds them grieving. A sorrowful wind again blows across the funereal landscape. Such visions are possible in this poetic landscape because the poet is full of grief. Taken as a whole, Chongxian's poem presents the vision of a monk who sees through the affairs of grieving as empty, and yet still he grieves.

As we have seen, at least two poetic strategies can be found in the laments by Chan abbots. First, Chan abbots would view the transformations of death as manifestations of the truth of things, a didactic mode akin to that of ritual verses. Second, Chan abbots could acknowledge their feelings in a way that did not attach to them. The poet could hold the conventional reality of mourning and the ultimate truth of emptiness in a kind of dynamic equilibrium.

Coda

In this chapter I have surveyed two distinct uses of poetic writing by monks in mourning. Throughout both modes of verse, Song-era monks sought to reconcile the powerful emotions of grief with commitments to monastic asceticism. I have argued that ritual verse as part of Chan funeral liturgies addressed communal mourning and, second, that the didacticism of such verses should be interpreted within the performative contexts of rites for encoffinment, cremation, and interment. The leader of a monastic community used ritual verses to offer religious succor to a grieving sangha. These same verses also initiated ritual care, such as commemorative veneration and merit-making, on behalf of the deceased. Burial songs and poems mourning the dead, on the other hand, were expressions of personal grief. This is not to say that personal poems were somehow separable from social performance. Just as literati would perform friendship after death in "a rhetorically private but textually public space" in order to affirm shared values, so, too, Buddhist monks in their personal laments would affirm relationships and values.[153] Unlike most literary expressions of grief by literati, however, monks' poetic laments reflect the Buddhist occupational commitment to equanimity.

Reading across these forms, we see the innovations that monks in the Song brought to their verse. Among Chan masters who served as abbots at public monasteries, some wrote laments that transposed the didactic strategy of ritual verses. Other Chan abbots, such as Chongxian, described the arising and passing of emotions without attachment. Qisong went so far as to say that, although as a monk he ought not be writing such poems, his passions needed to be let out in verse. Daoqian and Su Shi disagreed on the significance of being the kinds of people in whom feelings would collect. The layman arguing that the blissful stillness of insight and the emotions of poetry were not necessarily opposed to one another, while the monk was convinced that even if grief were unavoidable, the powerful emotion was of no benefit. The poems

---

153. Shields, *One Who Knows Me*, 310.

by Zhiyuan, meanwhile, directly subverted the broader monastic norms concerning emotions. I have suggested this as a parallel to Zhiyuan's non-dual view of emotions as expressed in his *Mahāparinirvāṇasūtra* commentary, which may have been part of a Tiantai literary subculture in the early Song. The numerous and diverse responses seen above reflect the expressive potential of funerary genres for monks of the Song.[154] Were this survey to inspire further study of monks' mourning poetry, I suspect we would find additional strategies by which Song monks responded to the inherent tensions between non-attachment and the genres of mourning.

---

154. Adapting comments from Shields, *One Who Knows Me*, 328.

Epilogue

THE CHAN MONK Yayu Shaosong 亞愚紹嵩 (fl. 1229–1232), while traveling, composed an incredible 367 "poems of gathered lines" 集句詩. This poetic practice flourished in the Song dynasty after Wang Anshi treated it as a serious genre.[1] Each poem drew together four or eight lines quoted directly from earlier Tang or Song poets, creating a kind of poetic bricolage. Shaosong was remarkably good at this practice and produced an unusually large collection, for which members of the literati wrote four colophons. One among these literati, the well-known Yang Mengxin 楊夢信 (fl. 1196–1233), wrote a laudatory poem, of which one couplet reads, "Studying poetry was never separate from practicing Chan; / a forest canopy of ten thousand images are all manifest right before us" 學詩元不離參禪，萬象森羅總現前.

The literati marveled at Shaosong's ability to appropriate the lines of others into new poems. The juxtapositions of his "gathered lines" revealed new and unexpected interpretations of well-known passages of poetry. Shaosong himself, however, understood his literary activity in terms of outer learning and therefore depicted it as a non-Buddhist practice. When another member of the literati, Chen Yingshen 陳應申 (n.d.), expressed to Shaosong his astonishment at the poems, it is said that the monk "heaved a great sigh" and replied,[2] "You've gone too far. The fundamental trait of the Way of Confucius and Mozi is usefulness. How could I have penetrated Buddhism by following the Confucians? Nor do I use Buddhism to rob the Confucians! [. . .] I merely use poetry in order to befriend gentlemen like you." 上人浩然歎曰：「君之言過矣。孔墨之道本相為用，況予由儒入釋也。非為釋而盜儒也。［ . . .] 予方以詩而與君友。」Shaosong, in other words, portrayed his poems as mere expedient means, a way to associate with members of the literati while traveling. Chen reportedly was impressed by the response and thus agreed to compose a colophon, dated 1231.

In 1237, a group of Shaosong's heirs sponsored the carving of woodblocks and the dissemination of the collection of poems.[3] Shaosong had by then composed his own preface for the fixed collection, which begins,[4]

---

1. Zhang Minghua, "Jijushi de fazhan jiqi tedian."
2. *Yayu Jiang Zhe jixing jiju shi*, ba/526.
3. Signed the first year of the Jiaxi 嘉熙 reign era (1237–1240). *Yayu Jiang Zhe jixing jiju shi*, 7.9b/525.
4. *Yayu Jiang Zhe jixing jiju shi*, xu/481.

274

In my view of the leisure time between *chan* and chanting, nothing surpasses poetry for expressing thoughts and feelings; however, all of my intoning is guided by my mouth. I have no skill for word craft, and so with my own compositions, as soon as I get one I toss it away. Now, these "gathered lines" were composed in response to things and to commit my thoughts [to verse], made after I set off in the fall of 1229, leaving Changsha and becoming an itinerant wanderer of the Jiang and Zhe river regions, traveling through villages and staying at inns, until in the fifth month of 1232, when the honorable Huang Yinyuan, magistrate of Jiaxing, offered me the empty abbot's seat at Dayun [Temple].

余以禪誦之暇，暢其性情，無出於詩，但每唫咏，信口而成，不工句法，故自作者，隨得隨失。今所存集句也，乃紹定己丑之秋，自長沙發行訪遊江浙，村行旅宿，感物寓意之所作。越壬辰五月中，瀚嘉禾史君黃公尹元以大雲虛席俾令承乏。

Shaosong used the remainder of the preface to narrate how he was eventually convinced to share his compositions and permit them to be arranged into a set text. According to Shaosong, he only composed these poems in periods of the day not dedicated to monastic activities, and judging from the contents of the collection, he appears to have stopped altogether once he had the responsibilities of an abbot.

Shaosong reportedly conceived of his Buddhistic inner studies and his poetry studies as separate endeavors. Despite suggestions to the contrary by members of the literati, he averred that he used poetry only to befriend them. Shaosong's protestations notwithstanding, he was a prolific participant in a mainstream Song-dynasty poetry game. It is clear at least that his unusual talent for combining poetic lines attracted positive attention from local officials, one of whom completed arrangements for Shaosong to receive an abbatial appointment. Had the discourse of outer learning become an affectation? Or was Shaosong sincere in acknowledging the tension? Did such a tension have impact on his poetic practices? Is it possible that his "poetry of gathered lines" exhibited "limpidity" (*qing*), for example, an aesthetic associated with refined works by poet-monks? Perhaps we could detect a didactic purpose lodged within some poems, but it also seems possible that Shaosong's portrayal of his poetry as expedient means was a polite fiction, an excuse for his indulgence in literary pleasure.

I have not come near to exhausting the genres that constitute the poetry of monks or their many poetic practices. It is my hope that future researchers will reconsider further genres, modes, and subgenres, or think further about the functions and rhetoric of monks' poetry. Some as-yet unexplored areas of study include monks' participation in another popular Song practice of "matching-rhyme poetry" 次韻詩,[5] mainstream topoi like "cherishing the

---

5. Chen Zhongxiu, *Tangdai heshi yanjiu*, 129–153, reviews the three types of *heyun* 和韻 poetry, including *ciyun*.

past" 懷古, as well as novel creations such as "poems of longing for the Pure Land" 懷淨土詩.[6] More work remains to be done on the poetry of Tiantai monks, especially to ground interpretations in Song-era exegesis and differentiate their discourse from that of Chan monks.

I have argued that the disciplinary apparatus of monasticism and the variegated practices of poetry intersected in complex relationships, which can be illustrated by critically thinking through genre. The result is a better understanding of the dynamics of Song China's Buddhist monastic literary cultures. I have argued further that it would be an error to take the prescriptions by critics and in legal codes of what Buddhist poetry *should be* and mistake them for descriptions of what Buddhist poetry *was*. The lives of monks were infused with verse. They often wrote poetry, sometimes bending literary norms toward Buddhist ideals, sometimes to curry favor and correspond with members of the literati, and sometimes to directly express the tensions between ideals of ascetic monastic deportment and the aesthetics of poetic emotions. We are enriched by paying close attention to the genres they constructed and put into practice.

When we discuss Buddhist poetry of the Song and on, we often conflate *jisong* by Chan monks with *shi*. *Jisong* and *shi* were neither mutually exclusive nor categorically equivalent. The appellation *jisong* (Chinese *gāthā*) signaled that the verse in question was primarily religious in nature. It was not limited to any poetic form; some *jisong* were written in *shi* form and some *shi* were treated as *jisong*. Across both the monastic and mainstream literary cultures, *shi* referred to the Chinese tradition of lyrical and personal poems, a vehicle for expressing deeply felt emotions. Song readers and writers used their terms for *gāthā* and poetry to distinguish between religious and literary ways of both writing and reading. The composition of *jisong*, which began in the late Tang, appears to have blossomed in the Song dynasty in part because the category of *jisong* expanded to include the manifold verses written by Chan abbots, some written in *shi* form, thought to be capable of awakening others.

In addition to considering how monks defined *gāthā* and propagated that normative knowledge, I examined how individuals and their textual communities would make *gāthā*. Manuscripts and paratextual evidence gathered from Song woodblock editions provide direct evidence of how norms were put into practice. When direct evidence is lacking, knowledge of poetic practice allows us to speculate about the contexts that might have surrounded poems. Although *jisong* often adhered to the regulated forms of *shi*, their authors, readers, and compilers treated these poems as religious objects.

If monks could treat their verse as *jisong*, it was equally true that some monks were writing *shi*. The study of *shi* as a worldly, non-Buddhist genre was connoted by the term "outer learning." Chinese poetry itself lay outside the Buddhist Way, according to numerous monastic prescriptive texts. The status of poetry as an outer art form was perpetuated in the Song through encyclo-

---

6. See Liao, *Daochui wukongdi*, 429–463.

pedias, Vinaya, "rules of purity," monastic primers, lexicons, meditation manuals, sūtra commentaries, and hagiographies. Monks' poems about poetry—on topics including the outer status of poetry and the poetry demon—demonstrate a widespread familiarity with the concept of outer learning. It was not just a concept in theory, but rather a concept that shaped the landscape of poetic practice. Moreover, terms such as *jisong* and "outer learning" made it possible for people in the Song to conceive of a monk's poetic writing as worldly poetry. Such worldliness was the implication of the term "literary Chan" (*wenzi chan*). *Wenzi chan* was not, as I have argued, a monastic movement, not a banner under which poetry was used to achieve liberation. Huihong instead used the term to refer to poetry that conveyed "feelings not yet forgotten." The term took on an ironic cast when Huihong used it in his braggadocio, because as a talented writer of poetry he was no mere "*gāthā*-scribbler," to borrow Mazanec's phrase.[7]

In thinking about "literary Chan," we should be careful not to mistake Ming-era interpretations of Song poetic practice as Song history. It was only in the seventeenth century in a Chan sectarian debate that Zibo Zhenke transformed Huihong's "literary Chan" into a lofty spiritual path. We need to keep in mind as well that Song-era rhetoric about what poetry was *supposed to be* does not describe directly what monks' poetry *was*. To more clearly articulate differences in practice, I compared in the preceding pages the writings of different types of Song monks, including Chan abbots, Tiantai masters, and literary monks. The exercise revealed that the differences in literary output corresponded to sociological differences between public and private Buddhist monasteries as well as the distinct corpora of Chan or Tiantai specialized learning among elite monks.

Song-era Tiantai monks seem to have had different commitments in their poetry. Zhiyuan, a Tiantai monk, faced similar tensions between Buddhist and Confucian learning but differed from Chan monks in his responses. He wrote *shi* and not *jisong*. I have argued in these pages that the differences in Zhiyuan's verse can be correlated with his own exegetical writing within the Tiantai tradition. Zhiyuan frequently embraced emotions in his poetry, consonant with his view that the refusal of ordinary human feeling would wrongly imply a duality where ultimately there is none. Our evidence for the poetry of Tiantai monks in the Song is significantly less diverse than for Chan. A future comparison of Zhiyuan's poems with those by Ciyun Zunshi may illuminate differences in their verse that reflect the intra-Tiantai doctrinal dispute. More research is needed to conclude the extent to which Zhiyuan's poetry is representative of a shared poetic culture of Northern Song Tiantai.

Song-era Chan monks, that is, the abbots and officers of Chan public monasteries, strongly distinguished between *gāthā* and poetry both in theory and in practice, a view that in part reflected the notion that a Chan master was an awakened person whose words had salvific power. The Chinese terms

---

7. Mazanec, "Medieval Chinese *Gāthā*," 143.

for *gāthā* signaled religious purpose, and such religious verses were not to be mistaken for mere poems. The lexicon *Zuting shiyuan* noted that "a poem (*shi*) follows from the affections (*qing*) and is sensuously intricate." A *gāthā* need not adhere to literary norms. Taking this idea further, some monks seemed to think that their poetic writing *should not* adhere to literary norms.

Still, we have seen that Chan monks wrote prodigious quantities of poetry. In the case of parting poetry, they often subverted the kinds of sentiments typical of mainstream genres. The *Yifanfeng* collection of parting poems is replete with disruptive humor, suggestions of spiritual attainment, and philosophical assertions about the emptiness of all phenomena as well as the universality of the awakened mind. These qualities were lodged within the form of a standard poetic quatrain and were presented in the customary manner before a traveler's departure. Common images of distance, such as the moon or the vast sea, are present in the poems. In *Yifanfeng*, these common topoi become opportunities to deny the ordinary pain of separating. Buddhist parting poems are made Buddhist by their participating within the mainstream parting poem genre and then inverting its conventions to affirm monastic values.

This kind of genre subversion was not practiced in the case of mourning poetry. Monks wrote in two distinct genres: ritual verses and poetic lamentations. Chan abbots wrote verses to be intoned together with formal parallel prose as part of modular funeral liturgies. These verses were formal, intended to be recited publicly before a grieving community, and aimed at affirming didactic truths. The ritual result of performing these solemn hymns was karmic merit that could be dedicated to the benefit of the deceased and assist the processes of death and rebirth. Such verses also offered religious succor to the survivors. With these performances, survivors publicly affirmed their own role as a disciple, dharma brother, or coreligionist on the path, and situated the dead in their new post-liminal status of "ancestor." Funeral verses were created not only to do this ritual work but also to fulfill a distinct aesthetic imperative. The verses by necessity could not resemble too closely mainstream poetry; they instead needed to sound and feel like scriptural language, what Zürcher has called Buddhist church language. Thus were created new generic forms, such as "offering a lamentation," that were Buddhist from their conception. These verses intentionally re-created religious aesthetics, were performed to do ritual work, and are preserved in anthologies marked as religious—not literary—texts. Although not categorized as literary, such texts were carefully composed, and our combined use of both literary and doctrinal analyses can reveal their combined ritual and sociological significance.

In contrast to ritual verse, when monks wrote lamentations, they were participating in a tradition of expressing personal grief. Qisong wrote that, as a Buddhist monk, he should refrain from such expression. For him, the distance between his monastic identity and his grief over lost friendship could not be seamlessly woven together. He felt compelled to write burial songs and at the same time had to note that he should deny his impulse. This double movement, to intone a poem that acknowledges that one "ought not," is a way of affirming one's Buddhist identity while poeticizing. When Qisong implied that to write of his grief was inherently antithetical to the idealized form of life for a monk he was expressing a tension. This widely felt tension between poetry and piety prompted multiple strategies.

The "poetry demon" is another example of how monks imagined their poetic passions. Here, poetry became a karmic habit, an urge that welled up unbidden. Poetic impulses that rushed into the mind could interrupt religious practices. A sudden insight into the right words in the right order and then crafting the sequence of lines to complete a poem was not in and of itself a practice that led to Buddhist liberation. It was for members of the literati that such poetic concentration was, in a loose sense, religious. But elite monks, too, were attracted to this textual spirituality. For example, Daoqian traveled and wrote together with Su Shi and Qin Guan and was part of the fabric of the literati class. There was, in fact, an entire class of monks who lived in non-public temples or small public monasteries, relied on private patronage, and often wrote poetry. In these circumstances, learned monks were not bound by sectarian "rules of purity" written for large public monasteries. They might instead adhere to basic Song monasticism. Basic monasticism often meant familiarity with the general knowledge evidenced in primers about Vinaya and might exclude the specialized knowledge of Chan lore or Tiantai exegesis. At the same time, evidence from normative texts, and *ex silencio* from *yulu*, shows that the metaphoric uses of Buddhist language by the literati to describe the satisfactions enjoyed when composing poetry, calligraphy, or painting were not Buddhist practices prescribed by Buddhist monks for other monks. Daoqian disagreed with Su Shi about whether poetry obstructed dharma. For Huihong, *wenzi chan* was an ironic reference to poetry and its worldly feelings. One connotation of the term "outer learning" was that poetry should be studied for the purpose of converting non-Buddhists. In and of itself, mainstream poetry was not the path to awakening for those in the priesthood. The syncretic use of Buddhist terms as analogues for literati writing did not fundamentally alter the established norms of Buddhist monastic learning in the Song.

Song-era monks were sometimes depicted as having instrumental relationships to poetry. They used poetry to correspond with lettered laypeople, a kind of pastoral outreach that was surely important for some monks during fundraising or when currying patronage. Sincere authorial intentions in literature cannot be demonstrated conclusively; however, it is difficult for me to imagine that the numerous actors involved in constructing and maintaining the Buddhist culture of the Song were acting with uniform cynicism in a quest for personal material gain. I think we can imagine that some monks sincerely wished to turn lettered men to the Buddhist path.

Looking ahead to future research, what were the impacts of Song monastic literary culture on later dynasties, and how did later monks' practices differ? My impression is that a general contiguity with regard to monks' poetry extended from the Southern Song to the end of the Yuan. At the same time, the works of numerous Southern Song and Yuan Chan figures have not yet been closely analyzed, and there are still exciting topics awaiting future discovery. Nonetheless, monks' poetry in the late Ming appears radically different from these earlier periods. This difference is visible in textual practices and can be seen even across earlier and later editions of texts for individual figures. For example, only in a newly re-compiled 1627 recension of works by Shiwu Qinggong 石屋清珙 (1272–1352), his poetry was placed *inside* his *yulu*.[8] The newly altered paratexts indicate the entire contents should now be treated as part of the *yulu*, whereas earlier, the monk's *shi* were separated from his explicitly religious writing. Similarly, the *shi* by Tianru Weize 天如惟則 (1286–1354) appear to have been collected separately from his other writings at first and placed inside his *yulu* only in the late Ming.[9] Such textual reorganization seems to have been a common practice in late Ming editions of *yulu* for Yuan-era Chan masters.[10] Despite such general continuities between Song and Yuan texts, further research will likely reveal innovations and deviation from Song precedents in the poetry of monks from the Yuan and early Ming.[11] By contrast, late Ming and early Qing *yulu* for contemporaneous Chan masters regularly included explicit sections of *shi,* sometimes in addition to *jisong.*[12] Some Ming compilers even created a novel genre to use as a section heading with the compound phrase *shiji* 詩偈. This could denote "poems and *gāthā*" (*shi* and *ji*) as well as "poetic *gāthā*" (*shi-ji*). These late-Ming departures from earlier Song textual practices would parallel the rehabilitation of the term *wenzi chan* in the late Ming. The broader changes in Buddhist literature of the late Ming and early Qing, including an embrace of *shi* as a Buddhist path and Buddhist playwriting for ritualized performance, have begun to be docu-

---

8. The structure and sequence of the earlier *Shiwu chanshi shanju shi—jizan—yulu* were altered in the late-Ming *Fuyuan Shiwu Gong chanshi yulu.* In the earliest edition of the former, the preface dated 1382 was carved to appear like brushwork. For more in English and a complete translation, see Red Pine, *Zen Works of Stonehouse.*

9. Further research may clarify the history of the disparate texts agglomerated in the ten-fascicle *Tianru Weize chanshi yulu.* My assertion that Tianru Weize's *shi* were collected separately is based on colophons in the nine-fascicle Edo edition of *Shizilin Tianru heshang yulu,* the Ming edition of *Shizilin Tianru heshang Jingtu huowen,* and the *Taishō* edition of *Jingtu huowen.* Each of these works is listed in the bibliography.

10. Poetry appears in the late-Ming editions of *Shuzhong heshang yulu* of Shuzhong Wuyun 恕中無慍 (1309–1386) and *Dai'an Zhuang chanshi yulu,* of Dai'an Puzhuang 呆菴普莊 (1347–1403).

11. For example, the "expanded records" 廣錄 of Zhongfeng Mingben in thirty fascicles, *Tianmu Zhongfeng heshang guanglu* 天目中峯和尚廣錄, contains poetry and prose. The 1334 petition appended to the beginning of the Qisha canon edition indicates that the *guanglu* was compiled from several separate texts, one of which was a ten-fascicle *yulu* that did not include a section entitled *shi.* Nonetheless, the comprehensive collection anticipates the inclusive editorial practices of the late Ming. On editions of this text, see Heller, *Illusory Abiding,* 22–23.

12. Numerous examples from *Jiaxing dazangjing* include *Fushi chanshi yulu* 浮石禪師語錄, *Linye Qi chanshi yulu* 林野奇禪師語錄, *Xiangtian Jinian chanshi yulu* 象田即念禪師語錄, and *Jiewei Zhou Chanshi yulu* 介為舟禪師語錄.

mented in recent and emerging scholarship.[13] Details about the transformations of the late Ming will need to be charted elsewhere.

In conclusion, I would like to return briefly to some of the factors that shaped the environment in which monks wrote poetry, to wit: insistence by monastic leaders that poetry should only consume a small portion of a monk's day; the dangers of poetry as a karmic obstacle on the path, or distraction from practice; disparagement of the written word by Chan leaders; and, most of all, an expectation that monks express emotions differently from others. To some extent we see all of this in the poetry itself; and when we don't, these expectations nonetheless may contribute to our making sense of monks' poetry. Verse was part of the fabric of daily life in a Chinese monastery, even as monastic life seemed to the monks themselves to be at odds with parts of the Chinese poetic tradition. I have not sought to compile an exhaustive inventory of Buddhist poetry, and indeed much research and reading remains to be done with regard to the Chinese poetry of Song-era Buddhist monks. I have tried, rather, to present ways of reading. Monks' poems selectively employed generic forms, sometimes adhering to mainstream norms and sometimes subverting them, and thus can be read against the landscape of genres. At the same time, monks' poetry fulfilled social and ritual functions specific to the ways that monastics lived. Doctrines and monastic norms shaped the rhetoric of monks' poems, whether it was parting poetry about the emptiness of movement or was casting poetic sentiments as the activity of Māra, a demon of poetry.

---

13. See especially the works by Liao Chao-heng listed in the bibliography; Bell, "Genuine Anguish, Genuine Mind;" and Mengxiao Wang, "Building a Pure Land Lineage."

Appendix

Poems by Title

AUTHOR'S NAME APPEARS in parentheses. If the title refers to a poetic sequence, the number in that sequence is given in square brackets. An asterisk before the Chinese title indicates the translation is an excerpt from a longer poem.

Bibliography

Note on Citation Styles and Digital Sources

The following citation styles are used in the notes for certain primary sources and reference works listed in this bibliography.

Taishō shinshū daizōkyō: Citations to the title appear as T, followed by volume number, page number, register, and line number(s). Example: T51.222c20–22 indicates vol. 51, p. 222, 3rd register (c), ll. 20–22.

Shinsan Dai Nihon zoku zōkyō: Citations to the revised Tokyo edition appear as ZZ, followed by volume number, page number, register, and line number. Example: ZZ56.934a24 indicates vol. 56, p. 934, top register (a), l. 24.

Traditional xylographic printed texts: Citations use a period (.) between the fascicle number and original printed page number(s), followed by recto (a) or verso (b). Example: *Canliaozi shiji,* 10.4a indicates fasc. 10, p. 4, recto.

Texts in *Sibu congkan* (SBCK), *Siku quanshu* (SKQS), and other sinological collectanea: Citations follow the same format as that used for traditional xylographic printed texts.

Modern critical editions: Citations use a slash (/) between the traditional fascicle number and modern page number. Example: *Bai Juyi ji,* 39/885–887 refers to fasc. 39, pp. 885–887.

Modern multivolume editions: Citations follow the conventional style, with volume and page numbers separated by a colon. Example: *Quan Song shi,* 23:154.

Rare books from the Kunaichō and National Diet Library were accessed using the online systems, *Kunaichō shoryōbu shūzō kanseki shūran,* and *Kokuritsu Kokkai Toshokan Dejitaru Korekushon.* In addition to print editions of the Buddhist texts, I used the digital edition and search functions of CBReader V5.3 (2016 ed.) by CBETA.

Primary Sources and Reference Works (listed by title)

Apidamo dapiposha lun 阿毘達磨大毘婆沙論. Translated by Xuanzang 玄奘 (602–664). T27, no. 1545.

Bai Juyi ji 白居易集. Bai Juyi 白居易 (772–846). Edited by Gu Xuexie 顧學頡. Beijing: Zhonghua shuju, 1979.

Baizhang qinggui zhengyiji 百丈清規證義記. Yirun 儀潤 (19th c.). ZZ63, no. 1244.

Banreki-ban daizōkyō (Kakō-zō/Kinzan-zō) Dejitaru-ban 万暦版大蔵経（嘉興蔵/径山蔵）デジタル版. University of Tokyo General Library, Council for Promotion of Study of Daizokyo, and the SAT Daizōkyō Text Database Committee. Citations begin with division (*shō* 正, *zoku* 続, or *ho* 補), followed by box (*chitsu* 帙) number, then folio (*satsu* 冊) number. Page references are to fascicle (*kan* 巻) number, followed by page number with recto or verso. https://dzkimgs.l.u-tokyo.ac.jp/kkz/.

Baojue Zuxin chanshi yulu 寶覺祖心禪師語錄. Huitang Zuxin 晦堂祖心 (1025–1100). ZZ69, no. 1343.

Baoqing Siming zhi 寶慶四明志. Luo Jun 羅濬 (fl. 1227) et al. *Song Yuan fangzhi congkan*, vol. 5.

Baozhenzhai fashu zan 寶真齋法書贊. Yue Ke 岳珂 (1183–1241?). SKQS.

Beijian heshang waiji 北礀和尚外集. Beijian Jujian 北礀居簡 (1164–1246). Kunaichō no. 556.113. Southern Song edition dated 1252. Digital photographs accessed via *Kunaichō shoryōbu shūzō kanseki shūran*. Citations are to page number, followed by recto or verso. For a critical edition of the text, see Xu Hongxia, *Zhenben Song ji wu zhong*, 1:1–97.

Beijian heshang yulu 北礀和尚語錄. Beijian Jujian 北礀居簡 (1164–1246). Kunaichō no. 556.111. Partial Southern Song edition dated 1252. Digital photographs accessed via *Kunaichō shoryōbu shūzō kanseki shūran*. Citations are to page number, followed by recto or verso. An early Gozan edition is reproduced in *Gozan-ban Chūgoku zenseki sōkan*, 7:385–434. Another Gozan edition dated 1370 is related to ZZ69, no. 1365.

Bianjing yiji zhi 汴京遺蹟志. Li Lian 李濂 (1488–1566). SKQS.

Biyanlu 碧巖錄. Yuanwu Keqin 圓悟克勤 (1063–1135). T48, no. 2003.

Bukkyō daijiten 佛敎大辭典. Edited by Oda Tokunō 織田得能. Tokyo: Ōkura Shoten, 1928.

Bukkyō go daijiten 佛教語大辞典. Edited by Nakamura Hajime 中村元. Tokyo: Tōkyō Shoseki, 1975.

Bushui tai ji 布水臺集. Daomin 道忞 (1596–1674). *Jiaxing dazangjing*, vol. 25.

Bussho kaisetsu daijiten 佛書解說大辭典. 14 vols. Edited by Ono Genmyō 小野玄妙. Vols. 12–13, edited by Maruyama Takao 丸山孝雄. 2nd ed. Tokyo: Daitō shuppansha, 1964–1978.

Butsugoshinron 佛語心論. Kokan Shiren 虎關師鍊 (1278–1346). In *Nihon Daizōkyō* 日本大藏經, edited by Nakano Tatsue 中野達慧 et al., 5:175–527. Tokyo: Nihon daizōkyō hensankai, 1916.

Buttoku Daitsū Zenji goroku 佛德大通禪師語錄. Guchū Shūkyū 愚中周及 (1323–1409). T81, no. 2563.

Canglang shihua jiao shi 滄浪詩話校釋. Yan Yu 嚴羽 (ca. 1191–1241). Edited by Guo Shaoyu 郭紹虞. Beijing: Renmin wenxue chubanshe, 1961.

Canliaozi shiji 參寥子詩集. Daoqian 道潛 (1043–after 1111). Citations first give the fascicle and page numbers found in the Northern Song edition, reproduced in *Zhonghua zaizao shanben* 中華再造善本 (Beijing: Beijing tushuguan chubanshe, 2003), and corresponding to SBCK; after a semicolon are page numbers for the annotated modern edition *Canliaozi shiji biannian jiaozhu*.

Canliaozi shiji biannian jiaozhu 參寥子詩集編年校注. Daoqian 道潛 (1043–after 1111). Edited and annotated by Chen Xiaohui 陳小輝. Nanchang: Jiangxi renmin chubanshe, 2017.

Chanlin baoxun 禪林寶訓. Jingshan 淨善 (S. Song). T48, no. 2022.

Chanlin beiyong qinggui 禪林備用清規. Zeshan Yixian 澤山弌咸 (fl. 1286–1311). ZZ63, no. 1250.

Chanlin sengbao zhuan 禪林僧寶傳. Juefan Huihong 覺範惠洪 (1071–1128). ZZ79, no. 1560.

Chanlin shuyu kaozheng 禪林疏語考證. Yongjue Yuanxian 永覺元賢 (1578–1657). ZZ63, no. 1252.

Chanmen yishu 禪門逸書. Edited by Mingfu 明復. 20 vols. Citations denote the series *chu bian* 初編 (Taipei: Mingwen shuju, 1980) or *xu bian* 續編 (Taipei: Hanshen chubanshe, 1987) and volume number, followed by page number(s).

Chanmen zhu zushi jisong 禪門諸祖師偈頌. Zisheng 子昇 (S. Song). ZZ66, no. 1298.

Chanyuan mengqiu yaolin 禪苑蒙求瑤林. Zhiming 志明 (fl. 1225). ZZ87, no. 1614.

Chanyuan qinggui 禪苑清規. Changlu Zongze 長蘆宗賾 (d. 1106). ZZ63, no. 1245.

Chanyuan zhuquan ji duxu 禪源諸詮集都序. Guifeng Zongmi 圭峰宗密 (780–841). T48, no. 2015.

Chanzong songgu lianzhu tongji 禪宗頌古聯珠通集. Faying 法應 (12th c.) and Puhui 普會 (fl. 1318). ZZ65, no. 1295.

Chanzong zaduhai 禪宗雜毒海. Re-compiled by Meigu Xingyue 梅谷行悅 (1620–1685) and Jialing Xingyin 迦陵性音 (fl. 1714). ZZ65, no. 1278.

Chenghua Hangzhou fu zhi 成化杭州府志. Xia Shizheng 夏时正 (1412-1499). 1475 ed. photoreproduced in *Siku quanshu cunmu congshu* 四庫全書存目叢書 (Jinan: Qi Lu shushe, 1997), *shibu* 175.

Chijue heshang yulu 癡絕和尚語錄. Chijue Daochong 癡絕道沖 (1169–1250). ZZ70, no 1376.

Chixiu Baizhang qinggui 敕修百丈清規. Dongyang Dehui 東陽德輝 (fl. 1329–1335). T48, no. 2025.

Chuiyuji. See *Weimojing lüeshu chuiyuji.*

Chu sanzang jiji 出三藏記集. Sengyou 僧祐 (445–518). T55, no. 2145.

Chushi Fanqi chanshi yulu 楚石梵琦禪師語錄. Chushi Fanqi 楚石梵琦 (1296–1370). ZZ71, no. 1420.

Cijue chanshi yulu 慈覺禪師語錄. Changlu Zongze 長蘆宗賾 (d. 1106). In Shiina Kōyū 椎名宏雄, "*Jikaku zenji goroku* honkoku" 『慈覚禅師語録』(翻刻). *Komazawa daigaku zen kenkyūjo nenpō* 20 (2008), 169–224.

Cishou Huaishen chanshi guanglu 慈受懷深禪師廣錄. Cishou Huaishen 慈受懷深 (1077–1132). ZZ73, no. 1451.

Conglin jiaoding qinggui zongyao 叢林校定清規總要. Jinhua Weimian 金華惟勉 (fl. 1274). ZZ63, no. 1249. Citations to Gozan edition give the page number in *Gozan-ban Chūgoku zenseki sōkan*, vol. 5.

Conglin shengshi 叢林盛事. Daorong 道融 (fl. 1197–1199). ZZ86, no. 1611.

Congshu jicheng 叢書集成, *xinbian* 新編. 120 vols. Reprint, Taipei: Xinwenfeng, 1986.

Da banniepan jing 大般涅槃經. Translated by Dharmakṣema 曇無讖 (385–433). T12, no. 374.

Da banniepan jing 大般涅槃經. Translated by Faxian 法顯 (337–422). T1, no. 7.

Da banniepan jing shu 大般涅槃經疏. Guanding 灌頂 (561–632). T38, no. 1767.

Da fangdeng daji jing 大方等大集經. Translated by Dharmakṣema 曇無讖 (385–433). T13, no. 397.

Da fangguang Fo Huayan jing 大方廣佛華嚴經. 80 fascs. Translated by *Śikṣānanda 實叉難陀 (652–710). T10, no. 279.

Da fangguang Fo Huayan jing shu 大方廣佛華嚴經疏. Chengguan 澄觀 (738–839). T35, no. 1735.

Da Foding rulai miyin xiuzheng liaoyi zhupusa wanxing shoulengyan jing 大佛頂如來密因修證了義諸菩薩萬行首楞嚴經. T19, no. 945.

Dahui Pujue chanshi pushuo 大慧普覺禪師普說. Dahui Zonggao 大慧宗杲 (1089–1163). *Manji Daizōkyō* 卍正藏經, vol. 59. Taiwan reprint, Taipei: Xinwenfeng, 1980.

Dahui Pujue chanshi yulu 大慧普覺禪師語錄. Dahui Zonggao 大慧宗杲 (1089–1163). T47, no. 1998A.

Dai'an Zhuang chanshi yulu 呆菴莊禪師語錄. Dai'an Puzhuang 呆菴普莊 (1347–1403). 1630 ed. *Banreki-ban daizōkyō, zoku* 189.1; and photoreproduction in *Jiaxing dazangjing*, vol. 25. The late Ming recension is the antecedent to ZZ71, no. 1418.

Dai Nihon Bukkyō zensho 大日本佛教全書. 150 vols. Tokyo: Bussho Kankōkai, 1912–1922.

Dai Nihon zoku zōkyō. See *Shinsan Dai Nihon zoku zōkyō*.

Daoju fu 道具賦. Lingzhi Yuanzhao 靈芝元照 (1048–1116). ZZ59, no. 1100.

Da Song seng shi lüe 大宋僧史略. Zanning 贊寧 (919–1001). T54, no. 2126.

Da Tang Xiyuji 大唐西域記. Xuanzang 玄奘 (602–664). T51, no. 2087.

Dazang yilan 大藏一覽. Chen Shi 陳實 (12th c.). *Jiaxing dazangjing*, vol. 21.

Dazhi dulun 大智度論. T25, no. 1509.

Dongjing Huilin Cishou guanglu 東京慧林慈受廣錄. Cishou Huaishen 慈受懷深 (1077–1132). Kunaichō no. 556.78. Woodblock print dated 1135. Digital photographs accessed via *Kunaichō shoryōbu shūzō kanseki shūran*.

Dongpo wutai shi'an 東坡烏臺詩案. *Congshu jicheng, xinbian*, vol. 27.

Ecang Heishuicheng wenxian: Hanwen bufen 俄藏黑水城文獻:漢文部分. 6 vols. Shanghai: Shanghai guji chubanshe, 1996–2000.

Entsū Daiō Kokushi Goroku 圓通大應國師語錄. Nanpo Jōmin 南浦紹明 (1235–1308). T80, no. 2548. 1372 ed., National Diet Library no. WA6–43, info:ndljp/pid/2543586.

Fachang Yiyu chanshi yulu 法昌倚遇禪師語錄. Fachang Yiyu 法昌倚遇 (1005–1081). ZZ73, no. 1448. Northern Song imprint dated 1105, entitled *Hongzhou Fenning Fachang Chanyuan Yu chanshi yulu* 洪州分寧法昌禪院遇禪師語錄. Harvard-Yenching Library (Hollis no. 990079147810203941). Microfilm.

Fahua jing helun 法華經合論. Juefan Huihong 覺範惠洪 (1071–1128). ZZ30, no. 603.

Fahua jing sandabu buzhu 法華經三大部補注. Shenzhi Congyi 神智從義 (1042–1091). ZZ28, no. 586

Fahua jing yaojie 法華經要解. Wenling Jiehuan 溫陵戒環 (fl. 1120s). ZZ30, no. 602.

Fahua jing yiji 法華經義記. Guangzhai Fayun 光宅法雲 (467–529). T33, no. 1715.

Fanwang jing 梵網經. References to Funayama Tōru 船山 徹, *Higashiajia bukkyō no seikatsu kisoku* Bonmōkyō 東アジア仏教の生活規則 梵網経 (Kyoto: Rinsen shoten, 2017), with cross-reference to T24, no. 1484.

Fanwang pusajie jing shu zhu 梵網菩薩戒經疏註. Yuxian 與咸 (d. 1163). ZZ38, no. 678.

Fanyi mingyi ji 翻譯名義集. Fayun 法雲 (1088–1158). T54, no. 2131.

Faxi Yin chanshi yulu 法璽印禪師語錄. Faxi Zhengyin 法璽正印 (fl. 1660s–1670s). *Jiaxing dazangjing*, vol. 28.

Fayan Chanshi yulu 法演禪師語錄. Wuzu Fayan 五祖法演 (1024?–1104). T47, no. 1995.

Fayuan zhulin 法苑珠林. Daoshi 道世 (d. 683). T53, no. 2122.

Fenyang Wude Chanshi yulu 汾陽無德禪師語錄. Fenyang Shanzhao 汾陽善昭 (947–1024). T47, no. 1992. 1709 edition, National Diet Library nos. 821–197, info: ndljp/pid/2537745.

Fo chui ban niepan lüeshuo jiao jie jing 佛垂般涅槃略說教誡經. T12, no. 389.

Foguo Keqin chanshi xin yao 佛果克勤禪師心要. Yuanwu Keqin 圓悟克勤 (1063–1135). ZZ69, no. 1357.

Fojian chanshi yulu 佛鑑禪師語錄. Wuzhun Shifan 無準師範 (1178–1249). 3 fascs. Southern Song edition, dated 1251. Kunaichō no. 556.57. Digital photographs accessed via *Kunaichō shoryōbu shūzō kanseki shūran*. Page numbers are discontinuous. Citations first give the section title, followed by fascicle number, page number, and recto or verso. Gozan edition dated 1370. National Diet Library no. WA6–1, info:ndljp/pid/2543481. Citations give the running page number and recto or verso. One other edition listed under *Wuzhun Shifan chanshi yulu*.

Fo shuo Mulian wen jielü zhong wubai qingzhong shi jing 佛說目連問戒律中五百輕重事經. T24, no. 1483b.

Fo yijiao jing 佛遺教經. See *Fo chui ban niepan lüeshuo jiao jie jing*.

Fozu tongji 佛祖統紀. Zhipan 志磐 (13th c.). T49, no. 2035.

Fuxing. See *Zhiguan fuxing chuan hongjue*.

Fuyuan Shiwu Gong chanshi yulu 福源石屋珙禪師語錄. Shiwu Qinggong 石屋清珙 (1272–1352). Newly organized 1627 edition. *Banreki-ban daizōkyō, zoku* 180.1; and photoreproduction in *Jiaxing dazangjing*, vol. 25. A late Qing edition (preface dated 1887) derived from this 1627 recension is the source for ZZ70, no. 1399. For information about the earlier recension, see the listing entitled *Shiwu chanshi shanju shi—jizan—yulu*.

Gaofeng Longquanyuan Yin shi ji xianyu lu 高峰龍泉院因師集賢語錄. Deyin 德因 (b. 1236). ZZ65, no. 1277.

Gaoseng zhuan 高僧傳. Huijiao 慧皎 (497–554). T50, no. 2059.

Genben shuo yiqie youbu pinaiye zashi 根本說一切有部毘奈耶雜事. Yijing 義淨 (635–713). T24, no. 1451.

Genkō shakusho 元亨釋書. Kokan Shiren 虎関師錬 (1278–1346). *Dai Nihon Bukkyō zensho*, vol. 101.

Gongkui ji 攻媿集. Lou Yue 樓鑰 (1137–1213). SBCK.

Gozan-ban Chūgoku zenseki sōkan 五山版中国禅籍叢刊. Edited by Shiina Kōyū 椎名宏雄. 12 vols. Kyoto: Rinsen shoten, 2012–2018.

Gozan bungaku shinshū 五山文学新集. Edited by Tamamura Takeji 玉村竹二. 8 vols. Tokyo: Tōkyō daigaku shuppankai, 1967–1981.

Guang hongming ji 廣弘明集. Daoxuan 道宣 (596–667). T52, no. 2103.

Guanxiu geshi xinian jianzhu 貫休歌詩繫年箋注. Guanxiu 貫休 (832–913). Beijing: Zhonghua shuju, 2011.

Guishan jingce zhu 溈山警策註. Shousui 守遂 (1072–1147). ZZ63, no. 1239.

Gu zunsu yulu 古尊宿語錄. Shouze 守賾 (mid-to-late 12th c.). ZZ68, no. 1315. Citations beginning "CBETA" refer to the online digital edition of the 1267 Southern Song recension held at National Central Library (Taiwan). Page numbers refer to vol. 48, no. 8939, of the CBETA *Guojia tushuguan shanben fodian*. Some footnotes also refer to an early Southern Song (likely 1138–1144) imprint of *Gu zunsu yuyao* 古尊宿語要, Kunaichō no. 556.107, accessed via *Kunaichō shoryōbu shūzō kanseki shūran*.

Han Changli shi xinian jishi 韓昌黎詩系年集釋. Han Yu 韓愈 (768–824). Shanghai: Shanghai guji chubanshe, 1984.

Hanshan ziliao leibian 寒山資料類編. Taipei: Xiuwei zixun, 2005.

Hanyu da cidian 漢語大詞典. Edited by Luo Zhufeng 羅竹風. 12 vols. Shanghai: Hanyu dacidian chubanshe, 1986–1993.

Hongzhi chanshi guanglu 宏智禪師廣錄. Hongzhi Zhengjue 宏智正覺 (1091–1157). T48, no. 2001.

Houshan jushi wenji 後山居士文集. Chen Shidao 陳師道 (1053–1102). Song edition reproduced in vol. 88 (of 120 vols.) of *Beijing tushuguan guji zhenben congkan* 北京圖書館古籍珍本叢刊. Beijing: Shumu wenxian chubanshe, 1987–2000. Citations give the traditional fascicle and page number(s), followed by the page number(s) in the modern edition.

Houshan shihua 後山詩話. Traditionally attributed to Chen Shidao 陳師道 (1053–1102). SKQS.

Huaihai ji jian zhu 淮海集箋注. Qin Guan 秦觀 (1049–1100). Edited by Xu Peijun 徐培均. Shanghai: Shanghai guji, 1994.

Huanglong Huinan chanshi yulu 黃龍慧南禪師語錄. Huanglong Huinan 黃龍慧南 (1002–1069). T47, no. 1993.

Huang Tingjian shi ji zhu 黃庭堅詩集注. Huang Tingjian 黃庭堅 (1045–1105). Edited and annotated by Liu Shangrong 劉尚榮. Beijing: Zhonghua shuju, 2003.

Huanzhu'an qinggui 幻住庵清規. Zhongfeng Mingben 中峰明本 (1263–1323). ZZ63, no. 1248.

Huayan jing. See *Da fangguang Fo Huayan jing*.

Huayan jing tanxuanji 華嚴經探玄記. Fazang 法藏 (643–712). T35, no. 1733.

Huilin lu. See *Dongjing Huilin Cishou guanglu*.

Jianzhong jingguo xudenglu 建中靖國續燈錄. Foguo Weibai 佛國惟白 (fl. early 1100s). ZZ78, no. 1556.

Jianzhong jingguo xudenglu mulu 建中靖國續燈錄目錄. ZZ78, no. 1555.

Jiaoding qinggui. See *Conglin jiaoding qinggui zongyao*.

Jiaojie xinxue biqiu xinghu lüyi 教誡新學比丘行護律儀. Daoxuan 道宣 (596–667). T45, no. 1897.

Jiaoyuan qinggui 教苑清規. Yunwai Ziqing 雲外自慶 (fl. 1347). ZZ57, no. 968.

Jiatai pudenglu 嘉泰普燈錄. Lei'an Zhengshou 雷庵正受 (fl. 1171–1204). ZZ79, no. 1559.

Jiatai pudenglu zongmulu 嘉泰普燈錄總目錄. Lei'an Zhengshou 雷庵正受 (fl. 1171–1204). ZZ79, no. 1558.

Jiaxing dazangjing 嘉興大藏經. 40 vols. Taipei: Xinwenfeng, 1987.

Jingang bore shu 金剛般若疏. Jizang 吉藏 (549–623). T33, no. 1699.

Jingde chuandenglu 景德傳燈錄. Daoyuan 道原 (fl. early 11th c.). T51, no. 2076.

Jingtu huowen 淨土或問. Tianru Weize 天如惟則 (1286–1354). T47, no. 1972. The *Taishō* edition based on a 1692 Japanese edition. A Ming edition of this work is listed under *Shizilin Tianru heshang Jingtu huowen*.

Jingtu shi yao 淨土十要. Chengshi 成時 (1618–1678). ZZ61, no. 1164.

Jixiu Qiliao Chanshi shiyi ji 即休契了禪師拾遺集. Jixiu Qiliao 即休契了 (1269–1351). ZZ71, no. 1408.

Ji zhujing lichanyi 集諸經禮懺儀. Zhisheng 智昇 (act. 8th c.). T47, no. 1982.

Jōwa-shū. See *Jūkan Jōwa ruijū soon renpō shū*.

Jūkan Jōwa ruijū soon renpō shū 重刊貞和類聚祖苑聯芳集. Gidō Shūshin 義堂周信 (1325–1388). References to *Dai Nihon Bukkyō zensho* are to vol. 143 and page number. Otherwise, citations are to the fascicle and page number in the likely 1388 edition (see Kawase, *Gozan ban no kenkyū*, 1.167, and vol. 2, no. 269), National Diet Library no. WA6–10, info:ndljp/pid/2543495.

Jushi zhuan 居士傳. Peng Shaosheng 彭紹昇 (1740–1796). ZZ88, no. 1646.

Juzhou wenji 橘洲文集. Baotan 寶曇 (1129–1197). *Xuxiu siku quanshu*, 1318:61-131.

Kaiyuan shi jiao lu 開元釋教錄. Zhisheng 智昇 (fl. 730). T55, no. 2154.

Kenninji Ryōsokuin zōsho mokuroku 建仁寺両足院藏書目錄. In *Shōwa hōbō sōmokuroku* 昭和法寶總目錄, vol. 3. Tokyo: Taishō Issai-kyō Kankōkai, 1929–1934.

Kokuritsu Kokkai Toshokan Dejitaru Korekushon 国立国会図書館デジタルコレクション. Digital photoreproductions from the National Diet Library. http://dl.ndl.go.jp/.

Kokuyaku Keigen-fu Setchō Myōgaku daishi Soei-shū 國譯慶元府雪竇明覺大師祖英集. In *Kokuyaku Zengaku taisei* 国訳禅学大成, vol. 5. Tokyo: Nishōdō shoten, 1929.

Kokuyaku Reigen Oshō Hitsugo 國譯靈源和尚筆語. In *Kokuyaku zenshū sōsho* 國譯禪宗叢書, series 1, vol. 2. Tokyo: Kokuyaku zenshuū sōsho kankōkai, 1919.

Kunaichō shoryōbu shūzō kanseki shūran: Shoshi-shoei zenbun-eizō dētabēsu 宮内庁書陵部收藏漢籍集覽: 書誌書影・全文影像データベース. Digital photoreproductions from the collection of Kunaichō (Imperial Household Agency). http://db.sido .keio.ac.jp/kanseki/.

Lanpen xiangong yi 蘭盆獻供儀. Lingzhi Yuanzhao 靈芝元照 (1048–1116). ZZ74, no. 1500.

Laozi Dao de jing 老子道德經. SBCK, a Song edition of the Heshang Gong commentary.

Lebang wenlei 樂邦文類. Zongxiao 宗曉 (1151–1214). T47, no. 1969A.

Lebang yigao 樂邦遺稿. Zongxiao 宗曉 (1151–1214). T47, no. 1969B.

Leishuo 類説. Zeng Zao 曾慥 (1091–1155). SKQS.

Lengqie abaduoluo baojing 楞伽阿跋多羅寶經. Trans. Guṇabhadra (394–468). T16, no. 670.

Lengyan jing helun 楞嚴經合論. Juefan Huihong 覺範惠洪 (1071–1128). ZZ12, no. 272.

Liao'an Qingyu chanshi yulu 了菴清欲禪師語錄. Liao'an Qingyu 了庵清欲 (1292–1367). ZZ71, no. 1414.

Lidai minghua ji 歷代名畫記. Zhang Yanyuan 張彥遠 (9th c.). SKQS.

Liezu tiwang lu 列祖提綱錄. Daiweng Xingyue 呆翁行悦 (1619–1684). ZZ64, no. 1260.

Liji ji jie 禮記集解. Sun Xidan 孫希旦 (1736–1784). Beijing: Zhonghua shuju, 1989.

Lingyuan heshang biyu 靈源和尚筆語. Lingyuan Weiqing 靈源惟清 (d. 1117). *Gozan-ban Chūgoku zenseki sōkan*, vol. 10.

Lin Hejing shiji 林和靖詩集. Lin Bu 林逋 (967–1028). Edited and annotated by Chen Youzheng 沈幼征. Hangzhou: Zhejiang guji chubanshe, 1986.

Linquan laoren pingchang Danxia Chun chanshi songgu Xutang ji 林泉老人評唱丹霞淳禪師頌古虛堂集. ZZ67, no. 1304.

Liuzu dashi fabao tanjing 六祖大師法寶壇經. Edited by Zongbao 宗寶 (fl. 1291). T48, no. 2008.

Luancheng ji 欒城集. Su Che 蘇轍 (1039–1112). Shanghai: Shanghai guji chubanshe, 1987.

Luohu yelu 羅湖野錄. Xiaoying Zhongwen 曉瑩仲溫 (12th c.). ZZ83, no. 1577.

Luoyang shike ji ji 嵩陽石刻集記. Ye Feng 葉封 (1623–1687). SKQS.

Lushan ji 廬山記. Chen Shunyu 陳舜俞 (d. 1076). T51, no. 2095.

Meng Haoran shiji jianzhu. Meng Haoran 孟浩然 (689–740). Edited and annotated by Tong Peiji 佟培基. Shanghai: Shanghai guji chubanshe, 2000.

Mi'an chanshi yulu 密菴禪師語錄. Mi'an Xianjie 密庵咸傑 (1118–1186). T47, no. 1999.

Miaofa lianhua jing 妙法蓮華經. T9, no. 262.

Mingjue chanshi yulu 明覺禪師語錄. Xuedou Chongxian (980–1052). T47, no. 1996. Citations to the Gozan edition dated 1289, based on a lost Southern Song recension, give the page number in *Zengaku tenseki sōkan,* vol. 2.

Mohe zhiguan 摩訶止觀. Zhiyi 智顗 (538–597). T46, no. 1911.

Mozhuang manlu 墨莊漫錄. Zhang Bangji 張邦基 (12th c.). SKQS.

Nan Song Yuan Ming Chanlin sengbao zhuan 南宋元明禪林僧寶傳. Huanjin Zirong 幻津自融 (1615–1691). ZZ79, no. 1562.

Nenggai zhai manlu 能改齋漫錄. Wu Zeng 吳曾 (fl. 1141–1162). SKQS.

Nian Bafang zhuyu ji 拈八方珠玉集. Fojian Huiqin 佛鑑惠懃 (1059–1117) et al. ZZ67, no. 1310. See also *Gozan-ban Chūgoku zenseki sōkan,* vol. 12.

Niepan jing shu sande zhigui 涅槃經疏三德指歸. Gushan Zhiyuan 孤山智圓 (976–1022). ZZ37, no. 662.

Ouyang Xiu quan ji 歐陽修全集. Ouyang Xiu 歐陽修 (1007–1072). Beijing: Zhonghua shuju, 2001.

Pinaiye zashi. See *Genben shuo yiqie youbu pinaiye zashi*.

Pusa dichi jing 菩薩地持經. Translated by Dharmakṣema 曇無讖 (385–433). T30, no. 1581.

Pusa shanjie jing 菩薩善戒經. *Guṇavarman 求那跋摩 (367–431). T30, no. 1583.

Qiji shiji jiaozhu 齊己詩集校注. Qiji 齊己 (ca. 864–937). Edited and annotated by Wang Xiulin 王秀林. Beijing: Zhongguo shehui kexue chubanshe, 2011.

Qin Guan ji biannian jiaozhu 秦觀集編年校注. Qin Guan 秦觀 (1049–1100). Beijing: Renmin wenxue chubanshe, 2001.

Quan Min shihua 全閩詩話. Zheng Fangkun 鄭方坤 (*jinshi* 1723). SKQS.

Quanshi waiji 全室外集. Jitan Zongle 季潭宗泐 (1318–1390). SKQS.

Quan Song ci 全宋詞. 5 vols. Edited by Tang Guizhang 唐圭璋. Rev. ed. Beijing: Zhonghua shuju, 1995.

Quan Song shi 全宋詩. 72 vols. Edited by Fu Xuancong 傅璇琮. Beijing: Beijing daxue chubanshe, 1991–1998.

Quan Song shi dingbu 全宋詩訂補. Zhengzhou: Daxiang chubanshe, 2005.

Quan Song wen 全宋文. 360 vols. Shanghai: Shanghai cishu chubanshe, 2006.

Quan Tang shi 全唐詩. Peng Dingqiu 彭定求 (1645–1719) et al. Beijing: Zhonghua shuju, 1960.

Quan Tang shi bubian 全唐詩補編. Edited by Chen Shangjun 陳尚君. Beijing: Zhonghua shuju, 1992.

Quan Tang wen 全唐文. Beijing: Zhonghua shuju, 1983.

Reigen Hitsugo bekkōu 靈源筆語別考. Anonymous, undated Edo-period manuscript book. 2 fascs. Komazawa University Library, *Junkichō tosho* collection, H124/179.

Reigen Hitsugo bekkōu 靈源筆語別考. Kanzan Jitei 幹山師貞 (1676–1745). 2 fascs. Komazawa University Library, *Junkichō tosho* collection, H124/35 (dated 1761).

Rentian baojian 人天寶鑑. Yunxiu 曇秀 (fl. 1230). ZZ87, no. 1612.

Renwang huguo bore boluomiduo jing 仁王護國般若波羅蜜多經. Amoghavajra (704–774). T8, no. 246.

Ru lengqie jing 入楞伽經. Bodhiruci 菩提流支 (d. ca. 535). T16, no. 671.

Ru lengqie xinxuanyi 入楞伽心玄義. Fazang 法藏 (643–712). T39, no. 1790.

Ruzhong riyong 入眾日用. Zongshou 宗壽 (fl. 1209). ZZ63, no. 1246.

Sande zhigui. See *Niepan jing shu sande zhigui.*

Sekimon Mojizen Chū. See *Zhu Shimen wenzi chan.*

Seng shi lüe. See *Da Song seng shi lüe.*

Sheng Song gaoseng shixuan 聖宋高僧詩選. Chen Qi 陳起 (13th c.). *Xuxiu siku quanshu,* 1621:1–48.

Shidi jing 十地經. Translated by *Śīladharma (fl. 785–805). T10, no. 287.

Shidi jing lun 十地經論. Translated by Bodhiruci (6th c.). T26, no. 1522.

Shi feng gao 始豐稿. Xu Yikui 徐一夔 (14th c.). SKQS.

Shihua zonggui 詩話總龜. Ruan Yue 阮閱 (*jinshi* 1085). *Qianji* 50 fascs., *houji* 50 fascs. SKQS.

Shijia rulai niepan lizanwen 釋迦如來涅槃禮讚文. Jingjue Renyue 淨覺仁岳 (992–1064). T46, no. 1947.

Shilin shihua 石林詩話. Ye Mengde 葉夢得 (1077–1148). SKQS.

Shimen wenzi chan 石門文字禪. Juefan Huihong 覺範惠洪 (1071–1128). 30 fascs. References give traditional fascicle number, according to the the Wanli-era edition dated 1597, reprinted in SBCK; fascicle number is followed by volume and page numbers of the 2011 Beijing critical edition of *Sekimon Mojizen Chū* 石門文字禪 註 by Sōtō Zen monk Kakumon Kantetsu 廓門貫徹 (d. 1730). See *Zhu Shimen wenzi chan* for bibliographic information.

Shinsan Dai Nihon zoku zōkyō 新纂大日本續藏經. 90 vols. Edited by Nishi Giyū 西義雄 et al. Tokyo: Kokusho Kankōkai, 1975–1989. Revised and expanded from *Dai Nihon zoku zōkyō* 大日本續藏經. Edited by Maeda Eun 前田慧雲 and Nakano Tatsue 中野達慧. Kyoto: Zōkyō Shoin, 1905–1912.

Shinshū Zenke shokan 新修禪家書鑑. Edited by Zen bunka kenkyūjo. Kyoto: Zen bunka kenkyūjo, 1996.

Shiren yuxie 詩人玉屑. Wei Qingzhi 魏慶之 (fl. 1240–1244). Edited by Wang Zhongwen 王仲聞. Beijing: Zhonghua shuju, 2007.

Shi shi 詩式. Jiaoran 皎然 (720–ca. 795). *Congshu jicheng, xinbian,* vol. 80.

Shi shi jiaozhu 詩式校注. Jiaoran 皎然 (720–ca. 795). Edited by Li Zhuangying 李壯鷹. Beijing: Renmin wenxue chubanshe, 2003.

Shishi liutie 釋氏六帖. Yichu 義楚 (fl. 945–954). Undated Song edition based on 1103 recension. Citations provide the page number in *Zengaku tenseki sōkan,* vol. 6, pt. 2.

Shishi mengqiu 釋氏蒙求. Lingcao 靈操 (n.d.). ZZ87, no. 1623.

Shishi yaolan 釋氏要覽. Daocheng 道誠 (fl. 1009–1019). T54, no. 2127. A 1529 edition by Zonglin 宗林 (n.d.), based on a 1433 recension by Baocheng 寶誠 (n.d.). In the collection of Harvard-Yenching Library, accessed at nrs.lib.harvard.edu/urn-3:FHCL:25616094.

Shishi yaolan jiaozhu 釋氏要覽校注. Daocheng 道誠 (fl. 1009–1019). Edited by Fu Shipping 富世平. Beijing: Zhonghua shuju, 2014.

Shishuo xinyu jiao jian 世說新語校箋. Liu Yiqing 劉義慶 (403–444). Edited by Xu Zhen'e 徐震堮. Beijing: Zhonghua shuju, 1984.

Shisong lü 十誦律. Translated by Puṇyatāra 弗若多羅 (d. 404) and Kumārajīva 鳩摩羅什 (344–413). T23, no. 1435.

Shiwu chanshi shanju shi—jizan—yulu 石屋禪師山居詩・偈讚・語錄. Shiwu Qinggong 石屋清珙 (1272–1352). Undated Ming edition, likely produced around 1382, photoreproduced in *Siku quanshu cunmu congshu* 四庫全書存目叢書 (Jinan: Qi Lu shushe, 1997), *jibu* 195, 648–696. A 1615 recension in *Xuxiu siku quanshu,* 1324:381–406; *Chanmen yishu, chu bian,* 6:1–27. For the 1627 recension, see *Fuyuan Shiwu Gong chanshi yulu.*

Shiwu jiyuan 事物紀原. Gao Cheng 高承 (ca. 1078–1085). Beijing: Zhonghua shuju, 1989.

Shixi Xinyue chanshi yulu 石溪心月禪師語錄. Shixi Xinyue 石溪心月 (d. 1256 or after). ZZ71, no. 1405.

Shixi Xinyue chanshi zalu 石溪心月禪師雜錄. Shixi Xinyue 石溪心月 (d. 1256 or after). ZZ71, no. 1406.

Shiyi ji 拾遺集. See *Jixiu Qiliao Chanshi shiyi ji.*

Shizilin Tianru heshang Jingtu huowen 師子林天如和尚淨土或問. Tianru Weize 天如惟則 (1286–1354). 1646 ed. *Banreki-ban Daizōkyō, ho* 10.1. Cf. the received ed. entitled *Jingtu huowen.*

Shizilin Tianru heshang yulu 師子林天如和尚語錄. Tianru Weize 天如惟則 (1286–1354). Nine fascs. Undated Edo woodblock edition, based on undated late-Ming recension reprinted at Yunqi Temple 雲棲寺重刊. National Diet Library no. 821–822, info:ndljp/pid/2607218.

Shuo fu 說郛. SKQS.

Shoulengyan jing 首楞嚴經. See *Da Foding rulai miyin xiuzheng liaoyi zhupusa wanxing shou lengyan jing.*

Shuzhong heshang yulu 恕中和尚語錄. Shuzhong Wuyun 恕中無慍 (1309–1386). 1598 ed. *Banreki-ban daizōkyō, zoku* 185.1; and photoreproduction in *Jiaxing zang,* 25:103–36. The late Ming edition is the antecedent to ZZ71, no. 1416.

Shuzhou Longmen Foyan heshang yulu 舒州龍門佛眼和尚語錄. Foyan Qingyuan 佛眼清遠 (1067-1120). Kunaichō no. 556.66. Southern Song edition by Zhu'an Shigui 竹庵士珪 (1092–1146), based on an earlier 1125 edition. Digital photographs accessed via *Kunaichō shoryōbu shūzō kanseki shūran.*

Sibu congkan 四部叢刊, *chu bian* 初編, *xu bian* 續編, *san bian* 三編. Shanghai: Shangwu yinshuguan, 1919–1936.

Sifen lü 四分律. *Buddhayaśas 佛陀耶舍 (4th–5th c.) and Zhu Fonian 竺佛念 (4th–5th c.). T22, no. 1428.

Sifen lü shanfan buque xingshi chao 四分律刪繁補闕行事鈔. Daoxuan 道宣 (596–667). T40, no. 1804.

Sikong Biaosheng shi wen ji jian jiao 司空表聖詩文集箋校. Sikong Tu 司空圖 (837–908). Edited by Zu Baoquan 祖保泉. Hefei: Anhui daxue chubanshe, 2002.

Siku quanshu. See *Yingyin Wenyuange Siku quanshu.*

Song gaoseng zhuan 宋高僧傳. Zanning 贊寧 (919–1001). T50, no. 2061.

Songshi jishi 宋詩紀事. Li E 厲鶚 (1692–1752). SQKS.

Song Yuan fangzhi congkan 宋元方志叢刊. 8 vols. paged continuously. Beijing: Zhonghua shuju, 1990. Citations include the fascicle number of the original text, followed by the page number of the modern edition.

Songyuan Chongyue Chanshi yulu 松源崇嶽禪師語錄. Songyuan Chongyue 松源崇岳 (1131–1202). ZZ70, no. 1377.

Su Shi shiji 蘇軾詩集. Su Shi 蘇軾 (1037–1101). Edited by Kong Fanli 孔凡禮. Beijing: *Zhonghua shuju,* 1982.

Su Shi wenji 蘇軾文集. Su Shi 蘇軾 (1037–1101). Edited by Kong Fanli 孔凡禮. Beijing: Zhonghua shuju, 1986.

Taishō Shinshū Daizōkyō 大正新脩大藏經 (Revised version of the canon, compiled during the Taishō era). 85 vols. Edited by Takakusu Junjirō 高楠順次郎 (1866–1945), Watanabe Kaikyoku 渡辺海旭 (1872–1932), et al. Tokyo: Taishō issaikyō kankōkai, 1924–1932.

Tang Wudai yuyan cidian 唐五代語言詞典. Edited by Jiang Lansheng 江蓝生. Shanghai: Shanghai jiaoyu chubanshe, 1997.

Tanjin wenji 鐔津文集. Qisong 契嵩 (1007–1072). T52, no. 2115.

Tianmu Zhongfeng heshang guanglu 天目中峯和尚廣錄. Zhongfeng Mingben 中峰明本 (1263–1323). 1334 edition. *Qisha dazangjing* 磧砂大藏經, vol. 120. Beijing: Xianzhuang shuju, 2005.

Tianru Weize chanshi yulu 天如惟則禪師語錄. Tianru Weize 天如惟則 (1286–1354). ZZ70, no. 1403.

Tiaoxi yuyin conghua 苕溪漁隱叢話. Hu Zi 胡仔 (fl. 1147–1167). *Qianji* 60 fascs., *houji* 40 fascs. SKQS.

Wang Wei ji jiaozhu 王維集校注. Wang Wei 王維 (701–761). Edited and annotated by Chen Tiemin 陈鐵民. Beijing: Zhonghua shuju, 1997.

Wansong laoren pingchang Tiantong Jue heshang niangu qingyi lu 萬松老人評唱天童覺和尚拈古請益錄. ZZ67, no. 1307.

Weimojie suoshuo jing 維摩詰所說經. Kumārajīva 鳩摩羅什 (344–413). T14, no. 475.

Weimojing lüeshu 維摩經略疏. Jingxi Zhanran 荊溪湛然 (711–782). T38, no. 1778.

Weimojing lüeshu chuiyuji 維摩經略疏垂裕記. Gushan Zhiyuan 孤山智圓 (976–1022). T38, no. 1779.

Weimojing shuji 維摩經疏記. Jingxi Zhanran 荊溪湛然 (711–782). ZZ18, no. 340.

Wenxin diaolong 文心雕龍. Liu Xie 劉勰 (ca. 465–ca. 532). SBCK.

Wenyuan yinghua 文苑英華. Li Fang 李昉 (925–996) et al. Beijing: Zhonghua shuju, 1966.

Wenzhong ji 文忠集. Zhou Bida 周必大 (1126–1204). SKQS.

Wudeng quanshu 五燈全書. Jilun Chaoyong 霽崙超永 (fl. 1693). ZZ82, no. 1571.

Wujun zhi 吳郡志. Fan Chengda 范成大 (1126–1193). In *Song Yuan fangzhi congkan*, vol. 1.

Wulin fan zhi 武林梵志. Wu Zhijing 吳之鯨 (fl. 1609). SKQS.

Wushan Jingduan chanshi yulu 吳山淨端禪師語錄. Jingduan 淨端 (1031–1104). ZZ73, no. 1449.

Wuwen Yin 無文印. Wuwen Daocan 無文道璨 (1213–1271). Southern Song edition, National Diet Library no. WA35–5, info:ndljp/pid/2545283.

Wuzhun Shifan chanshi yulu 無準師範禪師語錄. Wuzhun Shifan 無準師範 (1178–1249). ZZ70, no. 1382. Other editions are listed under *Fojian chanshi yulu*.

Xianchun Lin'an zhi 咸淳臨安志. Qian Yueyou 潛說友 (1216–1277). In *Song Yuan fangzhi congkan*, vol. 4.

Xianju bian 閑居編. Gushan Zhiyuan 孤山智圓 (976–1022). ZZ56, no. 949.

Xiao zhiguan. See *Xiuxi zhiguan zuochan fayao*.

Xiatang Huiyuan Chanshi guanglu 瞎堂慧遠禪師廣錄. Fohai Huiyuan 佛海慧遠 (1103–1176). ZZ69, no. 1360. Kunaichō no. 556.63. Partial Southern Song edition dated 1177, entitled *Fohai chanshi yulu* 佛海禪師語錄. Digital photographs accessed via *Kunaichō shoryōbu shūzō kanseki shūran*.

Xihu you lan zhi 西湖遊覽志. Tian Rucheng 田汝成 (*jinshi* 1526). SKQS.

Xinfu zhu 心賦注. Yongming Yanshou 永明延壽 (904–976). ZZ63, no. 1231.

Xin Huayan jing lun 新華嚴經論. Li Tongxuan 李通玄 (635–730; alternatively, 646–740). T36, no. 1739.

Xin Wudai shi 新五代史. Ouyang Xiu 歐陽修 (1007–1072). SKQS.

Xisou Shaotan chanshi guanglu 希叟紹曇禪師廣錄. Xisou Shaotan 希叟紹曇 (d. after 1275). ZZ70, no. 1390.

Xiuxi zhiguan zuochan fayao 修習止觀坐禪法要. Zhiyi 智顗 (538–597). T46, no. 1915.

Xizhai jingtu shi 西齋淨土詩. Chushi Fanqi 楚石梵琦 (1296–1370). *Congshu jicheng, xinbian*, 25:568–589.

Xuedou si ji 雪竇四集. Xuedou Chongxian 雪竇重顯 (980–1052). SBCK.

Xueyan Zuqin chanshi yulu 雪巖祖欽禪師語錄. Xueyan Zuqin 雪巖祖欽 (1216–1287). ZZ70, no. 1397.

Xu gaoseng zhuan 續高僧傳. Daoxuan 道宣 (596–667). T50, no. 2060.

Xu Gu zunsu yuyao 續古尊宿語要. Huishi Shiming 晦室師明 (fl. 1238). ZZ68, no. 1318.

Xutang heshang yulu 虛堂和尚語錄. Xutang Zhiyu (1185–1269). T47, no. 2000. Citations to *Gozan-ban* refer to *Gozan-ban Chūgoku zenseki sōkan*, vol. 8. This edition from the Kunaichō collection printed in 1313 is nearly identical to the only extant 1269 Song imprint, per Shiina Kōyū's appended explanation in *Gozan-ban Chūgoku zenseki sōkan*, 8:741. Another copy of the 1313 Gozan edition is available online from National Diet Library no. WA6–26, info:ndljp/pid/2543543.

Xuxiu siku quanshu 續修四庫全書. 1,800 vols. Shanghai: Shanghai guji chubanshe, 1995–2002.

Xu Zizhi tongjian changbian 續資治通鑒長編. Li Tao 李燾 (1115–1184). Beijing: Zhonghua shuju, 1985.

Yayu Jiang Zhe jixing jiju shi 亞愚江浙紀行集句詩. Yayu Shaosong 亞愚紹嵩 (fl. 1229–

1232). Song edition, dated 1237. In *Beijing tushuguan guji shanben congkan* 北京圖書館古籍珍本叢刊, 86:481–526. Beijing: Shumu wenxian chubanshe, 1988.

Yifanfeng 一帆風. 1664 edition (44 poems) in the collection of Tokyo University Library. Undated Edo edition (69 poems) in the collection of Kansai University Library. Manuscript edition in the hand of Daitō Shūhō Myōchō 大燈宗峰妙超 (1282–1337): fragment in a private collection at Kitamura Bijutsukan 北村美術館, Kyoto; Taishō photograph of fragment formerly in collection of Ikeda Seisuke 池田清助; Taishō photograph of fragment formerly in collection of Masuda Nobuyoshi 益田信世. Taishō photographs in the collection of the Historiographical Institute of the University of Tokyo.

Yijiao jing lunji 遺教經論記. Xiao'an Guanfu 笑庵觀復 (fl. 1141–1152). ZZ53, no. 846.

Yingkui lüsui 瀛奎律髓. Fang Hui 方回 (1227–1307). SKQS.

Yingyin Mingta Tingyunguan fatie 影印明拓《停雲館法帖》. Wen Zhengming 文徵明 (1470–1559). 2 vols. Beijing: Beijing chubanshe, 1997.

Yingyin Wenyuange Siku quanshu 景印文淵閣四庫全書. 1,500 vols. Taipei: Taiwan shangwu yinshuguan, 1983–1986.

Yintong: Chinese Phonological Database. Compiled by David Branner. An electronic edition of *Guangyun* 廣韻 rhyme dictionary of 1008. http://yintong.info/.

Yiqie jing yinyi 一切經音義. Huilin 慧琳 (737–820). T54, no. 2128.

Yongjue Yuanxian chanshi guanglu 永覺元賢禪師廣錄. Yongjue Yuanxian 永覺元賢 (1578–1657). ZZ72, no. 1437.

Yuanjue jing da shu 圓覺經大疏. Guifeng Zongmi 圭峰宗密 (780–841). ZZ9, no. 243.

Yuansou Xingduan chanshi yulu 元叟行端禪師語錄. Yuanshuo Xingduan 元叟行端 (1255–1341). ZZ71, no. 1419.

Yuanwu Foguo chanshi yulu 圓悟佛果禪師語錄. Yuanwu Keqin 圓悟克勤 (1063–1135). T47, no. 1997.

Yuan Zhen ji 元稹集. Yuan Zhen 元稹 (779–831). Beijing: Zhonghua shuju, 1982.

Yucen shan Huiyin Gaoli Huayan jiaosi zhi 玉岑山慧因高麗華嚴教寺志. Li Zhu 李燾 (fl. 1628). *Zhongguo Fosizhi congkan,* vol. 56. Yangzhou: Guangling shu she, 2006.

Yuefu shiji 樂府詩集. Guo Maoqian 郭茂倩 (1041–1099). SBCK.

Yuejiang Zhengyin Chanshi yulu 月江正印禪師語錄. Yuejiang Zhengyin 月江正印 (1267–after 1350). ZZ71, no. 1409.

Yunqi fahui 雲棲法彙. Yunqi Zhuhong 雲棲袾宏 (1535–1615). *Jiaxing dazangjing,* vol. 33.

Yunwo jitan 雲臥紀譚. Xiaoying Zhongwen 曉瑩仲溫 (12th c.). ZZ86, no. 1610.

Yunxi ji 鄖溪集. Zheng Xie 鄭獬 (1022–1072). SKQS.

Yuqie shidi lun 瑜伽師地論. Translated by Xuanzang 玄奘 (602–664). T30, no. 1579.

Yuting ji 羽庭集. Liu Renben 劉仁本 (d. 1367). SKQS.

Zengaku daijiten 禪學大辭典. Tokyo: Taishūkan shoten, 1978.

Zengaku tenseki sōkan 禅学典籍叢刊. 12 vols. Edited by Yanagida Seizan 柳田聖山 and Shiina Kōyū 椎名宏雄. Kyoto: Rinsen shoten, 1999–2001.

Zengi gemon shū 禪儀外文集. Kokan Shiren 虎関師錬 (1278–1346). 1626 edition, National Diet Library no. WA7–132, info:ndljp/pid/2544423.

Zenrin bokuseki 禪林墨蹟. Edited by Tayama Hōnan 田山方南. Ichikawa: Zenrin bokuseki kankōkai, 1955. All cited figures are located in vol. 1 and give only the figure number (e.g., fig. 10). References to Vol. 3, *Zenrin bokuseki kaisetsu,* give the volume and page number (e.g., 3:106).

Zenrin bokuseki shūi 禪林墨跡拾遺. Edited by Tayama Hōnan 田山方南. Tokyo: Zenrin bokuseki kankōkai, 1977. All cited figures are located in vol. 1 and give only the figure number (e.g., fig. 10).

Zenrin shōkisen 禪林象器箋. Mujaku Dōchū 無著道忠 (1653–1744). *Dazangjing bubian,* vol. 19.

Zhiguan fuxing chuan hongjue 止觀輔行傳弘決. Jingxi Zhanran 荊溪湛然 (711–782). T46, no. 1912.

Zhiyuan ji 芝園集. Lingzhi Yuanzhao 靈芝元照 (1048–1116). ZZ59, no. 1105.

Zhizheng zhuan 智證傳. Juefan Huihong 覺範惠洪 (1071–1128). ZZ63, no. 1235.

Zhongguo fatie quanji 中國法帖全集. 17 vols. Edited by Qi Gong 啟功, Wang Jingxian 王靖憲, and Yu Lan 余瀾. Wuhan: Hubei meishu chubanshe, 2002.

Zhonghua chuan xindi chanmen shizi chengxi tu 中華傳心地禪門師資承襲圖. Guifeng Zongmi 圭峰宗密 (780–841). ZZ63, no. 1225.

Zhong Tianzhu Sheweiguo Qihuansi tujing 中天竺舍衛國祇洹寺圖經. Daoxuan 道宣 (596–667). T45, no. 1899.

Zhongwu jiwen 中吳紀聞. Gong Mingzhi 龔明之 (1091–1182). Zhibuzuzhai congshu edition, accessed via Scripta Sinica of the Institute of History and Philology at Scripta Sinica.

Zhu Shimen wenzi chan 注石門文字禪. Edited and punctuated by Zhang Bowei 張伯偉 et al. 2 vols. Beijing: Zhonghua shuju, 2011. A critical edition based on the 1710 edition of *Sekimon Mojizen Chū* 石門文字禪註, annotations by Sōtō Zen monk Kakumon Kantetsu 廓門貫徹 (d. 1730), available in *Zengaku tenseki sōkan,* vol. 5.

Zibo zunzhe quanji 紫柏尊者全集. Zibo Zhenke 紫柏真可 (1543–1604). ZZ73, no. 1452.

Zimen jingxun 緇門警訓. T48, no. 2023.

Zizhu lin Zhuanyu Heng heshang yulu 紫竹林顓愚衡和尚語錄. Zhuanyu Guanheng 顓愚觀衡 (1579–1646). *Jiaxing dazangjing,* vol. 28.

Zoku Zenrin bokuseki 續禪林墨蹟. Edited by Tayama Hōnan 田山方南. Ichikawa: Zenrin bokuseki kankōkai, 1965. All cited figures are located in vol. 1 and give only the figure number (e.g., fig. 10).

Zongjing lu 宗鏡錄. Yongming Yanshou 永明延壽 (904–976). T48, no. 2016.

Zongtong biannian 宗統編年. Jiyun 紀蔭 (fl. 1690–1693). ZZ86, no. 1600.

Zutang ji 祖堂集. Jing 靜 and Yun 筠 (10th c.). Edited and annotated by Sun Changwu 孫昌武, Kinugawa Kenji 衣川賢次, and Nishiguchi Yoshio 西口芳男. Beijing: Zhonghua shuju, 2007.

Zuting shiyuan 祖庭事苑. Mu'an Shanqing 睦庵善卿 (act. 1050–1108). ZZ64, no. 1261. Although I did not find textual variants in the Gozan edition, for the reader's convenience *Gozan-ban* citations give page number in *Gozan-ban Chūgoku zenseki sōkan,* vol 3.

Zuying ji 祖英集. Xuedou Chongxian 雪竇重顯 (980–1052). Citations provide internal fascicle and page numbers of the Southern Song edition, in *Xuedou si ji;* followed by citation to *Mingjue chanshi yulu.*

Secondary Sources

Adamek, Wendi. *The Mystique of Transmission: On an Early Chan History and Its Contexts.* New York: Columbia University Press, 2007.

———. "The Impossibility of the Given: Representations of Merit and Emptiness in Medieval Chinese Buddhism." *History of Religions* 45.2 (2005): 135–180.

Ahn, Juhn. "Malady of Meditation: A Prolegomenon to the Study of Illness and Zen." PhD diss., University of California, Berkeley, 2007.

———. "Who Has the Last Word in Chan? Transmission, Secrecy, and Reading during the Northern Song Dynasty." *Journal of Chinese Religions* 37 (2009): 1–71.

Anderl, Christoph. "The Semantics of *Qing* 情 in Chan Buddhist Chinese." In Eifring, *Love and Emotions in Traditional Chinese Literature*, 149–224.

———. "Zen in the Art of Insult." In *Studies in Chinese Language and Culture*, edited by Christoph Anderl and Halvor Eifring, 377–393. Oslo: Hermes, 2006.

———. "Zen Rhetoric: An Introduction." In *Zen Buddhist Rhetoric in China, Korea, and Japan*, edited by Christoph Anderl, 1–94. Leiden: Brill, 2012.

Andō Tomonobu 安藤智信. "Kozan Chien to Myōkyō Kaisū" 孤山智円と明教契嵩. *Ōtani gakuhō* 55, no. 3 (1975): 39–51.

App, Urs. "The Making of a Chan Record: Reflections on the History of the Records of Yunmen 雲門廣錄." *Zen bunka kenkyūjo kiyō* 17 (1991): 1–90.

Araki Kengo 荒木見悟. *Fukyōhen: Zen no goroku 14* 輔教編: 禅の語錄14. Tokyo: Chikuma shobō, 1981.

Asakura Hisashi 朝倉尚. "Gozan-ban *Shinsen Jōwa bunrui kokon sonshuku geshu shū* kō" 五山版『新撰貞和分類古今尊宿偈頌集』考. *Zen bunka kenkyujō kiyō* 28 (2006): 221–254.

———. *Shōmono no sekai to zenrin no bungaku: Chūka Jakuboku shishō, Tōzan renku shō no kisoteki kenkyū* 抄物の世界と禅林の文学：中華若木詩抄・湯山聯句鈔の基礎的研究. Osaka: Seibundō, 1996.

———. *Zenrin no bungaku: Chūgoku bungaku juyō no yōsō* 禅林の文学:中国文学受容の様相. Osaka: Seibundō, 1985.

———. *Zenrin no bungaku: Shikai to sono shūhen* 禅林の文学: 詩会とその周辺. Osaka: Seibundō, 2004.

Asami Ryūsuke 浅見龍介. "Kamakura: The Art of Zen Buddhism." Translated by Thomas Kirchner. In *Kamakura: Zen no genryū* 鎌倉−禅の源流. Tokyo: Tokyo National Museum, 2003. Exhibition Catalogue.

Barrett, Timothy. *Li Ao: Buddhist, Taoist, or Neo-Confucian?* New York: Oxford University Press, 1992.

Baxter, William, and Laurent Sagart. *Old Chinese: A New Reconstruction*. New York: Oxford University Press, 2014.

Bell, Corey. "Genuine Anguish, Genuine Mind: 'Loyal' Buddhist Monks, Poetics and Soteriology in Ming-Qing Transition-Era Southern China." PhD diss., University of Melbourne, 2016.

Benn, James. "Another Look at the Pseudo-Śūraṃgama sūtra." *Harvard Journal of Asiatic Studies* 68, no. 1 (2008): 57–89.

———. *Tea in China: A Religious and Cultural History*. Honolulu: University of Hawaii Press, 2015.

Berkwitz, Stephen. *Buddhist History in the Vernacular: The Power of the Past in Late Medieval Sri Lanka*. Leiden: Brill, 2004.

———. *Buddhist Poetry and Colonialism: Alagiyavanna and the Portuguese in Sri Lanka*. New York: Oxford University Press, 2013.

Berling, Judith. "Bringing the Buddha Down to Earth: Notes on the Emergence of Yü-lu as a Buddhist Genre." *History of Religions* 27 (1987): 56–88

Bielefeldt, Carl. *Dōgen's Manuals of Zen Meditation*. Berkeley: University of California Press, 1988.

Birnbaum, Raoul. *The Healing Buddha*. Boulder: Shambala, 1979.

Birrell, Anne. *Popular Songs and Ballads of Han China*. London: Unwin Hyman, 1988. Reprint, Honolulu: University of Hawaii Press, 1993.

Bodiford, William. "Zen in the Art of Funerals: Ritual Salvation in Japanese Buddhism." *History of Religions* 32, no. 2 (1992): 146–164.

Bol, Peter. "Chu Hsi's Redefinition of Literati Learning." In de Bary and Chaffee, *Neo-Confucian Education*, 151–185.

———. "The Sung Examination System and the Shih." *Asia Major*, 3rd ser., 3, no. 2 (1990): 149–171.

Bourdieu, Pierre. *Outline of a Theory of Practice*. Cambridge: Cambridge University Press, 1977.

Brashier, Kenneth. "Eastern Han Commemorative Stelae: Laying the Cornerstones of Public Memory." In Lagerway and Kalinowski, *Early Chinese Religion, Part One*, 1027–1059.

Brokaw, Cynthia. "Book History in Premodern China: The State of the Discipline." *Book History* 10 (2007): 253–290.

Brose, Benjamin. *Patrons and Patriarchs: Regional Rulers and Chan Monks during the Five Dynasties and Ten Kingdoms*. Kuroda Institute Studies in East Asian Buddhism 25. Honolulu: University of Hawaii Press, 2015.

Broughton, Jeffrey. *Zongmi on Chan*. New York: Columbia University Press, 2009.

Buckelew, Kevin. "Becoming Chinese Buddhas: Claims to Authority and the Making of Chan Buddhist Identity." *T'oung Pao* 105 (2019): 357–400.

Bushelle, Ethan. "The Joy of the Dharma: Esoteric Buddhism and the Early Medieval Transformation of Japanese Literature." PhD diss., Harvard University, 2015.

Buswell, Robert. "Ch'an Hermeneutics: A Korean View." In *Buddhist Hermeneutics*, edited by Donald S. Lopez, 231–256. Kuroda Institute Studies in East Asian Buddhism 6. Honolulu: University of Hawaii Press, 1993.

Buswell, Robert E., and Robert M. Gimello, eds. *Paths to Liberation: The Mārga and Its Transformations in Buddhist Thought*. Kuroda Institute Studies in East Asian Buddhism 7. Honolulu: University of Hawaii Press, 1992.

Byrne, Christopher. "Poetics of Silence: Hongzhi Zhengjue (1091–1157) and the Practice of Poetry in Song Dynasty Chan *Yulu*." PhD diss., McGill University, 2015.

Cabezón, José Ignacio, and Roger R. Jackson, eds. *Tibetan Literature: Studies in Genre*. Ithaca, NY: Snow Lion Publications, 1996.

Cai Lingwan 蔡玲婉. "Sheng Tang songbie shi de shenmei neihan" 盛唐送別詩的審美內涵. *Guoli Taibei shifan xueyuan xuebao* 16, no. 1 (2003): 25–54.

Cai Rongting 蔡榮婷. *Zutangji Chanzong shiji yanjiu* 祖堂集禪宗詩偈研究. Taipei: Wenjin chubanshe, 2004.

Campany, Robert. *Making Transcendents: Ascetics and Social Memory in Early Medieval China.* Honolulu: University of Hawaii Press, 2009.

———. "On the Very Idea of Religions (in the Modern West and in Early Medieval China)." *History of Religions* 42, no. 4 (2003): 287–319.

Cao Shibang 曹仕邦. *Zhongguo shamen waixue de yanjiu* 中國沙門外學的研究. Taipei: Dongchu chubanshe, 1995.

Capitanio, Joshua. "Portrayals of Chan Buddhism in the Literature of Internal Alchemy." *Journal of Chinese Religions* 43, no. 2 (2012): 119–160.

Cartelli, Mary Anne. *The Five-Colored Clouds of Mount Wutai: Poems from Dunhuang.* Leiden: Brill, 2013.

Chan, Chi-wah. "Chih-li (960–1028) and the Formation of Orthodoxy in the Sung T'ien-t'ai tradition of Buddhism." PhD diss., University of California, Los Angeles 1993.

Chan, Timothy Wai Keung. *Considering the End: Mortality in Early Medieval Chinese Poetic Representation.* Leiden: Brill, 2012.

Chen, Frederick Shih-Chung. "The *Deathbed Injunction Sutra.*" In *Buddhist Stone Sutras in China: Sichuan Province 2,* edited by Tsai Suey-ling and Sun Hua, 45–52. Wiesbaden: Harrassowitz Verlag, 2015.

Chen, Jack. "On Mourning and Sincerity in the *Li Ji* and the *Shishuo Xinyu.*" In *Memory in Medieval China: Text, Ritual, and Community,* edited by Wendy Swartz and Robert Ford Company, 63–81. Leiden: Brill, 2018.

Chen, Jinhua. "Family Ties and Buddhist Nuns in Tang China: Two Studies." *Asia Major,* 3rd ser., 15, no. 2 (2002): 51–85.

Chen, Song. "The State, the Gentry, and the Local Institutions: The Song Dynasty and Long-Term Trends from Tang to Qing." *Journal of Chinese History* 1, no. 1 (2017): 141–182.

Chen Fang 陳芳. "*Canglang shihua* Mingdai jieshou yanjiu" 《滄浪詩話》明代接受研究. PhD diss., Fudan University, 2013.

Chennault, Cynthia. "Representing the Uncommon." In *Interpretation and Literature in Early Medieval China,* edited by Alan K. Chan and Yuet-Keung Lo, 189–221. Albany: State University of New York Press, 2010.

Chen Zhongxiu 陳鍾琇. *Tangdai heshi yanjiu* 唐代和詩研究. Taipei: Xiuwei zixun keji gufen, 2008.

Chen Zili 陳自力. *Shi Huihong yanjiu* 釋惠洪研究. Beijing: Zhonghua shuju, 2005.

Cherniack, Susan. "Book Culture and Textual Transmission in Sung China." *Harvard Journal of Asiatic Studies* 54, no. 1 (1994): 5–125.

Chey, Jocelyn. "*Youmo* and the Chinese Sense of Humour." In *Humour in Chinese Life and Letters: Classical and Traditional Approaches,* edited by Joselyn Chey and Jessica Milner Davis, 1–29. Hong Kong: Hong Kong University Press, 2011.

Chia, Lucille. *Printing for Profit: The Commercial Publishers of Jianyang, Fujian (11th–17th Centuries).* Cambridge, MA: Harvard University Asia Center, 2002.

Chia, Lucille, and Hilde De Weerdt. "Introduction," in Chia and De Weerdt, *Knowledge and Text Production in an Age of Print*, 1–29.

——, eds. *Knowledge and Text Production in an Age of Print: China, 900–1400*. Leiden: Brill, 2011.

Chi Kuang-yu 吉廣輿. "Songchu jiuseng shiji kaoshu" 宋初九僧詩集考述. *Pumen xuebao* 2 (2001): 1–29.

Coblin, W. South. *A Handbook of Eastern Han Sound Glosses*. Hong Kong: Chinese University Press, 1983.

Collcutt, Martin. *Five Mountains: The Rinzai Zen Monastic Institution in Medieval Japan*. Cambridge, MA: Harvard University Press, 1981.

Collins, Steven. "On the Very Idea of the Pali Canon." *Journal of the Pali Text Society* 15 (1990): 89–126.

Conze, Edward. *The Perfection of Wisdom in Eight Thousand Lines and Its Verse Summary*. Bolinas, CA: Four Seasons Foundation, 1973.

Culler, Jonathan. *Theory of the Lyric*. Cambridge, MA: Harvard University Press, 2015.

Davies, Robertson. *A Voice from the Attic: Essays on the Art of Reading*. New York: Alfred A. Knopf, 1960.

Davis, A. R. *T'ao Yuan-ming, His Works and Their Meaning*. Cambridge: Cambridge University Press, 1984.

Deleanu, Florin. "The *Laṅkāvatārasūtra*: A Bibliographical Survey." *Bulletin of the International Institute for Buddhist Studies* 1 (2018): 15–43.

Demiéville, Paul. "Langue et littérature chinoises: Tch'an et poésie." Reprinted in *Choix d'études sinologiques (1921–1970)*, 274–289. Leiden: Brill, 1973.

——. "The Mirror of the Mind." Translated by Neal Donner. In Gregory, *Sudden and Gradual: Approaches to Enlightenment in Chinese Thought*, 13–40. First published in French as "Le miroir spirituel" in 1947 in *Sinologica*.

——. *Poèmes chinois d'avant la mort*. Paris: L'Asiathèque, 1984.

——. "Stances de la fin." In *Mélanges Offerts a M. Charles Haguenauer*, 11–29. Paris: L'Asiathèque, 1980.

de Bary, Wm. Theodore, and Irene Bloom, eds. *Sources of Chinese Tradition: From Earliest Times to 1600*. 2nd ed. New York: Columbia University Press, 1999.

de Bary, Wm. Theodore, and John W. Chaffee, eds. *Neo-Confucian Education: The Formative Stage*. Berkeley: University of California Press, 1989.

De Weerdt, Hilde. "The Cultural Logics of Map Reading: Text, Time, and Space in Printed Maps of the Song Empire." In Chia and De Weerdt, *Knowledge and Text Production in an Age of Print*, 239–270.

——. "The Discourse of Loss in Song Dynasty Private and Imperial Book Collecting." *Library Trends* 55, no. 3 (2007): 404–420.

Diehl, Patrick. *The Medieval European Religious Lyric*. Berkeley: University of California Press, 1984.

Du Songbo 杜松柏. *Chanxue yu Tang Song shixue* 禪學與唐宋詩學. Taipei: Liming wenhua shiye gufen youxian gongsi, 1976.

Ebrey, Patricia. *Chu Hsi's Family Rituals*. Princeton, NJ: Princeton University Press, 1991.

———. "Song Government Policy." In Marsone and Lagerwey, *Modern Chinese Religion*, 73–137.

———. "Zhu Xi's Colophons on Handwritten Documents." In *Visual and Material Cultures in Middle Period China*, edited by Patricia Buckley Ebrey and Susan Shih-shan Huang, 226–253. Leiden: Brill, 2017.

Ebrey, Patricia Buckley, and Peter N. Gregory, eds. *Religion and Society in T'ang and Sung China*. Honolulu: University of Hawaii Press, 1993.

Egan, Charles. *Clouds Thick, Whereabouts Unknown: Poems by Zen Monks of China*. New York: Columbia University Press, 2010.

Egan, Ronald. "The Northern Song (1020–1126)." In *The Cambridge History of Chinese Literature: Volume 1; to 1375,* edited by Kang-I Sun Chang and Stephen Owen, 381–464. Cambridge: Cambridge University Press, 2010.

———. "Ou-yang Hsiu and Su Shih on Calligraphy." *Harvard Journal of Asiatic Studies* 49, no. 2 (1989): 365–419.

———. *The Problem of Beauty*. Cambridge, MA: Harvard University Asia Center, 2006.

———. "*Shi* Poetry: Ancient and Recent Styles." In *How to Read Chinese Poetry: A Guided Anthology*, edited by Zong-qi Cai. 308–326. Honolulu: University of Hawaii Press, 2008.

———. "Su Shi's Informal Letters in Literature and Life." In Richter, *History of Chinese Letters*, 276–306.

———. "To Count Grains of Sand on the Ocean Floor: Changing Perceptions of Books and Learning in Song Dynasty China." In Chia and De Weerdt, *Knowledge and Text Production in an Age of Print*, 33–62.

———. *Word, Image, and Deed in the Life of Su Shi*. Cambridge, MA: Harvard Council on East Asian Studies, 1994.

Eichmann, Jennifer. *A Late Sixteenth-Century Chinese Buddhist Fellowship: Spiritual Ambitions, Intellectual Debates, and Epistolary Connections*. Leiden: Brill, 2016.

Eifring, Halvor. "Emotions and the Conceptual History of Qing." In Eifring, *Love and Emotions in Traditional Chinese Literature*, 1–36.

———, ed. *Love and Emotions in Traditional Chinese Literature*. Leiden: Brill, 2004.

Faure, Bernard. *Chan Insights and Oversights: An Epistemological Critique of the Chan Tradition*. Princeton, NJ: Princeton University Press, 1993.

———. *The Rhetoric of Immediacy: A Cultural Critique of Chan/Zen Buddhism*. Princeton, NJ: Princeton University Press, 1991.

Felstiner, John. *Paul Celan: Poet, Survivor, Jew*. New Haven, CT: Yale University Press, 2001.

Feng Guodong 馮國棟. *Jingde chuandenglu yanjiu* 景德傳燈錄研究. Beijing: Zhonghua shuju, 2014.

Fisher, Philip. *The Vehement Passions*. Princeton, NJ: Princeton University Press, 2002.

Fogel, Joshua. "Sino-Japanese Shipping Connections as Reported in Chinese and Japanese Sources." *Sino-Japanese Studies* 20 (2013): article 4.

Fong, Grace. "Private Emotion, Public Commemoration: Qian Shoupu's Poems of Mourning." *Chinese Literature: Essays, Articles, Reviews (CLEAR)* 30 (2008): 19–30.

Fontein, Jan. *The Pilgrimage of Sudhana: A Study of Gandavyuha Illustrations in China,*

Japan and Java. The Hague: Mouton, 1967. Reprint, Berlin: De Gruyter Mouton, 2012.

Foulk, T. Griffith. "*Chanyuan qinggui* and Other 'Rules of Purity' in Chinese Buddhism." In Heine and Wright, *The Zen Canon*, 275–312.

———. "Histories of Chan." Unpublished manuscript, spring 2011.

———. "Myth, Ritual, and Monastic Practice in Sung Ch'an Buddhism." In Ebrey and Gregory, *Religion and Society in T'ang and Sung China*, 147–208.

———. *Standard Observances of the Soto Zen School*. 2 vols. Tokyo: Sōtōshū shūmuchō, 2010.

Foulk, T. Griffith, and Robert Sharf. "On the Ritual Use of Ch'an Portraiture in Medieval China." *Cahiers d'Extrême-Asie* 7 (1993): 149–219.

Fowler, Alistair. *Kinds of Literature: An Introduction to the Theory of Genres and Modes*. Cambridge, MA: Harvard University Press, 1982.

Frye, Northrop. *Anatomy of Criticism: Four Essays*. Princeton, NJ: Princeton University Press, 1957.

Fukuoka-shi Bijutsukan Gakugeika, ed. *Daiō kokushi to Sōfukuji* 大応国師と崇福寺. Fukuoka: Daiō kokushi to Sōfukuji ten jikkō iinkai, 2007.

Fuller, Michael. *Drifting among Rivers and Lakes*. Cambridge, MA: Harvard University Asia Center, 2013.

———. *The Road to East Slope: The Development of Su Shi's Poetic Voice*. Stanford, CA: Stanford University Press, 1990.

———. "Why Form Matters: A Systematic 21st Century *Shihua* on the Song Dynasty Poet He Zhu." *China Review International* 18, no. 1 (2011): 1–6.

Funayama Tōru 船山徹. *Butten wa dō kanyaku sareta no ka: Sūtora ga kyōten ni naru toki* 仏典はどう漢訳されたのか ―― スートラが経典になるとき. Tokyo: Iwanami shoten, 2013.

Galambos, Imre. "Confucian Education in a Buddhist Environment: Medieval Manuscript and Imprints of the *Mengqiu*." *Studies in Chinese Religions* 1, no. 3 (2015): 269–288.

Gao Shentao 高慎濤. "Shiseng zhi 'shusunqi' yu 'suanxianqi'" 僧詩之「蔬筍氣」與「酸餡氣」. *Gudian wenxue zhishi* 136, no. 1 (2008): 50–57.

Gardner, Daniel. "Modes of Thinking and Modes of Discourse in the Sung: Some Thoughts on the Yü-lu ('Recorded Conversations') Texts." *Journal of Asian Studies* 50, no. 3 (1991): 574–603.

Genette, Gerard. *Paratexts: Thresholds of Interpretation*. Translated by Jane E. Lewin. Cambridge: Cambridge University Press, 1997.

Getz, Daniel. "Rebirth in the Lotus: Song Dynasty Lotus Sūtra Devotion and Pure Land Aspiration in Zongxiao's *Fahua jing xianying lu*." *Chung-Hwa Buddhist Journal* 26 (2013): 33–65.

———. "Siming Zhili and Tiantai Pure Land in the Song Dynasty." PhD diss., Yale University, 1994.

Ge Zhaoguang 葛兆光. *Zhongguo zongjiao yu wenxue lunji* 中國宗教與文學論集. Beijing: Qinghua daxue chubanshe, 1998.

Gimello, Robert. "Apophatic and Kataphatic Discourse in Mahāyāna." *Philosophy East and West* 26, no. 2 (1976): 117–136.

———. "Mārga and Culture: Learning, Letters, and Liberation in Northern Sung Ch'an." In Buswell and Gimello, *Paths to Liberation,* 371–438.

———. "Random Reflections on the 'Sinicization' of Buddhism." *Society for the Study of Chinese Religions Bulletin* 5 (1978): 52–89.

Grant, Beata. *Mount Lu Revisited: Buddhism in the Life and Writings of Su Shih.* Honolulu: University of Hawaii Press, 1994.

———. "Through the Empty Gate: The Poetry of Buddhist Nuns in Late Imperial China." In *Cultural Intersections in Later Chinese Buddhism,* edited by Marsha Weidner, 87–114. Honolulu: University of Hawaii Press, 2001.

Greene, Eric. "Meditation, Repentance, and Visionary Experience in Early Medieval Chinese Buddhism." PhD diss., University of California, Berkeley, 2012.

Gregory, Peter N. "Bridging the Gap: Zongmi's Strategies for Reconciling Textual Study and Meditative Practice." *Journal of Chinese Buddhist Studies* 30 (2017): 89–124.

———, ed. *Sudden and Gradual: Approaches to Enlightenment in Chinese Thought.* Kuroda Institute Studies in East Asian Buddhism 5. Honolulu: University of Hawaii Press, 1987.

———. "The Vitality of Buddhism in the Sung." In Gregory and Getz, *Buddhism in the Sung,* 1–20.

Gregory, Peter N., and Patricia Buckley Ebrey. "The Religious and Historical Landscape." In Ebrey and Gregory, *Religion and Society in T'ang and Sung China,* 1–44.

Gregory, Peter N., and Daniel A. Getz, eds. *Buddhism in the Sung.* Kuroda Institute Studies in East Asian Buddhism 13. Honolulu: University of Hawaii Press, 1999.

Gyatso, Janet. *Being Human in a Buddhist World.* New York: Columbia University Press, 2015.

Hallisey, Charles. *"Therigatha": Poems of the First Buddhist Women.* Cambridge, MA: Harvard University Press, 2015.

———. "Works and Persons in Sinhala Literary Culture." In Pollock, *Literary Cultures in History,* 689–746.

Halperin, Mark. *Out of the Cloister: Literati Perspectives on Buddhism in Sung China, 960–1279.* Cambridge, MA: Harvard University Asia Center, 2006.

Harbsmeier, Christopher. "The Semantics of *Qing* 情 in Pre-Buddhist Chinese." In Eifring, *Love and Emotions in Traditional Chinese Literature,* 69–148.

———. "Weeping and Wailing in Ancient China." In *Minds and Mentalities in Traditional Chinese Literature,* edited by Halvor Eifring, 317–422. Beijing: Culture and Art Publishing House, 1999.

Harrison, Paul. "*Buddhānusmṛti* in the *Pratyutpanna-buddha-saṃmukhāvasthita-samādhi-sūtra*." *Journal of Indian Philosophy* 6 (1978), 35–57.

———. "Canon." In *Encyclopedia of Buddhism,* edited by Robert E. Buswell, 111–115. New York: Macmillan, 2004.

———. "Commemoration and Identification in *Buddhānusmṛti*." In *The Mirror of Memory: Reflections on Mindfulness and Remembrance in Indian and Tibetan Buddhism,* edited by Janet Gyatso, 215–238. Albany, NY: SUNY Press, 1992.

Hasegawa Masahiro 長谷川 昌弘. "Butsugen Shōon no shisō" 仏眼清遠の思想. *Indogaku Bukkyōgaku kenkyū* 41 (1993): 552–556.

Hata Egyaku 秦慧玉. *Shige sakuhō* 詩偈作法. Tokyo: Komeisha, 1952.

Heim, Maria. *The Forerunner of All Things: Buddhaghosa on Mind, Intention, and Agency.* New York: Oxford University Press, 2013.

Heine, Steven. "Empty-Handed, but Not Empty-Headed: Dogen's *Kōan* Strategies." In *Discourse and Ideology in Medieval Japanese Buddhism,* edited by Richard K. Payne and Taigen Dan Leighton, 218–239. New York: Routledge, 2006.

Heine, Steven, and Dale S. Wright, eds. *The Zen Canon: Understanding the Classic Texts.* New York: Oxford University Press, 2006.

Heirman, Anne. *A Pure Mind in a Clean Body.* Gent: Academia Press, 2012.

———. "*Vinaya:* From India to China." In *The Spread of Buddhism,* edited by Ann Heirman and Stephan Peter Bumbacher, 167–202. Leiden: Brill, 2007.

Heller, Natasha. "Between Zhongfeng Mingben and Zhao Mengfu: Chan Letters in Their Manuscript Context." In *Buddhist Manuscript Cultures: Knowledge, Rituals, and Art,* edited by Stephen C. Berkwitz, Juliane Schober, and Claudia Brown, 109–123. New York: Routledge, 2009.

———. *Illusory Abiding: The Cultural Construction of the Chan Monk Zhongfeng Mingben.* Cambridge, MA: Harvard University Asia Center, 2014.

Hightower, James. "*Wen Hsüan* and Genre Theory." *Harvard Journal of Asiatic Studies* 20, no. 3/4 (1957): 512–533.

Hirakawa, Akira. *A History of Indian Buddhism: from Śākyamuni to early Mahāyāna.* Translated by Paul Groner. Honolulu: University of Hawai'i Press, 1990.

Hisamatsu, Shin'ichi. "On Zen Art." *The Eastern Buddhist,* n.s., 1, no. 2 (1966): 21–33.

Hollander, John. *Rhyme's Reason.* 3rd ed. New Haven, CT: Yale University Press, 2001.

Hori, Victor. *Zen Sand: The Book of Capping Phrases for Kōan Practice.* Honolulu: University of Hawaii Press, 2003.

Hsiao Li-hua 蕭麗華. *Tangdai Shige yu Chanxue* 唐代詩歌與禪學. Taipei: Dongda tushu, 1997.

———. "*Wenzi chan*" *shixue de fazhan guiji*「文字禪」詩學的發展軌跡. Taipei: Xinwenfeng, 2012.

Hsieh, Ding-hwa. "Poetry and Chan *'Gong'an':* From Xuedou Chongxian (980–1052) to Wumen Huikai (1183–1260)." *Journal of Song-Yuan Studies* 40 (2010): 39–70.

Huang, Harrison Tse-Chang. "Excursion, Estates, and the Kingly Gaze: The Landscape Poetry of Xie Lingyun." PhD diss., University of California, Berkeley, 2010.

Huang Ch'i-chiang 黃啟江. *Bei Song Huanglong Huinan chanshi sanyao* 北宋黃龍慧南禪師三鑰. Taipei: Taiwan xuesheng, 2015.

———. "Canfang mingshi: Nan Song qiufa Riseng yu Jiang-Zhe Fojiao conglin" 參訪名師:南宋求法日僧與江浙佛教叢林. *Foxue yanjiu zhongxin xuebao* 10 (2005): 185–234.

———. *Nan Song liu wenxue seng jinian lu* 南宋六文學僧紀年錄. Taipei: Xuesheng shuju, 2014.

———. *Wuwen Yin de misi yu jiedu* 無文印的迷思與解讀. Taipei: Taiwan shangwu yinshu guan, 2010.

———. *Yiwei Chan yu jianghu shi: Nan Song wenxue seng yu Chan wenhua de tuibian* 一味禪與江湖詩:南宋文學僧與禪文化的蛻變. Taipei: Taiwan shangwu yinshu guan, 2010.

Huang Yi-hsun 黃繹勳. *Integrating Chinese Buddhism*. Taipei: Dharma Drum Publishing, 2005.

———. *Songdai Chanzong cishu Zuting shiyuan zhi yanjiu* 宋代禪宗辭書《祖庭事苑》之研究. Kaohsiung: Fo Guang, 2011.

———. *Xuedou qiji zhi yanjiu* 雪竇七集之研究. Taipei: Fagu wenhua, 2015.

———. "*Zhimen Guangzha yulu* zhi yanjiu" 智門光祚語錄之研究. *Hanxue yanjiu* 30, no. 4 (2012): 35–64.

Hucker, Charles. *A Dictionary of Official Titles in Imperial China*. Stanford, CA: Stanford University Press, 1985.

Hu Jianming [Ko Kenmei] 胡建明. *Chūgoku Sōdai Zenrin kōsō bokuseki no kenkyū* 中国宋代禅林高僧墨蹟の研究. Tokyo: Shunjusha, 2007. Chinese ed., *Songdai gaoseng moji yanjiu* 宋代高僧墨迹研究. Hangzhou: Xiling yinshe, 2011.

Hu Xu 胡旭. *Daowang shi shi* 悼亡詩史. Shanghai: Dongfang chubanshe, 2010.

Hyers, Conrad. "Humor in Zen: Comic Midwifery." *Philosophy East and West* 39, no. 3 (1989): 267–277.

Iriya Yoshitaka 入矢義高. *Baso no goroku* 馬祖の語錄. Kyoto: Zen bunka kenkyūjo, 1984.

———. "Chinese Poetry and Zen." Translated by Norman Waddell. *The Eastern Buddhist* 6, no. 1 (1973): 54–67.

———. *Gozan bungaku shū* 五山文學集. Tokyo: Iwanami Shoten, 1990.

———. *Gūdō to etsuraku: Chūgoku no zen to shi* 求道と悦楽：中国の禅と詩. Tokyo: Iwanami Shoten, 1983. References to *Zōho* 増補 edition; Tokyo: Iwanami shoten, 2012.

Ishii Kōsei 石井公成. "Baso ni okeru *Ranka kyō, Ninyū shigyōron* no iyō" 馬祖における『楞伽經』『二入四行論』の依用. *Komazawa tanki daigaku bukkyō ronshū* 11 (2005): 109–125.

Ishii Shūdō 石井修道. "Denpō ge" 傳法偈. In Shinohara and Tanaka, *Kōza Tonkō 8 Tonkō butten to zen*, 281–305.

Jackson, Roger. " 'Poetry' in Tibet: Glu, mGur, sNyan ngag and 'Songs of Experience.' " In Cabezón and Jackson, *Tibetan Literature*, 368–392.

Jamentz, Michael. "The Buddhist Affirmation of Poetry and Locating a Thirteenth-Century *Fugen kōshiki* in Liturgical Literature." *Japanese Journal of Religious Studies* 43, no. 1 (2016): 55–88.

Jia Jinhua 賈晉華. *The Hongzhou School of Chan Buddhism in Eighth- through Tenth-Century China*. Albany, NY: SUNY Press, 2006.

———. *Jiaoran nianpu* 皎然年譜. Xiamen: Xiamen daxue chubanshe, 1992.

———. "The 'Pearl Scholars' and the Final Establishment of Regulated Verse." *T'ang Studies* 14 (1996): 1–20.

Jiang Jing 江靜. *Ri cang Song Yuan chanseng moji xuanbian* 日藏宋元禪僧墨跡選編. Chongqing: Xinan shifan daxue chubanshe, 2014.

Jin Chengyu 金程宇. "Songdai Chanseng shi zhengli yu yanjiu de zhongyao shouhuo—du *Songdai Chanseng shi jikao*" 宋代禪僧詩整理與研究的重要收穫—讀《宋代禪僧詩輯考》. *Zhonghua wen shi lun cong* 109 (2013): 375–390.

Jin Jianfeng 金建鋒. "Shi Zanning *Song gaoseng zhuan* yanjiu" 釋贊寧宋高僧傳研究. PhD diss., Shanghai Shifan Daxue, 2009.

Kagamishima Genryū 鏡島元隆. *Yakuchū Zen'en shingi* 訳註禅苑清規. Tokyo: Sōtōshū shūmuchō, 1972.

Kageki Hideo 蔭木英雄. *Gozan shishi no kenkyū* 五山詩史の研究. Tokyo: Kasama shoin, 1977.

Kaji Tetsujō 加地哲定. *Chūgoku Bukkyō bungaku kenkyū* 中国佛教文学研究. Kyoto: Kōyasan daigaku bungakubu chūgoku tetsugaku kenkyūshitsu, 1965; references to the "revised and expanded (Zōho)" edition, Kyoto: Dōhōsha shuppan, 1979.

Kamens, Edward. *The Three Jewels: A Study and Translation of Minamoto Tamenori's Sanbōe.* Ann Arbor: Center for Japanese Studies, University of Michigan, 1988.

Kao, Yu-kung. "Chinese Lyric Aesthetics." In *Words and Images: Chinese Poetry, Calligraphy, and Painting,* edited by Alfreda Murck and Wen C. Fong, 47–90. Princeton, NJ: Princeton University Press, 1991.

Kawasaki Michiko 川崎 ミチコ. "Shūdō ge ni" 修道偈2. In Shinohara and Tanaka, *Kōza Tonkō 8 Tonkō butten to zen,* 263–280.

Kawase Kazuma 川瀬一馬. *Gozan ban no kenkyū* 五山版の研究. 2 vols. Tokyo: Nihon Kosho Shosekishō Kyōkai, 1970.

Keene, Donald. *Seeds in the Heart: Japanese Literature from Earliest Times to the Late Sixteenth Century.* New York: Columbia University Press, 1999.

Keyworth, George. "'Study Effortless-Action': Rethinking Northern Song Chinese Chan Buddhism in Edo Japan." *Journal of Religion in Japan* 6, no. 2 (2017), 75–106.

———. "Transmitting the Lamp of Learning in Classical Chan Buddhism: Juefan Huihong (1071–1128) and Literary Chan." PhD diss., University of California, Los Angeles, 2001.

Kieschnick, John. *The Eminent Monk: Buddhist Ideals in Medieval Chinese Hagiography.* Kuroda Institute Studies in East Asian Buddhism 10. Honolulu: University of Hawaii Press, 1997.

Kinugawa Kenji 衣川賢次. "*Guchū Shūkyū nenpo* to Isshō Zenkei *Nenpo shō*" 愚中周及年譜と一笑禅慶『年譜抄』. Published in 3 parts: *Zen bunka* 249 (2018): 127–136; *Zen bunka* 250 (2018): 80–88; *Zen bunka* 251 (2019): 117–129.

———. "Sōbetsu shishū *Yippanfū* no seiritsu katei" 送別詩集『一帆風』の成立過程, *Komazawa daigaku zen kenkyūjo nenpō* 25 (2013), 149–162.

———. "Sodōshū no kiso hōgen" 『祖堂集』の基礎方言. *Tōyō bunka kenkyūjo kiyō* 164 (2013), 165–230.

Kirchner, Thomas, ed. *The Record of Linji.* Honolulu: University of Hawaii Press, 2009.

Kishino, Ryoji. "A Study of the Nidāna: An Underrated Canonical Text of the Mūlasarvāstivāda-vinaya." PhD diss., University of California, Los Angeles, 2013.

Klein, Lucas. "Indic Echoes: Form, Content, and World Literature in Tang Dynasty Regulated Verse." *Chinese Literature: Essays, Articles, Reviews (CLEAR)* 35 (2013): 59–96.

Klein, Susan Blakely. "Wild Words and Syncretic Deities: *Kyōgen kigo* and *honji suijaku* in Medieval Literary Allegoresis." In *Buddhas and Kami in Japan:* Honji Suijaki *as a Cominatory Paradigm,* edited by Mark Teeuwen and Fabio Rambelli, 177–203. London: RoutledgeCurzon, 2003.

Knechtges, David. "Wit, Humor, and Satire in Early Chinese Literature (to A.D. 220)." *Monumenta Serica* 29 (1971): 79–98.

Knechtges, David, and Taiping Chang. *Ancient and Early Medieval Chinese Literature: A Reference Guide.* 4 vols. Leiden: Brill, 2010–2014.

Kobayashi Taichirō 小林太市郎. *Zengetsu Daishi no shōgai to geijutsu* 禪月大師の生涯と藝術. First published 1947 by Sōgensha. Reprinted as vol. 3 of *Kobayashi Taichirō chosakushū*. Kyoto: Tankōsha. 1974

Kodera, Takashi James. *Dogen's Formative Years in China.* Boulder, CO: Prajna Press, 1980.

Komjathy, Louis. *Cultivating Perfection: Mysticism and Self-Transformation in Early Quanzhen Daoism.* Leiden: Brill, 2007.

Kong Fanli 孔凡禮. "Song shiseng Daoqian shengping kaolüe" 宋詩僧道潛生平考略, *Xuelin manlu* 18 (2011): 127–182.

Kroll, Paul. "Daoist Verse and the Quest of the Divine." In Lagerwey and Lü, *Early Chinese Religion, Part Two*, 953–985.

———. "Li Po's Transcendent Diction." *Journal of the American Oriental Society* 106, no. 1 (1986): 99–117.

———. *Meng Hao-jan.* Boston: Twayne, 1981.

———. "Verse from on High: The Ascent of T'ai-shan." *T'oung-pao* 69 (1983): 223–260.

Kyūshū Kokuritsu Hakubutsukan 九州国立博物館, ed. *Chūgoku o tabishita zensō no sokuseki* 中国を旅した禅僧の足跡. Fukuoka: Kyūshū kokuritsu hakubutsukan, 2014.

LaFleur, William. *The Karma of Words: Buddhism and the Literary Arts in Medieval Japan.* Berkeley: University of California Press, 1983.

Lagerway, John, and Marc Kalinowski, eds. *Early Chinese Religion.* 2 vols. Leiden: Brill, 2009.

Lai, C. M. "The Art of Lamentation in the Works of Pan Yue: 'Mourning the Eternally Departed.'" *Journal of the American Oriental Society* 114, no. 3 (1994): 409–425.

Lee, Thomas H. C. "Books and Bookworms in Song China." *Journal of Song-Yuan Studies* 25 (1995): 193–218.

Levering, Miriam. "Dahui Zonggao and Zhang Shangying: The Importance of a Scholar in the Education of a Song Chan Master." *Journal of Song-Yuan Studies* 30 (2000): 115–139.

———. "A Monk's Literary Education: Dahui's Friendship with Juefan Huihong." *Chung-hwa Buddhist Journal* 13, no. 2 (2000).

Lei Hanqing 雷漢卿. *Chanji fangsu ci yanjiu* 禪籍方俗詞研究. Chengdu: Ba Shu shu she, 2010.

Levine, Gregory. *Daitokuji: The Visual Cultures of a Zen Monastery.* Seattle: University of Washington Press, 2005.

———. "The Faltering Brush: Material, Sensory Trace, and Nonduality in Chan/Zen Buddhist Death Verse Calligraphies." In *Sensational Religion: Sensory Cultures in Material Practice,* edited by Sally M. Promey, 561–579. New Haven, CT: Yale University Press, 2014.

———. "Two (or More) Truths: Reconsidering *Zen Art* in the West." In *Awakenings: Zen Figure Paintings from Medieval Japan,* edited by Gregory Levine and Yukio Lippit, 52–61. New York: Japan Society; and New Haven, CT: Yale University Press, 2007. Exhibition catalogue.

Liao Chao-heng 廖肇亨. *Daochui wukongdi: Ming Qing Fojiao wenhua yanjiu lunji* 倒吹無孔笛—明清佛教文化研究論集. Taibei: Fagu wenhua, 2018.

———. "Huangbo zong yu Jianghu zhongqi sengshi lunxi: Yi sengshi xuanji wei jinlu de kaocha" 黃檗宗與江戶中期僧詩論析：以僧詩選集為進路的考察. *Guowen xuebao* 62 (2017): 33–58.

———. *Zhong-bian, shi-chan, meng-xi: Mingmo Qingchu Fojiao wenhua lunshu de chengxian yu kaizhan* 中邊・詩禪・夢戲：明末清初佛教文化論述的呈現與開展. Taibei: Yunchen wenhua, 2008.

———. *Zhongyi puti: Wan Ming Qing chu kongmen yiming jiqi jieyi lunshu tanxi* 忠義菩提：晚明清初空門遺民及其節義論述探析. Taibei: Zhongyanyuan, 2013.

Lin, Nancy. "Adapting the Buddha's Biographies." PhD diss., University of California, Berkeley, 2011.

Lynn, Richard John. "Orthodoxy and Enlightenment: Wang Shih-chen's Theory of Poetry and Its Antecedents." In *The Unfolding of Neo-Confucianism*, edited by Wm. Theodore de Bary, 217–269. New York: Columbia University Press, 1975.

———. "The Sudden and the Gradual in Chinese Poetry Criticism: An Examination of the Ch'an-Poetry Analogy." In Gregory, *Sudden and Gradual*, 381–427.

Mair, Victor. "Buddhism in *The Literary Mind and Ornate Rhetoric*." In *A Chinese Literary Mind: Culture, Creativity, and Rhetoric in Wenxin diaolong*, edited by Zong-qi Cai, 63–81. Stanford, CA: Stanford University Press, 2001.

Mair, Victor, and Tsu-lin Mei. "The Sanskrit Origins of Recent Style Prosody." *Harvard Journal of Asiatic Studies* 51, no. 2 (1991): 375–470.

Makita Tairyō 牧田諦亮. "Sannei to sono jidai" 賛寧とその時代. In *Chūgoku kinsei bukkyōshi kenkyū* 中国近世仏教研究, 96–133. Kyoto: Heirakuji shoten, 1957.

Marsone, Pierre, and John Lagerwey, eds. *Modern Chinese Religion I: Song-Liao-Jin-Yuan (960–1368 AD)*. Leiden: Brill, 2014.

Martin, François. "Buddhism and Literature." In Lagerwey and Lü, *Early Chinese Religion*, 891–952.

Maspero, Henri. "Sur quelques texts anciens de chinois parlé." *Bulletin de l'Ecole française d'Extrême-Orient* 14 (1914), 1–36.

Mather, Richard. *Shih-Shuo Hsin-Yü: A New Account of Tales of the World*. 2nd ed. Anne Arbor: University of Michigan Press, 2002.

Matsubara Akira 松原 朗. *Chūgoku ribetsu shi no seiritsu* 中国離別詩の成立. Tokyo: Kenbun shuppan, 2003.

Matsuura Shūkō 松浦秀光. *Zenshū kojitsu gemon no kenkyū*. 禪宗古実偈文の研究. Tokyo: Sankibō busshorin, 1971.

———. *Zenshū shoyō kyōten no kenkyū* 禪宗所用經典の研究. Tokyo: Sankibō busshorin, 1993.

Mazanec, Tom. "How Poetry Became Meditation in Late Ninth-Century China." *Asia Major*, 3rd ser., 32, no. 2 (2019): 113–151.

———. "The Invention of Chinese Buddhist Poetry." PhD diss., Princeton University, 2017.

———. "The Medieval Chinese Gāthā and Its Relationship to Poetry." *T'oung Pao* 103, nos. 1–3 (2017): 94–154.

———. "Networks of Exchange Poetry in Late Medieval China: Notes toward a Dynamic

History of Tang Literature." *Journal of Chinese Literature and Culture* 5, no. 2 (2018): 322–359.

McDermott, Joseph. *A Social History of the Chinese Book*. Hong Kong: Hong Kong University Press, 2006.

McLaren, Anne. *Performing Grief: Bridal Laments in Rural China*. Honolulu: University of Hawaii Press, 2008.

McMahan, David. *The Making of Buddhist Modernism*. New York: Oxford University Press, 2008.

McMullen, David. "Han Yü: An Alternative Picture." *Harvard Journal of Asiatic Studies* 49, no. 2 (1989): 603–657.

McRae, John. "Encounter Dialogue and the Transformation of the Spiritual Path in Chinese Ch'an." In Buswell and Gimello, *Paths to Liberation*, 339–369.

———. *The Northern School and the Formation of Early Ch'an Buddhism*. Honolulu: University of Hawaii Press, 1986.

———. *Seeing through Zen: Encounter, Transformation, and Genealogy in Chinese Chan Buddhism*. Berkeley: University of California Press, 2003.

———, trans. *The Vimalakīrti Sutra*. BDK English Tripiṭaka Series 4, no. 353. Berkeley: Numata Center for Buddhist Translation and Research, 2004.

Miller, Stephen. *Wind from Vulture Peak: The Buddhification of Japanese* Waka *in the Heian Period*. Ithaca, NY: Cornell University East Asia Program, 2013.

Minford, John, and Joseph S. M. Lau, eds. *Classical Chinese Literature: From Antiquity to the Tang Dynasty*. New York: Columbia University Press, 2000.

Monius, Anne. *Imagining a Place for Buddhism: Literary Culture and Religious Community in Tamil-Speaking South India*. New York: Oxford University Press, 2001.

Morrison, Elizabeth. *The Power of Patriarchs: Qisong and Lineage in Chinese Buddhism*. Leiden: Brill, 2010.

Murai Shōsuke 村井章介. "Chūsei Nitchō kōshō no naka no kanshi" 中世日朝交渉のなかの漢詩. In *Higashi Ajia ōkan: Kanshi to gaikō* 東アジア往還　漢詩と外交, 115–181. Tokyo: Asahi shinbunsha, 1995.

Murck, Alfreda. *Poetry and Painting in Song China: The Subtle Art of Dissent*. Cambridge, MA: Harvard University Asia Center, 2000.

Myrhe, Karin. "Wit and Humor." In *The Columbia History of Chinese Literature*, edited by Victor H. Mair, 132–148. New York: Columbia University Press, 2001.

Nakajima Kōshō 中島晧象. *Shodōshi yori miru zenrin no bokuseki* 書道史より見る禅林の墨蹟. Kyoto: Shibunkaku shuppan, 1990.

Nattier, Jan. *A Guide to the Earliest Chinese Buddhist Translations*. Tokyo: The International Research Institute for Advanced Buddhology, 2008.

Newsom, Carol. *The Book of Job: A Contest of Moral Imaginations*. New York: Oxford University Press, 2003.

———. "Pairing Research Questions and Theories of Genre: A Case Study of the Hodayot." *Dead Sea Discoveries* 17, no. 3 (2010): 241–259.

Nishio Kenryū 西尾賢隆. *Chūsei zensō no bokuseki to Nitchū kōryū* 中世禅僧の墨蹟と日中交流. Tokyo: Yoshikawa kōbunkan, 2011.

Norman, K. R. *A Philological Approach to Buddhism*. London: School of Oriental and African Studies, 1997.

Nugent, Christopher. *Manifest in Words, Written on Paper*. Cambridge, MA: Harvard University Asia Center, 2010.

Owen, Stephen. *The End of the Chinese "Middle Ages": Essays in Mid-Tang Literary Culture*. Stanford, CA: Stanford University Press, 1996.

———. *The Great Age of Chinese Poetry: The High T'ang*. New Haven, CT: Yale University Press, 1981.

———. "How Did Buddhism Matter in Tang Poetry?" *T'oung-pao* 103, nos. 4–5 (2017): 388–406.

———. *Just a Song: Chinese Lyrics from the Eleventh and Early Twelfth Centuries*. Cambridge, MA: Harvard University Asia Center, 2019.

———. *The Late Tang: Chinese Poetry of the Mid-Ninth Century (827–860)*. Cambridge, MA: Harvard University Asia Center, 2006.

———. *The Making of Early Chinese Classical Poetry*. Cambridge, MA: Harvard University Asia Center, 2006.

———. "The Manuscript Legacy of the Tang: The Case of Literature." *Harvard Journal of Asiatic Studies* 67, no. 2 (2007): 295–326.

———. *Readings in Chinese Literary Thought*. Cambridge, MA: Harvard University Press, 1992.

———. "Spending Time on Poetry: The Poetics of Taking Pains." In *Recarving the Dragon: Understanding Chinese Poetics*, edited by Olga Lomová, 157–178. Prague: Kaolinum Press, 2003.

———. "Transparencies: Reading the T'ang Lyric." *Harvard Journal of Asiatic Studies* 39, no. 2 (1979): 231–251.

Pan, An-yi. *Painting Faith: Li Gonglin and Northern Song Buddhist Culture*. Leiden: Brill, 2007.

Pan Jianguo 潘建國. "*Shishuo xinyu* zai Songdai de liubo jiqi shuji shi yiyi"《世說新語》在宋代的流播及其書籍史意義. *Wenxue pinglin* 2015, 4:165–176.

Park, Doyoung. "A Vehicle of Social Mobility: Utilitarian Factors in the Rise of Neo-Confucianism in the Early Tokugawa Period." PhD diss., University of Illinois at Urbana-Champaign, 2013.

Parker, Joseph D. *Zen Buddhist Landscape Arts of Early Muromachi Japan (1336–1573)*. Albany, NY: SUNY Press, 1999.

Plutschow, Herbert Eugen. "Is Poetry a Sin? *Honjisuijaku* and Buddhism versus Poetry." *Oriens Extremus* 25, no. 2 (1978): 206–218.

Poceski, Mario. *The Records of Mazu and the Making of Classical Chan Literature*. New York: Oxford University Press, 2015.

Pollock, Sheldon. Introduction to *Literary Cultures in History: Reconstructions from South Asia*, edited by Sheldon Pollock, 1–36. Berkeley: University of California Press, 2003.

Protass, Jason. "Buddhist Monks and Chinese Poetry." PhD diss., Stanford University, 2016.

———. "The Flavors of Monks' Poetry: On a Witty Denigration and Its Influences." *Journal of the American Oriental Society* 141, no.1 (2021): 125–150.

———. "A Geographic History of Song-Dynasty Chan Buddhism: The Decline of the Yunmen Lineage." *Asia Major*, 3rd ser., 32, no. 1 (2019): 113–160.

———. "Returning Empty-Handed: Reading the *Yifanfeng* Corpus as Buddhist Parting Poetry." *Journal of Chinese Literature and Culture* 4, no. 2 (2017): 383–419.

Qian Zhongshu 錢鐘書. *Tanyi lu* 談藝錄. Supplemented and corrected ed. (*bu ding* 補訂). 2 vols. Beijing: Sanlian Shudian, 2001. First published 1948 by Shanghai shudian (Shanghai).

Qi Gong 啟功. *Shi wen shenglü lungao* 詩文聲律論稿. Beijing: Zhonghua shuju, 2000.

Raft, Zeb. "The Space of Separation: The Early Medieval Tradition of Four-Syllable 'Presentation and Response' Poetry." In Richter, *History of Chinese Letters*, 276–306.

Rambelli, Fabio. *A Buddhist Theory of Semiotics*. New York: Bloomsbury, 2013.

Red Pine (Bill Porter). *Poems of the Masters: China's Classic Anthology of T'ang and Sung Dynasty Verse*. Port Townsend, WA: Copper Canyon, 2012.

———. *The Zen Works of Stonehouse: Poems and Talks of a Fourteenth-Century Chinese Hermit*. San Francisco: Mercury House, 1999.

Richter, Antje, ed. *A History of Chinese Letters and Epistolary Culture*. Leiden: Brill, 2015.

Robson, James. "Introduction: 'Neither Too Near nor Too Far'; The Historical and Cultural Contexts of Buddhist Monasteries in Medieval China and Japan." In *Buddhist Monasticism in East Asia: Places of Practice*, edited by James A. Benn, Lori Meeks, and James Robson, 1–17. New York: Routledge, 2010.

Roth, Harold. "Text and Edition in Early Chinese Philosophical Literature." *Journal of the American Oriental Society* 113, no. 2 (1993): 214–227.

Rouzer, Paul. "Early Buddhist Kanshi: Court, Courier, and Kūkai." *Monumenta Nipponica* 59, no. 4 (2004): 431–461.

———. *On Cold Mountain: A Buddhist Reading of the Hanshan Poems*. Seattle: University of Washington Press, 2015.

Ruegg, David S. *Ordre spirituel et ordre temporel dans la pensée bouddhique de l'Inde et du Tibet*. Paris: Collège de France, Institut de civilisation indienne, 1995.

Saitō Takanobu 齊藤隆信. *Kango Butten ni okeru ge no kenkyū* 漢語仏典における偈の研究. Kyoto: Hōzōkan, 2013.

Salomon, Richard. "Aśvaghoṣa's Saundarananda 4–6: A Study in the Poetic Structure of Buddhist Kāvya." *Indo-Iranian Journal* 52, no. 2/3 (2009): 179–196.

———. "An Unwieldy Canon: Observations on Some Distinctive Features of Canon Formation in Buddhism." In *Kanonisierung und Kanonbildung in der asiatischen Religionsgeschichte*, edited by Max Deeg, Oliver Freiberger, and Christoph Kleine, 167–207. Vienna: Verlag der Österreichischen Akademie der Wissenschaften, 2011.

Sargent, Stuart. *The Poetry of He Zhu (1052–1125): Genres, Contexts, and Creativity*. Leiden: Brill, 2007.

Satō Seijun 佐藤成順. *Sōdai Bukkyō no kenkyū: Genshō no Jōdokyō* 宋代仏教の研究: 元照の浄土教. Tokyo: Sankibō busshorin, 2001.

Satō Shūkō 佐藤秀孝. "Kidō Chigu no Shihō monjin ni tsuite" 虚堂智愚の嗣法門人について. *Komazawa daigaku bukkyōgakubu kenkyū kiyō* 64 (2006): 1–117.

———. "Kidō Chigu to Nansō matsu zenrin" 虚堂智愚と南宋末禅林. *Komazawa daigaku daigakuin bukkyōgaku kenkyūkai nenpō* 13 (1979): 97–108.

Sawada, Janine. *Practical Pursuits: Religion, Politics, and Personal Cultivation in Nineteenth-Century Japan*. Honolulu: University of Hawaii Press, 2004.

———. "Religious Conflict in Bakumatsu Japan." *Japanese Journal of Religious Studies* 21, no. 2/3 (1994): 211–230.

Scheible, Kristin. *Reading the Mahāvamsa: The Literary Aims of a Theravada Buddhist History.* New York: Columbia University Press, 2016.

Schlütter, Morten. *How Zen Became Zen.* Kuroda Institute Studies in East Asian Buddhism 22. Honolulu: University of Hawaii Press, 2008.

———. "The *Record of Hongzhi* and the Recorded Sayings Literature of Song-Dynasty Chan." In Heine and Wright, *The Zen Canon,* 181–205.

———. "Vinaya Monasteries, Public Abbacies, and State Control of Buddhism under the Song (960–1279)." In *Going Forth: Visions of Buddhist Vinaya,* edited by William M. Bodiford, 136–160. Kuroda Institute Studies in East Asian Buddhism 18. Honolulu: University of Hawaii Press, 2005.

Schmidt, J[erry] D[ean]. *Stone Lake: The Poetry of Fan Chengda 1126–1193.* Cambridge: Cambridge University Press, 1992.

Schopen, Gregory. *Buddhist Monks and Business Matters: Still More Papers on Monastic Buddhism in India.* Studies in the Buddhist Traditions. Honolulu: University of Hawaii Press, 2004.

Shaku Seitan 釋清潭. *Hochū Wa-Kan kōsō meishi shinshaku* 補注和漢高僧名詩新釈. Edited and annotated by Ariga Yōen 有賀要延. Tokyo: Kokusho kankōkai, 1998.

———. *Kozen rishi* 狐禪狸詩. Tokyo: Heigo shuppan, 1913.

Shang Haifeng 商海鋒. "*Xuedou lu* Song Yuan ben jiumao xintan" 雪竇錄宋元本舊貌新探. *Wenxian* 149, no. 3 (2015): 3–15.

Sharf, Robert. *Coming to Terms with Chinese Buddhism: A Reading of the Treasure Store Treatise.* Kuroda Institute Studies in East Asian Buddhism 14. Honolulu: University of Hawaii Press, 2002.

———. "How to Think with Chan *Gong'an.*" In *Thinking with Cases: Specialist Knowledge in Chinese Cultural History,* edited by Charlotte Furth, Judith T. Zeitlin, and Ping-chen Hsiung, 205–243. Honolulu: University of Hawaii Press, 2007.

———. "The Idolization of Enlightenment: On the Mummification of Ch'an Masters in Medieval China." *History of Religions* 32, no. 1 (1992): 1–31.

———. "On Pure Land Buddhism and Ch'an/Pure Land Syncretism in Medieval China." *T'oung Pao* 88, no. 4 (2002): 282–331

———. Review of *Eloquent Zen: Daitō and Early Japanese Zen,* by Kenneth Kraft. *The Journal of Religion* 74, no. 3 (1994): 432–433.

Shields, Anna. "Defining the 'Finest': A Northern Song View of Tang Dynasty Literary Culture in the *Wen cui.*" *Journal of Chinese Literature and Culture* 4, no. 2 (2017): 306–335.

———. *One Who Knows Me: Friendship and Literary Culture in Mid-Tang China.* Cambridge, MA: Harvard University Asia Center, 2015.

———. "Words for the Dead and the Living: Innovations in the Mid-Tang Prayer Text (*jiwen* 祭文)." *T'ang Studies* 25 (2009): 111–145.

Shi Guojing 釋果鏡. "Ciyun Zunshi yu Tianzhu si" 慈雲遵式與天竺寺. *Fagu foxue xuebao* 1 (2007): 103–175.

Shiina Kōyū 椎名宏雄. "*Busso sangyō chū* no seiritsu to shohon" 『仏祖三経註』の成立と諸本. *Indogaku Bukkyōgaku kenkyū* 47 (1998): 28–33.

———. "Chōro Sōseku sen *Jikaku zenji goroku* no shutsugen to sono yigi" 長蘆宗賾撰『慈覚禅師語録』の出現とその意義. *Indogaku Bukkyōgaku kenkyū* 57, no. 2 (2009): 172–178.

———. "*Jikaku zenji goroku* honkoku"『慈覚禅師語録』翻刻. *Komazawa Daigaku Zen Kenkyūjo nenpō* 20 (2008): 169–224.

———. *Sō Gen ban zenseki no kenkyū* 宋元版禪籍の研究. Tokyo: Daitō shuppansha, 1993.

———. "Tōdai zenseki no Sōdai kankō ni tsuite" 唐代禅籍の宋代刊行について. In *Sōdai Zenshū no shakaiteki eikyō* 宋代禅宗の社会的影響, edited by Suzuki Tetsuo, 513–541. Tokyo: Sankibō busshorin, 2002.

———. "*Zenmon shososhi geju* no bunken-teki kōsatsu"《禅門諸祖師偈頌》の文献的考察. In *Zengaku kenkyū no shosō: Tanaka Ryōshō Hakushi koki kinen ronshū*, edited by Tanaka Ryōshō Hakushi Koki Kinen Ronshū Kankōkai, 221–242. Tokyo: Daitō shuppansha, 2003.

Shimada Shūjirō 島田修二郎 and Iriya Yoshitaka 入矢義高. *Zenrin gasan: Chūsei suibokuga o yomu* 禅林画賛 : 中世水墨画を読む. Tokyo: Mainichi shinbun, 1987.

Shimao Arata 島尾新 and Kojima Tsuyoshi 小島毅監, eds. *Higashi Ajia no naka no Gozan bunka* 東アジアのなかの五山文化. Tokyo: Tōkyō daigaku shuppankai, 2014.

Shimizu, Yoshiaki. "Zen Art?" In *Zen in China, Japan and East Asian Art*, edited by H. Brinker et al., 73–98. Bern: Peter Lang, 1985.

Shinohara, Koichi. "Illness and Self: Zhiyuan's Two Autobiographical Essays." In *Self, Soul, and Body in Religious Experience,* edited by Albert I. Baumgarten, 276–297. Numen Book Series 78. Leiden: Brill, 1998.

———. "Zhiyuan's Autobiographical Essay, 'The Master of the Mean.' " In *Other Selves: Autobiography and Biography in Cross-Cultural Perspective,* edited by Phyllis Granoff and Koichi Shinohara, 35–72. Oakville, ON: Mosaic Press, 1994.

Shinohara Hisao and Tanaka Ryōshō, eds. *Kōza Tonkō 8 Tonkō butten to zen.* Tokyo: Daitō shuppansha, 1980.

Shi Shuting 施淑婷. "Su Shi wenxue yu Fo Chan zhi guanxi" 蘇軾文學與佛禪之關係. PhD diss., National Taiwan Normal University, 2008.

Shklovsky, Viktor. *Theory of Prose.* Elmwood Park, IL: Dalkey Archive Press, 1990.

Sichuan daxue guji zhengli yanjiusuo 四川大學古籍整理研究所, ed. *Song ji zhenben congkan shumu tiyao* 宋集珍本叢刊書目提要, vol. 108. Beijing: Xianzhuang shuju, 2004.

Silbergeld, Jerome. "Origins of Literati Painting in the Song Dynasty" in *A Companion to Chinese Art,* edited by Martin J. Powers and Katherine R. Tsiang, 474–498. Chichester, UK: Wiley Blackwell, 2016.

Skonicki, Douglas. "Viewing the Two Teachings as Distinct yet Complementary: Gushan Zhiyuan's Use of Parallelisms to Demonstrate the Compatibility of Buddhism and Ancient-Style Learning." *Journal of Chinese Religions* 38 (2010): 1–35.

Slingerland, Edward. *Confucius Analects.* Indianapolis, IN: Hackett, 2003.

Smith, Wilfred Cantwell. *What is Scripture?* Minneapolis: Fortress Press, 1993.

Snyder, Gary. *Myths and Texts.* New York: Totem Press, 1960.

Stevenson, Daniel. "Buddhist Ritual in the Song." In Marsone and Lagerwey, *Modern Chinese Religion,* 328–442.

———. "The 'Hall for the Sixteen Contemplations' as a Distinctive Institution for Pure

Land Practice in Tiantai Monasteries of the Song (960–1279)." In *Buddhism in Global Perspective*, edited by Kalpakam Sankaranarayan, Ravindra Panth, and Ichigo Ogawa, 147–204. Mumbai: Somaiya Publications, 2003

———. "Protocols of Power: Tz'u-yŭn Tsun-shih (964-1032) and T'ien-t'ai Lay Buddhist Ritual in the Sung." In Gregory and Getz, *Buddhism in the Sung*, 340–408.

———. "Where Meditative Theory Meets Practice: Requirements for Entering the 'Halls of Contemplation/Penance' 觀/懺堂 in Tiantai." *Tendai gakuhō: tokubetsugo, kokusai tendai gakkai ronshū* (2007): 71-142.

Struve, Lynn. "Deqing's Dreams: Signs in a Reinterpretation of His Autobiography." *Journal of Chinese Religions* 40 (2012): 1–44.

Sturman, Peter. *Mi Fu: Style and the Art of Calligraphy in Northern Song China.* New Haven, CT: Yale University Press, 1997.

Sugano, Marian. *The Poetics of the Occasion: Mallarmé and the Poetry of Circumstance.* Stanford, CA: Stanford University Press, 1992.

Sun Changwu 孫昌武. *Chansi yu shiqing* 禪思與詩情. 2nd ed. (*zengdingben*). Beijing: Zhonghua shuju, 2006.

Suyama Chōji 須山長治. "*Gōkofūgetsu shū* no Zensōtachi" 『江湖風月集』の禅僧たち. *Komazawa tanki daigaku bukkyō ronshū* 4 (1998): 51–57.

Suzuki, Daisetz Teitaro. *Studies in the "Laṅkāvatāra Sūtra."* London: George Routledge & Sons, 1930.

Suzuki Tetsuo 鈴木哲雄. *Tō Godai Zenshū shi* 唐五代禅宗史. Tokyo: Sankibō busshorin, 1985.

Swanson, Paul. *Clear Serenity, Quiet Insight: T'ien-t'ai Chih-i's Mo-ho Chih-kuan.* 3 vols. Honolulu: University of Hawaii Press, 2018.

Tackett, Nicolas. *The Destruction of the Medieval Chinese Aristocracy.* Cambridga, MA: Harvard University Asia Center, 2014.

Tam, Wai Lun. "The Life and Thought of a Chinese Buddhist Monk Zhiyuan (976–1022 CE)." PhD diss., McMaster University, 1996.

Tan, Zhihui. "Daoxuan's Vision of Jetavana: Imagining a Utopian Monastery in Early Tang." PhD diss., University of Arizona, 2002.

Tanaka Ryōshō 田中良昭. "Shūdō ge—ichi" 修道偈 1. In Shinohara and Tanaka, *Kōza Tonkō 8 Tonkō butten to zen*, 245–262.

———. "Zenshū tōshi no hatten" 禅宗燈史の發展. In Shinohara and Tanaka, *Kōza Tonkō 8 Tonkō butten to zen*, 99–123.

Tanaka Ryōshō 田中良昭 and Tei Sei [Cheng Zheng] 程正. *Tonkō zenshū bunken bunrui mokuroku* 敦煌禪宗文獻分類目錄. Tokyo: Daitō shuppansha, 2014.

Tan Zhaowen 覃召文. *Chanyue shihun* 禪月詩魂. Beijing: Sanlian shudian, 1994.

Taylor, Charles. *Sources of the Self: The Making of the Modern Identity.* Cambridge, MA: Harvard University Press, 1989.

Ter Haar, Barend J. "Buddhist Inspired Options: Aspects of Lay Religious Life in the Lower Yangzi from 1100 until 1340." *T'oung Pao* 87, no. 1/2 (2001): 92–152.

———. *White Lotus Teachings in Chinese Religious History.* Leiden: Brill, 1992.

Thurman, Robert. *The Holy Teaching of Vimalakīrti.* University Park: The Pennsylvania State University Press, 1976.

Tian, Xiaofei. *Beacon Fire and Shooting Star: The Literary Culture of the Liang (502–557)*. Cambridge, MA: Harvard University Asia Center, 2007.

Toleno, Robban. "Skilled Eating: Knowledge of Food in Yichu's *Shishi liutie*, a Buddhist Encyclopedia from Tenth-Century China." PhD diss., University of British Columbia, 2015.

Tsuchiya Taisuke 土屋太祐. "Xuansha Shibei sanju gangzong yu Jianfu Chenggu sanxuan de bijiao" 玄沙師備三句綱宗與薦福承古三玄的比較. *Pumen xuebao* 33 (2006): 93–134.

van der Kuijp, Leonard. "Tibetan Belles-Lettres: The Influence of Daṇḍin and Kṣemendra," in Cabezón and Jackson, *Tibetan Literature*, 393–410.

Waley, Arthur. *The Life and Times of Po Chü-i, 772–846 A.D.* London: G. Allen & Unwin, 1949.

Walshe, Maurice, trans. *Long Discourses of the Buddha: A Translation of the Digha Nikaya*. Boston: Wisdom Publications, 1995.

Wang, Mengxiao. "Building a Pure Land Lineage: A Study of Zhida's Play *Guiyuan jing* and a translation of its Three Paratexts." *Journal of Chinese Buddhist Studies* 33 (2020): 1–47.

Wang, Yugen. "The Limits of Poetry as Means of Social Criticism: The 1079 Literary Inquisition against Su Shi Revisited." *Journal of Song-Yuan Studies* 41 (2011): 29–65.

Wang Fanzhou 汪泛舟. "Zan zhen 贊箴." In *Dunhuang wenxue* 敦煌文學, edited by Yan Tingliang 顏廷亮, 97–107. Lanzhou: Gansu renmin chubanshe, 1999.

Wang Xiulin 王秀林. *Wan Tang Wudai shiseng qunti yanjiu* 晚唐五代詩僧群體研究. Beijing: Zhonghua shuju, 2008.

Wang Zhipeng 王志鵬. *Dunhuang Fojiao geci yanjiu* 敦煌佛教歌辭研究. Beijing: Gaodeng jiaoyu, 2013.

Watson, Burton. *Po Chü-i: Selected Poems*. New York: Columbia University Press, 2000.

———, trans. *The Vimalakirti Sutra*. New York: Columbia University Press, 1997.

———. "Zen Poetry." In *Zen: Tradition and Transition*, edited by Kenneth Kraft, 105–124. New York: Grove Press, 1988.

Welch, Holmes. *The Practice of Chinese Buddhism, 1900–1950*. Cambridge, MA: Harvard University Press, 1967.

Welter, Albert. *The Administration of Buddhism in China: A Study and Translation of Zanning and the Topical Compendium of the Buddhist Clergy (Da Song Seng shilüe)*. Amherst, NY: Cambria Press, 2018.

———. "A Buddhist Response to the Confucian Revival: Tsan-ning and the Debate Over Wen in the Early Sung." In Gregory and Getz, *Buddhism in the Sung*, 21–61.

———. "Buddhist Ritual and the State." In *Religions of China in Practice*, edited by Donald S. Lopez Jr., 390–396. Princeton, NJ: Princeton University Press, 1996.

———. *The "Linji lu" and the Creation of Chan Orthodoxy: The Development of Chan's Records of Sayings Literature*. New York: Oxford University Press, 2008.

———. *Monks, Rulers, and Literati: The Political Ascendancy of Chan Buddhism*. New York: Oxford University Press, 2006.

———. *Yongming Yanshou's Conception of Chan in the "Zongjing lu": A Special Transmission within the Scriptures*. New York: Oxford University Press, 2011.

Williams, Nicholas Morrow. "The Brocade of Words: Imitation Poetry and Poetics in the Six Dynasties." PhD diss., University of Washington, 2010.

———. *Imitations of the Self: Jiang Yan and Chinese Poetics.* Leiden: Brill, 2014.

———. "Pan Yue's 'Study of a Widow' and Its Predecessors." *Journal of the American Oriental Society* 132, no. 3 (2012): 347–365.

———. "The Taste of the Ocean: Jiaoran's Theory of Poetry." *Tang Studies* 31 (2013): 1–27.

Winfield, Pamela. *Icons and Iconoclasm in Japanese Buddhism: Kūkai and Dōgen on the Art of Enlightenment.* New York: Oxford University Press, 2013.

Wong, Dorothy. "The Huayan/Kegon/Hwaŏm Paintings in East Asia." In *Reflecting Mirrors: Perspectives on Huayan Buddhism,* edited by Imre Hamar, 349–396. Wiesbaden: Harrassowitz Verlag, 2006.

Wright, Dale. *The Six Perfections: Buddhism and the Cultivation of Character.* New York: Oxford University Press, 2009.

Wu, Jiang. *Enlightenment in Dispute: The Reinvention of Chan Buddhism in Seventeenth-Century China.* New York: Oxford University Press, 2008.

———. "From the Cult of the Book to the Cult of the Canon." In *Spreading Buddha's Word in East Asia,* edited by Jiang Wu and Lucille Chia, 46–78. New York: Columbia University Press, 2015.

Wu Ching-yi 吳靜宜. "Huihong wenzi chan zhi shixue neihan yanjiu" 惠洪文字禪之詩學內涵研究. Master's thesis, Taiwan Shifan Daxue, 2004.

Xu Hongxia 許紅霞. "Ri cang Songseng shiji *Yifanfeng* xiangguan wenti zhi wojian" 日藏宋僧詩集《一帆風》相關問題之我見. *Zhongguo dianji yu wenhua luncong* 13 (2011): 150–166.

———. *Zhenben Song ji wu zhong: Ri cang Song seng shiwenji zhengli yanjiu* 珍本宋集五種: 日藏宋僧詩文集整理研究. 2 vols. Beijing: Beijing daxue chubanshe, 2013.

Yamada Shōzen 山田昭全. "Poetry and Meaning: Medieval Poets and the Lotus Sutra," translated by Willa Jane Tanabe. In *The Lotus Sutra in Japanese Culture,* edited by George J. Tanabe, Jr., and Willa Jane Tanabe, 95–118. Honolulu: University of Hawaii Press, 1989.

Yampolsky, Philip, trans. *The Platform Sutra of the Sixth Patriarch.* New York: Columbia University Press, 1967.

Yanagida Seizan 柳田聖山. "Goroku no rekishi" 語録の歴史. *Tōhō gakuhō* 57 (1985): 211–663.

———. "*Kosonshuku goroku* kō" 古尊宿語録考. *Hanazono daigaku kenkyū kiyō* 2 (1971), 1–48.

———. "Mujaku Dōchū no gakumon" 無著道忠の学問. *Zengaku kenkyu* 55 (1966): 14–55.

———. "The 'Recorded Sayings' Texts of Chinese Ch'an Buddhism." In *Early Ch'an in China and Tibet,* edited by Lewis R. Lancaster and Whalen Lai, 185–205. Berkeley, CA: Asian Humanities Press, 1983.

———. *Shoki Zenshū shisho no kenkyū* 初期禪宗史書の研究. Kyoto, Hōzōkan, 1967.

———. *Zen no bunka: Shiryōhen: Zenrin sōbōden yakuchū* 禅の文化 : 資料編: 禅林僧寶傳譯注. Kyoto: Kyōto daigaku jinbun kagaku kenkyūjo, 1988.

———. "Zenseki kaidai" 禅籍解題. In *Zenke goroku* 禅家語録, edited by Nishitani Keiji and Yanagida Seizan, vol. 2. Tokyo: Chikuma Shobō, 1972.

Yanagi Mikiyasu 柳幹康. *Eimei Enju to Sugyōroku no kenkyū* 永明延寿と『宗鏡録』の研究. Kyoto: Hōzōkan, 2015.

Yang, Jingqing. *The Chan Interpretations of Wang Wei*. Hong Kong: Chinese University Press, 2007.

Yang, Zhiyi. *Dialectics of Spontaneity: The Aesthetics and Ethics of Su Shi (1037–1101) in Poetry*. Leiden: Brill, 2015.

Yang Jun 阳珺. "Songseng Cijue Zongze xinyan" 宋僧慈覺宗賾新研. Master's thesis, Shanghai Shifan Daxue, 2012.

Yang Zengwen 楊曾文. *Dunhuang xinben Liuzu tan jing* 敦煌新本六祖壇經. 2nd ed. Beijing: Zongjiao wenhua chubanshe, 2001.

———. *Song Yuan Chanzong shi* 宋元禪宗史. Beijing: Zhongguo shehui kexue chubanshe, 2006.

Yang Zhifei 楊志飛. "Zanning *Gaoseng zhuan* yanjiu" 贊寧高僧傳研究. PhD diss., Zhejiang Daxue, 2013.

———. "Zhonghua shuju ben *Shishi yaolan jiaozhu* de banben wenti" 中華書局本《釋氏要覽校注》的版本問題. *Tushuguan zazhi* 36, no. 7 (2017): 103–109.

Yifa. *The Origins of Buddhist Monastic Codes in China*. Honolulu: University of Hawaii Press, 2002.

Yoshikawa Kōjirō 吉川幸次郎. *Introduction to Sung Poetry*. Translated by Burton Watson. New York: Columbia University Press, 1967.

———. *Sōshi gaisetsu* 宋詩概説. Tokyo: Iwanami shoten, 1962. Expanded edition, Tokyo: Iwanami shoten, 2006. Citations are to the 2006 edition.

Yu, Anthony. *Comparative Journeys: Essays on Literature and Religion East and West*. New York: Columbia University Press, 2009.

Yü, Chün-fang. "Ch'an Education in the Sung: Ideals and Procedures." In de Bary and Chaffee, *Neo-Confucian Education*, 57–104.

———. *The Renewal of Buddhism in China: Chu-hung and the Late Ming Synthesis*. New York: Columbia University Press, 1981.

Zhang, Cong Ellen. *Transformative Journeys: Travel and Culture in Song China*. Honolulu: University of Hawaii Press, 2011.

Zhang, Yunshuang. "Porous Privacy: The Literati Studio and Spatiality in Song China." PhD diss., University of California, Los Angeles, 2017.

Zhang Fuqing 張福清. "Cong Shaosong *Yayu Jiang Zhe jixing jiju shi* kan Songren dui Tang Song shiren shige de jieshou" 從紹嵩《亞愚江浙紀行集句詩》看宋人對唐宋詩人詩歌的接受. *Zhongguo yunwen xuekan* 26, no. 4 (2012): 79–84.

Zhang Gaoping 張高評. *Chuangyi zaoyu yu Song shi tese* 創意造語與宋詩特色. Taipei: Xinwenfeng, 2008.

———. *Shiren yuxie yu Songdai shixue* 《詩人玉屑》與宋代詩學. Taipei: Xinwenfeng, 2012.

———. *Tiaoxi yuyin conghua yu Songdai shixue dianfan: Jian lun shihua kanxing jiqi chuanmei xiaoying* 苕溪漁隱叢話與宋代詩學典範：兼論詩話刊行及其傳媒效應. Taipei: Xinwenfeng, 2012.

———. *Yinshua chuanmei yu Song shi tese* 印刷傳媒與宋詩特色. Taipei: Liren shuju, 2008.

Zhang Liang 張良. "Songdai Tiantai zong sengshi jiyi 77 shou" 宋代天台宗僧詩輯佚 77 首. *Guji zhengli yanjiu xuekan* 172 (2014): 32–37.

Zhang Minghua 張明華. "Jijushi de fazhan jiqi tedian" 集句詩的發展及其特點. *Nanjing Shifan daxue wenxueyuan xuebao* 4 (2006): 24–29.

Zhang Peifeng 張培鋒. *Song shi yu Chan* 宋詩與禪. Beijing: Zhonghua shuju, 2009.

Zhang Ruolan 張若蘭. "Shi Zhongshu de renge tezheng jiqi ci chengjiu de qude" 釋仲 殊的人格特徵及其詞成就的取得. *Pumen xuebao* 36 (2006): 129–142.

Zhou Yukai 周裕鍇. *Chanzong yuyan* 禪宗語言. Hangzhou: Zhejiang renmin chuban-she, 1999.

———. *Fayan yu shixin: Songdai Fo-Chan yujingxia de shixue huayu jiangou* 法眼與詩心: 宋代佛禪語境下的詩學話語建構. Beijing: Zhongguo shehui kexue chubanshe, 2014.

———. *Songseng Huihong xinglü zhushu biannian zongan* 宋僧惠洪行履著述編年總案. Beijing: Gaodeng jiaoyu chubanshe, 2010.

———. *Wenzi chan yu Songdai shixue* 文字禪與宋代詩學. Kaohsiung: Foguangshan wenjiao, 2001. First published 1998 by Gaodeng jiaoyu chubanshe (Beijing).

———. "Youxi sanmei: Cong zongjiao jietuo dao yishu chuangzao" 游戲三昧:從宗教 解脫到藝術創造. In *Zhongguo dishijie Su Shi yantaohui lunwenji,* edited by Zhuge Yibing and Su Biquan, 269–291. Jinan: Jilu shushe, 1999.

———. *Zhongguo Chanzong yu Shige* 中國禪宗與詩歌. Shanghai: Shanghai renmin chubanshe, 1992.

Zhu Gang 朱剛 and Chen Jue 陳珏, eds. *Songdai Chanseng shi jikao* 宋代禪僧詩輯考. Shanghai: Fudan daxue chubanshe, 2012.

Ziporyn, Brook. *Evil and/or/as the Good.* Cambridge, MA: Harvard University Asia Center, 2000.

Zürcher, Erik. *Buddhism in China: Collected Papers of Erik Zürcher,* edited by Jonathan A. Silk. Leiden: Brill, 2013.

———. "Buddhism and Education in Tang Times." In Zürcher, *Buddhism in China,* 297–337.

———. "Buddhist Chanhui and Christian Confession." In Zürcher, *Buddhism in China,* 609–635.

———. *The Buddhist Conquest of China.* 3rd ed. Leiden: Brill, 2007.

———. "Late Han Vernacular Elements." In Zürcher, *Buddhism in China,* 27–61.

———. "Vernacular Elements in Early Buddhist Texts." In Zürcher, *Buddhism in China,* 513–537.

Index

Bold page numbers refer to figures and tables.

About the Author

Jason Protass is assistant professor of religious studies at Brown University.

**Kuroda Institute
Studies in East Asian Buddhism**

Studies in Ch'an and Hua-yen
Robert M. Gimello and Peter N. Gregory, editors

Dōgen Studies
William R. LaFleur, editor

The Northern School and the Formation of Early Ch'an Buddhism
John R. McRae

Traditions of Meditation in Chinese Buddhism
Peter N. Gregory, editor

Sudden and Gradual: Approaches to Enlightenment in Chinese Thought
Peter N. Gregory, editor

Buddhist Hermeneutics
Donald S. Lopez, Jr., editor

Paths to Liberation: The Mārga and Its Transformations in Buddhist Thought
Robert E. Buswell, Jr., and Robert M. Gimello, editors

Sōtō Zen in Medieval Japan
William M. Bodiford

The Scripture on the Ten Kings *and the Making of Purgatory
in Medieval Chinese Buddhism*
Stephen F. Teiser

The Eminent Monk: Buddhist Ideals in Medieval Chinese Hagiography
John Kieschnick

Re-Visioning "Kamakura" Buddhism
Richard K. Payne, editor

Original Enlightenment and the Transformation of Medieval Japanese Buddhism
Jacqueline I. Stone

Buddhism in the Sung
Peter N. Gregory and Daniel A. Getz, Jr., editors

*Coming to Terms with Chinese Buddhism:
A Reading of* The Treasure Store Treatise
Robert H. Sharf